"The mystical feminine has a vital part to play in the present work of global healing and transformation. Feminine Mysticism in Art awakens us to HER central role. These images and mystical writings speak directly to the soul, reminding us of her eternal presence, her power, and beauty."

Llewellyn Vaughn-Lee, Ph.D, Sufi teacher,
author of numerous books on the Divine Feminine

"This exquisite book of astonishing and often haunting images of the Divine Feminine and Sacred Union created by contemporary artists will encourage us to embrace a new reality--that an exclusively masculine image of the Divine is not, and can never be, whole without HER."

Margaret Starbird, M.A, author of
The Woman With The Alabaster Jar

"In this masterpiece, the editors Victoria Christian and Susan Stedman, a mother/daughter team, give us a vision of where we are going as a human species--to a more integrated consciousness where the excuses of dualism no longer hold us hostage. This rare collection of new spiritual art demonstrates how artists are once again leading the way into uncharted territory of human evolution. It is tremendous contribution to the women's spirtuality movment and is a must read for any women's studies, transpersonal psychology, sociology, or transcendental art programs."

Debra Giusti, Founder of Harmony Festival,
Wishing Well Productions

"The reclaiming of the Divine Feminine is not just a means to women's wholeness, but a necessity for men's completeness and overall societal balance as well. Our ability to envision the Divine is a pathway towards bringing it back into practical daily life. And in this beautiful book and DVD project, the marriage of exquisite sacred art and words combines into a beautiful, inspiring vision of that Divinity."

Brooke Medicine Eagle, author of *Buffalo Woman Comes Singing*
and *The Last Ghost Dance*

Celebrating the wondrous diversity of the global visionary culture in a refreshingly feminine light, Victoria Christian's encyclopedic and scholarly book shares a profound menage of arts and mystical writings. This uniquely post-postmodern media is overflowing with magic and is sure to charge up your creative chi. This visionary primer is a must-have for any arts aficionados and scholars. It will no doubt inspire imaginations everywhere."

Delvin Solkinson, PhD, Managing Editor of
CoSM Journal of Visionary Culture

"If Victoria Christian's Feminine Mysticism in Art were nothing more than the reproductions of stunning and provacative images that she collected, you'd have yourself and artbook of extraordinary beauty and depth. But it's so much more. If you can accept her invitation to bring your "beginner's mind" to this book, you have in store one of the most profound journeys into appreciation of divine mystery that you'll ever experience. What a vast achievement of art and language."

Jeff Golden, Politician, Sacred Activist, and creator and
host of public television's, Immense Possibilities

Previous Page Artwork: Synergenesis, Amoraea Dreamseed

FEMININE MYSTICISM IN ART
ARTISTS ENVISIONING THE DIVINE

Edited by Victoria Christian and Susan Stedman

Awakening Soul Wisdom
www.**mysticspiritart**.com

FEMININE MYSTICISM IN ART: ARTISTS ENVISIONING THE DIVINE

Designer: Kelly Harding, Sunshine Design

Library of Congress Cataloging in Publication Data

Christian, Victoria

Feminine Mysticism in Art: Artists Envisioning the Divine

ISBN 978-1-7326924-1-1 Hardback

ISBN 978-1-7326924-0-4 Paperback

Credits for artwork appear in the body of text adjacent to respective images.

Published by Awakening Soul Wisdom
Ashland, Oregon
www.mysticspiritart.com

Cover Artists:

David Joaquin, Martina Hoffman, George Atherton,
Autumn Skye Morrison, Amoraea Dreamseed, Mark Henson,
AfraShe Asungi, Krista Lynn Brown, Blaze Warrender

This book is dedicated to the primordial sacred union and the renewal of Gaia. May the flame of the Divine Feminine burn bright again.

CONTENTS

Acknowledgments

As a co-creative vision, this book involved the synthesis of many brilliant cultural creatives. First and foremost, I want to acknowledge my mother, Susan Stedman, for her wisdom and steadfast devotion to the project. Not only was she my confidant, she was also an enormous source of emotional support and a fastidious editor. I simply couldn't have done this project without her. I would also like to acknowledge Michael Slavenski for believing in me and for his generous investment in the DVD. He literally gave me hope in the darkest hour and has been a monumental hero in my life and in the lives of so many others who know him.

A book like this, which is documenting a genre of visionary art, takes a considerable amount of time and devotion. This book took over twelve years to complete and went through many stages of evolution. I am most grateful to all of the artists for their unwavering patience and devotion. My soul was continually nourished by their precious art, music and writings, which hung on my walls, rotated through my altar and appeared on my computer screen. I am honored to have befriended several of the artists, not to mention having the opportunity to see their studios, original paintings and even watch them paint. I am in complete awe of all of their creative genius and learned so much from them.

I would particularly like to thank Mark Henson for all of his inspiration and support over the years. I consider Mark to be a crucial "hub" in the transcendental art movement. Not only has he done a lot of service work for the visionary art community, but for the last ten years he has organized one of the best visionary art shows in California called The Transformational Art Show at the Harmony Festival in Santa Rosa. I was fortunate to show my art there which allowed me to meet some of the best California visionary artists of our day. I also want to thank Paul Heussenstamm for his savvy business advice and abundant perspective. And I am most indebted to Suzanne Deveuve, Andrew Annenberg, Theresa Sharrar, Leslie Gibbons and Krista Lynn Brown for their friendship and emotional support.

One of the most fascinating things about the creative process is the mysterious unfolding of the journey and the synchronicities that occur along the way. There were indeed many mountains to climb and at times I felt completely lost in the woods, not knowing where to go next. To my surprise, an angel would appear. This project was literally done on a shoestring budget and I was fortunate to have a few angels who sponsored the project and me financially. I want to acknowledge Cory Jones, Kent Schoch, Tim Kohler and my favorite sociology professor, Kooros Mahmoudi. These men saw the social importance of this book and understood the sacrifice I made in my life to make it happen. I would also like to acknowledge Abba Yahuda and Brian Lloyd for assisting me financially in a time of great need. A new warrior brother by the name of Cliff Scheick saved the day on numerous occasions. Not only did he come into my life when I needed a friend, he sponsored the project with a computer and excellent business advice. I would also like to thank an amazing angel by the name of Jerry Schneider. He mysteriously came into my life during a time of great need and commissioned me to do a painting for his mother. He also sponsored the project with a new Macintosh laptop, which came nearly a week after my computer died. Ironically he didn't even know this had happened.

And in conclusion I want to thank all the people who helped me with editing: John Grimshaw, Greg Marchese, Ian Luepker, Matt Fawcett and Eric Alan. And also the gang at White Cloud Press—Gary, Steve and Steve Scholl—for all of their excellent advice and for believing in the project from the beginning. Last but not least, I should acknowledge Dave Emrich and Kelly Harding whose book design so fully realized my original vision of text and images. And a special thanks to John Grimshaw for assisting with the revisions to the book which required a tremendous amount of tedious editing and design work. He was the wind beneath my wings at the end of the project when my creative juices were all dried up. He blew his creative fires on me and reawakened a tired and wounded warrioress avatar suffering from temporary amnesia. I could not have finished this book without his help.

Forward

Gloria F. Orenstein
Professor Emerita Comparative Literature And Gender Studies
University of Southern California Los Angeles

It is my privilege to open the portal for your first glimpse of *Feminine Mysticism in Art.* As we step over the threshold into the universe of this amazing collection of works by women and men from diverse backgrounds, we must be cautious in thinking that we have seen this all before from the seventies Goddess art movement and from Ecofeminism as it developed through the nineties and into the new millennium. What you will find here is an enlarged, more inclusive, and more evolved interpretation of Goddess art for the twenty-first century. Having written about the earlier Goddess art movement in a book titled *The Reflowering of the Goddess,* I am stunned by how rapidly and organically this new movement has sprung forth from the seeds planted by the feminist "Goddess artists" of the 'second wave' and, more importantly, how the visionary aspect of this art literally transports the viewer to expanded states of consciousness. I feel extremely honored to present this expanded vision of Goddess art to you as a potent legacy of the evolving revolutionary scholarship and creativity of today's Feminist/Feminine mystical movement in art.

I want to begin by reflecting upon Goddess art in the context of its early beginnings back in the late sixties and early seventies, and continuing on through the nineties. In those days, when I taught Women's Studies (now known as Gender Studies) my students had one question that came to be the bottom line of our inquiry. What my students wanted to know most of all was whether there had ever been a civilization, a culture, or a society that was non-patriarchal. Had there ever been one in which the gender of the deity was female rather than male? (Here the inquiry was focused on western civilization). While there have been examples of cultures that were matrilineal and matrifocal, our search to uncover examples of a bonafide matriarchy or of a religion in which God was a female proved extremely daunting until, to cite an important landmark in our quest *When God Was a Woman* by Merlin Stone was published and filled us in on the history and mythology as well as the reality of centuries of Goddess-centered civilization. She informed us of how thousands of years of the history of pre-patriarchal civilization had been omitted from all books and courses on history and art in the western canon. As Merlin taught us, when one image of *The Venus of Willendorf* was found in an art history book, we were told that it represented a Goddess cult, suggesting that one image sufficed to represent such a minority's beliefs.

Merlin Stone's revolutionary findings, having poured through the anthropological and religious texts as well as the archeological logs that the general public would never see, led her to conclude that the plethora of Goddess images from a variety of pre-patriarchal cultures suggested the existence of a widespread and long-lasting Goddess centered civilization, not a cult, that preceded the historical erasure of the pre-existing Goddess religion. Soon after that, Marija Gimbutas' multiple volumes of archeological scholarship covering the language of the Goddess, and the myths of the Goddess reinforced our understanding of this civilization that had lasted for millennia. According to Gimbutas, it was gender egalitarian, peace-loving, reverent of the natural world, and devoted to the spiritual source of the Creatrix.

The early Goddess art movement was known for the works created by women artists; such as Mary Beth Edelson, Ana Mendieta, Betsy Damon, Judy Baca, Judy Chicago, Bettye Saar, Monica Sjoo, Afra-She Asungi and many others who made pilgrimages to ancient Goddess sites and sanctuaries, and enacted rituals and ceremonies at these places of power in order to experience what it might have felt like to participate in the rites of a woman living in a Goddess culture. This movement focused on performances, rituals, and imagining the female self living within the context of the life of a Priestess or a wise woman healer from the ancient past, empowered by her status in a non-patriarchal society. They sought to reclaim many of the ancient rites in revised forms, and introduce them into their present artistic and spiritual practices.

A welcome revision of the second wave of Goddess art by its contemporaries is the inclusion of male artists and writers as a part of the Goddess art movement. We had just begun to become familiar with pro-feminist men, and now we are encountering Goddess-revering men who are also visionary artists. The most important transformation brought about here by both female and male artists is the creation of work from a spiritually evolved visionary state of consciousness. These works often depict the energy pathways to spiritual evolution and union with Source through the chakra system as it aligns with the energies of the cosmos. These new works often express a clairvoyant perception of energy currents in the body as well as indicating the paths the energy follows in diverse spiritual meditative journeys to enlightenment. They raise important new questions and bring into focus themes that needed further elaboration such as the reclaiming of Shamanism as a direct path of revelation.

In addition, Goddess artists of the third wave are exploring the birth of a new world view of sacred activism. They are interested in learning about the role played by sacred geometry in creation and manifestation. They are working to create new social systems such as the gift economy. Many of the artists featured in this section of the book also have websites in which they connect with visionaries working in different fields in order to collaborate in the hastening of a major shift in culture and consciousness to take place, both on the spiritual plane as well as on the material level. This shift on the material plane will involve the development of permaculture, and eco-housing.

It is empowering and inspiring to encounter the new works of these ecstatic, futurist visionaries, who are seeking to give birth to a new, purified, and ecologically sustainable culture. Their communal vision is being energized by their networks, consciousness, art, meditations, and their newly evolved green technologies. For them, what used to be known as science fiction is a world whose magic is attainable through these new techniques of spiritual evolution as they are brought into practice here on Earth, and are used to bring about a loving relationship between all forms of sentient life in the universe.

I am thankful to Victoria Christian and to her mother, Susan Stedman, whose art, editing, writing, hard work and dedication enabled the birthing process of a work that undoubtedly will continue to inspire re-vision and re-birth for many generations to come. Now is the moment to step through the portal and begin the next phase of the journey. The Great Shift is upon us and it is clear that these visionaries have a lot to say about the evolution of feminine wisdom that will need to be absorbed into the fabric of our beings as it will inevitably bring humanity to a more harmonious and balanced place within ourselves and in the world at large.

Introduction

In every age there have been prophets, shamans, visionaries, mystics and transcendental artists who have attempted to envision the divine through an assortment of mediums and spiritual practices. They have seen through the surface of ordinary consciousness and looked directly into the interior. They reveal what lies beyond the boundary of the senses to bridge the gap between the sacred and the profane, while simultaneously instilling a sense of hope, reverence and awe of the Great Mystery.

Artists Envisioning the Divine is a co-creative effort between a number of contemporary mystics and visionary artists who have united in their mission to assist humanity in awakening to a new mode of consciousness—a symbiotic union of God/Goddess and ultimately an awakening to the Great Mystery, the Divine Infinite Consciousness, the Source, the Tao, the Ground of Being, the Ultimate Reality, the Nameless One—there are endless names for the Beloved. However, in alignment with the women's spirituality movement, we believe that imaging the divine as female is essential to our spiritual evolution, for we won't be able to shift into a new paradigm until the harmonious autonomy of the feminine principle is fully established in human consciousness.

In order to move into the new paradigm of integration between God/Goddess, it is imperative that we start to reevaluate traditional images of the all-powerful monotheistic male God in the Jewish and Christian religious heritages of Europe and the United States. While images of Father God are valid and empowering, the lack of a divine female image has not only justified and maintained male dominance, it has also caused severe damage to the psyches of women, as well as to the psyches of men. As several feminists, thealogians, archeologists and psychologists have already noted, the lack of divine female images not only supports an imbalance in our consciousness that diminishes our sense of wholeness as individuals, but has also conditioned us to undervalue the feminine principle within ourselves and in the world around us.

Given this situation, it is important for women, as well as for men with feminist goals, to both recover and create new empowering female symbols to help balance the ones that support the patriarchy and a one-sided view of humanity. Since the masculine side of God has been so heavily portrayed in Western culture, a large number of people are yearning for images of the Goddess, as they would provide alternatives to the conventional view that men are the primary purveyors of God in religion and society. In contrast, the Goddesses show us that the female can also be symbolic of all that is creative and powerful in the universe as well as provide an orientation that can help us save the planet from ecological destruction. As Carole Christ, a pioneer of the Women's Spirituality Movement informs us, "The real importance of the symbol of the Goddess is that it breaks the power of the patriarchal symbol of God as male over the psyche." [1]

Imaging the divine as female is essential to our spiritual evolution—one that transforms our current conceptualization of the divine and includes all of God's creation. As feminist art historian Elinor Gadon said, "Artists who are reclaiming the sacred iconography of the Goddess are creating a new perception of reality that is representative of their experience as spiritual women and men." [2] This book is an attempt to create this new vision of reality by filling the void of sacred imagery of the Goddess and the Primordial Sacred Union in the West. By merging the creative visions of a group of contemporary mystics and visionaries, it is our intention to cultivate a deeper awareness and reverence for the divine so that we can begin to move beyond gender associations and embrace the Eternal One.

We understand that there are many interpretations and theories about what needs to occur in order for humankind to evolve into a new paradigm and, therefore, we don't profess to have all the answers. There is nothing new under the sun. While the rebirth of the Goddess is just now beginning to emerge into the consciousness of a large number of Westerners, she has been with us from the beginning of time. We acknowledge the long history and lineage of mystics, visionaries and heretics who have come before us, many of whom were severely persecuted in their mission to keep the Goddess's flame alive. We commend and honor these individuals for their courage to uphold truth and justice in the midst of stark repression, for they paved the way for contemporary mystics, visionaries and heretics to carry the sacred flame of the Goddess into future generations where she could make herself known to humanity on deeper levels. However, keepers of the Goddess's flame continue to be up against a deeply entrenched system of denial that is sometimes as volatile today as in the past. Thus, it is imperative that we support each other in Her mission and not fall prey to ego and competition. It doesn't matter who came into an awakening of the Goddess first. What matters is that we are blessed to have this awakening now.

Those who are beginning to awaken to Oneness as it unfolds in current times are ushering in the dramatic shift into a new paradigm, a merging of science and mysticism,

East and West, male and female, God and Goddess. While the majority of people still cling to a scientific, nihilistic and materialistic world view, those who are aligning with the shift in consciousness will discover that they are in the process of their own rebirth and remembrance of what it all means, and will feel exhilarated by this awareness. However, personal growth is never easy. In fact sometimes it is downright uncomfortable. Ultimately, though, it is a thousand times easier to face our shadows than to stay stuck in belief systems that are keeping us spiritually stagnant. It is natural that new efforts to create a vision of God/Goddess will be mistrusted at first, for there are no familiar contexts to place them in. Thus it will be important to seek guidance from those who have already gone through the awakening process, as they will serve as spiritual midwives and provide the nourishment that our souls need during this time of transformation. It is our hope that this book will serve as a beacon of light to those who are seeking truth and understanding on deeper levels.

Although paradigm shifts can be a slow process, people are beginning to wake up to the realization that they have been denied access to the other half of their humanity. However, many feminist theologians, and even some mainstream theologians, agree that it can take years of living with images of the Goddess before the feminine face of god settles fully into human consciousness.

Much attention has and will continue to be given to this topic in the various strata of society, yet it is important to evoke a reawakening of the Goddess through art and religious symbolism as these media can trigger on an unconscious level a universal, archetypal remembrance of the Goddess. Since we are on the verge of a major breakthrough in the evolution of human consciousness, it is important to get as many images before the public as possible, for art is her most powerful form of communication and has the potential to spark an initial awakening.

The lack of Goddess imagery is an obvious sign that her embers are weak in the West. While the majority of Westerners are still unaware of the Divine Feminine, there is a wave of awakening that is rekindling the flame of Her eternal essence. The Goddess is ringing true in our hearts, as if we are motherless children who on some deep level always suspected that if humanity was truly created in God's image there should have been both a Father and a Mother involved in the original act of creation. On some deep, unconscious level, many of us have been longing for something that calls to be remembered. We've sensed that something has been missing, that there is an enormous imbalance, but we've not been able to discern what it is. I'm convinced the Great Mother is the missing link and that we have all had a long-lost love affair with her compassionate and loving essence.

While the re-emergence of the Goddess will inevitably cause many to change some of their deepest held beliefs, it is important not to go from one extreme to the other such that we abandon our understandings and love for the Father. While the pendulum may need to swing more in Her direction to counterbalance the overemphasis on the masculine principle and its war-like effects on our society, the Mother's return is meant to fulfill the divine partnership within human consciousness so that we can move into a new paradigm—a consecrated polarity between the masculine and feminine principles. The purpose of this book is to transcend either/or positions so that we can begin to cultivate balance and harmony. Whether you are ready to embrace the Mother's teachings or not, She is an essential part of the Godhead. We simply have yet to fully acknowledge her role in the Divine Plan. We are indeed undergoing the most extensive paradigm shift in consciousness that this planet has ever known. This shift needs a certain critical mass, a merging of complexity, crisis and consciousness in order to awaken. It is now happening. May you have the eyes and the ears to receive Her message of love and wisdom within these pages.

Feminine Mysticism in Art

Artists Envisioning the Divine reveals a myriad of ways contemporary visionary artists and mystics have experienced the direct, mystical experience of the Goddess and ultimate reality through various modes of knowing. This book is an attempt to explore on a deeper level the spiritual, mystical realms of the Sacred Feminine through art, creation, nature, meditation, prayer, relationship and community.

The intention for this book stems from the heart of feminine mysticism--a deep passion to experience the feminine face of God through various levels of awareness; physical, emotional, mental and spiritual. While some of these experiences have occurred through religious institutions, most did not. They are mysterious, immanent experiences that originated in the heart of the individual as they were engaged in various creative endeavors. They give us a glimpse of the transcendent mystery beyond this universe and present us with a different reality and truth than we ordinarily experience in everyday life.

To better clarify what I mean by feminine mysticism, I am referring to a spiritual movement devoted to the re-enchantment of the feminine principle or the feminine side of God. Mysticism is meditation, prayer, creativity or theology focused on the direct experience of union with Divinity, God or Ultimate Reality. This unity with the Divine is the heart of all mystical teaching. It is awareness of non-duality and non-separation, of no distance between your self, the ultimate mystery and all other beings.

Feminine mysticism is a spiritual movement devoted to the re-enchantment of the feminine principle or feminine side of God. It is a spiritual journey that has been lost to many Westerners but is beginning to resurface in various ways. The great treasures associated with feminine mysticism are a part of a universal mystical tradition, and our evolution as a human species depends on our willingness to not only integrate them into our own experience as spiritual beings, but to honor them as gifts from the Great Mother.

In the past thirty years, scholars from various disciplines have documented the ancient cultures and religions of the Goddess and the ways in which these had been intentionally subjugated by the patriarchal religions of Judaism, Christianity and Islam. The most concrete evidence we have that recounts the demise of the Goddess cultures can be found in the archeological record. Marija Gimbutas's archeological studies have given the highest scientific authority to our knowledge of ancient Goddess civilizations. Her book, originally published in 1974 with the title *The Gods and Goddesses of Old Europe: 7000 to 3500 B.C., Myths Legends and Cult Images*, [3] provided a full iconographic lexicon of pre-patriarchal images and symbols.

By examining the surviving historical evidence, it has been ascertained that God was conceived of as female for at least the first 200,000 years of human life on Earth, a far longer reign than that of the patriarchy. Archeological, mythological and historical evidence all reveal that for thousands of years matriarchal religions and patriarchal societies existed simultaneously in Old Europe, and that over a long period of time matriarchal or "pagan" religions were the victims of centuries of persecution and suppression by warlike patriarchal societies, usually referred to as Indo-Europeans, which imposed their male-dominated hierarchy and the worship of their sky gods on Goddess cultures wherever they settled.

Gimbutas summed up the difference between the two cultural systems: "The first was matrifocal, sedentary, peaceful, art-loving, Earth and sea-bound; the second was patrifocal, mobile, warlike, ideologically sky oriented, and indifferent to art." [4] Continuing waves of suppression by Indo-European culture eventually put an end to the Old European Goddess cultures roughly between 4300 and 2800 B.C., changing from matrilineal to patrilineal cultural traditions. As a result of continual suppression, the Goddess religions went underground or were assimilated into Indo-European culture, but the old European sacred images and symbols were never totally eradicated. "Many of these symbols are still present as images in our art and literature, powerful motifs in our myths, and archetypes in our dreams." [5]

While there is speculation as to whether matrifocal societies were truly egalitarian, Gimbutas as well as an assortment of other archeologists profess that they were, since no archaeological, historical, or anthropological evidence can be found for any widespread female dominant cultures in which males were oppressed. Gimbutas suggests that Old European culture was "matrifocal"—that is, woman-centered—and matrilineal, where descent was through the mother. However, it's important to note that woman-centered does not imply a matriarchy that is the opposite of patriarchy, a society in which one gender exercised power at the expense of the other. As Gimbutas notes, "The Goddess-centered art, with its striking absence of images of warfare and male domination, reflects a social order in which women as heads of clans or queen-priestesses played a central part." [6]

Archeologist Merlin Stone, in her book *When God was a Woman*,[7] explains that studies of indigenous cultures over the last few centuries have led to the realization that some indigenous peoples did not yet possess the understanding of the relationship between sex and conception. Thus, the concepts of paternity and fatherhood would not yet have been understood. Though probably accompanied by various mythical explanations, babies were simply born from women. If this were the case, the mother would have been seen as the singular parent of her family, the lone producer of the next generation. There are a number of theories and lines of evidence that speculate as to whether or not matrilineal cultures were indeed egalitarian. However, if this theory is indeed correct, one might be led to assume that in putting the Goddess on a pedestal as the creator of life, men could have been reduced to mere protectors of her powers.

The historical shift from matrifocal cultures to patriarchal cultures is, in my opinion, one of the most fascinating shifts in human history. While the transformation is fascinating and worthy of investigation, it is perhaps better left to more academic endeavors. There are a number of feminist thealogians, mystics, artists and scholars who have made enormous contributions to the women's spirituality movement and interspirituality movement and have laid a solid foundation for this book. I am greatly indebted to them for pioneering a path through education and a fierce commitment to truth and justice. The brilliant work of Carl Jung, Robert Briffault, Carole Christ, Charlene Spretnak, Marija Gimbutas, Rianne Eisler, Mary Daly, Jean Shinoda Bolen, Mircea Eliade, Judy Chicago, Vicki Noble, Mary Beth Edleson, AfraShe Asungi, Betty La Duke, June Singer, Gloria Orenstein, Elinor Gadon, Starhawk and Anne Baring (to name just a few) has made this book possible.

The impetus to organize this book was in many ways inspired by the visionary efforts of the Feminist Art Movement. As feminist and art historian Gloria Orenstein noted in her influential article, *Recovering Her Story: Feminist Artists Reclaim the Great Goddess,* [8] the reclamation of the Goddess was situated at the heart of the second wave of the feminist movement (1970s to the present) as well as within the newly developed field of women's studies scholarship. Several feminist artists of the 1970s, such as Judy Chicago, Ana Mendieta, Mary Beth Edelson, Donna Henes, Betye Saar, Penny Slinger, AfraShe Asungi, Max Dashu, Karen Vogel, and Betsy Damon, attempted to reclaim the ancient Great Goddess through images, rituals and performance art in an effort to reestablish a female perspective that has long been absent in world religions. The Goddesses in these works embodied images of women of power in domains other than those traditionally associated with stereotypic femininity in the West. Instead of images of women as mothers or in domestic roles, we see women of power in religious roles, as warriors, as athletes, Earth workers, as political leaders and as symbols of compassion and creativity.

The Heart of Mysticism: The Inter-Spiritual Age

In alignment with the philosophy of the Inter-Spiritual Age, this book is intended to assist humanity in our ability to move beyond religious exclusivism so that we can be re-united in the heart of mysticism, the common thread that weaves together a myriad of spiritual perspectives. While the majority of the book is devoted to the Goddess, it is not our intention to promote paganism or goddess worship as the only way to Truth. On the contrary, this book acknowledges a myriad of spiritual perspectives and spiritual paths, all of which make up the ultimate One. As contemporary mystic Wayne Teasdale so brilliantly put it, "We require a spirituality that promotes the unity of the human family, not one that further divides us or maintains old antagonisms. The truth itself is big enough to include our diversity of views. They are all based on authentic inner experience, and so are all valid. The direct experience of inter-spirituality paves the way for a universal view of mysticism--that is the common heart of the world." [9]

The mystical tradition which underpins all genuine faith is the living source of religion itself. Everything stems from mysticism, whether it comes in the form of revelation or a mystical state of consciousness. The heart of mysticism and spirituality embraces the paradoxical belief that truth is both relative and absolute. In other words, truth is the unification of a diversity of perspectives (unity in diversity) and acknowledges the jewels of truth in an assortment of spiritual traditions across the globe. When multiplicity is valued, diverse perspectives complement and augment each other, each lending a facet of the truth, an aspect of reality, an equally valid experience of the world. Each adds another color to the rainbow of life. Many mystics teach that understanding the relativity of knowledge is the highest task of the rational intellect. But there is one step beyond that. There is an intuitive level of understanding that is responsible for mystical or transcendent experiences that allow us a glimpse of Oneness in the cosmos—a oneness that all spiritual paths teach is the love that connects us with the vast matrix of life.

Aldous Huxley in his book, *The Perennial Philosophy*,[10] examines an assortment of spiritual traditions and reveals how Hindu, Taoist, Buddhist, Islamic, Pagan and Christian mystics all describe the human spiritual essence united with the divine Ground of All Being. In other words, at the core of the world's great religions there is a common thread of universal truth, which is the heart of mysticism. Thus, as Wayne Teasdale and the Dali Lama have already confirmed, we might say that inter-spirituality—the sharing of ultimate experiences across traditions—is the religion of the third millennium. "Inter-Spirituality is the foundation that can prepare the way for a planet-wide enlightened culture, and a continuing community among the religions that is substantial, vital and creative."[11]

There is certainly much to reflect upon, and a multitude of ways to perceive the divine. The diversity of perspectives is indeed a beautiful thing; however, problems arise when the human ego claims that its world view is absolute truth, when in fact it is only a small piece of the puzzle. Anytime a particular world view, such as science or religion, claims it has absolute authority on knowledge and truth, people should be extremely suspect since, as the saying goes, "absolute power corrupts absolutely." Since there are a diversity of perspectives within the Christian tradition and the disciplines of science as well as alternative movements and new paradigms emerging within the scientific disciplines, it is difficult to make any broad generalizations about those fields. Yet both ideological systems have had an enormous amount of power to define the very foundations of life and truth as we know it. In the third millennium, a clear understanding of science's limitations is developing, and most scientists, particularly the cutting edge ones, realize this truth.

We currently live in a culture where the greatest portion of intellectual and scientific thought continues to be dominated by the scientific method. Prior to the Enlightenment of the seventeenth and eighteenth centuries, institutionalized religion in the Western world had maintained its stronghold as "truth bearer." But in the development of the rational sciences, particularly classical physics and mechanistic science, the most dramatic split from religion occurred. The scientific method, or empiricism, which is knowledge based on factual evidence received through the five senses, came to be seen as the only way in which truth could be known.

There is a healthy skepticism inherent within science that is necessary and shouldn't be overlooked. However, when disbelief becomes so severe that it strips humanity of deeper meaning and purpose, it becomes counterproductive and potentially even dangerous, as evidenced by the state of the Earth today. The mechanistic, materialistic world view proposed by predominantly male scientists asserts that the entire universe and the miraculous biodiversity of our natural world are the result of a series of accidents. Furthermore, human beings are nothing more than a machine composed of material elements. Persons are thus reduced to mere sub-patterns of an inherently meaningless and purposeless universe so that when a person dies, there is no soul, spirit or afterlife. What exists in the material, empirical world is all that there is, and all information that exists in the invisible, non-material world cannot be used in the construction of knowledge. Therefore, any information that cannot be objectively, rationally and/or systematically known—concepts such as soul, the unconscious, intuition and the emotions—was deemed illusionary. The mechanistic and materialistic view of nature was a denial of divine immanence in nature as well as any natural immanence of God in the human mind, since nothing can be present in the mind except what enters through the physical senses.

Religion, like science, still continues to have a powerful influence on the way we define the world in the West. "Christianity and Islam are the two largest religious communities in the world, with some 1.8 billion adherents. Together, Christians and Muslims make up almost one-half of the world's population."[12] Looking back through the history of Christianity, we find that it has been used in both positive and negative ways. History reveals the ways in which noble acts of love, self-sacrifice and service to others have been rooted in deeply held religious world views that have been used for positive social change.

At the same time, religion has also been associated with the worst examples of human behavior. Muslims, Christians and Jews who advocate rigid exclusivism, such that their religion is the only truth and all others must be banished, do a great disservice to the possibilities for world unity and peace. Ironically, as professor of religion Charles Kimball revealed in his book *When Religion Becomes Evil*, "These tenets often feed attitudes and actions that are diametrically opposed to the heart of the religion being espoused."[13] Church history reveals continually the gap between the ideal, as exemplified by the teachings of Jesus, and the way Christians have lived and actually behaved. It has been said that more wars have been waged, more people killed, and these days more evil perpetrated in the name of religion than by any other institutional force in human history.

At this point in time, Westerners are beginning to wake up and see the shadow sides of both science and Christianity, particularly fundamentalism. However, most people acknowledge the functional role that religion and science have played in Western culture. Rather than throw the baby out with the bath water, the majority of Westerners acknowledge the value of religious and scientific traditions, even though they sense that there might be more to life than has yet been presented by either of those traditions. At this point in human history we have evolved into highly intelligent beings, and science and religion have contributed to human evolution in positive ways. On the other hand, humanity is also devolving at an accelerated rate as a result of the prevalence of old paradigms within the scientific community and traditional Judeo-Christian communities.

It has become evident to many that we are on a suicide mission that at times feels unstoppable—the denial and resistance to change seems too immense to tackle at this point in time. We have been so heavily conditioned with and bombarded by patriarchal religious fundamentalism and orthodox science that people don't seem to know what to believe anymore. To make matters worse, there is a growing fatalistic awareness that we might be doomed as a species and planet unless we have a radical change of consciousness. We now face the potential damage to our planet and ourselves in the form of nuclear and environmental threats such as toxic wastes, pollution, global warming and destruction of the Ozone layer—all made possible as the outgrowth of a masculine-oriented science and technology that have become synonymous with progress.

The process of dissecting patriarchal ideologies, such as mechanistic science and Judeo-Christianity, in order to glean the jewels of truth from the cancer of arrogance and fear is going to be a long and complicated process. Keepers of the Goddess's flame are up against resistance born of an entrenched and volatile patriarchal social structure that continues to benefit a certain small segment of society, especially the power elite. Furthermore, the process of deconstruction will be extremely complicated, as many of us will be forced to question the very hand that feeds us; meaning our jobs and security could be at stake. Immersion in the constructed knowledge of patriarchy is extremely difficult to recognize as such, especially when it is all that you have ever known. Many of us have had to completely reprogram ourselves, which has been a constant process of reconstructing our deepest-held values and beliefs.

As more women's voices are heard and validated, we have been able to unite and challenge the hegemony of masculine objectives and their authority over truth, power, women and minorities. After thousands of years of patriarchal warrior cultures that have ravaged and polluted the Earth, She is beginning to break down. To make matters worse, there is a growing feminization of poverty worldwide, which describes the trend by which women represent an increasing proportion of the poor, especially in the Third World where women's livelihoods and lands are being taken from them. Between the demise of nature and the gross exploitation of women and minorities, Western culture is in for some serious trouble if it does not wake up and start respecting the Goddess and all that She represents.

It seems that the more intelligent and evolved we become, the more we realize how little we actually know. This is actually a very humble place to be. As humans we can detect parts and pieces of the vast whole, but neither the rational mind nor any single ideological system is capable of fully grasping the concept of absolute truth. Intuitively we have the capability of sensing the vast oneness of creation through an assortment of mediums such as meditation and creativity, but at some point we have to admit our inability to comprehend the Great Mystery. Yet in our growing respect for the ways of the Goddess, perhaps we can allow her the dignity of her mysteries while working towards treating Her with greater care.

About the Sacred Art and Writings

For thousands of centuries, art has been a way for humankind to better understand itself and the world at large. While some art is more representative of the physical, material world around us, there is a particular kind of art that forces the viewer to envision a dimension beyond the material word. This type of art, otherwise known as transcendental art, satisfies a deep need for spirituality within the viewer, and thus has powerful transformative qualities. The sacred images in this book fall into the broad category of transcendental art, as they have the capacity to evoke visionary or mystical experiences in the viewer. However, the images also fall into other genres such as goddess art, eco-feminist art, magical realism, surrealism, shamanism, fantastic and visionary art.

The art and writing in this book are of superb quality. The artwork alone is unique, exquisite, political and provocative, communicating a message of hope for the post modern era. It is important to note that my emphasis was definitely on representational art as opposed to abstract art. Also, because my expertise is in painting, the majority of contributors are painters, but there are a few photographers and graphic designers in the mix. In addition, the diversity of writings and poetry by experts in women's spirituality, mysticism, eco-feminism, mythology, transcendental art and transpersonal psychology provide a conceptual foundation for the images. Susan and I were looking for mystical writings with creative flair that engaged the reader. Some of the writings are more intellectually challenging, while others are written with a language of the heart that is easy to absorb.

In a culture that is becoming more and more art illiterate and left brain oriented, it was important to use concepts and words to help people understand the sacred imagery. However, rational modes of knowing weren't championed over intuitive modes of knowing in choosing the images. Traditionally, western science has tended to stress the importance of rationality and objectivity as a source of knowledge. As a result, feelings, intuition and mystical experiences have been underemphasized as a valid source of knowledge because they are perceived as vague, inherently subjective qualities of thinking.

In our attempt to explore and envision the divine through concepts and words, we found that mysticism inevitably lies beyond the grasp of reason and beyond the limits of language to describe its ineffable and elusive nature. Since there are innumerable things beyond the range of human understanding, we often have to use symbolic language, such as mythology and art, to represent concepts that we cannot define or fully comprehend. We need forms, symbols and images to help us relate to the divine, as they are the universal language of the soul. This is one reason why all religions rely on mythological language and sacred symbolism; they are much less restricted by logic and therefore serve a vital role in their ability to instantly trigger people on emotional and spiritual levels.

When viewing the images inside these pages, we predict a number of responses to occur, ranging from disgust to utter reverence. All of these are valid responses. Some might accuse us of worshipping false idols. These kinds of responses occur because we have no reference for the Divine Mother in our minds. How can we feel reverence for something that we have never known? If you really think about it, our brains have no way of making sense of the information being thrown at us, simply because we have no concept of who She is, and our Judeo-Christian backgrounds might even predispose us to fear or even hate Her.

Furthermore, when reading about the mystical experiences in this book, we ask that you come with a beginner's mind and tread lightly in your judgments about these ineffable experiences. The unpredictable, spontaneous and subjective nature of intuitive, mystical experiences, coming as sudden flashes, can't always be broken down into its component parts to be studied; however, this doesn't negate its validity. It is important that we honor mystical experiences as a valuable source of knowledge even if we don't always have the words to describe them.

We are all created for the spiritual journey and have the capacity to feel the incredible gifts of the mystical connection, and it is important that we open the space to share these experiences with one another in a non-critical way. Not only will voicing these experiences serve as a source of validation and courage to those who still question their transcendental nature, they will also help to shine some light on these experiences so they can grow and evolve in a healthy way. Our mystical experiences deserve to be honored, for they are our lifeline to God.

How This Book Was Created

When I think about how this book evolved over the years and all the magical synchronicities that happened along the way, I could easily write another book about how it was created. However, for purposes of this introduction, I will summarize it briefly and leave the rest for the documentary.

The impetus to do this book project began in Flagstaff, Arizona, after six years of study in the sociology of art, gender and women's spirituality. I did my thesis research on Women Artists and Identity Formation at Northern Arizona University, which is being compiled in another book. At that time, I had also been delving into my own creative process and started bringing through archetypal imagery of the Goddess that I didn't totally understand at the time.

One afternoon I was taking a nap and had a powerful dream about the Muse who was summoning me to bring enchantment and mysticism to the world. I quickly jolted out of bed as if hit over the head, and asked Great Spirit what the dream meant. After meditating on it for a while, the message was clear. I was to publish an art book that documented a genre of contemporary Goddess art. It was also clear that this book wasn't going to be my vision alone, but was to include the creative voices of other artists and mystics.

I immediately went to the computer, wrote a rough book proposal and began contacting women artists in my area. Upon interviewing several female visionary artists in the Southwest, it was evident that we were all being summoned for a very important mission—to bring powerful images of the Goddess into the world so that we could complement the masculine energies and eventually create a new paradigm of peace and harmony on Earth.

Similar to the creative process, the book evolved over time, and different artists brought unique pieces of the larger story that I could never have fathomed on my own. I was later introduced to several male visionary artists, such as Mark Henson, Paul Heussenstamm, Daniel Holeman, Carey Thompson, Amoraea Dreamseed and Andrew Annenberg, all of whom were bringing the Goddess through powerfully in their art. I realized it was imperative to bring these male voices on board as well, since the Great Mother is reaching out to men just as strongly as she is speaking to women. Furthermore, the male voices in this book are essential, since She wants to reach a large male audience because they are the ones who need to witness the Goddess in Her myriad forms the most. This project desperately needed men who were aligned with emancipation and have experienced the benefits that come from integrating their own feminine sides, for these are the men who will serve as powerful leaders and spiritual mentors to those who are still asleep.

Another impetus to publish this book is to expose the blatant denial and subjugation of visionary art and artists in the conventional art world and society at large. Upon talking with a number of artists (both male and female) and other laypersons, it has been confirmed that a large number of people are highly disillusioned by the art world and its overall lack of socially redeeming art—more specifically, spiritual or transcendental art. Ironically, this dominant trend in the art world directly contradicts current social research that reveals that many people in the United States are in search of deeper meaning and spirituality in their lives. While some are seeking out traditional organized religions, many people are longing for alternative forms of spirituality because they don't resonate with the exclusivity and narrow conceptualization of God that some organized religions embrace.

In response to the larger spiritual malaise in the art world, visionary artists have had to find alternative routes to get their work noticed by a large population of people. Artist Alex Grey realized early on that the traditional gallery route was not his path. Rather than sacrifice his principles and morals, he knew he would have to carve out a path for himself. He recognized that new movements in the arts create friction, just as the introduction of new paradigms in science challenge the existing scientific establishment. Unfortunately, not all art critics and gallery directors are tuned-in to these new movements in art, despite the power they wield as gatekeepers into the elite art circles.

One would assume that the art world would be acceptant of a broad definition of art, simply because the very nature of art is so diverse and expansive. However, just like any discipline, there is usually a dominant paradigm that governs. And while these gatekeepers may have some valid knowledge of art, often it is a narrow definition of art that's chosen for its cosmetic suitability. The conventional art world has negatively labeled visionary art as "outsider art." In other words, it is art that goes against the grain of the traditional art world and therefore doesn't get much gallery space or attention in the media. In my opinion, the fact that it challenges the status quo makes it all the more authentic and potent. A true artist is one who has the courage to challenge old paradigms in art and push the boundaries of the imagination and creativity. I think you will find that we do that quite well in this book.

As pioneers of the transcendental art movement, the contributors to this book felt it was necessary to join forces with all the other brave artists who have refused to strip themselves and their art of spiritual meaning. Because some of the more powerful images in this book have been censored by various galleries, museums and media publications, it was imperative that we combine our individual artistic missions and publish the map, so to speak. We quickly realized that the opportunity to do so was not going to come to us; thus, we needed to carve out an alternative route for ourselves in order to reach those who thirst for sacred art, particularly images of the Goddess.

About the DVD

This colorful and inspirational animation of transcendental art, synchronized to uplifting music, is a stunning collaboration of artwork by over fifty contemporary visionary artists from an assortment of spiritual traditions. The purpose of the DVD is not only to document a genre of art referred to as feminine mysticism, but also to reveal powerful images of the Divine in his/her myriad forms. The DVD gives the reader more of the genre, as we couldn't publish all the images in one book, and includes inspirational music as well.

The musicians include Sasha Butterfly Rose, Elijah and the Band of Light, Kan' Nal, Montana Soul, Heather Noel, Prema Mayi, Duane Light and Susan Garret and Nancy Bloom.

The DVD was released to market in 2007 and has sold over 1,000 copies. It is currently being distributed by Amazon. The DVD is now on tour and is being used for promotional purposes at spiritual conferences and sacred music/art festivals around the world, such as Dance International, The Glastonbury Goddess Festival, The Gaia Festival, The Oregon Country Fair, The Harmony Festival, Faerie Worlds, Burning Man, Women of Wisdom Conference and many more.

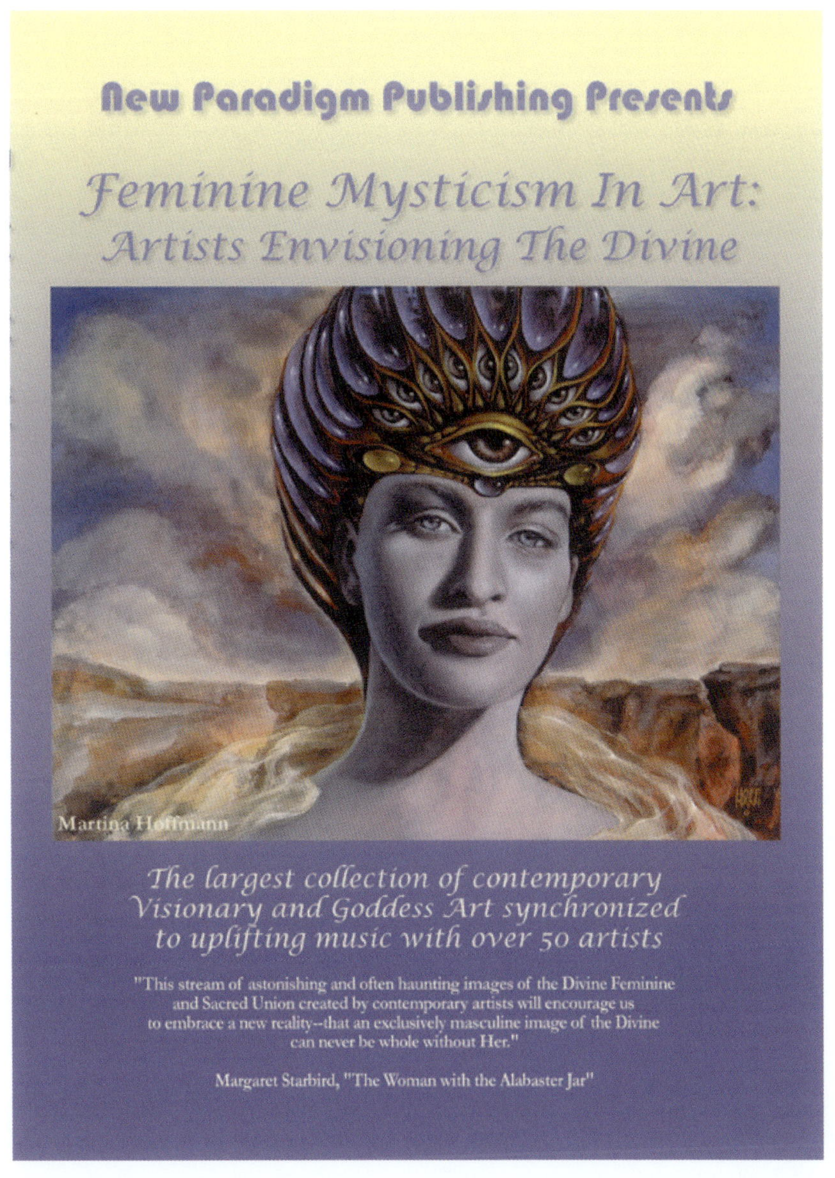

PART ONE:

The Primordial Sacred Union

The Loss Of The World Soul and Its Return

World Soul, Robin Baring, 24″x24″ oil on canvas, www.annebaring.com

By Anne Baring

Once upon a time, in a past so distant that we have no memory of it, the invisible and visible dimensions of life were imagined and instinctively experienced as a sacred unity. In the great civilizations of the Bronze Age (c.3000 BCE), particularly those of Egypt, India and China, the whole cosmos was envisioned as a living being and the manifest world was seen as an epiphany or showing forth of an unseen source which breathed it into being, animating and sustaining it. The air itself was experienced as the invisible presence of that world—an "awesome mystery joining the human and extrahuman worlds."[1] Just as the stars emerged each night from the darkness of the night sky, so the visible universe was born from the dark mystery of the invisible. Everything—plants, trees, animals and birds as well as moon, sun and stars—was infused with divinity because each and all were part of a living, breathing web of life.

Although this ancient way of knowing was once experienced in many different places (and may still be found today), Egypt has bequeathed to us one of the clearest images of it. Two goddesses were of particular significance for an understanding of the origins of the later concept of a World Soul: Hathor—often interchangeable with Isis—and Nut. Hathor was Egypt's oldest goddess, imagined as the nurturing Mother of the universe and as the creative impulse flowing from the cosmic immensity of her being. More specifically, Hathor was imagined as the Milky Way, whose milk nourished all life, yet she was

> *"You could not discover the boundaries of the soul, even if you travelled by every path in order to do so, so deep a measure does it have."*
>
> —Heraclitus

immanent within the forms of life, immanent in the statues that stood in her temples and in the beautiful blue lotus that was daily laid at her feet. As Divine Mother, she received the souls of the dead at the entrance to her sacred mountain.

Visionary artist Jonathan Weber created a powerful painting titled *Isis* (Hathor) sitting on a gold thrown, nursing her baby. Two magnificent lions with eyes of gold lay at her side, protecting her from harm. On her head she wears bull horns, a symbol of fertility. Behind her a Phoenix bird rises from the ashes, symbolizing the rebirth of the Goddess in human consciousness.

Nut was the night sky, whose vast cosmic body contained all the stars. The sun vanished into her body on its nightly descent into the underworld and was reborn from her at the dawn of a new day. Nut's image was painted on the inside of coffin lids and sometimes on the base as well, as if to enfold the soul entrusted to her care in her cosmic embrace. A moving inscription to her on a fragment of stone in the Louvre reads:

> *O my mother Nut, stretch your wings over me;*
> *Let me become like the imperishable stars,*
> *like the indefatigable stars*
> *O Great Being who is in the world of the Dead,*
> *at whose feet is Eternity, in whose hand is the*
> *Always,*
> *O Great Divine Beloved Soul who is in the mysterious abyss, come to me.*[2]

Presided over by the Great Mother, this era was characterised by a consciousness which participated in the deepest imaginative sense with the life of the cosmos and the life of the Earth. It was a fundamentally different way of perceiving and relating to life than the one we have now. Today we look back on our "superstitious" past with some contempt, not realising that our present consciousness has grown out of a far more ancient and instinctive way of knowing.

That knowing could be described as lunar, because the moon rather than the sun was of supreme importance in that distant time. It is possible that the image of a world or cosmic soul arose out of lunar mythology because

Isis, Jonathan Weber, 24‴x30″ oil on canvas, www.jonathanweber.org

the moon was our earliest teacher and the inspiration of some of the greatest myths of the ancient world: the Egyptian myth of Isis and Osiris, the Sumerian myth of the Descent of Inanna, the Orphic and Eleusinian Mysteries of Greece, and the later Christian myth all carry the same lunar theme of death and regeneration.[3]

We are just beginning to recognize the magnitude of profound wisdom brought forth during Egypt's greatness. Rich in culture, Egypt inspired artists and mystics to ponder the elusive, ethereal quality of the soul. Fascinated by the ancient mysteries of Egypt, Andrew Annenberg painted a master-work titled *Egyptian Enigma.* One of today's foremost visionary artists, Andrew is acclaimed for his meticulous detail, imagination and wit. He merges elements of architecture, archeology, mythology and mysticism into a mandala-like composition. Andrew describes his painting:

> *A timeless mystery is revealed in Egyptian Enigma as gateways to super-consciousness are opened. From the center of the world, the temple of time emerges, energizing the sacred structures of ancient Egypt. A prime focus for this civilization was to bring about fourth dimensional consciousness through the cosmos and etheric force fields, which they believed lifted mortal man out of his profane nature and into the sacred realms of consciousness. Egyptian Enigma is a gateway into a land where spirit and matter converge, where time and space effortlessly melt away, opening the doors to a transcendent realm of pure soul bliss.* [4]

Ancient Egyptian culture and so many others the world over have an important message for postmodern civilization. They are suggesting that we reclaim the ancient wisdoms of lunar consciousness so that we can come back to a state of balance and harmony. If this is the case, what does the moon have to teach us? The emergence of the crescent moon from the three days of darkness that preceded it gives us the image of the visible world emerging from an invisible one, the time-bound world from an eternal one. The moon nourished the creative imagination, teaching us to observe and to wonder, helping us to make connections between what was above in the heavens and what was below on Earth – a theme that is carried through into Hermetic philosophy and Alchemy.

For hundreds of generations, people watched the circumpolar movement of the stars and the changing yet stable course of the luminous moon. They observed the connection between the cyclical rhythm of the four phases of the moon's life and the rhythm of growth, maturation, death and regeneration in the life of the crops. They experienced the phases of their own lives – childhood, youth, maturity, elder hood and death – as woven into the rhythm of that greater life. The constant return of the crescent moon after three days of darkness laid the foundation for trust in the survival of the soul and the renewal of life after apparent death, and may have been the original inspiration for the belief in reincarnation. From this lunar pattern constantly speaking to the mythic imagination, birth and death became a rite of passage for the soul as it journeyed to and from the visible and invisible dimensions of life, a journey that was symbolised by the path through a labyrinth. The ancestors were not lost to the living but were close by, available to counsel and guide. Therefore, no final demarcation line between life and death existed.

The constant rhythm of the moon waxing and waning held both light and darkness in balance to each other, because the totality of the moon's cycle embraced both light and dark phases and therefore symbolically included both life and death. Light and darkness were not polarised as they were later to become in a solar culture, but were phases of the total cycle, so that always an image of a unifying whole which included both polarities prevailed.

Over countless thousands of years, shamanic rituals and myths kept alive the sense of connection between this world and another world. Poets, artists, philosophers and musicians received their inspiration from the invisible dimension that Henri Corbin, the great scholar of Sufism, named the *mundus imaginalis* (imaginal world), carefully drawing the distinction between the imaginal and the imaginary.[5] The words spoken, the music heard, the dreams and visions seen, came not from "inside" us, but from the cosmos, from goddesses and gods, from daemonic beings and the spirits of animals. The original role of the philosopher was a shamanic one—to journey to the Otherworld or Underworld and bring back what was seen and heard to help the human community harmonize its life with the sacred life of the cosmos. Fairy tales like Sleeping Beauty may be the residual fragments of that forgotten participatory experience where forests were inhabited by creatures who would help or hinder us; where spirits of tree and mountain, stream and sacred spring could speak to us; where bears or frogs might be princes in disguise and shamans living in the deep forest might offer us wise counsel, or birds bring us messages and warn us of dangers. There are countless tales which describe how the hero or heroine who responds to this guidance wins the reward of the treasure

Egyptian Enigma, Andrew Annenberg, 60"x60" oil on canvas, www.andrewannenberg.com

and the royal marriage.

Ancient Celtic mythologies speak of a time when magic abounded and the spirits of the Earth made themselves known. Much of Celtic mythology is captured in folklore, music and art, revealing a rich and mysterious history. Perhaps one of the most epic pieces of Celtic Lore is by Andrew Annenberg titled *The Enchantment.* The painting combines elements of lore, symbolism and mysticism, all woven in an exquisite tapestry of wonderment.

Ancient Celtic people honored the fairy realms because they were an important part of the maintenance of nature, bestowing magical blessings and harmonious delights unto humans and the natural world. They walked between the worlds and vibrated at a high frequency. The Celtic people would give offerings at sacred springs hoping they would bless their crops with nourishment. They would await the annual procession of nature spirits as they made their journey through the land during equinoxes and solstices. Most of the knowledge about these precious beings has been lost to us, but some of the ancient sites speak of the magic of a bygone day, when humans and the spirits of nature walked in harmony to prosper the Earth. It has been said that the faerie spir-

The Enchantment, Andrew Annenberg, 60" x 60 " oil on canvas www.andrewannenberg.com

its still roam the Earth and make themselves known to those with a childlike spirit. They love children as their hearts are still pure and open to receiving magic. However, they can only roam in places on Earth that have a strong heart vibration.

Other ancient cultures performed shamanic rituals. For example, Orphic and Eleusinian Mysteries in Greece strengthened the sense of participation in an unseen reality and gave initiates an experience of the immortality of the soul. People spoke with goddesses and gods in dream and vision. Birds were recognised as messengers of the invisible, very possibly because people dreamed about them in this role or even heard them as a voice inside themselves, speaking to them. Intuitive sensibility and the ability to communicate with the spirits of plants taught people to gather, grind or distill certain herbs and plants for healing illnesses.

Rites of incubation and healing were practised in many sanctuaries. Dreams and visions were of great importance in the diagnosis and healing of disease. Music was used to invoke the presence of a world that was the foundation of this world and as real as this one; everything was connected, everything was sacred. The shaman-healers who guided these cultures were trained to enter a state of utter stillness and listen and observe what they heard and saw in an altered state of consciousness. This lunar culture was primarily feminine in character—receptive to the presence of the eternal.

This, therefore, is the foundation upon which the concept of a World Soul developed. Plato (429-347 bce) was the first to name it as such in his *Timaeus*. Was it from the participatory experience of an earlier age that he drew his concept of the Soul of the World – *psyche tou kosmou?* He speaks of a great golden chain of being connecting the deepest level of reality with its physical manifestation where every particle of life is a revelation of creative spirit, but there is in his work a distancing of the sensory world from the world of spiritual or archetypal forms.

There is a fading of the feeling of participation in an ensouled world, a disjunction between rational mind and sensory experience, an objective definition of Soul rather than the experience of it so intrinsic to the earlier time. Plotinus (204-70 ce), who was steeped in Platonic thought, developed further the concept of a Universal Soul that he called All-Soul or Soul of the All *(anima mundi)* but in his philosophy as well as in Plato's there is the idea that this material world is the lowest level in the hierarchy of divine emanation.[6] Implicit in this immensely influential definition of reality, is the idea that nature is "lower" than spirit, body "lower" than mind and that animals and plants are "lower" in the scale of being than humans.

Aristotle (384-322 BCE) took this distinction further, defining matter as something inanimate—separate and distinct from spirit and soul – leading eventually to the modern idea that matter is "dead." While Plato and Plotinus had a strong influence on the development of Christian doctrine, the mainstream teaching of Western philosophy and science followed Aristotle. His philosophy draws a clear demarcation line between an ancient way of knowing and a new way whose emphasis is on the rational human mind distancing itself from what it is observing rather than participating in its life.

The increasing separation between these two ways of knowing was henceforth profoundly to influence the development of the philosophy, religion and science of the West. However, the sense of being within an ensouled cosmos lasted until the end of the Middle Ages when the School of Chartres, influenced perhaps by the brilliant Islamic scholars and architects of Moorish Spain, initiated the building of the great cathedrals of France. It found new expression in fifteenth century Florence when Marsilio Ficino translated Plato and recovered the texts of the Hermetic tradition, and it survived in Kabbalah and Alchemy. However, the older vision faded rapidly with the Reformation and the scientific revolution which succeeded it. What was lost was an imaginal, participatory and visionary way of knowing, grounded in shamanic experience.

Having described a lunar culture where people lived within a sacred cosmos, we may ask what wider cultural influences led to the demise of the World Soul? Why did D.H. Lawrence[7] despairingly write, "We have lost the cosmos?" To answer that question we have to look back some 4000 years. From about 2000 BCE, we begin to see developing a new phase in the evolution of human consciousness – a phase whose focus is the sun rather than the moon. As this process develops, solar mythology begins to displace lunar mythology: linear time begins to replace cyclical time, and a linear, literal and objective way of thinking slowly replaces the older imaginal and participatory way of knowing. Concurrently, the human psyche draws away from nature and as it does so, the predominant image of spirit changes from Great Mother to Great Father. The greater the withdrawal from nature, the more transcendent and disengaged from nature becomes the image of deity: divine immanence is lost. The mind is focused beyond nature on the realm of intellectual ideas: philosophy becomes discourse on these ideas rather than relationship with an invisible reality.

A second major influence was the impact of literacy

on our way of thinking. The written word replaced the oral tradition that had carried the wisdom and insights of the older culture. David Abram has shown in his book, *The Spell of the Sensuous,* how the new emphasis on the written word contributed to the loss of the older participatory consciousness: "Only as the written text began to speak would the voices of the forest, and of the river, begin to fade. And only then would language loosen its ancient association with the invisible breath, the spirit sever itself from the wind, the psyche dissociate itself from the environing air." [8]

Perhaps because literacy distanced us from nature, creation in the Judeo-Christian tradition is now believed to arise from the word of the transcendent Father, no longer from the womb of the Mother. This is a crucially important distinction because the unity of life is again broken: invisible spirit no longer animates and inhabits nature. The Earth is desacralised. Religious belief replaces shamanic experience. Ancient ways of connection are forbidden. With this shift in archetypal imagery, everything formerly associated with the feminine archetype (the Great Mother) is downgraded in relation to the masculine one (the Great Father). The lunar way of knowing is subjugated to the solar way and, under the influence of solar mythology, first nature, then cosmos, are ultimately de-souled.

As the sun becomes the new focus of consciousness, the cultural hero is no longer the lunar shaman who ventures into the darkness, assimilating its mysteries and returning from it with the treasure of wisdom, but rather the solar hero, often a king, warrior or outstanding individual, who is celebrated as the one who conquers and overcomes darkness. The emphasis is now on ascent to the light and repudiation of whatever is identified with darkness. Iron Age mythology (from c. 2000 BCE) celebrates a great contest between a hero-god and a dragon or monster of the underworld (see the Epic of Gilgamesh and the Greek myth of Apollo killing the she-dragon at Delphi). Contemporary artist Victoria Christian reveals this well in her image *The Slaying of the Dragon*, which draws meaning from ancient mythology, but brings it into contemporary times. It tells the story of a number of Goddesses from the Bronze and Iron Ages who were slain or made subordinate to the new gods of the patriarchal warriors, and how this has been played out in modern times by the clear-cutting of the forests and other acts that stem from a devaluing of the feminine principle.

Throughout history the myth of the slaying of the Goddess has been interpreted in an assortment of religious traditions and creation myths. However, one of the earliest representations of the slaying of the Goddess is the Babylonian creation myth, the Enuma Elish. In it, the primordial Creatress of Sumerian religion, Tiamat, the Goddess of the Salty Sea, is slain by the new god Marduk. A number of versions of the myth of the slaying of the Goddess can also be found later in Greek mythology. Victoria's painting is based on the story of Apollo's conquest at Delphi, told in the Homeric Hymn "To Pythian Apollo" (C. 700-600 BCE). [9]

Archeological evidence suggests that the Earth Goddess Gaia was worshiped at Delphi, later conquered by the Greek warrior Apollo, who also desecrated the sacred river Telphusa. As Carole Christ reveals, the female dragon, or large snake, and the sacred river are part of the language of the Goddess, and it is clear that the Goddess is the intended victim of the god Apollo. The dragon, often portrayed as a snake-like body, was once the guardian of the shrines of the Earth Mother. Just like the slaying of Tiamet in the Enuma Elish, the story of Apollo's slaying of the dragon was regularly performed at Delphi in a liturgical drama called the Septerion.[10] Victoria describes the motivation for the painting in more detail:

> *In this painting I wanted to capture the pain and agony of thousands of years of patriarchal subjugation of the ancient Goddess religions in one culminating moment of time. I depicted the Earth mother Gaia as a tree, fleeing in terror because the dragon, her last remaining protector, is about to be slain by Apollo. In the background the forest has been clear-cut, completely raped of its sacred beauty and harmony. I painted the trees gold, portraying their sacred value as opposed to being reduced to mere dollar bills. While I understand that trees are a renewable resource, old growth forests are not, and should be protected as if they were precious jewels.*[11]

The theme of conquest and victory becomes the dominating ethos of the hero myths of the Iron Age and so it is even today in our modern hero myth and the battle against "the axis of evil". In this solar phase, good and evil, light and dark, life and death are drawn as opposites inimical to each other and become increasingly polarized. The emphasis is no longer on relationship with the invisible world but on the light conquering the darkness. George W. Bush's words "Those who are not with us are against us" are a modern re-statement of solar mythology.

For over 4000 years, under the influence of this mythology, war and conquest were glorified as the noblest activity for man; victory and the spoils of war the coveted treasure to be won in battle, courage in battle the supreme virtue in the warrior. Wherever today we find the tendency to om-

The Slaying of the Dragon, Victoria Christian, .3' x 4' diptych oil on canvas, www.victoriachristian.com

nipotence and grandiose ambitions of empire and world domination, whether religious or secular, we can discern the influence of solar mythology and the inflation of leaders who unconsciously identify themselves with the archetypal role of the solar god or hero.

Solar mythology reflects an immense change in human consciousness, the formulation of an entirely new perception of life, one where, as technology advances, nature becomes something to be controlled and manipulated by human ingenuity, to human advantage. It had a dramatic influence on Greek, Hebrew, Persian and Christian cultures. The imagery of opposition and conflict between light and darkness, good and evil pervades the Old Testament and other mythologies. As people move to cities and cities become states, and as more and more men are conscripted into armies which obey a warrior leader, the cosmic battle is increasingly projected into the world: a fascination with conquest and dominance possesses the psyche and leads to the creation of vast empires (Assyrian, Persian, Greek, Roman). It is as if the heroic human ego, identified with the solar hero, has to seek out new territories to conquer, has to embody the myth in a literal sense. The terminology of conquest and dominance still influences our own modern culture with its focus on the conquest of nature, of space, of our enemies. It is as if we have been conditioned by this powerful mythology to think only in oppositional terms – victory or defeat—never in terms of dialogue and reconciliation.

Solar mythology is, above all, the story of the heroic individual. In the West, it has been the driving inspiration behind the Promethean quest for freedom, justice, knowledge and power. A major theme of solar myth is escape from the bondage of the body and ascent to the light and, by association, release from the bondage of mortality and ascent to spiritual enlightenment. In the West, we find it first in Plato in his metaphor of the cave. It carries with it the human longing to go beyond all constraints and limitations, to reach higher, progress farther, discover more. It is overwhelmingly male because the male psyche has been the dominant influence in most cultures over some 4000 years and it is the achievements and discoveries of exceptional men which have inspired other men. A strong sense of self and a focused ego, that was ultimately identified with the conscious, rational mind can be acknowledged as the supreme achievement of the male psyche during this solar era. However, the voice of women, who were denied access to education, the priesthood and the healing profession, was silenced throughout this era.

The influence of solar mythology gradually created a fissure between spirit and nature, mind and body which has defined our way of thinking and influenced the way we behave. During this solar phase, the male psyche unconsciously identified itself with the supremacy of spirit and mind over nature, woman and body and came to relate the former to the image of light and order and the latter to the image of darkness and chaos. Woman was named as an inferior creation: woman and body were a danger, a threat, a temptation to man.[12]

The religions of the solar era carry this polarization within their teaching wherever this is associated with the ascetic subjugation of the body, the mistrust of sexuality and the oppression and persecution of women. Because nature and instinct became something dangerous and threatening to the supremacy of the rational mind, much effort was expended in eradicating all vestiges of goddess-worship and of animism or belief in "spirits". Farther to the east, in China, Confucianism replaced the older Taoist vision of an ensouled and conscious nature. The sages of India, with certain exceptions, turned away from the body and sensory experience and held the phenomenal world to be an illusion.

All this had the effect of disconnecting us from nature and denying us access through the mythic imagination to that mysterious and all-embracing dimension of Soul. As the ego and rational mind grew stronger and more powerfully controlling, so, increasingly, did we lose the ability to relate instinctively and imaginatively to Earth and cosmos. The Judeo-Christian myth of the Fall describes this process of estrangement and loss and, in the story of the Expulsion from the Garden, discloses a total reversal of the way of knowing which had guided older cultures.[13]

The shamanic way of knowing survived in Kabbalah and Sufism as well as in certain Gnostic sects, the Hermetic Tradition and Alchemy but for centuries these had to remain hidden for fear of persecution.

With the psychological insight that has become available to us over the last hundred years, particularly through the depth psychology of C.G. Jung, we can understand that this solar phase of our evolution reflects a radical dissociation within the human psyche between the growing strength of the ego (the hero) and the older and greatly feared power of instinct (the dragon).[14]

As this dissociation gathers momentum, so the feeling of containment within a cosmic entity and the sense of relationship with an invisible dimension of reality fades, and with it the participatory consciousness of an earlier time. The legacy of the Platonic and Aristotelian emphasis on reason and the rational mind, together with the solar emphasis on ascent to spirit and light and the deep suspicion of sexuality and sensual experience, hastened the demise of the lunar way of knowing.

The danger of this solar phase is that the human mind, breaking away from its instinctive ground and its relationship with nature and cosmos, begins to assimilate a god-like power to itself, seeing itself engaged in a great struggle to attain mastery of nature. The priceless evolutionary achievement of the solar era and its masculine culture was the emergence of a strong ego from the matrix of instinct and the creation of the conscious, rational mind. But, tragically, this was won at the expense of repressing and denying whatever was perceived as threatening to it. The inner conflict between the two aspects of the psyche was projected into the world as the drive for power and control over others, whether in the religious or political fields.

The influence of solar mythology was to divide life into two halves: spirit and nature, light and dark, good and evil, mind and body, subject and object. These oppositions became fixed in our consciousness as an actual belief system. The solar myth is carried in all ideologies which strive to reach the light and split off the darkness. It entered not only into the sacred texts of Judaism, Christianity and Islam but into our behaviour towards the "dark" and so-called primitive races or anyone different from ourselves. As time went on religions took on the mantle of solar mythology in a struggle for supremacy and are tragically engaged in it to this day: the split between Catholic and Protestant in Christianity and between Shia and Sunni in Islam may be traced to the polarizing influence of this mythology. Finally, it is reflected in the secular totalitarian ideologies which ravaged the last century because these separated the heroic race or "chosen" social group from those they demonized as inferior or expendable. These ideologies justified the elimination of racial or class enemies just as Christianity and Islam had justified the elimination of heretics and apostates.

From this long historical process, it is possible to see that the belief system of scientific reductionism which has so powerfully influenced modern secular culture may be understood as the end-result of the long-standing dissociation between spirit and nature, mind and matter but, above all, the sundering within us of thinking

Land of the Free, Home of the Brave, Mark Henson, 48"x64" oil on canvas, www.markhensonart.com

and feeling, rational mind and instinctive soul – the conscious and unconscious aspects of our nature. It has concluded that the universe is indifferent to us, that we are the products of impersonal forces operating on inanimate matter: atoms are not living elements of divinity but lifeless particles, floating randomly in an inanimate universe. We are the outcome of genetic, social and environmental conditioning. Consciousness is an epiphenomenon of the physical brain: there is no such "thing" as soul; when we die, that is the end of us.

This belief system reflects a situation where we have become so estranged from nature that we believe that we have the right to exploit it for our own material advantage – even the right to control space in order to protect ourselves from attack by our enemies. Although we may profess a belief in God, nothing is sacred save our own survival or the survival of our group and our religion.

To sum up: over the four millennia that solar mythology became the dominant influence on world culture, we have achieved an extraordinary advance in scientific and technological skills and their application to improving the conditions of human life on this planet and a phenomenal expansion of the ability to express ourselves as individuals in myriad different fields of endeavour. But at the same time, we have suffered a catastrophic loss of soul, a loss of the ancient instinctive awareness of the sacred interweaving of all aspects of life, a loss of the sense of participation in the life of nature and the invisible dimension of the cosmos, a loss of instinct and imagination.

So we come to the present day where, in a secular culture, the rational mind has established itself as the supreme value, master of all it surveys, recognizing no power, no consciousness beyond itself. It has lost its connection to soul; not only soul in the individual sense but Soul as a cosmic matrix or field in whose life we participate. In its hubristic stance, the rational mind has become disconnected from the deeper instinctive ground out of which it has evolved which, ultimately, is the life of the cosmos. Cut off from its roots, it stands like a tyrant over and against nature, over and against the Earth, over and against whatever it defines as threatening to its supremacy. This leaves the human heart lonely and afraid and the neglected territory of the soul a barren wasteland. The rage and despair of denied inner needs confront us in the world as the enemies who seek to destroy us and whom we seek to destroy. We struggle to contain the effects of a dysfunctional way of thinking—believing that ever greater power and control will enable us to eradicate the evils we bring into being.

Yet, beneath the surface of our culture, the ancient concept of Soul is returning. The challenge of the immense problems now facing humanity is urging us to change our current understanding of reality and jettison the mechanistic paradigm we have inherited from the secular beliefs which shape the ethos of our culture. A deep human instinct is attempting to restore balance and wholeness in us by articulating values rooted in a different way of knowing: the ecological movement is restoring sacredness to the Earth; compassion is growing for those suffering from poverty, disease and the obscene effects of war; shamanic methods of healing are being recovered; a new image of reality is struggling to be born. We are beginning to understand that we are poisoning the Earth, the seas and our own immune systems with toxic chemicals and pesticides and inviting our destruction as a species through our predatory behaviour. Many individuals are awakening to awareness that we and the phenomenal world that we call nature are woven into a cosmic tapestry whose threads connect us not only with each other at the deepest level but with many dimensions of reality and multitudes of beings inhabiting those dimensions. Beyond the present limits of our sight an immense field of consciousness interacts with our own, asking to be recognised by us, embraced by us.

What is emerging at the cutting edge of science is a grand unified theory of quantum, cosmos, life and consciousness where physics is reunited with metaphysics. As this deep soul-impulse gathers momentum, the "marriage" of the emerging lunar values with the ruling solar ones is changing our perception of reality. The image titled *Lovers,* by visionary artist Mariela de la Paz, eloquently captures the sacred alchemy of lunar and solar wisdoms. If we can recover the ancient way of knowing in a modern context, without losing the priceless evolutionary attainment of a strong and focused ego, we could heal the fissure in our psyches. In the words of D.H. Lawrence, "The great range of responses that have fallen dead in us have to come to life again. It has taken two thousand years to kill them. Who knows how long it will take to bring them to life."[15]

Anne Baring is a writer and retired Jungian analyst, is author and coauthor of five books including *The Myth of the Goddess: Evolution of an Image*, *The Mystic Vision*, *The Divine Feminine*, and a book for children, *The Birds Who Flew Beyond Time*. Anne's website www.annebaring.com explores the deeper issues facing us at this crucial time of choice

The Lovers, Mariela de la Paz, 5'x5' oil on canvas, www.marieladelapaz.com

Artists Envisioning the Primordial Sacred Union

Maha Shri Yantra, Paul Heussenstamm, 24"x24" oil on canvas, www.mandala.com

By Victoria Christian

The profound spirit of the primordial sacred union is just beginning to reemerge in the minds and hearts of a large population of people, despite the fact that it is older than history itself. Mystics have speculated that the primordial sacred union began in a mythic time long before the birth of creation. It is present everywhere and within all things, and is the wellspring from which all creative inspiration is born. It has nourished an assortment of disciplines, from religion to literature, from the arts to the sciences. Human beings, however, sometimes have difficulty comprehending the mystery of this dynamic union, this passionate love affair between light and dark, the unconscious and the conscious, mother Earth and father sky, God and Goddess. There is certainly much to reflect upon and a multitude of ways to perceive such a phenomena.

In our attempt to explore and envision the archetype of the primordial sacred union, we find that it inevitably lies beyond the grasp of reason, and we quickly reach the limits of language to describe its ineffable and elusive nature. We may attempt to conceptualize the primordial sacred union, or the "Divine," but there is a point where reason must admit its incompetence. When reason has been pushed as far as possible, it eventually has to be suspended, and the wisdom of the non-rational subconscious must be allowed to express itself. Since there are innumerable things beyond the range of human understanding, we often have to use symbolic language, such as mythology and art, to represent concepts that we cannot define or fully comprehend. We need forms and images to help us relate to the Divine, as they are the universal language of the soul.[1] As we penetrate deeper and deeper into the reality of the beloved, we have to abandon more and more of the images and concepts of ordinary language and replace them with a mythical, symbolic language that is full of magic, rich in archetypal images and paradoxical truths. This is one reason why all religions rely on symbolic images and sacred symbolism. Mythical language, such as symbols, poetic images, similes and allegories, is much less restricted by logic and common sense.

In every age there have been prophets, shamans, visionaries, mystics and transcendental artists who have attempted to envision the primordial sacred union through an assortment of artistic mediums and spiritual practices. They have seen through the surface of ordinary consciousness and looked directly into the interior. They serve as teachers for those who don't know that it is possible to transcend the ego world and to cultivate a higher vision of reality than the mundane world. Music and art serve as gatekeepers into the ineffable realm of the invisible world. By releasing the individual from the strictures of words, they allow the imagination to swim into the deep, dark depths of the Great Mystery. Transcendental artists, visionaries and mystics attempt to reveal what lies beyond the boundary of our senses, to bridge the gap between the sacred and the profane, with intent to instill a sense of hope, reverence and awe of the great Mystery. Through dreaming, trance or other altered states, the artist attempts to see the unseen, attaining visions that transcend our regular modes of perception. The mystical or visionary experience more often than not involves a sense of unity with the vast web of life. "With unity comes a sense that ordinary time and space have been transcended, replaced by a feeling of infinity and eternity."[2]

Though artists and mystics may try to write or paint about the Divine, most acknowledge that it is beyond all concepts or theories. True mystics are imbued with a sense of humility, as they know it is impossible to explain the great mystery. Most experience it as similar to the moment of awakening from a deep dream: they remember only fragments and feelings, but know with serene certainty that there was more that they have forgotten. In this sense, no static symbol or image is an adequate picture of God, because the absolute reality is always changing and in flux, like a graceful dancer. "A symbol may point to God, but it cannot capture the transcendent, elusive intricacies of the Divine."[3] Nonetheless, this doesn't negate the power that art and symbolism have on human beings, or their role in society. Art can convey the nature of the mystical experience because it is a media not limited by reason and language.

While mystics and visionary artists are often misunderstood and devalued in the West, they continue to point humanity towards wholeness and healing. They are also aiding in our ability to transcend oppositional dualism and awaken to a new mode of perception, which I refer to as consecrated polarity. Consecrated polarity is another way of describing the sacred relationship between yin and yang. It expresses the notion that opposites, while distinct and separate, are also intertwined; interconnected and interdependent; that their duality is not necessarily born of hostility, but of symbiosis. Thus, consecrated polarity is a mode of perception that allows both the autonomy of each element and recognition of mutual support. The synthesis comes out of an acceptance and acknowledgment of the other's position as essential to its own. Spirit and matter are seemingly autonomous entities, yet they are also interconnected, just as in the yin/yang symbol there is an element of the feminine in the masculine and the masculine in the feminine.

Some have argued that the answer to oppositional dualism is integration, or for that matter, a complete eradication of dualism. Yet there is beauty in the dance of dualism when opposites attract, such as in electro-magnetism. However, an overabundance of synthesis (yin) without an understanding of autonomy (yang) would stifle originality, diversity and creativity. As June Singer once said, "The vital point is that there must be opposition between two differentiated entities in order for the dynamic process of evolution to occur. The clear difference is what attracts, for the mystery of the "other" promises to fill a longing for completion, in the world as in the self."[4]

In order to visualize the concept of consecrated polarity, imagine a coin with two sides. On one side of the coin is spirit and on the other side is matter. Both sides are autonomous and different, but they are also interdependent such that one can't exist without the other. Each side possesses a unique energy and emits a charge that is the opposite of the other. In this sense they are both autonomous entities. Spirit shapes matter and matter shapes spirit. The deep glue of primordial love for one another binds them in a symbiotic relationship. In a grander sense, the concept of dichotomy can be applied to an assortment of dualisms. Consciousness often draws on the unconscious through dreams, art and mystical experiences, and the unconscious reaches for the light of consciousness in the process of self-reflection. On a simple yet profound level, each polarity needs the other in order to exist in a state of equilibrium and equality.

In a world where consecrated polarity was the dominant paradigm, men and women would recognize their deeply symbiotic relationship and neither would attempt to dominate the other. The profound truth of consecrated polarity sunk in for me one day while working on my car. Not only did this experience help to ground the concept of consecrated polarity in a way that I could grasp, I also was better able to apply this concept in my everyday life, from relationships to work-settings. My boyfriend was educating me on the electrical function of spark plugs. He explained to me that the polarity between the positive and negative charge served as the catalyst that created the spark needed to run the engine. However, it was essential that a certain degree of space or gap existed between the two polarities in order for a spark to occur.

What was particularly fascinating to me about the spark plugs was the notion that a spark couldn't occur if the negative and positive charges were too close together. In other words, the two polarities needed to be autonomous, separate and differentiated from each other in order for the spark to occur. However, each charge remained dormant by itself, and needed its opposite before a spark could occur. This is also very similar to the way neurons function in the nervous system of our bodies. Neurons can't transmit impulses if they are touching each other. Rather, they need a gap or space in order to transmit synapses or electrical impulses throughout the body. It also applies to the two hemispheres of our brain that are bridged by the corpus callosum, making it possible to integrate different modes of learning within each part of the brain.

When this epiphany occurred, I had been doing some personal investigation into eastern spiritual traditions, particularly Buddhism and Taoism. I remember reading about dualism and the void or gap between the two extremes. While it didn't make sense to me at the time, I suddenly grasped the concept of consecrated polarity amidst the grime and grit under the hood of my car. It was the most profound concept I had ever come across, yet it was simple and easy to grasp. When visualizing the yin and yang symbol, for example, the void that exists between the two extreme polarities of black and white is a neutral state such that it is difficult to detect where black begins and white ends.

After several years of investigation into the concept of consecrated polarity on both micro and macro levels, I began to see how the gap between the two extremes serves as the glue or primordial love that binds the two opposing energies. It is the heart balance, or love affair between the two polarities, that allows for the spark of creative energy. Opposition or space must exist between the two differing entities in order for the dynamic, creative, consecration to occur. Once this concept really sunk in, I was able to understand its role as a fundamental principle in nature, in the human body, in relationships, in society and in the universe.

The consecration of the two opposing energies is a sacred polarity that exists at the micro/cellular level and the macro/universal level. In this sense it is a sacred, universal blueprint that transcends all biological, social and cultural barriers. Therefore, dualism isn't something that can be simply discarded or tossed into the boneyard of history. It is the antagonism and lack of integration, the domination of one element over the other that causes imbalance, not the fact of duality in and of itself. It is important then to realize that dualism is a precious concept. Furthermore, we won't be able to awaken to oneness as a human race until the autonomy of each position, the masculine and the feminine, is firmly established within each individual.

An awareness of consecrated polarity is therefore an exercise in paradox—what is true in one world is not always true in the other, but one world cannot exist without the other. Consecrated polarity is a willingness to embrace paradox and integrate ambiguity so that we can take the first step toward breaking out of the imbalance that limits our vision. In order to heal the split at the epistemological level between spirit/matter, intellect/emotions, religion/science, unconscious/conscious, male/female and God/Goddess, we need to retain dualism as a universal and fundamental aspect of human consciousness, but get rid of the antagonism, domination and lack of understanding between the two polarities that have been a hallmark of Western society.

On a simple yet profound level, each polarity needs the other in order to exist in a state of equilibrium and equality, and in order for there to be a spark that ignites the creative dance of life, leading to the sacred union. Each position must be seen as equally necessary, and neither should be championed over the other. The polarity in the archetype of the primordial sacred union is a fundamental and universal blueprint that exists on the tiniest of micro levels and the largest of macro levels. It serves as a catalyst for social change, creativity and natural evolution. It is the primordial glue or love that binds all things and spurs our evolution as parts within the whole.

A modern day mystic and new paradigm scientist, Fritjof Capra wrote a book titled, *The Tao of Physics: An Exploration of the Parallels between Modern Physics and Eastern Mysticism*, which expounds on the concept of consecrated polarity. In this book he brilliantly reveals the parallels between modern science, or "the new physics," and that of traditional mysticism, particularly Buddhism and Taoism. In Western consciousness, science and mysticism have always been perceived as two opposite poles of human experience--like oil and water, they simply don't mix. However, Capra reveals the common thread that binds them. In other words, he applies the concept of consecrated polarity to science and eastern mysticism, and reveals the mutually interdependent relationship between the two modes of perception. He also explains the various ways Eastern mysticism is assisting the West, which grossly tends to be more yang- oriented. When describing the valuable role mystics play in an assortment of cultures, he says:

> *Mystics transcend the realm of intellectual concepts, and in transcending it become aware of the relativity and polar relationship of all opposites. They realize that good and bad, pleasure and pain, life and death, are not absolute experiences belonging to different categories, but are merely two sides of the same reality; extreme parts of a single whole. The awareness that all opposites are polar, and thus a unity, is seen as one of the highest aims of man in the spiritual tradition of the East.*[5]

Mystics and transcendental artists play a fundamental role in all cultures, despite some people's inability to receive the gift they have to offer. Jung has taught us that myths and symbols are the universal language, and that the artist, shaman and mystic helps us to bridge the gap between the conscious and the unconscious so that we can understand that language on deeper levels. Through poetry, art and music, we are reminded of a realm beyond the physical; the realm of the soul, that has become lost to some Westerners. In a world rampant with fatalism, we desperately need sacred images of the Divine in order to reignite a deeper awareness of our connection to spirit and our purpose in the great web of life. However, these kinds of sacred art images are rare, especially in the United States. As with good music, art with depth and meaning must be sought out amid the mediocrity of the art world. This is a complex phenomenon, intricately bound to a deeply entrenched system of patriarchal oppression in the art world that has stultified and denied the artistic voices of an assortment of visionary artists, particularly female mystics.

What is of greater concern, and a problem directly

linked to the marginalization of mystics and visionary artists in the West, is that the sacred images available to us communicate that the Divine is exclusively male. Feminist Theologian Carole Christ says, "Religious symbol systems focused around exclusively male images of divinity create the impression that female power can never be fully legitimate, or wholly beneficent."[6] Furthermore, Feminist writer Sue Kidd Monk writes, in her transformative book, *The Dance of the Dissident Daughter*, that "The image, language and metaphor of God as male has been used so exclusively, for so long (about five thousand years) that most people seem to believe God really is male." [7]

The lack of a divine female image has unfortunately caused severe damage to the psyches of women, as well as men. As several feminists, thealogians, archeologists and psychologists have already noted, the lack of divine female images not only supports an imbalance in our consciousness that diminishes our sense of wholeness as individuals, we have also been conditioned to undervalue the feminine within ourselves and in the world around us. Women in particular have suffered both mentally and physically from misconstrued images of God, "... in whose name they have been informed that birth control and abortion are unequivocally wrong, that they should be subordinate to their husbands, that they must be present at rituals and services in which men have all the leadership roles and in which they are degraded not only by enforced passivity, but also verbally and symbolically." [8] Furthermore--and this is the deep affront--impoverished images of God as only male legitimizes and maintains patriarchal power in the culture at large. Feminist theologian Mary Daly, author of *Beyond God the Father (1973),* reveals that there is an undeniable link between the repression of the feminine in our deity and the repression of women. She writes, "The entire conceptual systems of theology, developed under the conditions of patriarchy, have been the products of males and tend to serve the interests of sexist society." [9]

In other words, patriarchal religions have served to justify and maintain gender inequality on a global level through ideology, language, symbolism and sex role socialization—a deep conditioning process that occurs throughout one's process of development. Furthermore, an unconscious internalization of sexism continues to shape perceptions even by those who don't profess to be associated or bound by religious creeds.

For these reasons and more, imaging the divine as female is essential to our spiritual evolution, for we won't be able to transcend gender associations in Western culture until the autonomy of the feminine principle is fully established in human consciousness. A consecrated polarity between the masculine and feminine principles can't occur until the feminine principle is understood and valued as a fundamental aspect of life. In the realm of spirit, one's gender is a non-issue; rather, it is one's heart and intentions that are of greater importance. But, for us Earth-bound humans, the gender war will continue, despite its irrelevance in the spirit world, until we can grasp as a people the concept of consecrated polarity.

In order to combat the imbalance of masculine energy in the West, we desperately need visionary artists and mystics to create images and symbols that not only dislodge images that reflect and reinforce the prevailing social arrangements, but enhance our ability to envision the Divine in a more holistic and inclusive manner. In our fast-paced and fragmented society, a work of art has an instantaneous impact on the viewer, and when coupled with simple words, the power is doubled. Art also bridges the gap between cultural and ideological barriers. As artist historian Elinor Gadon said, "Artists who are reclaiming the sacred iconography of the Goddess are creating a new perception of reality that is representative of their experience as spiritual women and men."[10]

The Primordial Sacred Union in Psychology, Religion and Mythology

The concept of the primordial sacred union has come to us by way of world religions, especially in elements of Hinduism, Taoism and Buddhism, as well as in the Platonic traditions of the West. An assortment of disciplines has also attempted to conceptualize this symbiotic union. The writing of Carl Jung is filled with examples from myth and culture that point to the importance and value of recognizing the qualities of the primordial sacred union within each individual and the world at large. Humanity was meant to be modeled after this divine union, but has somehow fallen away or become severed from its original wholeness, and has digressed into the fragmented world we see all around us.

In his book, *Man and His Symbols*,[11] Carl Jung proposed that, in addition to our immediate, personal consciousness, there exists a second psychic system of a collective, universal and impersonal nature, which is identical in all individuals. He referred to this as the collective unconscious, which does not develop individually but is inherited. The contents of the collective unconscious, Jung argued, manifest themselves in the form of symbolic images, or archetypes, representing the primordial events that shaped human history. These archetypal images, which include such symbols as the mother and father, the warrior, the seeker, the sage and the child, are common to all people. Jung's theory of the feminine principle as a universal archetype, a primordial, instinctual pattern of behavior deeply imprinted on the human psyche, has assisted humanity in its ability to both understand and ground the concept of the Goddess as existing within both individual and collective psyches. In this sense, archetypal symbolism of the primordial sacred union is an international form of communication because it bypasses the barriers of language, race and culture. It is perhaps the most effective form in which sacred concepts can be given expression.

Carl Jung's studies of alchemy, Taoism, and the work of new paradigm scientists led him to become one of the first modern male scientists to value the feminine in equal measure to the masculine. His concept of wholeness, the goal of the process of individuation, included the integration of the masculine and feminine principles. He recognized the feminine as the source of receptivity and relatedness, and called for its integration into a Western culture that had gone too far in development of the rational, the materialistic and the masculine.

Jung proposed that the primordial sacred union, otherwise referred to by him as "androgyny,"[12] is a universal archetype inherent in the collective unconscious and similar to the sacred marriage. Humanity was supposed to be modeled after this divine image of Creator/Creatrix, but somehow mankind fell away from and was severed from the original wholeness. While this sacred union is as old as creation itself, we have come to know about it through traces left in myths and the sacred traditions of many indigenous peoples. Jung proposed that androgyny, which refers to the anima (feminine) and animus (masculine) aspects within a single human being, regardless of sex, may be the oldest archetype inherent in the human psyche. Both are present within every human psyche, regardless of physical gender. Thus, there are masculine and feminine qualities in both men and women.

Jung believed that the anima (feminine) and animus (masculine) had to be in balance before a person could achieve psychological individuation, or psychic wholeness. Thus, women, at some point in their individuation process, need to integrate within themselves the masculine qualities, such as assertiveness and objectivity, in order to become whole persons. Conversely, men need to integrate the feminine qualities that reside within their psyches, such as compassion and non-resistance or passivity, in order to become psychically whole. Jung was not proposing that men become women. On the contrary, Jung believed that in order to bridge the gap between male and female, we need to be able to empathize with the opposite sex. The movement towards becoming androgynous persons implies a radical change in human consciousness and different styles of human behavior than what has been deemed normal. It demands that we resist traditional sex role stereotypes and the forms of sexual identity that force men and women into exploiting their differences rather than working together in equality and interdependence.

The concept of androgyny also proposes new ways of thinking about sexual identity. Rather than viewing sexual identity as only male and female, androgyny proposes that we begin to view sexual identity as existing on a continuum, which includes recognition of the multitude of sexual permutations that exist in the gray area, such as gays, lesbians and bisexuals. Biologist and feminist Anne Fausto-Sterling wrote a brilliant book titled *Sexing the Body: Gender Politics and the Construction of Sexuality,*[13] which challenges the notion that there always has been and can forevermore only be two human sexes; male and female. With examples drawn from daily life and from history, sociology, biology and anthropology, Fausto-Sterling demonstrates that these dualisms are neither natural nor cultural universals, but arise from our society's insistence on seeing people that way. If sexual identity indeed exists on a continuum, and male and female are universal energies, then it makes sense that there is an enormous gray area that has been severely denied in our culture.

After reading this book and gaining an understanding of the universal archetype of androgyny, my sense of male versus female was radically changed. I began to understand why some women I know exude more masculine than feminine qualities, and conversely, why some men appear more feminine than masculine. I have been fortunate to know several gays and lesbians who helped to solidify these ideas for me, for they carry a great burden and some have experienced extreme wounds from the internalization of repressive patriarchal ideologies. However, they have so much to teach the heterosexual community about free will, non-judgment and the full continuum of sexual chemistries, for androgyny is what our souls are yearning to seek. It is the sea of oneness that transcends all dualisms, including sex.

In addition to individual, personal experience, the concept of androgyny demands a meeting of the opposites in our external, socio-cultural environment as well. Jung proposed that once we have learned to recognize and accept the seemingly contradictory aspects within ourselves, it naturally follows that we need to extend this attitude of mutual interdependence to the wider human community. Change and wholeness happens from the inside out; therefore, we cannot expect to have equality in the external, socio-cultural environment until each individual first works on becoming integrated within his/herself. The power of the individual to change the world is a profound concept if, and only if, one is committed to her/his personal and spiritual growth. Too often people try to save the world when in fact what they really need to do is examine their own false beliefs and internal imbalances.

Images of the Sacred Union and Cosmic Mother

The intertwined histories of religion, myth and art reaching back to prehistoric times are the record that our ancestors left of the symbols that were meaningful and moving to them. Even today, as contemporary art reveals, the interplay of spirituality, myth and art is still alive. In the following pages I have chosen an assortment of sacred images created by contemporary visionary artists who have attempted to envision the primordial sacred union as well as the cosmic Mother. What is particularly fascinating about these images is the unique way in which each of these artists envisions the sacred union, reflecting the diversity of cultural and religious perspectives. However, I have no intention of exhaustively discussing the vast array of perspectives in this book, as there are too many.

All cultures around the world have collectively attempted to conceptualize the beginning of creation, and each one of them has pointed to the primordial sacred union that existed long before creation. Creation mythology has existed wherever people have questioned their origins. It is in the nature of humans to wonder about the unknown and search for answers. Since the beginning of time we have tried to imagine what it might have been like before anything had come into existence, yet the language tends to vary from culture to culture. Science too has focused on understanding what happened seconds before the Big Bang.

Despite being separated by geographical barriers, Carl Jung and his protégés discovered that many cultures have developed creation myths with the same basic elements. One of the commonalities is the belief that in the beginning there was a dark void. Chaos is the potency that exists in the void. No entities of any kind were in awareness, and then, in some mysterious way, some bright spark emerged out of nothingness. Within that spark were energies that would eventually be distinguishable as opposites, separating then into the masculine and feminine principles. In the old myths, the idea of this divine union stems from the belief that in the beginning there was a primordial unity, "the eternal one" in which all the opposites are contained. In other words, the "One" ultimately transcends gender. It can be defined as the genderless "One" which contains the Two; namely, the male and the female. At some point in time the primordial unity is broken open and separated into two opposite energies. Those polarities are expressed in an assortment of ways: light and dark, positive and negative, hot and cold, mind and body, art and science, war and peace, etc.[14]

When analyzing an assortment of creation myths, one will also find that many of them begin with the theme of birth. This may be because birth represents new life, and the beginning of life on Earth may have been imagined as being similar to the beginning of a child's life. This is closely related to the idea of a mother and a father who, through their love for each other, co-create the world together. Ancient mythology is saturated with tales of a time when the eternal male and the eternal female were locked in an unending embrace.

Contemporary visionary artist Jonathan Weber illustrates the sacred union in his painting Emperor and Empress. His vision is inspired by a combination of five tarot cards from the major arcana, an ancient form of divination that uses allegorical images to relate esoteric meaning. The tarot images used are the Emperor/Hierophant, the Empress/High Priestess, and the Universe cards. He writes:

> *A common theme in my work is the alchemical balancing of opposites: sun/moon, male/female, fire/water, light/dark, hot/cold, above/below. Like the black and white fish of the yin/yang symbol in Taoism, both figures wear the color of the other on their inner blouse, representing the interconnectedness of opposites. This enlightened quality of harmony within dualism is symbolized by the rainbow connecting the sun and moon. This ultimate unifying principle is also symbolized by the Earth and galaxy, containing a diversity of perspectives within the greater whole. The merging of the Emperor with the Hierophant (priest), and the Empress with the High Priestess, is symbolic of the spiritual leader ideal, transcendent and enlightened, yet also immanent and active in the world. The Empress represents the loving mother in tune with the cycles of life who acts with compassion and empathy. The Emperor represents the wise father who is aware of transcendent knowledge and acts with virtue and discipline. The combination of the two coming together is the heart and mind working in unison toward the peace and harmony of all things.*[15]

Emperor and Empress, Jonathan Weber, 24"x36" oil on canvas, www.jonathanweber.org

Double Helix, Mark Henson, ,38"x52" oil on canvas, www.markhensonart.com

The primordial sacred union is indeed a beautiful model of the love that binds all things. It is the gift of Eros, the divine, cosmic love affair embodied and reflected in two human lovers. Contemporary visionary artist Mark Henson, captures the primordial gift of Eros in his image *Double Helix*. In this painting, he powerfully depicts the dynamic union in the DNA molecule that carries hereditary messages. The DNA molecule looks like a spiral ladder where the rungs are formed by base molecules that occur in pairs. Each person, possessing both the masculine and feminine aspects within their DNA, also has his or her unique combination of qualities programmed into them at birth. When describing the image, Henson says:

> *The spiral of evolution or the double helix is the perfect representation of the Divine Union. The source of creation spews forth millions of forms of life, each unique and capable of reproduction. The secret of divine creation is its ability to create in love and release in love. Once creation is birthed, we are set free to be who we are.*[16]

Another profound image of the sacred union is by Amoraea Dreamseed titled *Synergenesis*. He views this painting as a living altar or sacred gateway that taps directly into the spiritual wisdom of creation, exploring the soul's ultimate mission to become one with the Divine. Amoraea writes:

> *Synergenesis expresses the glorious collective ascension of our spirits back into the Infinite Godhead. The Geometry of souls reveals the perfect symmetry of God's design. Eternal wisdom communicates that all things are interrelated by the sacred geometry known as the Golden Mean Spiral. Hidden within its infinite mystery is pure consciousness. In Synergenesis, the golden spiral is found in the matrix of eyes, weaving back and forth until it reaches the Great One Source. All of creation is imprinted with the sacred blueprint of the spiral, for it is the union of the two in the one. The culmination of this divinity is conveyed by the sacred marriage of the masculine/feminine, consecrated in the holy chalice of love. Sometimes referred to as Twin Flames or Soulmates, the magnetism or polarity between the two souls emerge from the same androgynous source. The individual and collective raising of consciousness that occurs as humans awaken to oneness is the process of Synergenesis—the path that leads us home to the Beloved.*[17]

Another image of the Sacred Union that is deserving of recognition is by Abba Yahuda titled *The Gathering*. Born in Jamaica and raised in a family of artists, Abba vowed to devote himself fully to art at a young age, making everything he did a creative exercise. Abba has an eclectic portfolio of both abstract and representational work. His abstract paintings are delightfully playful, spontaneous and original. You can clearly see the influence of African American painter Basquiat in his work, one of his greatest inspirations. Layered with bright colors, shapes and symbolism, each painting has its own imaginative story to tell. His enormous paintings of the Sacred Union and Divine Feminine are painted with precise technical skill, harmonious compositions, ornate borders, and a lot of cute little cherub angels. Abba is currently writing his own book about the Divine Feminine and is producing his own music as well. He was generous to let me include an excerpt from his book, which discusses his intentions

Synergenesis, Amoraea Dreamseed, 24"x 36" acrylic on canvas, www.divine-blueprint.com

for the painting. He writes:

The Gathering of the one hundred forty-four thousand of the Book of Revelations has been the subject of discussion for centuries. This painting depicts the enthroned primordial Divine aspect of humanity as mother and father, with the human family as children. The Emperor and Empress sit in union on one throne, representing the power of the Holy Trinity, as male and female through the power of the same unseen energy of spirit. Their union is represented in the eclipsing sun and moon with the consequent rebirth of the Earth through an African consciousness, namely Ethiopia.

It is the conscious awareness of our spiritual umbilical ties to our first parents from our African roots that we as humans will have to foster for our return to the very source of our spiritual and physiological existence. Archeological findings confirm the African origins of the human species, which is now common knowledge. The writings in the Book of Genesis, Chapter 2, verses 7-13, also place Adam and Eve in the geographical location of the garden paradise in Ethiopia, making Africa the mother of the biblical first parents. This fact speaks audibly of the Divine birthright of the African womb and the right of every individual to be reborn through the recognition of Her in order to come full circle to Divinity.

It is out of the denial, suppression and oppression of the African woman's Divine motherhood that the term Black Madonna or even the Black Christ is derived. Over five hundred years of internalized African oppression has catalyzed a number of self-destructive reactions to the forced assimilation of colonial Christianity. For example, when we as Africans exalt God with European images (depicting the holiest symbols, such as the Madonna and Child and the Holy Trinity) we automatically deny our own mothers, but we also deny our own birthright as first fruits of the Earth's womb. The Bible, with all its icons, has become the ideal for many of us still under the disillusioning force of colonialism and Christianity. However, if we continue to be distracted by false ideologies and ignore the reality of images which do not empower us as individuals, we will remain divided and conquered as a people.

The White Madonna or the White Christ, for lack of a better term, is the accepted norm of the dominant Christian world, even though the historical evidence proves otherwise. This illustrates that there is no dispute of color when it comes to the images of the Christ and his mother until they are painted brown, and then they all of a sudden become the Black Madonna or the Black Christ. This is ironic because the icons should convey the highest, as well as the first, of human ideals. This being so, all humanity should be able to trace their spiritual and biological roots to them as the prototype. How is this possible unless they represent in image and likeness of the primordial parents? How can the African woman identify her redemption through any other womb but her own?

As the mother of humanity, her womb becomes our common denominator and point of reference. The word, prototype, was coined by St. Basil in the fourth century to mean sacred personage, but the word soon evolved to mean the first or earliest icon of that per-

The Gathering, Abba Yahudah, 24‴x 36″ acrylic on canvas, www.abbayahudah.com

sonality. Applying this concept to humanity would amplify in an extraordinary light the sacred personage of the African W.O.M.B.M.A.N. as the earliest icon that we can literally draw from. Our enlightenment will come when we as humans can surrender to our true African nature from within, which is our natural birthright. As long as the idea of Black Madonna exists even as a language among us, it simply means that we are in denial of the reality that the mother of humanity is God, which happens to be African by nature. [18]

A sacred union image that is more Earth bound, yet equally profound is by visionary artist Atmara Rebecca Cloe titled *Mother Earth/Father Sky*. Beautifully illustrating the symbiotic overlap where Earth and sky bleed into each other, Atmara superimposes an eagle flying in the sky above an enchanted landscape. Subliminally embodied in the landscape is a woman's face, illustrating Mother Earth. Stories and myth portray the Earth Mother as having many faces, as numerous as her diverse landscapes, and all of her children affirm their kinship with her. The eagle serves as a bridge, or the primordial glue that binds Earth and Spirit. Half of the eagle's body blends into the landscape, portraying the interdependence of Mother Earth/Father Sky. While each are autonomous entities, there is a point where spirit and matter completely blend into each other, where their separate identities become non-existent. So, while the Earth is the embodiment of the Goddess, there are masculine elements in Mother Nature, and feminine elements in spirit, or Father Sky.

The Ogallala Sioux often speak of the Great Spirit, Wakan Tanka, as the grandfather of all things, but they also speak of the Earth as the grandmother of all things. Some Native American mythologies provide this female Earth with a mate. For the Yuma people of southern California, the Earth's husband is the sky. After a primordial embrace between Earth woman and sky man, the Earth conceives and gives birth to twin sons. As their first task, the twins rise up from their mother's body to lift up the sky.[19]

Images of the Cosmic Mother

Some ancient creation myths propose that the process of giving birth originated in the womb of the Universal Mother Spirit. All life was born out of the dark cosmic womb of the Great Mother. People have long identified the feminine as the source of all being. Just as our ancestors honored a woman's ability to create life, they also

Mother Earth Father Sky, Atmara Rebecca Cloe, 24"x30" digital media, www.nwcreations.com

honored the Earth as the Great Mother who nourishes us and from whose body we are all created. Therefore, some feminist artists, in accordance with a number of creation myths, envision the Great Mother as the original creator of life.

Feminist and mystical artist Monica Sjoo examined an assortment of creation myths in her book *The Great Cosmic Mother*. In resonance with an assortment of creation myths and feminist art historians, she proposed that, "The ancient Great Mother of all gave birth parthenogenetically to herself and the entire cosmos. Parthenogenetic means self-generating, without the help of male insemination. The Mother, therefore, was the world egg containing the two halves of all polarities or dualisms."[20] In other words, Monica strongly believes that the Great Mother is the creatrix of life and that it is from her that all life precedes, and to her that it returns.

The imagery Monica Sjoo uses in her paintings often makes reference to birth, the female body and nature. All of her images are central to her beliefs regarding her cosmic Mother. This respect and honoring of the Goddess is not only found in her art images, but also in two texts that chronicle her journey. Monica Sjoo made her paintings of women in the act of giving birth in the early 1960s, representing childbirth as a powerful and spiritual act. In fact when she exhibited the painting *God Giving Birth* in St. Ives, Cornell in 1970 and in London in 1973, it was deemed blasphemous by the authorities concerned and was attacked by members of the public, as well as attracting great support from some women artists. The painting questions the absurd myth that the creative force is "only" male and phallic.

Perhaps one of the more surreal and cosmic images of the universal womb is *The Tunnel of Love, Where We Came From* by visionary artist Mark Henson. While many of us have forgotten the Great Creatrix, she is encoded in every cell of our bodies. Each one of us was born of her sacred womb and will return, once again, to the tunnel of love when we die, possibly reincarnating into another life form in an entirely different dimension. Mark Henson writes, "A tiny spirit peers into the *Tunnel of Love.* All the nurturing powers of the universe await its presence."[21]

Mark Henson painted another image of the Universal Mother titled *Wonders of Nature.* In this image, we see the Crone aspect of The Great Mother, fully ripe in her wisdom years. Above her head is the universal womb, spiraling down to her third eye of psychic intuition. Looking down with eyes of compassion, she is captured by the beauty of her creation—a beloved lotus flower. Crystalline water cascades down from her cupped hands, and returns once again to the endless flowing chalice of the universal unconscious, the birthing place of creativity. This image clearly represents the transcendent and immanent aspects of the Mother, or, as above so below. It also communicates to us a message of hope—that the Goddess is alive and magic is afoot. While she has never left us, we have forgotten her eternal presence in the Godhead.

It is now time for humanity to fully embrace an Earth based spirituality that honors Gaia as a living organism that deeply loves its creation. The intelligence that guides evolution is not outside nature, but embodied in it as the body wisdom of the Earth. The great Gaia being knows itself in the same sense that our bodies know themselves, having the body wisdom to take care of themselves and keep on evolving. The split between spirit and matter must be healed so we can begin to explore the rich treasures of the Divine Feminine permeating so many aspects of our lives, for the Goddess' love is fully embodied in the Earth and in our bodies. We no longer need to feel the pain of separation, born from the illusion that God, man, and nature are separate and distinct categories. Humans were never meant to be separate from spirit or nature, nor were we meant to dominate and control one another and the Earth.

The cosmic womb or matrix is indeed a fascinating concept, one that I can't seem to get enough of. It's interesting that new paradigm scientists are beginning to learn more and more about the birthing of planets in the universe; however, there is still so much to be known. I fell in love with an image by visionary artist Paul Nicholson titled *Dance of Veils.* Here we see the cosmic Mother in full swing, casting out her web of interconnectivity from the dark void of nothingness, for she is the glue and interrelatedness of all things. Her message is one of community, harmony, cooperation, compassion and unification. However, it must be made clear that to live in awareness of the deep connection of all beings in the web of life does not mean that all is absorbed in a sea of oneness where the masculine principle of difference and autonomy is denied. Difference and diversity are the great principles of nature, but so are unity and interconnectedness. Maintaining the balance between chaos/harmony, diversity/unity, expansiveness/contraction is a delicate dance that only the primordial sacred union truly understands. We have so much to learn about the dance of veils as we clumsily dance through life, ignorant of the beautiful symmetry and graceful intelligence of the Creatress.

God Giving Birth, Monica Sjoo, 3' x 5', charcoal on paper, www.monicasjoo.weebly.com

The last image of the Cosmic Mother that I want to share with you is by Beth Avary, titled *Madonna.* Beth was a good friend and confidant. She has a lifetime of work that needs to be in a museum where people can witness her brilliant paintings. Beth's current images are mostly colorful landscape settings; however, some of her earlier work illustrates her passion for fantasy art. When describing the painting, she says, "The Madonna embodies the feminine principle. As Queen, she carries the weight of our problems. The light she holds symbolizes new life, consciousness and wisdom." [22]

While Beth's image is a powerful representative of the cosmic queen, I particularly like this image because she has a disturbed expression on her face that, for me, captures the Goddess' ambivalent feelings of sorrow and love for humanity. When you look into her eyes, you can feel her sadness and grief, but you can also see the flame of rage that refuses to accept the alienation that pervades our culture, especially in the West. Nonetheless, her presence is strong, despite our inability to receive her love. It is through the bright light of her emerging presence that we will be forced to evolve in our understanding of God as inseparable from the Goddess. In this sense, she is the light of truth, the ultimate redeemer of compassion who will guide us into a new phase of evolution.

Images of the primordial sacred union and cosmic Mother are not only powerful, but also redemptive and radical, as they cannot help but call into question the credibility of traditional religious symbolism in our culture. They literally demand an evolution of sacred symbolism. While the intention behind them is to inspire a more inclusive image of God, they can also potentially generate anxiety and even rage in viewers, as they demand nothing less than equality and justice. Images of the primordial sacred union inevitably challenge both an extreme male bias as well as an extreme female bias. They also communicate that a domination of yang over yin, male over female, and God over Goddess (or vice versa) is not only farcical, but also a denial of the power of partnership.

Tunnel of Love, Mark Henson, 36" x 46", oil on canvas, www.markhensonart.com

Wonders of Nature, Mark Henson, 36" x 66", oil on canvas, www.markhensonart.com

Feminist Artists Calling into Question the Male Bias

In our current postmodern society, masculine/yang energy is clearly championed over the feminine/yin energy. Images of the primordial sacred union not only disrupt male dominance as a keystone of the Judeo-Christian ideology, they also question male-oriented values and demand a radical shift in the patriarchal social structure. On the other hand, the shakers and movers of the women's movement should not go to the other extreme of a female bias. We are at a point in human history where we cannot afford anything less than equality between the sexes. Rather than repeat historical cycles of reactionary movements to one extreme or the other, we must begin to apply the concept of consecrated polarity (yin/yang) to all aspects of our lives. Fortunately, an assortment of postmodern feminists have exposed the truth about the construction of knowledge and the way it has been controlled by a white, male, eurocentric bias that has largely excluded the viewpoints of women and minorities. Contemporary feminist artists (male and female) both participate and expand upon the ground breaking work of not only postmodern feminists, but a long history of feminist artists, mystics, heretics and visionaries who came before them. With intent to expose the male bias at the fore in Western culture, a number of contemporary artists have mustered up the courage to challenge dominant patriarchal ideologies that have denied the voices of women and visionary artists, but especially minority women.

There are a number of talented visionary artists who have devoted their lives to the rebirth of the primordial Sacred Union in Western consciousness, one of whom is Martina Hoffmann. Known for her wild imagination and commitment to the sacred feminine, Martina's unique iconography has been greatly inspired by expanded states of consciousness: the realms of the imagination, meditation, shamanic work and the dream state. Much of her imagery shows a deep connection to the Great Mother, and her sculptural work is undeniably influenced by African cultural traditions. German-born, Martina spent her childhood in Cameroon, equatorial West Africa, where she grew up surrounded by three different cultures: the German heritage in her home, French schooling and social life, and the indigenous African culture which informed and enriched her life at the deepest instinctual levels.

Several of Martina's images will be discussed throughout this book, but there is one image in particular that deserves to be acknowledged for its sheer power, titled *Female Crucifixion*. In this image, a woman hangs from a cross similar to the one Jesus was crucified on, signifying the demise of the sacred feminine in the Judeo-Christian tradition. With all the gross exploitation and subjugation of the sacred feminine worldwide, one would be justified in saying that the Goddess was and still continues to be crucified, just as Jesus was, over and over and over for thousands of years by the patriarchal establishment. While so much attention and emphasis has been placed on the crucifixion of Christ, very few symbols exist today that capture the annihilation of the Goddess from human consciousness. This is not to berate or demean the crucifixion of Jesus; rather, it is an attempt to reclaim important information about human history that has been omitted out of ignorance by the priesthood.

Looking closely at the image, we notice the woman is menstruating, which Hoffman claims is representative of the stigmata or wounds believed to duplicate the wounds of Christ's crucifixion. However, rather than appearing on the hands and feet, and sometimes on the side and head, Hoffman places the wound on her yoni (vagina), signifying menstruation as a primordial wound. In ancient Goddess religions, menstrual blood was valued for its power. "Women's menstrual blood always was and continues to remain the essence of the creative power of the Great Mother."[23] Menstrual blood is both sacred and biological—within it dwells the life spirit. However, under patriarchy, menstruation has been viewed as a punishment rather than a gift. "Menstruation was seen by biblical men as the curse of God laid upon woman for her sin in Eden--and it is still called "the curse" today.."[24] Perhaps menstrual blood has been so degraded because it represents the creative power of the evolutionary female that has been so denied by the patriarchy. This explains why much of women's sacred blood rites, so vital to Goddess religions, were stolen or repressed by the patriarchal priesthood.

Dance of Veils, Paul Nicholson, 30" x 40", oil on masonite, www.fineartamerica.com/profiles/paul-nicholson

Madonna, Beth Avary, 24" x 36" acrylic on canvas

I created an image titled *An Homage to Women's Suffering* which portrays not only my own suffering as a woman, artist and mystic, but the collective suffering of women throughout history. When I painted this piece, I was in the midst of a deep depression. As a sociologist, I was well educated in social problems, particularly the sociology of gender. I had a solid understanding of feminist theory, particularly postmodern feminism, but I hadn't done much reading in feminist theology. I have always had a deep concern for women's issues, especially minority women—nurses, teachers, social workers, maids, cooks etc.—who work tirelessly in the trenches of our culture, mending and piecing together the broken spirits of a world gone mad, with very little respect or a decent paycheck in return for their efforts. My depression deepened when I thought about the women in third world nations, such as Africa, who are so suppressed by Patriarchy that their clitorises are cut out of their bodies, or the women in Thailand who are forced into prostitution in order to put food on the table.

In the early stages of this book project, I did a lot of research in the women's spirituality movement and eco-feminism. In a relatively short period of time, I dove deep and absorbed a lot of knowledge about the repressed "Herstory" of the Goddess. At this time in my life, I was in a relationship with a man who had very little respect for the wisdoms I brought to the table. I felt continually devalued and denied by him regarding my sociological insights and spiritual understandings, which over time weakened my spirit. While I didn't understand it at the time, I now know that he was threatened by my fascination with the Goddess. He would often tell me "the Goddess stuff is a bunch of poppycock" and that "I shouldn't bring it up anymore, especially around our friends."

I was living in Arizona at the time, away from my spiritual family in Oregon and had little social support and few mentors to guide me through the final initiation into the Goddess awakening. As a result, I fell into a deep depression and was feeling suicidal. Not only was it the end of my relationship, it was the end of a cycle of relationships with men who never fully understood or valued my spiritual side. I'll never forget the night I fell into the dark abyss. Pregnant with rage, I drove myself to Lee's Ferry on the Colorado river. I stood by the river, screaming at the top of my lungs "Why, why, why do we create so much pain for ourselves?" I thought about Virginia Woolf and how she must have felt before she committed suicide, so misunderstood and marginalized. I was fortunate to have many angels come to my rescue that night who gently talked me out of suicide. I felt Virginia Woolf's spirit with me, as well as Monica Sjoo's. They spoke to me of spiritual warfare and how the shadow of accumulated denial and human suffering is too much for anyone to take on. They said that the collective denial is threatened by souls who shine too bright because it doesn't want to be exposed for what it is, and that I would be letting the shadow of denial get the best of me if I took my life.

I cried a river of tears that gently flowed into the Colorado like a creek yearning for mama ocean. La Luna bathed me with her luminous light and the ancestors of the Navajo and Hopi performed healing rituals on my heart, for they knew the depths of my pain, as did the Mother, for Her tears were my tears and our tears. I called in Quan Yin, Kali and Tara to protect me from the collective shadow as it was too big to confront on my own. I was fortunate to have my biological mother come to my rescue. She flew to Arizona the next day and helped me make the transition from Arizona back home to Oregon. For the next three years, I would endure the darkest night of the soul that I have ever experienced. If it weren't for my spirit guides and loving family and friends, I would have been yet anoth-

Female Crucifixtion, Martina Hoffmann, 24"x30" oil on canvas, www.martinahoffmann.com

er female mystic in the history of humankind to take her life.

After receiving counsel from several wise women, I learned that the pain of the feminine wound is too deep to take on alone. It is extremely harmful if one doesn't have a spiritual midwife, particularly one who has gone through the initiation into the feminine wound, to guide them through the underworld and back again. It can drive one to insanity and even death if one doesn't have a strong support system of conscious people to help them process the pain and rage. I think this may be why so many women have been diagnosed with depression and mental illness. It takes great courage to wake up in the midst of a volatile monster of denial that feeds off people's fear and apathy. And it takes even more courage to stare it in the face and demand that it release you as a prisoner.

During this dark time of catharsis, I needed a way to funnel the pain and depression into a source of healing and strength as opposed to letting it debilitate me any further. I decided to do this painting as an homage to women's suffering, an altar of healing and transformation in my own life and women's lives. What is particularly fascinating about this painting is that I captured the distressed face on the woman in one try, which is quite rare for even a master painter. Faces usually take me three or four times to get right, but this one came out of the darkest depths of my soul in one full swoop. When I was finished, I stood back and took in the horror on her face, which triggered a surge of tears flooding my painter's palette. I then mixed my salty tears into the paint and began painting the sacred altar in the foreground, which contains an assortment of Goddess symbolism such as the snake, seashells (containing the spiral), a bird feather, flowers and deer antlers.

Homage to Women's Suffering, Victoria Christian, 24" x 24" oil on wood.

In the center of the altar I painted a lit candle, representing the Goddess's burning flame. When I think about all of the women who came before me who endured worse conditions of oppression, I am amazed at their courage and strength to guard the Goddess's flame in the most dire of circumstances. This piece is an offering of gratitude to myself, but also to all of the courageous, awakened women in an assortment of disciplines who have devoted their lives to the re-enchantment of the Great Mother and the healing of the planet.

Many women have made great sacrifices for equality, but they wouldn't have been successful if they let their pain and rage get the best of them. Having had the time to reflect on this dark period, I realize that I tapped into the larger female pain body so intensely that I let it take me down as opposed to releasing it up to God/Goddess. I dove way too deep into the shadow and experienced a death of the ego that was so shattering that I nearly died. And while I gained a tremendous amount of compassion from the luminous wisdoms of the Dark Goddess, I don't believe it was wise to take on the full burden of Her pain, for it was too much to bear. Nonetheless, I wear this experience like a badge of honor, symbolizing an important initiation into the underworld, which I believe is a requirement of all Goddess Warrioresses. I've developed effective coping mechanisms to deal with the internal fissure and fragmentation that occurs as a result of waking up in a world that is still very much in denial of the Great Mother. Perhaps the greatest blessing that came out of my underworld mission was compassion for myself and others. It is absolutely imperative that women learn to support one another in their awakening process as opposed to falling prey to competition and ego, for the path of the visionary is steep and arduous; thus, we must be compassionate and patient with one other if we are going to heal the feminine wound.

There is one more breathtaking crucifix painting that demands recognition. It was painted by a brilliant and beautiful soul residing in Olympia, Washington by the name of Heather Taylor. I met Heather at Mystic Garden Party in 2009 and was absolutely ecstatic to see her painting titled *The Living Cross: A Crossroad to Transformation.* Heather's painting is imbued with a cathartic message of transformation through the cross, which exists on the micro and macro realms of life. It is dripping with the Great Mother's grace and her message of hope for our time. Heather writes:

> *The sacred cross is a living form, a progressive and dynamic equilibrium forged by the unfolding of space in time—the DNA sequence of creation. A vision of our manifest nature, we bear the cross in likeness and in Truth, as we are crucified through karmic incarnations, the wheel of involution and evolution. This is not a tragedy, but a triumph. It is not divine torture, but holy grace as the crucifix enables us to ascend to greater and greater realms.*
>
> *A circle with a point connected by a cross (the most ancient of symbols) foretells the geometry of transformation. An axis of magnetic North, South, East and West corresponds to the four cardinal points. Our physiology recapitulates our divine orientation as our brain structure is a cross of dualistic hemispheres joined by the corpus callosum, which bridges the energies of yin/yang, intuition/rationality, unconscious/conscious. It is a divine imprint, an embodiment of the sacred union that will allow us to bridge heaven and Earth, and ultimately, rise to our perfection. Much like the saying, "as above, so below," the sexual chakra in our body grounds us in the Earth, while our crown chakra connects us to higher dimensions beyond the physical world. Like the Kabalistic cross, we are a living tree. When a tree is cut to form a cross, it has been falsely perceived as a symbol of suffering born from the illusion of separation. We remain a tree, but our etheric form is always whole and perfect. The Kundalini serpent power comes up through the Earth activating the portals of ascension. The various bird wings are symbols of transformation, such as the phoenix rising from the flames.*
>
> *The eternal axis of Teoleos (vertical time and Heavenly Father), Logos (central word, consciousness and Divine Child) and Hylos (horizontal space, manifest creation and Earthly Mother), represents the holy family. Crucifixion is a means of intercession through intersection, a grid overlay that connects all life through a ladder of analogy and pillars of polarity. We carry the cross in the very cells of our being—the crystaline lattice of our structural DNA. And it is through the Divine imprint of the cross in our cellular structure that we will become one human race—the sacred family of which all life is a part, for upon the cross we are Oned. We are Father, Mother and Child. We are the point radiating out to form the circle, united by the cross in ever widening ripples. Above all, the cross signifies the liberation of matter, the fulfillment of the Sacred Feminine and the resurrection of form. Long may She live...for her very existence is the key to our transcendence into a new paradigm of peace on Earth. We simply can't rise to our perfection without her.* [25]

The Socio-Political Satires of Mark Henson

Expanding on the feminine voices of emancipation in the women's movement, a number of male scholars, mystics and visionary artists have committed their artistic vision to the rebirth of the feminine principle in the West. One of these is the beloved Mark Henson. Aside from the sensual, mystical, erotic and goddess art that Mark Henson is most known for, he has also painted a number of social-political commentaries that brilliantly critique American culture, particularly male-biased values such as progress, consumerism, the domination of nature and rationality.

In *Sharing the Wealth*, Henson captures the reality of social inequality in America and globally. While every society is marked by social inequality, a major reason social hierarchies endure is because of ideology, which is a set of cultural beliefs that justify social stratification. For example, the idea that the rich are smart while the poor are lazy is ideological to the extent that it defines the wealthy as worthy and suggests that poor people deserve their plight.

In *Sharing the Wealth,* the canvas is divided in two halves, illustrating the "haves" and the "have nots," which, as Karl Marx has revealed, is characteristic of social stratification and hierarchical thinking. The left side of the canvas illustrates the United States, which on a global level is one of the wealthiest countries in the world, while the other side represents a Third World country. The left side is a quintessential image of the opulence and wealth of America—the shiny red apple. Henson comically captures a typical Hollywood or Las Vegas scene, where beautiful people ostentatiously dress in expensive clothes and drive around in exotic cars. The setting is reminiscent of the strip in Las Vegas—colorful, bright, clean, alive, and abundant with material possessions. In the upper left hand corner, floating across the sky, is a blimp that reads, "Buy," subliminally illustrating the material god of consumerism so prevalent in American culture. In the foreground is a stereotypical Hollywood couple driving away in their exotic, status symbol car. With no hint of mercy or guilt in their eyes, they look ahead as they toss a hamburger and French fries to a poor, starving, ethnic man on the "other side" of the canvas.

The right side is a portrait of a typical Third World country, most likely Bangladesh, Asia, India or Africa, where most people are very poor. The setting is much more dismal and bleak. Low-income countries cover thirty-five percent of the planet's land area, but are home to half its people. Population density, therefore, is generally high. [26] A desperate woman with a baby strapped to her back hurls herself towards the scraps of junk food being tossed by the wealthy Americans. She is most likely a poor peasant, representative of half the world's population. People living in affluent nations such as the United States find it hard to grasp the level of human suffering in much of the world. From time to time we get shocking glimpses of famine in countries like Ethiopia and Bangladesh, where every day is a life-and-death struggle. While poverty is indeed a problem in the United States, poverty in poor countries is both more severe and more extensive. Furthermore, in poor societies women and children are the poorest of the poor.

The true motivation behind Henson's painting is an attempt to reveal the historical exploitation of poor societies by rich ones. While there are an assortment of theories as to the cause of global inequality, Henson believes—along with conflict theorists and proponents of dependency theory—that poor societies are not simply lagging behind rich ones on the path of progress. Rather, the prosperity of the most developed countries has come largely at the expense of less developed nations. Some nations, such as the United States, became rich only by making other nations poor. This is mostly the result of colonialism, which has enriched the lives of high-income countries by funneling raw materials from around the globe to the United States and Western Europe, where they fueled the Industrial Revolution.[27]

Today, multinational corporations operate profitably worldwide, channeling wealth to North America, Western Europe, Australia and Japan. Very recently, we have witnessed the growth of multinational corporations and their obsessive compulsion to use human labor to accumulate enormous wealth for a small minority of elite white males at the top. Engineering and science have been their right hand men, as they aided in the replacement of labor with machinery, factories and technology. The multinational corporations, therefore, have taken advantage of Third World countries and its laborers. Not only do they have access to huge labor pools, they can also pay the laborers cheaper wages than what they would have to pay American laborers. When describing the meaning of the painting, Henson says, "This image reveals why people across the globe are mad at the United States. Our wealth is the result of the domination, exploitation and colonization of third world countries. We export illusion. We will kill to do this. There is something extremely wrong with this picture. Run for office! Vote! Recycle! Boycott sweatshop products and all tools of violence. Have compassion for our planet and global family."[28]

The Living Cross: A Crossroad to Transformation, Heather Taylor, 24"x36" oil on canvas. www.fullcirclemandalas.com

One of Mark Henson's more horrifying political commentaries is *The March of Progress*. In this image, Mark explains:

> *A woman with a child flees in terror from the progress monster. An assortment of animals flee with panic-stricken faces from the toxic waste spewing from the man-made tower of denial and greed. Nuclear power plants stand on top of the monster's head like antennas. Death masks of toxic waste and poisons spew from a missile studded face. Mindless military tanks herd corporate clear-cutting loggers towards the garbage-filled beach, as a whale lies bleeding on the sand. Fiery nuclear mushroom clouds fill the sky as attack jets fly over the darkened seats of global government. The entire monster forms a dollar sign, capitalism, greed, materialism devoid of anything but primal survival dynamics run amok.* [29]

In America we have held tight to the belief that we should always strive to improve our situation, and that if we continue to work hard, our plight will improve in the future. In modern societies, people link modernity to progress, a continual state of improvement. While the growing scale of modern life has some positive aspects, there are enormous costs that don't become evident until much later. In a capitalistic and technologically-oriented society birthed from a strict protestant work ethic, we have manifested a lot of material wealth, but with great costs to the human soul and the Earth. An ever-expanding capitalistic economy not only produces greater social inequality and feelings of alienation amongst individuals in the United States and globally, but it also severely taxes the Earth and its inhabitants. The increasing scale of affluence in the first world is a direct result of the insatiable appetite of capitalism. Since a capitalist economy pursues ever-increasing profits, both production and consumption steadily increase; however, the gaps between the rich and the poor also increase.[30]

Henson's painting, *March of Progress*, portrays the ugly monster that we have manifested as a result of our cherished value of progress. Western culture's rationalistic paradigm has promoted an ethic of compulsive doing and is reflected in our persistent trumpeting of physical labor/work, with little acceptance for rest and meditation. This type of work ethic and the valuing of progress, as social

Sharing the Wealth, Mark Henson, 66"x48" oil on canvas, 2000, www.markhensonart.com

theorist Max Weber revealed, has its roots in the protestant ethic, which has continued to influence our conception of human labor, work and economic activity.[31]

While political leaders look to the future, promising that our lives will improve in significant ways, people continue to experience stark pessimism in what the future holds. The confident belief that science and technology will make life better is also being seriously reexamined as environmental degradation and social inequality become more pronounced. Technological and economic progress has definitely promoted rapid transportation and effective communication, but they have also increased the speed and complexity of modern day society and increased feelings of fatalism, powerlessness, depression and alienation amongst sensitive individuals.

Both the women's movement and the ecology movement are sharply critical of the uncontrolled growth associated with capitalism, technology and progress. The vision of the ecology movement has been to restore the balance disrupted by industrialization and overpopulation. It has emphasized the need to live within the cycles of nature, as opposed to the exploitative, linear mentality of forward progress.[32] In investigating the roots of our current environmental dilemma and its connection to science, technology and the economy, it is important to also reexamine the ways in which science and rationality have contributed to the accelerating exploitation of human and natural resources in the name of progress.

One of the results of expanding population, deforestation and toxic waste pollution is the dwindling biodiversity of the planet. The last three hundred and fifty years, and particularly the last forty years, have seen the extinction of tens of thousands of species of flora and fauna. While the history of the Earth reveals periods of mass extinction, the twenty-first century seems to be the first time that much of the diversity of evolutionary development has been destroyed primarily by the expansion and rising population of humans.[33] Mark Henson captures the horrific reality of extinction in *The March of Progress,* and asks people to wake up, get educated and be aware of the delicate balance that needs to occur in nature so that the Great Mother can continue to abundantly nurture us. For if we don't make drastic changes in our lives, she will be forced to do it for us. And whether or not we are able to receive her help, it will be the most compassion-

The March of Progress, Mark Henson, 38"x56" oil on canvas, 1995, www.markhensonart.com

ate move She could make for her beloved children, for her unconditional love continues to bless us even though the majority of humanity consciously and unconsciously disrespects Her.

Questioning Scientific Ideology: My Socio-Political Commentaries

The critique of the history of knowledge and its influence on ideology is central to the problem of gender inequality. The connection between science, power and truth has led feminists to critique the devices that the dominant group uses to deny other people access to power--be it political power or the power to create facts, knowledge and define truth. A number of postmodern scholars have begun a critical review of the history of science in order to pinpoint the ways in which male perspectives have been championed over female perspectives. What feminists have discovered is that, from its inception, men hailed science as a purely masculine construction.[34] The language and metaphors of science reflect the masculine ideal of objective, rational, logical, linear thinking. The outright preponderance of men's voices in many fields of study, but especially science, reflects the lack of valuation of feminine wisdom and consciousness. The implications of this one-sided perspective of the world and ourselves is far-reaching, since the power to define truth not only affects our lives materially, but forms the very concepts we internalize about reality.

There is no doubt that science has provided remarkable knowledge about the universe and the Earth. The benefits of science touch every aspect of our lives, from communication to technology. Yet, caught up in the tremendous success of the objective, reductionistic approach, other paths of knowing, particularly subjective modes of knowing, about nature and ourselves have been devalued. After a thorough dissection of the history of western knowledge, feminists have targeted the philosophy of science, which has been male-dominated from the start. Postmodern feminists have uncovered the tendency of modernist philosophers of science to use oppositional dualism as the basis of knowledge, which is believed to be one of the root causes of all domination, inequality and environmental degradation. They have found that in each of the dualisms on which enlightenment thought rests, such as reason/nature, rational/irrational, subject/object, mind/body, intellect/emotion, masculine/feminine and spirit/matter, the male is associated with the first and the female with the second, and in each case the masculine, rational and objective elements are privileged over the female, subjective and emotional elements. As a result, the message that women receive is that the stability, continuity and order of systematic thought is maintained by including only objectivity, and repressing the feminine, the emotions and the subjective, as the ground upon which theories of knowledge develop.[35]

These discoveries have been an enormous source of emancipation, not only for women and minorities, but for artists as well. Postmodernists and feminists have finally been able to deconstruct patriarchal ideologies that have invalidated the tools, or subjective modes of experience and knowing, that visionary artists use in order to create, such as the emotions, intuition, the unconscious, visionary experiences and other spiritual guides. The demise of the feminine principle in the Western consciousness explains why all things associated with the feminine, such as intuition, the arts, eroticism and nature, have been deemed irrational and, therefore, in need of being controlled. It also explains why female mystics and visionary artists have been so heavily devalued in Western culture, and why they have experienced difficulty in forming artistic identities.

As a woman, artist and sociologist disillusioned by the overemphasis of rationality in Western culture, I painted *The Iron Cage of Rationality,* a concept coined by one of the greatest sociologists of our time, Max Weber. In the movement from traditional to modern societies, otherwise referred to as modernity, Weber claimed that a traditional world view was replaced by a rational worldwide. The continual rise of bureaucracy in modern societies rests on what Weber termed "rationalization,"[36] a matter-of-fact calculation of the most efficient means to accomplish a particular task. As Western society continues to progress, it would become increasingly characterized by "formal rationality" which would inevitably obliterate personal autonomy and constrict creative capacities. Modern society, Weber claimed, has become "disenchanted" as sentimental ties give way to a rational focus on science, complex technology and the organizational structure of bureaucracies. While bureaucracy is an organizational strategy that has promoted efficiency, it risks potentially dehumanizing the people it is supposed to serve by reducing human beings to "a small cog in a ceaselessly moving mechanism."[37] Weber predicted that the emphasis on rationalization, especially in bureaucracies, would erode the human spirit with endless rules and organizations. He rejected the idea of progress, believing that Western culture would eventually become a highly rational and bureaucratically organized social order, an "iron cage" that would cage our imagination and crush the human spirit.

In this painting, a man in a business suit sits in an iron cage, with a perplexed look on his face. While this person could easily be male or female, I decided to use a man, as he best symbolizes the "suits" of the patriarchal establishment, but also the scientist, the capitalist and the bureaucrat, all of whom tend to be male and rationally-oriented. However, the iron cage ultimately symbolizes the imprisonment of humanity by too much emphasis on thinking. It also represents our self-created limitations and contingencies of ignorance.

Expanding on Weber's ideas, spiritual teacher Eckhart Tolle in his book The Power of Now, pointed out that people seem to be overly caught up in their minds, which he believes is another form of disease. We have become obsessed and even addicted to thinking, which prevents us from finding the realm of inner stillness that is inseparable from our soul. "The compulsive thinker, which means almost everyone, lives in a state of apparent separateness, in an insanely complex world of continuous problems and conflict, a world that reflects the ever-increasing fragmentation of the mind." [38]

As a result of our addiction to thinking and fear consciousness, we have divorced ourselves from our souls, from nature and from our bodies--in other words, we have created a living hell for ourselves. Yet, paralyzed by a victim mentality, we fail to realize our power to change the situation. The man in the suit is sad because he doesn't see a way out of his situation. Like most people who have internalized a materialistic and fatalistic world view, he isn't able to see past the physical world of the five senses to a higher, spiritual dimension. He has fallen prey to a deterministic, scientific world view that has taught him that he is a victim of his environment as opposed to being a powerful agent who possesses the power to create his own reality. He has forgotten, along with a large population of people, that there is more to life than making money and seeking the shiny red apple of prestige. He doesn't understand that his fear and obsession with control have blinded him to the overflowing cup of abundance being handed to him by God/Goddess. It is this kind of scarcity thinking that has led to a state of disenchantment--a state that has blinded him from seeing the abundance, magic and hope in the world.

The open doors in the sky represent multiple dimensions of reality, universal archetypes or opportunities available to him and humanity by choice. In one of the doors, a voluptuous woman, symbolizing the sacred feminine, serves as an unconscious archetype influencing our psyche. She is helping us to open our hearts, as our hearts have grown cold and cynical, forgetting the true meaning of compassion. An old wizard with a long, white beard pointing to a city of gold appears in another door. This is the old mystic, the prophet, the visionary, trying to get us to see that there is the possibility of a much richer life if we would let go of the false belief that we are separate from the Divine, and begin to evolve as spiritual beings.

Another door reveals an ape scratching his eyes, flipping off "civilized" society as he waves the American flag. I understand that using the American flag in a demeaning way is offensive to some people, especially considering that we have it so good in America in many ways. While I am passionately in love with many aspects of my country and the freedoms that come with it, there is a shadow side to the United States that isn't apparent until you live here. In the process of moving from a traditional to a modern society, an attitude of arrogance and disdain for so-called "primitive" cultures has developed along with our wealth. In so doing, our sophisticated, Christian civilized society has completely severed itself from nature, from identification with our bodies, our souls and our animal roots. Ironically, it is only in the recent reclaiming of ancient knowledge that we might be able to save ourselves from mass suicide. We are only now beginning to accept the validity of ancient wisdom, never lost to indigenous peoples and animals, that the Earth is not merely a lifeless material body, but is inhabited with a spirit that is its life and soul. Just as we have denied the concept of soul and its power to influence our lives, so we have ignored the living forces that are not human--the

The Iron Cage of Rationality, Victoria Christian, 24"x30" oil on canvas, www.victoriachristian.com

power of the animals and their message of wisdom.

Atom bombs, nuclear warfare, death and disease portrays yet another dimension of potential reality. Modern military technology, coupled with science, divorced from ethical values, ushered in the Nuclear Age with the creation of atomic bombs capable of wiping out entire populations of cities at one blow. At this point in time, we have the means to completely destroy the Earth many times over. The patriarchal warrior energy, while functional and necessary in its place, has gotten far out of balance in the United States and needs to come back into balance before it manifests our worst nightmare.

The next painting I want to discuss has two titles: *Mechanization of Wo/Man* and *Alert... She is Waking Up*. Depicted in the painting is a gingerbread factory, with laborers (the proletariat) in orange suits working on an assembly line, cranking out mass quantities of gingerbread cookies. But these laborers aren't human, at least not anymore; rather, they have all turned into gingerbread men (aside from the woman in the foreground, which is me). Looming in the background is a giant machine, gobbling up the gingerbread cookies as they run down the assembly line. In the central control station are gingerbread men in blue suits, consisting mostly of white men. They represent the bourgeoisie, those who own the means of production.

The men in the blue suits are upset because they just discovered that one of their workers has woken up to the fact that she is human, with a mind and a unique personality of her own. A loud alarm has been triggered, which reads *Alert... She is Waking Up*, sending one of the "controllers" out the door to stop the process of awakening. The woman in the foreground, who is awakening to the realization that she is being used for the benefit of the owners, is a representation of myself, but also of all people who work for "The Man," especially those who work "pink-collar" jobs. If you look closely, you'll notice that on all of the uniforms is the company name "McMan Co." In all of the jobs I have had, men were always in top management positions, and it was a rare occasion when they sought the advice of female workers below them. I have been busting my ass all of my life for the man who owns the big machine.

I have worked a lot of physically laborious and emotionally draining jobs, at low pay and with no benefits, in order to pursue my calling as an artist. I've worked as a baker, maid, waitress, retail sales assistant, social worker and teacher, all of which have been categorized as "pink collar" jobs because they tend to have a high percentage of women working them and they are generally low paying jobs with minimal benefits. The inspiration for this painting came while working as a pastry chef. After years of doing social work and having my heart broken many times by the system, I decided to take a job as a part-time baker in order to have enough creative energy to pursue art and writing--or so I thought. On a daily basis, one of my job duties was to crank out a large number of what we called ginger peeps (short for people), with smiley faces on them. I made so many ginger peeps that I literally felt like I was turning into one. Over time my spirit began to weaken and my back began to ache. Thinking about my situation as a poor, white female in debt was simply too painful, and it was a lot easier to just numb out, succumb to the machine and forget about the deep calling within my soul. I thought to myself, "If I could only be a cookie-cutter individual, without an ego, a brain or a heart, life would be so much easier."

Furthermore, finding the energy to create art was always a challenge, due to the physical and emotional exhaustion that these kinds of jobs produce. When you are dehumanized on a day-to-day basis by the directives of bureaucracies, institutions and stale work environments, your creative spirit begins to shrivel like a dried-up raisin. The insatiable appetite of capitalism to produce more and more goods seems to be sucking up people's life force to the point that they don't have the time or energy to pursue their creative passions. This is a tragic phenomenon and is a leading cause of suffering and depression for all creative individuals, which includes everyone. Adding to this point, social theorist Herbert Marcuse[39] and Max Weber[40] argued that as a result of the rationalization of society and the alienation that went along with it, the uniqueness of the individual would be replaced by a mechanistic conception of humanity which would inevitably strip individuals of personal identity, purpose and deeper meaning.

In order to illustrate the tyrannical colonization of the imagination and creativity by rational, linear modes of thinking I painted *Creativity Under siege*. While there is a lot of personal and social meaning in this painting, it speaks about how we are socialized to shut our creative centers down and become emotionless, apathetic drones in order to assimilate to a mechanistic society. It is similar to what Madeleine L' Engle said, "All children are artists, and it's an indictment of our culture that so many of them lose their creativity, their unfettered imaginations, as they grow older."[41] Not only are we physically deformed in the process of socialization, so that our bodies can no longer express themselves in natural, harmonious movements, we are also psychically deformed because we are taught to conform to a social concept of normality that excludes individuality and

Alert...She is Waking Up, Victoria Christian, 24"x30" oil on canvas www.victoriachristian.com

free expression.

I intended to paint *Creativity Under siege* as a way to come to terms with the fear and anxiety I, and a large number of women artists, have felt in the process of developing an artistic identity in a complex, postmodern society. Although the modernization of society has brought about freedom to express individualism by creating more opportunities for determined women to develop artistic identities, the extensive social diversity, complexity and rationalization of society has made it difficult for many women artists to establish any coherent identity at all. Furthermore, the culturally constructed binary which portrays the artist as subjective and irrational and the scientist as objective, removed and rational has not only led to a hierarchical portrayal of science as "better than" or "more valuable" than the arts; it has justified and maintained the marginalization of the arts and artists. Not only are the arts continuing to be portrayed as dispensable luxuries that must prove their worth in an impersonal mass market, but an increasing number of schools are opting to eradicate the arts and extracurricular activities in order to focus instead on what a scientific and technologically-oriented culture views as society's major priorities.

In *Creativity Under Siege* the claustrophobic feeling of population density and urbanization encroaches on the sacred space of my studio as a constant distraction and disruption to the conditions needed in order to get out of my rational, linear mind and into an intuitive mode conducive to creativity. In the narrow hallway in the background, under the golden eye of psychic intuition, is an insane person representative of Edvard Munch's famous painting *The Scream*, which was intended to capture the essence of modern emptiness, fragmentation and insanity as a result of mass-society.

The decision to pursue an artistic identity brings with it an enormous amount of conflict, specifically about whether to conform to societal expectations or deviate from them. For example, while contemporary culture values conformity, competition, rationality, practicality, and security, art and the life of the artist are in some ways antagonistic to Western values--stressing individuality, freedom of thought, spontaneity, risk, subjectivity, originality, and diversity. As Rollo May sees it, "The very fact that creativity and the arts are unpredictable, chaotic processes are an inevitable threat to bourgeois rational order."[42] The creative act itself requires that one take risks and allow that which does not yet exist to manifest itself--to recreate the world from scratch, to defy order and to be critical of existing forms. Therefore, to some extent, artists, as well as mystics, are taught to approach life in a way that is sometimes contradictory to the values western society triumphs. For this reason, mystical artists have typically been defined by western society as "non-conformists" and "deviants." Yet interestingly enough, "it is those who break the conventional apart that inevitably perpetuate the emergence of new value systems." [43]

The scream character symbolizes the internal torment and fragmentation the artist in all of us experiences as a result of being silenced and forced to conform to the alienating directives of capitalism. In *Creativity Under Siege,* the tape on my mouth is representative of being silenced as a woman, artist and mystic. People often make the assumption that because one is an artist, one has the freedom to say whatever one wants to say and get away with it. This is simply not true, especially if one hopes to make a living as an artist. Once one becomes a professional artist who has to make ends meet, the luxury of creating art for personal satisfaction is rare. As a result, the conventional art world consisting of galleries and museums is filled with mediocre, decorative art that blends into the woodwork and lacks spiritual meaning and a political edge.

The scream character is also representative of a dark, unloving energy lurking in the background, just waiting to steal away my passion for art. Throughout my artistic career, there has always been something or someone, whether it be a lack of money or jealous individuals that

Creativity Under Siege, Victoria Christian, 24"x30" oil on canvas, 2004, www.victoriachristian.com

have attempted to constrain my ability to be an artist. The paranoia that often comes with creativity can be extremely stifling, as a mystical artist needs to feel safe in order to explore the realms of the imagination. It seems that there have been more constraints as opposed to supportive influences in my artistic career, which is why I've had to become extremely jealous of my creative time.

The scream figure also portrays my self-imposed limitations; self-hatred and fears that want to put me out whenever I shine too bright. The Angel praying behind my easel is representative of my higher self calling me to remember my soul purpose. My process of identification as an artist has indeed been an arduous path that I've had to carve out myself with the guidance of my spiritual family and higher power. While some artists' paths are more direct, mine has been rather circuitous. I had a difficult time accepting that I was an artist as a result of false beliefs I had internalized via external social and cultural influence. Because I was conditioned to believe that being an artist wasn't a practical choice that would support me monetarily, I chose other, more realistic paths that gave me life skills that eventually turned out to be dead end roads.

The internal desire to be an artist was imprinted on my soul and wouldn't stop bothering me until I pursued the path. I came to realize that denying this drive was more difficult than just accepting it. It took me a long time to admit that in the core of my being I was an artist. In fact, it wasn't until I did research on women artists and identity formation that I was able to admit to others and myself that I was an artist. Like so many women artists in the West, I had internalized a lot of conflicting messages about myself throughout my socialization process that resulted in internal fragmentation and internal conflict. Through massive amounts of education, personal counseling and spiritual growth, I have been able to break through this false conditioning and embrace my heart's desire. However, that choice has brought with it great compromises. While I have become more confident about my soul purpose and mission in life as I evolve spiritually, on a day to day basis I continue to be plagued by an enormous amount of social and monetary constraints.

The Primordial Sacred Union: Revealing the Female Bias

Images of the Primordial Sacred Union are controversial because they challenge a similar female bias, which is sometimes more difficult to detect because women's voices have been so denied in the construction of knowledge. However, as I offer my critiques on the female bias, I need to make something clear. I have ultimate respect and admiration for the courageous women in all disciplines who have carved out a path of emancipation for women of today. For this reason, I am hesitant to be too critical of the women's spirituality movement when it is still in its infancy. When I reflect on the thousands of women who challenged patriarchal ideologies in much more severe conditions of oppression, I am instantly humbled. I envision warrior women with enormous swords, cutting away the thick forest of ideological oppression. Therefore, the critiques I have to offer the women's spirituality movement come not from ego and competitiveness, but rather from good intention and a commitment to make the movement stronger.

In my educational years as a student of sociology, particularly feminism, and years of professional training as a counselor, the dynamics of the victim/victimizer relationship has always fascinated me because it is so evident in human relationships. Yet, what I find so ironic is that each position sees the other as the source of its problems. For example, women haven't always been able to see the ways in which they've contributed to the dynamic system of human suffering because in pointing the finger at "the patriarchy" as the evil victimizer, they have assumed the position of the innocent victims. I am not denying the fact that men have used warfare and physical violence to dominate women. On the contrary, I am merely making the point that there is a complex dynamic occurring here that reflects the dysfunctional role of the victim also. Women seem to know what "men's issues" are, but have we really owned our roles in the human drama? As humans who suffer from fragile egos, women are just as likely to abuse their positions of power if the tables are turned. Having had the experience of working under several power-tripping women, I'm convinced that women are equally capable of abusing their power and have the capacity to emotionally castrate a man with the glance of an eye.

I am cognizant of the diversity of feminist perspectives or "feminisms" within the women's movement as well as the varied perspectives within the neo-pagan and Wiccan groups and, therefore, I make no broad generalizations about any particular group. Exposing the female bias is indeed a complex topic, with multiple layers and perspectives that deserve a thorough analysis. Unfortunately, I am not able to delve into the complexity of these issues in this article. However, I will offer merely a superficial explanation of my own observations regarding the female bias. As a sociologist who is aware of the dialectics model of social change, history reveals the tendency to go from one extreme to another, which in some respects can be considered a defense mechanism or reactionary survival instinct. The pendulum doesn't need to swing to the other side in order to find a place of balance. While feminism has been a powerful tool of emancipation for women, there is a tendency in radical feminist and some pagan groups to go to the other extreme; thus, falling prey to a "female bias."

I agree with Carole Christ who so brilliantly noted that, "The Goddess is emerging at a time when women, women's bodies, and nature have been devalued and violated for centuries, and that a re-membering of the Goddess has the potential to bring healing to humanity."[44] At this point in time, it seems natural that both women and men should take the time to get reacquainted with the Great Mother. It might take a number of years, perhaps centuries, before the sacred feminine has attained a place of autonomy equal to men. However, in the process of awakening to the Goddess, it has become evident to me that some people have gone from one extreme to the other--from father worship to strictly mother worship, without a true appreciation of consecrated polarity, or the sacred union (particularly for those who have been severely damaged by patriarchal religions).

The tendency for the mainstream to go from one extreme to the other is all too evident in human history. The sexual revolution of the 1960s, immediately following the McCarthyism of the forties and fifties, is a perfect example of a pendulum swing from sexual repression to sexual liberation; however, we see now that neither extreme served us. This is also true of God and Goddess ideation. When speaking about the Divine, one simply can't talk about God without talking about the Goddess. For this reason, it is of particular importance that feminists not go the other extreme and succumb to a female bias, especially when they are openly disgusted and judgmental of a "male bias." The primordial One demands that at some point we transcend gender--the totality of the One is the void - it is pure potentiality, neutral and genderless.

Perhaps my biggest concern with feminist critiques of gender inequality is the tendency to make generalizations, which in many respects is an inevitable human phenomena that stems from a lack of deeper understanding on a particular subject or a lack of awareness of one's own bias. Making broad-brushed and overly simplistic statements shows not only a lack of motivation to fully explore the complexity and diversity of perspectives about a particular argument, but an unwillingness to apply a sense of reason and logic when exploring topics. Most of my concerns about feminists are tendencies that I also succumbed to in my own process of awakening; therefore I am not placing judgement on these tendencies. I merely wish to help women to be more aware of their own contingencies of ignorance. I was fortunate to have people in my life, particularly scientific men, who challenged my ideas and brought me back to a more balanced place. While I can't say that I am a fully integrated individual, free from my own bias, I have worked hard to bridge the masculine and feminine energies within myself so that I might be more effective in seeking balance in society.

When women take a position of blame and point the finger at men, men are more likely to become defensive and reactionary, when in fact women need the opposite to occur. Women need men to be more open and willing to receive the reflection they have to show them, as opposed to pushing it away. Women won't be able to penetrate the denial and resistance of men if they are coming from a place of blaming rage. The rage that emerges when a woman comes to realize the extent to which she has been wounded by the patriarchy is indeed a valid emotion, and must be embraced. But rather than venting this rage on men in general, it is important to work through it in personal counseling or with other women. Venting rage on men will only make them defensive and unwilling to examine the ways in which they have contributed to the problem. Feminists have, consequently, been stereotyped as "raging man haters" because of the few who didn't have the tools to deal with their rage in a healthy manner.

Women also need to be more specific as to what kinds of men and male behaviors perpetuate and maintain gender inequality. As far as I'm concerned, it is the really insecure men in positions of power, who tend to be more traditional and conservative in their views about gender roles, that are the biggest contributors to the problem. However, there are also those who openly admit they don't condone gender inequality, yet unconsciously contribute to the system of oppression on a day-to-day basis without even realizing it. There are also men who have worked hard to break through their conditioning and are open supporters of the women's movement.

After long hours of discussion with both men and women on the topic of feminism and women's spirituality, I witnessed the horror, pain and guilt felt by some men who professed they had nothing to do with "the patriarchal" establishment or social inequality. Upon hearing their voices of resignation and guilt for something they don't feel a part of, I came to realize that there are plenty of men who are open to healing and who recognize the value of integrating their feminine side within themselves and in the world at large. Men who openly embrace feminist interests will serve as valuable and positive role models for the large majority of men who either refuse to or simply don't understand the benefits of embracing the feminine principle.

Revealing the Shadow Side of Goddess Religions

There is, without exception, a shadow side to all social constructions; therefore, it would be ignorant of us to disregard the ways in which ancient matrifocal societies fell prey to their own contingencies of ignorance. After a critical evaluation of an assortment of perspectives within the women's spirituality movement, I have noticed the tendency of some feminists and theologians to paint ancient matrifocal societies in a simplistic and utopian light, as if they were perfect, egalitarian societies. However, as much as we would like to view them in this light, inevitably there is a shadow side to Goddess religions that might not be so easily detectable. While it is possible that these cultures may have been less violent and warlike, and maybe even more egalitarian, I don't believe it's right to assume this as "total truth" when in fact it is impossible for us, as outsiders from a different epoch, to truly discern the reality of a historical period.

Feminist thealogian Rosemary Radford Ruether makes some interesting claims in her book *Gaia and God: An Ecofeminist Theology of Earth Healing.* I am impressed by Ruether because she is careful to not oversimplify or make broad generalizations about ancient matrifocal societies and the reasons for the shift into patriarchy. I appreciate her cautious and balanced approach when analyzing the Goddess hypothesis. She is critical of feminists who tend to come off as separatists, such that the sacred masculine is negated. She writes, and I agree, that "A separatist vision of demonization of men offers no real hope for resolving the male-female conflict in society."[45]

She is critical of feminist thealogians who tend to paint a perfect picture of matricentric society because they fail to recognize the problems of an insecure male adult identity. Matrifocal societies that "fail to develop an adequately affirmative role for men, one that gives men prestige parallel to that of women but prevents their assuming aggressive dominance over women, inevitably risk developing the resentful male, who defines his masculinity in hostile negation of women."[46] Radford doesn't agree with some of the original mothers of the women's spirituality movement,that we can simply return to a Neolithic matricentric system. However, she does agree that reclaiming the memory of these earlier cultures can be immensely valuable to the wholeness we seek as a society today. But she strongly advises that we take into consideration the weaknesses of the matricentric core of human society that made it vulnerable to patriarchy.

It is difficult to know the downside of a particular ideological social structure until one has actually lived in it. Nonetheless, it is our human right to make humble, educated guesses as to what some of these might have been. While I can't say I have thoroughly investigated all theories as to how the shift from matrifocal to patriarchal societies came about, I know there is no simple explanation. When I try to recall a particular phase in my earlier development of consciousness, it is impossible to be totally objective. I find that I inevitably project some of my more "mature" or "developed" states of mind onto my earlier phases of psychic development. When examining ancient cultures or earlier phases in human consciousness, it is equally difficult for modern humans to revert back to ancient modes of knowing without projecting our modern day perceptions and beliefs.

When I intuitively reflect on the shift, the one thing that continues to come to mind is the pendulum swing, which seems to effectively reflect the rhythms of social change throughout history. On some deep level, I sense that there were necessary developments in consciousness that came out of matrifocal and patriarchal social systems. However, I think that in each phase we developed totally different modes of knowing, and that each phase eventually reached an extreme point that became dangerous--the shadow that lurks in all social constructions. In this sense, each phase was necessary in order for human evolution to occur; therefore, one phase isn't "better" than the other. In the West we have taken rationality and yang energy to an extreme state of imbalance, which is why it is important to now reclaim ancient intuitive knowledge that has been lost to us so that we can come back to a place of balance and equilibrium. However, it is unrealistic to think that we can simply go back in human history and manifest an earlier phase of human consciousness. This would be analogous to a mature adult trying to revert back to childhood--it is simply impossible. It seems that what we really need to do is awaken the inner child, the simplicity and the innocence of an earlier phase of human consciousness, but also retain the adult understandings that we have in the modern world.

In modern society we have experienced the damage caused by the separation of spirit and matter; we have been taught that they are two totally different realities that don't mix, despite how things function in nature. Our inability to integrate the invisible world of spirit and the visible world of matter has resulted in not only severe fragmentation and damage within the human psyche, but also a contradictory and divided understanding of the world and our relationship to it. An assortment of scholars claim that in ancient Goddess-oriented societies, spirit and matter were considered to be one and the same. There was no separation between this world and the other world, or the sacred and the profane. Supposedly, the separation into two autonomous and distinct polarities arose much later in human consciousness, and is considered by some scholars to be a tragedy brought on by the patriarchy.

When I apply the concept of consecrated polarity to the dualism of spirit and matter, I can't help but wonder if the two polarities were so intertwined in early human consciousness that they needed to establish a sense of autonomy before they could once again unite. Developmental psychologists have observed that a human in its infancy has no separation between its internal and external world, and that in order for self-development to occur, the polarities between self and world need to be established. Because the micro world of the individual and the macro world of society are reflections of each other (the individual is in society and society is within the individual), I propose that the evolution of human consciousness as a whole evolves in a similar way to that of an individual's psychic development.

If, in the infancy of human consciousness, spirit and matter were one and the same, it would make sense that in order for us to evolve, the separation between spirit and matter, or "this world" and the "other world," had to occur. From a Jungian perspective, the feminine principle of relatedness, without an understanding of the masculine principle of autonomy, would promote a sea of sameness that would deny the unique beauty of diversity. Remember that in order for consecrated polarity to function correctly, both polarities need to be autonomous; however, they also need to be interconnected in order for creative evolution to occur. Like the spark plugs in an engine, the positive and negative charges need a gap in order for the synapses or creative spark of evolution to occur.

Healing Our Wounds through Consecrated Polarity

The hectic pace of modern life may be a strategy that our culture uses to overwhelm and shut down our ability to get in touch with our soul's wisdom and the brilliance of our bodies. The patriarchal values of progress, workaholism, and an emphasis on results are just a few examples of a yang oriented society in desperate need of feminine, yin wisdom—particularly, that of Eastern mysticism. Unfortunately, the price paid for the banishment of the invisible world of soul from the scientific community, and the Goddess from the Judeo-Christian community (aside from Gnosticism) has been more costly than we have realized in terms of a deeper understanding of our true nature.

In order to heal the current imbalance, women and men are attempting to reclaim feminine values, such as compassion, cooperation and interdependence. Yet, beyond the contest of dominance, beyond the polarization of masculine consciousness and feminine consciousness, lies the intuition that there must be something else, a further development in human consciousness. I'm convinced it is a return to the primordial sacred union that we are all consciously and unconsciously seeking. Yet, because the voices of women, especially minority women, have been so silenced by men of science and religion, now is the time for women to speak their truth and reclaim the feminine soul that has been stolen from them. However, it is equally important that men awaken to the ways in which they have been wounded by the denial of the sacred feminine as well, for it is these men who will be extremely influential in assisting the women's movement in their mission create equality between the sexes. The women's movement, in all its forms, will be extremely influential in our ability to deconstruct the existing power structures that have sought to control the way in which truth has been defined. However, it is important for women to realize that an ideological battle is being fought, and for years to come it is likely to be a struggle.

As we move into the postmodern era, it is time for our fragmented perception of ourselves and of the world to undergo transformation. A radical restructuring needs to occur; transformation out of oppositional dualism and into a new mode of perception, which I call consecrated polarity, modeled after the primordial sacred union. This shift is necessary in order to heal the split at the epistemological level between the visible and the invisible worlds, masculine and feminine, God and Goddess.

In order to heal the split at the epistemological level between spirit/matter, intellect/emotion, male/female, we need to retain dualism as a universal and fundamental aspect of human consciousness, but end the antagonism and domination between the two polarities. The polarity in the archetype of the primordial sacred union must and will be retained, as it is a fundamental and universal blueprint that exists on the tiniest of micro levels and the largest of macro levels. It serves as a catalyst for social change, creativity and natural evolution. It is the glue or love that binds all things and spurs our evolution as parts within the whole.

The current movement to restore the sacred balance

of God/Goddess will inevitably require each individual to thoroughly examine deeply held beliefs that are no longer serving them. A radical awakening needs to occur on a massive level. We must be taken apart so that we might be built up again. While the future changes may provoke fear and discomfort, Western culture needs a dark night of the soul in order to reflect on the ways in which it has become imbalanced. The emergence of the archetype of the primordial sacred union is constructive, but also revolutionary. It is spiritual, but also political. It is a much more inclusive way of conceptualizing the Divine. However, it is important to remember, as the Taoists so humbly remind us, that the great One can never be named, for once it is named, it is confined within a box which imprisons its essence. In this sense, it is the never-ending Great Mystery that is beyond our ability to conceptualize—and for good reason.

Victoria Christian is a sociologist, social worker, counselor, artist, writer and sacred activist. She holds undergraduate and Masters degrees in Sociology. She also has a Masters of Social Work, with an emphasis in the sociology of gender, social theory, the sociology of art and ecofeminism. For more information about her art, books and DVD's, you can view her website at www.victoriachristian.com. To learn more about this book, see the website: www.mysticspiritart.com

Imaging the Divine Complements

God/Goddess, Claudia Connelly, 52"x13" oil on linen, www.claudiaconnelly.com

By Margaret L. Starbird

It has been a long journey—a journey I never intended to take. In the nineteen eighties, as a cradle Catholic raising a family of five children, it hadn't yet occurred to me that God did not resemble the athletic patriarch painted by Michelangelo on the ceiling of the Vatican's Sistine Chapel. Like Briar Rose in the Sleeping Beauty fairy tale, feminine images of the Divine had been asleep for nearly two millennia in the Western World.

My awakening to troubling distortions inherent in Christian dogma was a rude one. On a golden late-autumn Sunday in 1987 while attending the Feast of Christ the King Mass, I was confronted with a large banner newly displayed over the altar of my parish church in Franklin, Tennessee. Depicted against a black background near the outline of a church with a large steeple, the yellow orb of the sun was rising, spreading its bright rays in all directions. Gaudy orange lettering proclaimed an exultant message: "Every day is Son day."

Throughout the Mass I was uncomfortable, pondering the implications of the banner, gradually awakening to ramifications of its masculine orientation, wondering how little girls in the congregation might be responding to its proclamation. And how did the mothers of those daughters feel? Christianity was not only about sons, for according to St. Paul's epistle, in Christ "there is neither male nor female, Jew nor Greek, slave nor free, but all are one."

Mass ended the parishioners filed out of the church, greeting the pastor on their way to the parking lot. I paused in front of the priest and then blurted out that I was very uncomfortable with the banner above the altar. Father was surprised, explaining it was an historical fact that God had sent his Son. He laughed and made what he thought was an amusing joke: "Maybe next time God will send his daughter." I could feel the blood rising to my face. I knew he was laughing because he thought the idea ridiculous that God could ever have a daughter. "God sends His daughters every day, just as He sends His sons," I replied, as I turned away and walked toward my car.

During the spring semester at Vanderbilt Divinity School, where I was enrolled as a student, I became ever more conscious of the "sun-pun" in Christian communities. Driving through the streets of Nashville on my way to class one morning, I encountered the reader board of a local church that proclaimed, "SONday worship here at 10 A.M." Another sign, "Sun Worship here," struck me across the face. How true! The orientation of the Western World, under the hegemony of Christian faith, is solar. The architects of Christianity called Jesus "the Sun of our Righteousness." And according to the Christian Creed, Christ is "Light from Light." His mythology is that of the "Rising Sun" and its eternal return, born at the winter solstice when the descent of the sun is reversed and the light returns in the northern hemisphere, rising to its summer zenith in June.

As I contemplated the solar aspects of Christ-worship, I became more conscious of the distortion of reality it implies. Christianity has placed its "God of Power and Might" on a throne in heaven. But in exalting the masculine/solar principle embodied in the "Son/Sun," we have a 24/7 solar orientation that distorts reality since it denies the feminine/lunar complement. In the real world, day is followed by night. The sun has to allow darkness equal time, and the winter solstice in December meets its equal-opposite in June. There is a balance in the created cosmos and nature that is denied by the all-male trinity of Christian doctrine.

In Hebrew the Holy Spirit is feminine, but in Latin, "Spiritus Sanctus" is masculine. For two millennia, the Western World has been laboring under the influence and hegemony of exclusively male-oriented doctrines, the "faith of our fathers." Like the dark bride in the Song of Songs, the feminine lunar principle has been "laboring in her brother's vineyards," serving in bondage to the masculine principle, swarthy from her labor in the sun.

What we call "God" is the ultimate Force and Source behind Reality. But let us be very clear: God is not a patriarch with sculpted muscles and a flowing gray beard. Christian traditions provide a false image of God. Michelangelo's painting depicts a supreme patriarch—the Father God. But if we look very closely at the Creation, where God reaches out to give life to Adam, we see the Sophia, the spouse of God and mirror of divinity, tucked gently under his left arm. She is a young blond woman possessively clasping God's arm. In Scripture, the Sophia is the Wisdom of God, sought as a Bride by King Solomon and extolled in the Hebrew Proverbs and in the apocryphal Book of Sirach (Ecclesiasticus):

> *Come to me all you that yearn for me and be filled with my fruits; you will remember me as sweeter than honey, as better than the honeycomb. He who eats of me will hunger still, he who drinks of me will thirst for more; he who obeys me will not be put to shame, he who serves me will never fail.(Sirach 24:18-21).*

In Michelangelo's fresco, God and Sophia are surrounded by cherubim and enclosed in a cloud shaped like a human brain. Perhaps Michelangelo was suggesting that the Creator God, his Sophia, and their heavenly entourage are really the products of human consciousness, manifested in an attempt to explain human existence.

The image above titled *God/Goddess* by visionary artist Claudia Connelly is a contemporary rendition of Michelangelo's fresco. It beautifully captures God and Sophia as autonomous individuals, gazing into each other's eyes. She writes:

> *In my painting, Western man's most revered image of God now includes his divine partner, the Goddess! God and Goddess face each other as equals. Behind them is the backdrop of the universe, part of their dual creation of All That Is. Rather than reaching his hand down to man, this God entwines his fingers with Goddess as his partner in creation. With the return of the Goddess to her rightful place beside God, the true equation is being reinstated and spirituality is coming full circle.*

Aramaic, the spoken language of the Jewish people in the time of Jesus, is very poetic, each word loaded with several layers of meaning. When one examines the Lord's Prayer in Matthew 6:9-13 from the perspective of spoken Aramaic, one finds that the words "Our Father" can have many possible translations, with amazingly fluid meaning. One such meaning, translated by Neil Douglas-Klotz in his ground-breaking work *Prayers of the Cosmos* is: "O Birther! Father-Mother of the Cosmos!" What if the legacy of the Christian Gospels had been conveyed to us in Aramaic rather than Greek? What form might our image of the Divine have taken? I'm reminded of the little girl who tugged on her mother's sleeve during Mass. "I love hymns, Mommy; but are there any hers?"

That spring of my awakening in Nashville, Tennessee provided a stream of powerful synchronicities. Many occurred while I was driving my car, which is not surprising since I spent many hours commuting to classes and ferrying my children to their endless soccer, baseball, and track events. One day I was contemplating the modern state of the church. What happened? I thought. The institutionalized version of the twentieth century couldn't be what Jesus had intended! I looked ahead along Murfeesboro Road and was struck by a huge billboard advertising a new residential community, "Chapel Homes."

Exactly! The early church had been established on a model of "table fellowship"—people gathering with friends in their homes to share a meal and discuss the good news that Jesus Christ was risen from the dead and that his spirit was with them still, guiding and encouraging the believers. They celebrated the indwelling of the Spirit with their neighbors in "chapel homes."

On another day, a radio newscaster reported that a college woman had tossed her illegitimate newborn infant down a trash chute in her dormitory. Horrified, I stared out the window, noticing the trash along the highway, distraught that people could so casually toss away their trash and unwanted children in a nation that claimed to have Christian values. My attention was gradually drawn back to the radio. The newscast was over and a country singer was crooning, "When the sun always shines, there's a desert below. It takes a little rain to make the flowers grow."

Somehow I understood the message. I "knew" with my heart that the sun/son worship inherent in a solar/masculine orientation stripped of its feminine counterpart results in materialism, hedonism and violence, just as it did in ancient Babylon and in pagan Rome. A wasteland ensues, burned out under the relentless rays of unmitigated sunlight—the "desert below." And it seemed to me that the ultimate consequence of the Christian worship of a "God of glory, victory, power and might" would be holocaust.

The balance in nature requires rain and darkness in proper measure. Cosmic reality is a delicate dance of the polarities, just as a beautiful life is the integrated balance of head and heart. But the "Faith of our Fathers" has denied feminine gifts while praising and promoting only masculine ones: "Every day is Son day." Across the globe, this orientation manifests in a preference for male children, and catering to masculine priorities. The environment is ravaged and hopes of future generations "trashed" in a rush to satisfy rampant materialism and selfish hedonism.

A Celtic legend tells of a land where nine beautiful maidens guarded the springs. Every visitor to one of the springs was offered a drink from a golden cup borne by one of the maidens. Peace and prosperity flourished and everyone was happy. But the king lusted after one of the maidens and raped her, and following his example, his friends raped the other maiden-guardians of the springs. Then the land fell into a dismal gloom. The springs dried up, the vegetation died and the land became deserted.

A similar wasteland legend evolved in Christian Europe: the Grail King suffers from an incurable thigh wound and cannot be healed until the Holy Grail is found and restored to him. His domain reflects his misery by becoming a parched wasteland. Perceptive Grail scholars have suggested that the "Grail"—the vessel that once contained the blood of Christ—represents the lost feminine principle in Western civilization rather than an artifact or a chalice. That principle is embodied in Mary Magdalene, the archetypal "Bride in Exile," hidden for her own protection and then lost to posterity, her voice silenced when she was proclaimed a prostitute.

The image titled *Mary Magdalene*, by visionary artist Jonathan Weber: There is something about this image that resonates so deeply in the human heart. You can almost feel her sorrow, yet she has a look of peace on her face that instills a sense of hope and a deep reverence for divine justice. Jonathan writes about the painting:

She is seen in this painting at the tomb of Jesus, where she had come to anoint his body with oil, represented by the jar. She places her hand over her heart, where she feels her connection and devotion to Jesus. Having witnessed his painful and tragic crucifixion, and now realizing his ascension into the kingdom of heaven, she is immersed in the rapture of profound sadness and joy. As portrayed by the contrast between dark and light, she has come from a place of great suffering to realize the glory and greatness of spirit everlasting.

How, after two millennia, does one heal the wasteland—the desert caused by unmitigated solar orientation? An interesting story is told of Thomas Merton, an American mystic, who attended a conference on comparative religion in Tokyo. One of the Zen monks present at lunch one afternoon told Merton that he had always wondered why Christians had to memorize so many prayers and doctrines. Merton asked, "Why? What do you do?" The Buddhist smiled, "Oh, we dance!" How delightful!

The Buddhists celebrate the gift of life by dancing. The "Dance of the Cosmic Energies" is at the heart of the Cosmos. Ultimate reality is a dance of wave and particle, creating the visible and tangible universe. The dance represents a relationship between matter and energy manifested in the orbiting planets and constellations, the changing seasons, the infinite variety of created matter, flora and fauna. This principle is celebrated in the mythology of Shiva and Shakti in India and in other god and goddess mythologies expressing the Life Force, the source of all that lives. And the dance is about celebrating life. Jesus said that he came to bring "life abundant"—not sitting on a cloud looking down at the Earth, but fully participating in the "kingdom of God" already in our midst and all around us! How appropriate that the Buddhist prayer takes the form of dancing—matter in ecstatic motion, celebrating life.

So archetypal is the honoring of the symbiosis of the opposite energies that we find pagan cults from the Neolithic period honoring the Earth as Mother Goddess, and the sun as her heavenly consort. An ancient Earth temple was built about five thousand years ago at New Grange, just north of Dublin, Ireland. Massive standing stones line the circumference of an enormous man-made mound. A shaft, also lined with standing dolmens, runs from the entrance to an interior central chamber. At the winter solstice, a shaft of light from the rising sun penetrates to the center of the interior chamber, apparently symbolizing the sun's impregnation of the Earth. New Grange appears to be a Temple honoring the eternal return of the sun, the masculine energy of the Life Force, as eternal partner of the Earth Bride.

In ancient cultures in the Middle East, the Life Force was celebrated in fertility rites honoring both masculine and feminine energies personified as god and goddess. Rites of *hieros gamos* (sacred marriage) were often celebrated early in the New Year. The bride (usually a royal priestess) selected her consort from among the available men in the domain. He became king by virtue of his marriage in those matrilineal times. The anointing of kings is an echo of these ancient rites, when the bride's ritual anointing of the king was a pre-figuring of the anointing during the consummation of their nuptials in the bridal chamber. When the royal bride and bridegroom rejoined the community, the whole nation feasted and celebrated with lavish banquets often lasting an entire week. And they danced. The joy generated in the bridal chamber spread into the crops and herds and, as in our fairy tales, "everyone lived happily ever after."

Well, not quite. There is more to the story. Later in the liturgical year, the anointed king was arrested. He was tortured, mutilated, executed--sacrificed for the welfare of the people to ensure continued fertility and prosperity in the realm. He was entombed. After a short period, often of three days duration, his wife and her entourage of attendants came to the tomb to mourn the death of the "Bridegroom King." Imagine the joy of the bride when she found her beloved resurrected in the garden! They were reunited at the spring equinox in celebration of the eternal return of the Life Force.

Those who study the mythologies of the gods and goddesses of the Middle East will recognize the names of many divine couples celebrated in a similar myth: Inanna and Dumuzi in Sumer, Ishtar and Tammuz in Babylon, Adonis and Aphrodite in Greece, Isis and Osiris in Egypt; Ba'al and Astarte in Canaan. The liturgical poetry of these ancient fertility religions survives, including one very familiar version found in the canon of the Hebrew Bible—The Song of Songs. This erotic poem is a redaction of ritual incantations honoring Isis and Osiris, published under the title, The Burden of Isis, with which it shares lines that are verbatim and others that are similar.

Faced with the similarities of these ancient rites of the Sacrificed King with the Passion story in the canonical gospels of Christianity, how can we fail to include Jesus, the Sacred Bridegroom of the Christian story, and his bride, Mary, called "the Magdalene," on this list of deities? Clearly they too are cast in the role of Divine Complements in the Passion story, beginning not at Gethsemene, but at the banquet at Bethany when the sister of Lazarus anointed Jesus and wiped his feet with her hair (John 12:3).

In this significant passage, Mary was proclaiming Jesus as the long-awaited Messiah of Israel in the role of the Sacred King. In that role, she represented her land and people as Bride of the Sacred King. Her fragrance of nard is the fragrance also of the bride in the Song of Songs; it "fills the house," and the bridegroom in the canticle praises the fragrance of his bride's ointments. In the version of the anointing story found in the Gospel of Mark and repeated in Matthew's Gospel, Jesus admonishes his disciples not to complain about her action, saying, "She has done me a favor. She has anointed me in advance for my burial…and wherever this story is told, it will be told in memory of her" (Mark 14:8-9). Any pagan convert to Christianity would have immediately understood that Jesus and Mary Magdalene embodied

Mary Magdalene, Jonathan Weber, 22"x32" acrylic on canvas, 2006, www.jonathanweber.org

the ancient myth of the sacrificed god/king and his bride.

The New Testament insists that Jesus was of the royal lineage of King David and that he was the legitimate heir to the throne of his ancestors in Jerusalem. And the Hebrew word for messiah means "anointed." It seems clear that the authors of the Christian Gospels styled Jesus as the sacrificed King of Israel and an incarnation of the Divine as Bridegroom of the nation.

Many ancient Hebrew prophecies associate the Bridegroom with Yahweh, styling the nation of Israel as his Bride, a frequent theme in the Hebrew Bible: "No longer will she be called forsaken, or her lands desolate, but she shall be called 'Beloved' and her lands 'espoused" (Isaiah 62:4). In the book of Ezekiel, Yahweh finds Israel a desolate orphan child, and espouses her. But she is unfaithful, prostituting herself before foreign gods. And in the book of Hosea, the prophet is told to take the prostitute Gomer to wife as a sign of Yahweh's love for his people. For even when the people are unfaithful, God remains true to the covenant made with Abraham and affirmed

Mary of Magdala, Andrew Annenberg, www.andrewannenberg.com

to David and Solomon. The Temple in Jerusalem was built as a dwelling place for Yahweh and his feminine partner, and the Holy of Holies was their Bridal Chamber. So the "sacred marriage" was indigenous, not just to pagan cults of the ancient Near East, but also to the Jewish people. Apparently these people understood the intimate balance of Earth and heaven, matter and spirit, flesh and divinity, femininity and masculinity. The archetypal symbol used to express the harmonious union of Masculine and Feminine is the yod, an ancient symbol representing the metaphysical truth "as above, so below," the "chalice and the blade," and is found also in India, where it represents the "Cosmic Dance" of Lord Shiva and his consort Shakti.

Inspired by the sacred iconography of India, particularly the symbol of Shiva/Shakti, visionary artist Paul Heussenstamm painted *Jesus and Mary as One (previous page).* If you hold a piece of paper over each side of the face, you will clearly see both Jesus and Mary.

From the Christian Scriptures we receive powerful testimony to the egalitarian nature of earliest Christianity. Jesus walked and spoke with women, cherishing their companionship. Paul asserts (1 Cor. 9:5) that the brothers of Jesus and the other apostles all traveled around with their "sister wives." Another Scripture passage mentions a "sister" and "wife": "How fair is your love, my sister, my spouse" (Song of Songs 4:10) and "You are a garden enclosed, my sister, my spouse; an enclosed garden, a fountain sealed" (Song of Songs 4:12). Who is this "sister spouse" if not the twin flame of the Archetypal Bridegroom, his Complement and Beloved?

In the Egyptian myth of Isis and Osiris, the god and goddess are brother and sister as well as husband and wife—their intimacy and kinship is at all levels, manifested on every plane of existence. They embody the Divine as Sacred Complements. Apparently this loving partnership of couples was the unique model in the early Christian community as well. Yet two millennia of patriarchal overlay have persuaded us that Jesus' disciples traveled as pairs of male missionaries. Paul's epistle, however, testifies that they traveled as missionary couples, spreading the good news that the kingdom of God is already within us and in our midst.

I have become convinced that the wife and partner of Jesus in his ministry was the Mary called "the Magdalene." She is the pre-eminent woman in the Gospels, the most passionate and most loyal of all, present at both the cross and tomb. She is styled in the ancient role of archetypal Bride coming to the garden to mourn the deceased king. In the book of the Hebrew prophet Micah, we find a passage that appears to be the source of Mary Magdalene's title of honor, a title that affirms that she is Bride and "First Lady," the representative of her people:

> *As for you, O Magdal-eder, Watchtower of*
> *the Flock Stronghold of the Daughter of Sion*
> *Unto you shall the former dominion be restored,*
> *The kingdom of Daughter Jerusalem.*
> *Now why do you cry? Have you no king?*
> *Has your counselor perished ....?*
> *For now you shall go forth from the city*
> *And dwell in the open fields.*
> *To Babylon shall you go,*
> *and from there you shall be rescued.*
> *Now many nations are gathered against you.*
> *They say 'let her be defiled.'*
>
> *Micah 4:8-11*

Of all the passages in the Hebrew Bible, this one best sums up the story of Mary Magdalene; crying at the tomb of the deceased King and counselor sent into exile, defiled and defamed. The passage calls her the "tower" or "stronghold" of the Daughter of Sion. She represents the people as Bride, and the Church as the New Jerusalem. Micah's prophecy has her name on it. How can we fail to recognize her as the woman weeping at the tomb of Jesus when he asks her the question, "Why are you crying?" There is only one Mary who cries in the Christian Gospels: she cries over her brother's death, and Jesus is moved by her tears to raise Lazarus from the dead (John 11). She cries at the feet of Jesus, and wipes them with her hair (John 12). And like the woman called the "Magdal-eder," she cries at the tomb of her beloved king and "Rabboni" (John 20). Even her use of that Hebrew word, translated "my little teacher," shows a special intimacy between them. The image above titled *Yeshua and Magdelena,* by Christina Miller, reveals a teary Mary. The chalice holds the waters of life from which they both will drink.

One does not need any Gnostic Gospel to provide evidence that Jesus and Mary Magdalene were perceived as the Divine Complements in the Christian mythology. Their story has been told and retold in the canonical Gospels. Every pagan convert to Christianity would have recognized the bride crying at the tomb of the sacrificed god/king, and every Jewish convert would have recognized the "Magdal-eder"—the watchtower/stronghold "Jerusalem" personified as bride.

Every year Christians celebrate the return of the Easter Mysteries, named vicariously for the Goddess Ishtar, who seeks her deceased Bridegroom Tammuz in the underworld. Every year we celebrate the eternal rebirth

Jesus and Mary as One, Paul Heussenstamm, oil on canvas, 2007, www.mandalas.com

and regeneration of life and the immanence of a passionate Deity who loves Creation with an everlasting love that is stronger than death. And the model for the "sacred partnership" of the human soul seeking union with the Beloved Other has always been Mary, the one called Magdalene, searching for Jesus and being reunited with him. This story at its heart is not about a bloodline descended from Jesus and Mary—the "sangraal"/blood royal of medieval legend. Rather, it is about the paradigm of sacred union that was to have been our heritage. Sadly, the model was broken in the cradle: the very earliest Christian heresy was the denial of the Bride.

So what happened? How did we lose the Bride of Jesus? My personal belief is that the friends of Jesus, knowing that the Romans tracked the families of the men they crucified as insurrectionists, would have done everything possible to protect his wife, especially if she was pregnant. They would certainly have insisted that she be taken to a place of safety, probably in a secret location in foreign exile. The Book of Acts never mentions Mary Magdalene, nor do any of Paul's Epistles. She simply vanished. Legends place her in Ephesus and also on the Southern Coast of Gaul (France). The French legends are much more detailed than those of Turkey, stating that she and her siblings and friends arrived on the Mediterranean coast in a boat with no oars, bearing with them the "Holy Grail." Mary Magdalene is believed to have preached the Gospel in Marseilles and to have retired to the cave of Ste. Baume, living out her life for thirty years as a hermit. This implies that she lived out her life in total obscurity.

Over the centuries, the Magdalene was identified with the sinner who anointed Jesus at the banquet in Luke 7. Instead of being celebrated as the beloved wife of Jesus, she was given the epithet of "penitent prostitute," a slanderous assertion which has no basis whatever in scripture. Thus was her true role suppressed, her voice stolen, her royal status denied.

In February 2004 I was invited to give a lecture at my father's retirement home. Just as I was entering the auditorium, one of his friends slipped me a note with a quote from the prophet Joel. My father's friend had gone to his missal to preview the readings for Ash Wednesday. The line he slipped to me said, "Let the Bride come out of her closet" (Joel 2:16).

It is time to image the Divine as Sacred Partners who model the integration of polarities (masculine/feminine; spirit/flesh) and the harmonious wholeness of Creation. Mary Magdalene is standing at the threshold, after three millennia, waiting to take her proper place as the partner, the archetypal Bride and Sacred Complement of Jesus in the Christian myth of origin. In reclaiming Mary Magdalene as the Holy Bride, we will begin to heal the wasteland.

The Book of Revelation promises that streams of living water will flow from the throne of God for the healing of the nations. Perhaps the patriarchs will set aside their crutches at last to dance with the Bride!

Margaret Starbird holds BA and MA degrees from the University of Maryland and did further graduate study at the Christian Albrechts Universität in Kiel, Germany and at Vanderbilt Divinity School in Nashville, TN. A "cradle" Roman Catholic, she taught religious education and Scripture classes for many years. Starbird lectures and leads retreats worldwide. She is the author of several widely acclaimed books centered on the Sacred Feminine in the Christian tradition: *The Woman with the Alabaster Jar and The Goddess in the Gospels: Reclaiming the Sacred Feminine* and her latest book, *Mary Magdalene, Bride in Exile,* published in 2005. Starbird has two further titles: *The Feminine Face of Christianity and Magdalene's Lost Legacy,* both published in 2003. Please visit www.margaretstarbird.net

Antahkarana, Amoraea Dreamseed, 24 x 36 acrylic on canvas, 2006, www.divine-blueprint.com

PART TWO:

Rebirth of the Great Goddess

CHAPTER ONE:

The Goddess of Creation

Tree of Life, Victoria Christian, 2"x3" oil on canvas, www.victoriachristian.com

Envisioning the Divine in Nature

By Victoria Christian

As I sat in the midst of some of the last remaining old growth in Oregon, I sensed a peaceful tranquility slowly permeating my body. Distant but familiar memories of a deep enchanted forest swirled around in my mind like wine in a glass. The healthy redwoods stood tall and wide, like gentle green sentinels shooting up into the heavens to form an illuminated cathedral glowing with dappled light. Ocean mists gently floated across the lush green ferns as the low hum of a foghorn sounded off in the distance. The fresh scent of pine permeated the damp breeze as I took a long, deep breath of oxygenated air. I sat in utter silence, listening to the sounds of nature. I thought about what it might be like to feel this kind of peace all the time. Off in the distance a bird hummed its intricate song, sending me into a state of complete ecstasy. I felt so present, yet simultaneously far away. It didn't take long, however, before my mind began to engage in its usual chatter, obsessed on figuring out the never-ending human drama.

How have we become so disconnected from ourselves and from nature? And why is it that some people can't feel the sacredness of the Earth even while in the presence of her most profound beauty? Deep within my soul I sense a vast overall plan for the Earth, but to comprehend its total nature is beyond my limited and fragile human capacity. So I decided to go back into the stillness, and quieted my mind once again.

A soft wind gently brushed against my face as the still small voice within whispered "Open your heart and let me heal your wounds, for it is in your heart and body that you will be able to receive my wisdom." As I took another deep breath of pure oxygen, my heart expanded wide open as if it had suddenly grown little wings. Tears of pure love started to pour down my face. It had been too long since my last visit, and I didn't realize how thirsty I was to drink in this beauty, this love. Within an instant of being in the presence of nature, my worries evaporated into the mists. I had just felt what it was like to be embraced by the Great Mother, and I suddenly felt safe. Something inside me just knew the Earth was greater, stronger and more resilient than I could even begin to imagine. I had underestimated the Great Mother's strength, and was being reassured that she had an evolutionary plan of her own, one that was far larger than my ability to comprehend.

At this point in time we are all being called to acknowledge the primordial experience of the Great Mother, whether we are conscious of it or not, for it is from her womb that all life is born and sustained, and to which it eventually returns. The fertile Earth is clearly symbolic of the creative powers of the Source. "The Goddess is the life force which is nurturing, compassionate, beneficent, and also the terrifying force of death and destruction which inevitably regenerates what it has destroyed." [1] The first arts and religions, the first crafts and social patterns, were designed in recognition and celebration of her. She is the greatest artist of all, inspiring the creative endeavors of humans for centuries.

The Goddess as the giver of life is also referred to as the "Creatrix," since she gives birth to plants and animals as well as human beings. In the world's oldest creation myths, she is the Earth Mother, Gaia, the Goddess who creates the world out of her own body. In the Neolithic era, animals, birds and serpents were all symbols of the Great Mother. She was also *The Mother of Wild Animals* or the *Lady of the Beasts*. We first encounter her with her animals at Catal Huyuk where, as the life-giver, she sat between two leopards to give birth. She was her-

Creatrix, Suzanne De Veuve, 18" x 24", Oil on Canvas, www.suzannedeveuve.com

self an animal, and all the animals were embodied by her. In many of the Paleolithic images, she wears an animal mask. This means that she is symbolically any tree, beast, bird, fish or insect and must, therefore, be related to with magic and respect.

While eco-feminists vary in their beliefs, they all tend to build on the Gaia hypothesis of Lynn Margulis and James Lovelock which views the planet as a living, dynamic system designed to maintain and nurture life, and that the Earth itself functions as a unified self-regulating organism.[2] Eco-feminist Elisabeth Sahtouris states that, "The intelligence that guides evolution is not outside nature, but embodied in it as the 'body wisdom' of Earth. The great Gaia being knew itself in the same sense as our bodies know themselves, having the body wisdom to take care of itself and keep on evolving."[3]

In her book, *The Rebirth of the Goddess*, Carol Christ speaks of the Goddess as fully immanent:

> *The power of the Goddess is the intelligent embodied love that is the ground of all being. She is known in rock and flower and in the human heart, just as in thealogies of immanence. As the organism uniting the cells of the Earth body, the Goddess is the firm foundation of changing life. As the mind, soul, or enlivening power of the world body, the Goddess is intelligent, aware, alive, a kind of 'person' with whom we can enter into relation. Thus, the Goddess can 'speak' to us through the natural world, through human relationships, through communities, through dreams and visions, expressing her desire to manifest life ever more fully in the world. And we can 'speak' to her in song, meditation, prayer, and ritual, manifesting our desire to attune ourselves with her rhythms, to experience our union with the body of the Earth and all beings who live upon it.*[4]

What is particularly exciting about the concept of the Goddess as intelligent embodied love is that she truly is the root of everything we are and we experience her love in every cell of our body. In other words, we are so fundamentally rooted in the Earth that it is as intimate to us as our own bodies. We simply would cease to exist without our grounding in the Earth. To say that the love of the Goddess is embodied, adds Christ, "means that her love is grounded in the emotions and passions that arise from the senses.... It is rooted in deep feeling, and in this sense, is erotic."[5]

I have definitely felt the sensual eroticism of the Goddess while painting in nature. In fact, several of the artists and writers in this book have had profound experiences of the Goddess revealing herself to them in a variety of ways, through relationships, art, prayer, meditation, song, dreams, poetry and visions. In this article I will share with you some of these experiences, images and poetry by both male and female mystical artists.

Envisioning the Sacred Union in Nature

In reclaiming the sacred feminine in creation, it is equally important that we not overlook the androgynous and masculine aspects of nature as well. Eco-feminist Stephanie Leland explains the androgynous origins of life. She writes:

> *Research into our earliest history has revealed the possibility that psychologically, as well as biologically, we began as unconscious hermaphrodites, reproducing parthenogenetically. In the simplest life forms, reproduction took place asexually. As we move up in the evolutionary ladder, in very primitive life forms, such as ostracod crustaceans and nematode worms, the mode of reproduction is carried out by the female alone, parthenogenetically, or in pairs as hermaphrodites.*[6]

In addition, biologists have observed and recorded a number of masculine traits in nature, particularly in the process of fertilization and pollination. An assortment of trees, particularly conifers, reproduces by seeds that are attached to the surface of the pine cone. Typically, pollen develops from spores in the male cone, and pollination occurs in the spring when the pollen is blown into the female cone containing the ovules that develop and produce eggs. Many flowering plants also need pollen in order to reproduce. The great variety of flowers we enjoy today have come about by the coevolution of flowers and various pollinating agents such as the wind, insects and birds. There are also a number of plants that reproduce asexually, meaning they don't require pollination from the male species.

The egg and the seed are powerful symbols associated with the Goddess, fertility and cosmic creation; however, the egg remains stagnant unless fertilized by the semen of the male. In the ancient Goddess civilizations of the Neolithic era, particularly that of Catal Huyuk in Anatolia, images of the Goddess were found beside bull's horns, which symbolized male fertility.[7] In neo-paganism, the Horned God, or Cernunnous, is the male role or part in the male/female polarity. The horns of the Horned God are believed to represent his domain over the woodlands and his association with the bull and the ram, the animal consorts of the Goddess. His horns also symbolize the crescent moon —the symbol of the Goddess— and fertility.[8]

The ancient Sumerians understood that many gods

and goddesses were involved in assuring the fertility of the land, and the cooperation of all forces of nature was needed for success. Every year they performed an ancient ritual called The Sacred Marriage, which dates back to prehistoric times. In Sumer and the whole of the Near East, the symbolic mating of the Goddess Inanna with the King (a mortal representing the God Demuzi), would ensure fertility and the abundance of the land. Through her union with the King, the mystery of human sexuality was connected to the fecundity of nature.[9]

While the Earth has typically been associated with the feminine in an assortment of creation myths and is clearly representative of the creative life-giving aspects of the Great Mother, there are indeed masculine traits in nature that mustn't be overlooked. In order to avoid dualistic categories that polarize Creator/Creatrix into distinct categories, embracing the androgynous nature of Source will help us to avoid seeing things as only separate and divided when in fact they are also intricately connected. The Creatrix is indeed an autonomous entity, and needs to be established as such in human consciousness, for it is from her womb that we are all born.

Nonetheless, there is an element to the Goddess that is intricately connected to the Creator. There are elements of the sacred masculine reflected in manifest creation, just as there are elements of the sacred feminine in the invisible world of spirit. The Goddess can't be reduced to a position of immanence only in nature when her essence is also transcendent and present in the realm of spirit as an aspect of the One. Furthermore, God the Father shouldn't be relegated only to the spirit world when he is also immanent and visible in creation. In other words, the Divine One is both immanent and transcendent, impregnating the manifest world and the world of spirit at the same time, transcending gender.

The Erotic Landscapes of Mark Henson

The oil paintings of California artist Mark Henson passionately portray the sacred union in nature. Although delightfully diverse in his subject matter, a central theme of Henson's has been erotic landscapes portraying a man and a woman, God and Goddess, making love in various natural settings. Deeply inspired by the sheer complexity of the Earth in all of its pain and glory, Henson's imagery serves as a reminder of both the sacred union and the polarity nature it reflects. Mark views eroticism and the sex ritual as a natural and exalted state of consciousness. He sees the merging of souls as the manifestation of the cosmic design inherent in all living things. He calls upon our divinity as natural sensual beings in harmony with our environment by depicting lovers in all forms.

Henson offers an assortment of erotic landscapes, and his painting titled *Ravine Rapture* beautifully portrays the sacred union in nature. In this image two lovers nestle in a waterfall amidst a lush jungle setting, most likely in Costa Rica where Henson has a small farm. He is inspired by the pristine setting of the cloud forest and the essence of *Pura Vida* that permeates nature there. Henson writes:

> *If you spend enough time in the forest, you will begin to see the fecundity of the place. You learn about the birds and the bees by direct observation. Every life form is a marvel of seduction, and the jungle is covered with life forms from the micro to the macro level. Glorious flowers entice the insect world to participate in an orgy of genetic exchange. Amazingly colored birds shamelessly flirt in the branches overhead, and choruses of frogs announce amphibian orgies. Scent, color, flavor and sound fill the horizon of sensual experience. Seeds, eggs, pods, cocoons--you name it--the evidence of reproductive behavior is everywhere one looks. The force of life is erupting in such an eternal timeless climactic frenzy of sexual activity that it can only be balanced by mortality.* [10]

Another image by Henson, titled *Tree Incarnation*, shows several trees comprised of mating couples, with a central tree fashioned as a woman beckoning to a spiral galaxy overhead. In the foreground beneath the tree is a pair of human skeletons embracing on the ground where the tree is rooted. Henson beautifully captures the great mystery of life in this painting--that life and death are intertwined. The death aspect of the Goddess is integral to an understanding of the Goddess as giver, taker and renewer of life. The fundamental rule of Gaia is that everything is born, everything will die, and everything will be transformed. Henson gracefully portrays the transformation of death into new life with the remains of the two lovers and the recycling of their spirits back into the great universal matrix, while their bodies are recycled back into the Earth, transformed into molecules of nutrition for new life to emerge. "Hand in hand they gently lay their bodies down to become the playful forest. Gently, the Earth consumes their forms, freeing their spirits." [11]

It is his deepest desire to share his mystical experiences in nature with those who live in cities where the connection to nature is obscured by the demands and pressure of life in the contemporary world. Mark says, "These magical places are quickly disappearing in our lifetime, as the uncontrolled human urges of technological progress and procreation threaten our delicately bal-

Ravine Rapture, Mark Henson, 86" x 48" Oil on canvas, 1996. www.markhensonart.com

Tree Incarnation, Mark Henson, 48" x 60", Oil on canvas, www.markhensonart.com

anced position in the web of life." [12] In the process of differentiating ourselves from nature, we have lost touch with our primordial feelings of unity with nature. By viewing humans as separate from nature, the Earth has become objectified as that which should be subdued, controlled and manipulated, as opposed to a living organism to be revered.

The Mystical Fantasy Art of Jeffrey Bedrick

Many traditions celebrate the myth of a golden age, where magic, myth and mysticism guide our lives and there is no sense of separation form the Earth or one another. Some artists are able to tap into this golden age and invoke a sense of innocence and wholeness. Jeffrey Bedrick is one of these artists whose paintings take the viewer to another world of fantasy that bridges heaven and Earth. Born in Providence, Rhode Island in the 1960's, Jeffrey moved with his family to Northern California in the early 1970's. His artistic ability was recognized early as it developed in the Bohemian world of 1970's hippie culture.

"At thirteen, he spent time visiting the studio of his neighbor, renowned surrealist Norman Stiegelmeyer who coined the term 'Visionary' to describe a contemporary art movement that focused on spiritual and utopian visions experienced in altered states of consciousness - whether through drugs or meditation. Later at sixteen, Jeffrey met his idol, Gage Taylor, a painter of fantastic landscapes and a colleague of Steigelmeyer. Taylor accepted Bedrick as a private apprentice. By eighteen, Bedrick was accepting invitations to exhibit his work alongside his mentors. He continued his studies at the College of Marin with Bill Martin, another renowned Visionary landscape painter. For over 20 years since, Bedrick has produced art in a wide variety of genres and media." [13]

While Jeff has an enormous portfolio of paintings and digital animation, there are two paintings that capture his imagination: *The Immortal Light* and *Meadow Magic*. Upon viewing Jeff's work, there is a sense of innocence, or a message of Paradise lost and Paradise regained that speaks to our continual attempt to realize the ideal in the actual, the "fall" of the inevitable failure, and the renewed effort to try again. His painting, *The Immortal Light* speaks of the unwavering sense of innocence—the part of us that trusts life, our selves, and other people.

The Immortal Light, Jeffrey Bedrick, 30x40, Oil on Canvas, www.jeffreybedrick.com

It is the part that has faith and hope, even when on the surface things look impossible.

Many traditions celebrate the myth of the Fall from innocence. In Christianity, it is the myth of the Fall from Eden into a world of pain and suffering. But as with all versions of the myth, it does not end there, since the myth also says that a redeemer will come and save humanity—at least those who retain their faith in God—and take them back to heaven. Having faith in the unwavering light of love is the only thing that will help us through the storms of life. The rainbow bridge is the heart of mysticism that binds all things in love. And while we may feel the treacherous pains of this world, we must always retain the part of us that is whole and perfect. This is God's promise to us, that Love is Victorious and will be restored on Earth and in the hearts of humanity. This knowledge helps awaken in us the innocent pure child that believes as only a child can believe. Because we do not know what is coming, we have to trust.

In *Meadow Magic* we see the magic of Gaia in all her beauty and splendor. In the foreground are three little faeries or deva's, frolicking about in the meadow. They are a reminder that miracle's can happen if we take time to connect with ourselves in nature, embraced in solitude. It is only in the state of innocence that miracles happen. The faeries remind us that it is safe to trust. Our faithfulness will be rewarded. Our job is simply to have faith. Doing so opens the doors for miracles.

Meadow Magic, Jeffrey Bedrick, 30x40, Oil on Canvas, www.jeffreybedrick.com

Nature and Art as Spiritual Path: Andrew Annenberg and Paul Heussenstamm

For some people, nature is a spiritual path. Nature often lifts our spirits and provides inspiration, renewal, and experiences of awe. Being in nature is a spiritual reward in itself. Some artists feel more comfortable painting in nature as it helps them connect to the web of life. It makes them feel alive and inspired—to be fully immersed in the elements is to saturate your senses with intoxicating smells, sounds, tastes, and profound visual experiences.

Painting in nature has been a spiritual path for world-renowned artists Andrew Annenberg and Paul Heussenstamm. Both of these artists are incredibly prolific and have contributed a large number of art works to the transcendental art movement. Not only are they master painters, they are devotees of the Divine, forever thirsting for soul wisdom. They have devoted their lives to creating profoundly exquisite works of visionary art, not to mention Goddess Art. However, they have not limited themselves to nature art alone. Authentic artists don't like to be pigeon holed in one expression. Both of these artists have eclectic portfolios that capture the diversity of mythological and spiritual traditions, symbols, archetypes, and iconography.

Andrew Annenberg

Andrew Annenberg is an internationally renowned master artist who has a special affinity for natural and etherial wonders. Inspired by his many adventures and world travels, Andrew's art has evolved throughout his lifetime, leading to award winning masterpieces. Created from his own immersion in natural, mythical and spiritual experiences, his masterful creations share "world's within worlds" of awe and wonder."

Andrew's enthusiasm and zest for life flow freely through his art. His sensitivity and masterful renditions have earned him the recognition and respect as one of today's foremost visionary artists. Andrew invokes a strong sense of the European tradition present within his paintings from Breughel to Dali, but, in fact, his roots have drunk deeper from the well of the universal unconscious. The talent with which Andrew has been endowed is a royal gift that is shared with joyful appreciation for all that is magnificent, all that is sacred, a simple and yet profound statement for the benefit and pleasure of all mankind. Andrew summarizes it well:

> *Perhaps the most important quality that I aspire to, and which when successfully achieved raises a painting above the ordinary, is that subtle thing we call atmosphere. The soft haze in the distance; the bright reflection, the subtly blended skin tones and play of light and soft shadow that delineate every plane and curve and hollow of a face to produce a stunning illusion of actual three dimensional substance and weight and heft. These are the things I strive for.* [14]

Andrew has painted a diversity of landscapes from tropical ocean settings of Hawaii to the rolling landscapes of California. Andrew resided in Maui for over twenty five years and was inspired by the vast and colorful tropical landscapes. His paintings are ridiculously detailed and referred to as Visionary Realism. Much of his artistic inspiration comes from the Lemurian feeling of the Hawaiian Islands, his enchantment with the tropical version of paradise, as well as his fascination with the ancient civilizations of Egypt, Greece, and Atlantis.

The majesty and mystery of the sea is represented in his painting *Guardians of the Grail.*

> *Amidst the essence of medieval art and Gothic architecture, the curiously elusive Grail myth is represented. According to tradition, Arthur was crowned King of Britain and soon after founded the Circle of the Round Table, its shape reflecting eternal perfection because the table had no beginning and no end. Twelve guardian Dolphins symbolize the Knights each so great in dignity and power that none could occupy a more escalated seat than another. The Dolphins surround the sacred table, as 'Guardians of the Grail'. Just out of reach, the radiant chalice looms above the Knights. The Grail is the symbol of purity, faith, heroism and charity.,* [15]

Andrew also had the honor of residing in Northern California in his later years, particularly Sonoma County. He lived in a cute little farmhouse in the grape orchards just outside Sebastopol. As a humble admirer of nature, he went on numerous walks and absorbed the magical lighting and magnificence of the old oaks groves. His painting *Laguna Autumn* portrays the enchantment of this land. He writes, "On one particular walk through the orchards, the golden rays of sunshine were falling on the oak trees and the beauty was so magnificent it literally brought tears of joy to my eyes." [16]He saw the earth with the eyes of a child, full of excitement and wonder, as if seeing things for the first time.

Andrew has a fascination for ancient civilizations, architecture, sculpture, and sacred artifacts. He was fortunate to have the opportunity to travel to ancient ar-

Guardians of the Grail, Andrew Annenberg, www.andrewannenberg.com

Laguna Autumn, Andrew Annenberg, www.andrewannenberg.com

Venus Triumphant, Andrew Annenberg, www.andrewannenberg.com

cheological sites and cultures that revered the Goddess. Another one of Andrew's Master works is titled *Venus Triumphant.* This painting was inspired by a trip to Italy and Greece. He visited the city of Pompeii, which was an ancient Roman city near modern Naples. It was mostly destroyed and buried under 4 to 6 m (13 to 20 ft.) of ash and pumice in the eruption of Mount Vesuvius in 79 AD. It was in Pompeii that the idea for *Venus Triumphant* was born. [17]

Venus triumphant represents the rise of the feminine on a global scale and the VICTORY of Venus—a Goddess of Love, beauty, and the arts. She holds up the apple, which is a symbol of fertility. In Greek mythology the apple is associated with Aphrodite, the Goddess of Love. The root of the word apple is associated with the sun god Apollo. In Chinese mythology the apple is the symbol for peace and the apple blossom is a symbol of feminine beauty.

Paul Heussenstamm

Paul Heussenstamm is a visionary artist residing in Laguna Beach, California. Though originally aspiring to be a plein air painter, Heussenstamm's spiritual and artistic journey led him from landscape paintings, to flower paintings, and on to discovering his passion for mandala paintings. He was introduced to the healing potential of mandalas through the work and mentorship of Dr. Beverly Sheiffer. With permission, he adopted her method of painting mandalas for spiritual revitalization. [18]

A prolific and recognized artist, Heussenstamm's work has been featured in numerous religious and spiritual centers, including: Unity, Agape, and Church of Religious Science. His art is also featured at healing centers such as Deepak Chopra's in La Jolla, California; Esalen, in Big Sur, California; and Oglethorpe University Museum in Atlanta, Georgia.

Paul is well known for his capacity and clarity in helping others discover the "language of the soul." A fourth generation artist, Paul's formal education and degree in fine arts could not have prepared him for the ultimate revelation of his life's work: The artistic sharing and teaching of an ancient language and powerful symbol, the Mandala. For many, Paul's intensely colorful paintings are for and from the soul, and serve as a pathway to self-realization, healing, and wholeness. In addition to his art, Paul travels throughout the United States and around the world teaching "Art as a Spiritual Path" workshops. [19]

In his mandala workshops, he provides a safe container for people to explore the artists within each individual. A mandala represents wholeness, a cosmic diagram reminding us of our relation to infinity, extending beyond and within our bodies and minds. Mandalas are circular designs symbolizing the notion that life is never ending. They can be created by individuals to symbolize their journeys through life. Paul Writes:

> *The mandala, for me, more than any other teacher in this lifetime, has opened the doorway into the symbolic language of the soul. As I began to open up this ancient doorway, I received access to and understanding of a soul language that has powerfully changed my life and the lives of all those who come into contact with this level of intuitive knowing. One of the true gifts of this language is a deep understanding of the patterns, symbols, and currents in nature and how they relate to my own soul's enfoldment and development.* [20]

Paul has painted numerous mandalas, which are used for meditation purposes allowing the individual meditating to become one with the universe and make a connection with the higher self or soul. The design of the mandala is supposed to be visually appealing so as to absorb the mind in such a way that irritating thoughts are unable to get through and a spiritual essence surrounds the individual observing the mandala, which in turn allows the individual a higher consciousness or awareness, almost as though being hypnotized. This allows the busy mind to take a break while the creative mind is allowed to run free (see 3 sample mandalas on next page).

Paul's painting *Buddha Wisdom Tree* taps in to the deep spiritual roots of Buddhism and the Bodhi Tree. The Buddha is in deep meditation, quieting the mind, and breathing with the pulse of the earth. The Bodhi Tree was a large and very old Sacred Fig tree. It was at the Mahabodhi Temple at Bodh Gaya. Siddhartha Gautama, the spiritual teacher and founder of Buddhism, achieved Bodhi (spiritual enlightenment) while sitting under this tree.

In the tree, Paul has carefully placed various Sanskrit mantras and mandala portals that invoke the subtle realms of spiritual wisdom whispering in the wind. It is a call to quiet the mind and drop in to our hearts and bodies, as there is a vast inner landscape that is available to all of us if we are willing to be silent. Meditating in nature and allowing our bodies to come in contact with the earth's magnetic pulse is a revitalizing experience that has the potential to recharge our entire being and bring peace of mind.

Another painting is *Twilight Dancer*, a stunning representation of Guanyin in the zen garden. With open arms and downcast gaze, the Asian Goddess of compas-

Womens Movement Mandala, Paul Heussenstamm, www.mandalas.com

Kali Mandala, Paul Heussenstamm, www.mandalas.com

sion, kindness and love, revered since Buddhism's introduction in the first century, welcomes all who seek her virtues. She is standing on an orange lotus flower in a complete state of balance and harmony with nature. He eloquently captures the golden light of twilight on the bridge, water, and trees.

Paul is a proponent of the inter-spirituality movement, whose mission is to bridge the gaps between all spiritual traditions and ideologies. Our divisions as a human race are at the root of all war and suffering. Paul has painted sacred iconography from numerous spiritual traditions such as; Hinduism, Christianity, Buddhism, and Shamanism-- in order to reveal the symbolic oneness of all things, from the microcosm to the macrocosm. When we drop in to our hearts, we see that there is a universal thread of mysticism that binds all people, plants, animals (all our relations).

Oceans of Change Mandala, Paul Heussenstamm, www.mandalas.com

Buddha Wisdom Tree, Paul Heussenstamm, www.mandalas.com

Twilight Dancer, Paul Heussenstamm, www.mandalas.com

Women Artists Envisioning the Divine in Nature

We are in a time of intense shift in consciousness, and women artists-- particularly female mystics, visionaries and eco-feminist artists--play a fundamental role by creating sacred feminine imagery of the Earth and of women's bodies. As the domination of mankind continues to erode the balance and beauty of the Earth, it is of the utmost urgency that women rise up and restore a sense of reverence for the Earth. The time has come for women to take leading roles in the rectifying of this balance. Let me now introduce you to some of my images and experiences, as well as the work of a few contemporary female artists whose mission it is to heal the split between spirit and matter.

The Magical Realism of Victoria Christian

Being an artist means fulfilling a deeply rooted part of my soul and acknowledging my unique interpretation of the world. My passion is to create in material form the ways in which I interpret my reality through visionary insights. As a magical realist, my art sensitizes people to the element of magic working in their personal lives and in the world at large--a dynamic which is highly tied to our need for spirituality and emotional connectivity. The goal is to tap into the sensation of awe aroused in me when I'm in nature, and translate it onto the canvas in a way that reaches peoples' hearts and rekindles their desire to commune with nature. Too often we feel disconnected and trapped in the prison of our minds, making it difficult to be in the moment, where magic and mystical experiences occur.

My artistic mission is also to produce sacred images of the Great Mother and all that she represents. Highly influenced by the long tradition of mystics and Goddess artists that have come before me, I both participate in and expand upon this tradition in a way that is uniquely my own. As a young girl I first experienced my mystical connection to nature and my body through art, dance and biking. Having had the good fortune to grow up in the quaint little town of Ashland, Oregon, I was surrounded by forests, rivers and mountains in my childhood. Nature was always right in my backyard, beckoning me to come and partake in her glorious wonderland. Later in life, in the midst of education and work, I rode my bike and hiked all over the Pacific Northwest and Hawaii, eventually ending up in the Southwest.

Upon exploring a diversity of landscapes in the Four Corners region, I've had a number of mystical experiences in nature, yet I find it hard to put these experiences into words because they don't adequately capture the multitude of influences that coalesced into a sudden gestalt of spiritual and mystical awareness in those moments. I've found that putting these experiences on canvas with paint captures the essence of this experience in a way that words cannot.

Having lived in the Southwest, I've been fortunate to experience a variety of desert landscapes. Upon visiting the slot canyons in Utah and Arizona, I was inspired to paint *Towards the Within*. In this painting a woman sits cross-legged meditating in a canyon, with sagebrush burning in an abalone shell in front of her. She is in a state of complete inner focus and tranquility. Rising above her head into the heavens is the universal consciousness, an umbilical cord connecting her to the realm of the cosmic spirit. The Southwest is saturated with breathtaking caverns and caves, some of which have been designated as sacred sites to the Navajo and Hopi Indians. There are certain times of the day that the light shines through, illuminating the curvaceous and spiraling canyon walls. The peaceful tranquility of the canyon is truly enchanting, similar to standing in a giant cathedral with high ceilings shooting up into the heavens. The scent of spirit permeates the dry, cold air. The utter silence of the canyon is stultifying, urging you to stop and listen to the still small voice of your being within.

When I painted *Towards the Within* I was deeply yearning for a spiritual path that would incorporate the use of sacred ceremonies, ritual, meditation and a connection to nature. Upon delving into an assortment of spiritual traditions, I had come to the realization that there are jewels of truth in all religious paths. Within the funnel of universal unconscious, I painted various religious symbols, such as yin/yang, the infinity symbol, the third eye, the Star of David, and the cross, representing a synthesis of the world's religions and sacred iconography.

I didn't fully understand why I painted this piece until much later when I happened to read about the symbolism and meaning of the cave in ancient Goddess religions. For the people of the Stone Age, and continuing into the Neolithic Era, spiritual ceremonies were often performed in a cave. Symbolizing the womb of the Great Mother, the cave was considered by the ancients to be the primary holy place of mystic influences. Caves also were associated with childbirth and the maternal nature of the Goddess. In the original cosmology, a cave was the symbol of the whole world, providing passage for the dead and for the rebirth of souls. This is where one went to commune with the deepest, most resonant and awesome powers. In fact many tribal people and Native Americans still hold the belief that their first mythic an-

Towards the Within, Victoria Christian, 2.5" x 3.5", Oil on Wood, Gems, 2004. www.victoriachristian.com

Grace, Victoria Christian, 2 "x 2", Oil on Wood, Gems, 2004. www.victoriachristian.com

cestors emerged from caverns or "the underworld."

Also, much to my surprise, deep within the canyon walls a yoni (vagina) began to emerge, which was later covered up by the funnel to the universal consciousness. Next, the faces in the canyon walls began to emerge, along with the breasts. Although I was a bit frightened at first by the experience, I felt an enormous amount of love flowing through my body, which helped me to relax and move with the experience. I feel strongly that the Goddess was revealing herself to me in this painting in one of her many forms. Yet at the time, I knew nothing of what the cave symbolized in ancient matristic societies; that it was a place of spiritual rebirth. In many respects I went through a spiritual rebirth or possibly an initiation into the deep dark mysteries of the Great Goddess in the process of painting *Towards the Within*.

The exquisite grace of the Goddess is represented in a painting titled *Grace* . In this painting an elegant dancer kneels in the foreground, amidst a field full of brilliant red poppies juxtaposed on emerald green grass, carrying a red scarf above her head. Flying above her head is a white dove, symbolizing peace. In the background are three white Arizona Sycamore trees amidst a blue lake. Embedded in the trees are crystalline jewels that sparkle when the sun hits the painting. In my opinion, this painting beautifully captures the graceful elegance of the Goddess. There were many birds that were sacred to the goddess in Neolithic cultures--among them dove, crane, swan and owl. In dreams, birds often appear as messengers of the soul.

The lush field of red poppies represents the rich beauty and creative inspiration the Goddess bestows. Her beautiful, fragrant flowers bring joy and color to our lives and are offerings of her loving compassion and deep love for us. Without her magical touch, our lives would be drab, for she is the canary in the coal mine, singing her sweet, sweet song of hope. The dove is a universal symbol of peace and innocence. In ancient Greek myth it was associated with the goddess Athena and represented the renewal of life. In the Biblical story, Noah releases a dove from the Ark, and she returns with an olive branch in her beak to demonstrate that the flood is over. Ever since, the dove has symbolized deliverance and God's forgiveness. This is what I conceptualize when I think of God's grace.

The Sunflower Goddess, Victoria Christian, 2" x 5", Acrylic on Canvas, 2002. www.victoriachristian.com

It is a concept beyond this world, and one that Earth-bound minds cannot fully comprehend. It's a simple and elegant kind of love, and at the same time, complex and profound. May you have the eyes to see the Goddess's grace amidst all the suffering in this world, for she has nourished our souls from the beginning and has always been a symbol of peace and hope despite our ability to receive her gifts.

Since I am on the topic of flowers and their association with the Goddess, I should also talk about my painting, *The Sunflower Goddess*. This painting is very special to me because she appeared to me in a vision after years of struggling with self-esteem issues. When I think about what it might be like to have authentic self-confidence, I just look at sun flowers, how they stand so tall and raise their heads to the sun with glee, and I understand. Having been raised with Christian values, I was taught to be humble and contrite at all times, and that pride is a sin. While humility is indeed a good quality to cultivate, there were times when the pressure to be humble felt self-abasing.

The Sunflower Goddess is a representation of authentic self-love simply because she is able to fully receive God's love. As humans we are constantly seeking a grounded sense of self—a place between shame and arrogance. Too often we are taught to feel shame about our God-given gifts, or we assume an attitude of arrogance. Either posture is destructive and not how God intended us to be. At some point in our lives, each of us needs to come to a place of acceptance and learn to view ourselves as God does. The sunflower Goddess is just who she is, and she is able to shine in all her splendor and glory without feeling arrogant or shameful. She is proud to be God's unique and beautiful expression of love. May she be an affirmation to you in your own search for authentic self-love.

Francene Hart: Healing Self and Earth Through Sacred Geometry

The visionary art of Francene Hart speaks to me in a unique way as her images dive deep into the heart of humanity, exposing a hidden dimension lost to most Westerners. Based on the wisdom and symbolic imagery of sacred geometry, Francene produces images of multidimensional reality, serving as "a bridge between this reality and a metaphorical world of healing, continuity, and transformation." [21] The vast and complex discipline of sacred geometry has become a spiritual journey for her, with new facets revealing themselves to her along the way. "Sacred geometry can be described as attributing a religious or cultural value to the graphical representation of the mathematical relationships and the design of the man-made objects that symbolize or represent these mathematical relationships." [22]

The golden mean, or ratio, was often used in the design of Greek and Roman architecture. Shapes proportioned according to the golden ratio have long been considered aesthetically pleasing in Western cultures, and the golden ratio is still used frequently in art and design, suggesting a natural balance between symmetry and asymmetry. Francene writes:

> *It is with great humility, from an ever-opening heart space, that I embrace this sacred journey. My intention remains to follow my passion and life path as an artist and to continue to create paintings that bring forth healing and transformation for myself and for the planet.* [23]

Listening to the voices of nature helped Francene to find her unique artistic voice. "The trees and animals, the water and rocks, sun and wind, moon and stars all speak clearly to us if we take the time to listen. I seek to honor this connection by creating works of art that celebrate these experiences of nature's wisdom." [24] Francene's complete awe and reverence for nature is evident in her stunning piece titled *Forest Cathedral.* The trees are symmetrically arranged like the columns of a church nave. Perfectly constructed arches form the canopy of the trees, and a dove flies into the sanctuary, blessing the space with the symbol of peace. Meandering through the forest is a pathway that leads to a distant light.

The tree, like the Goddess, represents abundance and regeneration. Rooted in the Earth, it sprouts flowers, ultimately withers and dies, only to rise again from its own seeds. As Anne Baring so eloquently states in describing the Goddess, "She is like an immense tree, whose roots lie beyond the reach of our consciousness, whose branches are all forms of life we know, and whose flowering is a potential within us, a potential that only a tiny handful of the human race has realized." [25] The Tree of Life is an important symbol in nearly every culture. With its branches reaching into the sky and its roots digging deeply into the Earth, it dwells in three worlds, forming a link between heaven, Earth, and the underworld, uniting what is above and below.

Conveying her mystical connection to the Earth and the cosmos, Francene painted *Above and Below.* In this image a woman sits meditating in front of a large redwood tree. Rays of light and energy move from the sky, to the tree, through her body, and down into the Earth. Enveloping the woman are three hands spiraling throughout the painting, symbolizing the movement of

Forest Cathedral, Francene Hart, 18″x24″, Watercolor on paper. www.francenehart.com

Above and Below, Francene Hart, 18" x24", watercolor on paper. www.francenehart.com

energy from the heavens and the Earth. Francene says, *Above and Below* is a tree meditation intended to tap into the flow of life force in the tree. It is about being a kind of connection between Earth to heaven and back again to Earth."[26]

The union of heaven and Earth, or above and below, is an important aspect of our spiritual evolution as humans. The descending spiral from heaven is the materialization or grounding of spirit. The spiral moving upward towards the sky represents the spiritualization of humankind, which then descends back into the Earth, representing the materialization of humankind. The intersection of these two vortices within the body represents a sacred marriage of the polarities within the individual and a state of balance and equilibrium occurring at the axis mundi--God as both transcendent and immanent. The axis mundi (world axis) in religion or mythology is the center of the world and/or the connection between heaven and Earth. Many of Earth's indigenous peoples have designated a particular point on the Earth as the center of the Earth for their tribe, often pictured in drawings as a rope, tree, vine, ladder or staff.

In *Above and Below,* the woman harnesses the power of cosmic energy and grounds it in her body so that the natural movements of energy around and within her are in complete harmony. This piece exudes enormous power--an electrical current of energies pulsing through her body and soul. The woman understands that it is essential to stay grounded and conscious; remembering that the energy is coming through her but is not her. She is humble and respectful of the cosmic energy coursing through her body, and because of this she is able to increase her ability to heal and create beauty in the universe.

The Magical Landscapes of Theresa Sharrar

Residing in the heart of Oregon on a beautiful piece of property in a quaint little town nestled against the foothills of the Cascades lives a visionary and magical realist by the name of Theresa Sharrar. Her work speaks of the connection that exists between humans, nature and animals, beyond war and politics. It only takes viewing one of her original impressionistic landscapes to sense the aliveness and energy in her paintings. Having spent a good part of her life exploring the rich green forests and rolling pastures of Oregon, Theresa successfully communicates a world of magic, connectedness and compassion in her paintings. Well known and loved in her small community, although mostly unacknowledged by the larger art world, Theresa has an amazing body of work just waiting to be seen and appreciated. She is content with a simple life of mothering, painting and teaching, but also yearns to join her vision with a growing number of artists worldwide whose work sews the seeds of love that will one day flower into a garden of world peace. She writes:

> *As I hold within myself the inner knowing of a world without violence, I paint my brushstrokes and feel a sewing together taking place of the practical world we live in and of the inspired reality that I know exists. It is a world where solitude can be a rich experience, and simple beauty can just be, where the gifts of nature are embraced and held sacred. As we strengthen our connections, not only with our loved ones, but with the fragmented parts of ourselves, we sew a new reality based on love and wholeness.*[27]

The ritual of gardening and painting on location has triggered several mystical experiences, some of which are portrayed in Theresa's paintings. An image, titled *Ceremony of Spring*, depicts a pregnant woman in a garden setting, fertilizing the soil. In a serene, blissful state, she tends to her garden in the spring, renewing her connections to the Earth amongst a field of pink and purple cherry tree's in full bloom. For Theresa, as well as for many women and men, gardening is a vehicle for spiritual and emotional connection. The entire process of creating a garden--tilling the soil, digging into the Earth, planting seeds and watering--make us co-creators with nature. There is something heartening about growing a plant from seed and seeing it flower, or eating a tomato grown on your own vine. Planting seeds makes us active participants in the cycle of life, while tending our gardens teaches us about larger patterns of the cycle that are beyond our control.

Ceremony of Spring portrays the fecundity of the Earth mother in all her abundance and bounty. She is both the fertile womb and the fertile field. Throughout history, women's wombs were considered analogous to the Earth's; a seed of grain, left dormant for the long winter months, flowers in the spring becoming the harvest that nurtures the community. Women were generally credited by prehistorians with the discovery of agriculture. Experimenting with the natural seeds, women developed and cultivated grains that were to become the chief foods. They learned to husk, to grind, and to bake wheat barley into bread.

Another fertility image by Theresa is titled, *Guardian of the Seeds or Demeter*, depicting the ancient Greek Goddess who brings forth the fruits of the Earth, par-

Ceremony of Spring, Theresa Sharrar, 24"x30", acrylic on canvas, www.lunariagallery.com

Guardian of the Seeds or Demeter, Theresa Sharrar, 24"x30", oil on canvas, www.lunariagallery.com

ticularly the various grains. There are, consequently, many myths dealing with Demeter in her capacity as a fertility goddess. As the Goddess of grain, Demeter played an important role in ancient Greek society. Her association with grain also translated into a close relationship with human fertility, as this was another crucial part in our continuing survival. She was also said to have taught mankind the art of sowing and ploughing so they could end their nomadic existence. In ancient art, Demeter was often portrayed (sitting) as a solemn woman, often wearing a wreath of braided ears of corn.

All of Theresa's images possess a magical and mystical quality about them, imbuing a sense of reverence for the Earth. Her commitment to her children and her creative life has been a difficult task, yet she manages to protect and nurture her creative life and those closest to her with a fierce determination. She brings passion, color and beauty to her world and openly honors the Goddess for her creative gifts. She is wise, humble and kind in her ways. While the two images in this book in no way represent the diversity of landscapes she has painted, her portfolio can be viewed at Lunaria Gallery in Silverton, Oregon. She takes impressionism to the next level--to a translucent realm of organic light, impregnated with spirit. I have some of her mystical landscapes in my home and I am always amazed at their dreamy, timeless quality, for they are alive and literally look as if they are breathing, an amazing sight to witness and the sign of a true master.

The Luminous Landscapes of Beth Avary

Nestled in the Santa Cruz Mountains of California, lives a phenomenal visionary landscape artist by the name of Beth Avary. Her studio shares a border with Big Basin Redwoods State Park's nineteen thousand acres of wilderness. It is here that she comes to remember the Divine, the higher power underlying all physical and spiritual reality. While Beth prefers not to envision the Divine as male and female but as genderless, she fully embraces the Divine as manifested in the radiant beauty of nature. She writes, "I understand that most people need to personify this manifestation in the form of a God or Goddess, but I am content to feel a connection to the ineffable through the contemplation of natural beauty."[28]

For a long period in Beth's life, she was an atheist. However, later in her life she fell into a severe depression that almost killed her. It was early childhood memories of her connection to nature that eventually helped to cure her. Like most individuals in the West, she had been socialized to adhere to a scientific world view of nature--that it is lifeless, dead and unintelligent--as opposed to seeing the divinity and organic wisdom that exists there. Like most people, when she was a young girl she naturally felt a strong connection to nature. However, in the process of socialization, those magical feelings are not reinforced and many people conform to the directives and values of our science-as-god society. So in order for Beth to survive in a technologically and rationally oriented society, she felt forced to sever her connection with nature and keep her mystical experiences to herself. She writes:

> *Many people today are depressed and take drugs to compensate for their feelings of alienation and loneliness. While there may be some cases where these drugs are absolutely necessary, I think most people have simply lost touch with their connection to the spiritual side of life, the love of life that can be inspired by beauty. I don't believe it is possible for an individual to feel depressed if they feel connected to the great matrix of love, which is why is it so important to nurture one's connection to the Earth and the need for transcendental experiences.*[29]

Beth's artwork is an attempt to capture some of the radiance in nature, to create a physical manifestation of the beauty that points to the transcendental and immanent aspects of the Divine. Aside from the rolling hills of California, one of Beth's favorite places to paint is Yosemite National Park because it never fails to inspire a renewed sense of awe with its spectacular array of beauty. Her painting, titled *By the River,* was inspired by one of Beth's visits to Yosemite. It is reminiscent of a special place where she has painted several times in the pristine air. Beth's paintings fall under the category of magical realism because through her use of color and contrast she is able to portray the magical and mystical qualities of nature. The gestalt of sensory influences--the smells, tastes, sounds and sensations--all have to be communicated in order for a painting to capture the divine essence of nature. As a painter working with a flat surface, this is a difficult thing to accomplish because it requires that the artist communicate a complex mystical experience through a single visual reality, and Beth's luminous landscapes capture the transcendental experience in nature in a way that is uniquely her own. There is a Biblical verse from the Psalms that captures the essence of these two paintings for her: "The one who meditates on the Divine is like a tree planted by streams of water."[30]

Beth also likes to paint mountains because they personify the awesome power of the Earth's evolutionary cycle, taking millions of years to form and develop. Contemplation of the Earth's evolution and the evolution of

By the River, Beth Avary, 30"x40", Acrylic on canvas, 2004

Silent Chapel, Beth Avary, 30"x40", Acrylic on canvas, 2004

The Maiden Tree, Atmara Rebecca Cloe, 16"x20" digital image, 2006., www.nwcreations.com

the universe is an extremely humbling experience as it juxtaposes the length of a human lifetime against the backdrop of eons of time, and ultimately, eternity. Beth says, "This contemplation is important to me because it has a way of putting my life into perspective." [31] The holiness of the mountains is portrayed in an image titled *Silent Chapel*, which doesn't require any explanation as it speaks for itself.

Atmara Rebecca Cloe

The Visionary Art of Atmara Rebecca Cloe has it's own unique style and is literally jaw-dropping. She has an enormous breadth of subject matter, including goddesses, angels, visionary landscapes, the beauty of nature, dolphins, images of spirit and light, fractals, crystals, mandalas and more. Atmara began her work as a digital artist in the fall of 1995 after taking some computer classes at a graphic arts school. She had taken a few art classes in college, but did not have much success utilizing traditional artistic media. Once she obtained her own computer and computer technology advanced sufficiently to facilitate full expression of her artistic vision, she found her medium and her artistic expression took on a life of its own. Atmara says:

> *Creating art is an ecstatic experience for me. My inspiration comes from a variety of sources, but ultimately from the Universe--the All That Is--of which we are all a part. I feel that there is an energy, another dimensional 'beingness,' that wants to be expressed through me and be given a form in this dimension. Sometimes it guides me very specifically as to what form to create and other times it just develops organically over time. At its best my work is a wonderful form of channeling and I feel so honored to be able to do it.* [32]

While Atmara has a whole plethora of breathtaking visionary landscapes, some of which can be viewed in other parts of the book, her image titled *The Maiden Tree*

Moon and Water, Atmara Rebecca Cloe, www.nwcreations.com

captures the tranquil, almost surreal, qualities of nature. Having lived on a lake for a good part of her life, she witnessed some beautiful moments, particularly the calm stillness of the water in the early morning hours. Upon viewing this image for a long period of time, I seem to become entranced by the maiden tree juxtaposed on the soft pastel mountains and lake. It has a medicinal, dreamy quality to it, similar to the peaceful feeling one has when one first wakes up in the morning. It conjures up memories of a distant past, shrouded in the mists of the unconscious, a time when magic and mysticism abounded on the Earth and in our hearts.

Atmara has a moon series that is really spectacular. Her image *Moon and Water* is truly magnificent. Compositionally it is harmonious and balanced. The reflections of the moon on the water are masterfully done and the color scheme is soothing to the eyes. Atmara is a true master of color and uses it therapeutically in her mandala series, which can be viewed on her website as well.

Rebirth, Cynthia Ré Robbins www.art4spirit.com

The Magical World of Cynthia Ré Robbins

Cynthia Ré Robbins is a visionary artist who paints in oils and tempera, using the Mische (Mixed) Technique. Her colorful artwork has a beautiful refinement of detail and a rich, shimmering appearance. She has an eclectic portfolio, which includes mystical landscapes, sacred springs, animals, goddesses, fairies, flora, mermaids, and marine life.

Cynthia studied at the Cleveland Institute of Art for three years and then received a Bachelor of Fine Arts degree at Instituto Allende in Mexico. For 20 years she lived in Key West, Cozumel, Playa del Carmen, and the Virgin Islands. She later moved to Colorado and was fortunate to have the opportunity to study with Robert Venosa, a master of Fantastic Realism painting. Learning his adaptation of the Mische Technique had a transformative effect on her work. Alternating layers of oil glazes and white tempera rendering give an ethereal, luminous quality to the colors called "optic tones." In addition, this method of painting creates an effect where light reflects from within the painting. 33

Her painting *Rebirth*, portrays a "mermaid emerging from the waters of a quiet lagoon at dawn. The surrounding jungle is teaming with life. She is exulting in her well-being, as if just breaking free from a cocoon."[34]In folklore, a mermaid is an aquatic creature with the head and upper body of a female human and the tail of a fish. Mermaids appear in the folklore of many cultures worldwide, including the Near East, Europe, Africa and Asia. Mermaids are famous for their incredible beauty which humans believed surpassed all mortal beings. Legends claim that the beauty of a mermaid is so great that it could mesmerize men and lure them into the sea. Myths claim that the mermaid's gorgeous appearance could lure entire ships onto the rocks.

Cynthia also has a series of paintings called Fairies of the Forest. Her painting *Shooting Star Faeries* is sparkling with magic. Two playful faeries frolic amidst the wild flowers in joyous delight. A Faerie is a type of

Shooting Star Faeries, Cynthia Ré Robbins, www.art4spirit.com

mythical being or legendary creature in European folklore, a form of Spirit, often described as metaphysical.. What is particularly masterful about this painting is how she captured the evening moon ligh reflecting on the water and misty river air.

Pixies of Nickel Creek, Jim Thompson, 33.5X23 Digital Image, www.art-mind-soul.com

Jim Thompson: Envisioning the Great Mystery in Art

A brilliant visionary artist and writer who has devoted his life to the intersection of art and metaphysics is Jim Thompson. He began his artistic career in advertising as a technical illustrator and then moved into fine art. His works span a broad range of subjects such as; realism, fantasy,, and extraterrestrial landscapes. His works have been published widely in various articles, books and magazines, as well as exhibited in numerous shows. Possessing a keen fascination and sense of "awe" for the Great Mystery, Jim has produced numerous art works that capture a glimpse of the infinite ways to envision the intersection between the micro world of the physical plane on Earth and the Cosmos. Jim is also a devotee of the Goddess and had been deeply healed by HER compassion and wisdom.

Jim created a masterful digital image titled *Pixies of Nickel Creek.* In folklore a faerie or "pixie" is one of a class of supernatural beings, generally conceived as having a tiny human form and possessing magical powers. Faeries and Pixies have often been associated with magic and enchantment. Generally faeries are highly connected to nature and take care of the natural world or what some might call the elemental world. Jim expounds on his digital painting:

> *Here such creatures live in an old tree, deep in the enchanted woods. They all come spilling out of the old tree, as though part of a great family of pixies that have existed for thousands of years. They seem to respond to the full moon and take delight in their favorite creek with its little falls and pools. Their innocent, child-like nature evokes the side of ourselves that may abandon the strictures of social norms. And boy do they glow--each with a personal color that may be as much a signal to who they are as individuals.*

Awakening of Reena Centore, Jim Thompson, Digital Image, www.art-mind-soul.com

Jim created a series of extraterrestrial landscapes that are out of this world. His appreciation for surrealism is evident in two imaginative images *Awakening of Reena Centore* and *The Temple of Rengye*. Jim writes

Aliens come to the temple and are blessed into the ranks of more advanced fellow beings. The echelons of initiation are shown in their different colored garb, all wearing the logo manifested in the temple emblems. This may be an expression of universal intelligence, spirituality and a sense of the Divine. Here is a gesture of the possibility of communion with the broader scope of art, mind, and soul. Within the great golden dome of Rengye Temple there is a transcendent beacon or portal that connects with other intelligent life in the cosmos. A sort of teleportation device.

Victoria Christian is a sociologist, social worker, counselor, artist, writer and sacred activist. To learn more about this book, see the website: www.mysticspiritart.com

Temple of Rengye, Jim Thompson, Digital Image, www.art-mind-soul.com

Mother Nature, Andrew Annenberg, 20"x24", oil on canvas, www.andrewannenberg.com

Artists Reclaim the Body of Earth and Mother

By Victoria Christian

It is time for women and men to create a new vision for society--one that is in harmony with the life on the planet as a whole. As the patriarchal structure and military warriors threaten to destroy the Earth and her beings, we are being called to awaken to the wisdom of the sacred feminine, to have the courage to embrace our own denials on a personal level so that we will be better equipped to heal the reflection of our self-hatred in nature.

We can no longer sit back and watch in silence as the military industrial complex wreaks havoc on the immune system of the Earth and on its inhabitants. We need awakened individuals to take action in any way that they can to protest war based on greed and exploitation of women and minorities. As Ynestra King so powerfully put it, "War is the violence against women in all its forms--rape, battering, economic exploitation and intimidation--and it is the racist violence against indigenous peoples here in the U.S. and around the world, and it is the violence against the Earth." [1]

I am horrified that six of my closest women friends and several more acquaintances have been raped, molested and/or physically abused by men. We know that twenty-five percent of all women in this culture are raped within their lifetimes, and another nineteen percent have to fend off rape attempts. We know that as many as forty four million American women have been molested by relatives, with twelve million of those molested by their fathers.[2] Furthermore, increasing numbers of women, particularly single moms, are in poverty despite the fact that they work more hours per week than men, a phenomenon known as the feminization of poverty. There continues to be a severe income gap between men and women as well as a lack of women in positions of power and authority.

Despite the groundswell of women's actions for peace, women still lack power and authority when it comes to peace negotiations. Those sitting around the peace table are almost exclusively men. Furthermore, a number of recent studies have shown that depression is high amongst women, and is more common in working-class women than in middle-class women. With all the suffering that women have to endure on a day-to-day basis, it is no wonder we suffer from high levels of anxiety and depression. Yet some so-called experts still want to turn it around and place judgment on women for being passive, dependant and insecure, in essence blaming the victim.

It is due to the ground breaking work of an assortment of feminist thealogians, eco-feminists, feminist artists and other cultural creatives in an assortment of disciplines that women now have more opportunities to become fully empowered, autonomous and confident in their voices. Not only have feminists revealed a history where knowledge has been controlled by a white, male, eurocentric perspective or "androcentric bias" that has excluded the viewpoints of women and minorities; they have also exposed a history of tyranny in which patriarchy, power, knowledge and discourse have all been linked together, creating a complex system of justification for social inequality.

They have exposed a lack of sacred imagery of the Goddess in the West and how that lack has justified and maintained gender inequality and disrespect of the Earth and her animals. Imaging the divine as female is essential for the larger vision of emancipation and equality, because it not only empowers women but also gives them a sense of hope that they will be freed from the destructive impact of our culture's pervasive negative imaging of the female. As Carole Christ, a pioneer of the women's spirituality movement informs, us, "The real importance of the symbol of the Goddess is that it breaks the power of the patriarchal symbol of God as male over the psyche." [3] Therefore, it is through symbolic imaging in the arts that we will be able to take the first steps in our efforts to bring about social change.

At this crucial time in human history, the Great Mother is revealing herself to all cultures, including the West. We in the West simply have yet to acknowledge her presence as much as other cultures, and as a result have tended to neglect the thousands of images of the Goddess created by artisans in the United States. While this is a complex problem that has been occurring for quite some time, it is partly due to the censorship of Goddess images by the majority of galleries, museums and various media outlets. This trend of censorship is the result of a multitude of factors as well as an overall lack of awareness, but it is slowly beginning to improve as alternative routes are carved out by visionary artists and cultural creatives in an assortment of disciplines. More often then not, powerful gatekeepers in the art world aren't as sensitized to new movements in art as they think they are. It is the artists and mystics who are the true visionaries, inspiring a sense of hope as they midwife the birthing of a new mode of consciousness--the death of the old beliefs, values and limited perceptions of God that are no longer working for us--and a rebirth into a new paradigm of consciousness that is more aligned with the diversity of creation, the Earth and animals.

I also draw inspiration and courage from the extended history of female mystics from numerous disciplines constituting a long matrilineage of women who, through powerful mystical visions and divine revelations, acquired the authority to challenge the sexism and misogyny of their own patriarchal societies and religions. Many of these women put themselves at great risk as they swam against the current of mainstream culture. Not only were they severely marginalized by society and told that they were crazy, many of them also experienced grave poverty, psychological and physical torture and even death as a result of their selfless vision for social justice.

In order to honor these brave women and keep the flame of their vision for equality alive, I feel drawn to carry the torch, so to speak, for the brave women who have fought for justice, truth and equality before us. In this article, I hope to share with you some of the more cutting edge, "eco-feminist" art by several contemporary female artists who have devoted their artistic visions to the reemergence of the Goddess. What is particularly exciting about the discipline of eco-feminism is the way it has been used as a theoretical tool--a broad sword of truth, if you will--that has sliced through the thick forest of ideological oppression to reveal the ways in which women and nature have been mutually associated and devalued in Western patriarchal culture.

Reclaiming Goddess Iconography in Art

The rise in the United States of feminist religious movements that focus on female images of the divine Goddess suggest that many women, in addition to men, find Goddess symbolism appealing. Many feminist artists, too, claim to have found inspiration in symbols of the Goddess, as they evoke feelings of a lost and distant past—a vague, yet familiar reality, lost to many Westerners. Feminist critiques of religion and some postmodernists have taken issue with traditional images of God, arguing that male hegemony in Western cultures can be correlated directly with the centrality of a single, all-powerful male God in the dominant strands of the predominately Jewish and Christian religious heritage of Europe and the United States.

Many would argue further that given this situation, it is important for women, as well as for men with feminist goals, to recover or create empowering female symbols to help combat the ones that support the patriarchy, the denial of the feminine principle and a one-sided view of humanity. While Protestantism, Catholicism and Judaism can and often do affect women in myriad positive ways, these religions also can and often do cause women great pain, and they can do great damage to a woman's self esteem. These religions all have histories of being patriarchal in both doctrine (God as Father; woman brought sin into the world; women are less holy then men) and in practice (only men can administer the Catholic sacraments; only men can be priests; only men count to make up a quorum in temples).

In seeking spiritual resources upon which to draw, some Jewish and Christian feminists, as well as an assortment of other spiritual thinkers and artists, have turned to religious traditions other than their own. While there are indeed glimpses of the Goddess in Christianity that were never entirely eradicated, such as in Kaballism and Gnosticism, feminist and green movement ideologies have challenged the tenets of several established faiths, particularly the subordinate role traditionally ascribed to women and the value polarizing between spirit and matter in Christian dogma.

The rebirth of the Goddess in western consciousness is inevitably challenging Biblical and traditional ideas about the nature of God as well as domineering perceptions about the Earth and animals. While there are a diversity of perspectives amongst eco-feminists, many believe that the destruction of the Earth and the mistreatment of women are the result of Patriarchal ideologies that have justified and maintained a dualistic view of the world that has severed our ties to the Earth, to our feelings and to our bodies. According to feminist theaologian Carole Christ, the severing of divinity and humanity from nature was one of the decisive characteristics of monotheism that led to viewing "God," "man" and "nature" as separate and distinct categories

In her book, *Rebirth of the Goddess: Finding Meaning in Feminist Spirituality,* Carole Christ reveals the ways in which the Christian theological tradition has typically identified rational control with men and sensuality and emotions and nature with women. She explains that in patriarchal religions, divinity has typically represented rationality, order and transcendence, as opposed to the alleged irrationality, immanence and chaos of the finite changeable world of nature, women and the body.[4] In other words, the male priesthood that existed long before Christianity socially constructed the association of men with reason and transcendence, and women with irrationality, immanence and nature.

In my opinion, where the Western Judeo Christian view went wrong was not in its differentiation between the masculine and the feminine, but in its fixation on the transcendent, male-domination illusion. In separating the divine from matter, mind from body, man from woman, human consciousness has become fragmented, divided and totally out of whack. To counteract this imbalance, the hypothesis proposed by feminist thealogians, historians, archeologists and eco-feminists, that the Goddess is the equal and proper counterpart to God, is a way to assist Western culture, both men and women, in healing our psychological wounds so that we can then begin to manifest a more balanced and mutually respectful society.

A Brief History of Goddess Art:

If we examine the history of Goddess art, we find a number of female mystics and Goddess artists who have made it their life's mission to assist humanity in the larger awakening of the Goddess. However, this consciousness is just now beginning to sink in to the minds and hearts of a large number of Westerners. The feminist art movement in the 1970s in many respects paved the way for contemporary female mystics and Goddess artists as they challenged the dominant patriarchal ideologies of Western culture as well as the institutional discrimination of women artists.

An important aspect of the feminist art movement in the 1970s was to challenge the dominant patriarchal ideologies of Judeo-Christianity, particularly its overall subjugation of the feminine principle. Several feminist artists of the 1970s, such as AfraShe Asungi, Ana Mendieta, Judy Chicago, Mary Beth Edelson, Donna Henes, Betye Saar, and Betsy Damon, attempted to reclaim the ancient Great Goddess through images, rituals, and performance art in an effort to reestablish a female perspective that has long been absent in world religions.

Documenting the work of several feminist artists of the 1970s, art historian Gloria Orenstein wrote an influential article in *Heresies,* "The Great Goddess" issue (1978), titled *Recovering Her Story: Feminist Artists Reclaim the Great Goddess.*[5] In her well-researched article on Goddess art, Gloria Orenstein insightfully points out that the reclamation of the Goddess in art was, to a large extent, focused on the Goddess as a symbol of women's lost *Herstory* and as a path for women to recover their lost spiritual power. Goddess artists were inspired by an assortment of ground breaking discoveries in the social sciences and humanities.

Two of the more influential voices of the seventies were archeological scholars and historians Marija Gimbutas, who wrote *The Gods and Goddesses of Old Europe: 7000 to 3500 B.C., Myths, Legends* and *Cult Images,*[6] and Merlin Stone, author of *When God was a Woman.*[7] The work of these two female scholars documents an assortment of archeological images from pre-patriarchal Goddess civilizations, demonstrating that Goddess worshipping civilizations did indeed exist and that art is a potent transmitter of truths that were omitted from the patriarchal record of Western history.

Another major influence on Goddess Art of the 1970s, which predated Goddess scholarship, was the rediscovery of Carl Jung's concept of the archetype of the Great Goddess. The word "archetype" was freely used in those days and was taken from Erich Neumann's discussion of Jungian ideas about the archetype of the Great Goddess in his book *The Great Mother: An Analysis of the Archetype.*[8] Jungian psychology purports that the Great Mother represents the feminine in the human psyche, and that archetypes are internal images that exist in the collective unconscious and are at work in the psyches of everyone.[9] Many artists and scholars came to believe that the archetype of the Great Goddess is not only equally accessible to anyone, anywhere, but that images of Her transcend all patriarchal cultural barriers. As Orenstein noted:

> *Goddess art of the 1970s was perceived to be the one symbol that could transcend difference, diversity, and division, and that could harmonize women from a wide variety of backgrounds on a level that penetrated so deeply into human history and the collective psyche that the contemporary patriarchal, political and social constructions separating women from each other would be overcome.* [10]

In other words, through rekindling their memory of the Great Goddess, women from all over the world could begin to unite their wills to break the chains of social inequality and oppression. This was and still is a powerful realization that has the potential to invoke enormous change in the world. However, the transformation must begin at a grassroots level, through each woman's (and man's) commitment to healing herself and breaking free from the psychological bondage of patriarchal ideology.

Despite the golden ideals of several courageous feminist artists in history, many of them couldn't conceptualize how deeply entrenched patriarchy really was or how long it would take to see any liberating change within the social structure. Although there are now contemporary alternative spiritual movements that are awakening to the Goddess, we are at a crucial point in history where the evolution of human consciousness is dependent on our ability to integrate the masculine and feminine on personal and societal levels.

Contemporary Goddess and Eco-Feminist Art

Feminist scholars, female mystics and Goddess artists of the 1980s up through current times both participate in and expand on the feminist agenda of the 1970s, though they do so in different ways. As Gloria Orenstein notes, Goddess art of the seventies was primarily focused on the Goddess and the recovery of women's lost "Herstory" and spiritual power.[11] Contemporary Goddess art expands on these themes and takes them further. Due to the ever-growing awareness of the ecological devastation of our planet, nihilism and the trend of the feminization of poverty worldwide, the need for spiritual and socially redeeming art is enormous.

As artists slowly begin to awaken to their spiritual calling and fundamental role in the Goddess and Transcendental Art Movements, they are beginning to produce powerful images of the sacred feminine with a fierce passion. The explosion of Goddess iconography is just beginning to saturate the marketplace through an assortment of alternative publishing venues as it is filling a void and a thirst in humanity that has gone untended for too long.

Before I reveal some contemporary eco-feminist art, it is important to note that not all contemporary Goddess artists realize that it is the Primordial Sacred Union that we should be seeking to attain. While the rebirth of the Goddess is necessary in order to seek balance, there are some who have chosen to champion the Goddess. While these individuals have free will to do what they want, the Great Mother's true essence is not reactionary and exclusionary of the sacred masculine, but fully embracing of it; that is, if it is aligned with and balanced with her will.

Furthermore, it is important to note that there is a division within the feminist movement concerning the patriarchal association of women with nature and whether it is in our best interests as women to uphold this negative stigma created and perpetuated by the patriarchy. The association of women with nature is indeed evident in human history, and in many ways has been used by the patriarchal establishment to justify and maintain the oppression and mistreatment of both women and nature.

However, this important fact has led to a huge division amongst feminists about whether or not women should embrace and celebrate the relationship between women and nature or disassociate themselves from a patriarchal construct (man over nature, man over woman) that has been used as a source of oppression for women. Critics point to the problem of women's own reinforcement of their identification with a nature that Western culture degrades. Therefore, some feminists celebrate the woman/nature connection and seek to reclaim the lost spiritual heritage of the Goddess, while others reject it, claiming that women will only further validate the patriarchal construct by associating themselves with those concepts.

While it is not my intention to bridge the gaps within the feminist movement in this article, I feel it is important to acknowledge my awareness of this division within the movement. With this in mind, I will now reveal the work of several contemporary Goddess and eco-feminist artists who have made epic contributions to the women's spirituality and transcendental art movements. It is this type of work that transcends semantic and ego barriers and reaches into the heart of humanity. These works should go down in history as part of the third wave of feminist art, and will inspire generations to come. They are a major contribution to the women's movement because they validate women's experiences of oppression, and inspire women to reclaim their bodies as well as a connection to the Earth and the Great Goddess.

Hrana Janto: Faces of the Goddess

An astounding female artist who has devoted her artistic vision to the reclaiming of Goddess iconography in art is Hrana Janto. After graduating with a B.F.A. from the Cooper Union in New York City and studying at the School of Sacred Arts, she started her career as a professional artist and illustrator. Long inhabiting the realms of history, fantasy, myth and the sacred, painting the Goddess in her myriad of faces and forms has been an ongoing passion of hers for more than a decade.

As she was coming of age in the mid-seventies, her mother, Phyllis Janto, was involved with the women artists' evolution in New York City. She was part of a couple cooperative galleries and contributed to the *Environmental* issue of *Heresies* magazine. She was especially fascinated by *Heresies*'s *Great Goddess* issue in 1978. She had already been reading and painting mythological subjects when Merlin Stone's book *When God Was a Woman* (1976) was published.[12] She and her mother listened to installments on the radio together and then got their own copy. Hrana was searching for role-model images in art and culture and found that powerful images of women were few and far between, which inspired her to dive into her own research in ancient mythology and bring them back to life.[13]

Hrana has several images throughout the book that will strike your fancy, but there are two lesser known Creation Goddesses that I would like to speak about now. The first image, *Coatlique*, or the *Lady of the Serpent Skirt*,

Coatlique or Lady of the Serpent Skirt, Hrana Janto, 2'x2' acrylic on canvas, 1996. www.hranajanto.com

depicts an ancient Earth and Mother Goddess adopted by the Aztecs. In this image, Hrana eloquently portrays Coatlique in grief as she lifts the severed head of her beloved daughter Coyolxanuhqui, goddess of the moon, to the stars. The power of her love brings transformation as Coyolxanuhqui's head is transformed into the moon. "Her most famous images show her as the ruler of life and its end, garlanded with hearts and hands, wearing a skirt of swinging serpents, hung with skulls, vested in a flayed human skin." [14]

Another image depicting the Goddess of creation is *Lady of the Beasts,* known to the people of Sumer, Crete, and the Indus Valley (India). She was also known as the Cosmic Creatrix, the creative, fertile, life-giving force. Her special animals were held sacred as manifestations of the deity herself. She is depicted here pregnant, surrounded by her precious animals. In this image Hrana captures her nurturing tendencies, calming the wildest of spirits with her gentle touch. Speaking to her power as a fertility goddess, Hrana included the phases of the moon spiraling about in the night sky, which is closely connect to women's menstrual cycles. Hrana writes, "*Lady of the Beasts* evokes the body of the Goddess and the interconnectivity of all beings. In a dark cave deep within the Earth, a multitude of pregnant creatures support a Neolithic woman preparing to give birth. I was inspired

Lady of the Beasts, Hrana Janto, 2'x2' ft acrylic on canvas, 1994. www.hranajanto.com

by ancient Mediterranean images of Earth Goddesses seated on a throne and hands resting on the animal's backs."[15]

I was first introduced to Hrana's gorgeous feminine imagery on the cover of a *Sage Woman* magazine. Upon viewing her website, I was astounded by her prolific and diverse collection of Goddess images. Not only is she a master illustrator, she also has a piercing clarity of vision that is bright and bold, using all the colors of the rainbow. It is rare to see artwork that captures the essence of the Goddess in her multidimensional forms, but Hrana is one of those artists who does it with ease. She is a true visionary artist as she has a rare gift that enables her to pierce the abstract realms of the universal matrix and condense an enormous amount of information through her mind's eye and into her hand. Her work will shine like a beacon of light for future generations, emanating the Great Mother's truth and wisdom for those who have forgotten.

Suzanne DeVeuve: Art of the Mystical Divine

When I reflect on all the artists I have interviewed and befriended, Suzanne DeVeuve stands out as one of the most devoted, inspired and prolific painters I know. Her potent work graces the altars of many devotees, not to mention book and magazine covers. Residing in the San Francisco Bay Area for most of her life, she is a renowned visionary influenced by the feminist art movement of the 1970s and Carl Jung. Suzanne has been painting for over thirty years and literally has galleries of work spanning from Goddess themes to shamanic tribal art. Her paintings have appeared in numerous magazines and books. She illustrated covers for Z Budapest's, *A Holy Book of Women's Mysteries, Grandmother of Time,* and its sequel, *Grandmother Moon.* She has also designed covers for *The Return of Pahana* by Robert Boissierc and *The Alchemist's Almanac.* Her illustrations have appeared in *Women's Spirituality Calendar, Darshan, SageWoman, Sojourn* and other publications.

In her artist's statement she mentions one of her favorite quotes by Henry Miller, "To Paint is to love again." This is a truth she lives by, day after day, inspiring her heart song and creative dream seed. This falling in love with creativity is a sign of an authentic artist truly devoted to surrendering her life for a higher spiritual mission. It is an eternal love that pours from her heart like milk and honey onto the canvas with exuberant color and texture. She writes, "All of my paintings are like stepping stones to my awakening as well as the collective raising of consciousness. It is my intention that these works feed and nurture people's hearts and souls. May they invoke strength and courage to love, again and again, in joy and service to all of life." [16]

So many of Suzanne's paintings have inspired me, but there are a couple of paintings that have particularly nourished my soul. A painting that has a permanent place in my home and altar is titled *Bear Mama.* I have been fortunate to have many dreams and mystical experiences with bear, and Suzanne is one of the few that truly understands them. Bear Mama is my fierce protector and teacher of introspection. She has a powerful message of compassion, truth and wisdom.

In Native American mythology, animals are regarded as holy because they have powerful souls. They were often enlisted by people as their guardian spirits. Ancient priests and priestesses used animal totems to assist them in coming face to face with the spirit world. They would imitate the animals in posture, dress and dance, creating rituals around them so as to invoke and share in the energy manifesting in the world through that animal. The animal became a totem—a power or medicine. It became a symbol of a specific kind of energy. When they awakened to that totem and honored it, they released the archetypal energies behind it into their lives. Suzanne explains further below:

> *Bear Mama was inspired by a Haida Indian Myth of Bear Mother. I saw a picture of a sculpture cast in gold of the Bear Mother (Human) nursing two bear cubs. At the time, I was nursing my own new baby son, so decided to do a painting of Bear mother nursing one human child and one bear cub. In the original Myth from the Haida Indians, a young woman is out picking berries when she meets a bear. The bear makes this woman his wife and she gives birth to two bear cubs. In the story the woman later returns to her village to become the lawgiver of her community, a very important role.* [17]

Inspired by the rise of feminine power, Suzanne poured her heart and soul in to *Goddess Rising.* The human race is at a critical juncture. Women are rising up and speaking truth to power in defense of the planet, children, animals, elders, oppressed people, and disabled people. Women across the globe are feeling an urgent call to come in to feminine leadership. And the best leaders will be those who also know how to be led. We need women of all walks of life, class, race, and ethnicity

Bear Mama, Suzanne De Veuve, 20" x 24", oil on canvas, 1996.
www.suzannedeveuve.com

Goddess Rising, Suzanne De Veuve, www.suzannedeveuve.com

to come in to their power and speak their truth. She especially wants to here from oppressed people as they are the one's who can help create a partnership system that is beneficial for all.

Another eco-feminist painting is *Salmon Goddess*. In the Pacific Northwest, nineteen populations of wild salmon and steelhead are listed as threatened under the Endangered Species Act. What is particularly endearing about salmon (both male and female) is the great sacrifice they make to keep the future generations alive. At some point adult fish begin "homing"—migrating back to their natal stream, fighting their way upstream to spawn. The female digs a nesting pocket in the gravel streambed by lying on her side and whipping her tail. She lays her eggs, and the male, fighting other males for the privilege, fertilizes them. The female then covers the eggs with more gravel. After this once-in-a-lifetime mating, both male and female die. The carcasses of spawned-out salmon bring a load of nutriments from the ocean back to otherwise nutrient-poor rivers. Bears, foxes, wolves, eagles, wrens and ravens feed on salmon flesh.

Salmon Goddess, Suzanne De Veuve, www.suzannedeveuve.com

Martina Hoffmann: The Sacred Womb

Another epic contribution to feminist art is *The Goddess Triangle* by visionary artist Martina Hoffmann, which took several years to complete. It celebrates the unique ability of women to bring forth life, and the spiritual forces that are at play when such a step is taken. *The Goddess Triangle* is a 20' x 10' multimedia installation piece incorporating images of Earth Goddesses and pregnant nudes (Birthscapes) with sound that is composed of intra-uterine heartbeats and female voices reciting the many names of the Goddess. The central part consists of four panels depicting pregnant nudes. They tell the story of four women Martina encountered and their personal journeys into motherhood. The images portray the joy of carrying life and the strength, dignity and selflessness needed to become a perfect vessel for new life. In watching the bodies of the four women transform, she was reminded of their physical similarities with the Earth Goddesses of the Paleolithic and Neolithic ages. These women are indeed modern-day-Goddesses, and *The Goddess Triangle* explores the similarities that they share with ancient Goddess archetypes. Martina further clarifies the inspiration behind this epic piece:

> *This is my altar to the female principle and a reminder of a time when life was celebrated as miraculous and sacred. The Goddess Triangle was created as a tribute to all women who have selflessly chosen the path of motherhood to ensure our continued existence. It is not an easy path to walk on, and for most of human history this essential female contribution has been taken for granted. The Earth Goddesses depicted in the outer panels represent the virtues of wisdom and grace as well as the powers of life force and psychic knowledge.* [18]

The Goddess Triangle, Martina Hoffmann, 20"x10" multimedia installation piece, 1988-1995. www.martinahoffmann.com

This painting explores the deep, inseparable energetic bond between mother and child, whether our own mother or the cosmic archetype. All of Martina's Goddess imagery celebrates the female body--the great womb of life--and its life-giving powers, inspiring a sense of respect for mothers as nurturing providers. Her Goddess images resanctify the female body. They affirm the sacredness of Earth as the body of the Goddess and our own bodies, calling us to embrace life and to care for our Earthly bodies and the body of the Earth. Her contribution to feminist art will undoubtedly inspire and influence many generations to come.

Jane Evershed: Raising Social Consciousness Through Art and Poetry

In a world saturated with mediocrity and apathy, there are few artists who have the courage to challenge the status quo for fear they might be marginalized and risk financial despair. When an artist is true to her voice, even if it means swimming against the stream of dominant patriarchal values, she is, in my opinion, an authentic artist.

Jane Evershed's artistic mission is to raise the consciousness of humanity through art and poetry. She uses her art and poetry to invigorate the consciousness, not only of women, but of men too. However, reprogramming the socially conditioned belief that art is not as valid as the so-called rational ways of knowing has been a difficult process for her and for all others who have attempted it, yet expressing herself through art has enabled her to communicate to others what they already know and feel but perhaps lacked a vehicle to express.

She writes:

> *A woman with a vacuum cleaner in one hand and a crying baby on her hip does not have time to read the contents of a feminist manifesto dripping in footnotes. Children need to be fed, and bills need to be paid. The economic treadmill we walk each day can conveniently keep us away from meaningful spiritual pursuits, and we might be more easily controlled by authoritarian voices within the media under these circumstances.* [19]

Growing up in South Africa during the apartheid regime of white supremacy sensitized Jane to the dynamics of institutionalized oppression. On arriving in America in 1984, she sought to shed light on the injustices of the South African government and share them with Americans in the form of note-cards in her *Dream for South Africa* series. After that, her creative efforts were focused on the oppression of women worldwide as a much larger injustice. She moved into *The Power of Woman* series in 1985 and has been creating art related to women and oppression for over two decades.

What is particularly unique about Jane's work is not only her brilliant imagination, but also her clever and humorous way of getting loaded messages across. She creates poetry and images stolen from patriarchal iconography and reverses the meaning in order to awaken women to their authentic power. In other words, she takes effective psychological strategies from patriarchal indoctrination, turns it around and uses it for a healing agenda. For example, in her image titled *Raising of Women*, Jane usurps the patriarchal image of colonialism--the raising of the American flag by war heroes to claim

Raising of Women, Jane Evershed, 30"x40", acrylic

Who Let the Girls Out, Jane Evershed, 30"x40", acrylic

conquered countries-- and changes it to depict women raising the feminine symbol amidst a sea of Earth-devastation and poverty. The symbol of patriarchy, which is the double cross, is being torn down in the same way statues of dictators in foreign countries are torn down after an invasion.

Jane's artwork communicates her utter sadness at the lack of female voices in government, the judicial system and religious institutions. In an image titled *Who Let the Girls Out?* Jane draws attention to the beauty and innocence of girls at play juxtaposed against a patriarchal ruling body that hardly bats an eye at launching weapons of mass destruction. In this painting, a woman has sneaked in bottled "girl-power" and released it into the air above the conference table. In front of each representative is a piece of paper, which reads from right to left "Hell is our agenda." She writes:

> *The existing infrastructure of the current world order is bereft of the creativity, warmth and spontaneity of the divine feminine, and especially of the divine girl-child. Where are the images of the divine daughter? Instead, we are bombarded by testosterone-infused ruling bodies who are just as dangerous to the planet as they are to our psyches. Without the balance of feminine wisdom to mitigate the male bias, the traditional role of male-as-protector has gone beyond the bounds of reason and sanity and has created a global prison for women.* [20]

Expounding on the theme of gender oppression, Jane painted *The Fall of Patriarchy*, which portrays women fleeing en-masse to create their own definition of a sane existence. While Jane has work that is even more disturbing, this image is intended to motivate women to take their power back because we can't continue to sit back and pretend as if men, science and the military industrial complex will save the world. Jane feels strongly that:

The Fall of Patriarchy, Jane Evershed, 60" x48", acrylic.

Now is the time of woman! It is natural for women's wisdom to surface and be welcomed. Women's intuitive instinct for survival is being awakened on a massive scale, with infusions of female energy seeping into the consciousness of humanity. The atom has been split. Now is the time for women to put the planet back together. [21]

Reclaiming the Body and Eroticism in Art

A woman's right to control her body, her sexuality, and her reproduction is basic to the recovery of her full humanity. For these reasons and more, the body has been an image, an idea, and an issue of continuing significance in women's art. Feminist artists of the 1970s, up through current times, hope to use their art as a way to assist women in the reclaiming of their bodies and the natural eroticism that has been suppressed in America's puritanical/pornographic culture. With the rising consciousness of the feminist movement, a resanctification of the female body and sexuality as a source of power and pleasure has been a major concern, particularly since a majority of women in Western culture see themselves through the distorted gaze of a society dominated by men. As art historian and feminist Elinor Gadon informs us, "Our culture has been so constructed under the lens of male experience that women see themselves from the perspective of patriarchy. A woman's body is the object of male desire, fascination, and fear." [22]

Around the world, poverty forces many women and children into prostitution as a means of survival. Prostitution is greatest in poor countries where patriarchy is strong and traditional cultural norms limit women's ability to earn a living. Feminists and feminist artists have also raised concerns about pornography and its blatant dehumanization of women as the play-toys of men. Pornography rests on the assumption that women and sexuality should fall under the control of men, and has also been linked to violence against women. [23]

As a result of the patriarchal fear of and need for control of women's bodies and sexuality, a large percentage of women continue to be uncomfortable with their bodies. The barrage of messages about thinness, dieting and beauty tells "ordinary" women that they are always in need of adjustment, and that the female body is an object to be perfected. The overwhelming presence of media images of painfully thin women means that real women's bodies have become invisible in the mass media. The real tragedy is that many women internalize these stereotypes and then judge themselves by the beauty industry's standards. Women learn to compare themselves to other women and to compete with them for male attention. This focus on beauty and desirability as a way to attract men weakens the bonds between women and keeps us competing with each other rather than unified in a common goal.

Emma Gardner: Challenging the Beauty Myth

Perhaps most disturbing is the fact that media images of female beauty are unattainable for all but a very small number of women. In other words, the message that women receive is that if their bodies do not fall into the small definition of beauty espoused by the media, they aren't good enough. A contemporary artist out of Flagstaff, Arizona who has explored the influence Barbie has had on Western culture is a woman by the name of Emma Gardner. Her formal training began in high school and continued in college where she was trained in a program modeled after the Swiss School of Design, a perceptual and analytical approach to the visual arts. She went on to study advanced Chemistry and Art History in the Art Restoration and Conservation program at University of Delaware. After completing some independent studies in Florence, Italy, she moved to Flagstaff, Arizona, where she has a permanent gallery on the walls of Mart Anne's Burrito Palace, a locals' favorite. Well loved in the Flagstaff community, Emma is a creative soul with an enormous amount of talent.

She painted an entire Barbie series, but there is one image titled *American Beauty* which depicts Barbie as an American Icon. Emma's image speaks to the psychological bondage that women have endured as a result of the narrow, homogenized definition of beauty espoused by the media. Creating this image was a way for Emma to come to terms with a definition of beauty that has not only psychologically imprisoned women but has contributed to high numbers of health problems in women caused by plastic surgery, eating disorders and emotional disorders.

Expounding on this point, researchers generated a computer model of a woman with Barbie-doll proportions and found that her back would be too weak to support the weight of her upper body, and her body would be too narrow to contain more than half a liver and a few centimeters of bowel. A real woman built that way would suffer from chronic diarrhea and eventually die from malnutrition. Still, the number of real life women and girls who seek a similarly underweight body type is epidemic, and they often suffer equally devastating health consequences.

Perhaps some of her most intriguing work is a series of classic pin-up girls in evening gowns and in other poses of general fabulousness. It wouldn't be a huge leap to interpret Gardner's paintings as social commentary on the current fascination with extremely underweight models and super-skinny superstars. However, she sees her skeleton artwork as playfulness and likes the jolt of substituting a skeleton in such a sexy pose. She writes, "I did the pin-up girls because I thought about the contradiction of just the fleshiness, which was what was so sexy about them, of these robust women. To have them just be all bones I thought would be kind of funny. They could be all skinny, like the super models of today." [24]

Gardner's art is burlesque, a form of art that in its origins did not represent the strip-teases and bawdy commentary that we associate with that word today. Rather, it mocked the social attitudes of the upper classes by imitating them and, often, presenting them in ridicu-

American Beauty, Emma Gardner, 16"x20" acrylic on canvas,2004. www.emmagardner.com

Senorita, Emma Gardner 2'x6', acrylic on wood, 2006. www.emmagardner.com

Show Girl, Emma Gardner, 2'x6', acrylic on wood, 2006. www.emmagardner.com

lous scenarios.

Emily Kell: Alchemista of Feminine Strength

Revealing the intimate connectedness between women's body's, nature, and the reclaiming of feminine power, and the Goddess are strong themes in Emily Kell's work. While Western culture at large pays way too much attention to the surface appearance of women's bodies, Emily's imagery evokes the mysterious sacredness inherent in the female body and in nature. "Emily spent her childhood in Virginia, and gathered a lot of inspiration and wide-eyed wonder through the time she spent in nature, going to school on a farm and passing much of her time on a nature preserve in rural West Virginia. She graduated from Savannah College of Art and Design with a Bachelor of Fine Art in painting. She has painted at numerous art and music festivals, art events, and created a few large-scale murals in the United States, and one in Peru [25] Emily's experience of life as a woman has shaped her artwork through the years. She writes, "I strive to overcome restrictive modern concepts of female beauty and empower the women featured in the artwork to claim their own beauty and strength. Many of my paintings are very intimate and express the relationship of humanity to the sacred mysteries, divinity, and source. Using my own body and various women in my life as inspiration and models, I create paintings that speak to the entire human family; however, they also have a personal element to them. Much of my own personal journey is woven into my artwork through poetry, which is written in a secret language throughout the work." [26]

Her painting *The Great Mother Returns,* pays homage to the strength, wisdom, perseverance, and beauty of black women and women of color as they express their magic and talent. She writes, "The piece also honors our connection to the stars and the ancient wisdom-seeking

The Great Mother Returns, Emily Kell, www.emilykell.com

cultures; to the moon, and to crystals." [27]

The eroticism evoked in her paintings is categorically different than pornography in the ways in which is honors rather than debases the female form. Emily's nudes are so tastefully done and represent a diversity of body types, which is refreshing. There is a sense of the erotic in her work, which captures the raw and voluptuous landscapes of the female boy and it's connection to the cosmos. The word "Eros" comes from the Greek work Eros, the personification of love and creative power in all aspects. It is the life instinct innate in all humans, and we often feel a sense of eros engulf us when we are in nature. In that sense, it is a natural emotion that arises from deep instincts, and is the primordial glue that assures the continuation of the species.

The female body is the expressive vehicle of the creative life force and the primordial womb through which we are all born. Her painting *Rebirth of Mother Earth* is about self love, body positivity, and the healing of self and the earth. It represents her personal journey of empowerment—reclaiming her body, sexuality, sensuality, and creative expression through self-portraiture. She writes, "In this painting, I used my own physical vessel to depict an image of mother earth floating through the ether, about to be reborn. The pyramids on her chakras allude to the various temples and sacred sites across the energetic nodes on the earth. They speak to the connection of ancient earth based cultures and the renaissance of feminine wisdom emerging at this critical time." [28]

Another powerful contribution to the Goddess Art movement is *Return of the Primordial Goddess*. In a dark and desolate landscape, the primordial egg emerges with the sacred feminine hanging upside down in a cosmic primordial soup of intelligent design. Emily writes, "This piece speaks to the transformation of the earth and humanity, and the ancient cycles that the human family flows through. It is about the healing wisdom of ancient cultures and the primordial Goddess. It shows the Goddess sleeping, incubating, flowing through the ether, and waiting to be awoken to share her gentle wisdom with humanity." [29]

A lot of Emily's paintings contain symbolism from various cultures. Most systems of myth have an explanation for the origin of the universe and its components, otherwise known as creation myths. In a number of creation myths the formless chaotic egg is an example of the idea of a primitive chaos, or featureless, undifferentiated universe. It is symbolic of the unconscious, the primordial sea or universal womb. All creativity comes directly from the womb of the Creatrix. Emily is directly channeling the primordial soup of existence in her work. The wisdom of the egg is perhaps the deepest and most an-

Return of the Primordial Goddess, Emily Kell, www.emilykell.com

cient feminine wisdom there is, aside from death/rebirth.

A woman's right to control her body, her sexuality, and her reproduction is basic to the recovery of women's full humanity. As a result, women are waking up to the importance of reclaiming their bodies and reproductive rights from a scientific community that has been male biased from the start. As feminist Elinor Gadon writes, "There has been no place in our culture for ordinary women to turn for validation of bodily experience that is uniquely female. Conventional medicine has objectified and fragmented a woman's body, treating her organs and life processes with a 'scientific' detachment that excludes her psychological self. When medicine evolved as a scientific profession in the eighteenth century, the male doctors forced female practitioners—midwives, herbalists, traditional healers—out of the field and took over all aspects of health care connection with reproduction." [30] The social importance of feminist imagery that challenges a male bias is critical at this time when science and the medical model is still the dominant paradigm.

Rebirth of Mother Earth, Emily Kell, www.emilykell.com

Ashely Foreman: Riding the Wave of Shakti Power

Revealing the intimate connectedness between women's bodies and nature is a strong theme in Ashely Foreman's paintings. Our bodies are made from the earth and the cosmos, and therefore, will organically express the power of the erotic, which is acknowledged in many cultures. Shakti is the Sanskrit term for the female life force from which all existence originates. Expressions of this life force can come through a variety of ways-- sexuality, creating art, dancing, music, poetry, communicating deep love to a beloved, planting and cultivating a garden, etc.

The historical suppression of this powerful life-force has been an integral part of the exploitation of women. Reclaiming the power of our sexual chakras as our natural birthright and using this energy to fuel our liberation as brilliant creative women is what the Goddess is wanting us to do. Ashley is clearly tapping in to this powerful life force in her work, particularly in two of her paintings titled Fertility and Bloom.

In *Fertility* we see the power of the earth's Shakti coming up through the chakras of the woman's body and in to the cosmos and then spiraling back to the earth. In the foreground she taps into the universal unconscious, revealing dancers, crafts people, and devotees all entranced in the ecstatic dance of eros.

Ashely knows what it is like to be completely mesmerized by the creative trance of the dance of polarities. She is riding the wave of Shakti Power and it is amazing to watch. I had the opportunity to witness her do live paintings at the Harmony Festival in Santa Rosa and she was clearly drinking off a fire hose of creativity. She is incredibly gifted and will continue to bless the world with her visionary gifts in years to come.

In her painting *Bloom*, she captures the fierce passion of the sacred union, revealed in nature and in our bodies. We would not have the abundance of earth's bounty if the masculine and feminine polarities did not consecrate every year. In earth based spiritual traditions of the past, the ritual of Heiros Gamos was enacted every spring in order to pay homage to the Gods' and Goddess's of Fertility.

As an intuitive, she is alchemizing polar opposites from her flames of passion and sharing her unique vision of infinite creativity. She writes "making my art has granted me gradual access to a more integrated and multidimensional reality. I think the most powerful thing we can accomplish with our work is to inspire each other to accept responsibility for the liberation of oneself from the social conditioning of previous generations and the prevailing ignorance of our cultural story--to dismantle who we were falsely taught to be and find the unique creative identity within. My intention for my work, beyond personal healing, is to reflect a simple Truth -- that the universe is made of a profound Love beyond human categories, and that inter-collectively, we are One Being, One Consciousness." [31]

Bloom, Ashely Foreman, www.thirteentwentystudios.com

"From a young age Ashely's parents encouraged her creativity. At age fifteen she began painting in response to the conflict between her internal and external environment, and as a means for internal exploration. She attended Placer High School, in Auburn, California, and received the Jeanne Coppedge Joye Memorial Art Scholarship upon graduating.

She attended Humboldt State University in Arcata, California, where the natural beauty and power of the land continued to influence her work and personal explorations. She took a leave of absence in 2010 to travel, attend music festivals, and study the mischtechnik with the students of Ernst Fuchs, Laurence Caruana and Amanda Sage, in Torre, Italy. She also studied graphic design, and photography, graduating with a Bachelors of Art in Studio Art. " [32]

Fertility, Ashely Foreman, www.thirteentwentystudios.com

Autumn Skye Morrison: Resurrection of the Body and Ancient Wisdom

Women in search of themselves and the Goddess have been making sacred art as a deeply personal and cathartic process, involving the alchemical fusion of self and world, light and dark, intellect and emotion. In addition, reclaiming the body as a source of knowing and self-identification has been a major goal of the Women's Movement. A contemporary visionary artist who portrays the female body and ancient wisdom of the ancestors is Autumn Skye Morrison. What is particularly astonishing and unique about her work is the deep emotion and authenticity in which she portrays the female body, not as an object of male desire, but from the subjective lens of a woman.

Autumn says, "Through the exploration of 'being woman' and 'being human,' I express my journey and highest realization of who I am, through the language of paint." When I look at an artist's work, I want to be moved deep in my gut, but I also want to experience beauty. There is no doubt that Autumn's work is astoundingly beautiful; however, it is clear that her journey embraces the shadow aspects of life as opposed to only conveying the blissful states. She goes to the depths of darkness, but leaves a glimmer of hope, a butterfly messenger or a singing bird to ease the devastation of the dark night of the soul. Her style is original; her technique is highly developed and mature. It is always astonishing when a young painter is able to capture the wisdom of the Crone in her work.

Two paintings capture her process of development as an artist: *The Vital Commission and Work in Progress.* The enfoldment of self occurs much like a painting, one brush stroke at a time, and you never know where the creative process is going to take you. Forming an artistic identity in a scientific and rationally oriented society can be a difficult task for most women, but Autumn Skye is one of the lucky few that were supported in her creative path from a young age. However, this doesn't mean her path has been easy. Her vital commission has ultimately been the self-creation of her own artistic identity in a male dominated art world. This has always been an uphill battle for women artists, even in this postmodern era, which supposedly offers more opportunities to women artists.

Nature and art have clearly been a source of healing and self-empowerment for her. "Born in Nova Scotia, Autumn Skye moved with her family West across Canada. She spent her youth between the majesty of the Rocky Mountains with her Father, and the lush coastal rainforests with her Mother. Autumn Skye has been painting since she could hold a brush, developing a deep

The Vital Commision, Autumn Skye Morrison, 36"x36", Acrylic on Canvas, www.autumnskyeart.com

wonder for nature and the world around her. Amidst journeys to explore the world and share inspiration with the ever blossoming community, Autumn Skye otherwise lives and paints in her home north of Powell River on the Sunshine Coast of British Columbia, Canada. In her studio, she overlooks a sweeping expanse of ocean, islands, mountains, and sky."[33] In her artist statement, she speaks of the need for all of us to reclaim our divine right to create in whatever form that might take:

> *In this shifting and challenging time, I feel a deep stirring, a potent blossoming of creativity. It is all around us--gaining momentum and strength in one's self, in those of our family and community, and in the collective experience. It is our divine duty to create and share inspiration, especially at this time of change. As we honor our own personal creativity, we contribute vitally to the whole. We inspire those around us to celebrate, we empower them to create, and we manifest visual mirrors to the light, divinity, and potential of each viewer.*
>
> *As we release judgment, silence our mind, breathe deep into the process, and find bliss in each step, we realize that we are boundlessly assisted in our authentic and heart-centered expression. We step out of the way. We realize that Art is not born of us, but through us. And in this understanding, we are humbled, yet profoundly empowered. Each creation is an offering-- a reflection of ourselves and humanity, a celebration of evolving consciousness, an opportunity for healing and deepening, a vision of a brighter future NOW.*[34]

Work in Progress, Autumn Skye Morrison, 24"x48", acrylic, 2006. www.autumnskyeart.com

This brighter future that Autumn Skye is talking about is the promise of the Great Mother's return. For she is the Cosmic Creatrix—the transmitter of all energies and polarities. She is the supreme birth center, the cosmic void, the womb of the unconscious and intuition. Another painting titled *Divine Intervention p*ortrays the Cosmic Creatrix in her utmost brilliance. This painting speaks of the intelligent design of our minds, which are micro reflections of the universe. We have the universe in the genetic matrix of our DNA. We have been given the keys to the God Head, which includes the Great Mother, and we don't even know it. We also fail to realize that the return of the Goddess is the return of ART, and the feminine wisdom's of magic, mysticism, interconnectivity, the gift economy, and cooperation prevail. As the saying goes, "The Goddess has arrived and magic is afoot."

At this point in time, the Goddess asks us to have faith in her divine plan, for it is far greater than we could ever imagine. She is Queen Victorious--the Queen Bee, indeed! Working as drones for the patriarchal machine was never her intention for humanity. She wants to offer all of her creation equal opportunity and freedom to think and act creatively. These feminine values directly oppose a capitalistic and conservative agenda. Our creative energies have been drained because they have been invalidated by a male biased science and a mechanistic paradigm that is literally killing the soul of humanity.

Autumn's painting *Body Temple* portrays the intimate connection between our bodies and the larger body of Gaia and the Cosmic Creatrix. Every cell of our bodies is made up of divine intelligence; yet, more often than not, we tend criticize our bodies in one way or another. Women are socialized to be perfectionists and hold their bodies to an unhealthy standard of perfection, even when the body has aged. And the tendency for women to compare their bodies to other's can be destructive to one's self esteem.

We are so blessed to have the spirit of the Divine living within our bodies and the unique expression of various sizes and shapes should be celebrated. Using the world "temple" to describe Spirit's dwelling in our bodies conveys that idea that our bodies are a shrine in which the Spirit not only lives, but is worshiped revered, and honored. Therefore, how we behave, think and speak, and what we let into the temple through our eyes, mouth, ears, and yoni becomes critically important as well. One of my favorite articles is by a feminist Native American writer named Paula Gunn Allen titled "The Woman I Love Is A Planet." In this article, she talks about the rite of passage of the Earth into the crone stage. A time when she is giving birth to a new consciousness and her relationship to the other vast intelligences in the universe. Paula writes:

> *Now, now is the time when mother becomes grandmother, when daughter becomes mother, when the living dead are released from entombment, when the dead live again and walk once again in her ways. Together we all can rejoice, talk up the tasks of attending, take up the joy of giving birth and being born, of transforming in recognition of*

Divine Intervention, Autumn Skye Morrison, www.autumnskyeart.com

the awfulness of what is entailed, in recognition of what it is we together can and must and will do. I have said that this is the time of her new birth. I could also say it is the time of mutation, for transformation means to change form; I could also say it is the climacteric, when the beloved planet goes through menopause and takes her place among the wise women planets that dance among the stars.[35]

We are each and all a part of her, an expression of her essential being. The Goddess is inclusive of all the energies, even those souls that are young, ignorant, destructive and violating of Her. Her fires of passion and compassion can transform and awaken all beings, especially the weak, the poor and societies so-called "rejects." One drop of her compassionate waters will heal all suffering, for her wisdom is beyond anything we could ever fathom. The Goddess has a message for us—her Grace is the only thing we can bank on when all is said and done.

Krista Lynn Brown: Deva of Lunar Wisdom

Another extremely talented visionary artist who creates powerful images that portray a mystical relationship between humans and the Earth is Krista Lynn Brown. Her paintings are saturated with gaian, sophianic wisdom, urging the viewer to get out of their left-brain and into the deep well of their creative imaginations. With no formal art training, Krista has developed her creative expression through a mix of inspiration and experimentation. She writes, "I paint inner landscapes revealed to me through years of introspection, lucid dreaming and playing with psychedelics. I am voraciously interested in the underpinnings of how things connect-- bodies and psyches, religion and science, dreams and realities. I relate closely with the element of water, which allows me to stay creatively fluid, open to intuitive influence and at home in the wells of imagination."[36]

Krista's work is poetic and stylized. Her image titled *Sleeping Earth* is a potent representation of the Earth Mother, dripping with emotion, sensual passion and beauty. Offering sustenance and holding the seed of creation and potential, the great Mother nourishes us in more ways than we know. The female body is the vehicle of the creative life force-- the Shakti, erotic energy that activates our being. Every man also needs this connection to the vital feminine principle in nature. Krista has a way of channeling the erotic power of the earth, which arises from our deeper instincts and is our natural source of personal power and emotional connectivity. Krista ex-

Body Temple, Autumn Skye Morrison, www.autumnskyeart.com

Sleeping Earth, Krista Lynn Brown, 16"x20" acrylic on canvas, www.devaluna.com

plains this Gaian wisdom further:

> *My paintings are an invitation into a hidden magical reality shimmering beneath the skin of the ordinary—portals to a live interior landscape of dreams, visions and possibilities. In this supple place, plants awaken and dance, a woman becomes a river sighing to the moon, and a bird can embody the fleeting voice of intuition. I see this reality and paint it in a language of visual poetry, a tongue of archetypes woven into forms that echo the movements of nature, the undulations of waves, the growth of vines, the contours of flowers.*[37]

Another painting that is deserving of recognition is *Mother Power.* Here the Earth is nurturing and passionate, much like Pele, a fierce Hawaiian Dark Goddess. As she squeezes the nectar of milk from her breasts in compassionate service to all, she is holding a lighting bolt in her hand, a symbol of her tremendous power. While she gives of her love unconditionally, she will not allow humanity to destroy her. Because she is a symbol of self-love, she naturally has to set boundaries. If she needs to bring out her lightning bolt, she will, but it will be an act of compassion for our ignorance, as opposed to vengeance.

The Earth Mamma is continually evolving and changing. She wants humanity to ascend with her. She has been a container for our self-hatred for a long time now, but she needs us to respect her wisdom reflected in the cosmos and on the earth plane. She holds our rage and pain and then transmutes it in the fire of her hearts passion/compassion. As Carole Christ so eloquently puts it, "Human beings are so fundamentally part of the earth that the earth is as intimate to us as our own bodies. We could not live; we would not be, without our grounding in the earth."[38] As the ground of all being, every inch of my body yearns to return to her, like water yearns for the primordial ocean, for it was she who called every cell of my body to be recharged by her *primal* energy.

Mother Power, Krista Lynn Brown, 18"x24" acrylic on canvas, www.devaluna.com

Illumination—Between the Lines, Over The Edge, Krista Lynn Brown, 30"x40" acrylic on canvas, www.devaluna.com

Another monumental painting by Krista is *Illumination--Between the Lines, Over the Edge*. Nature and art have served as a means to experience the transcendental aspects of us as necessary and valid parts of the vast matrix of love still present on this earth. There is a sense of stillness, peace and organic wisdom residing in nature that is available to everyone. It is through a stilling of the mind that we are able to get in touch with our deeper selves and be illuminated with feminine wisdom. The compassionate nature of the earth will help to dissolve the feelings of unworthiness and alienation that keep us from true happiness if we will but attune ourselves to her grounding, her strength and her brilliant illumination.

Cathy McClelland: Dreaming Gaian Wisdom and Magic through Art

An important theme in ecofeminist art is the reclaiming of feminine wisdom and it's connection with the Earth. Another important issue is the willingness to deepen our experience of communion with nature. An artist who is dreaming this type of gaian wisdom back to the Earth is Cathy McClelland. Art has always been a healing refuge and literally an escape from day to day life, taking her into the realms of her imagination. A favorite quote of hers is by Gustave Flaubert, "The greatest achievement in art is not to bring laughter or tears, nor to be stirred with lust or fury, but to do as nature herself does and set men's minds into dreaming."[39]

All the indigenous elders are informing us that it is essential that we reconnect with Nature, for she will be our sanity through the great transition. We need to find our way out of the technocratic alienation surrounding us by cultivating and honoring our direct connections with nature.

At the age of five, Cathy saw the Nutcracker Suite ballet and was awed by the magic and stage colors of the performance. Her love for magical subjects was born, and the theme of fantasy and enchantment weaved its way into her artwork. She studied illustration at the Academy of Art College, in San Francisco. In 1979 she moved to the north shore of Lake Tahoe for the summer and never left. Lake Tahoe's beautiful environment is a constant inspiration for Cathy, bringing her close to the heart of nature. The mountains, water, forest, moon, animals and stars feed her creative spirit. Her work encompasses many themes, from the ethereal and magical, to animals, scenes of Lake Tahoe to lush jungles, deserts and places in between. Whether it is a mural, sculpture or painting, her artwork reflects her love of nature and mythical subjects. She writes:

> *Nature and the mystery of the universe play a big part with my inspiration. I like to weave the two together in my creations, hoping to inspire others to enjoy the beauty of nature and the wonderful creatures around us. Our world is full of miracles and magic—we just need to recognize the beauty and truth of this, and bring it into our lives and into our hearts. I hope that my artwork can be a contribution to others in that direction.*[40]

Cathy's art is imbued with magic and enchantment. It is a celebration of hope and rebirth through Goddess consciousness and a renewed appreciation for our own bodies and the Earth body. In response to the ecological crisis, a number of artists have been channeling their anger, pain and frustration into art. It is these kinds of images that have nourished our fragile hearts in these times of extreme fragmentation and suffering. An image by Cathy McClelland that has been a source of healing for the world and me is a painting titled *Prayer*. In this image a woman sits in deep prayer and meditation for the Earth and all of her beloved creatures. She prays for the awakening of the human race, for equality, social justice, healing and peace on earth. We know that we are one fabric with all life on this planet and that we have no right to destroy the integrity of the Earth's delicately balanced ecosystems, whose histories are far longer than our own.

There is a certain degree of trauma endured by the systematic removal of our lives from the natural world: from the tendrils of earthy textures, from the rhythms of sun and moon, from the spirits of the bears and trees, from the life force itself. This is also the removal of our lives from the kinds of social and cultural experiences our ancestors assumed when they lived in rhythm with the natural world. In order to survive, we have had to cognitively disassociate ourselves from the grief we feel over the demise of the earth and all the social injustices occurring in the world. However, suppressing this grief might not be the best solution. Ecofeminist and psychoanalyst Joanna Macy writes, "Just as grief work is a process by which bereaved persons unblock their numbed energies by acknowledging and grieving the loss of a loved one, so do we all need to unblock our feelings about our threatened planet and the possible demise of our species. Until we do, our power of creative response will be crippled."[41]

Cathy McClelland recently completed a Star Tarot Deck released by Schiffer Publishing. This has been a life dream and one that her fans are anxiously looking forward to. While all of the images are powerful and meaningful, there is one in particularly that speaks to a feminist agenda: It is titled *Justice*. Issues of social justice have been a major priority for feminists across the board as the feminization of poverty continues to grow in conjunction with globalization. When we start to understand that the earth is alive, she calls us to act to preserve her life and SHE CALLS US TO STAND UP FOR JUSTICE. Cathy explains her painting further:

> *Justice stands holding her scales in balance. The scales are part of her actual being. The scales symbolize her weighing out situations when it comes to decision-making. Her two-edged sword of righteousness and discerning intuition are lined up with her seven chakras, keeping her decision-making in balance and ready for action.*
>
> *The sword represents the creative mind directly applying and bringing realistic answers and solutions to the table. The sword also represents the strength that comes from Justice holding inner balance. Justice represents holding on to our inner balance while living in the chaos of the world. Justice wants us to look deep inside ourselves and identify our contradictions.By balancing what our intuitive side feels with what the conscious mind is speaking, one is able to work from a place of true reason, rather than confusion.*
>
> *Her crown is connected to the tree of life, allowing Justice to tap in to divine guidance and truth. Justice is associated with the astrological sign Libra, which has the ultimate goal of living in harmony and fairness. Justice represents the laws of nature, moral law, legal law and the laws of the universe. She reminds us that there is divine justice. Her purpose is to be fair and impartial while seeking truth and answers, which guides her to set her decision in motion. She encourages one to weigh matters carefully before making important decisions that will affect others.* [42]

The Goddess promises to bring justice back to the earth. She is refusing to be silenced any longer. She wants to empower all avatars—women, men and animals, who are committed to social justice. When we understand that everything is connected, we are called to cultivate compassion--the ability to literally feel with all living be-

Prayer, Cathy McClelland, 14"x20" acrylic on canvas, www.cathymcclelland.com

Justice, Cathy McClelland, 11"x17" acrylic on canvas, www.cathymcclelland.com

ings on earth. That feeling is the heart center or ground upon which we can build community and come together and take action.

In this article I have introduced you to an assortment of contemporary eco-feminists and Goddess artists who have devoted their lives to the re-enchantment of the sacred feminine in Western consciousness. I have also acknowledged a long lineage of female mystics and artists who challenge the misogyny of an arrogant white male perspective in times of great oppression. Through their ideas and imagery, they have attempted to re-envision a world that is more egalitarian, more connected and more compassionate.

As a way of honoring these women and the work they have done for the women's movement, I encourage all artists, and people in general, to rekindle their relationship with the Great Goddess, for it is through her resurrection in the minds and hearts of a large population of people that the marginalization of artists, gender and racial oppression, the mistreatment of animals and the destruction of the environment will be ended. The time has come to rise up and reclaim the body of Earth and Mother. If we don't act now, She may be forced to get our attention through earthquakes, tidal waves, volcanic eruptions and other natural calamities in order to end the imbalance that we ourselves have created.

Victoria Christian is a sociologist, social worker, counselor, artist, writer and sacred activist. She holds undergraduate and Masters degrees in Sociology. She also has a Masters of Social Work, with an emphasis in the sociology of gender, social theory, the sociology of art and ecofeminism. For more information about her art, books and DVD's, you can view her website at www.victoriachristian.com. To learn more about this book, see the website: www.mysticspiritart.com

Earth Blessing, Heather Taylor, www.fullcirclemandalas.com

The Oracle, Return of the Sun Goddess, Victoria Christian, 24"x24", oil on wood, www.victoriachristian.com

Contemporary Images of Spirituality and Resistance Among African Americans

By Arisika Razak

As a practitioner of women's spirituality, my sense of the sacred is inextricably bound to the embodied experience and physical realities of the female body. Our bodies are the gateway to life on this planet, and for millennia women's bodies have been revered as the source and sustainers of all human life. All over the ancient world, sacred images of women were carved in stone, painted on rock, incised in wood or lovingly formed in clay to honor the Sacred Feminine. These abundant images depict powerful, nude full-bodied women. Their bare breasts are often adorned with jewelry, while their prominent softly-rounded bellies are highlighted by knots, sashes and talismans of power. Their clearly demarcated vulvas are sometimes stained with red ochre. These images of the Sacred Feminine are as ancient as the Paleolithic and Neolithic eras, and as modern as today's woman. They stand as iconographic representatives of the life-giving power of the Great Mother, who rules over the abundant Earth, the life of the grain, birthing by women and animals, and the turning of the cosmos and the seasons.

Many of these images represent fertile or childbearing women, for childbirth is a primal female rite of passage connecting women to the Divine. As a midwife with more than twenty years of experience, I have tracked the path of active surrender, personal sacrifice, emotional empowerment, and spiritual transcendence that women traverse as they move through the birthing process. Standing as witness, companion and helper to women in labor has been a life-changing event for me, as was my own experience of a home birth. Nothing I had ever experienced prepared me for the holiness of the moment in which a laboring woman turns away from her preoccupation with the world outside to focus on the world-making within her body, a moment that reveals the face of the Goddess creating the world again.

Many scholars and practitioners of women's spirituality and Jungian psychology have documented the iconographic links between women and the natural world (e.g. the Earth, grain, animal life, and the celestial bodies of the moon and sun) as well as the primal forces of birth, death, and sexuality. [1] Contemporary artists of the modern era have continued this tradition in their depictions of Goddesses, sacred women, clan mothers, and grandmothers in patriarchal and women-centered cultures alike. However, patriarchal cultures of the West have greatly diminished this tradition which affirms the physical bodies of women. It has been severed from its connection to the bodies of ordinary women and to the "blood mysteries" – menarche, sexuality, childbirth, menopause – of the female body. Here in the United States, where hatred of the female body is endemic, we prize and sexualize the bodies of children, and reject and marginalize the bodies of mature women. This leads to low self-esteem, self-destructive behaviors, and women's exploitation at the hands of the cosmetic, health, and entertainment industries. Many women internalize cultural rejection of the female body, which is linked with hatred of female physiology and dissociation from physicality. These beliefs have led to a wide variety of personal, social and cultural ills, particularly in the West. [2] Some authors believe these to be especially marked among African-American women. [3]

Although modern society has moved away from degrading stereotypes of Black women as self-effacing mammies, lascivious Jezebels, and tragic mulattos, contemporary society still implies that Black women's bodies are socially and culturally unacceptable. [4] The absence of large, dark, full-featured, natural- haired Black women in popular media; the disproportionate use of Black bodies to illustrate social and cultural deviance in scientific and academic discourse; and the lack of our likenesses in mainstream religious iconography all contribute to our feelings of imperfection and marginalization. Living in a culture that defines "femininity" as small, fair, delicate and dependent, we find ourselves to be large, dark, independent women – women who are too large, too loud, too Black, and too nappy-headed! Every day we are assaulted by images which reinforce our perceptions of imperfection – and all too often our partners, parents, religious leaders, and health providers remind us that our natural bodies are inherently flawed.

Uncovering the ways in which African Diasporan women experience and resist oppression has been a prominent theme of contemporary Black feminist thought. [5] Modern scholars such as Audre Lorde, Patricia Hill Collins, Cheryl Townsend Gilkes, June Jordan, and Bell Hooks have all produced scholarly works that analyze and critique the social and cultural oppression of Black women. Visionary artists like Ntozake Shange, Nina Simone, Julie Dash, Alice Walker, Toni Morrison, Gloria Naylor and Bernice Reagon have not only documented our oppression, but offered us powerfully liberating re-visionings that point us towards a positive womanist [6] future.

Like many practitioners of women's spirituality, I believe that to be fully effective, this new cultural paradigm must be grounded in a spiritual vision of the body itself. In this article, I review visual images of sacred African women that have been produced by contemporary artists who create powerful visionary art that reframes and resists negative stereotypes of Black womanhood, and the distorted, discriminatory social practices these images support.

Spiritual images of African women have been produced for the last ten thousand years. Images of Black queens, priestesses, goddesses and sacred ancestors are found in Neolithic cave paintings in Algeria and Zimbabwe, and in the tombs and temples of ancient Egypt. [7] Sculptural and mask traditions of Eastern, Western and Central Africa document the moral authority and spiritual power of women in many African societies, and the work of the artists I have selected is informed by these ancient traditions. Even though the Christianity developed by Africans of the Diaspora was characterized by its rejection of racism and white supremacy, most of the artists I have selected create images outside of mainstream Christianity. Some of these artists have grown up in cultures where African-inspired or indigenous religious traditions are the norm. For others, the search for a liberating spirituality that supports the empowerment of women and the Black community has led directly to Afro-centric spiritual traditions. Sabrina Soujourner writes:

> *It was only as late as my parents' generation that countless Black women and men began leaving the church, no longer believing in the salvation offered by a white god and savior. Now, many women of my own generation are discovering that God is not only not white, She has never even been considered male until relatively recently.* [8]

Some of these artists celebrate Black women's cultural experience and mythic history. Others, who are practitioners of women's spirituality, create embodied female images to depict Black female Divinity. Their art subverts modern paradigms of racism and patriarchy by placing the bodies of Black women front and center in recognition of a god who is Black and female, embodied and divine. These soul-healing, woman-centered images are powerful tools for healing.

In the USA, the Black church served as a historic site for the generation of powerful, liberating African-American identities. It languaged our grief, supported our joys and wove a social network that embraced us mentally, spiritually, psychologically and physically. It named and resisted the racism of the outside community, for African-Americans re-visioned the Christianity of their masters to forge a religion of liberation. Rejecting racist notions of the times that defined us as ignorant, primitive, lascivious and repugnant, we defiantly created a spirituality in which we named ourselves "Sister," Brother" and "Child of God." Forbidden to write, own property or need anything of beauty, our songs claimed "I got a right. . . .you got a right . . . we all got a right to the Tree of Life." [9]

However, the lack of a liberating spiritual iconography that reflects the bodies of Black people has been a source of conflict for a growing number of African-Americans. As Marimba Ani notes, "Jesus, the symbol of perfection for the European Christian, is reinterpreted as white and similarly every symbol of purity is white. Even the ideal but unattainable sex object is blonde." [10] The Black church has also had an ambivalent relationship with Black women and their bodies. On the one hand, the church supported the creation of culturally appropriate female identities. Black churches sanctioned Black women's roles as missionary women, "mothers of Zion", and church/community organizers. [11] Even when Black women were formally denied the pulpit in many mainstream Baptist and Methodist churches, the sanctified church recognized Black women's right to pastor, preach, and found new churches.

On the other hand, the Black church has shared many of Western culture's sexist and patriarchal values. It privileged maleness over femaleness, and was ambivalent at best, and condemning at worst, towards female sexuality and the female body. As an institution, the church could embody sexist culture or mirror socio-cultural structures of Black internalized oppression, like classicism or colorism. [12] Most importantly for some, even though its language may call on God as Mother and Father, its most significant images of God are male.

As someone who came of age during the 1960s, at a time when there were virtually no images of Black people in the mainstream media, I remember the liberating power of the new aesthetic that proclaimed *"Black is beautiful,"* and urged us to *"Say it loud! I'm Black and I'm proud"!* My soul sang when I first read Ntozake Shange's famous lines: "i found God in myself/and i loved her/i loved her fiercely." [13] The artists I review offer new images of Black female beauty and Black female divinity. I honor and salute them, in recognition of their service as midwives for our souls' rebirthing.

Feminine Mysticism in African Diasporan Art

The four artists I have selected integrate themes of feminine mysticism with African Diasporan concepts of spirituality and liberation. Mass dispersions of peoples of a common culture, ethnic group, or national origin are commonly referred to as *Diasporas*. Historically, these dispersions are often forced or involuntary, reflecting pervasive economic, environmental, or political forces that separate people of a common origin from their homelands. While Western science states that all modern humans are descendants of an original African Diaspora which occurred between 125,000 and 65,000 years ago, the African Diaspora to which I refer, began in the early 16th century following European colonization of the Americas. [14] Tens of millions of Africans were brutally removed from their homes and forced to work as slaves in the households and plantations of the Americas and the Caribbean.

Although enslaved Africans came from various tribal nations of West and Central Africa, the Yoruba people and their spiritual traditions made a huge impact on the new cultures formed in the aftermath of the slave trade. The *orishas*, who are the traditional deities of the Yoruba people, travelled to the Americas with their enslaved devotees. New spiritual practices that disguised the worship of African deities by conflating each of the major *orishas* with a Catholic saint led to the creation of the syncretic religions of *Santeria* and *Lucumi* (Cuba), and *Candomble* and *Macumba* (Brazil). (A similar process occurred in Haiti where deities of the Fon and Ewe people – Ghana, Togo, Benin/Dahomey, and Nigeria – were syncretized with Catholicism leading to the religion of *Vodou*.) This process of syncretism, which also draws from indigenous spirituality, has become a major theme in the art and spirituality of contemporary Diasporan peoples.

Each artist I selected is part of the African Diaspora, and their art reflects Afro-Diasporan spiritual traditions. AfraShe Asungi and Liz Sykes create work reflecting Egyptian, Diasporan and/or Yoruba spiritualties. Yasmin Hernandez draws from the *Santeria* traditions of Puerto Rico while Lili Bernard documents the stories of her multi-cultural Cuban ancestors. Jamaican-American artist, Abba Yahuda, finds inspiration in the Diasporan traditions of Jamaica, especially Ethiopianism and Rastafarianism. This essay reviews selected images of sacred and empowered Black women as well as goddesses, since many traditional African cultures did not make divisions between the secular and spiritual realms. As women's spirituality affirms, we are all embodiments of the sacred – and our divinity is reflected not only in our spiritual practice, but in the everyday acts of love, service, and creativity performed by ordinary Black women engaged in the life-affirming tasks that nurture and support the community.

AfraShe Asungi: Resurrecting AfraGoddess Sistahood

I begin with the work of AfraShe Asungi, artist, priestess, writer and healer, who founded MAMAROOTS: AJAMA-JEBI an "AfraGoddess sistahood dedicated to Afracentric spirituality and cultural awareness." [15] Her art depicts Black women as mythic goddesses, historic queens and spiritual warriors. Their lush, dark, full figures are embedded in a cosmology that re-visions our ancient African past and points the way towards an empowered African womanhood. When I first saw her art in the 1980s, I remember thinking "*Her images' bodies look like mine!*" The rounded feminine forms, dark radiance, bare breasts and ease of posture suggest a time when Black women's bodies, sexuality and authority were honored. Her woman-centered images did not rely on male authority figures for validation, but were complete within themselves. They were clearly *spiritual* women, whose dress and adornment suggest ritual power and whole-

Dunham's Life Song, AfraShe Asungi, www.sistahpeace.com

Ochumare: Goddess Of Rainbows, AfraShe Asungi. www.sistahpeace.com

ness, while their bodies and skin tones reflect the diverse lineages of the Diaspora.

AfraShe situates many of her figures in ancient '*Kamaat*', which she translates as meaning "Sacred Sun-kissed lands where the Black-faced Mama of Genuine Righteous Truth dwells." [16] She rejects the term "*Afro-centric*" as patriarchal, and instead wishes to recreate a term that captures black women's perspective. She explains:

> *The goal is to transform what I consider the co-opted matriarchy in Africa and in the African tradition, and retrieve the essential elements of the unconquered female or feminist spirituality. A word that I developed in 1985 was 'Afracentrik,' which means we are going one step beyond feminists and one step beyond patriarchal African analysis to look for a unique vision where the Black female is placed at the center, revered as a norm and a valid perspective in the culture."* [17]

In her pastel painting, *Dunham's Life Song,* a dark, radiant, bare-breasted Black woman holds a snake in one hand and a unicorn in the other. A large pair of wings emerges from her back, and another set covers her eyes like a ritual mask. The orange, blue and soft magenta colors of her wings are in strong contrast to the starry night in which a dark moon dances. Her colors and symbols indicate a woman of authority. AfraShe writes about her piece:

> *Katherine Dunham is a great choreographer, anthropologist and priestess of the Haitian religion. She is represented by the snake and unicorn, both symbols of the mysterious positive life forces and ultimate powers of the universe. Other symbols are her golden arm bands, which give her the blessings of Ochun, the River Goddess. Her navel guard is the symbol of Isis, and the moon Goddess, Yemaya.* [18]

Another image titled *Ochumare: the Rainbow Goddess,* depicts a nude Black woman wearing a winged mask sitting in lotus position on a pad created from the starry night of the cosmic galaxy. The spinning Earth, with the continent of Africa foremost, sits at her navel. She wears golden armbands and balances the rainbow between her outstretched arms. Two pyramids rise behind her; a crescent moon sits at her left shoulder and her hair is an extension of the night sky. Asungi writes:

> *Ochumare, as the Rainbow Goddess, moves the sea waters between the heavens and the Earth. I see her as the cosmic channel amongst the Goddesses of the Universe and the Earth. Here, she rests in the beauty of self-awareness. She sits upon the Universal Waters and the Cosmic Lily Pads, symbolizing her ever-presence. She is nude, symbolizing her purity and ultimate pride of self. Her mask is a sign of strength and mystery. The Earth in her lap is spinning from the absolute energy that she provides from her navel, a source of Cosmic Power.* [19]

In her depictions of powerful Black goddesses, which are based on personal, historic *Afra-centrik* imagery, AfraShe has created a spiritual home for Black women seeking an empowering vision of themselves. She reclaims the sacred darkness of the night and the radiant darkness of our skins. She writes, "I needed to see strong, self-contained and focused Black wimmin, so I reached into our tales, myths, goddesses and other spiritual realities and created this series of paintings as my visual song, in praise of the wonders of the feminine spirits I found there. I recreate positive and powerful images of African Goddesses, so that every womin who looks at my work will connect to the Truth in its purest form, and the truth will create the Seeds of Transformation from the Depths of Her Great Unconscious." [20]

Lili Bernard: Celebrating a Multi-Cultural Cuban Heritage

Lili Bernard is a multimedia artist as well as a screen and theatre actress who was born in Santiago de Cuba. Her paintings skillfully blend political, artistic and spiritual themes which document the experiences of her Afro-Indigenous, Jamaican, Spanish, Chinese and British ancestors and their struggles to resist and survive genocide and enslavement. A prolific artist and the mother of six children, she has also founded youth organizations that provide community space for young artists of color. She writes:

> *I am interested in creatively exploring the impact of the ancestral upon contemporary life and the merging of the two as they relate to spiritualism and modern-day racism, from the standpoint of an Afro-Cuban-born woman of mixed descent, transplanted in the United States of America.* [21]

Bernard has created several large, stunningly colored oil paintings based on classical European art produced during the era of the slave trade. She has reinterpreted this work in order to tell the stories of her oppressed ancestors. She writes:

> *The concerns which inform my art-making practice stem from a feeling that I am divinely driven to tell the stories of my Cuban family and my Afro-Indigenous Caribbean*

The Sale of Venus, Lili Bernard, 96"x72", Oil on Canvas, 2011. www.lilibernard.com

ancestors' suffering, with a realization that I am their dream come true. I expose the suffering that our people have endured for generations, juxtaposed against the resilient faces and the splendid flora of the beautiful Caribbean island in which I was born.[22]

One of these paintings from her *Historical* series is titled *The Sale of Venus.* It's based on Botticelli's 15th century painting, *The Birth of Venus.* The central figure in this richly colored painting is a tearful and pregnant Black Venus who is the symbolic Mother of the Afro-Cuban people. Nude, violated and bleeding, she stands on a floating auction block, simultaneously evoking the waters of the Caribbean and the horrors of the Middle Passage. She is accompanied and protected by the twined figures of the Yoruba *orisha,* Shango, and his syncretized double, Santa Barbara; and she is protectively welcomed to Cuba by La Virgen de La Caridad Del Cobre, popularly known as "Cachita" (Little Charity), . . . the patron saint of Cuba", [23] who also represents *Ochun*. Details of this rich, lushly hued painting include Los Tres Juanitos (two indigenous Cubans and the enslaved African) who were the first to witness the appearance of Our Lady of Charity (or La Caridad Del Cobre) in 1612, as well as other figures drawn from Afro-Cuban spirituality.

While some might find this painting depressing, I view it as a poignant and deeply moving depiction of the suffering Black women endured during the era of the slave trade. Bernard writes:

> *I don't tire in telling our stories of suffering, for there is joy to be found even in suffering. It was through my mother's suffering in which I came into this world, and it will be in my children's suffering through which I will depart to heaven. As my friend, author Deborah Gregory once told me, 'Suffering is the touchstone of creativity.'*[24]

A second painting, *La Virgen de Regla-Yemaya*, depicts the Cuban Black Madonna, who has been syncretized with the Yoruba *orisha*, *Yemaya.* The original *Virgen de Regla* is found in Regla, Spain, where her dark-skinned image is housed in a Catholic sanctuary.[25] Spaniards colonizing Cuba established a city in Havana Bay, and named it after this Spanish port. *La Virgen de Regla* (and *Yemaya,* her *Lucumi* double) became its patron saint. Her name, *Yemaya,* is derived from her Yoruba title, *"Yeyeomo eja"*, meaning "The Mother Whose Children are Fish",[26] alluding to her children who are as numerous as the fish

Le Virgen de Regla—Yemaya arrives in Cuba, Lili Bernard, 36"x36", Oil on Canvas, 2007. wwwlilibernard.com

in the sea. In *Lucumi* tradition, *Yemaya* embodies the-spirit of motherhood, and she is linked to the ocean and the moon. She supported her enslaved children during the horrendous crossing known as the Middle Passage, and she is the owner of all the wealth of the oceans. Depicted as a fertile mother, a rich queen, and a beautiful mermaid, she dresses in blue and white and favors silver ornaments. Bernard's painting highlights the African origins of this divinity and her pre-eminent role as mother of the world; her blue and white colors link her both to *Yemaya* and to the Catholic Virgin Mary. Surrounded by the lush flora of Cuba, she epitomizes the syncretic deities who protected their children in their new homes.

Yasmin Hernandez: Celebrating the Beauty of the Feminine Spirit

Yasmin Hernandez is a Puerto Rican artist who celebrates the political, cultural and spiritual lives of the peoples of Puerto Rico. Often titled in Spanish, her images reflect the cultures of indigenous Taino people, Africans of the Diaspora, and Spanish colonizers and their descendants. Hernandez's work depicts the legacy and beauty of the feminine spirit, even as she documents the struggles that women endure. Her work depicts Yoruba and Taino goddesses, Puerto Rican liberation fighters, and women of her family lineage. She draws from Catholic, Santeria and 'Spiritist' beliefs, for her maternal grandfather was a medium in the Kardecian spiritist tradition. Art and spirituality have helped her reclaim her own identity and body:

> *When I first began painting as a teenager, I had major self-image issues. My art allowed me to develop a pride and appreciation for who I was physically and spiritually. By the time I got to college and started to research the spiritism and Yoruba faith traditions of my heritage, I realized the female Orishas were a potent source of empowerment and gave me a new understanding of my identity, culture, spirituality, gender and sexuality.* [27]

Her full-bodied images of Yoruba *Orisha* are balanced by images of everyday women and men, some of whom she depicts as deities. I was amazed by her vibrant palette of colors, which reflect the tropical colors of the Caribbean Islands. Yasmin challenges Catholic conventions restricting women to the narrow roles of virgins and whores through nude depictions of contemporary women's bodies that cry out against sexist violence and violation.

Hernandez's painting, *Miel De Abeja,* depicts the *Lucumi* goddess, *Ochun*, as a nude woman crowned with peacock feathers who stands in a river. The title, *Bee's Honey,* refers to the offering that is Ochun's favorite, and to the body and sensuality of the goddess herself. Hernandez portrays her as a beautiful and voluptuous woman whose feathered crown evokes indigenous and Afro-Diasporan imagery. Five gold bracelets embody her sacred number, five, while gold – her special color – shimmers in her honey-colored skin, in the sky behind her and in the flowers around her neck.

The radiant grace of her full figure is a stunning antidote to the shame that I was taught to feel towards my body. She embodies and radiates self-love, self-acceptance and pride in her natural beauty. The round curves of her body have never diminished her worth; they are emblematic of the abundant gifts of nature and of the feminine. When I look on her, my body fills with the healing power of self-love. This full-figured goddess is a tender representative of the divine radiance of our natural forms – and of a natural world that embraces our womanhood.

Another image, *Abuelita Pelando Grandules* (Grandmother Peeling Pigeon Peas), shows a large dark-skinned woman seated in front of a pot, peeling fresh peas. Her white hair frames a face radiant with light and alive with curiosity. Her elder status is marked by drooping breasts, white hair, and a receding hairline. Hernandez painted her after an encounter with "a beautiful elder woman" in the Dominican Republic as they sat and peeled peas together. She says "I offered to help her peel the peas, but in the time it took me to crack one pod, she got through

Miel De Abeja, Yasmin Hernandez, 24"x30", Acrylic on Canvas, 2003. www.yasminhernandezart.com

Abuelita, Yasmin Hernandez, 30"x48" Oil on canvas, 1997, www.yasminhernandezart.com

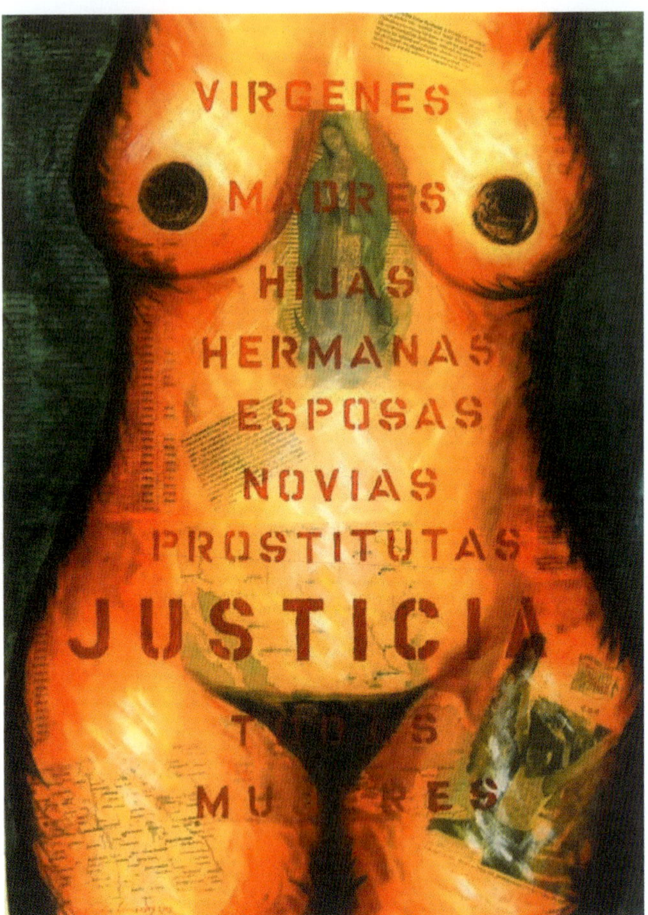

Todas Mujerous, Yasmin Hernandez, 36" x24", Mixed Media on canvas, 2004. www.yasminhernandez.com

ten .... We had a good laugh together. I painted her to remember what a beautiful spirit she was.[28]

This image portrays a working class woman of the African Diaspora who is aging into grace. She represents our ancestral mothers whose African blood lines live on, in spite of centuries of shame and denial. This abuelita (grandmother) has struggled, suffered, loved and lived joyfully. As the picture's title attests, she has borne children and lived long enough to see her children bear children. Her large, big-boned body is strong and capable and she is not afraid of work. Life has taught her that she can open to the new with the wisdom and strength that comes from experience; she embodies wise aging, connection to community, compassion and service. She bears the life-sustaining gifts of the Crone or the Matriarch – and her stance, her grace, and her commitment to life remind us to reject patriarchal fears of aging.

Hernandez's choice to portray "ordinary" working class women is also reflected in the image titled *Todas Mujeres (All are women)*, which is part of her political gallery. This painting illustrates a naked female torso inscribed with the words: "virgenes, madres, hijas, hermanas, esposas, novias, prostitutas: todas mujeres (Virgins, mothers, daughters, sisters, wives, girlfriends, prostitutes: all are women)".[29] The word "justicia" (justice) is inscribed in the area above the pubic triangle. Hernandez says, "The purpose of this piece is to remind us that every woman is a beautiful human being with the right to live a long, safe life, free from sexual and physical violence".[30]

Abba Yahudah: Honoring the Primordial African Mother

An African Jamaican male with a feminist perspective, Abba Yahudah is a conscious, visionary heart brother who is deeply committed to the rebirth of the Goddess and expresses a deep empathy for the suffering of black women, but also the larger pain body of African people. His art and writing is highly inspired by the African Diaspora, Ethiopianism, Symbolism, and the Rastafarian experience. While he ultimately believes in the Unity of all spiritual traditions, as a Jamaican who couldn't escape the Catholic missionaries, he was highly influenced by Christianity. However, he could be considered a "Gnostic Rastafarian" in the sense that he has retained the jewels of truth in Christianity, but has radically dissected the false patriarchal ideologies that subjugate the feminine principle. He prefers to take history all the way back to the lands of Ethiopia, where humanity originated from the primordial womb of the Mother.

It is imperative to include the powerful voices of men who see through the illusion of the dominant patriarchal ideologies and are consciously digging into the deep recesses of their personal psyches to reclaim their own wounded feminine, as well as the collective feminine consciousness that has been lost to us. He has felt the pains of his heritage and has spent most of his life developing an artistic identity as an African American male, which isn't an easy task.

Born in St. Catherine, Jamaica to a family of artists and builders, Abba Yahudah vowed to devote himself entirely to art, making everything he did a creative exercise. By the age of ten, he developed a very detailed eye, showing remarkable skill with the pencil and could draw the identical likeness of anything he saw. Abba Yahudah migrated to the United States in 1981 and took his first job as a sign painter, which intimately exposed him to typography and layout. Several of his works were published in local and national media; such as *Sights and Sounds*, *The Apprentice Write and Student Voice*. While living in New York in 1985, he attended Parson's School of Design, majoring in graphic design. A year later, he enrolled in The School of Visual Arts, majoring in design and illustration. In 1987 Abba got a job working as an art director/graphic designer for one of the larger design firms in Manhattan, New York. He designed and illustrated for companies such as; Sony, Sharp, Revlon, Maxwell House, and Pepsi, to name a few. In 1996, he opened the first Rastafarian gallery in Park Slope, Brooklyn, called *Lalibela* (named after the monolithic churches of Ethiopia's New Jerusalem).

Abba Yahudah currently resides in the San Francisco Bay Area and Oregon. His art has traveled internationally to Ethiopia, exhibiting at the Habesha and Lela Art Galleries. He also exhibited at the University of the West Indies in Jamaica, the Smithsonian Museum of Natural History in Washington, D.C., as well as at numerous galleries in the San Francisco Bay Area. He is in the process of writing his own book titled, *A Journey to the Roots of Rastafari: The Essene Narzarite Link*, which is due to be released soon. He has graciously given me permission to use two paintings and excerpts from his book.

The first painting to be discussed is *The First Supper*, which is a contemporary spin-off of Da Vinci's painting, *The Last Supper*. Abba Yahudah writes:

> *Leonardo Da Vinci's painting, 'The Last Supper,' the symbolic final Passover meal of Yahowshua and his disciples, is the most famous representation of the ceremonial feast before his crucifixion. 'And he took the bread and broke it, and gave it unto them, saying, this is my body which is given unto you: do this in remembrance of me.' And after supper, he said, 'This cup is the New Testament in my blood, which is shed for you' (Luke, ch. 22, vs 19). The ceremony of the* Last Supper *is considered by some theologians to be the embodiment of his love and compassion, as well as the prelude to his final and ultimate act of selflessness. However, in our preoccupation with the meaning of the* Last Supper, *we've forgotten the sacrifices made by the mother in preparation for the* First Supper, *which are obviously her M.I.L.K., Mothers Illuminating Love and Kindness.*
>
> *The First Supper is the most fitting title for this piece as it portrays the youthful and voluptuous nursing mother, reminiscent of the Goddess Auset (Isis), breastfeeding her messiah-son Heru (Horus). The mother and child image, representing Miriam and Yahowshua, the Son of God, is a universal image and is in no way unique to Christianity. The Sun, as the sustaining element of the globe, has a consistent harmonious relationship with Mother Earth. We, as humans, have come to recognize the significance of both polarities in creating our existence; Mother Earth and Father Sun. The First Supper is symbolic of the primordial Mother as the Tree of Life, sacrificing her essence and body as food for her offspring made from her blood. The 'blood of Christ' is the blood of his mother and the flesh he gave was also hers. It was she that was crucified in him. As the Queen Mother, her lap symbolizes the throne and her milk represents wisdom as she nurses her man-child with enlarged protective hands--a symbol of her strength and guidance. She is a Nazarene, as is her son, which is seen in her locks and her vow as a vegetarian. The First Supper represents the fundamental food prescribed by nature for humans. The first-born son from the Divine Mother's virgin womb through milk was able to fulfill the Last Supper. Her so-called 'Blackness' represents the primordial womb, the genesis of the human race. All things emerge from the dark void or the dark womb. She embodies the totality of the homosapien species, placing her first in the line of motherhood.* [31]

Another monumental painting to be discussed is *Revelation 12*. The painting is inspired by a quote in Revelations, Chapter 12:

> *"And there appeared a great wonder in heaven, a woman clothed with the sun, and the moon under her feet, and upon her head a crown of twelve stars; and she being with child cried, traveling in birth, and pained to be delivered . . . and when the dragon saw that he was cast unto the Earth he persecuted the woman, which brought forth the man child."* [32]

The people of the Law of Moses—as Ethiopians call themselves—commemorate their legacy as children of Israel, honoring Mary as the Mother of Zion. Each year, tens of thousands of Ethiopians celebrate one of Ethiopia's holiest days, Mariam Zion, or May of Zion. They focus their attention on a modest shrine that is actually part of a cluster of churches all dedicated to her. The chapel houses Ethiopia's greatest treasure, the Ark of the Covenant. They believe the Ark of the Covenant, which enshrines the Ten Commandments, has been in Ethiopia since their first king, Menelik, the song of King Solomon and the Queen of Sheba, took the Ark from Jerusalem. Mariam Zion therefore celebrates God's presence in the Ten Commandments and honors Mary as the New Ark. Abba explains the painting in more detail:

> *The woman in this painting is the geographical mother of the anointed child, literally Zion, the embodiment of the Shekinah and home of the Ark of the Covenant. According to esoteric Judeo-Christian theology, the Ark of*

First Supper, Abba Yahudah, 57"x43", Oil on canvas, 1999. www.abbayahudah.com

Revelation 12, Abba Yahudah, 57"x43", oil on canvas, 2002. www.abbayahudah.com

the Covenant is Miriam, Mother of Zion and the Holy Grail. She is the source and container of his bloodline and only through her could he be reborn in order to ascend the promised throne. The expectant Mother, pregnant with unlimited potential, poses a threat, as her child is the epitome of the law contained in the golden vessel called the Ark of God.

After enduring tribulation and countless self-sacrifice, she conceived, nurtured, and protected her progeny, giving birth to the revolutionary change of a new age. The rose she holds so delicately symbolizes the promise of her chief city, Addis Ababa, meaning 'new flower.' The scars on her palms are stigmata turned into pearls; across her bosom is painted in Amharic (the Ethiopian national language) the word Ethiopia. Six angels plus one guards her, signifying the seven spirits of the Most High. Clothed in the glory of her ascended son and with the moon under her feet, she is crowned with twelve golden six-pointed stars, a sign that she has triumphed above the perils of the dragon and the beast, which is destined to be slain by her son, the lion king. [33]

The quest to depict the inherent sacredness of black women's bodies in contemporary art takes many forms. Women (and men) of the African Diaspora have a long history of resistance to images generated by white supremacy, color prejudice, and patriarchy. Unfortunately, some of us succumb to the messages encoded in the negative images that surround us. But many of us resist, choosing to reject, transform and ultimately transcend racist depictions that deny our inherent humanity, intelligence and beauty. The task of combatting negative stereotypes through the review and re-creation of our actual past in Africa and the lands of the Diaspora has revealed that we are the descendants of powerful, spiritual African women. As we re-create and re-vision the worlds that they inhabited, we honor their spirits, which live again in us.

The images I have reviewed encourage us to change our social and spiritual perspectives and adopt new ways of viewing the world – internally as well as externally. They ask that we love our bodies as Black women – recognizing the Goddesses, Spirits, and Sacred Women that we once were, are now, and will be once again. We are the daughters of Africa. Our skin is black, brown, ivory, caramel, cinnamon, and honey. Our hips are strong, like trees growing in the Earth, round like the curves of the hills. The broadness of our noses declares our strength of character; our hair is a wilderness holding sunlight, rain, and the spiral patterns of the universe. I close with the words of Mari Evans: [34]

I

am a black woman

tall as a cypress

strong

beyond all definition still

defying place

and time

and circumstance

assailed

impervious

indestructible

Look

on me and be

Renewed

Arisika Razak has been a midwife, healer and spiritual dancer for over thirty years. She has provided full scope midwifery care to indigent women and women of color in the inner city of Oakland, California for over twenty years, serving as a home and hospital birth attendant, hospital based CNM, health care administrator and health educator. She currently directs the Integrative Health Studies Program at the California Institute of Integral Studies, San Francisco, California, where she is also an Associate Professor of Women's Spirituality.

Arisika has led spiritual and healing workshops for women for over two decades, and her dance celebrates the physical bodies of women and the blood mysteries of childbirth, menstruation, sexuality and menopause.

She is a contributor to several books, and presents at numerous conferences on the subjects of multiculturalism and diversity, women's health and healing, and embodied spirituality and movement. Her film credits include: *A Place of Rage* by Prahtibha Parma, which showcases the work and struggles of African American women activists Alice Walker, June Jordan and Angela Davis; *Fire Eyes* by Soraya Mire, the first full length feature film by an African woman to explore the issue of female genital cutting; and *Who Lives Who Dies,* a PBS special on health care services to marginalized and underserved populations.

Hecate is the triple Goddess of the Greeks and Romans. She is a mistress of fate and the underworld. She sees the past, present and future. The virgin is white, the mother is red, and the crone is black. Hecate becomes the Greco-Roman Triple Goddess of crossroads, entrances, and sacred precincts. She holds swords of discernment and fires of transformation and stands on her entwined twin serpents. Hecate's origins are in Anatolia where her main temple was at Lagina.
Source: Engraved gem, Rome

Goddess Icons of the Dark Mother Around the Globe

By Lydia Ruyle

Female images have deep roots in time. Blackness is associated with the Earth and fertility as the source of life and death. That source as female comes to us with dark images of a sacred female from Africa, the Middle East, Old Europe, Asia and the Western Hemisphere. Some of her names are Isis of Egypt, Diana of Ephesus, Crow Mother of the Hopi, Aumakua of Hawaii, Kali of India and Palden Lhamo of Tibet. My interest in Dark Mothers helped me find them in many cultures of the world.

During the first millennium, Christianity, as it gained in power, took over the sacred images of previous cultures and religions. During the twelfth and thirteenth centuries, crusaders carried images of Notre Dame, Unsere Schwarze Frau, Santa Maria, Nuestra Senora, La Madonna on their journeys to and from the Holy Land. Over two hundred churches, shrines and cathedrals were built on the pilgrimage routes in Europe. In the fifteenth century, Europe discovered the New World. People brought their images with them to the Western Hemisphere where they joined with indigenous images and were exchanged and absorbed into new images and Herstories.

Our Lady is a sacred image--an icon. All people and cultures create icons to honor the sacred dimension. Images are powerful. There are many myths and stories of images that heal, comfort, and bring good fortune. And there are dark images that are fierce and wrathful, protecting those who seek their help. In the Christian tradition Notre Dame, La Vierge visualizes and embodies the essence of spirituality and religion as kindness, unconditional love and acceptance of human imperfection. In Tibetan Buddhism, a fierce dark mother is the image of compassion.

What is the Appeal of the Dark Mother?

I see images as sacred connections to the universal spirit. Since we come into the world through the body of a woman/mother, our first experience of connection with another is through that body. The yearning to keep that connection is a living, strong, natural, universal one. However, in order to develop our own human potential, each person must separate and individuate from the symbiotic mother bond, develop a sense of self, set boundaries and experience his or her life's journey. The human story of this experience is told infinitely through myth, science, psychology, religion, history, art, and life experience. Reverence and celebration of the bond between the mother and child is critical to the human condition. Your task in life may be to come from a place of reverence through the negative dark side of the mother with acceptance and forgiveness of her humanness and yours (the Black Madonna). Or you may have a loving, connecting, experience of your personal mother. In truth, most of us have a bit of both. Women are born from a mother and over time may become mothers, the creation story in action. The experience is both physically personal and universal, especially for women. The process also has powerful psychic and spiritual dimensions.

As a miracle worker, Dark Mothers support each individual in his or her search to develop their potential. For example, the Black Madonna of Poland was used as a badge of freedom by the Solidarity movement in the 1980's and the brown Virgin of Guadalupe is a symbol for change in this hemisphere. The Shrine of the Black Madonna is a growing community for African Americans in the United States. The essence of spirituality is kindness, unconditional love and acceptance of human imperfection. The Black Madonna, as the mother of us all, embodies this ideal. Earlier cultures and civilizations visualized the source of life and death as a Mother Goddess.

My personal search for a sacred female icon began originally out of my own interests and life experiences. I was born into a white, American, Protestant tradition, which did not have an image of the Divine Feminine, white or black. As an artist, I collected images and stories, which eventually led me on the path of the Black Madonna where I found other Dark Mothers.

Reading about sacred females and seeing images in books is part of the process of discovery. Experiencing the image in situ with other humans is quite another. Making a pilgrimage to a sacred site is a long tradition. I love being in the physical presence of art and images. The two dimensional image becomes a three dimensional, multi-sensory experience of color, smell, sound and touch. When the image becomes fleshed out and embodied with my experience, it becomes part of me and I participate in the ancient tradition of honoring the Divine Feminine. In celebration, I began creating icon banners and exhibiting them at sacred places around the globe as my humble gift to the Black Madonnas.

Spirit Banners of the Divine Feminine:

Goddess icon spirit banners are sacred images of the Divine Feminine from various cultures of the world. Icons connect to the deep soul expression of the divine mystery of life. Each image was created and revered at some time in human history. The first banners were created for an exhibition at the Celsus Library in Ephesus, Turkey. Since then, the banners have blossomed from 18 banners to over 400. I took the banners to sacred sites to empower, teach, and share their stories around the globe, such as: Australia, China, France, Germany, Greece, Malta, Finland, England, Italy, Czech Republic, Poland, Mexico, Canada, Peru, Russia, Turkey, Ghana, Nepal, Tibet, Bhutan, the U.S. and Hawaii. I published a book titled *Goddess Icons: Spirit Banners of the Divine Feminine*, which documents over 400 banners and their journeys across the globe.

Below are a few of the Dark Mothers:

Black Madonna of Czestochowa Poland, is the most well known Black Madonna in the world. She is Matri Polski, Queen of Poland and the symbol for change and freedom. She saved the Poles from the Swedes and wears her battle scars on her check. The Madonna is a painting on wood which is covered by a screen of precious metals and jewels that is ritually changed during the year. Her image is displayed for mass, then hidden behind a curtain. The walls of her chapel are covered with offerings or milagros asking and thanking Her for miracles and healing.
Source: Painting with gold & jewels, Black Madonna Chapel. Jasna Gorna, Poland

Black Madonna of the Andes stands on the moon and a stepped pyramid. The Inkas and earlier cultures were master builders, shaping stone into sacred ceremonial places like Machu Picchu and Sacsayhuaman. The Peruvian Black Madonna has the features of a native mother and child, not a European version brought by the Spaniards. She is surrounded by a k'uychi, which means rainbow, aura of light. Her crown is a golden stepped gateway of wisdom and compassion.
Source: Moche clay. 500-800 CE

Nuestra Senora Montserrat resides in a spectacular mountain landscape in northern Spain not far from Barcelona. She was found in a forest and is miracle working in her Baroque sanctuary today. Spain has a rich tradition of Theotokos / Mother of God Madonnas. Nuestra Senora sits on her wisdom throne with her divine child holding the world orb in his hand for you to experience as a gesture of divine grace. This is one of the images the Spaniards brought with them to the Americas.

Source: Sculpture. Pilgrimage Shrine, Montserrat, Spain

Nuestra Senora La Virgen Guadalupe is the present name of the Great Mother Goddess of Mexico. The Spaniards brought Black Madonnas with them to the western hemisphere where they joined Mayan Ixchel and Aztec Tonantzin of earlier Pre-Hispanic cultures. La Virgen spoke to Juan Diego, a simple peasant, asking him to build a church to her on Tonantzin's hill at Tepeyac. Miraculously, La Virgen's image appeared on his tilma wrapped around many red roses as proof of his vision. The tilma hangs in the Cathedral today in Mexico City. Guadalupe is the Goddess of the Western Hemisphere, Central and South America and the southwestern United States. My banner of Guadalupe has been exhibited in Mexico and around the globe since 1998. I duplicated two banners of her for the Mayan Women's Center in Puerto Morelos, Mexico and the Franciscan Sisters of Perpetual Adoration in La Crosse, Wisconsin.
Source: Guadalupe Cathedral, Tepeyac, Mexico City

Queen of Sheba: Known for her beauty, intelligence and wisdom, she is a popular subject in the visual art and stories of many of the world cultures for 3,000 years. In Ethiopia, where she is known as Makeba, she is the Great Mother foundress of the people. This image of the Queen of Sheba is from an Ethiopian story frame painting tradition similar to modern cartoons.
Source: Internet image

Crow Mother is the mother of all the katsinas who are spirits of the Hopi universe. The Hopi, which means peace, believe all beings in the universe carry energy. They are one of the oldest living pueblo cultures and reside on three mesas in northern Arizona. Crow Mother appears during the Powamu or bean ceremony. She offers corn to sustain life and switches for discipline and protection. She stands on a labyrinth symbolizing the human journey. Black crows hang out around humans and love corn.
Source: Wood sculpture, Hopi Kachina, Museum of Northern Arizona, Flagstaff

Rangda is the demon queen of the underworld in Bali. The name means widow. Rangda is depicted as a nude old woman, with unkempt hair, pendulous breasts, long fingernails and a flaming vulva. Her face is fanged and goggle-eyed, with a long, protruding tongue. Rangda appears in Balinese ritual dance-dramas as the opponent of the lion monster Barong. While Rangda is fierce as the personification of evil, she is also considered a protective force much like Kali. There are many temples to Rangda in Bali.

Source: Painted wood sculpture. 1800-1900. Asian Art Museum of San Francisco

Black Madonna is carved in dark wood. She resides in the National War Museum in Auckland, New Zealand where a label states she was a gift to a bishop. Her inlaid shell eyes see into the spirit world. The Black Madonna holds a small soul in her large claw like hands. Her skeletal body indicates she is an ancestress. The bones of Maori chiefs were buried in boxes with similar images for rebirth.

Source: Wood sculpture.19th CE. National War Museum Auckland, New Zealand

CHAPTER TWO:

The Goddess of Sexuality

Reclaiming Goddess Sexuality

Yoni Rose, Penny Slinger, www.pennyslinger.com

By Linda E. Savage, Ph.D.

For at least five thousand years, female sexuality has been defined, discussed, dismissed, maligned, and misrepresented in patriarchal societies. The term patriarchy refers to the prevailing male-dominated social and political structure that has been reinforced by legal systems and militant power. It does not in any way refer to all men. In fact, only the dominant males in high status positions truly benefited from the unequal distribution of wealth and access to resources. In these cultures, masculine traits were distorted by the idealized male image of violent and emotionally disconnected warrior heroes.

Under patriarchal law, the rare women who pursued and enjoyed sexual activity in their own way (neither concubine nor wife) were castigated, ostracized, and even killed for it. The word sex meant "intercourse," and it was something men "got" and women "gave," and the purpose of the whole business for women was simply to bear heirs (preferably male) for the legal passing on of inheritances. And God help the woman who gave it under the wrong circumstances! When medical texts began to say anything about sexuality, the knowledge imparted about women was ludicrous at best. Early marriage manuals exhorted women to submit to what had been reduced to a wifely duty. Female physiology was grossly misunderstood. According to Elaine Morgan, author of The Descent of Woman, "Men with the highest medical qualifications pontificated that the very concept of female orgasm was a fantasy of depraved minds and beyond belief." [1] This was less than 100 years ago!

Until the 1970s, psychiatrists considered the clitoral orgasm to be "immature," and assumed that intercourse was the only right way to experience sexual pleasure. Not more than fifty years ago, Kinsey had the groundbreaking notion of actually asking women what they experienced. Since the 1970s, some serious attempts have been made to define women's sexual responses from more objective data. Human sexuality experts Masters and Johnson published their research findings regarding women's sexuality in a book *Human Sexual Inadequacy* (1970). [2]They studied women responding sexually in a laboratory and proved that all women were capable of orgasms, originating in the clitoris. This ushered in the age of sexual pleasure for women. However, it did not suddenly free women of the internal bonds. In fact, it merely added the previously male issue of performance anxiety to women's sexual problems.

Knowledge of the physiology of female sexual functioning does not address the deeper mystery of female sexual desire. Most writing describes how to make orgasms happen, with detailed descriptions of oral and manual touching. These books and articles remind me of recipe cookbooks ignoring the big picture of thousands of years of cultural conditioning. Women's desire all too often remains elusive, to the frustration of the women as well as their partners.

All the effort to "give" women orgasms (as if we did not own them for ourselves) is missing the point. The genital orgasm as the ultimate goal in sexual functioning is still defining sex by a model limited to an essentially male viewpoint. Unless a woman is engaged of her own free will and feeling the desire, unless she is in touch with the power of her feminine way, all the efforts of her partner are for naught.

Men are often the ones to bring their partners to sex therapy. They buy the books and try to persuade women to try this position or learn that technique. These techniques are all empty exercises without the full and active participation of the woman: her body, mind, and soul. Sadly, many men will settle for a sexual encounter that engages a woman's body even if it is through manipulation, illusory promises, mental coercion, or even force. But once they have experienced even one encounter when a woman's whole being is engaged, they seek this transcendent experience like the search for the Holy Grail.

Nubial Bliss, Mark Henson, www.markhensonart.com

What is Goddess Sexuality?

Imagine living in a culture where sex was sacred and not a sin! The cultures that honored the divine feminine, existing for over 30,000 years, knew that women's sexuality was a life-affirming expression of spirit. Women's sexuality and especially their Yonis were sacred. Goddess sexuality reflects the ancient erotic paradigm integrating sexuality and spirituality. The ancient cultures understood that sexual pleasure honored the Goddess, connected us with spirit, and renewed the life force.

A central aspect of ancient celebrations at special times of the year was the enactment of the Great Marriage, or the Hieros Gamos, which was a sexual union between the High Priestess, who was the earthly representative of the Goddess and her consort. The rite honored the deeper mysteries of sexuality. The Great Marriage ritual was performed in a beautiful private setting, yet the whole community participated in processions, singing, and prayer that supported the success of their magical connection. It was believed that the powerful energy they released ensured the prosperity of the community. What followed was a whole day and sometimes week of great joyous celebrating—feasting, drinking, dancing, singing and open enjoyment of eroticism. At Beltane (May 1st), fires were lit at sundown and after many hours of celebrating, couples would melt away to enjoy a night of erotic pleasure. In fact, making love in the fields was a way to honor the Goddess and ensure the health of the crops.

Today, when sexual energy is perceived as purely genital sensations, it can be misunderstood as a simple physical release. However, sexual energy moves from the base of the spine and radiates through the whole body-mind system. The spiral of energy travels up and down the body through all the energy centers in a continuous, pulsing current. In essence, we are plugged into a cosmic "electric outlet" through the energy centers.

At the heart center, sexual energy is healing, and connects partners in conscious loving. Keep in mind that our ability to tell the truth about ourselves deepens our capacity for intimacy and intensifies sexual desire. By practicing conscious loving we can develop the pathway to the next level of sexual expression, consciousness expansion. There is infinite potential for transcendental sexual experiences that produce a sense of merging with the source of energy and loss of physical boundaries at the moment of orgasm. These ecstatic moments are often described as "being in the moment of boundless bliss." It is cosmic orgasm, the direct experience of the self as pure energy, in union with a divine source. (geo image)

Yab Yum Yantra George Atherton, digital image, www.geoglyphiks.com

The uniting of sex and spirit is an ancient memory now emerging in our collective consciousness. Today, we can re-affirm our deep instinctual understanding that our sexuality is both a healing energy and a pathway to raising our consciousness. Whether practiced with a partner or solo, we can use the preparation of sacred space, breathing techniques and visualization to bathe our energetic fields and release our desires into the Universe. Goddess sexuality is the acknowledgement that ecstatic union with the life force is our birthright. It offers us life-long permission to explore and enjoy sexual pleasure.

The Power of Sex

There is an irrefutable power in sexual energy. Although sexual energy can be misused, the energy itself is transforming. When sexual energy is experienced by fully conscious, consenting adults, it is empowering and healing. Sexual union is the best way to experience wholeness that humans can know. I believe that the power of a woman's sexual desire and responsiveness derives from her internal alignment with her core feminine energy. When a woman clearly understands and creates the conditions that enhance, for herself, the experience of her ecstasy, she has the ideal setting for her sexuality to blossom. When a woman can validate her core self and unique approach to her sexuality, magnetic power emerges from within. She feels energized, uplifted, affirmed, and transformed. Her partner will feel it as well. When a woman finds her I AM GODDESS self, she transmutes universal energy and aligns with Life Force. Her powerful sexuality flows through her to her partner. This is the magic. This magnetic force transmutes through her body connecting her with herself, her partner, and life. The resulting alchemical transformation raises energy beyond the physical. The body-mind-spirit is joined with the powerful source of all energy.

The Wisdom of the Goddess

In order to heal feminine desire, women must reclaim the core of the universal feminine variously called: The Great Goddess, The Great Mother, Earth Mother, Mother of All. The Goddess represents the feminine polarity of the Life Force. She is not outside our experience, but an eternal awareness inside us all. Ultimately there is no gender to Spirit. However, by using the image of the feminine, we can break up the judging, sex-negative image of the Divine that has dominated for the last five to eight thousand years.

Holy Union, Heather Taylor, www.fullcirclemandalas.com

Political and religious domination by patriarchy has led us down a false path, leading us away from sexual pleasure as a freely chosen, mutually beneficial partnership. In order for women and men to experience the divine healing power of sexual union, both must be aligned with their essential core. Long before it was thought that men owned the reproductive and sexual rights to their mates, women conceived and gave birth and engaged in sexual encounters based on their choice. Sexual desire was perceived as the will of the Great Mother Goddess. Children were considered a gift of the Mother, and their legitimacy was never in question. They were accepted and loved in their own right. Any pregnancy was a miracle, and no societal judgment was placed on the woman for her sexual choices.

The worship of the feminine Divine Force gave women an important role in all aspects of life. During the Golden Age of the Goddess, the High Priestess was the Earthly representative of the Great Mother. She always had a consort with whom she enjoyed her sexuality, which was considered sacred. Any child of that union was especially honored. These Goddess cultures were matrilineal (inheritance traced through the mother) and woman-centered, but they were not ruled by women--they were essentially egalitarian. According to Riane Eisler in *The*

Wisdom of the Ages, Autumn Skye Morrison, www.autumnskyeart.com

Chalice and the Blade, [3] they favored a partnership model of male and female relationships. How they viewed sexual relations between men and women is most important for our understanding of the feminine way.

In the female-positive cultures, all paths were open to women and were honored equally: mother, priestess, healer, craftswoman, farmer, surveyor, scribe, and hunter. The choices depended on their abilities and inclinations. Most women chose several roles, as they do now. They were valued in all three stages of their lives: Maiden, Mother, and Crone. They were not ignored once their reproductive capabilities were over. One can only conclude that female sexual desire was not the problem that it has become in patriarchal culture. I believe that in the old wisdom lie truths that will lead women out of the terrible sexual self-perception they have endured for millennia.

Psychological Domains of the Maiden, Mother and Crone

The ancient cultures that worshipped the Great Mother Goddess recognized three distinct phases of a woman's life: the Maiden, the Mother, and the Crone (which means Wise One). Women were closely associated with the moon because their menstrual flow aligned with the new, the full, and the dark phases. Their lives bore a similar pattern of division into triads, and so the tides of the moon, the tides of a woman's monthly courses, and the stages of a woman's life are three. Women's life phases are not only chronological stages but useful divisions of feminine function and task that offer more than rich symbolic meaning. The stages continue to reflect many aspects of female life experience, as each stage represents a profound psychological transformation. Each of the stages, Maiden, Mother, Crone, is also a domain (field of influence) within the feminine psyche with different types of sexual expression, potentially available to all adult women.

The Maiden within us is the playful child delighting in the wonder of pleasure and sexual exploration. She is longing to be loved. She is the source of our natural curiosity and sensuality. The psychological sets of readiness to awaken sexual energy and permission "to do what feels good for me" in safe settings are necessary for the Maiden to come out to play.

The Mother is the nurturer bestowing loving acceptance and lasting commitment on beloved partners. She is the source within us of our capacity to build communion with another in the act of giving and receiving love. The Mother in us takes responsibility for generating compassionate sexuality beyond self-gratification. She knows our personal, seductive conditions and can surrender to sexual desire.

The Crone is the wise woman within us who can consciously generate healing energy. She is the part of us feeling empowered to act on intentional desire in an honoring setting. The Crone is the adept within, listening to intuition and recognizing divine guidance. If we so choose, she is the part of us that accesses the sixth sense, discerning information from our body wisdom.

A New Model of Female Sexuality

Women's low sexual desire is largely a reflection of the limits that were imposed by patriarchy combined with their own life histories. Extremely sex-negative messages have been indoctrinated into male and especially female children for the last few thousand years. Women will

Sweet Honey Wine, Heather Taylor, www.fullcirclemandalas.com

need to internalize the sex-positive, permission-giving, life-enhancing messages of the Goddess cultures and then create the safe, seductive and honoring settings that work best. With knowledge of ancient mysteries, they can choose to pursue sexual mastery, which in turn leads into the realm of spiritual sexuality.

When a woman is in her I AM GODDESS self, her capacity for creativity increases tenfold. The new view of female sexuality is uniquely feminine, without reference to the male model. I invite you to join with women who are reclaiming their sexuality from this perspective. I encourage you to explore ancient wisdom, and recapture the essence of the feminine sexual perspective that existed before the patriarchal myth that woman was fashioned from Adam's rib merely to be his mate. Goddess sexuality reclaims the essence of female desire and women's unique pathways to ecstasy.

Once the feminine way is added into the equation in relationships, the healing, life-giving, transforming, sacred sexual pleasuring can be experienced and can sustain long-term relationships. As communities finally become truly egalitarian between the genders, the ensuing partnership can expand into enriching life on this planet. It is time.

Linda E. Savage, Ph.D. is a licensed psychologist and sex therapist exploring the mysteries of sexual healing for over 30 years. She is the author of Reclaiming Goddess Sexuality: The Power of the Feminine Way, a view of women's sexuality that blends the ancient wisdom of the Goddess cultures with current clinical knowledge.
www.goddesstherapy.com

The Sexual Shadow of The World

By Azra Bertrand M.D. and Seren Bertrand

The truth is, there is a hidden epidemic of sexual abuse in our world – that is eating away at our communities, destroying the heart of humanity, and ravaging our planet. We can no longer afford to look the other way or turn a blind eye. The recent sexual abuse scandals involving Harvey Weinstein in America, Jimmy Savile in the UK, and in the Catholic Church across the world, are part of a greater cultural apocalypse – a feminine root word which means 'unveiling what is hidden'. We are finally seeing the hidden rot behind the false surface image of our culture. And before we point fingers of blame and shame 'out there' – we must know that this unveiling is gathering pace in every sector, every industry, and even in the family home.

These revelations teach us one lesson about the reality of sexual abuse, one thing we must understand if we want to heal and rebirth our world: most rape and sexual abuse is denied, hidden, repressed, unrecognized and unreported. What we see is only the tip of the iceberg. If we want to know the truth we must look deeper, we must be prepared to face one of the longest, darkest shadows of the world.

The scandals also teach us that a few brave individuals who break the spell of silence, who speak up and challenge the businesses, churches, gurus, media organizations, legal structures, health care systems, and family members who are complicit in the culture of denial – can create a new culture of truth and transparency that leads to tremendous healing. Our voices and our truth, especially when we come together, create change powerfully and quickly. This is the way our world will heal.

5,000 Years of Rape Consciousness

It is important to note that the mass collective culture of rape consciousness is not new, but has dominated the planet for thousands of years. In past eras, it was not even a taboo, as some women, and young girls and boys, were openly used by male power holders, including priesthoods, state rulers, politicians and family members, as if they were objects. These are the ancestral legacies still living on inside us.

Overt, culturally sanctioned sexual abuse still happens in many cultures of the world, but in others – such as the western world – the essence remains hidden from sight, repressed and kept as a forbidden secret. No wonder we feel an immense sense of cognitive dissonance in our lives. On the surface we are told one story, of caring families, caring leaders, caring organizations. Underneath is a completely different story, held in deep shadow.

Lillith, Jonathan Weber, www.jonathanweber.org

We live in a tumultuous, difficult, yet important time in history in which the shadow is being revealed. Rather than a charming politician with slick wordspeak, our current epoch gives us an elected president of the United States who publically condones "grabbing 'em [women] by the pussy." [1] The air is thick with the stench of sexual predation and dehumanizing rhetoric. Actors cavalierly say in public they love their job as they get to "rape beautiful women." [2]

Sexual Abuse & Mental Health

The same tidal wave of unveiling and revelations will soon sweep the mental and physical healthcare fields, which, at the moment, are still choosing to stay in denial of the true scope of the problem. When this happens, there will be a complete revolution in the way we look at health – and the impact of these trauma legacies.

Based on my twenty years experience as medical doctor, healer, researcher and community leader, working with more than 25,000 people, I have come to a very controversial, but sadly very real conclusion: sexual abuse is a huge, unacknowledged contributing factor in much of our physical and emotional illness.

The truth is that childhood developmental trauma, including a startlingly high incidence of sexual abuse, is a contributing factor to both chronic somatic illness and to many psychiatric diagnoses listed in the DSM-V, the so-called "Bible" of the mental health fields. [3]This includes depression, anxiety, borderline personality, dissociative identity disorder, and many others. The more intensive the trauma, the longer its duration, and the younger the age at which it happened, the more severe and chronic the psychiatric condition will be.

The same is true in chronic physical health conditions. Childhood traumas, referred to by researchers as "adverse childhood events", including sexual abuse, account for a large percentage of physical illness, not just in childhood, but throughout our adult lives. A full account of this phenomenon deserves its own book, and indeed many good ones have now been written that detail the hundreds of medical studies supporting this conclusion (*Scared Sick*, by Robin Karr-Morse is one example).

Sexual Abuse Much More Common Than We Are Told

Conservative and well-respected medical studies state that around 25% of girls and 18% of boys have experienced sexual abuse before the age of 18. [4] But, it is widely known that these reported numbers do not represent the true amount of sexual abuse. The actual numbers are significantly higher than this.

In 2014, the National Academies of Science stated, "sexual assaults are grossly underreported." At least 80% of childhood sexual abuse goes unseen. [5] Beyond the issue of non-reporting, childhood sexual abuse is often not remembered, for a number of reasons. In many cases, childhood abuse is perceived as so frightening, overwhelming and shameful, that an instinctive, protective amnesia and dissociation kicks in, and the memories are immediately repressed and forgotten. Or children may be given sedative drugs, alcohol or over-the-counter cold medicine, which blur memory further, with events lost in the unknown recesses of the mind.

If sexual abuse occurs when children are young enough, typically under the age of four, they usually do not have the neurologic capacity to form clear conscious memories. The feelings remain, but they are encoded in body memories and vague states of upset or behavioral symptoms that are difficult to understand.

In my clinical experience with women seeking healing for physical and/or emotional issues, the numbers are around 70% or greater who consciously remember sexual abuse, or who carry the symptomatic, behavioral and energetic signature of someone who has been exposed to sexual abuse, or who have this memory buried in their family history and lineage. The abuse can vary in intensity, from unwanted or inappropriate touch, voyeurism, leering, fondling, oral sex, penetration and beyond into the unthinkable. The more violent the incidents, the longer the duration, the closer the relationship of the perpetrator, and the more powerless the child feels to find support and safety, the more disruptive the outcome is to physical and emotional health.

Sexual Abuse A Common Cause of Borderline Personality and Dissociative Identity Disorders

Of all the mental health conditions, borderline personality and dissociative identity disorder, formerly "multiple personality disorder", are the most closely linked with childhood sexual trauma (often compounded by other developmental traumas). A 2016 study showed approximately 45% of people diagnosed with borderline personality disorder had a known history of childhood sexual abuse. [6] An older study reports this number to be as high as 70%. [7]As shocking as these figures are, we know that they greatly underrepresent the actual percentages. Of course, not every case of borderline personality will involve sexual abuse, and many complex factors contribute to it, but we must explore this possibility, rather than ignore it.

DID and Ritual and Network Abuse

In dissociative identity disorder (DID), a condition in which multiple fragmented personalities are present in a person, a history of childhood trauma is nearly universal; it has been found in 97% of patients, with childhood sexual abuse found in as much as 90% of cases. [8]However, the patterns of sexual trauma in DID present an even darker and more disturbing picture. Psychotherapists report that 25-50% of their DID patients recover memories of systematic, ritual or network sexual abuse – abuse carried out by multiple people in an organized way. [9]

Psychotherapy professionals who come forward to speak about the presence of network abuse in their patients and communities are generally disbelieved,

The Rose Lineage, Chanel Baran and Shona Keeli Jones (model), www.chanelbaran.com, www.wombillumination.com

mocked, humiliated, excluded from professional societies, and stonewalled from publication. Academic researchers who are professionally or personally invested in the climate of denial, or who are hired by the systems of abuse, have launched what has been called the "Memory Wars" – writing scientific papers that claim recovered abuse memories are a result of "false memory syndrome", that these memories are not real.

But, 60-80% of practicing clinicians, psychiatrists and therapists believe in the reality of trauma-repressed memories, especially in sexual abuse. [10]They are supported by new neurobiological studies and PTSD (post traumatic stress syndrome) literature that proves the existence of repressed memories caused by emotional trauma, later recovered in a safe therapeutic setting. [11]It is now known that we can repress entire events or segments of time as a coping response to an emotional crisis.

Creating New Paradigms of Support

Because we live in a culture that is in such profound denial of the tremendous scale of sexual abuse currently happening on the planet, often, abused women do not receive support. Their traumatic pain has not been recognized, not held with love, not healed. Instead they have often been misdiagnosed, medicated or disbelieved.

Many men are also playing out their repressed childhood sexual abuse wounds, sometimes as victims, but also at times becoming the perpetrator, unconsciously inflicting their sexual pain on a new generation of children. Crippled by the toxic shame they feel, and lacking the emotional tools and cultural support to heal, they can perpetuate the cycle of abuse. We sometimes forget that young boys are also vulnerable, and almost as many boys are sexually abused as girls. In the Catholic Church scandal, 80% of the victims were boys, mostly between the ages of 10 – 14. [12]

Statistics of abuse for transgender women, women and families of color, and those in marginalized or low-income communities are also higher than national averages, and are compounded with complex cultural biases that hinder support.

Protecting Women, Protecting Earth

The magnitude of the consequences of sexual abuse are immense; not just personally, but collectively, culturally, financially, ecologically and spiritually. Anyone who has worked directly with women knows of the slow, painful, agonizing and courageous journey it takes to heal these wounds – how they are written in the body and the psyche, and how much time and energy it takes to reweave trust.

And beyond this, the Womb and genitals of woman – the sacred sites targeted and attacked by sexual abuse – is also the portal through which our vibrational blueprint as a race is birthed, our 'world womb'. A womb imprinted with pain, fear, and disconnection transmits this pain to the DNA of their future children, epigenetically modifying the expression of their genome – until these womb wounds are healed. [13]

We are literally birthing a world of pain and suffering through hidden sexual abuse.The developmental trauma (chronic childhood emotional wounding, or "Complex-PTSD") that is a result of this abuse epidemic, is at the root of much of the world's suffering, costing us trillions of dollars per year in health care expenses and lost productivity, disconnecting us from earth, and costing us the lived integrity of our true soul self. We don't feel safe in our bodies, in our culture, or in this world.

As the body of woman is raped, commodified, abused – so is the body of Mother Earth. We are raping the very energy source that created us and sustains us.Protecting women is about more than "women's rights" – it is about the very survival of our species. If we defile and destroy that which births us, we will soon die out.

This current crisis of sexual abuse is an incredible opportunity to make the shadow conscious, to speak out, to take action and to begin our healing journey together. Collectively, we are at a prophesized turning point. We have an amazing regenerative capacity within us, biologically, culturally and spiritually. Our experiences of the past do not need to define who we become. We can invoke a spontaneous, regenerative healing of our collective body, and return to balance.

By **Azra Bertrand M.D. and Seren Bertrand**, authors of the acclaimed book, Womb Awakening – Initiatory Wisdom From the Creatrix of All Life, as well as Sophia's Return: Healing the Grail Wound, and Sacred Womb Rituals. They are founders of the worldwide Womb Awakening movement, and the Fountain of Life Womb Mystery School. They hold annual in-depth Womb Awakening Apprenticeships, and share shamanic music on Sacred Sounds of the Womb, Elemental Awakening, and other albums. Visit www.thefountainoflife.org.

Sophia's Return, Seren's personal story of healing from sexual abuse, is offered as a free ebook on the website: https://www.thefountainoflife.org/sophias-return-healing-grail-wound/

Yeshe Tsogyal: Awesome Yogini and Tantric Consort in Tibetan Buddhism

Photo of a painting of Yeshe Tsogyal at the Samye Monastery in Tibet, Vicki Noble, 2007

By Vicki Noble, MA

Since my introduction to Tibetan Buddhism more than thirty years ago, I have been fascinated by the strong female subtext that runs through it like an underground stream. At the Nyingma Institute in the early 1980s there were images of Tara, but the female in general was still fairly invisible; women attended retreats at the center and helped prepare the Sunday afternoon public dinners, yet were explicitly NOT allowed to ring the dinner bell. Shortly after beginning my Buddhist practice there, I learned from reading Stephen Beyer's classic text, *The Cult of Tara*, that Tara was at the heart of Buddhist practice for Tibetans who, Beyer said, called on her every day for every kind of purpose. Over the past three decades, the Tibetan Goddess has officially arrived in America along with numerous Lamas and teachers whose unfortunate refugee status has been such a boon to the West. Almost anywhere in America now, one can receive direct authorized transmissions of Dakini practices or get Tara empowerments, and so on.

As a younger feminist, I experienced Tibetan Buddhist organizations as a roller coaster ride. Although deeply called to the dharma, I found myself infuriated over what appeared then to be hopelessly entrenched discrimination towards women. I signed up for a three-week retreat to study Kum Nye Yoga, a wonderful Tibetan form developed by Lama Tarthang Tulku, founder of the Nyingma Institute. Our retreat was interrupted halfway through when the Lama requested that everyone in the organization come up to Oddiyan (the retreat center they were developing in northern California near Sea Ranch) and help with completion of the stupa that was being built there. It was urgent that the stupa be finished in time for fire ceremonies to be performed on an auspicious date, the next Full Moon. Retreat participants were invited to come as well, and we happily consented to join the community for this exciting event.

The minute we arrived at the retreat center, all the men in our small group were sent down to the stupa to join in the construction work, while the women were sent to the kitchen to cook and clean. I told the person in charge of our group that I had changed my mind and was going home ("been there, done that") and he surprised me by calling a special meeting with the Lama, Tarthang Tulku, the outcome of which was that men and women were allowed to work anywhere they chose at the site without reference to gender. Thus began an exhilarating three days of working from morning till night on the completion of the first stupa to be built in California. In an almost preternaturally harmonious environment, men and women worked side by side in a focused way for as much as twenty hours a day, and without any observable antagonism or gender charge.

This was my first experience of participating in a group context where a guru was holding a spiritual vision, and the light from that vision was so strong that it held us all inside of its amazing vitality and high-voltage energy. When Tarthang Tulku himself spoke to the group on the final day of the consecration, I saw threads of light emanating out from his heart to the audience and found myself weeping as my heart opened in response. I was certain I had found the community I was seeking. Then as the much-awaited fire ceremony was about to begin, our group was counseled that women might not be allowed to participate in the ceremony! Like a ping-pong ball, back and forth my state of consciousness bounced between joy and anger, moving from moments of profound awe to equally profound cynicism. Now many years later I know that this triggering process belongs to the central tenet of Tibetan Buddhism, which says that it is precisely our attachment to these hopes and fears, desires and aversions, that causes our perpetual suffering — but at the time I took every nuance personally. Luckily for me that day, not only did this very flexible

Yin Yang Ecstacy, Paul Heussenstamm, www.mandalas.com

Photo of a painting of Yeshe Tsogyal, Samye Monastery, 2007.

Lama decide to let women participate in the important fire ceremony, he even asked his two young daughters to help officiate ("priestess") the event.

Three years later, Dharma Publishing in Berkeley released the first English translation of the biography of Yeshe Tsogyal, the female cofounder of Tibetan Buddhism whose image is so often shown intertwined in sexual union with that of Guru Padmasambhava in the traditional "yab-yum" (father-mother) thangkas painted by Tibetan artists. The first translation of Yeshe Tsogyal's story was Tarthang Tulku's *Mother of Knowledge: The Enlightenment of Ye-shes mTshr-rgyal*, which became my sacred text. I underlined almost every word in the book. In the late 1980s, when I created the Motherpeace School for Female Shamanism in Oakland, I used the book as a text for my students. In the publisher's introduction to the Tulku book, we're told that "all of Padmasambhava's teachings came to us through Ye-shes mTshro-rgyal," who "received all of (his) teachings, as if the contents of one vessel were poured into another.... Her accomplishments and realizations have seldom been equaled, and the merit of her actions is beyond description."[1] Most of the biography is a telling of her amazing yogic abilities ("siddhis") and "miraculous bodily transformations" that she exhibited through her long life of service.[2] Her awesome powers make her a more than adequate role model for contemporary yoginis.

From the time of her conception and birth, Yeshe Tsogyal's life consisted of wholly extraordinary events, accompanied by earth changes, signs, and omens. Beyond being merely precocious, by the age of ten she had "matured into a woman of extraordinary beauty in both face and form.... Soon large numbers of people were coming from the many lands of Tibet, China, Mongolia, Turkestan, Nepal, and more — just to look upon her."[3] But in 8th-century Tibet the status of women had fallen to that of chattel and Yeshe Tsogyal — although a princess of Chärchen and therefore of higher rank than others — still had to put up with the challenges facing the women of her time. Suitors came to ask for her hand in marriage and, to avoid conflict among the lords and rulers who wanted her, her father and mother decided she should choose. But she pleaded with her parents: "To go with either of these men would be to enter the prison of samsaric suffering, from which it is so very difficult to escape." Her father — angered by her refusal — sent her away, saying "whoever finds you first shall have you." She was led away, dressed in "fine silks," in a caravan of "one hundred laden horses and yaks to face whatever disasters lay ahead."[4]

Beaten bloody by the thorn whip of the man who caught up with her wanting to be her husband, she "fell before them like an arrow. The soldiers were delighted and danced around, singing with joy."[5] When the soldiers became drunk with beer and fell asleep, she fled, "running more swiftly than the wind... through valleys and mountain passes." After some time spent free in the wilderness living near a cave as a yogini, "wearing only cotton garments and living on fruit," she was again captured and carried off by one of the suitors.[6] More fighting amongst the suitors occurred; her father the King threw up his hands until the Sovereign King of Tibet asked for his "wonderful and beautiful daughter," to which her father agreed and Tsogyal, whether she liked it or not, was finally married off to the highest bidder.

This King encouraged Tsogyal to study the dharma and brought teachers for her, including the great Padmasambhava, to whom he made offerings (a mandala of silver with clusters of gold, and a mandala of gold with ornaments of turquoise), even offering "the whole of his realm as if it were a symbolic mandala..." The Great Teacher refused to "barter Dharma with material goods," but at the continued pleading of the King, came forth with the following proposition: "I myself am unsullied by desire or lust; and such faults as attachment do not exist in me. But a woman is a necessary accoutrement to the secret teachings..." Listing the necessary qualities in "such a one," he explained that without her, "the maturation and liberation practices are obstructed; the result, the achievement of the secret teachings does not occur."[7] The King, understanding the bargain, removed his crown, bowed low to the magician, and besides the usual gifts and offerings, "he gave Padmasambhava the Lady mTsho-rgyal." The guru and the Queen went off to

Photo: Chimpu is the Tibetan place known as the "clitoris-vagina" mentioned later in the essay and shown in the photo I took in Tibet

the meditation caves of Chimpu to engage in the "secret practices" wherein he would pour from his vessel into hers — kind of an archaic Eastern variation on the Western story line in which the prince marries Cinderella and they "live happily ever after."

So who is this "Precious Queen" and from what lineage does she derive? I contend that the more ancient "Shaman High Priestess" became the "Precious Queen" under patriarchal rule, and that she comes down to us today in the office of the "Secret Consort." The question is especially apt since the tantric tradition, as expressed through the words of Padmasambhava (in the biography of Yeshe Tsogyal), explicitly stated that without "such a one," the yogic accomplishments desired as the result of the secret teachings will "not be accomplished."

Yeshe Tsogyal, Vajrayogini and the Red Nectar of Life

Yeshe Tsogyal is clearly identified as a tantric consort, and images abound of Tibet's cofounders locked in a passionate sexual embrace. Yet her practices and sexual teachings have not come down to us from her. That's what's missing from the Tibetan Buddhist work being disseminated throughout the world today: any direct lineage of teachings from the expressed viewpoint of the woman.

Tsogyal was believed to be an emanation of Vajrayogini, the naked red Goddess often shown with a crescent knife (chopper) raised in one hand, while she drinks menstrual blood from a skull cup held in the other. In one of the most dramatic sections of Yeshe Tsogyal's biography in Keith Dowman's translation, *Sky Dancer: The Secret Life and Songs of the Lady Yeshe Tsogyel*, she describes being near death from her yogic practice of austerities and calling out for help from the deities. She writes, "I had a vision of a red woman, naked, lacking even the covering of bone ornaments, who thrust her bhaga against my mouth, and I drank deeply from her copious flow of blood. My entire being was filled with health and well-being, I felt as strong as a snow-lion, and I realized profound absorption to be inexpressible truth."[8]

She meditated naked for the next year after that direct transmission from Vajrayogini, healing herself with medicinal herbs and shrubs. Keith Dowman calls this transmission of menstrual blood the "red bodhicitta, the essence of the Dakini," and says it "carries the seeds of passion, thought and samsaric action that provide the

Photo of a painting of Vajrayogini, Samye Monastery, Vicki Noble, 2007.

Menstruation Sculpture, photo by Laura Amazzone.

modes of Awareness of Emptiness."[9]

The essence of the narrative is the innate teaching (transmission) contained within the menstrual blood itself. I wish to reaffirm what women's spirituality has investigated, confirmed, and encouraged for thirty years of research, practice, and teaching: Contemporary women need to regain positive contact and psychic alignment with the sacred cycle of menstruation and ovulation. I believe it was the female of the species who precipitated the evolutionary leap into humanity when somehow our fertility synchronized with the monthly cycles of the Moon. In the shift from estrus into a bipolar lunar monthly cycle, humans split off from the other primates and differentiated as a species.[10] During much of our adulthood, women are initiated into the lineage of the "red bodhicitta" every month through our menstruation, which in tantric scriptures is stated to be the "red time," the time of sexual initiation — not, as we have falsely come to believe, a time when women are "unclean" and to be avoided sexually.

Vajrayogini, whose *bhaga* provided the red nectar of life for Yeshe Tsogyal and "suffused her whole being with bliss,"[11] is the red lineage thread leading all the way back to human origins and transmitting through women, down through the ages, this ancient original spiritual understanding,"[12] (Grahn, 1993). In a tantric sexual encounter, the dakini blesses her partner "with her empty and radiant body, a direct transmission of her nature."[13]

Yeshe Tsogyal embodies Vajrayogini's lineage as the shape shifting Dakini par excellence. Dowman says, "Dakini is virtually synonymous with Tsogyel herself,"[14] characterized by joy, spontaneity, and generosity of spirit. An altar built to honor Vajrayogini traditionally includes a mirror facing upward to catch her menstrual blood. This harkens back to what David Gordon White describes as the original tantric sexual rites, involving actual bodily substances, especially female sexual fluids. "Most of the messy parts of tantric practice (at least outward practice) were cleaned up, aestheticized, and internalized in different ways."[15] Tibetan Buddhist visualization practices, especially those honoring wrathful, erotic, female deities like Vajrayogini, appear to be living examples of "all such transactions involving sexual fluids [becoming] wholly internalized and incorporated into the so-called subtle body."[16]

In the 1970s, Australian-born feminist, Germaine Greer, wrote (scandalously) in her book, *The Female Eunuch,*[17] that if a woman really wanted to be liberated, she should taste her own menstrual blood. That prescription is still just as applicable today.

The Womb of Origination

The earliest, most continuous, and most pervasive symbol of the matriarchal construct is the vulva. It has been carved, painted, inscribed, scratched, and sculpted all over the world for tens of thousands of years. It would not be an exaggeration to say that the "yoni" (vulva, cunt, *bhaga,* slit, hole, "secret place") is a short-cut signifier for the female, not just on a personal individual level, representing Woman, but in the larger sense, Goddess.

The tantric five-fold central mandala of Five Dakinis (with Vajra Varaji in the center) is known as the *"bhaga"* or vagina, used interchangeably with "circle of great bliss."[18] A red lotus inside a white downward-pointing triangle is the symbol for Dharmakaya, what Buddhists call the "womb of origination," the source or origin "equated with the female sex organ or womb *(bhagah, yonih).*"[19] The vulva is a euphemism for the center of the universe from which everything springs, and it takes us all the way back to our origins.

The most popular mantra used by Tibetans is OM MANI PADME HUM—"Homage to the Jewel in the Lotus," or as June Campbell has translated it, the Goddess Manipadme of the "clitoris-vagina." [20] Yet the woman herself (more precisely her body) functions as a largely absent referent in Tibetan Buddhism: Symbols, images, concepts, mantras, prayers, and whole practices point to her origins and even her centrality, though she herself is rarely to be seen in official expressions of the monastic state religion. The worldwide shift from matriarchy to patriarchy that has been voluminously documented elsewhere certainly did not spare Tibet, and women in Tibet are profoundly positioned as second-class citizens — pretty much out of sight, out of mind. Even Tibetan nuns have never received the support given to monks and have therefore languished in poverty; the Tibetan word for woman explicitly declares her "inferior birth"; and most practicing Tibetan Buddhists have been taught that to become enlightened, one must be born in a male body.

Tibetan scholar John Vincent Bellezza points to many pre-Buddhist sites where art and ritual have left traces of "multi-sensory experience(s)," including images of women engaged in ritual dances, wearing jewel-studded coiffures, in attitudes of "greeting or benediction."[21] Bellezza states that "women dominated political life across the entire breadth of northern Tibet prior to the Imperial era... until the matriarchal structure had declined and was being replaced by a patriarchal society."[22] He speaks of "vestigial memory of a great goddess who once ruled supreme... suggesting the existence of a matriarchal culture and the supremacy of female deities in prehistory."[24] Rock art, which he believes to be a precursor of temple frescoes, and sites he discusses have names like "Dance Concourse of the Dakinis" or "Vulture's Nest." He speaks of ancient "Sisterhoods" and "Lands of Women" that existed prior to the anchoring of Buddhism in Tibet in the 8th century.

Although the marginalized condition of women in Tibet today is unfortunate, even reprehensible, many indicators point to an earlier matriarchal social organization and female leadership, as described by Bellezza and other historians of Tibet. Matriarchal Studies scholar, Heide Goettner-Abendroth, links indigenous Tibetans to the matriarchal Khasi of northern India, citing the importance of Neolithic megalithic stone worship to both cultures, saying, "...even the most magnificent Buddhist stupas I witnessed in Bodnath (Tibetan culture) and Swayambhu Nath (Newar culture) in Katmandu are surrounded by ancient magic circles, consisting of a ring marked with the points of the four sacred directions."[25] When pilgrims climb the long, steep staircase to the site of Swayambhu, the first shrine encountered is devoted to Agima, the pre-Buddhist Grandmother Goddess. And in the courtyard of an old temple at the center of Katmandu, I photographed a "firepit" dedicated to Agima; the iconographic shape is identifiable to classic Tibetan mandalas used in tantric (Vajrayana) practices. Goettner-Abendroth calls old Tibetan marriage practic-

Photo of a fire pit in Katmandu, Nepal. The fire pit belongs to the pre-Buddhist Grandmother Goddess, Agima, Vicki Noble.

Two Buddhist Nuns at Chimphu, where they lived like hermits in a cave-like "nun's hut," Vicki Noble, 2007.

es "polyandry" and describes their "woman-designed and woman-implemented group marriage"[26], calling "well-organized group marriage…the oldest, longest lasting and, in former times, generally widespread form of marriage" in which "the clan—not the individual—was the deciding unit." [27] Such matriarchal structures can still be found today in nearby cultures related to the Tibetans, such as the Mosuo of China, described by ethnographers as "a society without fathers or husbands."[28]

In addition to the many relics of earlier matriarchal cultures in Tibet since ancient times, we must also factor into an investigation of Yeshe Tsogyal's ancestry the influx of foreign visitors and immigrants to Tibet from the West, which can be documented from around 2000 BCE. The revolutionary discovery in the last century of Caucasoid mummies in Tibet's Tarim Basin oasis sites, who brought weaving technologies from the area around the Black Sea confirms what my research and that of Goettner-Abendroth has so clearly shown: "…if the pressure becomes too strong, [matriarchal societies] choose struggle of resistance or *migration of the entire people*."[29]A second wave of such migrants—whose bodies the sand and salt have preserved for millennia—were dressed in the deep wine-colored woolen homespun fabric still worn by Tibetan monks and nuns today; they traveled along the Silk Routes, arriving in the Tarim Basin around 1200 BCE (the end of the Bronze Age in Europe), and are linked to an extinct Tocharian language, "most closely related…with Italic and Celtic," [30] but found only in Buddhist manuscripts hidden in the famous Dunhuang caves. Another migration around the 5th century BCE included the burials of three women wearing tall pointy hats, described by archaeologists as "priestesses, although their headgear would mark them out as witches in Western society."[31] This is precisely the time "when there occurred a mass migration of Iranians, from Sogdiana in north-east Iran, to the northern part of Tibet,"[32] according to June Campbell, who believes this represents the introduction of Bön into Tibet. Texts and biographies, including Yeshe Tsogyal's, speak of powerful

Bön Queens and priestesses.

These general matriarchal and shamanistic themes can be seen as a unifying link joining the Maenads ("wild women") of western Afro-Eurasian heritage, across the vast Silk Routes of Central Asia where the shamans were women, to the Yoginis and Dakinis of India and Tibet.[33] Ritual practices performed in honor of Vajrayogini "contain a surprising number of motifs found in the artifacts and murals of Crete and Thera (e.g. mandatory use of mantric formulas, conch shells, bread sculptures as offerings, mirrors, special vases, bowls, saffron, flowers, incense, lamps, feast food, necklaces, and jewels, 'loosed hair,' red powder, musical instruments, bone ornaments, silk scarves and clothing, and 'amrita' to alter consciousness)."[34]

When women are at the center of a culture and unmolested by the orthodoxies of organized religion and male dominance, they have consistently created societies that are peaceful, egalitarian, and artistic, and whose ritual celebrations are characterized by spontaneous dance, song, and joyful revelry in the service of healing and regeneration. I believe Yeshe Tsogyal holds the lineage leading back to this ancient type of society.

Vicki Noble is a feminist shamanic healer, author, scholar and wisdom teacher. Born in 1947 and raised in Iowa, she awakened to the Goddess and Women's Spirituality on her arrival in Berkeley, California in 1976. Through a "shamanic healing crisis", she opened psychically to the healing, art, yoga, and divination processes that led to the creation of Motherpeace. Since then she has written several books, developed a powerful ritual healing process, taught and lectured internationally, and led tours of women on pilgrimage to sacred Goddess sites around the world. Learn more at her website, vickinoble.com. Vicki raised two daughters, Robyn and Brooke, and her special son, Aaron Eagle, who has Down Syndrome and was the subject of her 1994 book, Down is Up for Aaron Eagle. She teaches in the Women's Spirituality Masters program at Sofia University (formerly the Institute for Transpersonal Psychology) in Palo Alto, California. She sees private clients for astrology readings and healing sessions, and facilitates private tutorials for women in shamanic healing arts and Goddess spirituality. In her teaching she combines Buddhism, feminism, yoga, art, shamanism, and Goddess worship with a special focus on the female lineage of healers and yoginis since ancient times. Vicki is the author of Motherpeace, Shakti Woman, Down is Up for Aaron Eagle, Rituals and Practices with Motherpeace Tarot, and The Double Goddess: Women Sharing Power (Inner Traditions, 2003).

The 64 Dakini Oracle

Vajra Yogini Penny Slinger, Digital collage, 9450 x 6300 pixels, www.64dakinioracle.org

By Penny Slinger

The 64 Dakini Oracle is a divinatory system designed to provide a map of Goddess energy and consciousness for our times. The Goddess is emerging in our culture and the 64 Dakini Oracle is her 21st century temple. It presents an integrated vehicle through which to directly access the aspects of the energy of the Goddess. While inspired by the 64 Yogini Temples of India and related to the I Ching, the 64 Dakini Oracle is its own unique system of divination. Based on an elemental codex, it draws upon archetypes of the Divine Feminine from across the spiritual history of the planet, including those specific to our current era.

The term Dakini is found in Hindu and Buddhist spiritual teachings. Originating in the yogic and tantric traditions of the East, a Dakini is an expression of feminine wisdom-energy. Distillations of archetypal emanations, the Dakinis represent those essence principles within the self that are capable of transformation to a higher octave. Their ultimate mission is to awaken and enlighten all sentient beings. They are able to shape shift and appear in whatever form they choose to help instigate and promote the awakening process. The number 64 is a powerful interface between macrocosm and microcosm. It figures centrally in computer systems, in the DNA and the division of the human cell. The human embryonic cell divides 64 times before it specializes and becomes a specific tissue type and body part, and the DNA has 64 codons. As such, this oracle represents a map of potential. The aim of the Dakinis is to activate and stimulate the potential of all sentient beings, so that they may awaken and reach self-realization. The mandala of their temple is a full spectrum palette of these potentials and qualities.

I have been working with this system now for 30 years. In 1977, I co-wrote and designed *The Secret Dakini Oracle,* which was published by US Games and Systems. The accompanying book to the set of cards was published by Destiny Books/Inner Traditions. It was re-published as a boxed set of book and cards in 2003 as *The Tantric Dakini Oracle* by Destiny Books, Vermont. In this work, based on the cycle of 64 Yoginis, we made correspondences with the Tarot. The 64 Dakini Oracle fully personifies each energy as a Dakini and is a system in its own right.

This cycle of 64 Dakinis/Yoginis represents a complete

Yogini Temple at Ranipur-Jharial, Orissa, India

cosmogram for the transformation of the self, embodying the total energy cycle of creation. The 64 Dakini Oracle is based on the ancient Tantric Temple system of the 64 Yogini Temples that flourished in India in the 9th-10th centuries. Resembling the classic image of a spaceship, the Yogini/Dakini temples were open, circular enclosures. 64 niches around the inner circumference housed 64 forms of Goddess energy as surreal female figures. All Yoginis were worshipped collectively and individually, each one enshrined in her special position in a circular temple open to the sky.

These temples were often erected in remote places, particularly on hilltops. They were built by Tantricas, specifically those dedicated to the worship of Shakti, the Divine Feminine energy. Adepts came to the temples in order to perform rites to attain certain powers that each Yogini embodied. These rites were secret and sometimes included sacred sexual union (maithuna) for the devotees. The temple relates to the chakra (energy vortex or wheel) at the solar plexus of the subtle body of Tantra, which is envisioned as having 64 flames and is seen as the transformation center of the subtle body. The sacred rituals were referred to as 'chakra puja' (worship) or 'Yogini chakra' and was seen as a yantra (mystic diagram). In the center was often a shrine dedicated to Shiva, Hindu God of Transcendence.

A Yogini is a female practitioner of yoga. In Hindu and Buddhist texts the term is used to refer to a female initiate, shaman, wisdom seer, sorceress or alchemist. Through their practice of Yoga (the pursuit of divine union through mental and physical disciplines and practices) they may have attained certain supernatural powers (siddhis). In this context, as the Yoginis appear in the 64 temples, they are all aspects of Devi, the Great Goddess.

The origins of the temples and the 'Yogini Cult' are shrouded in mystery. In Hindu cosmology, which is related to the cycles of Yoginis, they are said to have arisen when the Goddess Durga was battling the asuras (demons/lower inhumane forces). Eight Yoginis were said to emanate from Durga to help her. These eight are said to be the origin of the 64. In a related tradition, there are 8 major forms of Devi, the Goddess. These are known as the Ashta Matrikas (8 Mothers). Each of these has 8 attendants which equals 64. The names of the Matrikas often occur in the cycle of Yoginis and are intimately connected with the iconography of most of the temples.

It is believed that the animistic and folk traditions of the local people who worshipped female nature deities were blended with the cult of Shakti (those who worship the deity in her female form) and Tantrism. When I initially saw photos of the Temples in the mid-seventies, I was fascinated and inspired by them. The forms of the Goddess as Yoginis was entrancing. Naked and adorned, they often had animal or bird heads, some had multiple arms. I knew I wanted to make a contemporary version of these temples that spoke so deeply to me.

Why *Dakinis*?

I decided on the name *Dakini* instead of *Yogini* because I felt that people would have a limited association with Yogini, assuming it was about yoga positions. While Yogini has a much broader context, I chose to use the term 'Dakini' as the role of the Dakini is to help all sentient beings achieve liberation through self -realization.

Dakinis are embodiments of feminine wisdom principles. They are most prominently featured in the teach-

Yogini, Dakini Oracle, Penny Slinger, www.64dakinioracle.org

ings of Tantric Buddhism and are also part of the Hindu spiritual pantheon. Their name translates as 'Sky Flier' and they are known to travel between the realms. They are female enlighteners, inter-dimensional shape shifters, messengers surfing the waves of consciousness to awaken all beings to their innate potential. They are akin to the principle of Shakti, which in the Indian system represents the active force, the power that is the energy behind all manifestation.

Dakinis are usually depicted naked as they represent the naked truth. Their ornaments and decoration have symbolic significance—they play a magical role rather than one that supports vanity or worldly status. They live outside conventional reality and are unshackled by its restraints. They communicate with a secret twilight language and speak in tongues in their own special languages. The Dakini is understood in Tibetan Buddhism to be the protector of the yogic tradition of the subtle body, the energetic confluence of the psychophysical in human life.

The Dakinis communicated to me that they are shape shifters, meaning they can pour themselves into whatever form they chose. They said, "Find the forms most resonant with the transformation of our times." I have searched through all cultures and historical periods to recognize those archetypes of feminine wisdom that would best serve the planet now. As this is a temple of initiation for the planet, I have taken a universal approach, incorporating the embodiments of Divine Feminine energy that have manifested throughout the world in different cultures. Thus, our Temple is non-sectarian, non-dogmatic, trans-cultural and multi-ethnic.

In this circle, there is no distinction drawn between classes of Divine Beings. In other words, Goddesses, Dakinis, Yoginis, Elementals and Apsaras are all given a place in the circle for they all carry potent medicine. They are transmitters of human potential, self-organizing entities, embodying maps for evolution.

Although they appear in female form, Dakini energy transcends gender. As embodiments of Shakti, the inner female force that dwells within everyone, they are not gender specific. We approach the vastness and ineffable nature of Divine awareness through lenses of sexual identity. In Hinduism, consciousness (Purusha) is seen as masculine and manifestation (Prakriti) is viewed as Feminine. In Tantra, the fundamental principles are known as Shiva and Shakti. The whole dance of creation comes about through the joining of opposites-- the union of a

Tribali, Dakini Oracle, Penny Slinger, www.64dakinioracle.org

positive and negative charge, male and female, yin and yang. Thus, it makes sense to approach the infinite from a similar perspective.

To serve our selves and our planet, it is imperative that we awaken the Goddess within. She wants to press our heart buttons and wake us up from the bad dream of separation we have imposed upon ourselves. The dream that caused us to forget that we are all One. The Goddess does not want to be reborn to dominate the male principle in any way. On the contrary, she wants to restore balance, equality and harmony.

Consult The Oracle System

The system that has been used to organize the Dakinis is based on an elemental codex. The Dakinis are all etheric beings, existing as they do in the Mindsky and in the ether of consciousness. As such they are disincarnate. To bring their energies into the plane of reality, the four elements of air, earth, water and fire are placed at the four cardinal points of the circle to represent the building blocks of all creation, as we know it. As we are bringing a sky Mandela down to earth, the 4 elements are associated with the directions of north, south, east and west. The elements are combined in sequences of three. This system reflects the threefold nature of all life – creation, preservation, and dissolution. It also relates to the trigrams that form the basis of the hexagrams of the great oracle system of the I Ching.

Manifestation in general is a mixture of all four elements in its formation (air, earth, fire and water), except for the pure elements. The trigrams represent the first three elements in the longer sequence. Each element has 16 permutations of combination with the other elements, making 64 trigrams in all. There is definitely some affinity with the I Ching, but whereas the I Ching is the Book of Changes, where one hexagram leads to another in the natural cycles of change, this system is about essence principles that represent standing waves of energy. These, although subject to the laws of nature, exist in essence outside time. Their frequencies can form the foundation of any new system. They are the cosmic signatures of beingness in its various aspects or manifestations.

There is a 65th Dakini who holds the central position in the circle. She represents the element of ether, the zero point. In the Yogini Temples of the Tantrics there was generally a shrine to the God Shiva in this position. As Lord of Transcendence, Shiva is sometimes represented

Consult the 64 Dakini Oracle at www.64dakinioracle.org

as a pillar of fire, without top or bottom, infinite. The etheric Dakini of this cycle, this temple, is embodied as an extra-terrestrial being who serves as the energy hub for the system.

The Temples of India were made of stone. Our temple is fashioned out of clouds and nebula, a living organism, situated high in the Mindsky, day and night cycle around it. It is veined with gold and liquid light flows through it as its arteries and veins, its system of circulation. Its transparent floor displays transforming holographic mandalas. It is a living, breathing entity in its own right, made of the plasma, the ectoplasm of consciousness. It is the Mothership of these transformational energies, which wants to find a foot in our dimension to deliver the wisdom of awakening. My wish is that you will be gifted through this series of portals with all you need to become all that you truly are. All the Dakinis are you.

'God loves all equally, but the Goddess loves each for their uniqueness'. - Dr Christopher Hills

Penny Slinger is a surrealist artist. She produced *50%-The Visible Woman* (1971) and *An Exorcism* (1977), two collections of powerful and haunting collages. Her 2D collages and 3D installations incorporated images and life-casts of herself. Her media during this period included pencil and paint, printmaking, life casts and other 3-dimensional constructions, as well as photography, film and collage. Penny Slinger is also known for her erotic and Tantric work and her Caribbean/Amerindian work. She created t*he Secret Dakini Oracle,* re-released as the *Tantric Dakini Oracle.* In 2011 Penny released an on-line version of the project she has been working on for many years, *the 64 Dakini Oracle,* an evolution of *the Secret Dakini Oracle.* Visit her websites at www.pennyslinger.com and www.64dakinioracle.org

Enflami, Penny Slinger, www.64dakinioracle.org

Quetza kundalini, Penny Slinger, www.64dakinioracle.org

CHAPTER THREE:

The Goddess of Creativity

Creativity, Myth and Mysticism: Something Calls to Be Remembered

Far Memory, Claudia Connelly, www.claudiaconnelly.com

By Claudia Connelly

I hadn't expected it to happen this way, my venture into painting. At the age of forty-six I had a profound mystical experience as I stood in the Uffizi Gallery in Florence before Sandro Botticelli's painting, *The Birth of Venus*. In this masterpiece, the classical goddess Venus emerges from the sea on a shell, blown towards shore by the Zephrs, symbols of spiritual passion. She is joined by one of the Horae, goddesses of the seasons, who offer her a flowered cloak. As with many mystical experiences, mine was hard to define or put into words. I like to think that Botticelli and Venus had conjoined in that moment to inspire me from above. It was as if my fairy godmother had waved her magic wand over my head and imparted the knowing that I was to be a painter.

Upon my return from Europe, I mustered up the courage to embark on my first painting. After years of procrastination, I was about to jump over a self-imposed fear hurdle--one that had paralyzed my creative side for much too long. I was still afraid that I would discover that I had no talent and, thus, would have to face giving up my dream of being a painter. However, even more important to me at that time, I had to prove that my over-budget trip to museums in France and Italy had not been a wasteful indulgence. So I picked up the paintbrush with a newfound determination, not realizing that my life's course was about to take off in a new direction.

As I put paintbrush to canvas, I was surprised to find, almost from the inception, that the woman coming through the canvas seemed alive, urging first that her hair color change from blonde to red and that it be pulled neatly to the side, not flying wildly in the wind. Next, she insisted that her clothing be blue, white and red, not green. Then my planned background was incorrect. Her surroundings were not to be woods, but a more pastoral scene. Later, apples had to be added. Finally, she revealed to me that the symbol on the locket was not to be a fertility goddess, as I had anticipated, but a pink rose. By the time the painting was finished it had named itself *Sacred Promise* and I had come to realize that the woman in the picture had long ago made a promise to the Goddess, a promise that I was now supposed to remember. Heavens! This was not the way I had envisioned the painting process.

More often than not, I don't understand the purpose or meaning of what I have created until long after its completion, as bits of information come together to form a whole. Who was this mysterious redheaded woman beckoning me to remember something? It wasn't until I had painted three more pictures of her that I realized I was painting the same woman. Then I learned who she was. Even so, the significance of the pink rose on her locket was only revealed to me gradually. When she first introduced herself to me, I could not have anticipated that she would put me on a path of discovery--about myself, about the sacred feminine, about myth and mysticism.

By following my intuitive urges during the creative process, I continue to receive direction and guidance through symbols and mystical experiences -- even the titles of my paintings. My artistic path continues to be a challenging journey of mystical remembrance, traveling through misty terrain to awaken a lost memory.

Envisioning the Land of Myth and Mysticism through Art

Several years ago I was asked to write something about myself and my art. I explained that my work serves as a bridge from the past into the future, not knowing what that truly meant even as I wrote the words. Since then I have come to believe that myth and mysticism are bridges to ancient memories that hold the knowledge of our human lineage as spiritual beings. These memories offer us a framework in which to better understand ourselves; a blueprint to guide us toward our optimal evolution as human beings. Through symbolism and sacred proportion, art can evoke deep remembrances of who we have been and where we are going. This information is contained within every one of us, and can be accessed

Sacred Promise, Claudia Connelly www.claudiaconnelly.com

as we awaken to our mystical selves. It is my belief that the lands of myths are real, though somewhat distorted through the mists of time and veils of consciousness.

Mysticism is a personal way to reach these mythic lands, and is used by many artists as the vehicle to consciously or unconsciously communicate something about our spiritual heritage as humans. In the process of teaching myself to paint, I studied the pictures of the old masters. Eventually I came to the realization that many artists before me had tapped into a vein of knowing or remembrance and that they had left mystical, evocative jewels of knowledge along the path of time. Botticelli, of course, was one of them.

On a recent trip to ancient Egyptian sites, I learned that every image was made for the purpose of inviting a god, goddess or archetypal energy to inhabit our world and that artists were considered bridges between the two worlds. If mystics bridge the worlds, then myths, in the form of images and stories, may tell us of our ancient origins, give clues to our human makeup and point to the existence of life beyond our three dimensions.

We all know some of the mythic heroes and heroines, such as Venus, Mars, Zeus, Neptune, Athena and King Arthur, as well as the tragic figures, such as Daphne, Tristan & Isolde, Orpheus and Ophelia. Mythic stories cover the emotional gamut of what it is to be human, including the generation gap, the sacred quest, sibling rivalry, love and betrayal, revenge, friendship, abuse of power, good and evil, violence and kindness. Other myths may recount our history and tell us of our human evolution. Through symbols and allegory a single story can cover vast swaths of time or combine complex elements to give us a simple image. In their simplicity, they can evoke a remembrance or hold in place key aspects of who we are, hinting of our evolution through time, such as in the stories of Noah's Ark and Adam and Eve.

Myths, whether in the form of art, story or ritual, help us to understand ourselves on many levels through the avenue of the subconscious. I believe that myths have the potential to serve as windows or portals into distant lands buried in the archives of the collective unconscious, lands that actually existed in our ancient past, such as Atlantis, Lemuria/Mu, Pan, Tara or Gaia. These lands and their crystal cities were inhabited by powerful magical wizards, ancient wise ones, unicorns, dreamers, winged dragons, centaurs and mermaids--creatures and beings which were part of our evolutionary process, some an experiment in form.

It is ironic that while places of myth are dismissed as mere fantasy, at least some of them are being uncovered now by archeologists and shown to have actually existed. Quite recently the tomb of Ulysses or Odysseus was found in the location of his legendary capital of Ithaca on an island in Greece. And in the 19th Century, Henrich Schliemans uncovered Homer's Troy in an archeological dig. Today scientists recognize Pangea and its existence as a super continent until it split 180,000,000 years ago into the lands of Laurasia and Gondwanaland.

Most likely it is not only because we are children-at-heart that we, as adults, are deeply moved by stories such as *The Lord of the Rings*, *The Dark Crystal*, *Sleeping Beauty*, *The Wizard of Oz*, *Star Wars* and *Harry Potter*. It is more likely that they move us profoundly by interrupting the slumber of our subconscious memory and triggering a haunting sense of familiarity. That children are more re-

The Gift, Claudia Connelly, www.claudiaconnelly.com

ceptive to these stories than adults is not surprising since, until the age of seven, the right side of the brain, which controls imaginative function, remains open and active. Thus children have little resistance to subliminal reminders of whom they are and why they have come to Earth.

The Holy Grail: Something Calls to be Remembered

Of all the mythical stories, those of the Grail legends peak my curiosity the most, causing my blood to stir and my heart to beat a little faster. No other myths have quite the same impact upon me. Shrouded within the grail legends, as if lovingly protected, lies the essence of the divine feminine. There it was secretly preserved during the patriarchal swing of civilization until its wisdom could be openly expressed. Also contained within the stories of the Grail legend is the ancient memory of who we are as spiritual beings on planet Earth -- ancient knowledge that has long been forgotten. I feel the myth of the Holy Grail resonates deeply with our souls because it aligns humankind with its highest purpose and reminds us of our collective spiritual dream to be honorable stewards of our Earth Mother and strives towards spiritual ascension. The story of the quest for the Grail may seem vaguely familiar, because it is a story that has been enacted and re-enacted many times as earthlings have striven, failed, and striven again to reach that dream.

In my painting process, the five-petaled pink rose has repeatedly come forward as a symbol to express compassion, sacred knowledge, the hidden presence of the Goddess and Her part in this divine plan for humanity's spiritual enlightenment. Roses figure prominently in the myths and lore surrounding the Grail and are often red or white. Having dwelt in the realms of subconscious memory and intuition for many years, I shouldn't have been surprised when memories were pulled from deep within me to be translated onto the canvas through my brush. As I painted *The Gift*, the phrase "I am from the stars" burst into mind. Simultaneously, I felt compelled to add stars to the blue orb already held in the figure's hand. Next, it came to my attention that the space around her head was empty and needed to be filled with the stars of Venus -- twelve of them.

As I worked on the angel in the stained glass window, her story began to unfold. She told me about the rose, a gift bestowed by the angels to mankind so that we on the earth plane might subconsciously stay connected to the knowledge of who we are, aligning us to humanity's ancient pledge to the Grail Code. The dove in the center of the window brings the message of the Goddess

Sacred Moment, Claudia Connelly, www.claudiaconnelly.com

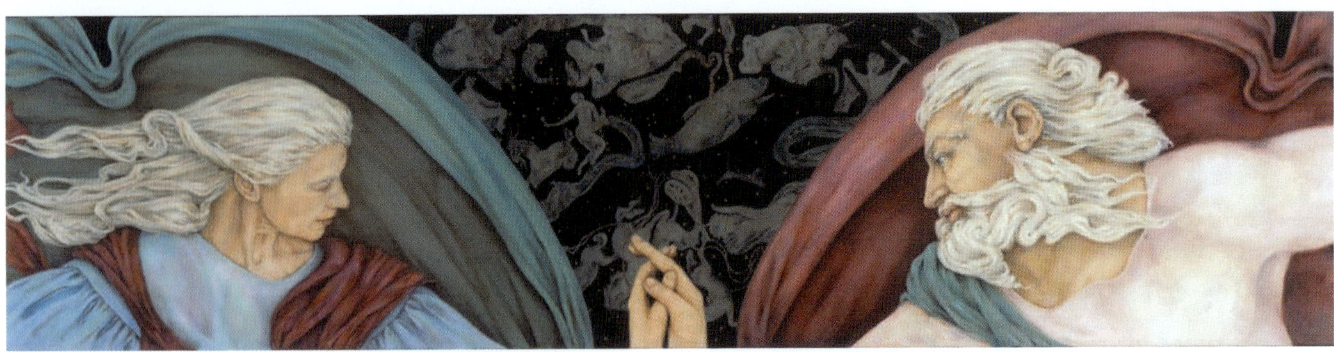

God/Goddess, Claudia Connelly, www.claudiaconnelly.com

-- peace, hope and wisdom. The rose serves to hold her remembrance through its unique beauty, color, and most of all, fragrant scent.

I don't always know where my images are coming from as I work on them. However, the identity of the young woman in *Sacred Moment* was revealed to me early in the creation process. As I was drawing out my concept, I was unsure as to whether she should hold a unicorn or carry a candle. Unable to solve the quandary, I decided to run some errands. As I was driving home, I suddenly felt the urge to stop at the local bookstore. As I entered the store I was drawn to a particular shelf in the back. Scanning the books, the binding on Caitlin and John Matthews' book *Ladies of the Lake* immediately attracted my attention. I picked it up and it fell open to a chapter on Igraine, the mother of King Arthur. Igraine was described as holding a candle, with a unicorn at her feet. Bingo! I knew in that moment that I was painting Igraine. I had not resolved my candle/unicorn dilemma, but I went away in awe of my discovery and the power of following my intuition in the creative process. Later I learned that this was the very woman who had come through in my first painting, and that I had already done three paintings of her. To my astonishment, I had not noticed the likeness.

As I worked on the painting, I gradually became aware that I was depicting the moment when Igraine was divinely chosen to be the sacred vessel to carry the baby who would become King Arthur. I knew that King Arthur was in some way aligned with Jesus and his mission, and I began to think of the twelve disciples and the twelve Knights of the Round Table. I also felt a strong connection between Igraine, Mother Mary, and Mary Magdalene, but I couldn't put my finger on it logically. Much later I came to learn that some people believe that they were all sacred vessels carrying the Grail line. Additionally, I felt that they were somehow linked to the 15th Century French tapestry, *The Lady and the Unicorn,* as well as the priestesses of Avalon, both of whom are portrayed in the robe. Certainly Igraine was the daughter of Vivianne, high priestess of Avalon, and presumably one of the holders of sacred knowledge.

I worked for several months on *Sacred Moment* which, to my surprise, would alternately name itself *The Princess*. To my dismay, the final three weeks of its completion were spent in grief over the death of Princess Diana. Painting, in those weeks after her passing, became a reverent ritual to her memory. Much later I learned that Princess Diana was of the royal Stewart line of Scotland whose symbol is the unicorn. The Stewarts are said to be descendents of the royal blood of Jesus and Mary Magdalene, including the sacred and charismatic Merovingian dynasty that includes King Arthur. I found it highly symbolic that Diana's body was laid to rest in the middle of a tiny lake much like the Isle of Avalon that was inhabited by the Ladies of the Lake. Diana too had been a vessel of the sacred bloodline of the Holy Grail.

In one painting thus far, the process has been mental rather than intuitive. In 1997 I was watching the news on TV. A woman being interviewed mentioned that most Westerners envision God as looking like Michelangelo's depiction on the Sistine Chapel. In that instant I said, "I must paint the Goddess as the equal and opposite partner to Michelangelo's God!". In my painting, *God/Goddess*, Western man's most revered image of God now includes his divine partner, the Goddess! God and Goddess face each other as equals in a sacred union. Behind them is the backdrop of the Universe, part of their dual creation of All That Is. Rather than reaching his hand down to Man, this God entwines his fingers with Goddess as his partner in creation. With the return of the Goddess to her rightful place beside God, the true equation is being reinstated and spirituality is coming full circle. The evolution of humankind can once again flower as it was meant to. *God/Goddess* celebrates this divine re-union.

Since the creative process often involves the feminine energy of the right brain with its access to intuition and the subconscious, it is not surprising that many writers, artists, poets, musicians and visionaries have come to be recognized as the mystics and prophets of our time, as the old masters were in their time. Not surprisingly then, I feel a special kinship to the painters who have gone before, and gratefully consider them my teachers. My heart is always moved by the mastery of Edward Burne-Jones, Botticelli, Leonardo Da Vinci, Eleanor Fortesque-Brickdale, John Waterhouse and John Duncan, among others. These mystics and dreamers were striving to communicate some elusive sense of the Goddess, who has always dwelt in misty worlds and mythic lands. Though many forgot her existence, she has always been there, reachable through the heart, intuition, inspiration, inner knowing, and distant memory, through mysticism, soulful reverie and prayer. We are once again awakening to her presence as the Goddess emerges from the mists that have enshrouded her for so long. There is a heightening sense that something calls to be remembered--something that dwells in the lands of myth and mysticism.

Out of the mists of time something sacred calls to be remembered. In her paintings **Claudia Connelly** touches that remembrance, evoking a sense of time and place long forgotten. Working intuitively, she draws inspiration from the Old Masters, especially Botticelli and the Pre-Raphaelites. Her archetypal images slowly evolve through the medium of oil paint on linen, canvas or panel. Claudia's paintings have been reproduced in books, magazines, cards and calendars. Visit her website: www.claudiaconnelly.com for more information about her work.

A Feminine Path in Art and Life

Gift From the Goddess, SoulCard, Deborah Koff-Chapin, www.touchdrawing.com

By Deborah Koff-Chapin

As a child I had an underlying sense that there was some purpose my life was to serve. In my search for identity, the closest role models I could find were artists. I sensed, in artists like Michelangelo, Van Gogh and William Blake, a sincere passion to bring into form a vision that pierced the veil of ordinary reality. These artists seemed to possess a fierce determination to let nothing come in the way of their creative path. As a young woman I remember thinking to myself, "Why are all these artists men?" The response I sensed from within was that it did not matter. If I felt a calling to pursue truth and beauty through art, being female would not get in the way. As my life was to unfold, surrendering to the feminine path actually opened the way to a new form of artistic expression as well as a more integral vision of life as the ultimate art form.

During the tumultuous upheavals of the sixties, while other teens were turning to drugs, politics or parties, painting was my mode of truth seeking. It was a vehicle for turning inward, as well as a means of communicating from the depths of my soul. My natural tendency was to reflect states of being and feeling through images of the human form. I recall a time in high school when I was frustrated with the authoritarian attitudes at school. I went home and painted a giant red face gazing down from the canvas with power and authority. Transforming my anger into image, I began to realize the healing power of creative expression.

Sometimes I would carry my painting materials into the forest. After a time of deep silence, I would begin to feel an emerging impulse and translate this sense of presence into an image. There was magic in these moments, a feeling of having helped God in the act of creation.

Thankfully I had parents who sensed that my art was a healthy expression, and gave me space to find my way. Upon graduating from high school, I attended art school in New York City. I enthusiastically leaped into the great mystique of the art world. However, it wasn't long before an existential nausea began to set in, as I started to question the meaning of art. The human form disappeared from my paintings as "art talk" became the high craft. Paintbrushes began to feel like obscure instruments, so I started to pour and wipe paint. I dove into the void, feeling my way into formlessness, searching for something underneath and unknown.

In the midst of this exploration, I was gifted with an ecstatic moment of recognition. One day, while on a retreat at my school's rural campus, I came across a willow tree swaying gently in the breeze. The tips of its branches were etching lines in the sand below, creating ever-changing patterns on the beach. I was witnessing the pure, uninhibited act of *nature* drawing. This touched me to the core, fueling my underlying search for a more organic way to express *human* nature.

By my last year of art school, I had become fluent in the language of abstraction. It was pure and essential, but foreign to the eyes of those not educated in the "esoteric knowledge" of the art world. One day I found myself doodling some silly little faces on a piece of paper. I wrote *"What's wrong with drawing faces?"* and tucked the embarrassing doodle away. But in that moment I remembered something simple and universal; the image of the human face. A seed was germinating in my psyche.

On my last day of school, as I was helping a friend

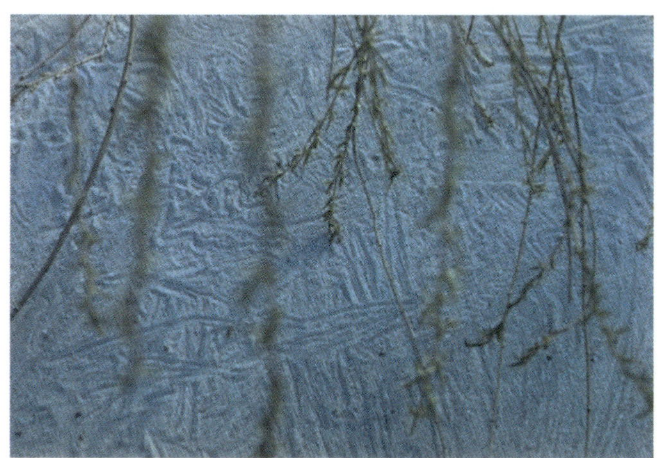

Willow Drawing in Sand, photograph, 1972, www.touchdrawing.com

clean up the print shop, I placed a paper towel over a plate of inked glass. But instead of wiping off the ink, I felt an impulse to playfully move my hands on the paper towel. Lifting the towel, I saw impressions that had been transferred to the underside by the pressure of my touch. I was thunderstruck. Lines were coming directly from my fingertips! I laughed ecstatically with this realization. My fingertips danced from one paper towel to another. The imprints that were created from the pressure of my touch were pure and natural. Like the willow tree drawing in the sand, they were a direct expression of my being on paper. Soon my fingertips were forming simple, childlike faces on the paper towels. The seed of my face doodles had burst into life.

Although this experience appeared to be simple play, from the inside it felt like a revelation. The moment my fingertips touched the paper, I felt circuits within me opening to something larger than my personal self, something that existed outside of time. I sensed that I was receiving an evolutionary creative process that people in the future might use to express the consciousness of their time. This inner knowing constellated in my psyche as a calling to share *Touch Drawing* with the world.

In the following months, I poured my soul into this direct drawing process. Alone with my newfound creative impulse, it became my main source of grounding. Whenever I felt pain, fear or confusion, I would turn to the drawing board to express my feelings. In releasing an emotion onto the paper, I was freed of its power and poised to move into the next state of being. I would then transfer the sensations of the next moment onto another page. Each drawing was a stepping-stone that led me deeper. Although the drawings were raw, primitive and personal, I trusted that the work I was doing was on behalf of the larger calling I had received. I soon realized that I was doing more than drawing; I was sculpting my psyche, bringing my soul into form. At the end of a drawing session I could step back and witness my process through a series of images conveying my internal transformation.

In those first months of *Touch Drawing*, another layer of realization transformed my path. At this time in my life I had identified with the myth of the isolated and potentially tragic artist's life. I felt alone in the drama of my newly discovered drawing process. I assumed this isolation was essential to fuel my creativity.

One day I was walking along the streets of New York City, creatively stimulated, yet unstable. Then a single word floated into my mind – *"health."* The epiphany that came with this word was that the natural world is essentially healthy, and embodies truth in its very being. If I was to find a path of truth in my life and art, I had to align myself with the health and interconnectedness found in nature. I had to find another way to be an artist. The isolation of my art world persona fell away as I shifted my gaze toward health and community. I moved out of the city and began to find kindred souls who were also opening to new ways of being. I explored places to share my images where they were not commodities for sale but integral components of collective experiences and sacred processes. Among these were Jean Houston's workshops and Elizabeth Cogburn's ceremonials. They generated communities of co-creation in music, dance, image and heartfelt sharing. In these settings, my wholeness could be expressed.

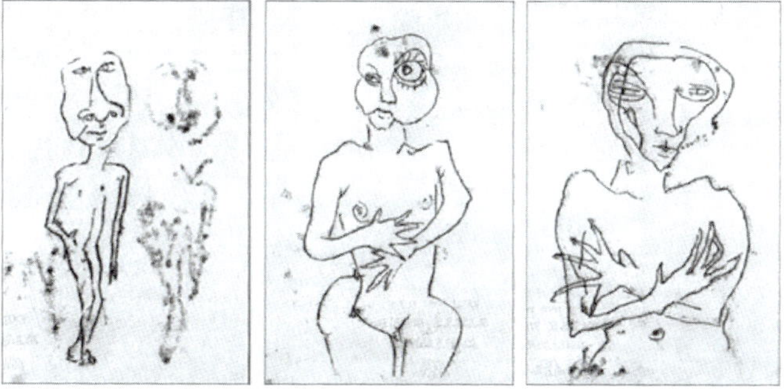

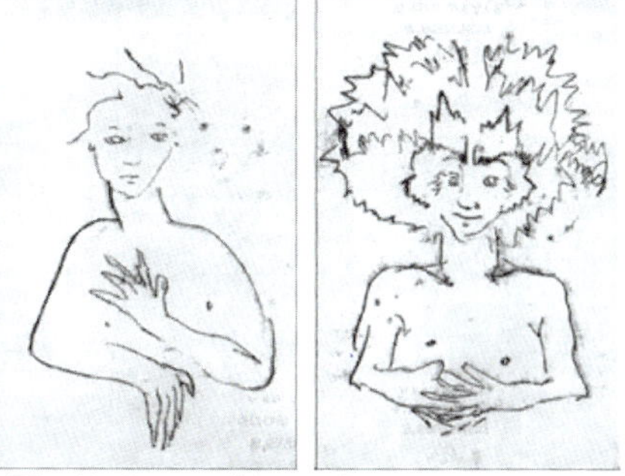

The Uglies, etching ink on paper, 1975, www.touchdrawing.com

By the mid 1990s I was married, had a child and was embedded in community life. By then, my *Touch Draw-*

Selections from SoulCards 1&2, Deborah Koff-Chapin, www.touchdrawing.com

Selections from SoulCards 1&2, Deborah Koff-Chapin. www.touchdrawing.com

ings were emerging from a quieter sense of interior attention. When completing a drawing session, it felt like I was disengaging from a deep communion. My images gradually blossomed into fullness, with layers of color and refinement of form. The seed of the earlier, child-like drawings had grown into a tree, abundant with fruit. It was time for the images to find their way into a greater relationship with the world.

A friend suggested I create a deck of cards. I felt a clear YES from the universe, deciding to take the leap and publish them independently. I sorted through hundreds of *Touch Drawings*, looking for the broadest range of human feelings that I could find. I wrote a booklet that offered creative ways to interact with the images, encouraging readers to trust their own perceptions and inner voice. I called the deck *SoulCards.*

SoulCards 1 & 2 have become sacred vessels through which my images have entered the lives of others. Rather than being seen by a select audience for brief times in a gallery, they are in people's hands and hearts during their most intimate moments of reflection. This is certainly a fulfillment of my original calling to find another path – to speak to the human soul through images. The cards evoke strong response and a sense of recognition. They empower people to access their inner wisdom and communicate with others from this place. *SoulCards* are used by therapists and workshop leaders; in creative writing groups, hospitals, and management teams. The broad range of people who respond to them is confirmation of their universality. By going deeply into my own being, I seem to have found a place we all know.

Over the years I have done my best to keep my artistic life vital. I am most inspired when I work in relationship. I go to conferences as *interpretive artist* where I translate the content into image. Some of my deepest work is in private sessions when I create a series of drawings inspired by someone's presence. But much of my life has been dedicated to actualizing the sense I had in those first moments of *Touch Drawing.* My work is to midwife the emergence of this dynamic creative process into the world. I began by sharing *Touch Drawing* with friends and demonstrating it when the opportunity arose. Over the years I have developed a workshop structure that holds the space for people to go deeply into the process. My experience with ceremony and ritual gave me the foundation to craft each workshop as a sacred space. While people draw, I create a live musical sound field with drums, chimes and voice. People gaze into the 'inner mirror' of the drawing board, hands tracing sensations onto paper. Pulling one sheet off the board and going to the next, they are immersed in their own inner journey. When their drawing series is done, they can reflect upon the transformations that have occurred. It is such a natural process. Like the willow tree drawing in sand, our human nature leaves impressions on the page.

Touch Drawing has sprouted up in a broad range of settings. It is used as a spiritual practice, as a way for "non-artists" to find their creative voice, and for experienced artists to open to deeper sources in their work. It is used as a therapeutic tool with at-risk youth, people with AIDS, depression, cancer, Parkinson's, Alzheimer's, sexual abuse and in Hospice. I have had the honor of introducing it to Palestinian therapists who work with traumatized children in Gaza, and Japanese therapists who work with people affected by the tsunami.

I recall my commitment from childhood to not let being female "get in the way" of being an artist. I realize now that following a more feminine path has actually *opened the way.* Touch Drawing is an embodiment of the feminine principle: the creation of images through the touch of open hands rather than the point of a singular stylus; the focus on process rather than product, on authenticity rather than artifice. The rising tide of the feminine is essential to the emergence of a vibrant, whole, interconnected planetary culture. It is my hope that the work of my heart makes a contribution to this essential shift, that we may regain a healthy and balanced relationship with life on Earth.

Deborah Koff-Chapin graduated with a BFA from Cooper Union in 1974. She has been practicing Touch Drawing since it came to her in an ecstatic awakening on her last day there. She teaches this simple yet profound process internationally, and has held the annual Touch Drawing Gathering since 1997. Deborah is the creator of best-selling SoulCards 1&2, timeless classic decks that are sold worldwide. She is author of Drawing Out Your Soul and The Touch Drawing Facilitator Workbook, and has published five SoulTouch Coloring Journals. Deborah has served as Interpretive Artist at numerous conferences including The Parliament of the World's Religions. She works with individuals to bring subtle dimensions of their soul into form through Inner Portraits.

The Fantastic Muse of Carrie Ann Baade

Dali, Carrie Ann Baade, 10"x10" oil on panel, 2005, www.carrieannbaade.com

By Victoria Christian and Carrie Ann Baade

Artists have a way of stretching the imagination, but Carrie Ann Baade takes her viewers on a magic carpet ride of fantastical, surreal vision. Inspired by the muses of literature and art history, Carrie Anne Baade's bizarre, colorful images are filled with allegorical details and layers of meaning. Carrie is a painter who enjoys plumbing the depths of the human condition. "Her autobiographical oil paintings are allegorical narratives inspired by spirit, literature, and art history. These parables combine fragments of Renaissance and Baroque religious paintings, resulting in surreal landscapes inhabited by exotic flora, fauna, and figures."[1]

Born in Natchitoches, Louisiana in 1974, Carrie spent most of her life in Colorado. She has traveled extensively all over the world and currently lives in Tallahassee, Florida, where she is a Professor of Painting and Drawing at Florida State University. "Baade received a Masters in Painting from the University of Delaware where she expanded her knowledge of materials and techniques under the guidance professors of art conservation. She received her B.F.A. from the School of the Art Institute of Chicago that included one year of study at the Florence Academy of Art in Italy. Baade was awarded the Florida Division of Cultural Affairs Individual Artist Fellowship in 2010, the Delaware Division of the Arts Fellowship for Established Artist in 2005, and was nominated for the prestigious United States Artist Fellowship in 2006 and the Joan Mitchell Grant in 2012. Her work has been exhibited in museums and galleries nationally and internationally, including recent solo exhibitions: the Museum of Contemporary Art in Jacksonville Florida, the Delaware Center for Contemporary Art, the Rosenfeld Gallery in Philadelphia, Billy Shire Fine Arts in Los Angeles, and the Ningbo Art Museum in China."[2]

She has exhibited widely with the Pop Surrealists and her paintings have been featured in Metamorphosis, a survey of the top, contemporary Visionary Surrealists including Ernst Fuchs, Alex Grey, Amanda Sage, and Kris Kuksi. "In the greater art world, 'Pop Surrealism' has been finding new acceptance in contemporary art criticism and in major urban art museums. Since 1994, this ground swelling of lowbrow, surrealistic, pop, figurative, narrative work has coalesced and found a voice in the pages of Juxtapoz magazine published in San Francisco. The foundation of this work relies on the artists' ability to describe the world realistically – in order to then subvert and distort it. Whether the artists' works are wickedly satirical, bizarre, humorous, fluently painted or crudely conceptualized, there is no doubt of their popular appeal."[3]

Despite her post modern, pop-surrealist flair, Baade is a steward of art history. She writes, "I consider myself to be steward and ax man to the legacy of art history by cutting and serving up the reinvigorated past to be contemplated in context of the contemporary."[4] Carrie is interested in creating a meta-narrative of a work, commenting on its original context as well as its contemporary relevance. She explains, "As an artist and subject in my work, I attempt to use and reuse art history for the purpose of reinvigorating the past for a contemporary audience. Studying with art conservators and looking at the old masters has informed my choice to revitalize the archaic traditions of both traditional oil painting and egg tempera. My subjects are adopted from religion and mythology; these are often cautionary tales that mirror my personal experience. In desiring to speak to the complexity of the human condition, I use the language of allegory and narrative to relate to my own story, which is at once an age old."[5]

The ideas for her work come from various muses that tantalize her in the fanciful and idealized world of her imagination. The subjects of her work include the gods, rulers, and demons as metaphors for the complexity of absolute states of the human condition. Myths and mon-

The Insomniac, Carrie Ann Baade, 14"x14" oil on panel, 2005, www.carrieannbaade.com

sters are commonly used to build intrigue around tales of morality and the human condition. Carrie says:

> *I see myself as a storyteller, telling my own tale while keeping alive the religious stories and myths of the past. For many of us, these visions are the language of God, connecting us to our spirituality. I believe that cultivating art and spirituality are essential for cultural renewal and understanding ourselves. When I was growing up with visions, the only books that talked about people having visions was in abnormal psychology. Supposedly, it was only the schizophrenics that had visions and magical thinking. This was not the place to look for answers as a young artist! It was so easy to question why I was making weird art and fall into the trap of self-doubt that says I must be crazy. Thankfully, I simply refused to believe it. My greatest accomplishment so far is being terrible at everything but painting and teaching. It was my one great, God given talent. I'm very proud that I suck at everything else, so I had no choice but to follow my heart's desire."*[6]

History is saturated with visionaries and artists who thought they were going mad when in fact they were having normal, visionary experiences. Unfortunately, there wasn't a safe container to talk about these experiences out of fear they would be burned at the stake. Thus, they were channeled into some form of artistic medium or expression. Artists have spoken of a love/hate relationship with their creative muses; while they can be alluring and quite inspiring, some have felt the psychologically torture of their wild imaginations as they get lost in fantasy and get sleep deprived as a result. Nonetheless, the intoxicating benefits of the muses often out weigh the demons, but they never go away. Carries painting titled *The Insomniac* captures this well. She writes, "I am an insomniac and feel most comfortable being alone while everyone else is asleep so that I can have the world to myself without distractions. I like the idea that if I laid down, the eye mask would hover in front of me. I repeated the eye mask to suggest all the sleepless time I have spent where I felt as though I was locked out of dreaming and could not get back in."[7]

Carrie has a large body of work with various themes such as "Intemperance," "Virtues and Vices," and "Tales of Passion and Woe" --to name just a few. Reminiscent of surrealists of the past, such as Remedios Varos, Frida Kalo, and Salvidor Dali, her work is incredibly imaginative, unique, rich, detailed and masterfully painted. In fact, she did an amazing painting of Dali that brilliantly captures his style and personality. While her style is definitely surreal, Carries creative process is quite unique as it is composed of snippets of pictorial fragments of which she turn into a collage and then paints. She speaks of her creative process in more detail:

> *To begin a composition, I start with scissors, clipping fragments, composing from snippets of several hundred pictures scattered about me on the floor. A prototype collage of layered scraps with cut edges is created that includes an array of photographs and images from art history. Looking at this collage, a painting is executed in a trompe l'oeil manner showing the multiple layers with cut edges which suggest the complexity of individual's psychologies – their masks and their hidden secrets. To create these paintings, I cut up and serve the reinvigorated past to be contemplated in context of the contemporary.*
>
> *The spark of the muse that could be called intuition is present when I make the collage for my work. I begin this process by covering the first floor of my house in photos and ripped out pages from books. After the floor is covered I walk around looking for images that fell on top of each other in an interesting manner. This is similar to reading tealeaves. Often I will have a question in mind while diving into the piles of picture images, such as, 'What can I say about the horrors of dating in Tallahassee.' The process reminds me of reading tarot cards and getting an answer through the cards that can sometimes be uncannily accurate. Looking for the divine spark to speak to me through the images, I collect and adhere together with cellophane tape to paint later. I know something is really working if*

I involuntarily laugh out loud at the juxtaposition. I alas use the collage to rearrange, and rearrange, and rearrange the visual elements of my work until they resonate and make a worthy subject to spend a 150 hours rendering. I am hopelessly committed to oil paint, so then I take those collages and slavishly paint them to look like the collage with a bit of trompe l'oeil. [8]

Carrie admits that her work is rather self-cathartic and autobiographical. Most of her paintings consist of self – portraits and an assortment of complex, bizarre, female characters dripping with emotion, allegory, humor, and of course demons and monsters. She writes, "My whole life I have comfortably taken my innermost thoughts and used symbolism and fantasy to obscure them. Myths and monsters are commonly used to build intrigue around tales of morality and the human condition. Perhaps it could be said that it is feminist or goddess based. Being female has definitely influenced my experience. I have found that the more personal I make my work, the more others could feel the intensity and relate. Art has the potential to narrate and be cathartic in the telling of something that would otherwise be unspeakable or incriminating."[9]

Speaking of demons, she has a number of self-portraits, but there is one that I would like to discuss titled the Temptation of Medusa. She has always felt a resonance with Medusa as her altar ego. In Greek mythology Medusa was a monster, a Gorgon, generally described as having the face of a hideous human female with living venomous snakes in place of her hair. Gazing directly upon her would turn onlookers to stone. Carrie writes, "In this self-portrait as my alter ego, I am painting and trying hard to stay on task as I am assaulted by several demons that wish to provoke me away from my work. This painting combines: The Penitent Magdalene, The Temptation of St. Anthony, St. Luke Painting a Portrait of the Virgin Mary, and Medusa. Medusa was an innocent, then punished by being turned into a monster, later rehabilitated like Magdalene; however, the demons may lure her back to evil ways against all her efforts to be pious."[10]

While Baade has always loved the strange and the unusual, sorrow has been a large theme in her art, which gives it more depth and authenticity. She did apiece titled *Lady of Sorrow* that I adore. In this painting, she portrays the grief of the Madonna, tears streaming down her face, holding a pink rose. The eyes of her characters are usually enlarged and have a mask-like quality to them. She expounds on this more in an interview:

The Temptation of the Penitent Medusa, Carrie Ann Baade, 12" x 18" oil on panel, 2010, www.carrieannbaade.com

In my older work (2002 to 2007), I used Our Lady Sorrow and Our Man of Sorrow as the foundation for my work. In the collage for these paintings, I would cut the eyes out of historic paintings, particularly from the Primitive Northern Renaissance. These would serve as masks--often for myself, so that only my nose and mouth were visible. Through this period of my life, I was dealing with my own sadness, which is shunned in our culture. I wanted to connect with the universal and the Christian archetypes of compassion, so that I might be removed from my own personal story. In a way this is hiding, but it is also protection. I didn't want to be petty and self indulgent about my personal pain, but to learn how to see through the eyes of universal compassion and suffering which is part of being alive. While sorrow is a constant, unending river that flows beneath us, I have also experienced the universal river of joy that flows above us. I am attempting a new and exciting challenge: how does one paint out of pure joy? Is it possible to continually extend these periods of joy? Or is it as Robert Frost suggests: 'Happiness makes Up in Height for What It Lacks in Length.'[11]

Our Lady of Sorrow, Carrie Ann Baade, 12"x9" oil on copper, 2005, www.carrieannbaade.com

Carrie has some paintings in her "Intemperance" series that are gut-wrenchingly sorrowful, ominously beautiful and a tad humorous. She writes, "The spirit of this series encompasses behavioral extremes. Plumbing the shallows of polite society and surpassing the boundaries of moderation have been my inspiration. Adultery, betrayal, blood lust, blasphemy, and suicide are among the subjects that I seek to provide a theater for public display. These are subjects that one might feel or imagine in private or experience in real life to their soul's detriment; my intention is that these paintings provide catharsis for the unmentionable."[12] There is one painting in particular that caught my eye *The Supposedly Shared Sorrow of Magdalene*. In this image Mary Magdalene is holding a crocodile with worried and sad eyes. She explains the painting in more detail:

> *This one is my favorite from this series. The eye on the crocodile is from a painting of Christ, Our Man of Sorrow. And the eyes on Magdalene are from, Our Lady of Sorrow, belonging to Mary. I fear this crocodile has a duplicitous nature. I suspect he, at times, really wishes the crying Magdalene well and enjoys the physical contact her sorrow has allowed him. However, his tears are borrowed... he IS a crocodile and eventually one can only anticipate that he will indeed devour her. It is true that Mary Magdalene was a redeemable person only in the eyes of Jesus Christ, yet it is the idea that one must be on one's guard in times of vulnerability. There are those that will seek to gain intimacy for their own purpose, which may turn out to have a detrimental hidden agenda.* [13]

Another painting in the same series is *The Perilous Compassion Of The Honey Queen*. Carrie also calls the painting, which uses themes of Catholic Madonna Dolorosa, but is actually about "her own ill-fated relationship with a man whom no matter how much "honey" she lavished on him, he would always be dead inside. No amount of my tremendous love could fill the void that was within him." She explains further, "The Honey

The Supposedly Shared Sorrow of Magdalene, 9"x12" oil on panel, 2009, www.carrieannbaade.com

The Perilous Compassion Of The Honey Queen, Carrie Ann Baade, 18"x24" oil on panel, 2009, www.carrieannbaade.com

The Teaching of Lilith, Carrie Ann Baade, 18"x12" oil on copper, www.carrieannbaade.com

Queen" pours over herself over a damaged soul in an attempt to make them whole. There are those individuals who cannot be redeemed by any act benevolence. There is something necrotic within them that can never be revived. Having a generous nature, can lead one into being trapped into an engagement that will cost them their virtue and vitality. It can come as quite a surprise to find out that blood letting, or energy giving can feel so good and nothing can come of it...outside of euphoria." [14]

A painting that is a powerful contribution to the Women's Spirituality Movement is *The Teachings of Lilith*. Carries speaks of the inspiration for this painting in more detail:

> *Set in a field of night flowers, a beautiful woman headed snake has congregated her devotees. This painting explores why women have been historically spliced with serpents in pictorial representations of the story of Adam and Eve. In this myth, Evil is represented as the serpent or 'Satan.' This story has originated or reinforced some cultural ideas including the doctrine of original sin and the subordination of women in many Christian denominations. Influenced by the writing of Elaine Pagels, I prefer the idea that the tree of knowledge gave humans free will as they ate from the apple. In this scenario, the serpent represents the bringer of wisdom as reinforced by pre-Christian mythology. I chose to build on this myth and create a world where more female-serpents will spread enlightenment and free will to more humans who are otherwise blissfully unaware that they are ignorant.* [15]

A recent painting deserving of recognition is *Butterfly Lovers*. This piece beautifully portrays the cathartic, transformative powers of the Goddess, particularly death and rebirth. Carrie explains, "*Butterfly Lovers* is more like the traditional intuitive High Priestess who represents the world from behind the veil, serving as the medium for reconciliation and resurrection into a higher plane. She holds the power to transmute the suffering made possible by her power of transmogrification. She is the spiritual power behind transcendence." [16] A beautiful quote by Alejandro Jodorowsky eloquently captures the intention of this piece: "Awakening is not a thing. It is not a goal, not a concept. It is not something to be attained. It is a metamorphosis. If the caterpillar thinks about the butterfly it is to become, saying 'And then I shall have wings and antennae,' there will never be a butterfly. The caterpillar must accept its own disappearance in its transformation. When the marvelous butterfly takes wing, nothing of the caterpillar remains."[17]

The butterfly is a graceful message of non-attachment, much like creativity, which ebbs and flows like a river. Carrie Ann Baade is a complex person indeed, extremely intelligent, profoundly deep and an inspiration to all of her students. She says, "I love to tell my students all of my mistakes so they don't do the same thing. I feel like someone should benefit from all my blaring ignorance. I try to give them advice but I think a wiser person lets others make their own decisions while giving them the tools to be their best. My current philosophy is: Be passionate and free yourself from the expectations of its outcome." [18]

Carrie's muses must be working overtime as she paints like she is drinking from of a fire hose of creativity. She is a true visionary art geek and one that will go down history as a highly driven and prolific artist with a dash of bizarre and an appreciation for the weird and strange. I will end with one last quote by Carrie: "Art is what makes the world go round for me. As an educator, I am connected to guiding my students through their work and their understanding of their greater role in the world. I see artists as ambassadors of culture, prodders of consciousness, and conduits for the furthest reaches of the human experience."[19]

Victoria Christian is a sociologist, social worker, counselor, artist, writer and sacred activist. She holds undergraduate and Masters degrees in Sociology. She also has a Masters of Social Work, with an emphasis in the sociology of gender, social theory, the sociology of art and ecofeminism. For more information about her art, books and DVD's, you can view her website at www.victoriachristian.com. To learn more about this book, see the website: www.mysticspiritart.com

The Butterfly Lovers, Carrie Ann Baade, 18"x24" oil on panel, 2012, www.carrieannbaade.com

CHAPTER FOUR:

The Goddess of Emotion

Aphrodite, Jonathan Weber, 24"x36", Oil on Canvas, www.jonathanweber.org

Bodhisattvas of Compassion: Awakening the Heart through Art

By Victoria Christian

Every heart is connected to the Great One Heart. It is from this heart of hearts that we are unconditionally loved, nourished, healed and redeemed. The Hebrew word for "compassion" is derived from the word for "womb." God is the primal matrix, the Great One from which all beings are born and all love streams forth. We experience on a very tangible level this immense love pulsating through our veins. This heart connection to source is our lifeline or umbilical cord.

While it is difficult for humans to fully grasp the immense love of the Great One Heart, we are all intimately connected to it and can learn to cultivate a deeper and richer understanding of this love if we so desire. Not all humans acknowledge Great Spirit as the ground of their being, but this does not stop the unwavering flow of love from source. We may choose to intellectually deny the Creator, but we continue to partake of divine love in each breath we take, for God/Goddess resides in every cell of our bodies and nourishes our souls on spiritual and physical levels. If we decide to cultivate and understand on a deeper level the compassion of the Great One Heart, we must first open our heart to receive Spirit's love, which requires a certain degree of reverence, surrender or transformation of the ego, for it is only when we surrender to the Beloved in our brokenness and pain that the Great One Heart can then fill our cups with unconditional love and forgiveness. This is what it means to claim our divine gift as the beloved. It is because of Great Spirit's compassion for us that we can then love ourselves and extend compassion to others.

When we know, deep in our hearts, that we are a reflection of God's awesome love, we are exhibiting authentic self-love. We have claimed wholeheartedly the gift of our belovedness which, as Jesus teaches, is available to all those who have the eyes to see and the ears to hear. The tendency to deny or reject one's self or elevate self above others usually stems from an insecure ego that has fallen prey to the illusion that its self-worth comes from worldly definitions as opposed to a direct connection to Source. Self-rejection is the greatest enemy of the spiritual life because it contradicts the sacred voice that calls us the Beloved. Our belovedness is the core truth of who we are. Every time we listen with great attentiveness to the voice that calls us Beloved, we will discover within ourselves a desire to hear that voice longer and more deeply. It is like discovering a well in the desert. Once you have touched wet ground, you want to dig deeper.

Winged Heart, Robby Donaghey, Digital image, www.artisticgenius.com

When we have been transformed and melted like butter by the love of the great heart, we can then choose to become a vessel of this love and commit our lives to assisting those who are still suffering. We might choose to become what Christians call stewards of God's love or what Buddhists call a Bodhisattva of compassion, a being (satva) committed to liberation (bodhi). This kinship with the suffering of others is the discovery of our soft spot, the discovery of Bodhicitta or Mercy. It is said to be present in all beings. If this is the case, everything that exists in creation does so because of the Great Mother's compassion. This love is so great that it moves us to explore what it means to live a compassionate life and seek enlightenment

A Bodhisattva of compassion is one who has empathy for the distress of others, coupled with a desire to alleviate suffering in the world. The word compassion is derived from the Latin words *parti* and *cum*, which together mean "to suffer with." Compassion asks us to go where it hurts, to enter into places of pain, to share in brokenness, fear, confusion, and anguish. It challenges us to cry out with those in misery, to mourn with those who are lonely. Compassion requires us to feel weak with the weak, vulnerable with the vulnerable and powerless with the powerless. Compassion requires us to withhold judgment and practice empathy. It also requires us to set healthy boundaries that honor our highest good as opposed to falling prey to a codependency that enables dysfunction. Compassion requires that we value the wisdom of grief and solitude. It also requires us to be humble and forgive those who have trespassed against us, so that even though we can feel the suffering of others, we also maintain the witnessing part of ourselves that allows us to see the bigger picture simultaneously.

We have much to learn from Buddha's and Christ's messages of compassion, for they are some of the deepest sources of strength and validation of the arduous path of the bodhisattva or faithful steward. Both Masters understood that life is filled with suffering and that we must learn to live in ways that reduce the suffering of those around us. We, too, must learn to find ways to alleviate our own suffering and transform it into well-being and peace. We need to look deeply into the nature of suffering to see the causes of suffering and to find the way out. This requires every one of us to focus on our own healing, as it is the only thing we can really control. We can't alleviate war and suffering in the world until we have first alleviated the war within ourselves.

We all have the capacity to feel compassion, but not all of us desire or choose to cultivate and implement it in our daily lives. For most humans, the practice of compassion is easier said than done since it goes against the grain of the ego, which is self-serving and competitive by nature. In Sanskrit, *bodhi* means "awakened" and *chitta* means "mind" or "heart." Bodhichitta -- "awakened heart-mind" -- is the compassionate wish to realize enlightenment for all beings, not just for one's self. Through bodhichitta, the desire to attain enlightenment transcends the narrow interests of the individual self. Bodhichitta is an essential part of Mahayana Buddhism. Without bodhichitta, the path to enlightenment is mired in selfishness. However hard we work, we are still wrapped up in our own heads, our own pain, our own wants. The path to awakening opens when we become aware of others as well as ourselves. One of my favorite Tibetan Buddhist teachers, Pema Chodron, explains the cultivation of bodhichitta in more detail:

> *Those who train wholeheartedly in awakening unconditional and relative bodhichitta are called bodhisattvas or warriors—not warriors who kill and harm but warriors of nonaggression who hear the cries of the world. These are men and women who are willing to train in the middle of the fire. Training in the middle of the fire can mean that warrior-bodhisattvas enter challenging situations in order to alleviate suffering. It also refers to their willingness to cut through personal reactivity and self-deception, to their dedication to uncovering the basic undistorted energy of bodhichitta. We have many examples of master warriors—people like Mother Teresa and Martin Luther King—who recognized that the greatest harm comes from our own aggressive minds. They devoted their lives to helping others understand this truth. There are also many ordinary people who spend their lives training in opening their hearts and minds in order to help others do the same. Like them, we could learn to relate to ourselves and our world as warriors. We could train in awakening our courage and love.* [1]

In our legalistic societies, we have been conditioned to believe that there is little incentive in the human world to cultivate compassion because it might make us too soft, and therefore, more likely to be eaten alive by those who have chosen to shut their hearts down. We have been taught to view suffering as something to be avoided at all costs. Hence the call to compassion is a call that goes against the grain and requires a total conversion of heart and mind. Why would we want to open our hearts when the world will just break them over and over again? In the midst of so much human suffering, we might assume that it would be easier to shut our hearts down and not have any expectations of hope for the future at all. Yet, in our heart of hearts we all know that a world without compassion would be a living hell, a human wasteland, and therefore the choice to uphold God's grace amidst great suffering and despair can be seen as a choice for a better world for all. We do this for one reason and one reason only, because it is at the very core of who we are as humans; it is the greatest blessing any of us could ever ask for. In embracing human suffering and healing our hearts, compassion breaks down walls and unites all of humanity in the Great One Heart. It is the gateway to our spiritual evolution as a human race. It is the true utopia that we all seek.

Those who choose to cultivate compassion in their lives soon come to learn of the spiritual riches in the Great One Heart, which makes the false riches of the socially constructed, egoistic material world look like plastic, disposable toys. When we come from a place of compassion, we are holding up an ancient light of truth that has been revered throughout history and can never be destroyed. It is the truth that we are One in the Great Matrix of Consciousness. It is the truth that each one of us is a reflection of the Ultimate Reality. This is the core message of the Bodhisattva and the central message of Jesus' teachings as well as many other teachers of compassion. Their teachings are designed to awaken each person to his or her Divine Self and to cultivate a direct connection to Source.

The path of the bodhisattva is indeed a radical call, a call that goes to the roots of our being. Those who choose to implement compassion in their lives are the weavers and the menders, the bridge builders, the integrators, the diplomats and the nurturers. They work in the trenches of our communities in an assortment of vocations. They have embraced their grief and experienced the redemptive power of God's unconditional love. They are the salt of the earth, the lighthouses in the storm that guide us back to our Divine Self. They are the true educators of spirit, the wounded healers, totally perfect in their imperfection because they have been touched by the healing powers of Grace. Their one wish is to awaken all souls to the power within themselves.

It is because of the Great One Heart that the Bodhisattvas of compassion come as humble admirers of the Beloved in others, grateful and joyous, for they know that Love is the only true power. They remind humanity that we have a lot to look forward to. However, we have an immense amount of healing work to be done, for the illusion is much like a weed that wants to strangle out the truth. Bodhisattvas are quite aware of the social injustices in the world and the human ignorance that produces those injustices. They are deeply pained by them all, just as God is pained by it all. However, rather than run from the places of poverty and despair, which most people tend to do, they go directly to these places where "angels fear to tread."

Most of them choose to serve without recognition, blue ribbons and purple hearts. They have chosen the difficult task of opening and healing their hearts so that they can then assist in healing what is broken on larger levels. They don't expect recognition because they know that those who are still suffering are experiencing a spiritual void—a starvation of the soul-- and therefore aren't coming from a place of gratitude. Most of them work in humble servitude and know their human limitations. They don't expect to save the world; this is too heavy of a burden for one person to carry. They do, however, wish to assist in the raising of human consciousness, even if it means working with just a few individuals in their lifetime, for awakening others to their Divine Self is the most powerful source of social change. In this sense, they are radical agents of social change. And while they are the very glue of humanity, most bodhisattvas will never be featured on the cover of a magazine for their humanitarian deeds. In keeping their eyes on God, they know where their true source of recognition comes from.

Some people say that it could take many lifetimes of practicing compassion before one can become an authentic, realized Bodhisattva. Therefore, one must be patient with one's self and practice forgiveness over and over, embracing imperfection and humbly asking for redemption. We can create struggle in our spiritual lives when we compare the images we hold of ourselves with those of enlightened teachers, of figures like Buddha, Jesus, Gandhi, or Mother Theresa. Our heart naturally longs for wholeness, beauty, and perfection. This can be very discouraging, for most of us are not yet masters. Spiritual evolution is a process that will inevitably reveal all of our faults, but this is meant to make us stronger, more humble and teachable.

While it is difficult for us to understand and make judgments about the nature of spiritual evolution, there are a number of paths of service and rites of initiation that one can experience in order to cultivate the Bodhisattva's state of consciousness. Some of the more obvious character traits of the Bodhisattva are humility, joy, empathy, kindness, patience, forgiveness, faith, surrender, gratitude and a commitment to service. Most Bodhisattvas have experienced a dark night of the soul, which is an experience of complete darkness, separation and despair, sometimes involving ego death and rebirth. It is a time of utter pain and disillusionment, where one's sense of self is shattered. However, it is in these places of darkness that the greatest healing can take place; that is, if one is able to see the compassion that lies underneath the pain. It can take many dark nights before one is able to truly see the luminous wisdom that exists in the darkness. Some of us may never embrace the wounded parts of ourselves that exist in the shadows, but if we seek the path of liberation from suffering, healing the wounds of the heart, mind, body and emotions is an essential focus to bring about real internal healing.

Bodhisattva's don't feel the need to draw attention to themselves, because they don't need any validation from others in order to be whole. Fully awakened to their complete and utter dependence on God, their cups are overflowing with love and ecstasy, yet they are intimately connected with experiences of pain and suffering as well as the suffering of others. They understand the weakness of the human spirit and are completely dependent on the Great One Heart. They pray a lot and ask that God will keep their hearts free from the illusion of competition and ego. More importantly, they know that the human race has been forgiven for its ignorance and that God has bestowed the ultimate gift of grace on us. Human suffering and pain are therefore inevitable manifestations of the human drama. Pain can either take us down a road of self-destruction or it can be used as a catalyst for redemption. More often than not, pain is used by God to wake us up so that we can be drawn closer to the central heart or the inner integrity, which is our true destiny.

Another important trait of the Bodhisattva is humility. Bodhisattvas generally avoid self-aggrandizement, a sign of spiritual weakness. They also stay away from self- deprecation, since feelings of both superiority and inferiority are signs of ego imbalance. They have great compassion for those who struggle with low self-esteem because they have experienced the psychological torture that it brings. They also know that it is extremely difficult to see through the illusion of fame and ego, because there are so many incentives on a day to day basis to worship the *maya* of the world. Even the most enlightened humans fall prey to the ways of an insecure ego at times, but they know that going back to source, to self-reflection, prayer and humility will return them to balance. This is the Goddess's promise to all of us; that if we respect and honor the compassionate boundaries that are set for us by our inner spiritual guides, we will not be thrown off-base by the demands of the world.

Awakening the Heart through Art

The world over, art has been used as a compassionate tool to raise consciousness and alleviate suffering. Musicians, writers and artists of all kinds have used their gifts to support the evolution of consciousness, whether by raising money for the poor or as a therapeutic modality to resolve conflicts, heal toxic emotions and bridge gaps in communities. All of the artists and writers in this book have in one way or another devoted their lives to a path of service through art and/or other healing modalities.

If we look at history, we see that most of the great visionaries and prophets were marginalized, particularly women and minorities. While all of the artists in this book have chosen a difficult path, they are also committed to their own spiritual and personal growth. Furthermore, they see the gifts that all of God's children bring to the healing of the planet, and therefore have made a conscious attempt to avoid competition or spiritual elitism. Most of them are doing their own shadow work and understand that awakening doesn't necessarily happen overnight. However, they also understand that the process of awakening involves cultivating a humble heart and what Buddhists refer to as "beginner's mind," which means that they are open to learning from all walks of life. We are all teachers and students in this life. It might take many lifetimes to reach enlightenment, and therefore we can come to accept learning experiences with gratitude. We can greet conflict with open arms and value the life lessons in all relationships. As a result of our ignorance, we need others to help us see our denials or our denied shadows. We simply can't evolve alone.

Heather Taylor: Art as a Sacred Service of Beauty and Goodness

Visionary art is a path of service that involves devotion, reverence and humility. Heather Taylor embodies these characteristics in every way. It is through the sacred geometry of the mandala that she channels and creates beauty, compassion and goodness.

Residing in Olympia, Washington, Heather is a devoted wife and loving mother of three boys. Trained in Art History and Psychology, Heather has always been drawn to the cross-cultural constants that intersect human history. The trinity and alchemy, sacred geometry and numerology—patterns large and small—reveal an innate order imbedded in the natural world. This is the code of creation, personally revealed as the light structure of the matrix of matter. Heather says, "I have seen the exquisite and intricate cathedrals of light that are the building blocks of creation. At times looking at the dirty clothes hamper, a bedroom light or at a sacred site, I could see a pattern so beautiful and complex it could not be conveyed. It lay behind the façade of the mundane world, all the more powerful, as if to say, this apparent chaos (hamper) is actually a profoundly ordered and beautiful miracle." [2]

This understanding of the majesty and mystery of life inspires Heather to listen and look for signs around her—to learn the method of creation from the natural order, rhythms and cycles of the world and to follow the path of service as it reveals itself. Her book, *Love is a Circle,* was written before 9-11 and illustrated beginning 11-11-11 as a demonstration of the light patterns of love that connect us and the cycle of life that is transitioning at this time.

Another fabulous project underway is the creation of 25 murals for the *Hands-On Children's Museum* in Olympia, Washington, where children are taught concepts of conservation based on an appreciation for and stewardship of nature. Heather explains, "Children must go into and identify with the natural world to wish to save it. What would the world be without birdsong, swimming salmon or the height of wind swept trees? There is no greater teacher in compassion than Mother Nature, our Beloved Earth. We must learn from her, sit at her feet with great gratitude in our hearts and humility in our nature." [3]

Heather's painting, *Green Tara Healing,* is an example of true compassion as it was inspired as a service project to support Tibetan nunneries after recent earthquakes. Indigenous women around the world traditionally work with the four sacred elements and the four kingdoms of

Green Tara Healing, Heather Taylor, 24"x36", watercolor, www.fullcirclemandalas.com

Robed Mother, Heather Taylor, 24"x24", watercolor, www.fullcirclemandalas.com

nature in an act of compassionate healing. The women are the intermediaries through prayer and a form of spiritual birthing. Green Tara exemplifies beauty and balance in harmony with the natural world. Through focusing on the serenity of her face, we see the transformative potential of suffering in the liberation of peace.

Another exquisite painting, titled *Robed Mother*, works with the four elements, colors and kingdoms of the manifest world, through a Western tradition—the mother protectress. It is she who shelters those in need, who speaks for the voiceless and champions the weak. The Mother is the intercessor who works on behalf of humanity and the natural world, offering a bridge to spirit and salvation. It is a salvation that is born of compassionate identification with all that is—a willingness to transcend shared suffering through nurturing. So we approach the Father through the compassion of the Mother—she is embodied grace. The Mother is the third aspect of the trinity, the circle divided into four quadrants of earth, air, fire and water.

Heather's iconic mandalas are incredibly potent, imbuing the ancient/future message of hope, catharsis and transformation. The word "mandala" is from the classical Indian language of Sanskrit. Loosely translated to mean "circle," a mandala is far more than a simple shape. It represents wholeness, and can be seen as a model for the organizational structure of life itself--a cosmic diagram that reminds us of our relation to the infinite, the world that extends both beyond and within our bodies and minds. Describing both material and non-material realities, the mandala appears in all aspects of life: the celestial circles we call earth, sun, and moon, as well as the conceptual circles of friends, family, and community. In addition, mandalas are healing for an individual's body, speech, mind and the environment. They are used to enhance the spiritual practice through image and meditation, to overcome suffering through compassion and loving kindness. [4]

Julia Mandala Weaver: Healing Ocean of Light

There are some artists who have taken their practice of loving kindness and compassion to a whole new level. They are messengers of the heart and are healing people on profound emotional levels through the artistic process. Julia Weaver is one of these "heartists," who uses her art as a medium for personal and planetary transformation, and an exhibiting artist who reveals the relationship within our collective consciousness and the interconnectivity of all life. Julia also works as an environmental arts educator, psychotherapist, creative consultant and workshop leader. She has more than thirty years experience combining the arts and cross cultural practices, particularly the creation of mandalas and gardens for individual, community education and global healing. Drawing from her personal experiences of the ocean's healing medicine, Julia urges us to wake up and cherish the ocean as the primordial womb from which we were all born..[5]

While swimming off the Hawaiian coast, Julia had a mystical experience where she spontaneously received mandala images, which took her artwork into deeper dimensions of healing and spiritual practice. An unexpected shamanic death and resurrection occurred, opening a visionary channel in which she received detailed, luminous mandalas. Two weeks later, she began studying with Dr. Judith Cornell, author of *Mandala: Luminous Symbols for Healing*.[6]Julia speaks of this profound visionary experience:

In February 1996, I made my first of many pilgrimages to the Big Island of Hawaii, fulfilling a lifetime desire to swim with dolphins. The first day, I had a mystical experience, which shifted my life and artwork into a deeper dimension of healing and awareness. Waking at sunrise, I went snorkeling at a natural marine sanctuary. The water sparkled and felt invigorating. Thrilled to be alive, I effortlessly swam into the middle of the bay, ever hopeful that the dolphins might appear. I turned to look back at the shore and realized that I was farther away from land than I realized. I was alone with the wild sea and felt so energized and deeply contented.

Moments later, the delight in my aloneness suddenly changed. Adrenaline began coursing through my body and for the first time I was afraid of the ocean. The fear of sharks consumed my attention. Paralyzed, I heard the voice of my spiritual teacher say, 'Let the shark have you!' Timelessly, I imagined my body being torn apart by a large grey shark. I experienced excruciating physical pain and a full range of emotions. The experience continued until I felt my body was utterly devoured. Nothing left. Complete silence. Stillness.

A great peace filled my being and my body was totally at ease. Upon closing my eyes, I had a crystal clear visionary experience. The most beautiful mandala spontaneously appeared before me, perfectly symmetrical and concentric, with rich, vibrant colors illuminating like a stained glass cathedral window. This was a truly profound experience as I never had visions before.

As I gazed into boundless, blue, liquid space, I felt I was given a glimpse of the Infinite. The gift of the mandala from the ocean goddess herself was a symbol of wholeness. Prior to this visionary experience, I had been praying for a vehicle to express my spiritual vision of the whole. Before this, drawing was difficult for me, but the experience of being in the ocean and releasing to her power literally opened my natural ability to create visual art, which I find exists in all my students when they allow the invisible force of life to guide their hearts and hands. [7]

Julia creates mandalas through an energetic visionary process, which combines intention, meditation, prayer, movement and sacred sounds. Visualizing does not come naturally to her. Sensations are translated into emotions, then visual images, and later psychological meaning. Mandalas are vehicles for journeying to the center of one's being. Bridging individual and collective consciousness, they invite participants to rest in the core of their own hearts and, simultaneously, in the heart of the world. Julia expounds on the artistic process:

> *I use black charcoal paper and white pencils. The vast black open space evokes the divine feminine, already pregnant with endless possibilities. For me, the black is synonymous with the ocean's dark mysterious depths, an enduring symbol of the great womb of the living earth.*
>
> *In all religious traditions, the Light of Consciousness (the white) desires to see and be seen. Each mandala is first drawn only with white, symbolizing Oneness. Later comes the colors, or as the Taoist say, 'the 10,000 things', which dissolve back into the white as an expression of the return home. Just drawing the circle on the paper inspires a feeling of relaxation. Now I have a place to rest: a nest for the mystery of my soul to reveal itself. Mandalas are tools for awakening into this present moment; step by step, one pencil stroke at a time, we directly touch here-and-now. For me, each mandala is an invitation to perceive and reveal the Light inherent in all of Life.* [8]

Julia's mandala *Mermaid Dakini (Resting in the Sea of Consciousness)* illuminates a Dakini, which means "Sky Dancer" in the Tibetan Sanskrit language. They are embodiments of enlightened feminine energy and are essential teachers on the path of awakening our Buddhanature. As keepers and revealers of secret teachings, they also permeate and transcend all dimensions. This mermaid Dakini arises from the sea of consciousness. In her upraised right hand, she holds a Dakini knife for cutting through illusion. Her left hand caresses a lotus whose bloom rises from the muddy waters of experience as pure "enlightened" being. She cradles a radiant Buddha child. Her heart, aflame with love, rests both in and on the water in her lotus throne. She celebrates the full sensual embodiment of all the elements: earth, water, fire, air and ether. She is Heaven on Earth.

Another mandala worthy of recognition is *Limitless Ocean of Chi.* Julia speaks of the inspiration behind this profound piece of work:

> *This mandala emerged during a healing crisis, which inspired new capacities of surrender to luminous source of Life. I sobbed my prayers for healing, I grabbed several pencils in each hand and let go of trying to control the outcome. (You can see the result on either side of figure). Soon after, I was guided to study and intensively practice Zhineng Qigong. I was immediately captivated when my teacher (Master Mingtong Gu) began each session invoking an 'Ocean Light' around us in all directions! After a ten- day retreat, I was symptom free of debilitating chronic fatigue for six months.* [9]

Limitless Ocean of Chi, Julia Weaver,
18"x18" pencil on black paper. www.juliamandalaweaver.com

Many of Julia's mandalas honor the ocean, along with dolphins and whales, modeling joy, altruism and healing. Nature has inspired flexibility and service in all areas of her life. As a mother, she often expresses the Goddess as protector, nurturer and healer. Love moved the goddess Tara to vow to reincarnate until all sentient beings experience liberation from suffering. Effortlessly, her vow is ours when we directly and viscerally feel our interconnectedness with all life. Julia intuits that as humans collectively attune to nature, we deepen awareness and respect for our relationship to the Earth and all sentient beings. She believes this transformation is occurring – even in the face of challenging times. Each mandala has been a gift of grace in her life and the lives of others.

Since 1996, Julia has offered mandala workshops for all ages across the US and in the UK, as well as dolphin-swim retreats in Hawaii. Her workshops were featured in *New Age Journal's Body and Soul,* and she co-facilitated a workshop for children with Julia Butterfly Hill and Jane Goodall at the Kinship With All Life conference held in San Francisco. A passionate environmental arts educator, Julia designs and facilitates rites-of-passage ceremonies and combines the mandala process with tree planting or gardens to promote community revitalization and ecological healing. She birthed a long time vision to fa-

Healing, 18"x18" pencil on black paper.
www.juliamandalaweaver.com

Nurturing, Julia Weaver, 18"x18" pencil on black paper.
www.juliamandalaweaver.com

Mermaid Dakini, 18"x18" pencil on black paper.
www.juliamandalaweaver.com

Sanctuary, 18"x18" pencil on black paper.
www.juliamandalaweaver.com

cilitate award winning community based environmental art, that she calls Healing Hearts/Healing Earth, which combines planting fruit trees, herb, and flower mandala gardens with heart-inspired drawings and prayers for personal, community and global healing. She created a series of mandalas to support environmental education organizations. In 2001 she created a 5' x 40' interactive series of peace mandalas called One World, One Heart, One Love, Peace Mandala, which served as a vehicle for community healing after the tragedy 9/11.

Eva Sakmar-Sullivan: Awakening to Love

Another visionary artist inspired by the ocean, Eva Sakmar-Sullivan's visionary art has the ability to elevate the spirit into realms of pure love, peace and joy. Eva is a visionary painter and environmentalist devoted to opening the heart of humanity through magic and mysticism. Her love of animals, the Earth and the Divine Creator is a constant theme in her paintings. She spent time in both the Atlantic and Pacific Oceans swimming with dolphins, sea turtles and observing whales. In fact, she had a profound experience learning to swim with the dolphins in Florida that changed her life forever, so much so that she decided to donate a portion of her art sales to support environmental, animal and humanitarian causes. Eva has won many honors and awards and has exhibited on a national and international level. Her work is on book and magazine covers, tapes, CDs, posters and in private collections. She has written and illustrated several children's books and presented them to local schools through her "Read and Draw with Me" program. [10]

Eva's paintings can be used as a meditative journeying tool for accessing one's own portal to higher dimensions. Eva's mission is that her artwork serves as inspirational tools to joyously facilitate personal and planetary healing, transformation and love. Subjects of her artwork include angels, dolphins, mystic creatures, fairies, goddesses, priestesses and lightworkers. Eva says, "I want to touch people's hearts with my artwork, with hopes of inspiring, empowering or just helping them feel good." [11] She undoubtedly achieves these goals with her artistic and spiritual/intuitive gifts.

Eva's visionary gifts and passion for the healing of the ocean is evident in a painting titled, *Earth Balance Planetary Healing.* Highly activated with intention and love, this painting is extremely powerful and makes one feel a sense of hope that the Goddess is doing her healing work on the planet. Images of the ocean and water can be traced back to the mythology of the Great Mother. Since the beginning of time, humans have identified the ocean with our first home, the maternal womb, birth, death and rebirth. For two-and-a-half billion years on earth, all life forms floated in the womb-like environment of the ocean. Cross-culturally, many creation stories describe the universe as originating within a cosmic egg and the ocean as the intra-uterine sea where the embryo dwells. "Just as the embryo is suspended in the amniotic fluid of the womb, so we are suspended in the invisible matrix of life - perhaps the vastness of 'dark' matter that underlies the phenomenal world" [12] Today the ocean contains an amazing array of life at every depth. Over one million known species of plants and animals live there, and scientists say there may be as many as nine million species we haven't discovered yet.

Another painting that speaks of the great soft spot is titled *From the Heart of God.* We all have experienced this divine love in one way or another, perhaps in meditation, swimming in the ocean with dolphins, taking a walk in nature, creativity, sex and dance. It is a profound unconditional love that no other human love can fulfill. Artists and musicians have portrayed this divine love affair with God, the heart song of longing for the beloved, for it is where our hearts yearn to go and be healed and renewed. This love is much like a child's heart or a dolphin's heart; pure and free of judgment. It is an unwavering love that never abandons or betrays us. It is steadfast and strong like a rock. It calls us the Beloved and invites us to drink from its well of peaceful tranquility. Upon meditating on this image on my altar, I felt the fourth chakra of my heart open on both physical and emotional levels. Profound grief, outpourings of compassion, and then laughter and joy may also arise as the emotional floodgates of the heart are opened. Issues of love, connection, loneliness, and great patterns of the heart surfaced. Eventually, sweetness and love filled my being. The opening of the heart can be slow or fast, occurring one petal at a time or with great explosions of feeling.

Sue Halstenberg: Opening the Heart with Visionary Art

Residing in the hills of Ojai, California, Sue Halstenberg is creating beauty and magic in her community and the world at large. Sue holds a Bachelor of Fine Arts Degree from the prestigious Art Center College of Design in Pasadena and a Signature Membership from the Pastel Society of America. Her original paintings were recently exhibited at Agape International Spiritual Center in Culver City, California, and at the Center of the Heart in Santa Barbara, California. [13]

Since 1992, Sue has been painting metaphysically inspired images with a healing intention. Along with creating and teaching art, she is an astrologer and Angel Therapy Practitioner®, certified by Dr. Doreen Virtue. Since 1996, Doreen has taught thousands of people worldwide how to engage in Angel Therapy. Many of these students have become Angel Therapy Practitioners, who have private practices and give workshops on related topics. "Angel Therapy is a non-denominational spiritual healing method that involves working with a person's guardian angels and archangels to heal and harmonize every aspect of life. Angel Therapy also helps you to more

Earth Balance Planetary Healing, Eva Sakmar-Sullivan, 24"x36" acrylic on canvas. www.stardolphin.com

From The Heart of God, Eva Sakmar-Sullivan, 24"x30" acrylic on canvas. www.stardolphin.com

clearly receive Divine Guidance from the Creator and angels. Everyone has guardian angels, and these angels perform God's will of bringing peace to us all. When we open ourselves to hear our angels' messages, every aspect of our lives becomes more peaceful."[14]

All of Sue's art speaks directly to the heart of the viewer, but there is an image of Kuan Yin that is absolutely breathtaking, titled *Pink Lotus Heart.* Sue speaks of the inspiration for the painting; "I envisioned Goddess Kuan Yin holding a pink lotus at her heart. Her emotion of pure unconditional love expands and unfolds (represented by the large lotus behind her) as it is energized with the focused intention of her clear mind. This unification of heart and mind is also symbolized by the painting's integration of the complimentary colors pink (red tint) and green."[15]

Quan Yin is one of the most universally beloved of deities in the Buddhist and Taoist traditions. Also known as Kuan Yin, Quan'Am (Vietnam), Kannon (Japan), and Kanin (Bali), She is the embodiment of compassionate loving kindness. As the Bodhisattva of Compassion, She hears the cries of all beings. Quan Yin enjoys a strong resonance with the Christian Mary, the Mother of Jesus, Mary Magdalene and the Tibetan goddess Tara.

In many images She is depicted carrying the pearls of illumination. Often Quan Yin is shown pouring a stream of healing water, the "Water of Life," from a small vase. With this water devotees and all living things are blessed with physical and spiritual peace. She holds a sheaf of ripe rice or a bowl of rice seed as a metaphor for fertility and sustenance. The dragon, an ancient symbol for high spirituality, wisdom, strength, and divine powers of transformation, is a common motif found in combination with the Goddess of Mercy.

Quan Yin, as a true Enlightened One or Bodhisattva, vowed to remain in the earthly realms and not enter the heavenly worlds until all other living things have completed their own enlightenment and thus become liberated from the pain-filled cycle of birth, death, and rebirth. Bodhisattvas are dedicated to the universal awakening or enlightenment of everyone. They exist as guides and providers of support to suffering beings. The qualities associated with Kuan Yin are kindness, gentleness, responsiveness, empathy and helpfulness. Below is an excerpt on Kuan Yin from Anne Baring 's book, *The Divine Feminine:*

The image of the primordial Mother was embedded deep within the soul of the Chinese people who, as in Egypt, Sumer and India, turned to her for help and support in time of need. She was particularly close to women who prayed to her for the blessing of children, for a safe delivery in childbirth, for the protection of their families, for the healing of sickness. Their mother goddess was not a remote being but a compassionate, accessible presence in their homes, in the sacred mountains where they went on pilgrimages to her temples and shrines, and in the valleys and vast forests where she could be felt, and sometimes seen. Yet, like the goddesses in other early cultures, she also had cosmic dimensions.

Guardian of the waters, helper of the souls of the dead in their passage to other realms, she was the Great Mother who responded to the cry of all people who called upon her in distress. She was the Spirit of Life itself, deeper than all knowing, caring for suffering humanity, her child. Above all, she was the embodiment of mercy, love, compassion and wisdom, the Protectress of Life. Although she had many names and images in earlier times, these eventually merged into one goddess who was called Kuan Yin - She who hears, She who listens.[16]

Another painting deserving of recognition is *Durga,* a Hindu Goddess who represents the power of the Supreme Being that preserves moral order and righteousness in the creation. The Sanskrit word Durga means a fort or a place that is protected and thus difficult to reach. Durga, also called Divine Mother, protects mankind from evil and misery by destroying evil forces such as selfishness, jealousy, prejudice, hatred, anger, and ego. Sue informs us of the creative process below:

In meditation, I saw Durga's arms merging with the stripes on her tiger's forehead. I painted that image, but the piece didn't feel complete. As I was researching yantras, I came across the 'Nava-yoni Chakra' with its interconnecting triangles. I knew immediately it would fit perfectly in the painting of Durga. The 'Nava-yoni Chakra' symbolizes the imperishable energies of Shiva-Shakti, the dance of opposites that unifies us with the cosmos. Durga's tiger and fiery red clothes signify her fearlessness, as she destroys illusions of separation using all the weapons bestowed on her by the Hindu Gods and Goddesses.[17]

The worship of Goddess Durga is very popular among Hindus. She is also called by many other names, such as Parvati, Ambika, and Kali. In the form of Parvati, She is known as the divine spouse of Lord Shiva and is the mother of Her two sons, Ganesha and Karttikeya, and daughter Jyoti. There are many temples dedicated to Durga's worship in India.

Pink Lotus Heart, Sue Halstenberg, 7″x22″ pastel on paper. www.sue-halstenberg.pixels.com

Durga, Sue Halstenberg, 24"x24" pastel on paper, www.sue-halstenberg.pixels.com

In Her images, Goddess Durga is shown in a female form, wearing red clothes. She has eighteen arms, carrying many objects in Her hands. The red color symbolizes action and the red clothes signify that She is always busy destroying evil and protecting mankind from pain and suffering caused by evil forces.

Melanie Gendron:
The Imaginative Delphic Oracle

Tucked away in the Santa Cruz mountains lives a fabulous artist by the name of Melanie Gendron. She is also a graphic designer and highly sought after spiritual intuitive. She created her own Tarot deck called *Gendron Tarot,* and gives divination card readings to people on a regular basis. She has shown her work in numerous shows and has published her art in books and magazine covers.

Art critics have called Melanie Gendron a "visionary surrealist," and rightly so. Among such surrealists are included the likes of Michelangelo, Tintoretto, Fra Angelico, Giovanni Bellini, Donatello, Jan Van Eyck, El Greco, Luca Signorelli, and a whole range of Late Gothic and High Renaissance artists. In truth, there has hardly been a time that visionary surrealism has not existed in Western and Eastern cultures. The visionary is someone who uses her/his intuition to see what the future may hold. The surrealist is able to perceive beyond what is real or presently embodied in physical form, and then is able to bring that perception into her/his art form. Melanie states; "Living art breathes through the symbiotic relationship of artist and observer, through awareness shared. I explore invisible subtleties inherent in physical manifestation, drawn by the infinite source of creation to express itself." She has this tradition behind her work both technically and philosophically. [18]

Throughout the course of history, a small number of metaphysician-artists have been moved to express their love and knowledge of the Tarot by creating their own Tarot deck. Melanie Gendron is among this group. She is an oracle of the awakened heart, a clear channel of the Ascended Masters and Bodhisattvas. The Tarot is a unique visual instrument that enables us to tune in to the divine and natural forces at work in our lives and the world around us. The Tarot and art go hand in hand. Simply, the Tarot cannot exist without some type of visual image. Furthermore, art, like Tarot, may be employed to represent, and has a way of stimulating, the human mind and imagination in a way nothing else can. It is known among mystics that if one meditates on a symbol long enough, the meaning of that symbol will become clear even if it has never been explained. Not only is Melanie Gendron an outstanding artist, she is also someone who has clearly spent a great deal of time in deep meditation, and as a result of her efforts, offers us an evocative, symbolic vehicle in *The Gendron Tarot.* [19]

Gaia Blessing, Melanie Gendron, www.melaniegendron.com

One of Melanie's masterpieces is a painting titled *Butterfly Woman.* She is an ocean or water goddess and assists with the healing of the heart during painful transitions. The butterfly is a symbol of transformation in various indigenous traditions and has potent medicine for healing. Melanie writes, "Feel the joy and the love that surrounds you when you choose to tap into the energy of the butterfly medicine, and revel in the opportunities and fresh new ideas that come your way. Butterfly signifies courage and a newborn willingness to usher in the changes that bring you closer to creating the new you and the new earth."

Scientific research has shown that the butterfly is the only living being capable of changing entirely its genetic structure during the process of transformation: the caterpillar's DNA is totally different from the butterfly's. Thus, it is the symbol of total transformation. Butterfly Woman's medicine is the never-ending cycle of self-transformation, reincarnation, and magic. To use Butterfly medicine, you must astutely observe your position in the cycle of self-transformation or transmutation. Like butterfly, you are always at a certain station in your life activities. You may be at the egg stage, which is the beginning of all things. This is the stage at which an idea is born, but has not yet become a reality. The larva stage is the point at which you decide to create the idea in the physical world. The cocoon stage involves "going within"; doing or developing your project, idea, or aspect of personality. The final stage of transformation or transmutation is the leaving of the chrysalis and birth. The last step involves sharing the colors and joy of your creation with the world.

Leslie Gibbons: Sacred Altars of Prayer and Peace

A visionary artist and healer who is a walking instrument of peace and loving kindness is a woman by the name of Leslie Gibbons. I am honored to have witnessed her beauty in my life and to be showered by the loving presence of her altars in my home. Not only is she a dear friend, she has also been a mentor and creative life coach, supporting and inspiring my artistic path. She has many fans as she is vibrating so much love, but I would like to think that I am her biggest fan. I have one of her altars on my desk, just under my computer, which has been a source of inspiration through the process of writing and editing this book. Inside a little gold box is an exquisite little butterfly, a symbol of transformation. On the bottom is an inspirational message that reads "Trust

Butterfly Woman, Melanie Gendron, 3'x6' oil on wood panel. www.melaniegendron.com

the Process." Whenever I feel overwhelmed by life or this book project, I look at the altar, take a deep breath and surrender over and over to the divine plan of my life. It is my mojo, so to speak.

There are so many blessings Leslie has to offer the world. She brings over twenty-five years of professional experience as a gifted healing arts facilitator, educator and artist. She has extensive training in indigenous wisdom traditions, Qi-Gong, energy medicine, Reiki, and Eastern meditative practices. She is a certified life coach and licensed Esthetician, offering a unique approach to cultivating a life of loving kindness every day. Leslie has served as an educational consultant in the fields of holistic health/wellness, creative arts and spirituality. She has offered seminars and workshops for schools, universities, hospitals, multicultural centers, wellness retreats, healing centers and health spas throughout the United States. [20]

Leslie's sacred altars and mosaics are some of the most potent I have seen. They deeply nurture the soul with messages of hope, peace, wisdom, transformation, grace and oneness. Altars serve as a sacred place for prayer, meditation and devotion. They are imbued with a collection of powerful symbols to honor Spirit and channel divine wisdom. The meaning of the word altar is "high place," which indicates the most important aspect of the altar – to serve as a connection point between you and the divine. Spiritually, altars should express and encourage a personal relationship with divine consciousness. Leslie's altars contain symbolism and earth elements that emit certain frequencies or vibrations, such as an animal totem, a statue of a guardian angel, or an amulet that has special meaning. Stones and crystals that are known to promote higher spiritual awareness (ametrine, amethyst, fluorite, opal, obsidian, etc.) are a wonderful and powerful element in her altars, as well as flowers, bones and sea shells. The center pieces are often statues of the Buddha, Mary Magdalene, the Virgin of Guadalupe, Tara and Quan Yin, to name just a few. Leslie talks about her altars in more detail:

> *I have always been deeply drawn and inspired by sacred art from around the world and the journey of creativity and awakening shared by all people and cultures. I invite you to experience my artwork as a meditative-gateway into the divine intelligence within and all around us. Altars exude a morphic field of consciousness and the symbolism transmits certain vibrational frequencies and archetypal energies. They tap into living libraries of consciousness and transmit teachings that assist with awakening and healing. If your intention is to cultivate more peace, meditating with a Buddha is the solution matrix—it will work on your subconscious to produce the desired result. When I am creating an altar, I meditate on the heart essence and set an intention for the piece. I am talking with my spirit guides and Ascended Masters and they transmit the codes of universal heart wisdom through my heart and hands. Their essence is embodied in the symbolism, and we play together. They wink at me when I am in my inner child, totally open and free. It is through the gift of the child's heart that they shine the brightest. I am so blessed to be a channel of this divine wisdom.* [21]

Leslie doesn't limit herself in her creative expressions, and she seems to be fueled by the universal heart medicine, as she is a gifted intuitive and emotional empath. The alter *Virgin of Guadalupe* is an exquisite example of the sweetness of the Beloved coming through Leslie's keen intuition. The Virgin of Guadalupe is a powerful cultural symbol of Mexican identity and nationhood. José Guadalupe Posada, the Mexican muralists and other artists have used this image for its liberationist and powerful meanings. In the 1960s César Chavez marched with the image when The United Farm Workers went on strike. There is an ongoing attempt to rediscover the "indigenous" origins of Guadalupe, depicting her as an embodiment of Tonantzin-Coatlicue, goddess of the cosmos, sacred guardian and mother image for the Mexican nation. [22]

Various female artists have mined its potential as a feminine symbol of empowerment. In the nineties, the appeal of Guadalupe/Tonantzin is evident in Chicana feminist writing in which the Virgin/Goddess has been enlisted against the patriarchy. In the 1996 collection *Goddess of the Americas,* the Virgin of Guadalupe is a complex, mystical and transcendent spiritual figure who evokes the pre-Hispanic cosmos and is also linked to African Orishas and other female deities. Mary is not only the Queen of Heaven and a source of emotive power, but she is the female goddess life-giver who empowers feminists who seek the female face of God. [23]

Another alter dripping with love is *Green Mother Mary, Divine Mother of Compassion.* This particular version of Mother Mary is highlighted by a sage green and gold mosaic embodying the energies of the earth and healing on the earth plane. Mary is integrating (prayer mudra) heaven and earth in her transmission/emanation. She radiates a pure, yet deeply grounded ancient wisdom related to Gaia and the healing frequencies of nature. She is crowned with a vintage jewel of green laurel and copper leaves, and veiled in a tapestry surrounded by embedded pearls (pearls of wisdom gained

Virgen of Guadalupe, Leslie Gibbons, 12″x 18″ Mosaic on wood, www.sacredcreativity.com

Green Mother Mary, Leslie Gibbons, 12x18" Mosaic triptych on wood incorporating vintage shards; pearls, buttons. www.sacredcreativity.com

through suffering) and shards of blue-green, symbolizing the heart broken open by compassion for all beings. She is offering the medicine of an awakened heart deeply inspired to serve humanity through healing actions in the world. She is a vibrant alternative to the more traditional "celestial-blue Mary of the heavens" in that she serves through direct earthy embodiment of living compassion in day to day life.

It is such a joy to witness the Great One Heart bursting forth in the hearts of so many gifted artists. It is this love that will save the planet. It is this love that will heal and redeem humanity. It is this compassionate love that we must offer to ourselves and to ot

Victoria Christian is a sociologist, social worker, counselor, artist, writer and sacred activist. She holds undergraduate and Masters degrees in Sociology. She also has a Masters of Social Work, with an emphasis in the sociology of gender, social theory, the sociology of art and ecofeminism. For more information about her art, books and DVD's, you can view her website at www.victoriachristian.com. To learn more about this book, see the website: www.mysticspiritart.com

Dark Night of the Madonna, Turiya Bruce, 91″ x 107″ oil on canvas. www.turiyabruce.com

Compassion

By Susan Stedman

One time amid the dark of night
My mind recalled an inner sight
A ragged child, with cries unfurled
Creates a scene, this little girl,
Amid my local grocery store,
Whilst I was shopping, doing chores
Her mom looks tired, her nerves are frayed
She looks at me and meets my gaze
Her shoulders heave and then she sighs
I turn my head and pass her by

Then off to get a bite to eat
I see a beggar on the street
His clothes are torn, his face unshaved
I knew 'twas but some coins he craved
But my heart closed, my mind recoiled
I would not touch his hands so soiled

Yet now I lie here wide awake
And toss and turn and contemplate
How little effort it would take
For me to smile and wish them well
In moments that for them were hell
And all they needed was a heart
That felt for them and took their part

For even if I did no more
Than smile at them and let them see
I honored their humanity
And knew that, just the same as me,
Their souls would live eternally,
That might have been just one small spark
To light that moment oh so dark
And let them feel for one brief time
The beauty of their souls sublime
Because they saw from my two eyes
A look that made them realize
That they were loved and not despised

The Heart of the Mother

By Grace Mantle Sorensen

Oh Great Mother, as I reveal myself, I unveil you.
May your features be maps to the Infinite
for searching fingers in the darkness.
May the heart of your radiance
be felt through the colors of my brushstrokes
and the ink of my pen.
I am made free through your reflection.

ReCall Totem: Red Tailed Hawk

I am one who has searched in desperation for the light, crying for rescue while all the while holding up a sword and shield to protect myself from it. Now here before you, in these paintings, is a mirror of my journey home into the heart of God. Through the process of their creation, and by God's grace, I learned to lay down my weapons and to trust in the infinite, nurturing love of the Divine Mother.

Knowing that I am a woman made in the image of God, I turned in my searching to the feminine aspect of the One. I reached out my hands and called her to me, asking for her love and healing to lift me from my misery. To my great surprise, she answered me by appearing directly in my dreams and in waking visions. I took up my skills as an artist and Reiki master, and set about to translate what I saw, heard, and felt into works of art in chalk, watercolor, ink, and pencil. God, in the form of Divine Mother, healed me and taught me as her images revealed themselves under my fingers. With each movement of my hand and eyes, she led me out of my illusions and fears and into her loving heart.

In awe, I gave back to her through my prayers, that the healing I was receiving would also be given to all of humanity and to the Earth herself. Creating these paintings was a deeply humbling and empowering way for me to awaken, and I offer these gifts in gratitude. This is only the beginning...

Let There be Peace in Our Hearts

I am the One, Remember Me?
I wrap my arms around your every wound
I breathe into your frozen places
I wrap you in my confidence.
Come; gather yourself and your tears,
Lay down your fears.
I am here again--never left--
To hold you.

Resurrection Totem: Vulture

Shattering my myth of godlessness, I was called out of my soul's sleeping the week after 9/11 by a powerful waking vision of transcended light. Not knowing where my journey would take me, I set out to answer the call as best I could. I pulled my art tools from storage, and with six feet of art paper nailed to the barn wall in which I was living, began my quest.

Words cannot begin to tell you the power of the winds that blew through me in those days of unfolding vision. I worked in tremulous awe at what I had been called to do. I rooted the energy in the painting's heart through Reiki and prayer, sealing its mandala as the seed frequency from which all else would evolve. From there, God revealed herself to me in ever-radiant forms. She appeared as all-encompassing love, non-judgment, and unshakable totality of Presence. Ultimately neither male nor female, yet both, this One that is God reached out with a powerful embrace, taking me in along with each one of the many souls who flew from their bodies on that morning.

The day came when I had to look at their faces--the many who ran to safety, and the many more who would never again be found in their physical form. For three days I dove into this underworld through photos in magazines and newspapers. Then through sage-smoke prayers and thick tears, I began to translate the images and emotions into chalk on paper. This experience became also my own agony, my own translation into dust and black. My own demons lay in that smoke and fear. Faced with such horror, I was forced to look deep into the eyes of my own petrified darkness, and to raise myself up through the fierceness of my determination. God bless the help that I was given, for I could not have passed through those veils alone. I was pulled from the cave of my false sense of self, out of the darkness of my personal misery, and was received by the enfolding heart of God.

The final prayer was the action of applying green henna from the Middle East to the olives of peace carried by the white dove--peace for the world, peace for myself, peace for the collective consciousness of humankind.

Then completion. With shattered illusions of self falling all around me, I raced to expose my discovery to a world that was not ready for me. I was received by some,

"Let There be Peace in Our Hearts", by Grace Mantle Sorensen, 3' x 6' pastel, ink, watercolor, ash,henna on sanded pastel paper, 2001. www.gracemantlestudios.com

rejected by others, and was eventually shown clearly that it simply was not the time for my co-creation with God to be presented on the scale that I had perceived. When I was able to release my beliefs, God took my hand, as a Mother to a child, and led me into a deeper search with her through my artwork.

Ma Mary

"Hail Mary, full of Grace,
The Lord is with thee.
Blessed art Thou among women, And
Blessed is the Fruit of thy Womb, Jesus.
Holy Mary, Mother of us all,
Blend with us, your Children of the Sun/Son,
For we have consciously won our Ascension,
Right now and Forevermore, I AM!"
Mary-Ma McChrist

Re-Search Totem: Golden Eagle

Spring came to me then in a mountain home, and with it came the desire for Mary. I ran to the Mother I had met at seventeen in the Paris Notre Dame cathedral. I had felt her there as I knelt before her statue, surrounded by candles and flowers, and the tears had moved down my cheeks as my heart remembered her. I knew her to be the Divine Mother of Jesus, the essence of the pre-Christian Great Mother, and a woman who had walked the Earth and known its griefs and fears. She would be able to understand me and take me in.

I prepared the paper, praying for her guidance. Her heart came to me first, a merging of East and West--Jewish, Buddhist, Christian, and Native American traditions. The crystalline core of her heart radiated out to me a peace I had only briefly touched in the past. Mary showed me her flaming sacred heart of love in a new way, one that promised healing to me as a woman.

She began to talk to me in a voice of love resonating in my heart that first terrified me, then soothed and grounded me. She spoke to me of her mission to heal love relationships between men and women, and to bring sexuality back to its sacred standing as God's gift of Unified One-ness experienced and realized. She spoke of the children of the world and of her desire that each one be fully embraced, loved, cared for and protected. She helped me to understand that the deepest purpose of human existence is joyous love, and that the path of marriage and family is meant to be a sacred and ecstatic experience with God.

As I began to relax, I found her heart to be vast beyond comprehension, and the depth of her giving washed over me in gentle waves of compassionate grace. Reaching out her hands to me, she offered me more than I could begin to imagine. I was compelled to move forward in a new way; that of surrender and of trust.

As my brush traced the outlines of her image and words, Mary's resonant frequencies traced the lines of my body and soul. She taught me the true meaning of the "Immaculate Conception"; that this really refers to the "Immaculate Concept". This is the vision of perfection that she holds within her heart for all of humanity, to lift up and embrace the individual and collective radiant truth of our Beingness as God's Divine Creations. Mary literally holds the blueprint of our perfection in her heart of hearts, as she did for her son Jesus while on his Earthly sojourn.

While creating the "Peace" painting, God drew me into the all-encompassing heart of love's presence. However, in painting the Divine Mother as Mary, her heart radiated out to meet me. She literally stepped out of the painting in etheric form and ministered to me in selfless mastery of love, as well as to others who were drawn to my studio during this time.

I began to experience compassionate grace beyond imagining, yet there were deeper layers for me to understand.

"Ma Mary", by Grace Mantle Sorensen, 39"x59" pastel, ink, watercolor, on sanded pastel paper, 2002.
www.gracemantlestudios.com

Makuahine o' ka La'a Aina/ Mother Maui

For I am the light of the world
I am the Divine Giver, the Radiant One.
I am Ascended Earth, Mama Gaia.
Deep within the crystal core of my blessed body I sit
Radiating goodness and light.
I emit signals of peaceful union in bliss,
Safe place to rest,
Radiance blessed.
Aloha e aloha e aloha e aloha

Re-Creation Totem: WhiteOwl/Pueo

My own darkness again enveloped me as questions surged up inside. My mind and memory fought with the mother of Jesus at the same time as she caressed me. I needed to know the Great Mother as the Earth Tribe people know her. My warrior self furiously demanded answers, as the resonance of violence by "Christians" vibrated in my being. Blackfoot, Wiccan, African--whether from past lives, genetic memory, or global consciousness, these and all Earth people's pain called to me in my blood and bones. I sunk down again, seeking truth.

The island of Maui called me this time, with ancient eyes in dreamtime's flight. Her jungle haven opened to me, and I slept and walked in respectful awe on her living body. Her pulsing waves of Earth energy rocked me, forcing me to let go of my pain, like a waterfall in an island rain. Mary's nurturing presence, too, was everywhere in this Christianized home of Earth Tribe peoples. I felt my body become one with the Mother and with the island—Aina, the bliss of Oneness--and the beginnings of understanding welled within me.

Twice above me, in magnificent, enormous form, the Mother appeared to me over her island, rainbows stretching out around her as jewels in sunlight. I was dumbstruck by her massive beauty. She led me to her mountaintop where, alone in the gap of her ancient volcanic flow, I rode her swelling Earth-frequency waves as best I could while I painted her image. Through the winds of her heart, this Mother took me hurtling through the genetic lines of my own and all Earth-people's pain, lighting up our collective DNA like blue liquid fire. A cosmic vastness of Being was revealed to me as I floated like a leaf on these overwhelming currents.

At the same time, Mary and Jesus spoke to me, and I soon came to understand what I had instinctively known; that there is no separation at all between the frequencies of Mother Earth and Christ consciousness. I was shown the truth, in gigantic beauty beyond words, that our precious Mother Earth is herself an ascending Angel.

The culmination of my understanding of Divine Mother's deep nature came in a moment of gentle bliss when in my heart I felt the union of perfect Love. Giving and receiving became one, as my heart and the Mother's heart met and merged in pulsing ecstasy. Her abundance met my desire, and together there was a harmony that surprised me in its quiet softness. In this moment I learned to rest in the Mother's compassionate grace and infinite power. At last, I chose to lay down my weapons of defense and to surrender to her loving care.

Throughout the creation of all of these paintings, I was given gifts beyond measure. I learned beyond a doubt that our Sweet Mother is present in every moment. She hears our hearts calling, and blesses us with her Love. Our task is simply to accept her and what she has to offer us. In the words of Mother Mary when first she appeared to me:

"Why are you so afraid, Daughter? You have called and I have come!"

Grace Mantle Sorensen is a natural artist who was blessed to have an artistic mother and so was drawing and painting as soon as she could hold a pencil. She was always encouraged to pursue her talent, and was given many opportunities to do so. She earned a Bachelors degree in Fine Arts from the University of Oregon, studied in France with Parsons School of Design NY, and apprenticed for eight years with NYC sculptor A. Bruce Hoheb. Grace's spiritual seeking led her to become a Tanran Reiki master with William Bagley, and this has deeply influenced her work. As a woman artist, Grace has sought to understand the Divine through the feminine, and knows that as she did this work for herself, she did it for all women who may not have had the same opportunities. Her work has been published and shown in many forms, including in the Wemoon calendar, the Ministry for the Arts catalog, and by Ascension Mastery International. She is honored to be a part of this book's collection. Grace currently lives in the Northwest with her husband and child. Visit her website: www.gracemantlestudios.com

"Makuahine o'ka La'a Aina/ Mother Maui", by Grace Mantle Sorensen, 30" x 40" pastel, watercolor on sanded pastel paper, 2004.
www.gracemantlestudios.com

Tara: The Savioress

Chenrezig, Buddha of Compassion, Sherab Khandro, 44"x44", acrylic on canvas. www.sherabkhandro.com

By Sherab "Shey" Khandro

Chenrezig, the Buddha of Compassion, sat in quiet meditation looking out at the world. His heart broke. Tears of compassion welled in his eyes as he contemplated the depth of suffering experienced by the countless beings he saw there. The Goddess Tara sprang forth from his tears, responding as a mother would respond to the needs of her children.

Through the centuries, artists have portrayed the image of Tara in many forms. She is the quintessential expression of motherly compassion; Goddess of prosperity, longevity, loving mother, source of comfort, relied on to help us overcome our fears. She is a wish- fulfilling source of profound blessing.

Tara might even be understood as the original feminist. The tale is told of a time many eons ago when Tara was a princess and followed the teachings of the Buddha with great devotion. She studied and prayed with much determination. The result of her efforts gave birth to the pure heart of the Bodhichitta: the compassionate motivation to attain Enlightenment for the sake of benefiting others. The monks observed the greatness of her potential and recommended that she pray to be reborn in a future life as a man to insure her spiritual accomplishment. Tara responded from the depth of her spiritual understanding saying:

> *"There is no man, there is no woman, No self, no person, and no consciousness. Labeling 'male' or 'female' has no essence, But deceives the world."*

Tara knew that in her time women who displayed the qualities of supreme accomplishment were rare. She vowed that she would always return as a woman, she would serve as an example to others of the truth of our equality.

It is important to note that from the Buddhist perspective male and female refers not merely to the distinction of our bodily form but to the more profound spiritual qualities of Wisdom and Compassion. The female expresses transcendental Wisdom, the recognition of the true nature of all phenomenon, free of any fixed, inherent existence. The male expresses universal Compassion or skillful means. This is the activity of Wisdom: generosity, ethics, patience, effort, and meditation. Together the pure qualities of Wisdom and Compassion are none other than the display of the Enlightened mind.

The mystical qualities of the divine feminine are multi-faceted and layered with meaning. The soft motherly aspect of Tara reflects a strength that is familiar and comforting. Her peaceful countenance and beatific smile calls forth feelings of warmth, safety and nurturing. Yet compassion in its Wisdom display has many faces. The wrathful aspect, Vajravarahi, reflects a fierce, fiery, passionate display of profound love. She will stop at nothing to save us from the poisons that bind us to our suffering. She is compassion in action; it's very movement through the shadows of our mind.

The creation of these images, whether they are female, male, peaceful or wrathful, is more than an artistic expression. According to the teachings of the Buddha, these images are in truth a living display of the Enlightened mind, an active wish to bring an end of suffering for all beings. The images are said to be the presence of the Buddha Himself (or Herself) in the world, a pure display of all the Buddha represents. The roots of these expressions extend deep into the Tibetan Buddhist tradition, tracing back to the time of Shakyamuni Buddha, over 2500 years ago. Proper proportions and details necessary to the composition are explained in the sacred texts that can be traced back through an unbroken lineage. Adherence to these prescriptions is said to be of inestimable benefit to the art, the artist and those who experience the work.

Having studied as a Buddhist nun in the Tibetan tradition for fifteen years, I have gained a deeper under-

Mother Tara: Angel of Peace, Sherab Khandro, 3'x 7' acrylic on canvas. www.sherabkhandro.com

Vajravarahi: Dance of the Red Dakini, Sherab Khandro, 3′ x 6′ acrylic on canvas. www.sherabkhandro.com

standing of the qualities and mindfulness this work requires. I adhere strictly to the instructions set forth by the tradi- tional masters with whom I formally trained. There are a number of "worthy qualities" the artist must cultivate. According to the text written by Tibetan master painter Gega Lama: "The artist must be skilled in drawing and well versed in correct proportions and they must maintain properly the lineage of artistic transmission and technique. They must understand the characteristics of the deities and portray all elements of the composition faithfully: ornaments, gestures and so forth. In addition to what might be expected, the artist must be restrained of disposition, having respect for the divine images. They must be compassionate and patient in all circumstances. Although they must be skilled in the arts, they must be without vanity regarding their skill. Slow to anger, have little concern for the wealth of others, bathe regularly and be scrupulous of conduct: no lying, stealing, or deceiving others, are qualities the artist aspires to. The artist is also expected to devote increasing energy to the creation of these images."

Before a painting or sculpture is begun, a ceremony is performed to purify the canvas and to bless the pigments and the brushes. The tools for creating sacred images of the Buddha are then considered sacred themselves. They are treated with respect, never left on the floor, left in a disrespectful state or stepped over. They are kept nicely as it is understood that the image of the Buddha arises from them, flowing through the artist, through the tools and into the world for the benefit of all beings. They are regarded as implements of spiritual practice.

I begin a painting by priming the canvas with four coats of gesso. Each coat is offered to one of the four sources of refuge within this Buddhist tradition: the lama (one's spiritual teacher in this life), the Buddha (the Enlightened mind), the Dharma (the teachings of the Buddha) and the Sangha (the spiritual community). Each coat is dedicated to the long life of our pure teachers and the swift spread of their miraculous activities. The canvas is lightly sanded between coats with prayers to smooth the way for all beings to find true happiness.

Work on the drawing begins on an auspicious day in the Tibetan calendar. The day is chosen based on the subject of the particular piece of art and its relation to the Tibetan liturgical calendar. The work is most often begun on the new moon, aligning one's efforts with the energy of the growing phase. Once the canvas is ready, a pale gold letter from the Tibetan alphabet (a seed syllable) is painted at the heart center of the deity. The syllables in the Tibetan language carry a profound blessing, as it is a language that was created for spiritual purpose.

This golden letter represents the essence of the image being created. As a practitioner, I visualize myself arising from this same seed syllable. Arising as the deity, I am then the deity painting the deity. Through this practice I seek to awaken the understanding of non-duality or inseparability of my own nature and that of the Buddha I paint.

The prescribed proportions are one of the significant elements that support the spiritual foundation of these images. They are linked to that which is ancient and profound. In this tradition we understand that these proportions were laid down by the Enlightened mind for the purpose of reflecting in the world the Enlightened qualities of the Buddha: compassion, loving kindness, equanimity and joy. The image is carefully sketched in place. Each element of the painting—color, ritual implements, facial expression, mudras (hand gestures)—are researched for accuracy and meaning. It is important that the artist understand the nature and meaning of this work. It is important that the artist understands that the image arises purely as a result of her/his altruistic intention and depth of understanding of the nature of this work. The creation of this work is a spiritual practice dedicated to the benefit of all. Whether the viewer understands it or not, the blessing is there and is received.

Once the drawing of the deity and the background are complete and I am satisfied, color is introduced. I have chosen the neo-impressionistic style of pointillism, tiny dots of color that create rich and vibrant imagery. There is a blending here of the Eastern philosophy and a western painting style.

I am blessed to be one of the early western artists to receive formal training in bringing forth this art in the traditional way they have been doing so in Tibet for cen-

Red Tara: Tara of the Bodhichitta, Sherab Khandro, 28"x34", acrylic on canvas. www.sherabkhandro.com

turies. As part of pioneering the western Tibetan art movement, I have developed a style using western techniques and materials. In both my pointillist paintings and bronze sculptures I have attempted to create a contemporary appeal, yet stay true to the Tibetan art philosophy. With each stroke of the brush comes a prayer of compassion. Each dot is offered as a jeweled universe, a prayer to the Buddha to end suffering in the world. Many layers of pure color are applied to the canvas. After months of finely crafting each element of the composition, the image of the Buddha arises as a rainbow display, appearing as colored points of light. Countless dots give the viewer a sense that the quality of the image is real but not solid. The rainbow display and the impression of insubstantiality are both qualities ascribed to the Buddha's divine appearance. The work becomes a meditation for artist and viewer, a mandala offering, an invocation to the Buddha to bring the blessing of his appearance to the world.

A truly sacred expression in the arts is a powerful force that brings great blessings and much benefit to the world. Among the many elements that contribute to the creation of sacred Buddhist art there are two that are essential. The first is that the artist must establish the intention that her work is being created for a purpose greater than herself, a purpose that will bring benefit to all beings. Prayers are made throughout the process of creation. The second essential element is that the painting or sculpture must be consecrated. This is done using the syllables OM, AH, HUNG in Tibetan or Sanskrit. For a painting, they are inscribed on the back, corresponding to the placement of the head, throat and heart. For a sculpture, they are placed inside as rolled prayers, also corresponding to the three places.

The presence of these syllables carries a profound benefit; blessings of the Body (OM), Speech (AH) and Mind (HUNG) of the Buddhas. Together they radiate the pure and profound qualities of the fully Enlightened mind. Resonating with our own pure qualities, they act as a catalyst, bringing forth the greatest potential of our own hearts.

Now the image is complete. Images of the Buddha in his/her many forms are regarded as living presences; therefore, they are treated with great respect. They are kept respectfully in a clean place. They are never placed where one's feet will point directly at them. These images are in truth a display of the pure qualities of Wisdom and Compassion in the world. They manifest solely for the purpose of guiding each of us, all living beings, to freedom, the ultimate end of our suffering.

Art is a voice, a sacred song, a prayer, a channel of energy taking form in the world. It is an expression of the heart. It stimulates our thoughts, stimulates our conversation. We ask ourselves, where is my compassion? Am I loving and kind? How do I speak to the needs of the world? Can I take action? Will I take action? This movement within our being, this stirring of the heart, this is the appearance of the true mother, this is Tara within each of us, goddess of compassion, angel of peace, divine mother, unfailing spiritual guide. This inspiration is the blessing of Tara bringing healing to the world.

Sherab "Shey" Khandro, a celebrated artist, speaker, and author of *Creating a Healing Universe,* is one of only a few Western artists to receive formal training in the spiritual arts from Tibetan masters. After spending 15 years as a Tibetan Buddhist nun, she served as artistic director for Kunzang Palyul Choeling, a Tibetan Buddhist center for practice and study in Maryland and Arizona. Many of Khandro's paintings and sculptures can be seen in private collections and galleries, or as part of sacred Buddhist monuments called stupas. To create the rich and vibrant imagery in her paintings, Khandro uses a neo-impressionist style of pointillism. As she deepens the intent of her Bodhisattva vow, each stroke of her brush holds a prayer of compassion. Each dot is offered as a jeweled universe, a prayer to end suffering in the world. Sherab Khandro is committed to living from her heart and inspires others to do the same through workshops and lectures on the spiritual arts and intentional living, which she leads across the country. Visit her website at: www.sherabkhandro.com

Green Tara, Sue Halstenberg, www.sue-halstenberg.pixels.com

CHAPTER FIVE:

The Goddess of Wisdom

The Sacred Feminine and Global Transformation

Gaia, Suzanne De Veuve, 20x24, Acrylic on canvas, www.suzannedeveuve.com

By Llewellyn Vaughn Lee

The feminine holds the mystery of creation. This simple and primordial truth is often overlooked, but at this time of global crisis, which also carries the seeds of a global transformation, we need to reawaken to the spiritual power and potential of the feminine. Without the feminine nothing new can be born, nothing new can come into existence—we will remain caught in the materialistic images of life that are polluting our planet and desecrating our souls.

We see around us a world being destroyed by greed and consumerism, and feel within us the hunger of our soul for a way of life that acknowledges the sacred within all of life. And deeper, there is the cry of the soul of the world, the primal cry that comes from the depths of creation when the divine light that belongs to life is being lost. At this time we need to reclaim what has been denied, what has been abandoned in the pursuit of our materialistic dreams. We need to return to the core of our being, to where the sacred comes into existence. And the mystical feminine holds the key to this work of redemption and transformation.

The last era has denied women access to their real power. The patriarchy systematically repressed the power of the goddess and the mystical teachings of the feminine. And yet this wisdom is still present, just as is the deep knowing every woman has of the interconnectedness of all of life. And every woman carries in her spiritual centers the sacred light of creation. Without this light she could not conceive and give birth, she could not participate in the greatest mystery of bringing a soul into life: giving the spiritual light of a soul a physical form out of the substance of her own body. Men do not have this sacred light within them in the same way; they have to purify and transform themselves to gain access to it. For a woman it is always present.

But women have to recognize their true spiritual nature and the transformative potential they carry within them, so that they can offer it back to life—for without its light the world will slowly die. The world needs the presence of women who are awake to their spiritual light, and who can work with the substance of life in order to heal and transform it. The last era has created a separation between matter and spirit, and so matter has forgotten its sacred nature, its ability to transform. Life itself has become caught in the abusive thought-forms of the masculine that seek to dominate through power. Life needs to be freed of these constrictions, and matter itself needs to be reconnected to its spiritual potential. This is a work that belongs to women, to those who know the sacred nature of life and how to bring light into matter, just as they instinctively know how to bring a soul into this physical world. For a woman the physical and spiritual worlds can never be separate: she carries the light of the world within the cells of her body; her sexuality is a sacred offering to the goddess. But she needs to consciously recognize this divine potential and deep knowing, so that she can live it in service to life and the need of the time.

For many centuries this spiritual knowing has been kept as a secret, hidden in order to protect it from the soldiers of the patriarchy and a church that repressed and persecuted the sacred feminine. Now many women are awakening to their natural spirituality, to their birthright, and also to the ancient tradition of feminine wisdom. They are seeking to reconnect to the sacred feminine in different ways, through creativity, healing, personal transformation, and other ways of empowerment.

Qualities of Feminine Wisdom

There are many different qualities of feminine wisdom, from the understanding of the healing power of herbs to the deep, lived knowledge of the feminine nature of the soul's relationship with God, the soul's true state of receptivity to the divine. So many of these qualities have been lost; so many priestesses have been killed, wise women burned. And yet the real wisdom remains, because it belongs to life itself. In the cells and in the soul of every woman this ancient knowing is waiting to be awakened, so that once again the sacred feminine can make her contribution, can help the world come alive with love and joy.

Women know the wisdom of receptivity, of holding a sacred space. They experience this in their bodies through the wonder of pregnancy; but the sacred feminine also knows how this works within the soul, how within the heart love and longing create a space for the divine to be born. Rumi describes this eternal mystery of longing:

Sorrow for His sake is a treasure in my heart.
My heart is light upon light,
a beautiful Mary with Jesus in the womb.

Safe In Her Arms, Atmara Rebecca Cloe, 12"x12" digital image.
www.nwcreations.com

The feminine mysteries of love—the sanctity of longing, the receptivity of the heart that is always awake, waiting for her Beloved, for that moment when love comes secretly and sweetly—need to be reclaimed and honored. Only through receptivity can we give birth to the divine as a living presence within ourselves and within our life.

Women also know the importance of being rather than doing. We are addicted to activity, and have lost access to the primal power that comes from the still center of ourself. We think that the problems of the world and of ourselves can only be solved through "doing," not realizing that it is this focus on ceaseless activity that has created much of our present imbalance. Rather than always asking, "What should I do?," we can learn to reflect, "How should I be?" From this quality of being we listen, are attentive and aware. Through this simple but essential attitude, balance can return and a natural healing take place.

Just as a mother instinctively knows how to listen to her children so that she can respond to their real needs, so does the sacred feminine know how to listen inwardly and outwardly to life, to experience and participate in this sacred mystery of which we are a part. Then we can make a real relationship to life and to our soul, learn to live the life of the soul rather than the illusory life of the ego.

An understanding of relationships belongs to the feminine. Feminine wisdom understands the way connections between people, and the interconnectivity of life itself, hold something essential. Without these connections life cannot sustain itself. The sense of separation and isolation that our masculine culture has created is damaging and deeply painful. Because women are closer to creation than men are, they are more awake to the sorrow of the earth and can hear more clearly its cry of despair as our present culture continues to desecrate and pollute it. They know that this cannot continue much longer, that the light that belongs to life's sacred nature is being lost and that without this light nothing new can be born, there can be no transformation of life or human consciousness.

The innate wisdom of the feminine is needed to repair the damage we have done and to reconnect with what is sacred and essential within ourselves and within life. We need to understand our part within the sacred web of life, and how to relate once again to this primal wholeness that is a direct expression of the oneness of the divine.

It may be painful to be fully present, to hold this sacred connection with life, the earth, and our own soul. But without the presence of the sacred feminine and those who honor it within themselves, an essential substance

Meditation, Cathy McClelland, www.cathymcclelland.com

will be lost to life. The spark of the divine that connects the creation to the Creator—the spark that holds the mystery of creation and the divine purpose of everything, every butterfly, every stone, the laughter of every child, and every lover's tear—will begin to dim.

Symbolic Consciousness

Listening is an essential quality of receptivity. We need to learn to listen, to be inwardly and outwardly attentive, watching the signs that tell the real story of life. In our present masculine culture we are often too busy to listen to what life and the Beloved are trying to tell us. Instead we are caught in superficial experiences, and so we miss the meaning, the real purpose of our soul's life. Life is a direct expression of the divine, but unless we listen to this hidden presence, we experience only the distortions of our ego-self, its desires and anxieties. Life and the soul are always beckoning us, wanting to share the real wonder of being alive.

When we really listen we find ourselves present in another world full of meaning and magic. Then the signs within our outer life and in our dreams can speak to us, and take us on a journey far beyond the limited world of the ego. They open a door to the symbolic world that is just beneath the surface. It is from this inner dimension of images and symbols that the soul is nourished. Recognizing and working with symbols requires an attitude of receptivity that allows the symbols to communicate in their own language. We come to know this ancient part of ourselves that is fully alive and knows the deeper destiny of our soul. And it is from this inner world that our everyday life too is nourished and we are given the direction we need.

When we work with the images of the inner world, a mysterious alchemy takes place as the conscious and unconscious come together, a coniunction of opposites. The symbolic world opens us to a depth of meaning beyond our conscious self, to the archetypal world of the gods, where we can gain access to the way these powerful energies can work within our inner and outer lives. Then we begin the real work of the soul, a transformation that takes place in the very depths of our being that expands our consciousness and enriches our daily life with a deep sense of purpose. Each of us has our own journey to make, our own exploration of the inner world, and we are drawn into this dimension through different doorways: dreamwork, painting, music, sacred dance, or just sitting and being present with the images that arise from the depths. But each journey follows the timeless path of alchemical transformation, turning lead into gold, revealing the light that is hidden in the depths of our being.

This is an individual inner work, and yet it takes us beyond our individual self into the archetypal world where the symbols that belong to all of humanity also change and transform. Here we may discover that we are working not just with the substance of our own soul, but with the *anima mundi,* the soul of the world. The light we discover in our own depths is a spark of the World Soul, and the world needs this light to evolve. When we make this connection within our consciousness and within our imagination, we begin to change the fabric of life.

Within the *anima mundi,* the primal forces of creation, the energies and powers that give form and meaning to all of life, are also being transformed. New symbols are arising from the depths to guide humanity on the next step of its evolution, for, in the words of Carl Jung, "The archetypal images decide the fate of man."

Symbols act as a bridge between the inner and the outer worlds, allowing the energy and meaning of the inner to flow into the outer. They can bring into life primal energies that have not been polluted or conditioned, which we can then creatively channel. Through our conscious participation, our inner work and creative imagination, we can recognize and help bring into life these images that are needed to heal and transform our world. In previous eras this has been the work of the shaman, someone who was initiated and trained to work

Flower of Life, Daniel Holeman, 16′x20″ digital image, www.awakenvisions.com

with the energies and images of the inner world. But at this time of global need this work is open to anyone whose attention is drawn inward, who is receptive and attentive to the images arising from the source of life.

Within each of us lies the knowledge of how the worlds work together, how the images of the soul come into being and determine the fate of humanity. This knowing is a part of life, part of the miracle of creation. And we may find that these new images are not the esoteric images that we have associated with the sacred, but are simple images that belong to life and to the patterns of interconnectivity and wholeness that are now making themselves known. For example, the Internet is a powerful, living image of life's interconnected oneness. As it becomes more and more present in our collective consciousness, it is more and more able to channel life's underlying energies in new ways. It is a power and life force of its own, able to evolve and adapt like a fast-changing organism, and, like other emerging images of our time, it is reconfiguring our consciousness, helping us to interact with life in new ways. And yet, like all symbols, it will only reveal its real potential when we relate to it with the correct attitude. If we see it just as a mechanical tool, its meaning and transformative potential will remain hidden.

It can be a shock to think that the sacred is revealing itself in something as mundane as the technology of the Internet. But we need to be alert, to realize that the symbols that will shape the dream of the next era are likely to turn up in the places we least expect them in ourselves, in the ordinariness of our daily lives. Then we can open ourselves to laughter and joy in the way the divine awakens us to a new way of being, turning our spiritual perception upside down once again!

Once we understand how these images arise from within life, we will give them the correct attention, and start a creative dialogue with the symbolic world. This is part of the co-creative relationship that humanity is being offered, in which the individual can interact directly with the whole. As we help bring into being the symbols that can heal and nourish the soul of the world, we begin to live this responsibility. We take on our role as guardians of the planet, and we do so with the consciousness of oneness that includes and connects the sacred and mundane, the inner and the outer, spirit and matter, the world's soul and body and our own, the individual and the planet.

The Need of the Time

At this time of global crisis and imbalance, women have a unique role. A woman feels the pulse of life as intimately as she feels her own blood pulsing through her veins. Her knowing is not abstract, but lived in her very body in a way that is inaccessible to men. In the cells of her body she carries the light of the consciousness of oneness, a light that is not present in men's bodies. In this light she knows the interconnectedness of life: how it is all a part of one living whole. This primal knowing needs to be given back to life, which is suffering under the masculine thought-forms of duality and separation. Our science has imposed upon life the image of the world as dead matter, something we can freely pollute and abuse. Feminine spiritual consciousness can reawaken the world to its sacred nature as a living being, and so help it to heal and transform. This simple acknowledgement of the divine within life is a powerful catalyst, transforming the life of the world just as a woman's awareness of the divine nature of the child growing within her can transform her own life.

To be aware of the divine within oneself and the divine within life and the world, and to know that it is all one, is a simple and powerful practice. It means to be present in life as it is—not as one would want it to be. And it means to live in the moment—there can be no transformation in the images of the past or the dreams of the future. Yet we are conditioned to look to the past and the future, rather than daring to live in the now. But only in the now can we participate in the creative mystery of life. Alive in the present moment, one can see the significance of newly forming patterns of relationship and the way in which they belong to life's organic nature—an Indra's net of dynamic possibilities.

All around us there are signs of life recreating itself in new configurations as people begin to come together in new and different ways. The Internet and other tools of global communication are an essential part of this process, connecting people together regardless of the barriers of race, nationality, or physical location. Different people in all parts of the world are linking together, forming networks of shared interests—networks outside the control of any hierarchy or government, belonging to life itself. And these patterns of connections are growing.

But we have yet to fully understand that it is these patterns of relationship themselves that are so essential, that will provide the simple answers to the complexity of the times. Their deepest meaning and purpose lie not in the information they convey, but in the new, fluid, organic interrelationship of individuals and groups they are

Tree of Light, Daniel Holeman, 16"x20" digital image. www.awakenvisions.com

creating. Something is coming alive in a new way. While masculine analytic consciousness sees only the separate parts, feminine consciousness sees the whole pattern, and thus allows us to recognize what is really happening, to grasp the meaning of these fast-forming patterns and understand their sacred purpose within their seemingly mundane appearance, to know these signs as all a part of the organism of life recreating itself from the matrix of global oneness.

And through this awareness a spiritual energy can be given to these patterns of relationship, an energy that is needed for life to transform. On its own, life evolves slowly over millennia. But the light of consciousness dramatically speeds up this natural process, just as a catalyst accelerates the process of chemical transformation. Through the light of direct feminine knowing, life can quickly reconnect with its own divine nature, and the divine can transform life in ways that we cannot imagine. With our own ordinary consciousness we cannot heal and transform the world of the effects of our pollution—it would take too long to redeem what we have destroyed. But the presence of the divine can awaken the world to its magical and miraculous power. If we welcome the divine back into life, if we acknowledge her divine nature, hen we can participate in life's recreation, in the miracle that is waiting to happen.

Women know the suffering of the world and also the secrets of its transformation. They feel this suffering in the cells of their bodies. And in the cells of their bodies lie also the sacred light and instinctual wisdom that are needed to help the world to change and awaken. How each woman lives this knowing is unique to herself, but connections are being created now that are an organic part of life's regeneration. Some of these are connections between awakened individuals and groups through which the light of the sacred feminine can flow, communicating the primal mystery of how the divine can come alive within creation. The ancient mysteries of the feminine were never written down, but passed from woman to woman. As this wisdom resurfaces, once again women will create connections of light that honor what is sacred within themselves and within life. They will not deny the suffering of the world, but recognize it as a part of the process of transformation, the way "the divine enters through a wound."

Each age comes alive in its own way. We are entering an era of oneness in which we have to return to the sacred source of life that is within each of us. We each have to recognize our own divinity and from this point of light make our unique contribution. And yet we are also one, part of an interrelated body of light we call the world. And in the core of creation a new light is being born, a light that carries the secrets of the future and of how the real miracle of life can once again be recognized and revered. This is the gift we are being given, the child of the future that is being born to each of us. And we are also the midwives of this destiny, this joy that is being returned to us, the primal joy of life celebrating its divine nature. Through the wisdom of the feminine we can all, each in our own way, give birth to this future.

Llewellyn Vaughan-Lee is a Sufi teacher and author. In recent years the focus of his writing and teaching has been on spiritual responsibility in our present time of transition, and the emerging global consciousness of oneness (see www.workingwithoneness.org). He has also specialized in the area of dreamwork, integrating the ancient Sufi approach to dreams with the insights of modern psychology. Llewellyn is the founder of The Golden Sufi Center (www.goldensufi.org). His most recent books are *Working with Oneness and Spiritual Power*.

Dreaming and the Longing for Feminine Wisdom

Dream Messenger, Cathy McClelland, Acrylic on illustration board, 24"x30", www.cathymcclelland.com

By Anne Scott

O God, the stars are shining:
All eyes have closed in sleep;
The kings have locked their doors.
Each lover is alone, in secret, with the one he loves.
And I am here too: alone, hidden from all of them....
with you. – *Rabia*

At night, when our conscious minds are at rest, our deeper wisdom, the holy wisdom, speaks to us through our dreams. Answers that we might be seeking are sometimes hidden in the darkness--answers that cannot be found in the light of day. They speak the language of the soul, opening wide the windows of our perceptions, helping us to respond to the urgent need of our time. Working with our dreams, we learn to listen with the heart, to work with the fluidity of the inner world, to stand at the doorway where love flows from the infinite emptiness into life. Feminine wisdom is so simple that we often overlook it. And when it is noticed, it is often undervalued. Yet there is nothing more important than feminine wisdom as it is revealed to us moment by moment—in our attention to what is in front of us each day, in our dreams at night, in the silence of nature, or while in meditation or prayer. This wisdom is the deep understanding that springs from and takes us back to what is real, to what nourishes and heals. Its waters come from a source that is always pure, a place of mystery and wonder that can renew our lives and help us to restore the earth itself.

Feminine wisdom lies so deeply hidden within us that we can barely remember what it feels like to live in relation to it. This wisdom lies underneath our beliefs and our perceptions of how life works, beyond our personality and desires. It is vital that we remain at the edge of the unknown, waiting, attending, listening and receiving, so that wisdom can speak to us from within. At times it is the suffering that life brings that can open us to this authentic wisdom, because suffering opens the heart. For it is only in the heart that we are able to perceive this deeper state of consciousness.

Our dreams give us direct access to this wisdom, to this healing, to this nourishment that we as a culture hunger for, and that women especially need in order for their hearts to be deep and open. Our culture offers little to nourish the hearts of women. We find in our culture no echo of the sacredness of wisdom or of the spiritual values of the feminine nature. If the hearts of women are not nourished, then the whole of humanity suffers. While this wisdom is alive in both men and women, there is a particular role that women play in weaving it into the fabric of everyday life. The feminine principle is essentially a unifying force, bringing together what has been split apart within us and in our lives. It calls to us to turn our attention inward instead of searching for answers outside of ourselves, and to live in relation to the soul. Life needs the feminine now, and it especially needs women to rediscover and reawaken to their own feminine souls. When women live their sacred relationship to life and to the Creator, they can help to clear and nourish the stream of life in a profound way.

The first dream that caused me to pay attention to my inner world was direct and simple. In the dream I was shown a circle with a dot in the center, a symbol I had seen before, carved into lava in Hawaii. I then heard a voice say, "If you would be that dot in the center, which is Love, then the problems with your family will cease to exist." With these words I began to feel into what this meant. I became the dot in the center and an ocean of love poured into me and through my body. It went on and on, streaming into every part of me, and then I woke up, amazed and in awe of what had just taken place.

This dream changed the course of my life. It awakened a longing to return to the experience of love, to live from the center of myself, although I had no idea what that even meant or how I would go about doing it. I only knew that I could no longer live my life as I had done before. For the next three years I stumbled in and out of this love. I then met a teacher of Sufism who specialized in dreamwork. Gradually I learned to access the wisdom I had experienced in my dream, to feel its source in my own body and soul.

Visionary artist Cher Lyn's painting, Grandmother, beautifully illustrates the ancestral quality of feminine wisdom that emerges when we learn to let go and trust the voices within. The process of this painting began with a dream in which the artist was wrapping a bundle of sacred sage in preparation for a ceremony. The next day, a small pile of sage then synchronistically appeared beneath her painting table. She felt compelled to explore its significance, and invited two women friends to participate in this exploration. Cher explains, "We began by sitting together in a circle and speaking from our hearts about the feminine re-emerging in our hearts, minds and the world. We also spoke of our places of pain… We spoke of our desire to heal and break free from the chains of shame that bound us. We recognized our role as women healers and the necessity to call upon ancient power and wisdom to help heal our wounds . . . and the world at large."

In whatever way we choose, whether it be through creativity, meditation, or sharing dreams, when women gather together for the sake of healing feminine consciousness, a connection is made both to the source and to each other, strengthening our inner knowing and trust. Later on, as the image of Grandmother had come forth on the canvas in luminous pastel colors, Cher was called upon to go deeply into this space of trust; she felt a strong inner prompting to lay dark paint over the entire canvas. She said, "Mind chatter and self criticism exploded in my mind, which made me feel doubtful and fearful. I silenced my mind again through meditation and again heard, 'Trust! This is a painting about trust!" Yielding to this intuition as she painted, she began to see forms of tribal ancestors emerging through the black as if in celebration of the return of the divine feminine. "The human tendency is to want to hold onto the pretty painting of an older woman," Cher explained, "but beneath the external beauty, in the deep, dark unconscious,

Grandmother, Cher Lyn, 39"x63"x2" Acrylic, blue corn, sage and tobacco on canvas, www.mysticartmedicine.com

emerged a powerful ancient elder, a carrier of light and feminine wisdom who brings healing to individuals and the planet." Listening to this place of knowing enabled Cher to experience her own connection to the ancient aspect of feminine wisdom within, a power and depth so easily rejected or denied for something "pretty" and more palatable. It took effort to keep out the voices of conditioning which wanted to criticize and analyze her work, but in so doing, she was blessed by the pure spring of creativity.

To let go and embrace this deepening, to allow this wisdom to nourish our lives, seems simple, but is not easy. It is like walking in the lava field, in the darkness, and being unable to do anything until the sun rises. It is like my stumbling around for three years, waiting for the real help that would enable me to find my way back to the state of being that was shown to me in my dream.

A friend, who had been experiencing difficulty in her life for many years, recently received a message in a dream that said, "You know nothing, and you are nothing." It was a phrase so simple that she barely noticed it. Only a week later did she realize that it was an answer to her prayers for understanding. Finally she was given what she needed to heal her relationship to life. To know nothing was to allow for the dream to be wiser than her fears and doubts. To be nothing was, for her, to give up her complaints and comparisons to others and to instead bow down before the sacredness of her life. She then had subsequent dreams revealing the hidden rich texture inside her life, imaged as brocade and green silk, indicating that she could now live in relation to this deeper aspect of her being rather than focusing only on what was lacking.

Another woman friend recently dreamt of a natural hot springs that had been covered over. It was only when she stopped cars from driving over this area that it would again become pure and rise to the surface, creating warm pools for women to bathe in. This pure water is real -- it comes from the source, from the innermost sacred place within us. There is an old Sufi saying about Khidr, who walks where the two seas meet, where inner and outer worlds come together. "That magic spring where Khidr once drank the water of life is in your own home, but you have blocked its flow."

This deep well of wisdom has always been with us. It is as vast and deep as the ocean, where the source of Divine Wisdom runs deep, waiting for us to remember it. This place where wisdom surfaces from the depths of our unconscious invites us to drink from its clear water. It is not personal, although it touches us in an immensely personal way. If we try to bring to dreams our preconceived ideas or any imposed rational way of thinking, it is like driving cars over the natural hot springs.

What do we do with a dream that opens us to a new way of being even though the outer framework of our lives remains the same? It is usually not a matter of changing our lives, but learning to be attentive to the new quality that has been born within us. This attentiveness is like standing at the doorway between the dream and our daily life as an expression of devotion to the emerging new life impulse. Gradually our daily life becomes infused with meaning that permeates everything that we do.

Another woman had the following dream at a time when she felt deeply troubled by the state of the world. Although she valued her life, there was a nagging sense that what she was doing was not enough. Her dream came like a bolt of lightening, waking her up to the womanly power of her being as a mother and career woman:

> *I dreamed I was walking in the pitch-black night of the world. The night was like all the darkness in the world right now. As I was walking, I saw a beacon of light that was surprising to me. Off in the distance I began to see thousands of lights shining bright in the darkness--beacons all over the world, each one a person holding her/his own portion of the light in the darkness. I got the sense that each of these beacons was outshining the darkness . . . they were more powerful than the darkness. The lights were like lighthouses or beacons for other souls in the world to gravitate to. They would be attracted, so to speak, to the light.*

Dreams are here to help us, to guide us, to bridge what has been cut off in our lives and in life itself. When we work with dreams for the sake of the greater whole, then the clear waters can flow into our lives. We learn how to work with the current of life where love flows out from the source, and those who are in service to life are given access to this love. For many, the knowledge of the ways of love lies beneath feelings of despair or anger or experiences of suffering, but through our yearning for truth and understanding we can learn to be receptive to what the dreams reveal. Feeling vulnerable or uncertain in our life makes our need for wisdom more acute, our heart more receptive. Just inside our own darkness is a light that is the very core of our being, and so it is within the darkness of the world.

In Western psychology, the dream world is interpreted in various ways according to various schools of thought, but most agree that is a mysterious place we go into when we are asleep. Often elusive, the images from our dreams can evaporate from our conscious awareness shortly after we awake, revealing them to be idiosyncratic. But there are ordinary dreams, and then there are are shamanic dreams, or, lucid dreams, in which one is fully awake and aware that they are dreaming. The modern visionary can learn to enter this level of experience while very much awake. These are visionary experiences of the transpersonal realms that may be accompanied by spirits, animal guides, and elements.

Like many women who are willing to face their own darkness, a greater realization grew in Uma as she painted; that the healing of her own wounds was for a purpose that went far beyond her individual self. Women are connected to life, and their own healing touches those around them -- and even beyond. The wisdom of the old woman became a guiding principle, as the painter entered the labyrinth of her old wounds, and helped her to take the next step; giving back the suffering as an offering to life, an offering to God. Real wisdom sings the ancient knowledge of transformation, of dying and rebirth, speaking to us in so many ways, in dreams and in intuitions that point us towards the dawn even in our darkest times.

Visionary artist Lindy Kehoe, is a master of dreaming awake and riding the magical wave of the imaginary realms. The gift of imagination is a gift that is highly underestimated and misunderstood. It is with our creative imaginations that we dream the world in which are living into being. She expounds on her creative process, her muse, and what it means to dream awake:

> *What does it mean to Dream Awake? There is a state that is accessible to the creative and open mind. A trance like state of peace that exists in a paradox of readiness to be completely surprised by magic. This kind of mind can conjure the ability to recognize everyday magic by the action of being sagacious. There are symbols all around that remind us that perhaps we exist inside a Great Dream. If this is so, then perhaps our socially conditioned limitations are illusions molded into our psyche that can fall away once we decipher the higher frequency codes of the dream world. How many movies has one watched where the ending was the person waking up and the whole plot was but a dream? 'Merrily We Row Along, Life is but a Dream.*
>
> *If one takes a look at my body of work, they will perhaps feel a sense of a dream-like state. In my paintings, there are no straight lines, only flowing rhythmic forms, almost cloud like landscapes of soft and bright colors. I feel most inspired to create such realms because I wish to exist there. These works are like windows and guides into this place, helping to amplify this awakening into the dream of 'wishes come true.' One may wonder where the people in my paintings come from. I feel most connected to the idea that before the great "fog of sorrow" we were light beings existing in higher dimensions. Perhaps we lived on prana and blood was never shed.*
>
> *Modern day myths talk about the ancient land of Lemuria. This resonates with me. I feel that we may still have access to this place through meditation, sound healing, and sacred art. My hope is that my art work can do this kind of service at this critical time. That the remembering of our magical enlightened selves can continue to be nourished and called forth, and that more and more will continuously awaken into this awakened dream.*

Learn to hold dreams and visions carefully. Allow them to unfold in their own time. Without knowing *how* to reach this love that will make life full, allow the freedom to follow the thread of the inner voice. Follow a dream's intimacy or terror, tenderness or power that you feel upon awakening, and wait. Slowly, the truth of these dreams becomes real, and a quality of wonder returns to life. We can remember again what has been forgotten; to be the dot in the center of the circle. And from this place, our real feminine wisdom can find its way in the world.

Foxcrow, Lindy Kehoe, www.lindykehoe.com

As the founding director of DreamWeather Foundation, **Anne Scott** travels around the United States to foster the knowledge of the innate feminine in everyday life. Anne Scott has worked for over 20 years supporting women in communities and organizations who long to reconnect with their forgotten wisdom. She recently initiated a program at The Living Room, Santa Rosa, bringing her work to women in a drop-in center for women who are homeless. She received a B.A. in Anthropology from Occidental College and worked for many years in Asia for business magazines and newspapers. Her experience living in different cultures gave her a global perspective that informs her work with women today. She has been a presenter at global conferences for women in India, Switzerland and Italy. Her training also includes dreamwork in the Sufi tradition since 1990. Anne is an author of several books, the most recent is *Women, Wisdom and Dreams: The Light of the Feminine Soul*, published in 2008. Visit her website: www.dreamweather.org

Dream Guardian, Lindy Kehoe, www.lindykehoe.com

Saraswati's Secrets: Singing the Waters for Personal and Planetary Transformation

Saraswati, Hrana Janto, 24"x24" acrylic on canvas. www.hranajanto.com

by Lotus Linton, Ph.D.

There is a mysterious and intriguing relationship between water and sound, which the ancients knew about and utilized in their spiritual and healing practices. In Hindu stories of creation, Love and Desire come together to form the first Cosmic Sound, which is hidden in the Word and in the Waters. In many cultures and religions we baptize ourselves in water, we bury each other with watery rites, believing that after death we cross over the waters to the otherworld. These watery rituals are often accompanied with the sounds of bells, drums, bowls and horns, hymns, chants and mantras. Although we may have forgotten the ancient relevance of the connection between water and sound, it is a sacred relationship.

It has become an integral aspect of my personal path to rediscover the transformative powers of the sound/water connection. In my morning meditation practice, I sing to the jars of water I have collected from streams and wells, rivers and waterfalls of the world. I seek out and intone sacred chants to the springs and waterways of my home region, the Pacific Northwest, and I take groups of fellow water singers with me to the holy wells of other lands. In many locations throughout the world I "Sing the Waters," continually discovering greater physical and metaphysical correlations between water and sound and their conjoined contribution to personal and planetary transformation.

My practice of water singing began in Bali many years ago, when I landed in the lap of the goddess Saraswati. Deluged with a series of personal problems in Bali, I went to a nearby yet unfamiliar village to seek the help of a traditional healer. My friend, Wayan, brought me to the door of the village priest who was also a traditional doctor. After allowing Wayan to translate my traveler's woes, explaining my inability to rid myself of an intimidating opportunist, Jero took me into his family temple, dedicated to Saraswati.

Nestled within the family living compound, Jero's tiny sanctuary room of concrete blocks opened to the melting light of the evening sky. It was decorated with numerous statues, thatched roofed altars, and fading cloths of black, white, and gold. Jero bade me to sit for awhile as he lighted incense and chanted into a vial of water, his deep singing accompanied by bell ringing and periodical splashes of water on my head. Jero then dotted my face and neck with the liquid and whispered to me while Wayan translated: "Be fearless. You will be all right. The goddess, Saraswati, is a good goddess for you. She favors you." As we took our leave, the air teemed with the poly-rhythms of frogs in the rice paddies and gamelan musicians at their practice in the village hall. Jero stood at the door in the light of a solitary electric bulb on his porch to wave until we were out of sight.

Thus did Saraswati, The Flowing One, become a beloved reference and refuge in my life, as Her holy water, splashed and dabbed on my face, initiated me into the ancient practice of Singing the Waters. As Jero had predicted, all my complaints vanished that night. Since then, he has become my dearest friend in all of Bali and I visit him often.

Bali is the land of flowing water, falling from the mountains, coursing through river valleys, trickling through levels upon levels of rice paddies. Bali's particular brand of Hinduism is known as *Tirtha Agama,* Religion of the Holy Water. It is the singing of the water, embuing it with the power of ancient chants, that renders it holy. It is fitting that I should meet Saraswati in such a watery Eden.

Although there are many angels and archetypes shining from within the religions of all cultures to guide and assist women in our awakening, Saraswati provides the personification of womanly wisdom itself, deep womanly knowing that our world desperately needs today. She is not only the oldest goddess known to India, but She is said to embody all the qualities of the other deities. Though Saraswati is commonly referred to as the goddess of education, learning and the arts, Her deeply feminine, "flowing" way of knowing takes us below mere mental knowledge and the accumulation of facts to the deep recesses and far more comprehensive intelligence of the Soul.

Saraswati is the dawn-goddess, dispelling the darkness of ignorance, chaos and confusion. The four sacred scriptures of the Vedas are her offspring. As in most cultural pantheons, She has been reduced in more recent history to the consort of a god -- in this case, the wife of the creator, Brahama. Yet, Saraswati's greater wisdom and spiritual superiority are still retained in the myths in which She serves as Brahama's teacher in all things, taming both the god's wandering mind and his entrenchment in material desires.

I believe Saraswati existed long ago as an actual human who attained an enlightened state. As often happens to such *rishis,* or Soul-realized ones, She was, over time, labelled a goddess by those of lesser understanding who were not yet able to grasp their own potentially divine nature. Still, I know Her personally to be a contactable Presence. Her wise and watery spirit, conveyed through image, story, and especially, the direct communion approached through sacred chanting, offers deeper understanding of the ineffable workings of the Universe for those of us who are growing toward wisdom.

Whether we acknowledge Saraswati as a genuine and contactable divine Presence, or merely as an inspirational archetype to educe our own divine qualities, Her power is palpable. If we can plumb the deepest meanings of the imagery associated with Her, we can discover transformative secrets lying within the physical and metaphysical properties of Her two greatest tools, sound and water, and the tremendous healing power of the two conjoined. As a wisdom seeker and as a sound healer with a penchant for the sacred waters of the Earth, I find in Saraswati a personalized, tailor-made doorway to the Divine Feminine within myself. In one translation of Her name, Saraswati is "She who gives the essence of our own Self." Saraswati bids us to ride the rhythmic waves of Creation, upon which we arrive at the fountain of our own wisdom. This beautiful, evolved personage can guide our womanly quest for our own spiritual moisture and help us finally and forever nourish our brittle, arid, overly-masculinized world.

So let us explore together Saraswati's mysterious depths and allow Her to help us fathom our own. Let us observe Her, as women can do so beautifully, from the combined perspectives of mind and heart. Let us create a rainbow bridge between the masculine and feminine aspects of our nature and plumb the relationship between the old myths and our modern scientific discoveries. Let us allow Saraswati to reveal to us the secrets and true power of Singing the Waters for spiritual awakening and planetary transformation.

The Goddess of Sound

Picture Saraswati as a beautiful four-armed goddess in a pure white garment, sitting upon a lotus, rooted in Truth, the Supreme Reality that the lotus signifies. She is simply adorned, needing no jewelry except Her simple rosary, signifying the deep contemplation, assisted by chanting, that leads to union with the Divine. In two of her graceful arms She holds her *veena,* or Indian lute, upon which She plays the music of love and life. The first Cosmic Sound of Love and Desire, is *OM.* This original sound of all Creation is Hers, as is also the syllable *Aim* (pronounced "ime"), which depicts all streams of energy flowing in and out of the deep Self. Chanting either of these two syllables or any number of mantras associated with Her brings one under Saraswati's direct influence. Because She exemplifies the potent quality of sound, both words and music connect us with Saraswati, for She is "the impeller of true speech."

Quantum physics now understands the entire Universe to be, at its core, infinite pulsations of vibrational frequencies. Despite the appearance of solidity, we are -- everything is -- essentially, vibration. Sound healing is the therapeutic art that most obviously utilizes this truth. Using rhythm, pitch and timbre of the voice, the drum and other instruments or previously recorded music, the sound healer helps synchronize the rhythms of body, mind and heart, thus serving to relieve many common maladies and open doors to the deeper Self, or Soul. Even such debilitating ailments as heart problems, chronic pain, autism, or depression have been helped or healed by these methods.

Music therapy and sound healing are emerging today as viable complementary forms of medicine, yet they are truly timeless healing arts known for at least 30,000 years by the shamans and physicians of ancient cultures who could perceive the vibratory nature of reality beneath the surface of physicality. The enlightened ones of old, the *rishis* who created the Vedas, the sacred texts of India, understood well the healing power of sound. Their primordial chants and mantras are designed to have enlightening effect. Sanskrit, itself the Vedic language, is

Saraswati, Paul Heussenstamm, 24"x32" acrylic on canvas. www.mandalas.com

mantric in nature, its every syllable consciously utilized for healing and teaching purposes.

One of Saraswati's secrets, as the Goddess of Sound and sound healing, is the principle of *entrainment*, a core aspect of our world and all Creation. As clocks in the same vicinity synchronize to one rhythm, and as little babies' hearts beat in double-time to the rhythm of their mothers' hearts, entrainment is a strong steady rhythm (or frequency) overtaking a weaker, less steady rhythm. This causes the lesser rhythm to rise to the occasion, becoming more pronounced and vital itself. The entire Universe operates on this principle of entrainment, as the rhythms of all bodies and all systems affect each other. Whether we are talking about the gyrations of planets or the movement of blood cells, we can observe entrainment at work.

Saraswati's Gayatri mantra, the oldest known healing song in human history, is considered by many to be an extremely potent force, precisely because of its power of entrainment. In Vedic teachings, mantras are designed to awaken deep states of consciousness that already exist within us, drawing them forth from our own cellular memory and bringing them to life.

As a goddess of the most ancient origins, Saraswati is undoubtedly a tantric goddess, meaning She embodies the primordial and divinely feminine power of *shakti*. *Shakti* is the raw, liberating, creative energy that surges through all vibrations in the Universe and gifts them with purifying vitality. *Shakti,* when awakened within humans, is the energy of Enlightenment. *Shakti* is the immanent presence of the Goddess -- not above, aloof and transcending the physical world, as so many deities are depicted, but throbbing within every aspect of the created universe, humming inside the very structure of our cells and all molecules.

Saraswati is usually portrayed with a peacock sitting next to Her. In this sacred imagery, the peacock signifies the ego and the mind, the more masculine, worldly forces. It is important to note that She is not riding the peacock, but has tamed it, knowing that knowledge dominated by ego can destroy the world. In modern culture, subjugated as it is by the left-brain and the eye as the preferred modes of knowing and perceiving, the egoic peacock still reigns. Brilliance of mind is not yet tempered and balanced by the intelligence of the heart, and thus, our current reality is far too often driven by ego's insatiable needs, creating strife, war, conflict and misery in its wake. Saraswati, on the other hand, provides the healing salve and the antidote for this left-brainitis with which we find ourselves afflicted.

Applying sacred sound in our daily lives, we can become more ear-oriented, and thus more attuned to the right brain, the feminine aspect in both men and women, which is, basically, the corridor to the Soul and the avenue to a more sacred way of being. Left-brain function is important, useful and valuable, but if it is not balanced by the softening qualities of the right-brain, we too often find ourselves in a violent, hierarchical world of human-caused pain. Orientating ourselves to the divine attributes of Saraswati, especially through singing the chants and syllables associated with Her, we can entrain our own frequencies of body, mind and emotion to the more refined, enlightened, and Soul-aligned energies of Her sacred being.

The Goddess of Water

"Through the ages pools, lakes, sacred wells and springs have been invested with magical properties. Many were believed to be the dwelling places of gods or supernatural beings, and so were seen as rich sources of both physical healing and spiritual transformation."
Jane Hope, The Secret Language of the Soul

Saraswati originates as the first of the world's many water goddesses. Perhaps it is because humans come from the watery womb, or that life evolved from the womb of the ocean, that we have always understood water to be a feminine element, representing spirituality itself.

Saraswati was once the name of a river, a mighty river with creative, purifying and nourishing properties, upon whose banks the entire Vedic civilization arose. The Saraswati River was the biggest and most important of the seven holy rivers mentioned in the ancient scriptures, yet it has long been dry, not unlike the dehydration of the Sacred Feminine for many long centuries in the majority of cultures upon the planet.

Although the Saraswati River exists no longer in the physical realms, it is remembered in the personification of this beautiful goddess, who is usually depicted near a flowing river with one or two swans at her feet. She often holds a lotus flower in one hand and a pot of sacred water in another, always clearly associated with the healing powers of water. One epithet for Her is "She having lots of pools." Saraswati is also known as the ocean of understanding, the vibration of consciousness itself from which all rivers of thought and energy arise and to which they all return.

We begin by acknowledging that water is the most effective carrier of vibrations. Sound travels through water four times faster than through air. It is this transmissional power of water that allows dolphins and whales

Water Goddess, Atmara Rebecca Cloe, 16"x20" digital image. www.nwcreations.com

Saraswati, Sue Halstenberg, 24"x48" acrylic on canvas.
www.sue-halstenberg.pixels.com

to communicate with each other through thousands of miles of water in a very brief period of time.

Science is also demonstrating that water has a memory, capable of retaining what it has "heard," or been exposed to. The ancient *rishis* and wisdom keepers understood this, for they had highly developed intuitive capacities to perceive subtle realms of electro magnetic energies, capacities that have all but atrophied in the modern mind. The Maori word for water, for example, is *wai,* which means "remembrance" and water is understood by them to be the container that holds the memory of all that has ever been and will be.

This knowledge that water has a memory has been recognized for over 200 years by homeopathic physicians who "potentize" water by exposing it to the specific frequencies of healing substances from the plant and mineral worlds. Homeopathy relies on water's ability to retain the subtle, electromagnetic information that becomes encoded in its memory container.

Water's powers of memory are made quite visable in the photographs of frozen water crystals in Dr. Masaru Emoto's two volumes of *Messages from Water*. His photos of the beautiful and brilliant six-sided crystals of frozen water, which have been "influenced" by the works of Mendelssohn or Vivaldi, stand in stark contrast to those from water which has been polluted by discordant rock music or toxic chemicals. Emoto's ground-breaking work vividly demonstrates that water's power of memory is especially sensitive to sound vibrations.

Water not only possesses the faculty to store information impressed upon it previously by a given frequency level, but it also is able to transfer such information to other systems. Evidently, it is the crystalline nature of water that renders it so potent in the storage and transmission of energy. Water researcher William Marks has pointed out that the water-filled cells within our bodies contain microscopic crystals that vibrate in harmony with the energies of the universe and our world.

Crystals, and thus water, are transducers as well as transmitters of energy, having the ability to take one form of energy and convert it to a higher form of energy. Crystals are also "acousto-luminescent," having the ability to convert sound waves into light.

Healthy water, or vital water, is beautifully structured, like the crystals of Dr. Emuto's photographs. It has a strong three dimensional microstructure that collects and transmits information. It is this structure which allows water to communicate and to nourish.

Water flowing through natural landscapes has similar properties and powers. Unimpeded, "living" water does what the wind does, what the sap of trees, the blood of creatures and nebulas do. It flows in spiral, vortexial patterns, becoming recharged and revitalized as it continually tumbles over itself on its journey downstream. Properly structured, living water, cradled in the forests, flowing down from the mountains, surging in the seas and bubbling up from the springs is the health-giving blood of Mother Earth.

Water that is channeled into straight pipes or polluted with chemical contaminants becomes damaged and dead. Damage to water goes hand in hand with a loss of vibration, since it is vibration that makes the difference between living and dead water. Thus, once again we are brought to the feet of the Goddess of Sound, the goddess

Magnetic Springs Spirits, Cynthia Ré Robbins. Oil and Tempera on Panel 16" x 20". www.art4spirit.com

Grotto Guardians, Cynthia Ré Robbins, Oil and Egg Tempera, 12" x 16", www.art4spirit.com

Grotto Guardians, Cynthia Ré Robbins: Eureka Springs was founded because of the popularity of its healing waters, which had been held sacred for many years by the Native Americans. With the growth of the town, the springs were covered, enclosed, forced through pipes, and polluted. In recent times, the townspeople have been doing a lot to bring back the health and beauty of the springs. Now there are lovely gardens and walkways. Groups of well-wishers visit, bringing crystals and chants to call back the power. My paintings in this series have the intention of revitalizing the waters. I mix sacred water from Lourdes into the paint to carry a high vibration onward to the viewer and back to the water.

of vibration.

As Viktor Schauberger, forester and brilliant inventor, once said, "What we do to water, we do to ourselves." We could add, "What we have done to our water goddesses, we have done to ourselves," for the abuse and neglect of our planet's waters, polluted now beyond measure, is co-incident with the denial of the Sacred Feminine and Her way of being that holds all the elements, all the gifts of life in deep reverence. For this we suffer on many levels, both individually and collectively.

As we continue to pollute the waters of the planet and to ingest non-living, stale, chemically treated, sterilized and pressurized water into our systems, we are playing with a time-bomb for ourselves and our children and all future generations. Even though we may improve contaminated water chemically and free it of bacteria, it will still possess the electromagnetic oscillations of certain wave lengths which can be precisely traced to that water's original contaminants. Thus, the water will still be energetically polluted. Water that cannot behave properly, that cannot attend to its infinite functions, affects the health of body, mind, society, and all of nature.

Physics now dances in the enlightening realm of the goddess. As Victor Schauberger has said, "The Upholder of the Cycles which supports the whole of life, is WATER. In every drop of water dwells a Deity, whom we all serve..." And as we know by now, one of Her names is Saraswati.

In the end, our discussion of water, sound, and Saraswati brings us back to our own spirit -- it is the very core of our consciousness that we must upgrade. To bring water back to life, *humanity* must come to life. We must see with new eyes, hear with new ears, sing with new voices. These are the attributes of the Divine Feminine through which we recognize that both our bodies and our planet are over 75% water and through which we can honor the beauty and holiness of that correlation. Water is not an ordinary commodity, but a magical, blessed foundation for all life on Earth. We must once again learn to relate to it, and to all life forms and elements, as sacred.

And by relating to water as sacred and holy, humanity can learn the methods by which we might maintain water's livingness. We have both the ancient teachings and the modern research, both the necessary spiritual and scientific knowledge already at hand. We know how to allow water to flow feely and regenerate itself without impediment. We can revitalize the polluted and stale waters we have inherited from technologies which do not serve our health or the health of the planet. In sacredness, with our hearts full of gratitude, we can Sing the Waters into health and ourselves into new ways of being.

Summoning the Spirit, Cynthia Ré Robbins, Oil and Egg Tempera, 16 x 20, www.art4spirit.com

The Goddess of Sound and Water

"A river sings a holy song conveying the mysterious truth that we are a river, and if we are ignorant of this natural law we are lost."
Thomas Moore

We know that sound is vibration, and vibration is sound. Saraswati's very essence reminds us that everything in Creation has its own vibration and thus its own sound. And we know that water is the rememberer, the transmitter and the transducer of this sound. When sound is used in healing the body of a person or the body of our Earth, it is water that responds most lovingly and completely to that vibration. Learning to understand water, we better understand how it is that sound "works" to balance and heal us and our natural systems. Spiritual growth is a movement into ever higher frequencies of consciousness, and water is both a transducer and a rememberer of that movement. In this sense, both the physical and metaphysical aspects of Saraswati's power transcend any notions of Her as an outmoded entity or superstitious tale. The Enlightenment She bestows upon us is that of increased energy, more spirit, higher frequency, improved fluidity, and greater light.

I participate in Saraswati's watery rites by giving thanks each day for the water I drink, bathe in, and look out upon in this world. I potentize clear, pure drinking water with sacred sounds, songs and chants of many cultures as well as with appreciative thoughts. I drink this revitalized water to enhance my physical wellbeing, helping the body to entrain to new rhythms of optimum health. I send sung water home with my friends, my family members, my clients. I sing to the waters in the bath, in the garden, or in the soup I stir.

Dr. Emoto tells of the Shinto priest in Japan who recently gathered numerous chanters to successfully purify the polluted waters of the temple lake. Drunvalo Melchizedek, reporting on avante-garde technologies, heralds Sufi masters from Turkey who are now mass-producing "chanted water" to clarify pollution on many continents. He describes how participants each brought jars of dirty, polluted water to a global ecology conference and watched them clear within minutes from the influence of the Sufi sung-water. Brooke Medicine Eagle, sharing the spiritual teachings of her Crow and Sioux grandmothers, imparts a "waterfall song" to her students, insisting that it is by singing to the aspects and elements of nature that we establish communication and become bonded at the heart level with All-Our-Relations in the elemental, mineral, plant and animal kingdoms. And Algonquin women are gathering sisters of all cultures on all continents to sing an ancient woman's water song for revivifying the planet's waterways.

Even science has now discovered its own version of Singing the Waters, demonstrating that we can erase contaminant information within water and revitalize it by returning it to its natural spiral motions or by exposing it to various energetic influences, especially sonar treatment. Vital, high-frequency water, reintroduced to polluted farm streams, entrains them to be living again. When used for irrigation, this revitalized water produces higher crop yields and stronger, darker, richer, more flavorful food. After drinking revitalized water, the coats of sheep grow curlier and softer. Revitalized water used in

Reflection, Mark Henson, 4'x6' oil on Canvas., www.markhensonart.com

Gateway of the Higher Heart, Tessa Mythos, www.artbymythos.com

industry rids pipes of slime, sludge, mold and incrustations. The world-renewing possibilities are endless, once we attune to Saraswati's song of wisdom that takes us into a new, soulistic realm of being where we truly love our planet and actually care for her resources.

When I sing to water -- rivers, oceans, waterfalls and springs --enhanced energy returns to me in the process, and I am propelled into ecstasy. Water sings back! And this is another of Saraswati's great secrets. This interchange of energies between voice and water is reciprocal and it is deep. I am transformed. I am renewed. I am edified by this ancient form of communion.

Having practiced sacred sounding for several years now, I have been witness to my own transformation in the increasing harmony arising in my emotional and mental fields and vast waves of spirit taking over the body itself. This is Saraswati's doing. Sounding the waters of the body with appropriate chanting, toning, humming and drumming, as well as employing both sound and water in ritual practice, enhances spiritual awakening. Singing the Waters of Earth contributes to human evolution and planetary survival.

The advanced practitioner of water-song magic wields the magnificent force of Sarawati's *shakti*, this ultimate power of the Divine Feminine. Aquarian energy is spiritual power. Women dancing in the light of the Goddess hold the keys to the kingdom (or queendom) in our healing voices and the waters of our cells. We rise up singing.

Dr. Lotus Linton has taught and facilitated spiritual growth seminars for twenty-five years. Lotus' doctoral studies at The Union Institute focused on spiritual transformation through the sacred arts of numerous cultures. As described in her book, *Soul Springs: Seeking Self in the Waters of the World,* her personal and professional life has taken her throughout the world to explore the global aspects of spirituality. Lotus is a sound healer, a sacred dancer, and a ceremonialist. She has worked with women and men of all ages and diverse walks of life, ranging from young people to elders, from professionals to prisoners. Lotus is also a public speaker, presenting to book stores, colleges, women's groups and churches throughout the United States and in Australia. In her classes and retreats, Lotus often calls upon the physical and metaphysical properties of Water to lead participants to the wells of the Soul within themselves.

Awakening Womb Wisdom

Womb Illumination, Chanal Baran and Shona Keeli Jones (model), www.chanelbaran.com, www.wombillumination.com

By Seren Bertrand and Azra Bertrand, M.D

In the global women's marches, the world witnessed the awe-inspiring, collective power of the new Feminine Awakening--an outpouring of solidarity from a diversity of feminine voices across the world. We are being catalyzed into action. Taboo subjects are coming out of the closet. Women want to unite and heal. We want to reclaim our power and voices. For centuries, women have had to adapt to patriarchal values and social systems; however, in this postmodern era we want the freedom to explore the unique power of the feminine, on our own terms.

We are in the midst of a radical revolution. From Naomi Wolf's groundbreaking and bestselling book, Vagina, to the explosion of Red Tents and women's circles across the country, to new movements to reclaim the sanctity of menstruation, childbirth and sacred sexuality--women are remembering our innate power and reclaiming the wisdom of our wombs. We are all born from a mother's Womb This sacred space unites us all. The womb holds a key to unity consciousness and can help humanity transcend our differences.

Womb Awakening is a new cosmology in which women are honored for their life-giving creativity. It awakens the sensual, intuitive wisdom of the Goddess in our bodies. This new paradigm also includes men--honoring their unique gifts and creative powers, as well. It aids in our ability to get out of our heads and in to our bodies. The goal is to become more embodied—to deeply honor the organic, somatic wisdom of our brilliant bodies.

Reclaiming Menstrual Power

Reclaiming our lunar and menstrual power is another element to this revolution. The world is experiencing a lunar crisis – we no longer cycle with the rhythm of the moon, and have forgotten the power of our holy Womb Blood, which is filled with life-enriching stem cells that have an astonishing capacity to heal and regenerate. Women often give their power away to patriarchal ideologies, using cancer-causing chemical-bleached tampons during their moon flow, or seeing their menses as

The Rose Lineage, Chanel Baran, Shona Keeli Jones (model), www.chanelbaran.com, www.wombillumination.com

an inconvenient curse they are ashamed of, whilst male scientists around the world are using this sacred blood to harness its amazing regenerative powers, documented in dozens of scientific studies on the healing power of menstrual stem cells.

In most ancient myths throughout the world, dating back hundreds of thousands of years, the power of rebirth and regeneration has always been a blessing of the feminine womb, embodied and gifted by sacred womb priestesses across many cultures. This sacrament has never originated in a man, although there are many legends about the menstrual powers of female shamans being stolen by male gods.

Restoring Our Primordial Womb Cosmology

We are in a time of cosmic renewal, remembering the ancient Womb Mysteries, the sacred feminine spiritual tradition once embraced across the world, dating back to the dawn of time. Followed by initiates of many lineages of Womb Shamans and Womb Priestesses, this primordial wisdom stream includes Mary Magdalene's pathways of the Divine Womb, an oracular, gnostic left-hand path of Christ that was passed down to the Cathar Priestesses of the Holy Spirit, and was said to be encoded in a lost gospel of the sacred feminine mysteries.

The shamanic womb mysteries were also practiced by the Yoginis and Devadasis of India, the pre-patriarchal Khandros and Dakinis of Tibet, the Egyptian Priestesses of Isis, the Celtic Swan priestesses of Avalon and by many indigenous cultures across the world. This wisdom path helps us reclaim the intelligence of the body, our connection to Mother Earth, our shamanic birthing wisdom, sacred menstrual rites, creative power and the magical possibilities of living within a unified cosmology, mythology, biology and ecology.

The awesome power of the Cosmic Womb and Earth Womb is held in in the Mystical Rose in the center of your own Womb. By taking a shamanic journey into the mystical Womb-Worlds within, we embody our oracular feminine consciousness, and open the magic doorway to reclaim our primordial creative power. Men also have an "energetic Womb" called the Hara.

When we connect with our spiritual Womb, we discover an inner oracle that communicates messages from our own intuition and gnosis, which is deeply rooted in the wisdom of Mother Earth, and divine transmissions from the Cosmic Womb.

On winter solstice, consulting our own inner Oracle, we received a message from the dreamtime, where we encountered magical spirit horses, vibrating with pulsing life-power, galloping through the worlds to bring us a message from the ancestral womb shamans, and Ancient Mothers of the world. They ask us to remember and follow the horse tracks, the sacred paths, the lost fairy-ways of earth consciousness.

The Earth spirit, the soul of the world, is singing to us – calling out, shouting loud. This song of beauty, this anguished cry, is reverberating across filaments of light that weave the world in a web of energy, flowering inside our sacred Wombs.

The gateway-time is at hand.
We are on RED ALERT.
Red is the color of our womb blood,
It holds our sacred birthing power.
It holds our wisdom memory,
In an unbroken genetic line,

Back to the Ancient Mothers.

We need to hold the line.

The Womb of woman must sing in tune with earth again

Our sexual energy and birthing power must root into the Womb of Gaia

It is time to awaken our Womb sovereignty, and plant our power deep

It is time to Re-wild the Womb and rebirth the world.

We must also hold the celestial lines
Our ancestors danced with the stars
We must remember the astrological waltz
And find our cosmic rhythm again
We must birth stargates through our Womb
The fate of our universe depends on it

Seren Bertrand and Azra Bertrand, M.D., authors of the acclaimed book, Womb Awakening – Initiatory Wisdom From the Creatrix of All Life, as well as Sophia's Return: Healing the Grail Wound, Sacred Womb Rituals, and their forthcoming Magdalene Mysteries. They are founders of a worldwide Womb Awakening movement, and the Fountain of Life Womb Mystery School. They share courses, journeys, retreats online and in-person, as well as shamanic feminine music on Sacred Sounds of the Womb, Elemental Awakening – Calling to the Mother, and other albums. Visit www.thefountainoflife.org. Sophia's Return, Seren's personal story of healing from sexual abuse, is offered as a free ebook on the website: https://www.thefountainoflife.org/sophias-return-healing-grail-wound/

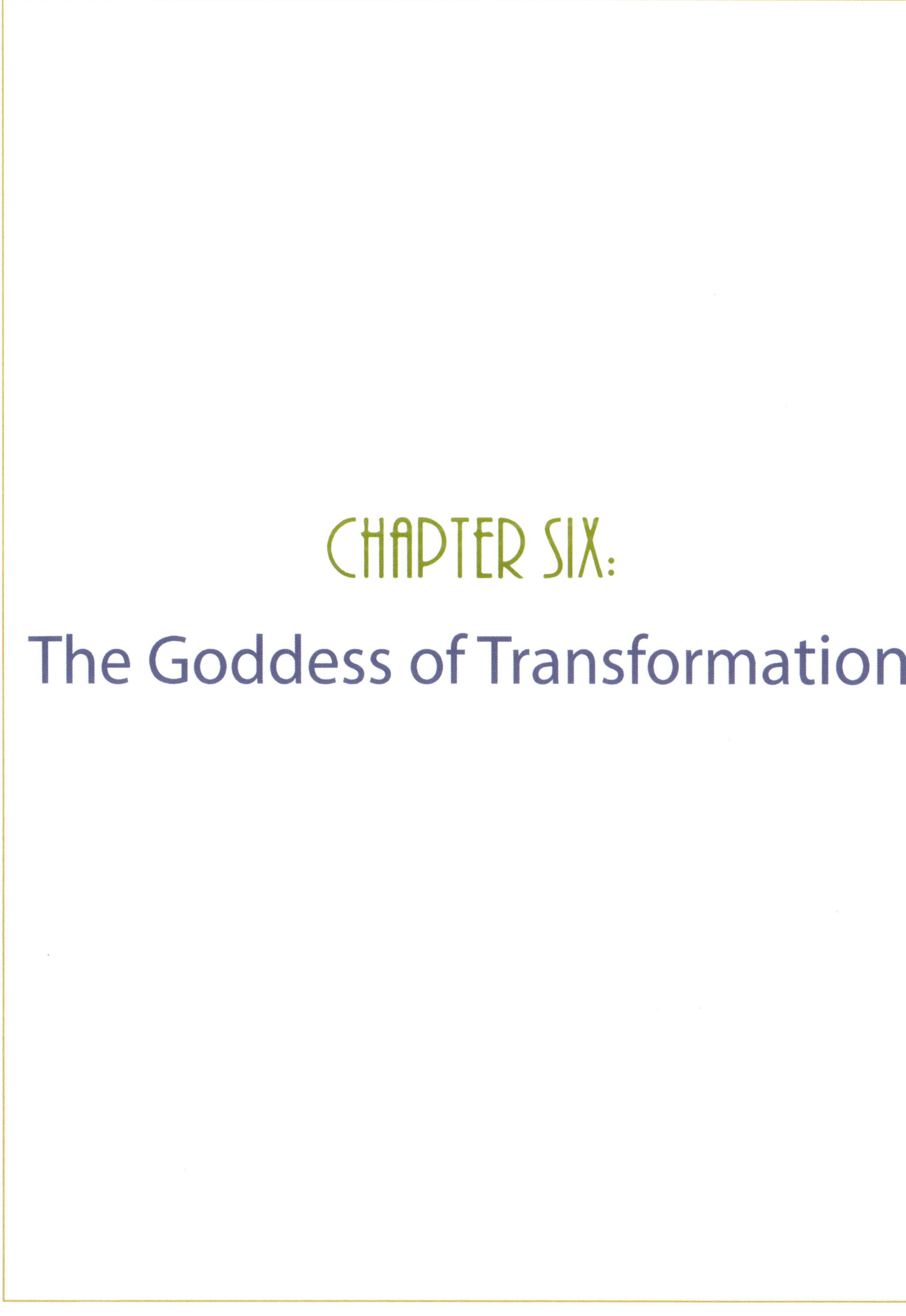

CHAPTER SIX:

The Goddess of Transformation

Psyche: The Goddess of Personal Transformation

Psyche, Hrana Janto, 16"x20" acrylic on canvas, www.hranajanto.com

By Jacquelyn Small

Psyche's story is the story of all of us. As the immortal goddess who chose to experience a fall from Mt. Olympus, the home of the gods, in order to become a human, Psyche's earthly incarnation begins by completely forgetting her goddess nature, believing she is only a mortal, just as we have all done. At its most profound level, the myth of Psyche is a spiritual parable of the transformational journey we must all travel to regain the memory that we are divine, and so become complete. As the archetype of the human soul, Psyche's journey through her incarnated life tells us of our soul's longing to be human, and of our human longing for spiritual transcendence. At the intersection of these two yearnings, our world comes into being. Psyche's experience on earth is the story of our own process of awakening from innocence to wisdom.

Her story begins on Mt. Olympus, of course, where Aphrodite becomes jealous of Psyche's youth and beauty, and furious with her for falling to earth to become a mortal, forgetting her universal duties as a goddess. To punish Psyche, she sends her son Eros to earth to prick Psyche with one of his arrows so that she will fall in love with any dreadful creature who comes to claim her as his bride. But as Eros draws his arrow from his quiver, he pricks his own finger and falls madly in love with the lovely girl himself. Eros, a silly god who loved to frivolously make people fall in love, had never felt love's potent sting himself. Now he must take responsibility for his actions and experience what he so blithely inflicts on others.

In their initial pairing, Psyche and Eros are like two children playing house in the dark, living in the night world of the creative imagination. Psyche has to promise Eros she will never see his face in the light or know anymore about him. Happily pregnant with his child, Psyche never dreams of questioning her lover god. And like the innocent Psyche, Eros is content to remain in the dark, seeking whimsical pleasure without accountability, coupling without commitment. There, in fantasy life, everything is done for them. They don't even have to think!

Psyche, however, begins to tire of living in ignorant bliss. So one night, after making love with Eros, she waits until he is fast asleep and lights a lamp, shining it on Eros's face to see for the first time that, indeed, he is a god! The light is symbolic of consciously awakening to reality. Yet Eros wants to remain an eternal youth and continue to shrink from knowledge and responsibility. So when the light startles him awake, he angrily flees, accusing Psyche of betraying their love.

Psyche's yearning to become conscious is representative of how our own human psyches work. She reminds us of what we all must eventually do in order to be fulfilled. Although it's natural for us to want to escape into fantasy from the harsh realities of life, especially in our romantic pursuits, doing so can become the seedbed for seeking chemical "highs" or for a romantic love addiction. Seen rightly, this is our journey, for all men and women embody both Psyche and Eros, the archetypes who had the courage to participate in and open the doorway to the greatest Love Story ever told, the marriage of the human with the Divine.

Your Psyche

Your psyche is your inner life, the voice that speaks to you inside your head. Your psyche is your consciousness. Everything you think comes through your human psyche. And since our feelings are responsive to our thoughts, then everything we feel is indirectly a result of our psyches as well. Without our psyches we'd be cut off from even knowing that we exist, since self-knowledge, or the ability to contemplate our own existence, is what sets us apart from the animal kingdom and makes us human. The human psyche gives us knowledge of the world and helps us function in three-dimensional reality.

In the original Greek, the word psyche means soul, breath, or the chrysalis that becomes a butterfly. You will sometimes see Psyche depicted as a human girl riding on the back of a butterfly, a symbol for the process of personal transformation. From caterpillar to chrysalis to butterfly, we have the perfect metaphor for the death/rebirth sequence of transformation. We die to the old way of being, sheltered in a quiescent, helpless condition in consciousness while the old self is disintegrated, its positive qualities absorbed. Then one day we emerge as an entirely new creature. This metamorphosis is similar to the creative process of bringing the unconscious into conscious reality in the way artists first envision what they create.

Psyche's journey through incarnation, which culminates in her marriage to a god, has much to teach us about our personal quest for psychological and spiritual wholeness. Her quest follows the path of direct knowing that can only come from experience. It is a harrowing journey, full of peril and promise, mysterious helpers, miraculous insights, tricks, stratagems, disobedience, despair and victory.

As you follow Psyche's story you experience her quest as she moves through her unconscious dream state to the wisdom of experience learned through the four labors of love she has to complete to remember she is divine. Every goddess has her unique divine purpose, and Psyche's is to travel the thorny road through the trials of initiation in order to purify her ego so that she can remember her immortal spiritual nature. She is the goddess of personal transformation who reminds us that when we make the decision to seek our true life's purpose and are willing to do the deep inner work of awakening from unconscious dreaming, she can become our guide. And anytime we lose our inspiration, Eros is there in our psyches to rekindle our fire.

Fortunately, for us, the road Psyche travels toward full consciousness is mapped, though not in the ordinary way. We can think of the path of personal transformation as a spiraling track marked by a trail of seeds scattered along its twists and turns. If we pay attention, these subtle signs will keep us on course, pointed in the right direction. We'll discover that though the twists and turns of each person's journey are unique, most of us on a path of transformation pass similar markers. To the extent that we can be conscious travelers looking carefully to spot the seeds of wisdom that appear at significant points along the way, we can speed our progress.

At the end of the journey, like Psyche of myth, we may arrive at a place we only dreamed possible, having grown gracefully into the soul-based Divine Self we were designed to become. In the end, the human Psyche not only marries a god but also is restored to the goddess that she originally was. Could this transformation be our sacred mission as well? Is our reason for living to become more godlike while simultaneously allowing the gods, through us, to experience being human? If so, the merging of psychological health and spiritual qualities that make up Psyche's nature could become the keys to fulfillment, not only for us as individuals, but also for the world.

Your Psyche's Initiatory Tasks:

Seen from the soul's overview, human trials always take on a deeper significance. Your soul unfolds in your inner life upon a larger canvass, undergoing rites of passage and initiations that carry you forward on a timeless evolutionary journey. Often while undergoing a soul-mediated experience we are unable to fathom its purpose; we must experience it first in order to know it. Only in retrospect does its meaning become clear. But Psyche's story can point the way. The four tasks Aphrodite forces upon Psyche are the four initiations we all must master in order to complete our human story and become whole.

Psyche's First Task: Sorting the Seeds

When Psyche comes out of her unconscious dream state where she was living with Eros in the night worlds of fantasy and immature love, she is then required to embark upon the journey of becoming a fully conscious human being. To that end her first guide is the earthy goat-footed god Pan, who symbolizes natural, sure-footed grounding in the physical world. As her first task, Psyche is required to "sort the seeds," a symbol for discerning the true nature of things here in the human world. She needs to recognize the true nature of each person or thing she comes into contact with in order to relate to it realistically.

Psyche is completely overwhelmed by this task. She is pregnant and terrified, knowing so little about this world. In her despair, she rushes to the river to drown herself. But the river refuses to drown her and throws her back on land, where a colony of ants appear and offer to help her. Ants know how to work instinctively and methodically to bring order and complete earthly tasks.

Psyche, whose destiny is to be the goddess who guides humans through personal transformation, first has to learn to be human herself. She learns that running away from the painful elements of life without examining them and decoding their hidden messages keeps her in an unconscious dream-state that lacks maturity. The path of self-knowledge is always fraught with paradox – love and hate, light and shadow -- and all these must be faced and recognized for what they truly are if one is ever to become whole. We all must learn that we are separate selves -- beings who can reason, make choices and take action. Psyche has to individuate from the Divine Feminine archetype, Aphrodite, and take responsibility for herself.

And this, too, is our own first task along our journey of maturation; becoming uniquely ourselves as we separate off from our mothers and fathers, who have made decisions for us thus far. Through the process of individuation we gradually learn to identify our unique talents and to use our human wills to bring order out of chaos.

You might want to reflect now on the ways in which you, like Psyche, allow confusion or a lack of discernment to keep you from moving forward. Here are some questions you can ask yourself:

Do I belittle physical reality as not being as important as the mental or spiritual realms?

Am I willing to live in my body and be fully present in this human reality, or do I excessively seek out-of-body experiences?

Do I often find that I've failed to do my required tasks because I tend to distract myself by scurrying about here and there unconsciously?

Do I still allow authority figures to tell me what to do or expect others to magically come to my aid rather than trusting my own powers of discernment?

To overcome our unwillingness to "sort the seeds" and set our lives on track, we must strive with all our rational might to give shape to our deepest yearnings, hopes, wishes, and fears. Once we can focus our grounded will and full intention on what's really important, new abilities will arise to assist us. An industrious inner "army of ants" will mobilize to help us create order, and progress toward our goals.

The task of sorting the seeds gives Psyche the opportunity to put these dormant human instincts to work. We learn to be active participants in our lives rather than passively waiting for events to "just happen" in the night worlds of fantasy and imagination.

Psyche's Second Task: Gathering the Fleece

Psyche's second initiatory task has to do with learning to balance her emotional nature and bring it to maturity. She is ordered to head straight into an open pasture of fierce, crazed rams in order to retrieve from their coats the golden fleece desired by Aphrodite.

Again Psyche is overwhelmed by this task until the swaying reeds along the riverbed tell her the secret of how to deal with this situation. She is told to observe how the rams draw their fierce power from the light of the sun and are only powerful during the daytime. She observes that at dusk, when the sun's brilliance begins to ebb, their energies dissipate and their wild frenzies cease. She realizes she can hide in the bushes until the rams are lulled to sleep by the gentle evening breeze, and when they are safely slumbering she gathers the fleece that clings to the bushes in the grove.

Psyche is learning that she doesn't have to directly combat aggressive masculine energy. Rather, she can meet her task in a harmless fashion through subtlety and careful planning. She is also learning to be brave and to keep in harmony with the rhythms of day and night.

Her inner helpers are the reeds. Water is symbolic of the emotions, and water, like our emotions, has many moods, from violent storms to glassy calm. Moreover, its surface appearance does not always reveal what goes on underneath. Though the reeds grow close to the water, their roots are in the earth, while they flow gracefully in the air, a symbol of the mind. Often in an emotional crisis we will feel we're in deep water and have "gotten in over our heads." What helps us then is "coming up for air."

Traditionally the emotional realm is considered feminine, while the mental realm is thought to be masculine. Thus, Psyche is learning to balance the masculine and feminine energies within herself -- head and heart -- as a central task of her journey into maturity. Up to this point Psyche's overly feminine emotions have been that of an immature girl, a benighted unconscious love for Eros, the desperate flights and impulses of a frightened child. She is now learning how to bring these girlish emotional responses into balance with the conscious drive and problem-solving power of the analytical, left-brained masculine principle of thought. At this point, then, she has learned to master her emotions and to use her head to outsmart the rams.

Many women fear that they will be annihilated or lose

their femininity if they come too close to this source of primal masculine power. However, we women must all learn, as did Psyche, to steal some of this magic solar god power for ourselves in order to balance our emotional tendencies.

Here Psyche is also learning about the human shadow that lives in our emotional body. The human psyche contains both light and dark. Our shadow side can sometimes move from docile to crazed in unconscious ways, making a mess of our lives. Therefore, we must come to terms with how the human shadow works so our lives are not driven by emotional over-reactions. In maturity we can eventually learn to emerge from the shadow of unconscious, impulsive emotionality into the clear air of willed intention and balanced action. Anytime you catch yourself getting too emotional about something, stop and ask yourself, "What part of my shadow is being triggered by this situation?" Then, take responsibility for healing your emotional wounds so that you can be balanced and clear in realistic ways. Developing a sound and healthy feeling nature is not easy. We have to strive to draw from both sides of the continuum – masculine and feminine, rational and emotional, outer and inner – and avoid the extremes on either side. So where do you fall along this continuum? Ask yourself these questions:

Am I so heartfelt, soft, and vague that I can't seem to cope with interpersonal problems without excessive emotionality?

Am I so analytical, rigid, and hard that I run roughshod over other people's feelings, not even realizing I'm doing this?

Am I able to know how I really feel about something and then act in a healthy, life-giving manner?

Am I afraid of my passions, not willing to risk being myself?

When emotionally upset, do I go also into my mind and get to the bottom of what's really bothering me, then own my unhealed shadow and/or negative thinking pattern so that I can behave appropriately?

Psyche's Third Task: Containing the Waters of Life

In Psyche's third task, Aphrodite makes her climb up a high mountain and look down on the dark waters of the river Styx that gush and swell with all of humanity's unhealed turbulence. On either side of the river, terrible dragons with fiery breath and unblinking eyes guard the waters. Poor Psyche is ordered to go at once into the middle of the river and fill a goblet to the brim with the dangerous waters, returning the filled goblet to the goddess.

All her life Psyche had been warned that she would perish if she ever approached this treacherous river, so she gazes at this awful scene with tears of sheer terror in her eyes. Just as she is about to give up, a majestic eagle, the royal bird of the high god Zeus, flies into her vision. "Give me the goblet," commands the bird, known for its sharp eyes and deadly precision in swooping down onto its prey. As it turns out, Zeus owed Eros a favor, and since Psyche was his former lover, Zeus turns himself into an eagle and rushes in to save her. Upon seeing the eagle and recognizing his royal nature, the waters quiet, the dragons relent, and the eagle dives into the river Styx, fills the goblet to the brim, and delivers it safely back to Psyche.

Now, how shall we interpret this initiatory task? What is the message here for Psyche and for us? Mythology tells us that the river Styx flows in a circular fashion around the entire earth. Swift-moving and menacing, it is the river of life and death. Seen in the light of depth psychology, we might think of the Styx as the human collective unconscious, a powerful floodtide of unprocessed and disorganized archetypes, images, and passions. Within these waters is all of life's vitality – birth and death, joy and suffering, triumph and disaster.

How can one fragile human being contain this onrush and not be shattered? It appears that this lesson is about learning to develop a strong enough ego to anchor our growing complexity so that we might learn what to take on and what to leave behind. The crystal goblet is symbolic of the human ego, the vehicle Spirit must use in order to embody here. Psyche's container must be sturdy enough to accommodate all that she is becoming without cracking apart.

By this time in her awakening Psyche is beginning to use both her human and her divine attributes, but she has no awareness of this quite yet. She does not realize that all this divine intervention she's been given arises from her own inner resources. She does not realize yet who she truly is. Yet the completion of this task will bring her great reward.

As the collective unconscious, the river Styx carries the generative seeds of all imaginative and creative endeavors. The task that Aphrodite gives her is to gather the waters and hold them in a fragile goblet, thus giving the waters form. Psyche is pregnant, remember, and therefore it is obvious that she is learning form making.

As her container strengthens to encompass both the inner feminine and masculine powers, both Aphrodite and Zeus come to her aid, because both are elements of Psyche's inner divinity.

And for us, too, the lesson is clear: We need a strong ego container in order to filter the collective unconsciousness, or the world of imagination, taking only what is usable and helpful in our daily lives. Like the eagle, we need to develop a discriminating bird's-eye view in order to see clearly what boundaries to set up, what parts to let in and what to shut out. And when we can access our soul's-eye-view, represented by the eagle form of Zeus, we empower ourselves to fulfill our soul's destiny here on earth. The questions then for each of us are these:

Does my ego filter out too much or too little of my soul's perspective?

Have I learned to take on only the tasks that are rightfully mine and let the rest go?

Am I in danger of being shattered by attempting to take on all of the flow of life, not only for myself but also for everyone around me?

Have I become a dysfunctional enabler or shield for another, keeping him or her from growing because of my neurotic need to be needed?

Have I found a balance between my head and my heart?

Can I accept the fact that I, like Psyche, am both human and divine?

Psyche's Fourth Task: Descending to the Underworld

In fairy tales there are usually three tasks. Psyche is given four. In the science of numerology, three is the number for creation, while four symbolizes manifestation--grounding creation into the physical plane. In her first three tasks, Psyche had help from the animal and plant kingdoms, unconscious aspects of herself represented by earth, water, and air. These are the elements that make up our physical, emotional and mental bodies. In all three of these tasks Psyche learns to use the masculine principles of grounding, logical problem solving, and discriminating vision to balance her overly feminine nature.

In this final stage of her initiation she must enter the mysteries of the inner divine feminine, represented by the great goddess Persephone in both her light and dark aspects. Psyche must once again face the question of whether she is mortal or immortal, and this task will teach her that she is both. This task will prepare her to undertake her divine function here on earth, to become the new Aphrodite, a goddess who has learned how to feel and think – not just universally, as all gods and goddesses do, but in a personal life on earth as well.

Aphrodite now gives Psyche the task of traveling down into the Underworld to gain from Persephone, the Queen of Hades, a box of her beauty ointment. She is ordered to bring this ointment to Aphrodite without opening it or putting it on her own face.

Now Psyche knows that she must surely die. Hearing Aphrodite's words, she remembers the ominous oracle given to her father, that his beloved daughter would be married to Death. It seems the prophecy is now to come true, for in Hades she must encounter Death consciously and with purpose. Psyche does not realize that the goddess Aphrodite, from the heavenly realms, and the goddess Persephone, from the Underworld, are two sides of the same Divine Feminine archetype. As the human link between these two goddesses, Psyche must discover that mature femininity contains both light and dark, creation and destruction, heaven and earth, life and death. To learn this, the human psyche must delve deeply into the dark inward places where the extremes of beauty and ugliness swim together in paradoxical chaos. There it will realize that only when it faces both the illuminated and the shadowed aspects of existence will it become grounded in solid reality.

The Tower is Psyche's guide for this horrendous adventure. While visiting in the Tower, she is taught all the rules she must follow in order to travel to and from the Underworld in one piece. The main warning she is given is that under no circumstances is she to put Persephone's beauty ointment on her own face! This ointment was made only for a goddess. And this time she must go alone, with no divine intervention.

On her way she is to pass three tests. First, she is to pay for her passage with barley cake and mead, not allowing anything to distract her from her mission. Second, she must leave a dying man drowning in the lake, because he was already lost and saving him would have deterred her from her path. And third, she is implored by three weaving women to help them find a needle they had lost, a request she must also refuse, for again this would deter her from her path. Clearly all these distractions were designed to tempt her away from her purpose.

The Alchemist, Emily Kell, www.emilykell.com

Reflect on this, for this, too, is your story.

Persephone is the perfect final teacher for Psyche, as she too was once an innocent, carefree young girl. Having been kidnapped and forced to marry the God of Death, Hades, Persephone has grown into a goddess who knows both the heights and the depths of feminine experience. She lives in the harsh winds of winter for half of every year in the Underworld, then ushers in the springtime for the other half on earth. This divided life makes Persephone wise to the ways of the human world, and she passes this wisdom along to Psyche, though Psyche is unaware of this gift until later, when it bursts forth spontaneously in her decision to put the beauty ointment on her own face.

How does her decision to violate the main order she was given come about? Well, we human girls can certainly relate. She was walking along, thinking of the time when she would once again meet up with her cherished lover, and her longing for him became so strong she could feel his arms around her and hear his sweet voice. As she reveled in this fantasy, she caught a glance of her reflection in a pond and, horrified at how bedraggled she looked, she could not bear to think of Eros seeing her in such a state. Wouldn't he turn away in disgust? Then suddenly she remembers the precious beauty ointment she is carrying and thinks: "If I can anoint my face with this divine beauty, my lord will find me irresistible for I will be as a goddess myself and fit to be his bride."

When she opens the box of ointment, out flows a noxious cloud of sleep, wrapping Psyche in a deathlike slumber. And there she lies, as though a corpse, her life force seemingly extinguished right at the time of her greatest triumph.

What shall we make of Psyche's new disobedience? Has she simply succumbed to vanity and self-forgetfulness, all her efforts for naught? Or, as when she disobeyed Eros and shined the lamp of consciousness upon his face, is there a higher purpose to this new disobedience? Yes, indeed. Psyche's actions are the kind of mistake known as a *felix culpa,* which means "a happy sin," one that pushes us towards a greater good. When Psyche falls asleep, she dies to her immature "maiden" identity. This is the kind of sleep that shifts us from one state of consciousness to another. The maiden Psyche must be sacrificed before the mature wife of a god can be awakened. Death will always precede rebirth into a new and greater form. We simply wait, as though dead, until some act of grace or new vision arrives.

Psyche's *felix culpa* has another meaning as well. By this action Psyche has announced her willingness to enter into personal love and raise it to the level of the sacred. This love is so strong it is felt by Eros, who flies to her rescue and kisses her awake from her death-like sleep. The Eros who awakens Psyche is no longer the silly boy nursing his wounded pride, hiding in his mother's house – the *puer aeternus,* or eternal youth, of Jungian psychology. Eros has now become a Redeemer God who can recognize, serve, and honor genuine love.

When Psyche awakens she is no longer an immature girl but a conscious woman who has claimed her life's purpose as the goddess who brings divine love and beauty from the archetypal dimension down to earth. This represents the opening of the heart chakra that bridges earthly and spiritual ways of being. Love and beauty awaken us to the element of fire, the spiritual aspect of our nature. Psyche has opened a new door for humanity; the possibility that divine love can live in individual human minds and hearts. And as for the gods, she brings them an awareness of personal experience, a life beyond the limitation of only knowing how to relate universally to the world.

Thus did Psyche, a mortal, become the wife of Eros, the immortal god of love and inspiration. Soon Psyche gives birth to their daughter, whose name in heaven is Joy, while on earth she is called Pleasure. She is the marriage of the soul's happiness with the earthly pleasures of the human senses.

So what can this last task teach us about our own journey home? In the classical sense, initiation connotes an expansion of consciousness, a wider opening of mind and heart to a remembrance of the inner divinity that is our essential nature. In her own initiation, Psyche did the sacred work of acting as a mediator between the human world and the world of spirit. She is the link between the divine principle of love and its manifestation in the world of human relationships. Psyche raises individual human love to the level of the gods, a marriage between the human and archetypal dimensions of consciousness.

Now it's up to us to bring divine love into all our human partnerships. When an archetypal occurrence of something happens in the psyche even once, it creates a pathway for others to follow. We humans now have the responsibility to treat love as a sacred mystery, as an avenue to spiritual transcendence.So ponder the following to gain more understanding of your own sacred purpose:

Ask yourself in what ways your current relationships fulfill your highest purpose for being on this earth. Acknowledging that each partnership serves a spiritual purpose can make your relationship a sacred pact.

Sanctuary, Ashley Foreman, www.thirteentwentystudios.com

Practice surrendering to love, realizing that surrender is not defeat but a conscious act of letting go and letting be. Surrendering to love opens your heart so that you become more loving and available to be loved.

See the divinity in everyone you love – especially when the going gets rough. Loving each other soul-to-soul is a path to creating heaven on earth.

Jot down or reflect on your own "big memories," those soul events that brought you significant dreams and inner visions. Do they suggest a unified theme? If so, what is your role? What purpose are you here to serve?

What are you doing in your life right now that expresses your spiritual gifts and highest purpose?

Never forget that Psyche is the archetype of our human psyches. Everything you've read about this goddess is about you and me. Just as Psyche has modeled for us how heaven and earth can marry within us, we can also model incarnation as the divine entities we came here to be. May your journey be fulfilled and completed by acknowledging both the dark and the light, by honoring as sacred both human pleasure and soulful joy in yourself and in your life.

Jacquelyn Small, LMSW, is a Phi Beta Kappa graduate of the University of Texas at Austin with degrees in Human Psychology, a Masters of Science in Social Work with a specialization in Clinical Social Work and a degree in Applied Music. She is a licensed nondenominational minister and a licensed psychotherapist who works with both spiritual and psychological concerns. Jacquelyn is a popular presenter and consultant in academic settings, new-thought churches and new paradigm conferences and mental health settings, known for her easy-going, self-disclosing, humorous style of intimate relating with her audiences. Jacquelyn has authored eight books about soul-based psychology and the process of personal transformation, some of which have become classics in the counseling and consciousness fields. She is also a regular columnist for *Science of Mind* magazine. For more information visit her website: www.eupsychia.com

Feminine Light in the Dark Night of the Soul

Dark Night, Uma Rose, 18"x24" acrylic on canvas.

By Uma Rose

The details of my life had lost definition Like Matisse's paintings of the lily ponds, I was floating in a world of grief, fear and self-hatred. Yet again I'd been cut free from a relationship, set afloat like some old boat without sails. I felt rejected, abandoned and devoid of light. I didn't want to have a future alone, without loving arms to hold me. Yet the only direction my boat seemed to go was inward, toward *the dark night of the soul.* Although at the time I felt bereft and abandoned, I was about to go through a huge transformation where I would find the shining beacon of Mother God to guide me home. I had already embraced the Goddess as a real presence in my life around this time, when I began hearing a woman's voice call my name as I walked down the street. This went on for some time before I finally mustered up the courage to tell a trusted friend about it. Having some knowledge of such things, she said, "Sounds like the Goddess has something to tell you."

The idea of facing the old woman inside me was terfying. She had already appeared in a painting, but when I first faced her in a vision, she appeared as Death; a skeleton in a purple satin cloak with red lining. I could barely understand her words, and her form would shift from skeleton to sweet grandma, then back to skeleton again. However, as elusive as she seemed beneath my eyelids, she wasn't so shy in bookstores, whispering in my ear, "Go here, go there!" Her urgency was often so powerful that books seemed to fly off the shelves in response to her suggestions, in order that I might receive their message.

One such book, *The Pregnant Virgin*, by Marion Woodman, helped me to better understand what I was going through. She used the image of the chrysalis to portray the inevitable process of death/rebirth of the human soul. Just as a caterpillar naturally goes into a cocoon state, the human soul must also go inward and die in order to gain enough self-love and understanding to transform into a vibrant butterfly. More often than not, people fear self-reflection or going inward, and avoid it until everything in their life falls apart. She said:

> *. . . a reason for fearing the chrysalis lies in our cultural loss of containers. Our society's emphasis on linear growth and achievement alienates us from the cyclic pattern of death and rebirth, so that when we experience ourselves dying or dream that we are, we fear annihilation.*[1]

While the nature of existence is ceaseless transformation, we are taught to deny or suppress the death process so as to avoid being socially ostracized. Spiritual growth requires that we discover the depths of our wounds, yet we often use denial to protect ourselves from difficulty and discomfort. We sometimes expend enormous amounts of energy fighting pain, death and loss, and hiding from the basic truths of the natural world and of our own true natures. In fact some of us use addictions to support our denials. Ours has been called the Addicted Society, with over twenty million alcoholics, ten million drug addicts, and millions more addicted to gambling, food, sexuality, unhealthy relationships, compulsive work and keeping up a constantly fast pace. As Buddhist and author Jack Kornfield says, "Until we are able to bring awareness and understanding to our old wounds, we will find ourselves repeating their patterns of unfulfilled desire, anger, and confusion over and over again."[2]

According to Carl Jung, the *shadow*, or unconscious parts of the self, are often repressed and hidden from the conscious personality. He says, "…man is, on the whole, less good than he imagines himself or wants to be. Everyone carries a shadow, and the less it is embodied in the individual's conscious life, the blacker and denser it is."[3] We all have a shadow that in part is comprised of those forces and feelings that we outwardly ignore and reject. The more strongly we believe something and reject its opposite, the more energy goes into the shadow.

This explains why, in my visions and dreams, the many aspects of my personality showed themselves as dark and light or good and bad in nature. It explains, for example, why the Crone Mother appeared as Death as well as someone who looked like my loving maternal grandmother. In mythology and dreams there are many archetypes that live in what Carl Jung called the *collective unconscious.* These figures can appear to us as helpers and can guide us through the death and rebirth process of a dark night of the soul.

Much later, long after my first dark night, I read an article that described my initial encounter with the Crone Mother quite well. It was an article in *Sage Woman* magazine, by Rebecca Vassy titled, *Wild Women don't Get the Blues or My Adventures With Baba Yaga.* I loved Ms. Vassy's description of the Crone:

> *My Grandmother is no ordinary grandmother. Her cheeks are gaunt and bony, not ripe and round as apples. She is (according to some) more likely to bake children than cookies; she tends a bone garden, not a rose garden; and rather than rocking quietly in her chair on the porch, she races through the night air in her mortar, steering with a pestle, the wind tearing through her iron gray hair and the thunder echoing her primal shrieking. This is Baba Yaga, my grandmother, my Patroness, my Crone Goddess, my harsh and healing Teacher.*[4]

After reading this article I was inspired to draw a picture of my Crone self, who called herself *Mama Yaga.* The softness of the Crone is what I wanted to draw though, with the intensity of her gaze and knowing smile. In my first meeting with Mama Yaga she appeared as a dark Goddess, not unlike her sisters Kali, Sekhmet and Ereshkigal. But rather than seeing my Crone in her shadow side as something to repress in myself, I embraced her and listened to what she had to tell me. Mama Yaga then guided me to take sacred healing baths. She taught me how to do emotional release sessions in the hot water, which helped me to clear the grief, heartbreak and rage I was holding in my body as a result of the trauma I'd experienced in my childhood with my abusive stepfather.

Many times during the release, through vibrating my emotions, I began to reclaim essence that had fragmented out of me because of the trauma. Mama Yaga encouraged me to embrace the images and visions I had, no matter how otherworldly and unbelievable they seemed, because this essence had long been lost to me and was now coming back into me.

The essence I reclaimed was a sister part of me that embodied my desire and strength to live. The name she called herself was Mira, and what she brought back to me was the ability to heal myself and others through massage therapy, energy work, and psychic abilities. With Mira's and Mama Yaga's presence and awareness, I was now able to take the next step into the unknown, while holding enough light inside me to guide the way.

Descent Into the Underworld

When I discovered the Sumerian myth of Inanna and her journey into the Underworld to face her shadow sister Ereshkigal, I felt like I had found a road map into the dark night. In a book titled *The Dark Goddess*, Marcia Starck and Gynne Stern discuss the importance of Inanna's descent into the underworld and how the dark goddesses are meant to assist us in our journey into the dark night. They write:

> *Inanna's descent is the classic heroine's journey--one that most of us take at some time in our lives. We are forced to make this descent when trauma plunges us into depression, when change catalyses us to make major life decisions, or when physical illness pushes us to look beneath the surface at emotions we have been suppressing.*[5]

In the story, Inanna is Queen of Heaven and Earth. Traditionally, in order to maintain her position as Queen she must have a King. However, Inanna's King, Demuzi, has abandoned her. Nonetheless, she is invited to go to her brother-in-law's funeral in the Underworld where, by tradition, Inanna must face her shadow sister Ereshkigal in order to obtain true power as Queen through the process of death and rebirth. In order to fortify herself for this descent into the Underworld, Inanna adorns herself with seven precious jewels signifying her identity as Queen. She wears her gold crown, her lapis beads, the gold breastplate and bracelet, with the indigo robe over her shoulders, and the lapis measuring rod in her left hand. She then goes into the Underworld, where there are seven gates she must pass through, each requiring her to give up one of her seven jewels of identity, and then finally even her skin, so that at last she stands before Ereshkigal as only a wraith of pure light.

When I went on this internal journey in a guided meditation, I found myself in a cave. I was instructed by

Mama Yaga, Uma Rose, 24" x30" acrylic on canvas.

Mama Yaga to plunge into a pool of lava, which burned off all my skin. I pulled myself out and onto a ledge, and realized that I had become the light of my true essence, glowing in soft pink and gold hues. I felt raw and vulnerable as I walked along the ledge deeper into the cave until I came upon a huge primordial Mother figure that was a part of the cave. She had long jagged teeth and appeared as a lion-headed woman-dragon. I let her devour me, sucking down my light like milk. I didn't mind. I felt the need to surrender and find relief from the heartbreak. But rather than eternal sleep, I was reborn, rushing out of her vulva into a cool stream. Mama Yaga was waiting there for me, and in my new body I climbed into the boat.

Integration of Shadow Sister

After embracing my shadow self, as Inanna had to do with Ereshkigal, I began to experience the rage that had been seething beneath all the heartbreak and tears I had cried. I wanted change! I wanted life! I began meditating, quit smoking, did yoga and took healing baths. I painted like a mad woman, went to massage school, and found good, paying clients and healing experiences I would never forget. I no longer felt collapsible. I felt mean, bloodthirsty, wise and powerful. Underneath that, however, I trusted no one, couldn't receive love very well, and didn't recognize how afraid I felt of everyone, because in my rage I no longer cared anymore--and not caring felt like relief from the pain of unrequited love or rejection.

When I painted *Kali-Ma*, I was waking up to the illusion of the world and getting in touch with my rage at the injustices I had experienced as a woman. The Hindu goddess Kali, otherwise referred to as Kali-Ma or Ma-Kali, is a powerful feminine diva or goddess who knows the horrors that are in the world. She is a fierce protector and is called upon during dramatic transformations in a person's life. In her dark side she is the destroyer, and is depicted as the black Kali, with blood on her lips and human skulls about her waist and neck. She commonly holds a knife in one hand and the severed head of a giant, dripping blood, in the other. Her body is naked except for her hideous ornaments, and she is dancing on the white body of the god Shiva. Kali is an archetype that, once evoked and felt, takes a woman into her dark side.

Another excerpt from *The Dark Goddess*, by Marcia Starck and Gynne Stern, explains how dark goddesses can help us go through cataclysmic transformations and gain strength through embracing our shadow side.

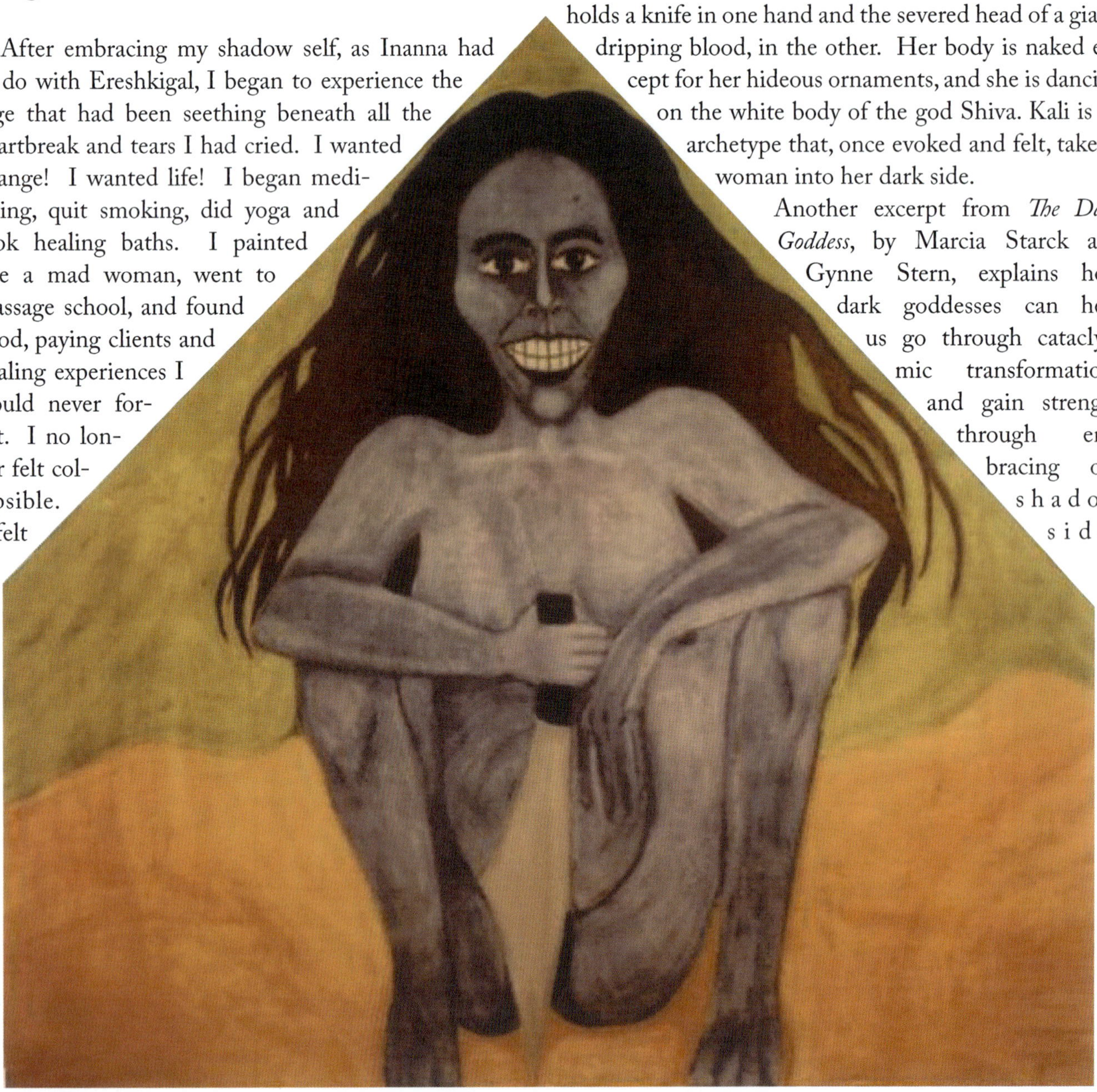

Kali-Ma, Uma Rose, 24"x 24"Acrylic on wood panel.

However, contacting these goddesses might require that we completely change our definition of ourselves. They write:

> *For women to contact Kali they often have to become violent and terrible--traits not considered feminine or associated with the "nice little girl" idealization that most of us grew up with.*[6]

An encounter with Kali can be shocking, especially if a woman has kept a lid on her negative feelings and thought of herself as a nice person, or she's someone who has internalized heavy judgments on anger. In her book, *Archetypes in Older Women*, Jean Shinoda Bolen writes, "It's deeply informative to find yourself capable of rage and fantasies worthy of Kali; not only do you discover a side of yourself you may not have known, but it gives you a better understanding of those who act on their rage."[7]

By the time I created *The Awakener*, I had met my ex-husband and was on the verge of marriage and motherhood. I had been integrating my shadow sister for about five years now and had come to resonate deeply with the Egyptian Goddess Sekhmet, the lion-headed daughter of Ra, who was believed to be the first king of the earth. Sekhmet was born of Ra's third eye, and was seen as a sun goddess with many lunar attributes; the solar disc above her head situated between two horns, her human body beautiful and lithe. Avenging the perceived slight of her father by humanity, Sekhmet devours humanity for no longer paying libations to Ra. She becomes drunk on the blood of humanity, and would have destroyed humans had her father and brother not tricked her with a concoction of wine. Sekhmet drinks the wine and becomes intoxicated with joy, no longer caring if she's drinking human blood or not.

My connection with Sekhmet inspired a painting of the lion-headed woman with wings. I called her *The Awakener*, not knowing the change she would create in my life. The lightening behind was a recurring theme in my visions, the purple and red colors reminding me of Mama Yaga's cloak. Like meeting the Crone that first time, I had no idea what was in store for me in my life. I was doing what I thought I should do, becoming a wife and mother. *The Awakener* was there to mark the end and the beginning of a new journey for me, but I could never have imagined what was about to unfold. Like Sekhmet or Kali or Baba Yaga, *The Awakener* is not a soft teacher. She is harsh and challenging. She is the Destroyer as well as the Illuminator. I feel lucky to have survived the events that followed my painting of her.

The Awakener, Uma Rose, 24"x36" acrylic on canvas.

Surviving the Dark Goddess

When my son was born, I almost died of blood loss. I was having a home birth and had to be rushed to the hospital. My son was separated from me there, replaying my own birth scenario. I had to have four pints of blood replaced, and as it turned out, we were fortunate to be at the hospital because my son choked on colostrum while there and had to be taken to intensive care. Later it occurred to me that this experience was an outer manifestation of being devoured by the Dark Goddess in my earlier vision, only this time I almost died physically and had to make a conscious effort to live. But having a newborn child gave me more incentive to live than anything ever had before.

This near death experience is part of what inspired *The Silencing of Mother's Heart*, along with visions that came later, after I'd recovered. In the painting I am suspended in Hell from the thread of a huge spider web, my body like a fetus, barely formed. If I made a sound, the spider in the light at the top of the painting would shoot down towards me to suck out my essence. It was hard not to make sounds, because in this place it got very hot and compressive, then freezing cold. I could hear women's voices wailing and screaming down below me, which made me want to make noise, but anytime I did scream out, the spider would come to torture me again.

The Silencing of Mother's Heart is just one of many images I've seen on my journey through the dark night. It's taken me a long time to allow myself to paint these dark places because they are so vivid and frightening to me. However, I also feel that they deserve recognition and acceptance as expressions of what Eckhart Tolle calls the "collective pain body of women". [8]

The journey into the dark night of the soul is a lifelong experience for some people, especially those battling major depression and other forms of dysfunction. Not everyone is equipped to handle the light of the Crone Goddess helping to reveal his or her deepest inner truth. For me the journey with the Crone Goddess as my guide was a life or death choice that has continued since I began this journey over eighteen years ago. The details of my world are still soft around the edges, like Matisse's lily ponds. I sometimes feel as if I'm waking up from a strange dream. It's a path that weaves between the worlds, one that is by nature dark and mysterious, and not without pain, as the gentle fire devours my armor and unfolds me like a flower, exposing my true fragility; the tender light of my soul.

Calm After the Storm, Uma Rose, 24"x30", acrylic on canvas.

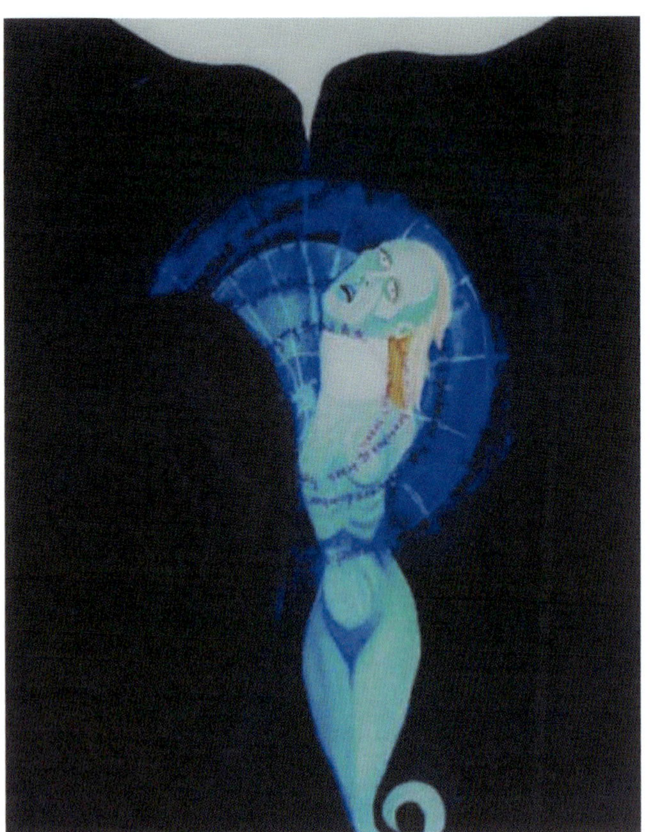

Silencing of Mother's Heart, 16"x20" acrylic on canvas.

Uma Rhiannon Rose attended Interlochen Arts Academy and Albion College in Michigan where she majored in Art and Literature. She is primarily self-taught in the areas of painting, archetypal psychology, and mythology. Her poetry has been published (under different names) in small literary magazines. Her art has been shown in coffee houses, local bars, and small galleries. Presently she lives with her mate in Ashland, Oregon, creating out of the depths of life--her best teacher. Her artwork and poetry can be viewed at www.rhiannons-visions.com.

In The Golden Warmth of Darkness
Poem and Image by Rose Sharrar

There is a presence you can hardly see
Ready to love you, each part of you

We have lost parts of ourselves in various places
That are real even if we don't know them
or think we havn't been there

You have to go into the darkness inside of you
and feel in order to reclaim these lost parts

In the golden warmth of darkness
you will find your lost and found soul
And you won't be steely, or cold no more

Reclaiming Initiation: The Priestess Path

Grandmother Moon, Suzanne DeVeuve, 20"x24" oil on canvas, www.suzannedeveuve.com

By Anyaa T. McAndrew

Initiatory rites and rituals are the domain of all religions and spiritual paths. The path of the female mystic, or priestess, can be seen in its own light in these times of great turmoil and change at the "Turning of the Ages." It is unique not only because it is a feminine path, but because it has been absent from our psyches for thousands of years. We have witnessed the shadow side of the Divine Masculine, the Patriarchy, gain ascendancy and foster myriad forms of oppression, including the suppression of women's rights, Holy Inquisitions, and the negation of feminine mysticism. Over millennia we've had priests but no priestesses; a male God, but no Goddesses. It has been out of balance, but things are changing.

One of the features of Patriarchy has been an emphasis on "solar initiations" or those that focus on transcending the body to join with Spirit. Fire-walking, warrior sweat-lodges, the Sun Dance, mental meditations, some martial arts, and many forms of vision quests use the mind and endurance to reach out of the body and thereby elevate consciousness. By contrast, the Divine Feminine employs "lunar initiations," or those that call Spirit into the body, a welcome alternative to jettisoning out into the universe to make a connection! The feminine loves the sparkle of life, the senses, getting down and dirty and into the pleasures and pains, joys and tears of earth.

Another feature of Patriarchy is our loss of soul connection to our bodies. The result is that most of us center ourselves from our neck up, denying the life-force energy that enlivens us and makes life worth living. We identify heavily with our thinking and action based on thought alone. But as women reclaim their Divine Feminine natures, the true feeling function of femininity gets to play and be re-membered. Shakti dances into ecstatic bliss. Aphrodite revels in sacred sexual pleasure. Pele fully runs the life-force energy of fiery passion. Inanna consciously surrenders to the death-rebirth mysteries. Baubo laughs her bawdy belly laugh. Kuan Yin cries her tears of compassion for all living things, while Gaia pours forth her infinite abundance. Priestess consciousness allows the many faces of the Goddess to be soulfully expressed, as the human woman learns to step into her spiritual power.

After a long suppression, the Divine Feminine and the priestess archetype are returning to cultural consciousness and acceptance. Women walk differently on a spiritual path when they are fully encouraged to express their soulful nature. They are wild, willful, chaotic, earthy, sensual, sweet, empathic, merging, deeply emotional, passionate and compassionate. These natural soul qualities are the qualities of the Divine Feminine seeking to awaken the priestess within the woman. Through our wild desires and intricate passions we find our soul stirring and our spirit calling. We stop silencing our deepest dreams and allow the voice of the Goddess to come through as our own. This awakening, through the various stages of Initiation, and finally Emergence, can result in the full empowerment of a woman as a priestess whose temple is the everyday world. She exerts her influence in all of her roles—as daughter, mother, lover, career woman, neighbor and in every interaction she has, moment to moment. At last, the divine feminine and the divine feminist are joined. Finally, we can embrace a movement of soul and spirit, human and divine. Finally, we can experience the sacred in our daily lives and express our life force energy in everything we do. We can include the very essential factors that make the new feminine mysticism grounded and practical, yet imaginal and sacred.

It is Divine Calling that awakens the inner sleeping priestess. For me, it happened in divine astrological timing. It was a cold summer night on the Isle of Lewis in the highlands of Scotland. The stones of Callanish

Pathways, Cynthia Ré Robbins, 13"x19" oil and tempera on Panel, www.art4spirit.com

The Healing, Cynthia Ré Robbins, 18"x24" oil and Plaka, www.art4spirit.com

haunted the landscape like the Ancient Ones of legend. My heavy red velvet cape was keeping me toasty warm as we ushered in the full moon on this auspicious night to ceremonialize with my teacher, Daniel Giamario, Shamanic Astrologer. It was 1997 and we were co-leading a group to visit the stone circles of Northern Scotland. Never before had I felt so connected to the land. I was re-membering my lineage, and in that moment I felt the priestess within me quicken and congeal. This part of me was longing to be re-born and to have her say in my life. I discovered the Priestess Process™ and later that year, I initiated as a priestess in a circle facilitated by Nicole Christine.

Receiving the Call is the first step toward *Initiation.* The Calling can be from childhood, when a woman simply knows or re-members past lives when she was witch, sorceress, shamaness, wisewoman healer, courtesan, oracle, or any number of ancient roles she has played. I remembered being a nun many times, and even attempted it in this life, but my sexuality was far too strong for me to seriously consider surrendering it to a disembodied Jesus. Some women are fortunate to have mothers who open the way for them to re-member. Children from the sixties and seventies had parents that may have passed on enough "pagan" spirituality to allow their daughters to feel comfortable exploring a feminine spiritual path. Many simply hear the word "priestess" and something gets triggered on a deep cellular memory, and if the opportunity to respond is given, they will follow it into Initiation.

Creating intention is the second step toward *Initiation.* It must happen consciously. As women, when we intend, we are calling back our right to be spiritual beings. We are calling back the power to call on the Divine, to do ritual and ceremony and magic, to manifest our own dreams and visions on earth. We are calling back power we may have never known in this lifetime or for thousands of years. This is heady stuff for most women and it can come with a certain amount of fear. What if someone hears, sees, and knows I am claiming my right to be spiritually powerful? It is a time where we must confront the Inner Patriarch who has limits and rules about being feminine in a man's world.

Intending to evoke our power then plunges us into the darkness that must be faced, and directed into a cathartic dying stage of the initiatory process. What we intend always has a shadow that stands in the way and must be traversed and integrated for us to fully be all that we are. Nicole Christine, creatrix of the Priestess Process™ and the Magdalene Mystery School™, taught that initiation always results in a psychic death. When we can get conscious of those aspects that must die, we consciously cooperate with Spirit in freeing ourselves from past patriarchal conditioning. We also realize that the abuse, betrayal and oppression of the past were what drove us to seek our lost feminine spirit.

It is helpful for women to find a way to tell their story. The telling of our stories allows us to surrender those aspects of self that must go, and to call back those aspects of soul that need to be retrieved. This may involve a format like therapy or a priestess circle, but the empathic presence of other women can hold an initiate in a womb of love that can never be experienced in the same way with men. Releasing, burning and cord-cutting rituals can be helpful to give greater intention and meaning to what we are dying to. Expressing and releasing emotion at the deepest levels is also called for. Tools like breathwork, trance or ecstatic dance, chanting, sounding or anything that allows free movement physically and emotionally is the natural feminine way to let go.

Re-birth always follows death in the great cycles of transformation. My soul sister, Linda Star Wolf, Shamanic Priestess, Visionary, and creatrix of Shamanic Breathwork™ and Venus Rising, describes the path of the shamanic priestess as one who is willing to walk these cycles consciously throughout her entire life. She is the "walker between the worlds" and embraces both the human and the divine. Death is always the death of some aspect of the ego, and connects us to our humanity once again, giving rise to compassion. Rebirth connects us to our archetypal or divine natures and allows us to walk as the goddesses walk. The priestess requires a connection to both worlds. If she embraces death or humanity without a connection to the archetypal worlds, she will have no greater purpose. She will not be able to see the overview. If she is too celestial, she will become arrogant with her power and lose compassion.

For the priestess, re-birth can also be about having the inspiration and vision to create heaven on earth, to seed her version of new Earth. Since she has traversed the underworld with Inanna, she now has what she needs to step into that vision. That vision can be carried out in the simplest way, such as a commitment to working with an altar or the Celtic wheel of the year holy-days or a medicine wheel. Or it can be a more complex commitment to express more of her feminine in her relationship(s), do volunteer work at the local women's shelter or create a

The Beloveds, Krista Lynn Brown, 18"x24" acrylic on canvas, www.devaluna.com

women's art guild. In this way the new priestess walks in the world while she stays enlivened and inspired by her spiritual connection.

Following re-birth, the priestess is ready for Sacred Marriage or the uniting of all polarities and dualities within. Isis/Osiris, the Magdalene and the Christ, Shakti and Shiva, and all the divine couples through time, hidden from our view as they have been, show us the way to open to God/dess within. The priestess is particularly aware of uniting these dualities because her sacred task is to bring Spirit into Matter. As Carl Jung noted, the "individuation" process or integration of polarities can take a lifetime of spiritual work and healing. We are always alchemizing and integrating polarities throughout the life cycle.

Consciously evolving, exploring and embracing our inner masculine is inner work that is essential to the feminine. Unless we walk with healthy inner masculines, we cannot walk safely and effectively in the world. The inner male's highest function is to be present, listen and make decisions based on what is good for all aspects of the Self. Because this is not how the masculine has been modeled for us, we suffer from not even knowing our own inner male's essence or Divine qualities. We can tend to push away the concept of the masculine both inside and out, while in fact, he longs to be known and to serve. Many women have become "animus-possessed" drivers, letting their immature male selves unconsciously run the show to the exclusion of their understated feminine selves. It is time for this inner patriarchy to change along with its outer manifestations!

Sacred marriage is another ongoing life process, just like the continual process of death/rebirth. We can find ways to ceremonialize the inner marriage to give power and potency to this essential aspect of *Initiation.* Priestess Circles in my lineage spend an entire weekend expanding their understanding, and then co-create a beautiful Sacred Wedding Ceremony where they make vows and declarations to themselves. In these times we cannot afford to exclude the Divine Masculine as we embrace the Divine Feminine. The ancient fertility rite of Hieros Gamos was played out every year by the Year King and the High Priestess to ensure prosperity for the land and the people. Our own Sacred Union or Sacred Marriage within is the spiritual foundation from which springs true personal growth and empowerment. It is the alchemical activity that engenders wholeness and balance.

At the end of *Initiation*, the new priestess *emerges.* She is ready to step into her newfound spiritual authority in an immediate and formal way. In my Shamanic Priestess Process, *Initiation* lasts nine months or the time it takes to gestate a "Self." Emergence can be a solitary experience of self-proclamation or a public proclamation/declaration with beloved friends and family. Sometimes a woman chooses to be ordained as a minister, and this can be a powerful way to proclaim herself a priestess. An Emergence Ceremony allows the priestess within to be seen and honored, even if only Spirit and Nature witness.

The ancient priestess was either called to the temple to serve or took on her sacred healing work as a special task recognized and valued by her community. The new priestess will not be so easily acknowledged by the world. This has the disadvantage of appearing to separate her

Priestess Graduation, Ashely Foreman, www.thirteentwentystudios.com

out from her spirituality but the advantage of shielding her from criticism in times that do not yet fully honor sacred functions. There are some lineages that will certify or train or anoint women as priestesses, but in fact, we are creating as we go. The temples are long gone, as is the Matriarchy that supported them. However, all women have the priestess archetype within them, ready to be awakened.

The new priestess walks everywhere and does everything within the ordinary flow of her life. The difference is that she is fully aware that where she walks is sacred, what she does is sacred and who she is, is sacred. The new priestess "priestesses" the planet.

Women's spiritual work calls for full embodiment if we are to co-create a New Earth with Spirit. We can no longer afford to be disembodied victims of a worn-out patriarchal system on any level: physical, economic, political, social or spiritual. As many have predicted for these times, it is women and the feminine that will have the greatest impact. The "New Priestess" archetype that is rising up in women is a sure sign that everything is happening in Divine Feminine Timing!

Anyaa T. McAndrew, M.A., L.P.C., N.C.C. psychotherapist and teacher, resides in a shamanic retreat community in the Smoky Mountains of western North Carolina. Her early work expressed through the lens of the women's movement, feminist therapy, and the rape and incest survivor's the Midwest. her website www.goddessontheloose.com .

Shakti, Suzanne DeVeuve, 24"x30" oil on canvas,
www.suzannedeveuve.com

CHAPTER SEVEN:

The Goddess of Interconnectivity

The Healing Power of Art

By Cher Lyn

Prepare your self for the ultimate flight
on the tail of a dragon
Fly through the dungeon into the light…
Know thee oh child of thy heritage; know ye are truly
the Spirit of Light…
Ancient secrets seeded… A leap of crimson rust…
in light that cast shadows of distant memories…
Breathe… I trust!

The healing qualities of art can take many forms, and art has been a monumental gift in my personal journey of deep inner healing and spiritual awakening. If not for the creative passion gifted me, I feel I may not have survived in this world. It is interesting that art is the last three letters in heart, so it is no surprise to me that pain in the heart and emotions do transform through art.

I remember seeing into what is considered the unseen worlds of Spirit early in my childhood. I found myself at times experiencing strange dimensions, sometimes light and sometimes dark. Now I have learned that the abusive childhood I endured perhaps caused a tear, shattering the boundaries of my mind, creating an opening into other worlds. It has proved a blessing, though, for I feel it has given me the ability to commune in the Spirit realms and has prepared me to be a messenger of sorts through my artwork.

Learning to embrace my gifts of keen sensitivity and recognize them as such has been a challenge. Most of my life, these sensitivities invoked a feeling that something was seriously wrong with me. As a girl, I heard multitudinous voices, not understanding them or being able to discern which voices were helpful and which were not. These experiences were frightening, and I felt myself to be different, thus becoming extremely introverted.

Yet in 1972, at thirteen years old, a blessing occurred for me when I discovered I could draw while in an art class at school. My first still life, compiled of natural earth elements, opened a door of realizations about texture, light and shadow. Fired with passion and dedication, from then on I drew every day. Art offered me, right from the beginning, a safe haven and an emotional healing tool.

The same year I discovered my artistic abilities, I also discovered Janis Joplin singing the blues wildly, as the creatively dressed tapestry woman with feathers in her hair depicts. I was enthralled by her spirit. She mirrored for me my own struggle for freedom. I wanted to express my deep inner turmoil in a creative, raw and honest way like she did. I loved her daring, adventurous nature. I loved that she stood out in a man's world, in the face of racialism, and that she belted out her truth in a time when it was not accepted or considered safe to do so. Her raw passion in speaking her truth completely captivated the gypsy part of me. I loved her and I wanted to help her out of her pain. The seed was planted then to one day paint her portrait and help heal her spirit.

However, it was not until much later in my life that *Mother Pearl* came into manifestation on my canvas. *Mother Pearl* marks the pivotal point in my paintings where stairways became a recurring symbol. Stairs represent ascension, always climbing upwards. For Pearl, it is a stairway into the mystical Faerie realms. In the process of painting her portrait, I began to think of her '65 Porsche painted in a tapestry of psychedelic hues that exhibited such a classy expression of who she personified herself to be. I was reminded of just how creative she was, so I invited Pearl to paint and play with me. The canvas was lying flat on the ground, so we splashed and swirled colors of green and maroon while singing "Combination of the Two." At one point I walked around and looked at the canvas upside down, and she had arrived! I was excited to see her image in a ghost-like figure taking shape within the painting. For facial details, I used a photo I found to be unusual to most of Janis' images. She was beautiful, she was a Goddess, and I painted her as such!

At fifteen years old I conjured up enough courage to run away from home, an event I'd first attempted when I was four years old. In San Francisco's Golden Gate Park, I found myself sitting in a tree, smoking a joint, pretending to be Janis, pretending to be free. It was in this moment I decided I was going to be a famous artist. I thought about my soul connection with Janis Joplin and our struggle towards freedom. Yet I soon found this new escape into a strange land of drugs and alcohol difficult for my sensitivities. My uncle, who was also an artist and lived in the bay area, took me in. He confronted me one day, saying he knew I was doing drugs and he did not approve. Still, it was my body and I was free to abuse it if I chose. Yet his words sunk in and shortly after I gave up my self-abuse, I felt respected by an adult for the first time. Ten months had gone by before I returned home to my family in Southern California, feeling I possessed

Mother Pearl, Cher Lyn, 24″ x 30″ Acrylic on Canvas, www.mysticartmedicine.com

Breakthrough, Cher Lyn, 24" x 30" Acrylic on Canvas, www.mysticartmedicine.com

new strength of command. My eyes turned from brown to green while I was a runaway, and secretly I saw this as a symbol of my liberation.

Until my late twenties, drawing Native American Indians was my sole subject and interest, a love and passion of mine since I was a young child. From the time I was seven years old until I turned thirteen, I ate dirt in the secret hope that it would help me become more like an Indian. In 1976 I discovered the artwork of Frank Howell. He was the first artist that inspired me to draw with a mystical flair. My love of Native culture eventually led me to the reservations, working with handicapped children. Years later, and to this day, I work as an activist and supporter of Native American culture through my art.

I received an art scholarship upon graduating from high school, but the structure of college was not the inspiration I had hoped it to be. Insecure from the beginning, I did not do well in that scholastic formal setting, as I still carried within me the scars of my childhood. In 1977, within my first semester of college, I became pregnant and ended my formal art schooling. Six months after my son was born through a C-section, unaware at the time that I was suffering from PTSD due to childhood abuse, I had an emotional breakdown and spent time in mental wards for serious suicide attempts. I finally came to the realization that God's angels were not going to stand by and let me die. I was sick of the mental institutions, saturated in medications, coffee and cigarettes, and I watched a girl lose her spirit through shock treatments there. Finally I was presented with two divergent paths. I could easily take the path of the victim and lose myself in a sea of pain, or I could choose to empower myself and "do life," or at least try it for a while. I chose life. I feel the painting Breakthrough depicts the choice I made at nineteen years old.

However, the day I began this enlightening piece of art, I was not feeling so very enlightened. Caught in a thick angry muck of illusion, I allowed myself to express it all out onto the canvas. My choice of colors and expressions of imagery, such as the boxed-in lines you see throughout the background, signify the prison I felt I had locked myself into. Painting has always proven cathartic for me as a way to work through deep emotions, and this time was no different. I felt much better afterwards.

For the next stage of the painting -- the enlightening part -- I used prayer and meditation, along with my didgeridoo and lots of cedar smoke, to clear the energies. I watched as healing colors and images emerged, such as the Tree of Life and cool water on the hot red color. The lion appeared for the medicine of courage through these difficult times. Her movement through the mucky dark is purposeful, with intent. Her eyes fill with love as she commands the top of her head to open in breaking through the illusion, remembering that we are the creators of our own circumstances. She remembers she is the Light, as the delusional doors of perception clear.

In the choice to "do life," my family encouraged me to re-enter a modeling career that I had begun at fifteen years old. Success came quickly, and at twenty I found myself traveling Europe as a fashion and commercial model with my son and husband. All the while sketching, I kept up a hectic pace as a professional model, mother and wife. However, the inside emotions were ignored; the pain was merely stored. And eventually the lifestyle, coupled with the emotional and psychological wounds of childhood, took its toll. I ended my marriage and fell head first into a downward spiral of self-abuse once again. However, this time, although the suicidal tendencies remained, I refrained for the sake of my son.

In 1985, still struggling with deep depression in an emotionally unfulfilling career, I met and married my second husband and birthed my second son. The circumstance of suppression in this marriage became the opportunity I needed to begin healing the deep core issues that had held me bondage for so long. I painted every day and almost every night, driven by passion and emotional necessity. Once again, art proved to be a tool for clearing my emotional baggage and a haven of escape.

In experimenting with paint, I found the play of colors had powerful healing qualities that I was just beginning to discover. The more I allowed the emotion to flow, the more developed my style of painting became. I recognized the profound therapeutic effect colors had upon my psyche, and I was fortunate to have the opportunity to daily dedicate my creative efforts towards healing. During the daylight hours I volunteered as an art teacher in my son's elementary school, and during the midnight hours I painted sometimes until the sun rose!

Early interest in my paintings from others was encouraging. Yet I did not sell my work, nor did I try. Insecure about receiving, I was more comfortable giving them away, and I always found a willing recipient. My confidence in the ability to produce "medicine art" grew as many people who spent time with my artwork felt something open within them. The dictionary recognizes that medicine is a synonym for magic, as applied to magical forms of healing. I believe this effect is due to setting my intention, through prayer, to offer healing through my art. My prayer has always been that my paintings go on to heal and inspire others as they have done for me.

I began painting my first spiritual portrait back in 1987 on the canvas that is now entitled *Blue Oracle Woman.* I had painted several portraits of friends and relatives, and realized that within the process I fell so deeply in love with whomever's portrait I was painting, it eventually occurred to me that it would be a good idea to paint my own portrait. My self-esteem and all aspects of my self-image were quite low on the totem pole, so the idea seemed to be worth a try.

Over a ten-year period I painted my portrait four times over on the same canvas, trying to find love for myself. Although each painting was beautiful, I never found the love I was seeking. Therefore, one more time, in 1997, I poured indigo blue paint over the whole canvas and began again. This time I dug into an area of shamanic spiritualism, which for me was

Blue Oracle Woman, Cher Lyn, 30" x40" Acrylic on Canvas, www.mysticartmedicine.com

much more interesting than attempting to love myself by painting me pretty. The effect of the indigo was exhilarating in the mysterious image rich in texture that took shape on the canvass. I felt a love for her right from the start. Each symbol has significant meaning. The sun and moon in the same sky, which can be found in many of my paintings, represents the masculine and feminine in balance. The stag antlers signify the ability to shape-shift into other dimensional realms. The Tree of Life weaves its branches into my hair and its roots into my veins. The Celtic cross is one I have worn in many forms. The hands are my handprints as spirals, representing coming from and going forth. The six-pointed star is an ancient symbol of Lemuria, representing creation, spirit and Earth, as well as a symbol that came to me in a vision, which I use in my Spirit Guided Soul Painting activations. *Blue Oracle Woman* is my first spiritual portrait, and she appears in my oracle deck as Shapeshift, since her ability is to shape-shift any situation into love.

In 1992 my memories began to surface in a prolific deluge; hence, I chose consciously to dive into exploring the dark corners of my mind with intent to heal. This has proven to be the threshold of my conscious spiritual quest as well. Already painting daily, I found a therapist I could trust and began my journey inward. I read many books in the areas of shamanism, journeywork and dreamtime. Haunted by nightmares, I was deeply inspired by Patricia Garfield's book Creative Dreaming, and discovered that many of our great teachers gathered information and gifts from the dreamtime. My chronic insomnia was cured as I indoctrinated myself into the mysteries and embarked on a new world of creativity within my art. I love the conscious exploration into the vast unknown, and it has proven invaluable to my healing process and the quality of my art.

Mystical experiences began for me as a young girl. At four years old, I saw the spirit of a deer jump into my heart while my father was gutting it. Silently I held it there, secretly thinking I was protecting it. I recall an incident at eight years old where I merged and became one with a large eucalyptus tree high above the ground, looking down upon the landscape. These are two of my secret "strange-to-the-white-man" Spirit journeys. The strength and confidence I gained from lucid dreaming as an adult on my healing journey inspired me to explore new levels consciously within these realms. I began to develop skills of journeying with plants and animals in meditation and exploring other worlds by choice. My art too began to express itself in new ways. The work became an amazing interdimensional adventure into various relationships between the many aspects of creation.

My style continuously evolves through the deep exploration of personal healing, dreamtime and my spiritual practices. I get to learn repeatedly to trust my own guidance and not worry about what others think; that is not what creating art is all about. I believe very deep aspects of who I am are coming through from other dimensions to bring about healing specifically for this moment in time. I have learned to allow these gifts to flow unadulterated, as I believe that is an artist's responsibility.

I begin every painting with prayer and meditation. I use holy water and sacred geometry. I burn sacred essences while using rattles, drum, didgeridoo and chants to cleanse, bless the space and bring in love energy. After spending many years on the Native American path, I have learned a deep reverence and honoring of all life as sacred. I watch in awe as Spirit emerges onto my canvas through me, showing me that a very sacred magic truly does exist. Over twenty years had passed since my modeling days and I found myself again traveling to Europe. I had come full circle, this time in a fulfilling career living my passion as a successful artist, painting and spreading my light.

Color plays such an important part in the healing process. My painting *Creation's Child* was created in 2001, painting all of my dark nights with a desire to heal my childhood without worrying what others might think about me revealing this. I experienced her pain, I painted her experiences and I wrote her transformation in the spoken word and rhyme. I walked her through the fire and we faced the shadows together. Now we are returning to love and compassion for all that has been and all that is to come. I started out using only red and black to express my pain. Digging deep into a primal space within me, I released a lot of tears and rage. Later, I felt an urge to use light blue to bring healing into this place within me as well as into the painting. I was guided to paint spirits blowing light blue smoke on me for healing, and the angels are carrying vessels that are also filled with this light blue healing essence. Light blue in this case represents God's healing. *Creation's Child* is one of my soul paintings, like *Blue Oracle Woman.*

In the year 2001 at an art show, when I thought her complete, I performed the spoken words, unveiling my blood, sweat and tears in my painting and rhymes. Afterwards a woman offered me an incredible amount of money to purchase Creation's Child. For me at the time, as a single mom, I really could have used the money, but I got a very strong message that I had to say no. I didn't know why then. I thought maybe she wanted to hang the painting in a museum where many people could view it, since so many people were deeply moved while

Creations Child, Cher Lyn, Acrylic/Mixed Media on Canvas, 50" x 50", 2001-2011, www.mysticartmedicine.com

Rainbow Activator, Cher Lyn, 30" x 40" Acrylic/Mixed Media on Canvas, www.mysticartmedicine.com

Rainbow Activator, Cher Lyn, 30" x 40" Acrylic/Mixed Media on Canvas, www.mysticartmedicine.com

in her presence. Yet now I know why I was not to sell the painting at that time: Her/my transformation was not yet complete.

Eleven years later, in 2012, she is arriving into fruition in her healing process. The spoken words were written in 2001, but bringing through the images the poem speaks to were not seen by me until one day in 2005 when I sat in front of the painting again in mediation. She had been in storage after my travels overseas, but I wanted to be with her again, not expecting to ever paint on her again. Yet this time I saw her angel wings and more of her transformation that I hadn't seen before. It took a lot of courage at first to lay more paint on her, since so many had already seen her as a masterpiece and I had been offered so much money for the painting; I feared I might ruin her. Again I had to put away ideas of other people's judgments and follow my inner guidance, not caring what anyone else would think. This was for me.

Today *Creation's Child* is filled with healing layers and rainbow hues. Angel wings and dolphins bless her. She is destined to become another deck of mine, a healing oracle card deck to assist others in transforming their trauma. I have used her image and words to help others lift off a layer of their own transforming trauma. Yes, I now know why I was guided not to sell her eleven years ago, and I'm grateful I listened.

> *"Innocence is found in the song of the dolphins' dance. The Rainbow snake transmutes the poisons, the shamans in a trance. Vessels filled, the tall ones bring, healing her womb, growing her wings."*

Now, as a mature visionary artist today, I am amazed at my awakening process and I'm truly grateful for everything I have experienced. Amazing realizations are unfolding to me about the power of God in art. I began doing personalized Spirit Guided-Soul Paintings in 2004, and I am discovering that in the process of painting a person's higher self, I can see into the wet paint like an oracle. I began to understand more about this healing work by doing my own soul painting; Rainbow Activation. After witnessing the power of this work, I now do soul portraits as a healing modality. I enter and explore that person's inner world and find energies that are seeking light, somehow making this transformation possible through focused intention and prayer. The painting then becomes a tool, with information gathered from insights gained through the journey.

Painting for me has become a powerful shamanic transformational tool that has assisted me in my personal healing process as well as my ability to help others. I feel as though I am pioneering new modalities, yet simultaneously remembering an ancient way of healing through art. Now that I have shifted more and more out of the fears I've carried all my life, I have been able to say yes to teaching my techniques to students, and have found great pleasure in sharing what God has shown me in the power of transformation and magic. It is my intention to pass on this gift to others who wish to use these techniques playfully and cathartically, transforming their pain into healing, creating mysticism in art.

In July 2010 I self-published my Mystic Art Medicine Cards deck, consisting of sixty-four vibrantly colorful images on cards, with an accompanying 158 page booklet printed on eco-friendly paper. This self-help tool reflects my intention to offer healing to all who gaze upon my images so that they might receive what they need for their highest good. I am honored and grateful to be the hollow reed for Creator to work through. I am a persistent seeker of truth, and because of that, a survivor too. I thank God/Goddess for my art and the blessing of the vision to perceive the magic and miracles all around me and know they truly do exist. Let it Be…ॐ

Cher Lyn is a visionary artist, writer and poet residing in Sedona, Arizona. Art has been a personal journey through deep inner healing and spiritual awakening for Cher Lyn. In preparation and during the process of painting, she uses meditation, sacred essences and shamanic instruments such as the didgeridoo; drum rattles and chanting to call in energies of love. She opens herself up to the grace and guidance of the Creator. Her images invite the viewer beyond the borders of the canvas into the multidimensional worlds of mysticism, myth, emotion and texture. While she paints to assist the transformation of herself and others, it is always with the intent that her paintings will illuminate and activate those who gaze upon them. Her mystical artwork can be viewed at www.mysticartmedicine.com

Her One Song
The Goddess of Interconnectivity, Shamanism and Art

Totem to Earth, Suzanne DeVeuve, 20"x30" oil on canvas, www.suzannedeveuve.com

By Sandra Ingerman MA, Hank Wesselman Ph.D, Martin Ball, Ph.D and Victoria Christian MA

The wisdom of our ancestors, wherever they come from, basically points to one truth: everything is in relation to you. Native Americans say, "all my relations," acknowledging their connection to everything that is alive. The ancient shamanic teaching that all beings in the web of life are deeply connected is also the central ethical vision of Goddess religion. The concepts of interconnectivity, relatedness and community are all aspects of the feminine principle revered by many ancient indigenous and goddess cultures that practice earth-based spirituality. And throughout history, it is through the medium of art that humans have explored and attempted to understand their connection to nature and the spirit world. The image of the earth as the body of the Goddess is a powerful symbol of oneness. All that we know, all that we do, occurs in and through Her One-Song. Goddess theology affirms that we all come from one source while stating that diversity is the great principle of the earth body. In other words, we are both different and related in the web of life (unity in diversity).

All shamans speak of this web or net that connects us to everything, everywhere, as well as to the spirits that live in all things. The idea that we are separate from other life forms is simply an illusion. All life lives and moves by virtue of oneness, what the *Nuu-chah-nulth* people call *hishuk ish ts'awalk* (everything is one). They hold a deep respect for all forms of life, with a humble awareness of our dependence on the plants, animals, and even inorganic matter of the planet. All of nature exists as an evolving web of consciousness. The shining sun floods the elemental networks of the planet with energy that builds the fractal realms of biological sentience and experience.

This world-creation is a sparkling summit of universal complexity. Yet modern Westerners often live in a state of distraction and fragmentation, lost within an exclusive secular faith in linear reason disconnected from the many modes of organic wisdoms that bring balance and health. This loss of harmonious participation in one's own bioregion has resulted in the tragic destruction of biodiversity and the diminution of quality of life. The pathos of this can be seen on any street where people are walking while talking or texting on cellphones, oblivious to the natural environment and even the people around them.

Re-cultivating our full humanness and interconnectivity can assist the wholeness and integrity of our communities and the ecologies within which we are inextricably united. Many existing nature-oriented communities retain traditions that maintain interconnection with the spirits and ancestors of their bioregion, for the ancient indigenous ways are expressions of the land itself, not merely human creations. Over many hundreds of thousands of years, the ceremonies, medicines, arts and stories generated through shamanic practices have assisted human groups in maintaining harmony between nature and culture, body and mind. In this article, we will provide a brief overview of some of the fundamental organic wisdoms of Shamanism and how they have been translated in art by various indigenous cultures of the past and by a number of contemporary visionary artists. We will also reveal the long hidden female roots of the world's oldest form of religion and medicine and how these roots have been denigrated by patriarchal values and ideologies.

What is Shamanism?

Shamanism is the most ancient spiritual practice known to humankind and is the "ancestor" of all modern religions. The word "shaman" comes from the language of the Evenki peoples, a Tungusic tribe in Siberia. However, there are many different names cross-culturally for people who initiate ecological and spiritual knowledge and healing within their communities. Some of these names include *Shaman* (Tungus, Siberia), *Vegetalista* (Mestizo, Peru), *Dukun* (Indonesia), *Kahuna kupua* (Hawaii). Such people cultivate esoteric knowledge and have extraordinary spiritual abilities such that they serve as intermediaries between the human and the spirit worlds. In Shamanic cultures, the word "shaman" has come to mean "the one who sees in the dark" or "the one who knows."

Most of what we know about the ancient practice of shamanism comes from ethnographic fieldwork done among the tribal peoples of Siberia, Asia, Africa, Australia, Greenland, from North, Central, and South America, and from cultures of northern Europe such as the Saami of Lapland. Technical papers, monographs and books about shamanism are only expanding, but suffice it to say that we have come to know that the shaman is a universal figure found in virtually all the world's cultures. There are certain commonalities in a shaman's worldview and practices across the world, which allows us to make certain broad generalizations about shamanism. However, this does not negate the unique differences that various animistic cultures exude. It is important to honor the diversity of original languages and traditions anchored in the experience of a community residing within its unique bioregion. All ancient traditions have arisen from a unique interconnection with the land and sky, and so it is the land and sky we must again look to for guidance.

Shamanism is an animist tradition, which posits that everything has a spiritual aspect or soul and thus everything is alive. Shamans don't follow the laws of man; they follow the laws of spirits. They don't dominate the earth and its creatures; they strive to live in harmony and balance. Animist cultures view plants and features of their ecosystem as fellow sentient subjects, not as merely material objects. Plants and fungi are revered in the many Amazonian cultures as plant teachers; non-human people who are fellow subjects in the universe, communicable and to be respected.

In the majority of indigenous cultures, the universe is viewed as being made up of two distinct realms: a world of things seen and a world of things hidden, yet no distinction is drawn between them. A shaman understands that these two worlds present themselves together as two halves of a whole. The shaman is the inspired visionary, a man or a woman who learns through practice how to enter into this "world of things hidden," and once there, he or she typically encounters extra-mundane personalities or archetypal forces that the indigenous peoples refer to as spirits, ancestors or even gods.

A shaman may engage in healing work at various levels—physical, mental, emotional, and spiritual—and he or she may be able to access information from "the other side" through enhanced powers of initiation, a practice known as divination. Some shamans are also gifted in their ability to guide the souls of the dead to where they are supposed to go in the afterlife. Some are even accomplished at reweaving and restoring the fabric of a person's damaged soul through the practice of soul retrieval.

Ceremonies and rituals are performed to honor the spirits, to celebrate life and changes in Nature, to acknowledge rites of passage, to give thanks and to create change. One of the most common ceremonies in the practice of Shamanism is the shamanic journey. Shamanic journeying is a method of direct revelation and it is the experiential centerpiece through which shamans make contact with their helping spirits to access empowerment, personal guidance and healing help.

Shamans and visionaries know that the non-ordinary reality of the "world of things hidden" is really a kind of parallel universe to the one in which we live. These hidden realities are inhabited by compassionate, helping spirits, who may offer guidance and healing on behalf of all life on Earth.

A shaman is one who goes into an altered state of consciousness at will. However, indigenous people know everything there is to know about their surrounding environment, and if there are psychotropic plants growing nearby, the ritual use of hallucinogens derived from these "plant teachers" is sometimes utilized for the purpose of expanding awareness and accessing the sacred realms. It is also generally known that the intensely physical stimulus of monotonous drumming and rattling, combined with culturally meaningful ritual and ceremony, prayer and chant, singing and dancing, can be equally effective in shifting consciousness into visionary modes of perception.

Research has revealed how the steady beat of the drum affects the brain to achieve visionary experiences. In this altered state, he or she makes a conscious choice to journey to another reality, a dimension outside of time and space. The Shaman is a universal figure found in all the world's cultures, and all shamanic traditions agree that the spiritual worlds are organized into three primary lev-

Beings Tree, Suzanne DeVeuve, 24" x 36" oil on canvas, www.suzannedeveuve.com

els: the Lower World(s), the Middle World(s), and the Upper World(s). There are also numerous levels within each world. The shaman is able to establish relationships with these spirits and to bring back information and healing for the community or the individual.

Shamanism and Art

Another doorway into the hidden realms is through shamanic artwork. Our uniquely human capacity to create helps dissolve the veil between ordinary reality and the spirit worlds, but acquiring a visionary state of consciousness through art acquires both practice and discipline. When a balance between the inner and outer worlds are achieved, the doorway through the heart opens and the created object can take on truly amazing levels of expression. These activities reaffirm the shaman or visionary as a person who can move out of the mental state and become a "hollow bone" or "hollow reed" through which the Navajos say the many colored winds may blow. By serving as the bridge between worlds, the visionary can literally merge with and act as a conduit for the power of the universe. One way to do this is through making art.

Most Shamanic cultures have traditions of using art for healing. As we look at the petroglyphs and pictographs on the walls of rock shelters and caves, and as we observe the paintings of ayahuasca visions from the Amazon and the visionary yarn paintings of the Huichol shamans in Mexico, we see imagery of the well-traveled territories of the hidden worlds as well as the powerful helping spirits who are so familiar to the shaman. There are a number of books that have documented the shamanic art of various cultures; however, the purpose of this article is to discuss the work of several contemporary shamanic artists.

Contemporary Shamanic Art

It is truly astounding to witness the powerful influence shamanism is having on the contemporary art scene. The reclaiming of ancient wisdoms seems to be the wave of the future as shamanism continues to be a powerful and liberating spiritual path for our time. The resurgence of interest in shamans and their practices may in fact represent the seeds of the next religious tradition in the West—one that will determine much of the Western world's spiritual focus and practice for the next two thousand years and beyond. In this section, we reveal the works of several contemporary visionary artists who are using shamanic principles, ritual and ceremony in the creation of their work. Some are incorporating the use of entheogens, while others are using traditional methods.

Blaze Warrender: Protector of Animals

One of the core messages of Shamanism is a deep respect and reverence for all living things. All animals have a purpose in the great web, and we must learn what the animals are seeking to teach us as well as how to take care of their habitats and how to offer healing when needed. Blaze Warrender is a shamanic visionary artist who has been called to consciously tend all our animal relations: the wild ones and the domesticated ones. An inspiring quote by Jill Robinson reflects her own philosophy and how she chooses to live her life: "Animals have emotions every bit as profound as ours—and our duty to them all is to recognize this, help them, and work for the day when we can look into their eyes without shame."

A self-taught visionary artist born in Australia, Blaze was highly influenced by the indigenous teachings from various cultures, particularly Native American. She started her career in London as an interior decorator with Colfax and Fowler. This eventually led her to paint interior walls in stately homes and castles in the UK and Europe. She learned the art of painting wall mosaics in

Italy, studied decorative furniture painting in Guernsey and spent nine months in Beijing, China studying the art of Chinese brushwork. Through these experiences, she developed the painting techniques that she employs in her artwork, intuitively creating 'faux' and 'fantasy' paint finishes and murals on canvas and walls.

In the late 1970s, on a visit to San Francisco, Blaze was drawn to a group of artists based in Sausalito. Their wildlife fantasias resonated deeply with her and so began her journey into visionary art. In the early 1990s, she was commissioned to create artistic fantasies for various high profile restaurants, a museum and various animal conservation groups.

Around this time, she made the transition from walls to canvas. She studied Transpersonal Art Therapy, a platform to further understand the transformative aspect of her art practice. As a result, Blaze created a process called *Vision Drawing*, based on her own intuitive art process. Over the past ten years, Blaze has exhibited extensively in Australia, the USA and the UK. Her artistic mission is devoted to raising awareness of wildlife protection. She is committed to cruelty-free living and her greatest hope is to make the world a better place for animals. She explains her artistic style and mission in more detail:

> *Essentially my imagery embodies the interconnectedness and reverence for all life. The women are symbolic of the nurturing aspect of the feminine. The animals symbolize nature in all her beauty. I have experienced deep connections with animals and nature. I have seen their underlying gentleness and beauty. Animals are unique beings with souls. They have emotions as valid as ours and are driven by the same passion for life. In my art, I paint from the souls of animals and hope my viewers will feel this connection too.*[1]

All of Blaze's images contain potent imagery of symbolism, animals and the sacred feminine. Each painting is imbued with the medicine that each animal brings. In the shamanic belief, everything is alive and carries with it power and wisdom. Power animals are an essential component of shamanic practice. These spirit guardians provide us with power, protection and support in times of crisis, illness and/or danger. They can also offer guidance and support in our day-to-day lives. Power animals often awaken our creativity as well as the ability to perceive the beauty and magic that surrounds us. Shamans may call upon their power animal(s) for many reasons: in the diagnosis of an illness, to assist the shaman in spiritual journeys through other realms of reality, to bring power to a ceremony or to provide needed information and teaching.

Shamanic cultures believe that when we are born, the spirits of at least two power animals volunteer to remain with us to keep us emotionally and physically healthy and to protect us from harm. According to the shaman, the power animal is not the spiritual essence of one animal but rather the essence of the group oversoul of the whole species. It is also understood that one power animal does not have more power than another. The spirit of mouse has just as much power as the spirit of tiger, but mouse does have different qualities and abilities as well as different lessons to teach from those of tiger.

A painting that speaks of the nurturing aspect of Mother Nature is titled, *The Healing Gift.* In this image an avatarian nature spirit nourishes a leopard with the precious gift of water. Blaze writes about the inspiration for this piece:

> *This painting was inspired by the return of the Sacred Feminine, nature and balance. It also came from a deep need for green in my life. Living in the city, surrounded by concrete, I ventured to my art supply store to immerse myself in the beautiful colors that jumped off the shelves. Cinnabar green light asked to be claimed, so I took it home and squished a big dab on the sparse white canvas, knowing well that the dark void of creation would birth the story into being. And soon came the moon, which started as a huge voluptuous flower. And then a large cross of equal proportions came into the background, something very new for me. The feminine spirit is sitting on the world ablaze with fire, symbolic of destruction and renewal. The ancestors (bottom right) dance their power and dream a new world of balance and harmony into being.*
>
> *As always in my paintings, there are seven moons symbolizing the many meanings behind the number seven. On the left, the burning forest is a metaphor for the biblical burning Tree of Life--the highest fire, or the fire of the mind, burning up those things in the lower nature of which it becomes increasingly aware. The birds, representing wisdom, fly upward into the mystery. The Goddess offers water as a healing gift to all her beloved creatures. Each drop is imbued with her nourishing compassion, dripping down to quench the fire.* [2]

Another painting deserving of recognition is, *In the Company of Bears.* This painting was inspired by a clay mask she created during a course she took on Transpersonal Art Therapy:

The Healing Gift, Blaze Warrender, 40" x 28", oils and mixed mediums, www.blazewarrender.com

In the Company of Bears, Blaze Warrender,40" x 28", oils and mixed mediums, www.blazewarrender.com

This painting captures the medicine of bear, which is introspection and hibernation. Bear suggests you go within to integrate experiences and incubate ideas. Everything you need to know is there. Cease searching outside of your inner wisdom for the truths you need. Bring your own knowing to the surface and share this knowledge with others.

The Mother or Guardian Bear watches from the background. The butterfly in her head symbolizes transformation. She is cloaked in fur, gifted by bear, who is gently touching and protecting her from harm. An eagle hovers on the left, encasing the ancestors and the sacred circle (the four directions).

In the bottom right of the canvas, there are all sorts of bear people, the river of life, the Mother Earth Turtle in the centre of the web of life, dragonflies and an owl. There are also shamanic elements--the mask and the owl near the eagle, transporting the shaman on his/her journey. On the far left side is a seed near the Tree of Life with the three worlds--lower, middle and upper.[3] Last but not least, Blaze created an important painting dedicated to her good friend and mentor, Susan Seddon Boulet, titled *Missing You SSB.* Blaze's style of painting is similar to Susan's in that they both intuitively channel shamanic visions. They also use a lot of animal totems and mythological symbolism in their art. In this sense, the visionary artist, like the shaman, becomes a hollow reed, totally egoless. They may not call themselves shamans *per se*, but visionaries can definitely go into a creative trance state easily. Blaze talks about the painting in more detail:

This is dedicated to Susan Seddon Boulet, who informed my life as a painter. Her mysticism inspired me to embrace the sacred in all that is.Here the goddess is Shaman, and like Susan, Protector of the Wolf. The eye in the throat is the all-seeing eye of wisdom gained from the cancer that invaded her life. The stairway to this wisdom comes through the wolf. The Moon Mother oversees and protects life. The emblem of the phoenix and the lotus are from one of her paintings and symbolize the resurrection to a higher plane. I/we miss you, Susan.[4]

Susan Seddon-Boulet is considered one of the founders of the visionary art movement in the United States. Working primarily in French oil pastels, inks and occasionally pencil, she developed a distinctive personal style characterized by the use of color applied in layers from which dream-like forms emerged. She drew her inspiration from a wide variety of sources: mythology and poetry, Jungian psychology and worldwide spiritual traditions, as well as a deep love of animal and the natural world. There is a fairy tale quality to her work, a sentimental recalling of childhood dreams of fairies and castles and magic. Her art exerted and continues to exert a profound influence on the lives that it touches.[5]

Missing You SSB, Blaze Warrender, 40" x 28" oils and mixed mediums, www.blazewarrender.com

Earth Goddess, Peter Eglington, 81" x 94" color pencil on canvas, www.petereglingtonart.com

Peter Eglington: Channeling Ancient Future Mythology and Symbolism in Art

A creative genius from Byron Bay, Australia, is Peter Eglington. His artwork synthesizes the ancient indigenous wisdoms with galactic, futuristic wisdom. He has been greatly influenced by the Aborigines of Australia, Native American cosmology, and Eastern mysticism. He doesn't feel inclined to "self proclaim" to be a "shaman" as he is not necessarily healing people with plant medicines. However, he has been on a shamanic personal path of revelation with plant medicines and other hallucinogenics, not to mention shamanic journeying through art.

His work is meticulously painted with an open heart of reverence and devotion. As he walked the shamanic path of direct revelation, he discovered that his personal consciousness was a part of a greater field of consciousness—an insight currently being illuminated by quantum physics. His fascination with art in conjunction with a devotional heart led him on a path of self-realization and spiritual empowerment. Peter had the great honor and karmic responsibility of raising his three children alone, which is a tremendous path of service, compassion, patience, strength, and loyalty. His kids are spiritual teachers that help keep Peter grounded as he could have easily transcended off the planet by now.

An exquisite painting by Peter is titled *Earth Goddess*. This painting came into manifestation over a three-year period and entailed over a thousand hours of work. Peter writes "It emerged from a deep sadness about the dire state of the world's ecology and man's inability to perceive the interconnectedness of all life on earth. The Goddess wears a headband in which a medallion features the sign of Hunab Ku, reminding us of our essential one-

Soma Tree, Peter Eglington, 94" x 83", www.petereglingtonart.com

ness with the source of all creation."[6]

All of the indigenous elders believe that Nature, or the Earth Mother, is prophetic and insightful; that wisdom is embedded in the very threads of creation. The spiritual power of the Earth and the heavens releases dormant wisdom and creates moments of transpersonal guidance. At this time, the indigenous Grandmothers say, "We are being nourished with a new, purer energy transmitted by nature and the universe, which will help us meet these challenging times with integrity and grace." [7]

Peter has several paintings that honor the wisdom of plant medicines; however, I can only mention a few. His painting, *The Ancient Soma Tree* portrays the spiritual and magical majesty of the tree. Soma is a Vedic Sanskrit word that literally means "distill, extract, sprinkle," often connected in the context of rituals. "In ancient India, the stalks of the plant were pressed between stones, and the juice was filtered through sheep's wool and then mixed with water and milk. After it was offered as a libation to the gods, the remainder of the soma was consumed by the priests and the sacrificer. It was highly valued for its exhilarating, probably hallucinogenic, effect. [8]

A painting inspired by his travels to Peru and shamanic journeys is *Holy Mother and Child Emerging from their Sanctuary in the Heart of the Amazon.* He was so deeply touched by the spiritual guides and healers that he dedicated this piece to them "Maestro Santiago Enrique Paredes Melendez, his wife, Curandera Ayme, and his family."

Another monumental painting that deeply honors the spiritual lineage and wisdom of Peru is *The Usko-Ayar Visionaries.* Peter has been so profoundly influenced by a number of amazing beings, particularly Don Emilio, Don Jose Coral, Apolinar, Don Basilio Gordon, Juan and Mauro Reategui Perez, Ake Hultkrantz, Raph Metzner, Terence McKenna, Richard Evans Schultes, and Reichel

Holy Mother and Child, 72" x 72", Peter Eglington, www.petereglingtonart.com

Dolmatoff. Peter's personal path with regards to both sacred plant medicines and the resultant expression of the realizations gifted through these teacher plants in the form of painting has been tremendously influenced by both the Colombian born anthropologist and researcher Luis Eduardo Luna as well as the master painter of shamanic visions, Pablo Amaringo.

The Usko-Ayar Visionaries, Peter Eglington, 94" x 83", www.petereglingtonart.com

David Joaquin: Honoring the Great Mother in Native American Culture

Art plays an important role in Native American culture. Art has been used as a form of expression in the Native American way of life for hundreds, even thousands of years. The rich art of Native American culture expresses a deep connection with the spiritual world, particularly with the animals they regarded as their ancestors and kin. Supernatural spirits, symbols and patterns were carved, painted, woven or sewn into everyday utensils, garments, as well as in sacred and ceremonial objects such as masks, totem poles and pipes. Myth was inseparable from daily life, and decorations represented, among other themes, thanks to the spirits, protection in warfare, or accompaniment of a spiritual journey.

David Joaquin is perhaps one of the greatest Native American visionary painters of our time. He was born in San Diego, California in 1968 and was raised for most of his life in Hawaii. His mother (who emigrated from Colombia) is a weaver and a wood carver. She became his first art teacher. David recalls, "When I was a child I was surrounded by art. My mother built our house by hand with recycled wood. All the cabinets, beds and moldings were beautifully carved and adorned with painted vines and flowers. In our room she carved a piece of dark wood and painted the star-sign characters of everyone in the family."

David's father was a librarian at the University of Hawaii and was connected to a number of Native American artists, mystics and healers. He built a sweat lodge in their back yard and invited shamans to lead ceremonies. David writes, "Having a sweat lodge in Hawaii exposed me to many different tribes (Lakota, Zuni, Ute, Crow) who would come to sweat with the family, each with different stories and ways, shared in the hot darkness. This is what I began to see in my dreams and in wood grains, which inspired me to study my own native heritage of Chibcha (Colombia) and Mi'kmaq (Quebec)."[9]

He began his visions and dreams working with exotic woods such as milo, koa, hau, and mango. Most recently, David has expanded his technique, using the palette knife with oils on canvas to create his works of Western scenes. His illustrations have appeared in such publications as *The Land and People of the Colorado Plateau*, *Dreams: Science, Art and the Unconscious Mind* and most recently *Mountain Spirit: The Sheep Eater Indians of the Yellowstone*.

David's artistic mission is supportive of the Goddess Movement. The majority of his paintings are feminine in nature, portraying women as shamans, oracles and pow-

Corn Mother, David Joaquin, www.theartofdavidjoaquin.com

Photographs by Marisol Villanueva, courtesy of the International Council of 13 Indigenous Grandmothers

erful earth mothers. He feels strongly that throughout history, women's power has been undermined--an extraordinary tragedy for all humanity. He is devoted to recovering the feminine in Native American traditions and shamanism in his art. He is quite aware of the various Native American prophecies and supports the efforts of the International Council of Thirteen Indigenous Grandmothers, for they have come to fulfill an ancient prophecy known by many of the world's indigenous tribes: "When the Grandmothers from the four directions speak, a new time is coming."[10]

An important book that documents their valuable message for the world is by Carole Shaeffer titled, *Grandmothers Counsel the World: Women Elders Offer Their Vision for Our Planet.* Here is a short excerpt from the book:

> *The council, which had been spoken of in prophecy and seen in visions since time immemorial, finally emerged in the aftermath of 9/11. The Grandmothers' participation in the council had been foretold to each of them in different ways. All of the Grandmothers had been invited long ago, in a time before time as we know it, to meet at the time of the Great Turning to become a force for peace in the world. Prophecy revealed to each one that they must now share even their most secret and sacred ways with the very people who have been their oppressors, as the survival of humanity, if not the entire planet, is at stake.* [11]

Prophecies of each of the Grandmothers' traditions state that we are entering the Purification Times. The purification process is a natural cleansing of all the accumulated negativity caused by being materially instead of spiritually oriented.

The urgency of the world's situation requires a global response. The Grandmothers, living legends among their people, are the wise women, curanderas, shamans, and healers of their tribes. They have come in council to share their prayers, rituals, and ceremonies to create global healing and forge an alliance creating one voice. They speak of ways of bringing about sustainability, sovereignty, and a unified alliance among all the Earth's people in the interest of life and peace.

Many American Indian tribes thought that the primary potency in the universe was female, and that understanding authorizes all tribal activities, religious or social. In accord with the inherent authority within a family,

White Buffalo Woman, David Joaquin, 24" x 36" oil on wood, www.theartofdavidjoaquin.com

Spirit Canoe, David Joaquin, 2' x 5' oil on wood, www.theartofdavidjoaquin.com

traditionally the women elders, the grandmothers, were the ones who were looked up to as guardians to watch over the physical and spiritual survival of the family, and thus the tribe. They were the keepers of the teachings and rituals that allowed the tribe to flourish, and they upheld the social order. In many of the tribes around the world, including the great Iroquois Nation, the Council of Grandmothers was always consulted before any major decision was made, including the decision whether or not to go to war. For without peace and harmony, which are the powers of a woman's heart, the powers of light, corn and ritual magic cannot function correctly.

At this point in time, a plethora of books have been published focusing upon 2012, the year that many indigenous traditions such as the Maya, the Inca, the Hopi, and others have predicted as the end of a great cycle. A powerful painting by David Joaquin depicting a Native American prophet is *White Buffalo Calf Woman*, a sacred woman of supernatural origin, central to the Lakota religion as the primary cultural prophet. Oral traditions relate that she brought the "Seven Sacred Rituals" to the Teton Sioux. According to legend, the buffalo were the gift of White Buffalo Calf Woman. The Sioux depended on the buffalo for food, clothing and housing, and so the buffalo were considered holy to the people. Tragically, in less than ten years, hundreds of buffalo were slaughtered for sport by encroaching settlers, pioneers who obviously had no concept of the sacred Oneness of Creation.

Nicholas Black Elk (Hehaka Sapa) was an Oglala Sioux medicine man and shaman who is well known for the story he told an anthropologist named John Neihardt—an account that was published as a book titled *Black Elk Speaks*. In this volume, Black Elk tells the story of his life, as well as a great prophetic vision that he was given in his childhood. Lesser known is Black Elk's second book, told just before his death to another anthropologist named Joseph Epes Brown, titled *The Sacred Pipe: Black Elk's Account of the Seven Rites of the Oglala Sioux*. Originally published in 1953, this book contains something that may have great relevance for all of us in our time.

At the beginning, Black Elk recounts the mythic story of White Buffalo Calf Woman and of her gifting of the first sacred prayer pipe to the people (the Sioux). At the end of the account, he relates that as the Holy Woman started to leave the lodge where this historical meeting took place, she turned and said to a man called Standing Hollow Horn: "Behold this pipe! Always remember how sacred it is and treat it as such, for it will take you to the end. Remember also that in me there are four ages... I am leaving now but I shall look back upon your people in every age...and in the end I shall return."[12]

According to Sioux philosophy, at the beginning of the "cycle of four ages," a buffalo was placed in the west in order to hold back the waters. Every year the buffalo loses one hair, and at the end of each age, he loses one leg. When all its hair and all four legs are gone, the Sioux believe that the waters will rush in once again and the cycle of ages will come to an end—an indigenous prophecy of more than just passing interest considering the polar meltdowns very much in progress and the predicted catastrophic rise in sea levels.

But Black Elk also predicted just before his death that with the closing of this cycle, the primordial spirituality would re-emerge and be restored, and on this foundation the next cycle of ages will begin again. This is highly significant because the primordial spirituality is the path of direct revelation—it was and is the shaman's path—and interest in Shamanism has increased dramatically over the last several decades as part of the widespread spiritual reawakening currently going on in our time.

Tessa Mythos: Shamanic Visionary Bridger of Worlds

The awareness that we exist in both the visible and invisible worlds at the same time brings the realization that everything is intertwined. The shamans of the Amazon and Andes believe that interconnectivity is the nature of the cosmos. This is why many native tribes refer to all living beings as "all my relation." Indigenous peoples lived in a communal system that was based on reciprocity—everyone sharing what they had and everyone taking care of every one else. There was no hoarding, thus no one in the tribe ever went without and all prospered equally. When everyone benefitted, the individual benefitted more. We can learn from the tribal system how all humans can thrive today.

Also common to indigenous people is an honoring and reverance for the Spirit World. Visions, dreams, prayer, ceremony, and ritual are the means to access the sacred Spirit World. Art is another means of accessing the nonordinary realm of Spirit. A visionary artist deeply inspired by the simple and brilliant complexity of Great Spirit is Tessa Mythos.

She writes, "Within the psyche is the universal existence of everything. Uni-verse = One–song."[13] This simple yet profound truth inspires and imbues her paintings with emotional depth and spiritual wisdom. When you tap into the "One-Song" you access what the psychiatrist Carl Jung called the collective unconscious, the aspect of your consciousness that participates in the shared awareness of all of creation, and recognizes your oneness with all beings and with nature.

When we engage with Spirit we discover that each of us has the ability to interact with the Divine directly. And it is a beautiful thing to witness the infinite ways Spirit can manifest in the imagination of artists, some of which are gifted alchemistas. "Tessa Mythos is a multidisciplinary artist from Victoria and Hornby Island B.C. Canada. As a self-taught artist with unique intuitive gifts, she has experimented with many mediums and methods from the illustration of her graphic novels, oil painting, acrylics, sculpture, murals, drawings and abstract work. Greatly moved by the ceremonial and ritualistic aspects of creation, Tessa is inspired by the realms of spirit, magic, faery tales, animals, nature, folklore, prophecy, medicine, the healing arts, infinity, love, death, evolution, and sacred symbolism."[14] In her artistic statement, she expounds on the inspiration for her work:

> *I feel that art is a bridge of the invisible and visible realms, which opens up an endless spectrum for transformation and healing for people and the Earth. Art is a healing practice that empowers the artist with inner guidance, intuition, and meditation on the deeper mysteries. In my experience, creativity nourishes positive ideas and growth, uncovers aspects of the psyche, and illuminates new and ancient ways of wisdom. It continues to inspire and evolve us individually and collectively to a greater understanding of the world we live in.*[15]

For Tessa, art has been a powerful tool for self-discovery, healing, and prophecy. It has been a means to make sense of her visionary experiences, which can be confusing and frightening at times. Art is also a cathartic tool of transforming negative emotions and traumas into something positive. In order to funnel her intense emotions of grief and anger about the destruction of Gaia and the subjugation of the Sacred Feminine globally, she painted *The Universal Mother*. Tessa expounds more on the painting:

> *The painting speaks of a time of awakening for humanity. She is Gaia, the Creatrix of all life. Her belly is the dark womb of the universe birthing the Divine child and lotus flower. She emerges from mother ocean where all life began. From the stars and seas she brings with her the next generations of humanity--those who will inherit the earth and what we leave for them.*
>
> *In her hand she grows the DNA strands of humanity's evolution mixed with the DNA of the healing medicine plants of the earth - the intelligent beings who help nourish us and allow us to more deeply understand and merge with the world we live in.*
>
> *The Universal Mother holds the medicine we need to reach our highest expression and evolution. If we keep destroying Her medicine, we will not be able to reach our highest form as evolved Divine Humans. She offers us the chance to grow into our true potential of expanding beyond our current awareness and into beings of endless possibility. The Universal Mother alchemizes the seed of creation and the star of consciousness.*

The Universal Mother, Tessa Mythos, www.artbymythos.com

The eagle and the condor that circle in the sky, represent a South American prophecy, specifically from the Ecuadorian and Peruvian shamans. The prophecy reveals humanity splitting into two paths--one path is the eagle in the North, representing the path of the mind, vision, intellect, industrialization, achievement, and the masculine principle of manifestation. In the South, the condor represents the path of the heart, love, compassion, community, nurturing children, and cultivating bonds with each other and the Earth. This represents passion, playfulness, warmth, joy, and the feminine principle.

The prophecy speaks of a time when it is possible for us to heal the connection of the North and South, forging a connection, from the mind to the heart. The prophecy states that in 1490, a 500 year period would begin, where the energy of the eagle (masculine principle) would become so strong that it would drive the energy of the condor (feminine principle) almost out of existence. However, the prophecy also speaks of a time, starting in the 1990's, when the eagle and the condor can fly in the same sky, coming together and creating a new level of consciousness

and healing for humanity. [16]

When one has the devotion to seek the ineffable wisdom of the Spirit realm, it is possible to tap into a well of ancestral knowledge that transcends time and space. When one is called by Spirit to use their talents to create sacred activist art, it is difficult to ignore the call. Inspired by Native American values and cosmology, Tessa had the honor of attending the *International Indigenous Leadership Gathering* in Lillooet, British Columbia. She had the honor of witnessing a rare gathering of elders and medicine people from all over the world, performing ceremonies for five days. It was at this gathering that the vision for her painting *Mni Wconi—Water is Life*, was born. It was a profound experience that deserves to be documented. She writes:

At the beginning of the gathering, the pipe of Crazy Horse (Chief, mystic, warrior of the Lakota tribe) was returned to the people and smoked in prayer for the first time in about 200 years. Of the many prophecies of Crazy Horse that have come to pass, he foretold that the return of his pipe to the people would signify the dawning of the 5th World of Peace. Within this prophecy, people from all corners of the Earth would come together in unity and gather at the great tree of life to heal the world and usher in a new consciousness of peace.

It was a great honour to witness the Elders go into the small round wooden house where the pipe was held. Around the sacred fire they sat, one by one, holding the pipe and praying, tears falling, hearts and spirits full of prayers. It was such a blessing to be a part of this moment and to offer my own prayers to the pipe and to the spirit of Crazy Horse.

Afterwards, I was told by Chief Phil Lane Jr. to go sit with the pipe, which was a deeply moving experience that led to many deep visions and healing connections. Since that time, I felt his spirit and know that the 'The spirit of Crazy Horse is alive and well.' Over the years, I made a number of sketches of this prophecy as he appeared to me in my inner vision. After holding the vision for many years, the time came to paint it just as the situation at Standing Rock began to heat up with protests against an oil pipeline passing through the land and putting the sacred water source at risk.

At this point, I heard Crazy Horse say NOW IS THE TIME. The painting came through very strong in tandem with the protest at Standing Rock. There were many

Mni Wconi, Tessa Mythos, www.artbymythos.com

interesting things that happened during the process. For example, when I was painting the White Buffalo among the ancestors in the image, I was pondering its place in the Spirit World. Later, I found out that during the same two days where I was working on this part of the painting, the white buffalo in North Dakota (named White Cloud and considered sacred among the Lakota) was passing to the other side.

These kinds of synchronicities happen to me often in the creative process, reassuring me that I am on the right path. Throughout history there have been many prophecies. Each year another facet and aspect of these prophecies appear and each year we come closer as a global tribe and community. Each year the Earth changes faster and faster, calling us to greater action. The Time is now. [17]

It was inspiring to witness people come together to support the cause at Standing Rock. As Tessa so beautifully professes--water truly is Life and we are so blessed to drink of these waters. The sacred waters were never meant to be owned by corporations that exploit and dominate the entire water supply. It is clear that we need a tidal wave of awakening if we are to continue to live on this beautiful planet who has been so generous with us.

We are fortunate to have wise elders, avatars, and ancestors on the other side that are ready to be spiritual midwives for us. They are the visionaries of the past who were marginalized, silenced and even put to death. In fact, there is a long history of the dark side of Christian history that annihilated pagan women. There was a 300 year period of witch-hunting from the fifteenth to the eighteenth century, what R.H. Robbins called "the shocking nightmare, the foulest crime and deepest shame of western civilization." [18](quote).The Church created the elaborate concept of devil worship and then used the persecution of it to wipe out dissent, subordinate the individual to authoritarian control, and openly denigrate women. In honor of the witch hunts, Tessa created *As Above, So Below*. She writes:

This painting is an expression of my feelings about the witch burnings, which have continued on in so many ways to this day. It speaks to a time of healing-- recognizing the wounds of the past and how they have brought us to where we are now. The painting is addressing the violence and injustice that is still happening against women, indigenous people, marginalized people, and people of color. It is for the lost and fallen sisters, and for everyone who is suffering and traumatized because of this patriarchal system of domination, oppression, and disrespect of the Earth. She carries a message of justice and healing saying All Will Be Held Accountable.

On one side of the painting there are witches on the burning pyre's and their grieving families and friends, traumatized and hiding, the spirits of the dead flying up into the sky in anger, sadness and confusion. On the other side, a healing scene unfolds, the spirits returning and finding harmony again with nature, gathering around the sacred trees. The central figure is the triple Goddess, she is Hecate or Diana, the milk and blood of life pour from her. She holds all the sacred symbols of the oracle Tarot—the cup (water/emotion), sword (air /intellect), wand (fire /creativity), and pentacle (earth /abundance). She is a magician and master of the elements, which aid in her ability to transform the situation.

The painting is also in honour of a dear friend of mine who was murdered by a psychopath--a man who was never caught and is likely responsible for the death of many other women. This condition of imbalance and violence has to end. We are facing a major shift on the planet--the equilibrium has to return in order to move towards a harmonious path for us all, and for life on the planet to continue. The ongoing violence against women is in direct correspondence of violence against the Mother Earth. She is calling for our help, asking us to step into our power, to find our strength and rise, for the love of all.[19]

The global trend of violence against women is a reflection of the sexual shadow of the world, which must be exposed and brought to justice. The demise of the Earth is directly related to the global oppresion of women. This is just another pattern that has to change if we are going to exist harmoniously on the planet.

Krystleyez: Shamanic Alchemista of Harmony, Symbolism, and Grace

The Goddess of Interconnectivity wants to us to know that each individual plays a very important role in the awakening and transformation process. She wants us to stop comparing ourselves with others and claim our unique, infinite, autonomous selves. However, she also wants us to transcend our individual egos and awaken to a state of oneness, which can occur in many different paths - yoga, meditation, art, dance, nature, various spiritual traditions, and even hallucinogens (if that is someone's path).

We can choose to be an alchemist of our own spiritual evolution. Alchemy is an ancient path of spiritual purification and transformation; the expansion of con-

As Above So Below, Tessa Mythos, www.artbymythos.com

sciousness and the development of insight and intuition through images. Alchemy is steeped in mysticism and mystery. The alchemists relied heavily upon their dreams, inspirations and visions for guidance in perfecting their art. In order to protect their secrets, they recorded diaries filled with mysterious symbols rather than text. These symbols remain exceptionally potent for changing states of consciousness. [20]

We are blessed to have contemporary, masterful alchemistas that exude the grace of a ballet dancer riding the spirals and waves of symbolic consciousness. Witnessing and feeling the vibration of their art is like listening to the most exquisite classical music. They have tapped into another dimension and brought back pearls of wisdom that are beyond words. It's like witnessing nature in all of her magic and glory, but adding an element of original creative imagination that is refined and pure.

"Through an ever-evolving process of intention and intuition, Krystleyez harnesses the power of art as a vehicle for personal and collective transformation. In a world stifled by the illusion of separation, she shares impacting visions of unity. Exploring the luminous landscapes of consciousness, her multidimensional paintings radiate transcendental light with balanced serenity. Pulsing and breathing with life, the etheric geometries that dance off her canvas disintegrate the boundaries between art and audience. Cosmic maps into the interconnected nature of existence, her artwork navigates the way between heart, mind, and the enchanting realms of spirit." [21]

Her painting, *Alchemy,* exquisitely portrays a feathered being in a state of harmony and balance. She is the Alchemista who uses the polarities to turn lead into gold. She also creates harmony from the chaotic realms. Krystle writes:

> *A winged being sits in contemplation in the center of a fountain of energy. Her left hand holds a blank palate while her right hand is poised to create. This mudra depicts the balance of giving and receiving which is essential to any creative process. In the center of the being's body is an energetic egg that holds a spiraling sphere of energy and a star tetrahedron within it, representing a womb of creative life force. Within this energetic cauldron, light is alchemized into new forms through the power of the imagination and focused intention. A dance of subtle energies flows through the space, energizing the environment with geometric codes of light.*
>
> *Below the fountain, a lotus blooms out of a heart-shaped seed. The lotus represents the flowering of consciousness. Spiraling strands of DNA emerge from the lotus and rise up the central channel of the painting. Star tetrahedrons ascend up the major energy centers, representing the bridge between dimensions of spirit and matter. Two hummingbirds hover on each side of the painting as guardians of the space and as messengers that carry harmonic blueprints of light.*
>
> *The process of alchemy transforms energy from one state to another, and this alchemical act is at the heart of the evolution of consciousness and the creation of life itself. This painting illuminates the creative nature of the soul to be the artist of one's reality and to co-create in harmony with nature.* [22]

Krystle's painting, *The Arc of Grace*, illustrates the gift of spiritual wisdom available to all of us at all times. We are unconditionally given air to breathe, food to eat, an amazing body with senses and somatic wisdom, a beautiful Earth to live in, a plethora of spirit guides ready to assist at any time, a universe within every cell of our bodies. If one has the desire to evolve in one's spiritual path, one has to cultivate a devotional heart and be willing to implement discipline and self-mastery through spiritual practice, yoga, meditation, diet, and spiritual counsel. Krystle expounds on her painting more:

> *Beyond the boundaries of the physical senses lies a vast, energetic architecture of the Cosmos. The Arc of Grace reflects the multidimensional nature of consciousness spanning from the universal to the personal. A totem of spirit-guides rises above a young woman as she anchors light into her body and into the Earth. Below her, a lotus blossoms into the "seed of life", which is a pattern that contains the harmonic proportions of light, music and life itself. As she breathes in harmony with the elements and the energies that surround her, the Goddess nurtures and protects the sacred womb of Creation.*
>
> *Two guardians hold space directly above her, representing her higher self as a balance of the divine feminine and masculine. A crystalline stairway above her leads into the mouth of a lion, which is also the entrance to a pyramid of light. The expansive universe is cradled and protected within the head of an elephant, representing universal wisdom and divine protection. This painting weaves connections between sacred geometry, astrology, ancient civilizations and archetypal symbolism, all which work in harmony as part of a universal cosmology.* [23]

Much like the artwork of the indigenous Shipibo tribe of Peru, her paintings contain prayers of healing frequencies. Shipibo designs are visual translations of

Alchemy, Krystleyez, www.krystleyez.com

The Arc of Grace , Krystleyez, www.krystleyez.com

sound frequencies that they perceive during medicine ceremonies. "Awareness of reality's subtle details allows Krystle to continually recognize the synchronistic flow bestowed by experience. Her artistic process also mirrors this natural tendency in her being--to connect the dots. Identifying threads of connection between the natural world, countless subjects studied by humankind, and the comprehension of life's purest meaning, her artwork aims to transcend the boundaries of polarized modes of consciousness by revealing the fundamental patterns that unite everything. Gathering inspiration from the enrapturing beauty of nature, sacred geometry, metaphysics, mystical experiences, ancient civilizations, meditation and music, she illustrates a celestial language of Oneness. " 24

The Goddess of interconnectivity unconditionally offers her gift of Divine Grace and cathartic healing prayers. Her redemptive powers of death/rebirth are a gift of grace that most people don't acknowledge as being an act of compassion. It is freely given with no strings attached. She offers protection to individuals, animals, and humanity at large. However, she can't control or violate free will. If one makes a conscious choice to go down a path of self-destruction, she has to honor that choice. She knows that we are at a turning point in the history of human consciousness, which is why she encourages us to seek out spiritual teachers and take the time for spiritual retreats, particularly silent retreats, as the silence can bring about powerful awakenings.

Entheogens and Shamanic Visionary Art

Throughout human history, spiritual seekers have used sacred plants and fungi for healing, visionary encounters, and mystical experience. Though this history has been largely obfuscated by prohibitionist attitudes and misinformation, entheogens, or substances that "generate the experience of God within," hold a special place in the development of world religions and countless spiritual traditions. "Psychedelics," as entheogens are often called, were not something discovered in the counter-cultural sixties, but in fact can be traced back to the very dawn of human cultures. Many of the earliest human artifacts – from mushroom shaman effigies in prehistoric African cave paintings to marijuana incense burners in shrines in ancient Europe - depict entheogenic fungi and plants with clear associations with ritual and religious activity. The "foods of the gods" have been with us from the beginning.

Art, in multiple forms, and altered/visionary states of consciousness have always gone hand-in-hand. This is certainly true of the representational arts. Archeological evidence shows that the earliest paintings and carvings that humans produced in caves and secret grottos related directly to altered states of consciousness, often through the ingestion of visionary plants and mushrooms. It is also clear that these representational art forms were expressive of early human societies' sense of "the sacred" or "the spiritual," however these terms may be understood. Representational art also marks the transition between pre-human and human consciousness, as it is a hallmark of culture, self-awareness, and a desire to communicate and express experiences and perceptions of the mysterious world in which humanity awoke to consciousness.

The first artists were the shamans – those who bravely journeyed into the unknown realms of consciousness and awareness in order to experience and learn. Among the most powerful of the shaman's tools to experience altered states of consciousness have been the mind-altering plants and fungi. While knowledge of the ancient, and often, ongoing, use of psychedelic and entheogenic substances is becoming more common and widespread, many are still largely ignorant of the primary role these substances have had in human cultures, religions and traditions throughout history, and their close connection to art.

Entheogenic Experience

Art that is the product of visionary states of consciousness and the entheogenic journeys of the artist, such as much of the art in this section of the book, has a great deal to communicate and has played a fundamental role in the development of human cultures and consciousness. In order to understand this art, we need to understand the role of visionary states of consciousness and entheogenic experiences and how they translate into imaginitive representations.

We can begin with a basic understanding of what entheogens are and what role they play in the human body. The word entheogen means, "generating the experience of god within," and was coined to replace the word "psychedelic," which was itself coined to replace the term "hallucinogenic." Entheogen is meant to be reflective of the "sacred" quality of the experiences that these substances occasion and their use in ritual and ceremonial practice among traditional cultures and religions, as briefly reviewed above.

There are several families of entheogenic plants and fungi, with the most significant for our conversation being the tryptamine family of entheogens. We will largely limit our discussion to this family as this is what is directly represented in the art that we are considering here, and therefore is most revealing of the connections between entheogenic experience and artistic creation and communication.

Perhaps the most significant feature of the tryptamines is that they are endogenous to the human body, meaning that all humans naturally have tryptamines in their bodies at all times. Though their roles are still not fully understood scientifically, both Dimethyltryptamine (DMT, or N,N DMT) and 5 Methoxy Dimethyltryptamine (5-MeO-DMT) are found in all humans. These compounds are found in our lungs, blood, nervous system and spinal fluid. Both compounds also function as neurotransmitters. Not only are they found in humans, but all mammal species as well. Given their ubiquitous presence, they have obviously played a role in mammalian evolution, and quite possibly a direct role in the evolution of human consciousness and self-awareness.

Ayahuasca is a DMT-containing brew made in the Amazon by indigenous cultures and is central to their traditions and lifeways. The DMT of the *Psychotria viridis* leaves is accessed through combining them with the monoamineoxidase inhibitor of the *Banisteriopsis caapi* vine and boiling them down together into a thick and pungent brew. DMT is also the base molecule for the psilocin and psilocybin found in a variety of psychedelic mushrooms.

When consumed in any form, DMT is a powerful chemical catalyst. Though it is already present in the human body, when consumed in relatively small amounts, in the range of 20 – 100 mg, it can radically change how one sees and understands the nature of the self and the world. Many in the contemporary Western world enjoy smoking DMT for a very fast, very powerful experience that begins almost instantaneously and comes to a conclusion within less than 10 minutes. In more traditional settings, with the ingestions of ayahuasca or mushrooms, the DMT can take up to an hour to really come into effect and then will last for several more hours, with mushrooms generally lasting several times longer than ayahuasca, despite the fact that ayahuasca tends to produce a more powerful experience. Smoked DMT, however, can be far more powerful experientially than either ayahuasca or mushrooms. Smoked 5-MeO-DMT is the most powerful and radical of all.

DMT experiences are extremely visual in nature, especially when eyes are closed. At times, the visual experience behind closed eyes is completely unique and has no relationship to what is seen with eyes open, and one can toggle between two completely distinct sets of visual impressions merely by alternately opening and closing the eyes. At other times, an immersive visionary scene might be identical regardless of whether one has open or closed eyes. And at other times, even when things appear "normal" with open eyes, or relatively so, vast and complex images can appear behind closed eyes.

Actual visionary content can vary tremendously from person to person and from experience to experience. However, there are some universal features of DMT experiences, regardless of culture, tradition or context, that reveal significant underlying features. At the most basic level, entheogenic experiences are experiences of energy. Such experiences are palpable within the body, visible to open and closed eyes, and synesthetic in nature. When one ingests an entheogen, one's ability to perceive and experience energy is greatly enhanced and amplified. Visually, the effect is quite dramatic.

The underlying foundation of the visionary experiences occasioned by DMT are experiences of perceiving energy. This energy can be both seen and felt in the DMT state. At the most basic level, consumption of DMT can be said to enhance an individual's ability to perceive and experience certain forms of energy, and this is clearly reflected in the universal perceptions of geometry, patterns, gradients and fractal and symmetrical forms.

Mariela de la Paz: Indigenous Visionary Plant Medicine Art

Mariela de la Paz is a Chilean artist who has researched the Mesoamerican, Andean and Amazon cultures for over twenty years, and has been channeling this art through sacred power plants. Her paintings reflect the traditions of ancient rituals, which invoke the ancestral memory of the universal soul. Mariela has been able to deliver, through her forms and colors, a timeless and sacred message that will remain in the eye of the beholder as a unique and non-repeatable experience. Mariela writes, "Sacred plants are entities of a female nature, and considered by the sages of these cultures as spiritual allies.

The substances within these plants cause information currents to pass through the body, which then arouses and resonates with a cosmic awakening. These are intimately related to the procreation of life on this planet, and they bring light and love. Sacred medicinal plants act as a meditative state that stills the mind so as to connect us with reality in all of its realms - taking us away from linear time and putting us in touch with multidimensionality."[25]

All of Mariela's work tells a potent story of female shamanism and interconnectivity. Her painting titled

La Machi is one that is close to her heart as it honors the powerful female shamans of the Mapuche society. A Machi is a traditional healer and religious leader in the Mapuche culture of Chile and Argentina. The Machi is a person of great wisdom and healing power and is the main character of Mapuche medicine. The Machi has detailed knowledge of medicinal herbs and other remedies, and is also said to have the power of the spirits and the ability to interpret dreams. As a religious authority, a Machi leads healing ceremonies, called Machitun. During the machitun, the machi communicates with the spirit world. Machies also serve as advisors and oracles for their community. Mariela describes the painting in more detail: La Machi is a devotional piece that took one year to complete.

> *This painting came through after dedicating many years to working in ritual and healing ceremonies with women from all over the world. I wanted to honor the most powerful figure of the Mapuche society: La Machi. She is the keeper of their ancient knowledge and of their millinery communion with the earth. She knows all of the healing properties of the plants of their rainforest. With the beat of her drum, she induces herself into a trance where she enters the spirit world to dialogue about the healing and the well-being of her people. This role is performed by women only and it follows a 13,000 year old matriarchal tradition.*[26]

Societies everywhere designate certain individuals as taking on the role of shaman for their group. Such people have the capacity to understand and change events in the ordinary world. They can accomplish this during normal waking consciousness, as female Machi or shamans in Chile do, by climbing a cinnamon-tree altar and playing a frame drum. More typically, they enter an alternative state of consciousness by fasting, undertaking a vision quest, engaging in lucid dreaming or ingesting hallucinogens. Shamans view ritual and ceremony as ways to create a deeper and more personal sense of connection with the earth and their communities. Ritual engages the spirit of a place, a circuit of energy in which the entire cosmos participates. Rituals and ceremony are a form of prayer, and our prayers for the world are our greatest contribution to healing and rebirth.

A woman who professes to be on the shamanic path, Mariela has been involved in many rituals and ceremonies. She has also developed her psychic intuitive abilities and gives private divination readings with the *Mother Peace Tarot,* created by Vicki Noble and Karen Vogle. In fact, it was Vicki Noble who encouraged her to come to

La Machi, Mariela de la Paz, 5′ x 5′ oil on canvas, www.marieladelapaz.com

the United States. She writes:

> *The strong women's spirituality symbols in my initial drawings called the attention of Vicki Noble, international teacher, author, and passionate feminist leader. I was invited by Vicki to travel to California and join her school of Contemporary Female Shamanism. I arrived in California in 1989, and settled there. I began elaborate oil paintings based on the original drawings I had designed alongside Pedro, my first teacher.*
>
> *In the last decade, my interests took me on the path of Amazonian plant medicine work. I was also initiated in the sacred path of Tantra. My recent paintings have picked up elements from both of these practices as they intertwine visions received in ceremony as a tantrika and yogini.*[27]

Another powerful painting to discuss is *Ayahuaska at the Gates of San Pedro,* which illustrates a plant medicine journey. There are more than two hundred plants that shamans around the world use to alter their consciousness so they can communicate with the natural and spiritual world, achieve artistic inspiration and self knowledge, know the future and the hidden past, and perform purification and healing rituals. These drugs blur the distinction between everyday reality and the world of dreams. They often create a subtle joy that blends with a feeling of timelessness, unity and comic consciousness. Ayahuasca, a mixture containing the bark of a South American vine and leaves of other forest plants, breaks up the visual field into kaleidoscopic images of yellow, red, purple, or blue.

Ayahuaska at the Gates of San Pedro, Mariela de la Paz, 24" x 24" oil on canvas, www.marieladelapaz.com

The New Moon Maiden, Mariela de la Paz, 40" x 40" oil on canvas, www.marieladelapaz.com

Mariela describes the painting in more detail:

This painting was channeled in less than an hour. I watched my hand in amazement as it moved in a serpentine fashion while it carried a graphite pencil knowing exactly what was next. I took this sketch to my studio where I turned it into an oil painting which took me about nine months to finish. This vision I saw as I journeyed in surrender to the spirit guides in plant medicine. I felt sperm of fire shooting out of the center of my hands. This was energy available and intended for healing. My feet released other type of energy, similar to roots going deep inside the earth. I was birthing, not my son, but all the love I have given to the men who have been my companions and merged with my flesh.

As I allowed this love to permeate me and to surround me, I felt a rose underneath embrace my whole body. There is a portal open only to those who participate in these sacraments. It is a place where a state of complete surrender to the divine plan can be reached. A place of timelessness, free of barriers. The mind and the body commune with the earth. Our channels of light open from the inside out and we are whole.[28]

Those of us who have taken an ecstatic spiritual journey with plant medicine know how physical and sensual the experience can be. The rose that Mariela felt underneath her is representative of the flower as the feminine life force and all sensual delights, including sexual love, art, music, singing and dancing. The visual relationship between the clitoris and a half-opened flower is a frequent motif in the art of many cultures, in part because flower petals unfold to reveal the pistil and stamen and its reproductive center. This painting is a powerful representation of the ecstasy one feels in the trance state.

A painting that captures another shamanic state of consciousness is *The New Moon Maiden*. In this painting we see a powerful warrioress with strong legs and arms raised to the sky. She is fully empowered, alive and connected to source. The energetic patterns on the desert floor and throughout Mariela's paintings reflect Ayahuasca's revealing of the energetic patterns and interconnectivity of all things. Every plant possesses an energy or life force of its own. They can also communicate with you and sing special songs.

Mariela describes the intention for the piece:

The New Moon Maiden is a piece that was channeled and executed fairly quickly. It took six months from beginning to end. I became aware of the power within the female body through the birth of my son. I wanted to convey this sacred union of the woman's bleeding cycle, her ability to become fertile and the moon cycles. I saw how through birthing all humans were connected, and women were linked together to their entire ancestry. I realized that there is a tremendous body of knowledge that lies dormant and ready to be unleashed in our DNA and through our blood. I painted 5 square feet with every pigment of red and red shade variations. It is named Copihue after Chile's national flower, which grows in a vine near the volcanoes of the Southern region. In this way, I honored the core of our planet, the molten lava and the blood of womb.[29]

A phenomenal book by Barbara Tedlock titled, *The Woman in the Shaman's Body: Reclaiming the Feminine in Religion and Medicine*, documents the blood mysteries of female shamanism. She writes, "Within the dark fluids of menstrual blood resides the vital essence of the most feminine form of spiritual energy. Concentrated and deeply mysterious, this force touches every woman and links her to a formidable shamanic tradition. Female hormones play a central role in women's shamanic abilities. Just before and during menstration women experience their strongest healing and oracular powers."[30]

The water of life, menstrual or postpartum blood, was held sacred to many Native American tribes as well. The blood of woman was in and of itself infused with the power of Supreme Mind, so women were held in awe and respect. Indian women valued their role as vitalizers. Through their own bodies they could bring vital beings into the world—a miraculous power unrivaled by mere shamanic displays. They were mothers, and that word implied the highest degree of status in ritual cultures.

Timothy White: Dreamer of the Imaginal Realms

Traversing the rich landscapes of visionary plant medicines, Timothy White is creating iconic portals that entice viewers into exploring the transformative mythic worlds of shamanic dreaming and entheogenic visions. He writes, "My desire is to depict provocative narrative images that speak to the archetypal patterns imbedded in our ancestral genetic memories and that help us align with our highest states of consciousness."[31] Born and raised in British Colonial India by American missionary parents, White grew up surrounded by a diverse mix of religious traditions and ethnic cultures. He was educated at a private boarding school located in the foothills of the Himalayas, where he learned to question authority and how to express his thoughts and feelings through the medium of creative writing. After returning to the United States in order to attend college, he explored several mainstream majors before deciding to pursue a career in photography and filmmaking.[32]

In 1985, following an entheogenic vision on Mount Shasta, White conceived and mid-wived the birth of *Shaman's Drum: A Journal of Experiential Shamanism*. For the following twenty-five years, White dedicated himself to editing and publishing the small but ground-breaking journal. As the journal's art director, White found himself gradually producing more and more illustrations for the magazine—initially out of necessity but later out of pleasure. Many of White's early paintings have graced the covers of *Shaman's Drum*, and his pen-and-ink illustrations have been published in several books, including *A Kayak Full of Ghosts*, an ethnographic collection of Inuit shamanic folktales compiled by mycologist Lawrence Millman.[33]

When *Shaman's Drum* officially folded in 2010, White took the opportunity to retire in order to pursue his love of painting. Despite having only recently launched his career as a visionary painter, his paintings and other artworks are exhibited by private collectors in Oregon, California, Washington, and Hawaii. White maintains a home base in southern Oregon, but he also likes to travel extensively, pursuing his interest in entheogenic sacraments and seeking inspirational material for his visionary paintings.[34]

"While many of White's iconic paintings are inspired directly by his active dream life and by his entheogenic visions, he also draws creative inspiration from the visionary art of the surrealists Hieronymus Bosch and Salvador Dali, the expressionistic art of Paul Gaugin and Gustav Klimt, the dramatic narrative art of Frida Kahlo and William Blake, and the expressive folk art of Henry Rousseau and Pablo Amaringo. Recently, he has been working on a series of "Wisdom Keeper" portraits that are intended to honor famous and lesser-known pioneers of entheogenic shamanism."[35]

Each painting is created with sacred intention and is imbued with a potent message of the heart. His colorful, vibrant, pointalist style is loaded with intention, each brush stroke is an offering or prayer to Great Spirit. His paintings have a dreamy quality that sings to the heart on subtle vibrational levels. If one quiets the mind and listens, they will hear the icaros of Gaia impregnating all of creation with her heart song. It is with our creative imaginations that we dream the world in which we live into being. This is what Timothy and all visionary artists are doing with their art—they are using their creative imaginations as a portal for Gaian wisdom to come through. Indigenous peoples universally refer to the dream world as a timeless archetypal field, which is not separate from the spirit world. "In Western psychology, the dream world is interpreted and understood in various ways according to various schools of thought, but most agree that it is a mysterious place we go into when we are asleep—a place where we have strange, numinous experiences and encounter people and localities that we may know, yet are always different in some way."[36]

Much of Timothy's paintings are inspired by visions that occur in the dreamtime. A painting titled *Nuestra Senora de las Aguas* is a gorgeous depiction of the Sacred Feminine bestowing her gifts of renewal and cleansing. Hummingbirds sip the sweet nectar from her vines and water flows from her hands into the earth. Timothy explains the intention in more detail:

> *The central image of a water goddess emerging from a flowering tree was inspired by a vision that came to me during a mushroom velada in Mexico with the Zapotec curandero Guadalupe Martinez. I saw streams of water flowing from the hands of the great goddess, while hummingbirds, which are associated with psychoactive plants in many cultures, drank nectar from the Morning Glory blossoms covering the stylized tree. Because the image of the goddess and the waters flowing from her hands reminded me of the famous Teotihuacan murals, which R. G. Wasson proposed were derived from mushroom visions, I included some symbolic motifs from those murals at the bottom of the painting.*[37]

Another fabulous painting is *Frida Kahlo's Resurrection*, which deeply honors Frida as one of the great feminist icons. Considered one of the greatest Mexican artists, Frida began painting after she was severely injured in a bus accident. Kahlo later became politically active and married communist artist Diego Rivera in 1929. Kahlo's folkloric style, influenced by Mexican popular art, and her fantastical imagery earned her recognition among the Surrealists, but her intriguing persona and unmistakable originality propelled her beyond the confines of a specific movement to become a leading figure in modern art.

In the background, Timothy painted Frida nailed to a cross, symbolizing the physical and emotional suffering she endured as a female mystic and artist. Timothy says, "This painting, which was inspired directly by an ayahuasca vision, revisits some of Frida Kahlo's well-known

Nuestra Senora de las Aguas, Timothy White, 24"x30", Acrylic on canvas, www.timothywhitefineart.com

Frida's Resurrection, Timothy White, 24"x30", Acrylic on canvas, www.timothywhitefineart.com

self-portraits depicting her physical suffering, but it also introduces a more optimistic theme of her rising from a coffin, wearing a necklace of thorns but vibrantly alive, accompanied by her favorite pet monkey and parrot. As a predominately self-taught artist myself, I have long appreciated Frida's intense expressive themes and her visionary poetic style."[38]

As a wounded healer, her spirit continues to live in and through the earth and contemporary artists who are inspired by her authenticity and courage to speak her deepest truth at a time when women were severely oppressed.

Morgan Mandala: A Microcosm of the Universe

Some visionary artists have the ability to bridge the sacred and the profane. Morgan Mandala is one of the gifted artists who has fully surrendered her ego to infinite imagination. She is well-known for her ability to live paint, which is not something all artists can pull off. It takes the ability to be in your right brain and surrender to the creative flow with absolute trust and non-attachment to results.

Morgan's art is painted on a circular canvas or mandala, which is a spiritual and ritual symbol in Hinduism and Buddhism, representing the universe. A "mandala" is a geometric pattern that represents the cosmos metaphysically or symbolically--a microcosm of the universe. She describes her art as "fantastic naturalism combined with geometric forms." [39]"Morgan earned a double BFA in painting and art History with a minor in philosophy at Colorado State University. Her studies sparked her interest in the relationship between art and spirituality, and how this relationship manifests itself throughout global cultures with a special interest in Shamanism and plant medicine." [40]She writes about her artistic mission:

> *I paint to visually explore our connection to the world, each other, and our inner selves living the conscious human experience. Mandalas are graphic representations of the universe - the multiplicity, and the singularity; the macrocosm, and microcosm. I re-interpret and merge objects and symbols in my paintings to create a metaphor for our seamless connection to the world, and open up a wider understanding (or questioning) of what we see and how we perceive.* [41]

Morgan's paintings are informed by her world travels, symbolic studies, and experiences with plant medicine. Two paintings that resonate with the Goddess of Interconnectivity are *Seeds of Life Within* and *Trinity.*

Seeds of Life Within, Morgan Mandala, www.morganmandala.com

The seed is a powerful symbol that holds the supreme intelligence of the cosmos and earth. Seeds are potent vessels of nature that contain ancient organic wisdom. As a beautiful metaphor for consciousness, a seed represents the divine design within all things. In the center of the painting is a seed and emanating outward is the flower of life. Found at the heart of an ancient pattern called the flower of life, there is an entire cosmology of consciousness encoded into this singular geometric seed.

Another image that resonates with the dark, chaotic, and cosmic void of the universal Mother is *Trinity.* The concept of death/rebirth is a powerful message of the Goddess --one that the indigenous people have always respected. Morgan explains the intention of the painting:

> *Trinity embodies the archetype of the Divine Mother. This archetype is honored and celebrated across many cultures, though the personifications may appear drastically different. Trinity is a combination of Kali (Hindu), Mary (Christian), and Morrigan (Celtic).*
>
> *The central figure in Trinity is based on Michelangelo's 'Pieta' pose, where typically Mary would be holding the body of Jesus. The central figure holds a skeleton. The skeleton represents humanity in its purest form - no gender, no race - just human. The Divine Mother cradles the skeleton with a gaze of compassion, knowing that humans have the fear of mortality, but also that you will be liberated through death. She holds the mortal through the struggle of the loss of ego.*

Trinity, Morgan Mandala, www.morganmandala.com

In her womb is a spiral galaxy. Her womb embodies the ever-expanding realm of infinite possibility and energy--the interconnection of everything with the cosmos. Her womb represents the ultimate source of creation. She has the blue skin of Kali, the embrace of Mary, and the wings of Morrigan, who shape-shift into birds to carry people from the realm of the living back through the cycle. Adorned on the crown of the Divine Mother and throughout the windows are symbols of dark blue stone, swirls, moons, and triangles.

The rosary window-like geometry behind the Divine Mother is the symbolic eight-petalled lotus from the outside of the Kali yantra, alluding to the cyclic world axis encircling the image (side note - this is one tiny facet of the symbolism behind the eight-petalled lotus and Kali Yantra!). Behind the central figure, the sky changes from window to window--representing time and the Divine Mother's transformative power of change.

The landscape in the background is filled with fertile land, flowing rivers, and rocky hills revealing faces of ancestors within them. Like the Divine Mother, the land holds the memory of the past, which creates the potential of the present and the foundation of the future.

As the eye moves upward from the figure, a light beam takes the viewer from the Divine Mother through the pure light of the sun, or, the light of the One Source Consciousness. The light of the One beams upward though the cosmic cloud yoni of rebirth; again beginning the cycle of life and death. [42]

Morgan's mandala's are powerful representations of the cycles of life, symbols, archetypes and intelligent design.

Martina Hoffmann: The Shamanic Priestess of Visionary Art

Martina Hoffmann, German-born, spent part of her childhood in Cameroon, West Africa. She majored in art and sculpting at the Johann Wolfgang Goethe University, in Frankfurt Germany. Hoffmann currently works as a painter and sculptress. Much of her imagery addresses the sacred feminine, while her sculptural work shows undeniable African influences, as reflected in her Goddess Sculptures, semi primitive representations of female archetypes. Her paintings fall within the realm of Visionary Art, and have been greatly inspired by the visual language generated in expanded states of consciousness, such as the dream state, meditation, spontaneous visions, and shamanic practices, including experiences with entheogenic plants.

She draws inspiration from the iconography and insights encountered in expanded states of awareness. Her paintings are split second glimpses of intricate and complex multidimensional visions. She considers them metaphors of the original experience, symbols translated into a three-dimensional world, which portrays the indescribable. Hoffman creates doorways, which instantly transport the viewer to "the other side," thereby manifesting higher truths in this reality.

Martina Hoffmann describes herself as a "magical realist" whose aim is to express visionary states of consciousness of dreams, entheogens, and meditation on canvas. She writes, "All my shamanic journeys as well as my meditative practice and dreams have been highly revelatory and produced insights that have transformed my consciousness and hence deeply affected my work." [43] Chief among these experiences has been her work with the profound visionary medicine of ayahuasca: "I greatly owe a large body of my work to the inspiration obtained through the usage of sacred plant teachers.

My extensive travels to the Amazonian regions of South America and my contact with a range of shamans in Brazil and Peru have allowed me to connect with the 'mother spirit' of ayahuasca especially, a medicinal drink composed of various plants such as Banisteriopsis Caapi (The Vine of the Soul) and Psychotria Virides (La Chacruna). This sacrament, used by the Amazonian indigenous people for millennia and legal in this part of the world in the indigenous context as well as within the Santo Dime and Uñoa Vegetal churches of Brazil, has allowed me to glimpse the indescribable, and presented me with a call of recreating aspects of its intensely beautiful visions in my paintings, basically a near impossible task. However, I continue to lend it my best efforts." [44]

For Martina, ayahuasca is an incomparable tool. "I feel that the journeys provide the most expedient and direct connection to 'Source Energy' and great travel access to the Universe. They are an immediate entryway into the realms of spirit." [45] Art representing such states of consciousness has a special role to play, according to Martina, both personally and publicly. For her own experience, art provides a mirror and a meditation: "While painting, the canvas becomes a mirror, which allows me to deepen my understanding of what I need to know about myself, how I perceive the world around me and what information needs to be made visible for All in this very instant," she writes. "It is my oracle way, my sharing with myself as well as my community and the world." [46]

The process of creation is itself an exploration into vision and self-knowing, much like the ayahuasca experience. With her art, Martina hopes to awaken similar glimpses into the greater reality in her viewers. She primarily paints for herself, not for public consumption, and this perhaps deepens the impact of her work. She sees her own self-exploration as serving others and inspiring change. "I'm an activist, like most artists, always pushing the envelope, and I wish to be a messenger for higher consciousness and Source Energy." [47] Personally, she is motivated by her perceptions of the Sacred, especially the Divine Feminine. "From the beginning of human history the urge to create has been sparked by a desire to communicate the deepest truths about who and what we are, and our connection to and within the greater reality." [48] As she sees it, images of the Goddess, Gaia, and the experience of interconnection are integral to this expression of the deepest truths.

The first painting by Martina Hoffmann that speaks of interconnectivity is *Caught in the Web*, a graphic and symbolic depiction of certain aspects of the ayahuasca experience. Visually, the scene shows a high degree of symmetry and balance, despite the wild profusion of elements. A woman lies on her back with her head to the viewer, her arms outstretched with hands open. She

Caught In The Web, Martina Hoffmann, 2′ x 3′ oil on canvas, www.martinahoffmann.com

Firekeeper, Martina Hoffmann, 3′ x 6′ oil on canvas, www.martinahoffmann.com

is vulnerable, surrendered, completely overtaken by the flood of visions, energy, and dramatic purging that ayahuasca gives rise to. Martina identifies "complete surrender as the most important prerequisite demanded of us while drinking 'The Vine of the Soul'." [49]

Though challenging, purging is an integral part of the ayahuasca experience and most drinkers find themselves required to submit to the ordeal sooner or later in their schooling with the master drink. "Engaging with the deeply transformational energy of this most powerful plant teacher, ayahuasca, will create a dynamic that works two ways: First there's the purging that opens the gate to other dimensions and makes the healing possible," writes Martina. [50]This is graphically represented in the image with the woman purging into the visions themselves, with little distinction between what emerges from the interior of her body and the interior of her visual realm of immediate experience. She is literally bound to the totality of the experience with vision serpents wrapping around her arms as more serpents writhe about her head. All of nature seems present to witness this profound cleansing and dramatic transformation. Second, "From the realms of higher consciousness, the plant spirits and animal totems of Anahuac (snake and jaguar) are entering our being through this portal in order to do the deep and necessary healing work." [51] As Martina describes it, this two-way action of purging and inviting in of energies is what allows for healing and transformation.

Also highly significant in this piece is the energetic nature of the ayahuasca visions. The overall piece shows clear bilateral symmetry, a common energetic perception with ayahuasca. Furthermore, energy radiates from the edges of the vision, reminiscent of electricity, which is also a common sensation within the body of the ayahuasca drinker, almost like pulsing waves of static electricity or electromagnetic vibrations. As Martina writes, "The 'energetic of everything' is a strong component of what I respond to. There is such irresistible beauty all around us and all pervasive." [52]

Another powerful painting by her is *Firekeeper*, which shows the divine feminine in a striking pose of poise and dignity. We see similar elements in this piece as in *Caught In The Web*: radiating waves of energy and an overall emphasis on balance and bilateral symmetry. Yet here, rather than surrendered and passive, the woman stands erect, proudly holding her ground with her hands protecting her wombspace, a guardian of the sacred. Martina describes this figure as an archetypal "female warrior." "Here woman turns into a truly awe-inspiring Goddess and asserts herself in a very active way." [53] Though nude, SHE is in no way vulnerable or an object of the gaze of desire. On the contrary, she is powerful and demanding. She is, "fueled by tapping into the powerfully transformative energies contained within the web of consciousness that are being channeled through her body. Her crown is made of pure, live energy," [54] writes Martina, allowing her to be a transmitter of wisdom and ancient knowledge. This energy is so powerful that it melts the ice of illusion and stagnation underneath her feet, allowing the new and dynamic to emerge and transform. Here the Goddess does not assure our continuation through the birthing of new life but rather by being a "Keeper of the Sacred Flame and Mysteries." A timely call and invitation for all women to embrace their power in whichever form and expression they choose.

The Fantastic Art Of Robert Venosa

Robert Venosa describes his process of discovering the images in the canvas, which he renders using the *mische* technique, as an exploration. Venosa studied with the modern masters of the Vienna School of Fantastic Realism, Mati Klarwein and Ernst Fuchs, in order to learn this complex technique of layering paint with glaze, thereby rendering the final piece luminescent and full of three-dimensional depth. As Venosa proclaims, "It was the perfect technique for me to try to manifest the visions that I was having," that inspired him to become an artist. [55]

It was exposure to psychedelics, and LSD in particular, that "turned my head around," says Venosa. His view of reality upended by his experiences, Venosa left a profitable business in advertising and design to pursue the manifestation of his visions in artistic form. He felt drawn to the work of the Fantastic Realists, artists who in the United States would be identified as "visionary" artists. The levels of perception opened up by psychedelic states of consciousness became the foundation for Venosa's artistic vision. Inspired by what he identifies as the superconscious that is accessible through dreams, visions, and meditations, Venosa has sought to use the process of art as a medium of expression for the deepest levels of being and awareness.

In order to let the superconscious express itself through his work, Venosa engages in a meditative process with his art that is perhaps best exemplified by *Ayahuasca Dream*. Venosa says, "That particular painting, as with most of my art, I didn't plan the imagery. What I do is I sit down and I start painting. You don't sketch or pre-plan anything. The sort of imagery I do, I let it come through me. I'll lay out some abstract colors and forms, and then I'll look into it. I'll look into what's sitting in the so-called 'abstraction."[56]

He goes on to say, "Let the painting tell you what it wants to be instead of one imposing one's ego on it. When one doesn't impose one's ego, the message that comes through is much clearer. It's more profound. It comes more from the depths of your spirit rather than the depths of your subconscious, your ego. In that way, painting is a constant surprise. The more you start looking into it, the more you see these forms, the more the painting opens up and becomes this narrative."[57]

With this piece, Venosa began with his usual process of laying down color abstractly on the canvass with no particular intention. Later, he had the opportunity to take part in an ayahuasca session. In the middle of that session he walked to his studio where he studied the canvas and let the images form before him. "I came down to my studio the next day and started painting it, and it came out exactly like I saw it on the ayahuasca. So in that case it presented me with this road map. It was very exciting. I couldn't wait to paint that. Six months later it was finished."[58]

A painting titled *The Enlightenment* shows Venosa's desire to render unique images that have common iconographic representation. Here, Venosa was commissioned to depict the Buddha at the moment of enlightenment. Not wanting to fall back on conventional imagery of the Buddha, Venosa began with the "crystal explosion" of the glazed background, upon which he superimposed a luminescent, meditating figure. It is recognizable as the Buddha only minimally, with maximum emphasis on the light-filled transcendent experience of awakening. It is almost as though Venosa is showing us the energy of the experience more than the iconography of recognizable form.

Ayahuasca Dream, Robert Venosa, 4' x 6' oil on canvas, www.venosa.com

The Enlightenment, Robert Venosa, 2' x 4' oil on canvas, www.venosa.com

Juan Benavides Perez

Mauro and Juan Perez: The Usko-Ayar School of Amazonian Painting

The Usko-Ayar School of Amazonian Painting in Pucallpa, Peru, was founded by the famous artist/shaman Pablo Amaringo. It is an institution dedicated to the preservation, through art, of the flora, fauna, and cultural lore of the Amazon. The Amazonian rainforest is the home to Native indigenous cultures that are rapidly becoming extinct. An anthropologist by the name of Louis Eduard Luna documented the work of Pablo Amaringo in a monumental book called *Ayahuasca Visions: The Religious Iconography of a Peruvian Shaman.*[59] For almost a decade, he engaged in an inter-disciplinary study of mestizo shamanism in the Peruvian Amazon.

In this profound book, he documents the indigenous wisdoms of the Peruvian natives and how their spiritual heritage has been highly misunderstood by various Christian missionary groups. Louis writes "Intense missionary activity still in effect today aims to deprive the Indians of their spiritual heritage; incapable of understanding and accepting an alternate world view."[60] In addition, numerous anthropologist and environmentalists have documented the rapid extinction of the Amazon, with its immensely rich and diversified biota, and the cultural richness of its inhabitants. Pablo writes "It has become sadly evident that unless profound measures are taken, our grandchildren will never be able to see any of the great rainforest that today covers large areas of the South American Continent."[61]

There have been massive efforts to preserve the earth-based wisdom of Native cultures, for the Amazon literally is the "Lungs" of the Earth. It is our breath of life and it is where many of the medicines of the Earth are found. These medicine are freely given from Gaia to heal our bodies, minds, hearts and souls. Yet, we continue to be on a path of self-destruction in order to fuel our gross addiction to consumerism, financial progress, and fossil fuels.

This incredibly heartbreaking reality is beautifully portrayed in the award winning film *Avatar*. Nonetheless, the life force of Gaia cannot be destroyed by human ignorance and the military industrial complex. In these times of vast ecological destruction in the Amazon, the shamans are trying to reveal through art that plants have an immensely important message for humankind. She is way too powerful to allow years of human neurosis to metastasize like cancer on her body.

The Peruvian shamans are incredibly tuned into the ancient wisdom of the Earth, ancestors, and the animals. They exemplify a much more harmonious way of living with ourselves, our communities and the Earth. They are calling us to reconnect with the Spirit world and heal our fractured psyches through art, nature and plant medicine.

It is a great honor to have in this book two Peruvian artists who have devoted their lives to the healing of the Earth. "Visionary Artists Mauro Reátegui Perez and Juan Benavides Perez are becoming two of the most visible and sought after Peruvian visionary artists. Having trained with the renown visionary artist, Pablo Amaringo, the shaman brothers have developed a distinctive style that has become known internationally and they have had shows throughout Europe and North America.

Mauro draws inspiration for the vibrant and rich detailed "cosmo-gaian" vision he portrays in his paintings from his own personal spiritual journey working with

Mauro Reátegui Perez, www.mauroart.com

Amazonian plant medicines and from interviews with shamans that he has made over the years. As well as being a talented painter, Mauro is also a teacher and guide and possesses an extensive knowledge of the cultural life of the Peruvian Amazon." [62]

His gallery of visionary paintings portray deep shamanic journeys and visions revealing an array of spiritual beings inhabiting the forest, the underwater and subterranean realms, and angelic realms. His paintings are divine messages from the plant-spirits containing visions of evolution, magic, creation, healing the jungle and love. Through "icaros," which are songs that heal and carry "the message" in sacred ceremonies with Mother Ayahuasca, visions become vivid and clear.

Juan Benavides Perez says, "My first experiences with painting were only about the jungle. I now paint visionary art with channeled messages regarding the life of healing medicinal plants. And, my love for nature shows in my canvasses as paintings for the healing of our Planet." [63]

Star Flower, Martin Ball, www.fractalimagination.com

Envisioning the Infinite Eye of Divine Imagination with Fractals (By Martin Ball)

As a fractal/digital artist, my work is mostly abstract. I resonate with a non-dualist perspective, which doesn't adhere to any particular religious affiliation and transcends binary gender associations. I see the Divine similarly: neither masculine nor feminine. However, both fractals and the divine hold the potential for all form and manifestation, so metaphorically speaking, we may speak of both as deriving from the "womb of creation," giving them a feminine resonance. As the cosmos infinitely births new planets, we also continually birth art, offspring, and creative ideas from the deep feminine well of our individual and collective unconscious--the infinite well of our creative imaginations.

My primary goal as an artist is to create images that are beautiful, inspiring, cosmic, and representational of not only the external world around us, but also the vast inner landscapes of visions, dreams, and entheogenic experience. Not only is the outside world made of fractals, but so are the inner realms of visionary and mystical experience. In my art, I portray complex fractals, tessellations, labyrinthine structures, hyper-dimensionality, movement, and the evolving nature of reality. The inner eye of the divine imagination is a vast and infinite reservoir of creativity, birthing one fantastical vista after another in an endless array of scintillating light, geometric form, and mind-boggling complexity. For those experienced with entheogenic states of consciousness, the shapes, forms, and colors should look familiar. For those who are merely curious, this is what it looks like when you let the mind go, transcend the ego, and pass into a unified field of consciousness.

To create a finished work, I first start with fractal flame software, searching for shapes, images, colors, textures, and patterns that I find pleasing and interesting. When asked about the process, I liken it to nature photography – moving through a landscape and looking for the details of interest that stand out to me and my artistic eye, and when I find something worth my interest, I take a snapshot. From there, I begin composing layers in Photoshop, adjusting colors, blending layers, and moving elements around until I have a finished product. As a fractal/digital artist, it is important that each image be a composite and not a single image that was rendered out of a software program. And when it works, I also like to add in some of my original photography as well, blending the inner and outer worlds into a unified field of infinite being.

I've chosen a few images that, depending on the viewer, may have more of a feminine association with them, given the imagery, colors, shapes, and textures. For example, I've include some images with flowers (all created through fractal mathematics), which, for me personally, I

Entrance to Love, Martin Ball, www.fractalimagination.com

associate with femininity and sexuality.

The image *Star Flower* is a very iconic image for me personally as I chose it for the cover of the second album that my wife, Jessalynn Jones, and I, released, "Flowers in the Dark." Together, we are known as "Fractal Love Jam," and when I was deciding on what to call our 2015 release, I chose the song "Flowers in the Dark," as the title track. Once that decision was made, this image immediately came to mind, for fairly obvious reasons, as the perfect image to grace the cover of the album. The concept of "flowers in the dark" is a somewhat obscure reference to the Aztec description of the psilocybin mushroom experience as the "flowery dream." When consumed and experienced in the dark, the inner light of the divine imagination blossoms into full view with either eyes opened or closed, as intricate geometries and fractals unfold into sweeping visions. The song lyrics capture my sentiments about this image:

Mystery calls to me in the shadows of the night
Secrets unfold to me in the petals of the light
The labyrinth I walk within is an ever-turning path
The ecstasy that surrounds me I know will always last
There are flowers in the dark, and they're blooming just for you

There are flowers, and they're blooming just for you
Now is the time to change: Let go of the past
Open our eyes and see the truth that will last
We are the ones who must be ones of the light and reality
This is the time of the change, to embrace life

One of the most difficult parts of making art for me is choosing a title, especially since I mostly work with abstract geometry. The image *Entrance to Love* feels particularly inviting to me with overtones of feminine sexuality. Yet love is not confined to either gender or sexuality – as the star-like background intimates, love is boundless, unconditional, and non-possessive. It is cosmic and universal in scope. The true entrance to love is the infinite well of love found within the heart, through which we are all connected to THE ALL.

Before starting to work as a digital/fractal artist, my favorite subject to draw was birds, and in particular, birds of prey. I have a deep love and fascination with our fine feathered friends, and regularly combine avian photography with my fractal art. In the image *Feathered Beings*, no such combination was needed as these variations on

Feathered Beings, Martin Ball, www.fractalimagination.com

Flower of the Cosmos, Martin Ball, www.fractalimagination.com

feather-like structures started showing up in my fractal flame generating software. Are they bird feathers, butterfly wings, bird-butterfly hybrids, angelic presences? That's all up to the viewer. In the beginning and end, they're just math, but that's part of the fun of working with fractals, and the fractal nature of reality in general. Colorized math can turn itself into recognizable structures from our experienced reality of the lived world, and also the world of the inner imagination and its cosmic spaces and inhabitants.

Conclusion

What the entheogenic experience reveals is that all things are united in their energetic natures. There is nothing that exists that is not energy in some form, and there is no real boundary to energy, for it is a continuum of interrelated spectrums. Within the infinite energy continuum of reality there is the experience of the self, the experience of being. What unites all spectrums and manifestations of energy is the unitary experience of "I am." This is knowledge that can never be destroyed, for it is the very ground of experience. Within the entheogenic experience, the knowledge that "I am" persists, even if the nature of that self is not understood by the rational or egoic mind.

The art here shows this expanded view of the self. It is presented "imagistically", sometimes as a scene, sometimes as a mirror image of the self as directly experienced in the entheogenic state. In "imagistic" form we are reminded that we are that sacred geometry, we are that energy, we are that connection between all things, and we are that experience of "I am." The art is calling us to awaken to who and what we truly are; energetic embodiments of the "I am." The conclusion is clear; we are the Divine Being. All of reality is contained within us, within our experience of "I am." We are the sacred.

Martin W. Ball, PhD, is an independent researcher focused on the interface between spiritual awakening and entheogenic experience. He received his Ph.D. from UCSB in Religious Studies with an emphasis on Native American traditions, shamanism, and comparative mysticism. He is the author of several books on entheogenic spirituality, including his latest, Entheologues: Conversations with Leading Psychedelic Thinkers, Explorers and Researchers, featuring interviews from his weekly podcast, "The Entheogenic Evolution." Martin's podcast can be found at www.entheogenic.podomatic.com and his books and music can be found at his web page, www.martinball.net

Spiral Dance, Martin Ball, www.fractalimagination.com

Sandra Ingerman, MA, is an award winning author of twelve books, including Soul Retrieval, Medicine for the Earth, Walking in Light, and The Book of Ceremony: Shamanic Wisdom for Invoking the Sacred Into Everyday Life. She is the presenter of eight audio programs produced by Sounds True, and the creator of the Transmutation App. For 35 years Sandra has been a world renowned teacher of shamanism teaching workshops internationally on shamanism and reversing environmental pollution using spiritual methods. www.sandraingerman.com

Hank Wesselman, PhD, is an anthropologist who conducts research with international expeditions in Eastern Africa's Great Rift Valley, in search of answers to the mystery of human origins. He is the author of nine books on shamanism including The Journey to the Sacred Garden, Spirit Medicine (with Jill Kuykendall), the award winning Awakening to the Spirit World (with Sandra Ingerman), The Bowl of Light: Ancestral Wisdom from a Hawaiian Shaman, The Re-Enchantment: A Shamanic Path to a Life of Wonder, and his Spiritwalker Trilogy. He offers workshops at the Omega Institute in Rhinebeck NY, the Breitenbush Conference Center in northern Oregon and Mosswood Hollow in Duvall WA and lives with his family on their organic farm in south Kona, Hawaii Island. See his website at sharedwisdom.com

The Search for a New Worldview: Co-Creating a New Golden Age on Earth

By Victoria Christian, M.A. and Gary Stamper, Ph.D

> *"No problem can be solved from the same level of consciousness that created it." - Albert Einstein*

This is an extraordinary time in the planet's history. We stand today on the threshold of a new era. Indigenous elders, visionaries and prophets throughout history all point to our current period as a time of great world transformation. Are we facing the end of the world or is a conscious revolution occurring? Perhaps we are both regressing and evolving at the same time. This purification time, as some call it, is the end of the world as we have known it: a world dominated by unbridled violence and insatiable greed, competition, egoistic hierarchy of values, corrupted institutions and corporations and irreconcilable conflicts between organized religions. Time appears to be going faster than ever and most people are in some sort of existential crisis as the economic, political and social systems fall apart. It has become evident to many that we are on a suicide mission that at times feels unstoppable -- the denial and resistance to change seem too immense to tackle at this point in time.

We in the West have been so heavily conditioned with and bombarded by patriarchal religious fundamentalism and orthodox science that people don't seem to know what to believe anymore. We now face potential damage to our planet and ourselves in the form of nuclear and environmental threats, such as toxic waste, pollution, global warming and destruction of the Ozone layer -- all made possible as the outgrowth of a masculine oriented science and technology that has become synonymous with progress. After thousands of years of patriarchal warrior cultures that have ravaged and polluted the earth, Gaia is breaking down. Between the abuse of nature and the gross exploitation of women and minorities, Western

Garden of Eden, Andrew Annenberg, 24"x30", oil on canvas, www.andrewannenberg.com

New Pioneers, Mark Henson, 48 x108" Oil on Canvas, 2010, www.markhensonart.com

cultures will continue to reflect this imbalance if they do not begin to embrace the Great Mother and all that she represents.

Looking around our world we can see the breakdown of multiple social and economic systems. This breakdown is also a spiritual crisis. These systems are failing because they are no longer serving humanity. These failing systems are a last call for humanity to wake up and step into its true nature. This is the death and rebirth of a new era, and however it turns out, we will bear the ultimate responsibility. We are on the bleeding edge of birthing a new human and knowing that we will step into a new way of BE-ing or perish. We have no choice but to become co-evolutionary partners if we want to ride this wave.

The dominant belief is that the existing social, economic and political order is both rational and inevitable. In other words, most people aren't critically questioning the unregulated system of patriarchy and capitalism, and as a result, are completely disillusioned by the matrix. The majority of humans are taught to accept the world as it is, and thus, unthinkingly reinforce and reproduce it. But we can challenge the larger trend of economic determinism. A number of social theorists agree that we enter a social world not of our own making, but we are able to act upon it provided we understand how it is made, and in doing so, we can develop a new revolutionary praxis to free ourselves, at least to some degree, from the hegemony of the power elite.[1]

Simultaneously, the birthing of a New Golden Era on Earth is occurring. We are in the process of a global consciousness shift. The vibration of the planet is rising and new energies are changing the paradigm on Earth. Amidst rampant fatalism, humanity is also evolving at an accelerated rate. Those who are beginning to awaken to Oneness, as it unfolds in current times, are ushering in a dramatic shift into a new paradigm, a merging of science and mysticism, East and West, male and female, God and Goddess. While the majority of Westerners are still clinging to a scientific, nihilistic and materialistic worldview, those who are aligning with this shift in consciousness will discover that they are in the process of their own rebirth and a remembrance of what it all means. However, this transformation may indeed ruffle the covers, so to speak. Personal growth is never easy -- in fact, it can be downright uncomfortable. Yet it is a thousand times easier than staying stuck in belief systems that are keeping us spiritually stagnant. It is natural that efforts to create a new vision of God/Goddess will be mistrusted at first, for there are no familiar contexts to place them in.

We are witnessing the unraveling of an old system of greed and ego that is no longer serving the evolution of human consciousness. It is this system of profit mentality that has enslaved the human spirit—capitalizing on our creative energies in order to line the pockets of the corporate elite. The great illusion of machines and ego structures has continued to exist because it is feeding off our denials, fear and human ignorance. However, the tides are now changing. Babylon the Great is falling and it is time for humanity to awaken from the mind control and lies that have served to devalue our divine purpose. We are being called to embrace our individual and collective shadows so that we can break the chain of illusion that binds us. We can no longer afford to be imprisoned by our denials. We have the power within to create Heaven on Earth if we so desire. This global dark night of the soul we are witnessing is happening for a very important reason; it is time for us to awaken as a human race and fulfill our destiny as the beloved---one with God/Goddess and all of creation.

More and more, people are awakening to oneness and will continue to experience the unification and completion of all natural, cultural, religious and prophetic time cycles. Noted scholar Daniel Pinchbeck writes, "As we complete this apocalyptic passage, we will conceive ourselves increasingly as fractal expressions of a unified field of consciousness and sentient aspects of a planetary ecology—the Gaian mind—that is continually charged by our actions, and even our thoughts."[2] In other words, each one of us holds the power to create positive change with our thoughts, feelings and actions. We are all a part of the Gaian mind. The Goddess of Interconnectivity believes that we all hold powerful medicine and she is inclusive of everyone. She needs all of us to wake up and stand in our power at this critical time. If you are choosing to be numbed out with drugs or remain in a "fake bliss," then that is your expression of free will. But you are missing out on a very important quest—the survival of the human race, which is a pretty sobering reality check.

The Gaian mind and heart is calling us to be more conscious of our thought patterns, particularly scarcity thinking and competition, for these patterns are keeping us divided, and therefore, conquered as a people. The dominant group in society has become very proficient at using competition to its advantage by playing one oppressed group against another and exacerbating tensions among them. This divide and conquer behavior on the part of the dominant group effectively obscures the commonalities of oppressed groups. Without unity, competition emerges among oppressed groups for resources and attention. A goal of social transformation necessitates a shared ideological position among various oppressed groups, which provides the glue for building and maintaining coalitions. Without a common ideology there is no common cause. The net result is that if any change occurs, it is only a minor change within the system and not a fundamental change of the system itself.

In this article, we explore in more depth what exactly this "new world-view" is. What might such an enormous paradigm shift look like, should we succeed? What are we dreaming into existence with the imaginal cells of this paradigm shift, this Great Turning, this metamorphoses as we begin to weave our cocoon? What will emerge? While this is an enormously complex subject that is occurring on multiple levels and in various disciplines, we will merely scratch the surface of several important topics, such as death and rebirth, co-creativity and sacred activism, awakening the new masculine, sacred economics and the gift economy, permaculture and the slow food movement. We will also introduce the visionary art of several male artists who are on the path of conscious evolution and supportive of a feminist agenda to create a new system of equality and liberation for all.

Death and Rebirth

On a global level, but particularly in the United States, we are witnessing the breakdown of multiple institutions. The system of unregulated capitalism is failing because it is no longer serving humanity. It is the last call for humanity to wake up and step into its true nature as compassionate, generous co-creators of life. The social transformation of a society characterized by domination and force will require a lengthy and difficult process, one that could take decades or centuries. The system is deeply entrenched in our psyches and will take time to deconstruct. Unfortunately, we don't have decades to make changes. A tidal wave of awakening has to occur on both the micro level of the human psyche and the macro, structural level. This will demand a radical and passionate humility, particular among those who "think" they have all the answers and are fixed in their positions of power and authority.

Our priorities need to drastically change from a profit mentality to passionate humanitarianism. Change is inevitable—it can either be preventative and organized, or it will manifest as massive amounts of people falling through the cracks in a failed system. The time is ripe to start choosing people over profits. We can't afford to buy into a system that is set up to self-destruct. The house of cards is falling and we need to start cultivating more compassion and cooperation if we are going to survive the coming changes.

If we aren't able to make these changes, they will inevitably be made for us. The massive baby boom generation is an enormous tidal wave that is about to hit our social and health care systems. And not just in the United States; it is a global aging population that will be needing services. Social researchers all agree that our systems aren't set up to handle the housing and health care needs of this globally aging population. As the overall population ages, the numbers of the most vulnerable will grow as well. A new report from the Center for Housing Policy, *Housing an Aging Population—Are we Prepared?*, claims that "By 2050 the 65+ population is expected to grow from 40 million today to more than

88 million; put another way, one in every five Americans will be 65+." Demand for housing will more than triple over the same period to 19 million."[3]

It is time for a new worldview to emerge. As the famous futurist and architect R. Buckminster Fuller said, "You never change things by fighting the existing reality. To change something, build a new model that makes the existing model obsolete."[4] One of our jobs at this Great Turning is to render these worn-out systems obsolete as soon as possible. However, there is considerable debate about how to go about changing the system, which we are not able to fully address in this article. If you are wanting cutting edge information about the transformation in the social system, we highly recommend Bob Mullaly's book, *The New Structural Social Work.*[5] In my opinion, it is one of the most informed books out there about the death of capitalism and rebirth of a new system that is more egalitarian, conscious and incorporates the wisdoms of Modernism and Postmodern social theory.

We can say that at its core, the death of the old paradigm is a spiritual crisis. Neale Donald Walsh, author of the nine-book series, *Conversations with God*, says, "The world is in serious trouble, if what humans choose is to continue their present lifestyle on this planet. There is a way out of this trouble, but the solution to the world's problems is not political, it is not economic, and it is not military. The solution is spiritual, because the problem is spiritual. That is, it has to do with what human beings believe." Beliefs, the book tells us, create behaviors. You cannot change behaviors over the long run without altering the beliefs that underlie them. The one-word solution is education. In two words, spiritual education. In four words, a new cultural story. We have to tell a new story to ourselves about ourselves. We have to tell a new story to ourselves about each other. And we have to tell a new story to ourselves about God."[6]

Waking Up from the Land of Make Believe

We are facing a global dark night of the soul and if our hearts aren't broken open with pain, then we are living in a land of make believe. A quote by Dr. Kathy McMahon confirms this point: "Panglossian Disorder: The neurotic tendency toward extreme optimism in the face of likely cultural and planetary collapse."[7] We don't have the time to be blissed out, pretending that everything is hunky dory. We need a reality check--one that will require a serious look at numerous addictions such as; greed, power, sex, drugs, violence, domination, materialism, social prestige, competition and oil (to name just a few).

Ecofeminist and psychoanalyst Joanna Macy writes, "Just as grief work is a process by which bereaved persons unblock their numbed energies by acknowledging and grieving the loss of a loved one, so do we all need to unblock our feelings about our threatened planet and the possible demise of our species. Until we do, our power of creative response will be crippled."[8] She also talks about the tendency for us to lead a double life. "On one level we maintain a more or less upbeat capacity to carry on as usual, getting up in the morning and remembering which shoe goes on which foot, getting the kids off to school, meeting our appointments, cheering up our friends. All the while, there is an unformed awareness in the background that our world could be extensively damaged at any moment. Awesome and unprecedented in the history of humanity, the awareness lurks there, with anguish beyond naming. Until we find a way of acknowledging and integrating that level of anguished awareness, we repress it; and with that repression we are drained of the energy we need for action and clear thinking"[9] This is a sobering statement and one that should not be taken lightly. It is a call to all humans to be authentic, which means doing their shadow work and possibly sobering up, as we need clear thinking to create a new world for ourselves.

But what is it that will drive a person to take on such an onerous commitment to take on the world as we now know it and attempt to transform his or her self and the larger social structure? The answer, I believe, is to use our anger as a catalyst for change—anger at the social conditions of millions of people in the less-developed countries and in capitalist countries; anger at governments that cater to the wishes of the wealthy at the expense of women, children, minorities and other marginalized groups; anger at the raping of the Earth and the violence against women and children; anger at the treatment of animals.

A number of psychologists contend that anger can be mobilized from internalization as anxiety and depression into externalization as collective resistance. Anger has been the driving force behind all great social movements. Social change can happen at Godspeed if we wake up and break the psychological chains of illusion and slavery that bind us. In this awakening process, we will all be called to speak our truth and become authentic avatars of social justice, but it is important that we educate ourselves about the issues and appoint leaders with radical, progressive views.

How long do we need to create suffering for ourselves when there are better and more humane ways of co-existing on this planet? The crux of the problem is that people will have to question the hand that feeds them, and this is a scary thing to consider, especially when our survival is at stake and we have families to support. However, the irony of the situation is that our survival is already at stake by our continuing choice to remain apathetic drones, cogs in the great machine of capitalism.

Perhaps the most difficult challenge to uniting in social causes is the deeply entrenched system of competition which continues to divide and conquer people. In addition, we are conditioned to buy into the overly "yang" work-a-holism that keeps people so exhausted that they don't have the energy or volition to challenge the status quo or be politically engaged. Not only is unregulated capitalism a living hell on Earth for the majority of people, it is also killing the soul of humanity.

All of this is happening while people work their lives away in some unfulfilling job only to come home to sit on the couch completely absorbed in the technocratic distractions created by science and big business for the purpose of keeping people distracted, consumer-focused and numbed out. Meanwhile, the world swirls into further chaos and fragmentation and more and more people start committing suicide. Is this what the world is going to have to come to before we start making people a priority? We are already seeing the teenage suicide rate go up and up, but we sweep it under the carpet and pretend like everything is just fine. What kind of future are we offering our children? A land of make believe?

A Call to Sacred Activism: Networks of Grace and Co-Creativity

A brilliant internationally renowned mystic, scholar and writer by the name of Andrew Harvey released a profound book titled *The Hope: A Guide to Sacred Activism*. This is another book that is a powerful call to social transformation and includes spiritual wisdom from various traditions. It is a simple yet compelling guide to help people respond to current global challenges. Harvey believes that the death we are going through is a blessing because it is a wake-up call that no one will be able to ignore. He writes, "It is a blessing also because it is an awakening, on a massive scale, a response of creativity and selfless service among those who recognize what a crucial time it is and see that anything is now possible—the best as well as the worst."[10] According to Harvey, this great birth will have to come about as the result of a massive grassroots mobilization of the hearts and committed wills of millions of people. The vehicle for this mobilization Harvey believes will be through what he calls "Networks of Grace." The following is an excerpt from his book:

> *Our sense of community is in disrepair. It is essential, therefore, that sacred activists, while pursuing their individual spiritual paths and embracing their own specific kinds of service, learn to work together and to form empowering and encouraging 'networks of grace' - beings of like heart brought together by passion, skill and serendipity to pool energies, triumphs, griefs, hopes and resources of all kinds. When people of like mind and heart gather together, sometimes miraculously powerful synergy can result.*
>
> *Such 'networks of grace' can only be as transformative as our crisis needs them to be, if those who form them work constantly on the seductions of power, glamour and celebrity, and develop ever-deeper discrimination. Learning to discern the real gold of authentic networks of grace from the false glitter of networks of power and self-importance is difficult and demands prayer, humility, patience and shadow-work, and the unglamorous ability to wait on results and not force them before the Mystery has had a chance to form them completely.* [11]

The economic, political, and spiritual global crisis that we currently find ourselves in is a call to action. Sacred activism embodies an integral, or holistic, approach that combines all the spiritual and wisdom traditions that have come before and provides a clear way forward. In the heart of the chaos of the modern crisis, an extraordinary lineage has arisen of ordinary people who have fused the wisdom traditions and deep spiritual knowledge with wise action for justice and peace. Having emerged against all odds, they accomplished the unimaginable. The vision of sacred activism is dedicated to honoring and continuing the tremendous work of extraordinary people such as Mahatma Gandhi, Martin Luther King Jr., the Dalai Lama, Nelson Mandela, Rosa Parks, and Desmond Tutu. Each of these individuals rose up to meet the challenges of his or her time with great spiritual grace and integrated inner contemplation with decisive action.

Sacred Economics: The Gift Economy

Voices like Charles Eisenstein, author of *Sacred Economics: Money, Gift & Society In The Age of Transition,* are bringing new ways to think about how social systems and money can function at later stage consciousness. Eisenstein champions a "gift economy" where the more you give, the richer you are. The way we now create money promises, even demands, scarcity. In addition, it also separates us from each other, because money is set up as a win/lose proposition. But besides that, our money system is based on perpetual growth and will eventually collapse. The need for endless growth has been institutionalized and is another system that is failing. At this time, the environment is paying the price for this continued growth, but it can't go on much longer. We have learned that the most successful cultures throughout history were not competitive, but cooperative. We must awaken and realize that we are a sub-set of a larger cooperative ecosystem, not its masters.

One of the most successful gift economies is Burning Man, and it all happens without capitalism. While not sustainable, it's a temporary zone of B.S. free living. Gift economies are about giving stuff away for free without expecting to get anything back. More generally, in hunter-gatherer societies, the hunter's status was not determined by how much of the kill he ate but rather by what he brought back for others. For example, antelope meat called for a gift economy because it was perishable and there was too much for any one person to eat. In gift economies, human beings are worth more than market items. Eisenstein says:

> *In former times, people depended for all of life's necessities and pleasures on people they knew personally. If you alienated the local blacksmith, brewer, or doctor, there was no replacement. Your quality of life would be much lower. If you alienated your neighbors then you might not have help if you sprained your ankle during harvest season, or if your barn burnt down. Community was not an add-on to life; it was a way of life. Today, with only slight exaggeration, we could say we don't need anyone. I don't need the farmer who grew my food—I can pay someone else to do it. I don't need the mechanic who fixed my car. I don't need the trucker who brought my shoes to the store. I don't need any of the people who produced any of the things I use. I need someone to do their jobs, but not the unique individual people. They are replaceable and, by the same token, so am I.* [12]

Not only does the reclamation of a gift-based economy hasten the collapse of the unsustainable growth monetary system, it also mitigates its severity. Our present monetary system is but one of many crises, all converging at the same time. And they all provide us with the opportunity to create new systems, a new relationship to Earth, more connectedness to each other and a new human entity to go along with the new creation story of who we are, where relationship is our new wealth.

Conscious Relationship: Awakening the New Masculine

By Gary Stamper

It is clearly time for men to wake up. Just a little over one decade into the twenty-first century we find ourselves in the biggest struggle of our existence—a struggle in which the outcome is still unknown. No longer faced with mere territorial struggles, the consequences humankind faces today are global, and we are faced with the very real possibility of our own demise as a species. To be sure, these are issues of patriarchal power and the light and dark forces on the planet facing off against one another. It is the oldest story on the planet. It's time for the patriarchy to be disassembled and for its sons and daughters to grow up. Never before in human history has humankind been this close to a global psychosocial and spiritual awakening. At the same time, never have we been in such danger of being swept into global totalitarianism, potentially more oppressive than any system known before. Technology in the hands of little boys pretending to be men has led us to this new geopolitical reality.

Never before have we been called to wake up on the scale that is required today. My work with men has been about awakening the sacred masculine and the sacred activist within the masculine. My latest book, *Awakening the New Masculine,* [13]and the *Integral Warrior* men's workshop series are both predicated on the premise that there is still much healing to be done and that men, and women, almost always need to do their own work on healing their own inner masculine and feminine essences before they can ultimately come together in sacred union.

We live in a culture where men have been raised and taught to compete with other men and the winner is determined by who accumulates the most. We've all seen the bumper sticker that reads, "He who dies with the most toys wins." It is in this culture of inadequate development, where most men remain boys, that men need to learn to trust other men. This is something we have regrettably not been taught to do and that can only happen within the safe container of a men's circle.

Organizations such as the *Mankind Project* have been effective at transforming men who are stuck in their beliefs about what it means to be a man. After an intensive retreat and workshop, they are involved in a sacred circle with other men to learn how to express their emotions in a safe and mature way. Alot of men have been through this training and it has given women tremendous hope in the emergence of the new masculine. It is a transformative program that is healing the gap between men and

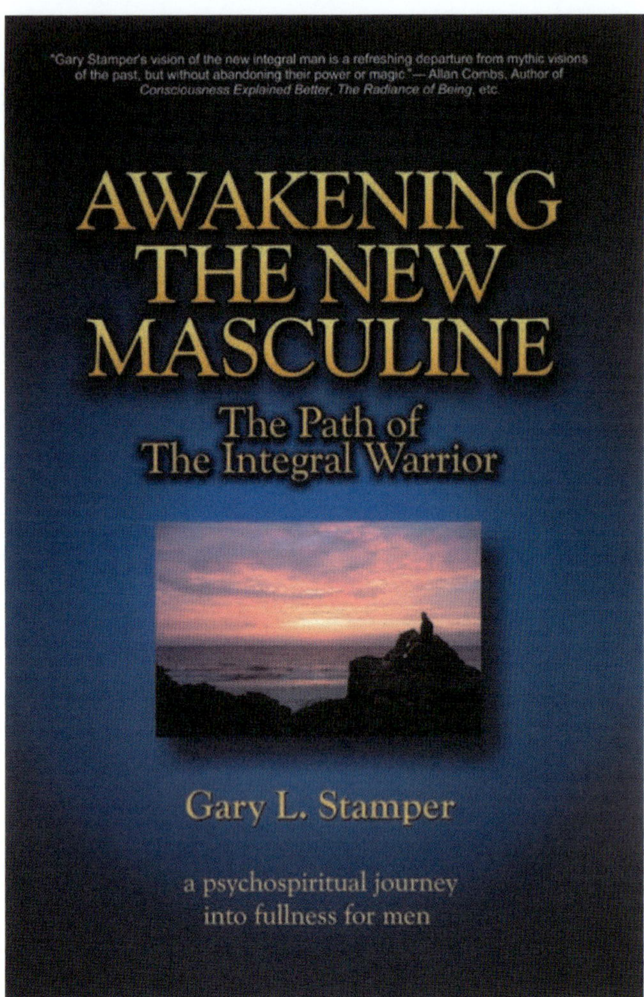

Book Cover, Gary L. Stamper
www.awakeningthenewmasculine.com

women in extraordinary ways.[14] (www.mankindproject.org)

Many women today are crying out for the Divine Masculine to show up and enter into sacred marriage with the Divine Feminine, both in external and internal realms; in the individual and in the collective. There is no doubt men are playing catch-up with the work women have been doing. We have surrendered to a hero image that we can't possibly attain, disregarding everything except our own egos and a false sense of power. Men are socially conditioned to be the wounded warriors, internalizing centuries of patriarchal values that have numbed our souls and our feelings.

With increasing awareness, men have come to believe that masculinity, men, and patriarchy are the same thing. Consequently, we sometimes deny and repress the power and the gifts of the Divine Masculine. Many postmodern men have adopted the softer, gentler, more caring aspects of their inner feminine, often because the masculine was so shamed that we denied even the healthy aspects of our masculine selves. The work I do with men in *The Integral Warrior Men's Process*, [15]helps integrate their healthy feminine and then re-integrate and reclaim the healthy aspects of the new masculine with a strong sense of purpose and mission.

When men and women, no matter what their sexual orientation, integrate their masculine and feminine essences, something magnificent happens--an internal "sacred marriage" occurs. Speaking only for men, this sacred marriage is a quality that enables a man to open his heart without giving up his essential masculine essence,without going soft or being so much in his feminine that he loses the ability to penetrate the heart of his beloved. At the same time, he retains the ability to move between the masculine and feminine poles as needed in whatever moment arises, with the intention of keeping the polarity, the tension between the opposites, active and alive.

Conscious relationship can occur when each of us remains conscious or present in our connections. It is also about honest communication, intimacy, being vulnerable, and providing a safe container for personal growth and healing. Conscious Relationship requires the courage to talk about what we are feeling and let down the defenses we've erected to keep ourselves safe. One of the great realizations of my life was understanding that I needed to become the kind of person I would want to be with. If both partners are committed to the relationship and their own personal and spiritual growth, a conscious relationship is one of the fastest ways to awaken.

The Integral Warriors of Visionary Art

By Victoria Christian

It has been a great blessing to witness a number of male visionary artists who have experienced the Goddess awakening and have felt a calling to pursue a spiritual path through art. And while the emphasis in this book is to reclaim feminine wisdom and allow mostly female artists a voice, the ultimate mission is to transcend the socially constructed binary of gender. The only way that we can do this is through a true understanding of the Goddess and all that she represents. This will require that men come to a full understanding and grasp of the feminine wisdoms within themselves and in the larger world. It behooves a man to integrate his feminine side, as more and more women are attracted to men who have empathy for the feminine wound. It is a great honor to discuss the work of some powerful new warriors of visionary art.

Daniel Holeman: Awakening Visions of Beauty and Truth

Daniel Holeman is a visionary artist consciously committed to his personal and spiritual growth. He has been envisioning the "golden age" his entire life and communicates this through his paintings. Daniel is a bridger of Heaven and Earth, attempting to bring enchantment, peace and sanity to the planet. "At a young age, Daniel had a profound spiritual awakening and experienced the nature of pure consciousness from which the manifested world is created. Since then his life has been about deepening that awareness and sharing it with others through art, lifestyle and conversation." [16]

"Daniel's primary role in life is that of a spiritual guide and messenger - and the art that comes through him is an expression of that role. He is here to assist others in remembering their connection to Divinity and living from that place - inspired to live their fullest potential, their unique possibility. His beautiful paintings have a strong impact on people and are loved all over the world. Many are deeply touched emotionally – sometimes brought to tears. He invites the viewer to dive into a deeper dimension of consciousness while viewing his paintings. The imagery stirs forgotten awareness of a place felt to be HOME – a warm, familiar and heartfelt state of mind – a welcome contrast to the day-to-day world we live in."[17]

Daniel created a painting called *Yoga Meditator*, which exudes the yin energy that all of us need to tap into in these chaotic times. As a result of the complexity and fragmentation of the hyper-rational technological era, people are losing their center as a result of being too much in their heads. More and more we will witness people moving into insanity and extreme neuroses. There isn't a single person who hasn't been damaged or wounded by the overly yang system of unregulated capitalism. It is a sick neurosis that has been deeply conditioned into westerners. Some say that it could take over a thousands years of just BEING to balance out the larger trend of "hyper-doing" in our culture. The Eastern traditions of yoga and meditation are a saving grace to the Western mind running amuck with incessant thinking, planning and strategizing. It's only through quieting the mind that one can come to a place of stillness, enabling the voice of Spirit to be heard and received.

Meditation is one of the Five Principles of Yoga. It is the practice by which there is constant observation of the mind. Through the practice of meditation you can achieve a greater sense of purpose and strength of will. It also helps to achieve a clearer mind, improve concentration and discover the wisdom and tranquility within you. Research has shown that meditation can contribute to an individual's psychological and physiological well-being. This is accomplished as meditation brings the brain wave pattern into an alpha state, which is a level of consciousness that promotes the healing state.

Another exquisite work by Daniel is *Bridging Heaven and Earth*, which speaks volumes about the need to resolve and heal all forms of separation from God and the heavenly realms. We can all look around and see that heaven is reflected on this beautiful planet of ours. It is also reflected in the holy temples of body, mind, heart and emotion. The illusion of separation from God, which came about in the scientific dualistic split between spirit and matter, is no longer serving us. This type of illusion exacerbates scarcity thinking, fatalism, meaninglessness, and social Darwinism, all of which are at the root of disease and mental dis-ease. Scarcity thinking is fear-based and assumes there isn't enough for everyone: For me to win, you have to lose. Furthermore, scarcity thinking cannot be assuaged by consumerism, that bottomless hole into which we throw stuff, only to be wanting more stuff soon thereafter. While much of commercial enterprise not only survives but thrives on this mentality, it is like a cancer that undermines society and leaves billions of people deprived of basic human rights. It is the driving force of a capitalistic agenda, and it can no longer be reinforced through social conformity.

Abundance thinking, by contrast, assumes there is more than enough for everyone – we can all win – and allows us to find win-win solutions for all. The fact is that we live in a world of abundance. There *is* enough for everyone to have their basic human needs met. It's not a question of whether there is enough to go around, but rather simply a question of priorities. In fact, in many cases in the developed world it would actually cost society less to eliminate poverty than it does to service it. And in the developing world it only takes a small fraction of what the world spends on militaries, as an example, to ensure that everyone has food, water, access to medical care, education and shelter.

Jose Arguelles: Society and Art in the Noosphere: From 'Time is Money" to "Time is Art"

Jose Arguelles is a gifted visionary stretching the boundaries of human consciousness with his art and writings. Jose's love of art and culture inspired him to obtain his Ph.D. in art history and aesthetics from the University of Chicago in 1969. His academic career led to professorships at Princeton University, the University of California at Davis, the Evergreen State College,

Yoga Meditator, Daniel Holeman, digital image, www.awakenvisions.com

Bridging Heaven and Earth, Daniel Holeman, Digital Image, www.awakenvisions.com

the Naropa Institute, San Francisco State University, San Francisco Institute of Art, University of Colorado Denver, and the Union Graduate School. Author of numerous philosophical and cultural essays, as well as poetry, his pioneering books were translated into many languages and include: *The Mayan Factor, Earth Ascending, Surfers of the Zuvuya, The Arcturus Probe*, *Time and the Technosphere: The Law of Time in Human Affairs,* the seven volume *Cosmic History Chronicles* (with Stephanie South) and *Manifesto for the Noosphere: The Evolution of Human Consciousness.* [18]

From 1992 until his passing in 2011, Argüelles had promoted and organized the annual July 25th *Day Out of Time Peace Through Culture* festivals throughout the world and promoted the circumpolar rainbow bridge meditation. He continued to travel the world several times over, giving numerous conferences and seminars and promoting the paradigm shift from "Time is Money" to "Time is Art."

According to the Law of Time, modern humanity is in crisis because it is immersed in an erroneous and artificial perception of time, causing civilization to deviate at an accelerated rate from the natural order of the universe. To remedy this self-destructive situation, a collective unification into galactic consciousness is required. For this reason, José Argüelles promoted the return to a natural time cycle through the regular measure of the 13-Moon 28-day calendar. Knowing that the Maya used up to 17 calendars simultaneously, and after experimenting with living many cycles at once, Argüelles found that the 13-Moon 28-day cycle was more than a calendar but a master synchronization matrix that all other systems and counts could be synchronized by. For this reason he called it a *synchronometer,* a tool for measuring synchronicity.

The 13 Moon, 28-day calendar is a new standard of time for all people everywhere who desire a genuinely new world. If the calendar and time we follow is irregular, artificial and mechanized, so becomes our minds. And as our minds are, so becomes our world. We see this in our world today: it is irregular, artificial and mechanized. But if the calendar we follow is harmonic and in tune with natural cycles, so also will our minds become, and so we may return to a way of life more spiritual and in harmony with nature; a time system that places creativity and art at the center.

This shift from "time is money" to "time is art" is a huge part of the paradigm or frequency shift. In going from the biosphere to the noosphere, we are literally passing from one time to another, from the old mechanistic time to a time altogether new and different, a time appropriate

Galactic Mandala, Jose Arguelles, 24"x24", acrylic on wood, www.lawoftime.org

to the noosphere, the time known by the Galactic Maya as the natural time of universal synchronization. We are at the time of the Great Synthesis of Knowledge, leading to Galactic Synchronization. But this is only the beginning. We are being rewired from within as old thought structures and conditionings give way to cosmic perceptions. This is also known as the biosphere-noosphere transition.

The noosphere is the planetary sphere of mind, or thinking layer, of planet Earth. To grasp the idea of the noosphere, we must elevate our consciousness and open ourselves to the most general, elemental and cosmic principles of life on Earth. As the mental sheathe of the planet, the noosphere characterizes mind and consciousness as a unitary phenomenon. This means that the quality and nature of our individual and collective thoughts directly affect the noosphere and create the quality of our environment—the biosphere.

As the Earth's mental sheathe, the noosphere represents a breakthrough to a new consciousness, a new time and a new reality arising from the biospheric crisis. This is known as the biosphere-noosphere transition. Just as the biosphere is the unity of all life and its support systems, the noosphere is the unity of all mind and its thinking layers. In this way the noosphere can be understood as the sum of the mental interactions of all life. Within the noosphere exists the evolutionary control panels known as the psi bank, the storage and retrieval system for all the mental programs.

While Jose created many illustrations for his books,

Radiant Woman, Radiant Man, Jose Arguelles, acrylic on wood door panel, www.lawoftime.org

for the purpose of this article we will discuss a couple of paintings from his *Doors of Perception Series*: *Radiant Woman* and *Radiant Man*. These paintings are one-of-a-kind works of classic psychedelic art from a true visionary of our time. Created to depict the sacred order of reality through their use of color, symbol, geometry and symmetry, a truly transcendent visual experience is invoked. These doors will turn any room into a truly cosmic space! The name is derived from an event that occurred when four of the original doors were on display at the Princeton University Art Museum in April of 1968. One of the invited guests, Humphrey Osmond, who is the man who coined the word "psychedelic," took a look at the four painted doors and exclaimed, "If only Aldous (Huxley) were here to see these! These are the Doors of Perception!"

The process of creating the doors is fascinating. As stated in Arguelles' biography *2012: Biography of a Time Traveler*, "He divided both sides of each door into three, two-foot-square sections and determined that the top and bottom sections would create mirror symmetry, each with a common overall geometrical design: as above, so below. The middle section would represent the place of change or the zone of transformation. His intention was to create what he called the 'cosmic change booth,' where one could sit in meditation surrounded by these mind-altering paintings and allow their perceptual shifts to work on the subconscious mind."[19]

Jose's vision of art and its role in the evolution of cosmic consciousness is right on the mark. He viewed art as one of the highest expressions of humanity. He said, "Art is the prelude to universal liberation." Before he passed away, Jose published an amazing book titled *The Manifesto for the Noosphere: The Next Stage in the Evolution of Human Consciousness.* I highly recommend this book to anyone interested in the possibility of humanity rising to the next level of consciousness. As Jose Arguelles says:

> *Art is the medium for collective and planetary fulfillment. It is the enactment of the noosphere as the supreme form of cooperation of the cosmic intelligence channeled by the human collective in co-creative interaction with the whole Earth, herself an embodiment of the divine self in its planetary order. With the noosphere engaged, the Earth becomes a psychic instrument of the cosmic consciousness. Transformed into a work of art, it takes its new place in the grand symphony of cosmic civilization. In the Noosphere we are going from 'time is money' to 'time is art.' We have to imagine that the structural basis of the entire planetary social order is reorganized so that the highest priority is given to artistic expression—not just individual artistic expression but to collective artistic expression as well. Art is not merely an activity practiced during leisure time, as in today's economic terms; on the contrary, it is the very essence of all human activity."*[20]

Envisioning The Divine Human

Written by Amoraea Dreamseed

Our species is in the beginning stages of a mutation and evolutionary leap from homo sapiens to homo universalis or "The Divine Human."" This is a shift from the egoic, subconscious personal self to the non-egoic, co-creative, divine Essential Self, and it is within each of us now as members of this crossover generation to become fully human and fully divine, recognizing this not as a dichotomy but as the crescendo-ing spiral of consciousness within form. This is the ultimate goal of the incarnational process, as we each emanate out from Source into Soul Essence, and then bring Soul into the very heart of matter to become self-aware of our God-nature and awaken from within the Creator's Dream as Individualized Immortal reflections of Itself.

Each being here in this vision represents one of the main root races, as well as one color of the rainbow. Below them is the region of the Earth their race is rooted from (beginning at top-center moving clockwise: Europe, North America, India, South America, Africa, and Asia). Each being is held in polar balance with its masculine or feminine counterpart across the circle. Three generations are also embodied within the group – a pair of younger beings, middle age adults, and elders (within the women's cycle; maiden, mother and crone).

Earth stewardship, enlightened service, God-focused awareness and recognition of global unity are the hallmarks of the Divine Human. In empty presence we become channels for the Light and the Will of the Divine to inseminate into the planetary membrane for the fulfillment of the evolutionary plan of our local home here. As we expand in compassion and consciousness, we graduate from the Genetic Mind of the planet into the universal and cosmic planes of existence, eventually merging with the Supreme Intelligence of Source and becoming co-creators of not only our own reality, but sacred architects birthing blueprints for new dimensions and spheres of consciousness within the playground of the material universe. These six beings are entirely linked into the Motherboard of Creation and surrender their personal identity to the Quantum Organizing Intelligence that pulses from the center of the Black Hole/ White Hole, the Alpha and Omega of Love.

Can you feel the higher dimension of Self that is peer-

Homo Universalis or The Divine Human, Amoraea Dreamseed, Digital image, 2013, www.divine-blueprint.com

ing through us, like a prism catching the light? We are holding the field for all of humanity to awaken through us because we are becoming a broadcasting station for cosmic and genetic wisdom. We merge with and emerge from the Akashic field and enter a state of Buddhic awareness. This is a return to the place within us that has already transcended and yet is the whole of creation as well. This painting represents the convergence point of consciousness crescendo-ing into full global awakening.

The Buddha or the Christed One contains all humanity's choices at once, with enlightened compassion, and experiences all trials and triumphs, all pleasures and pains as a witness and as an evolutionary agency within creation. Our evolving sacred being is a testament to the beauty of creation, and we learn to accept all as part of our own body, our own consciousness, embracing the whole of humanity and the whole of the universe as our greater Self.

The characters' interlocking bodies are actually creating a geometric mandala of energy and consciousness. Their tantric fusion creates the portal into infinite dimensional awareness that thrusts all mind and all matter into one. The Omega point is where spirit (or Divine Mind) and matter collapse back into one. When the psychic body and the primal matter of our physical universe merge as one, the Divine Human is born, informed by the Divine Intelligence of Creator.

We reside now in the accomplished deed - we enter into Zero time, where everything is pure potential and yet has already happened. We hold the planet from that state of Clear Diamond Awareness, the Heart of Perfect Wisdom. As we are blessed with God's Immortal Compassion, so too do we now hold the planet within that compassion. Eternal Compassion... Perfect Wisdom... Enlightened Mind.... The Womb of Creation gives birth to us perpetually. We surrender to that force… the Singularity that draws us towards it.[21]

Aaron Pyne: Activating the Cosmic Codes of the New Earth

Reverence is an attitude of honoring life in all of its manifestations. It is a deep appreciation for holiness and the sacredness of all things. The decision to approach life with reverence means acting and thinking as a spiritual person in a world that does not always recognize Spirit, and it often requires courage. Living life with reverence and gratitude is also a conscious choice that involves the cultivation of heart wisdom or intuitive wisdom, for it is the wisdom of the heart and soul that will guide us through the dark night and into the golden age on Earth. We have been heavily conditioned to shut our visions down, but it is through the opening of the third eye that we receive direct guidance from Spirit. Aaron Pyne is a clairvoyant who has worked on honing his intuitive channels, which has enabled him to be a dynamic artist, graphic and web designer, energy healer and meditation teacher.

"Since his youth, Aaron has been on a spiritual path and his reverence for Spirit is reflected in his devotion and life choices. As a child he made sketches of mandalas (without consciously knowing their deeper meaning) and had desire to be a teacher of subjects not taught in normal schools. When he turned seventeen he had various spiritual experiences that reconnected with his spiritual heritage and rediscovered these childhood gifts. At the age of seventeen he began his study of spiritual subjects with astrology. He has received certification in psychic development, Reiki, AHS, Reflexology, Theta Healing, and Crystalogy. Aaron has also studied and practiced astrology, yoga, sacred geometry, Qabalah, shamanism, and other spiritual practices with various teachers."[22]

"At the same time he began to study spirituality, he had a renewed interest in art and started to create images that reflected his spiritual studies and meditations. By the age of twenty-one, his art and writings were published in various local publications. He also became ordained as a Priest of Melchizedek (a non-denominational spiritual church). At the age of twenty-four he was initiated into Peruvian shamanism. Aaron has done a lot of world traveling seeking spiritual truths, mystical places and avenues for his art and messages. He now seeks to help others who might benefit from his spiritual understandings and variety of services to help uplift humanity to a positive, healthy, abundant and co-creative place."[23]

"Aaron's artwork is all created on the computer using art and photo editing software. Many of his artworks contain Aaron's photography as well. He was self- taught and guided by Spirit on using this software and creating his art. He has been making digital art since 2003. Most of the artworks take ten or more hours to make. During meditation or dreams, Aaron receives the images for his art as well as instructions on how to make it. Once an artwork is complete, he then receives from Spirit the message/description to go with each image."[24]

Aaron created a beautiful image of the Cosmic Goddess holding and manifesting the *New Earth* with her creative powers. She is asking that we set this intention as well—to simply focus on our own healing and spiritual connection to God/Goddess. We don't need to take on the whole burden of human suffering across the globe—it is too much for our fragile souls to handle. All we need to do is be responsible for our own part in it. As the Dine' people say, "walk the beauty way," which means walking your talk and living a life of integrity and self-love. This one intention—being humble enough to admit that you don't have all the answers and that you need Divine illumination and guidance--will serve as a catalyst for a spiritual awakening. As the saying goes; "Ask and thou shalt receive." As we begin to open ourselves to spiritual teachings, Aaron believes that cosmic codes are activated within our beings.

Another digital print by Aaron is *Keeper of the Cosmic Codes*. He writes:

> *Within each and every one of us is a vast ocean of atoms and particles. Within each of these atoms and particles is the Keeper of the Cosmic Codes. It is inherent in all. The Keeper protects these codes until we have come to the right point in our Soul's journey to begin the process of activating them. The Keeper is Divine Intelligence activating awareness to ever expanding levels.*
>
> *As we begin to open ourselves to spiritual awareness, the codes begin to unlock, allowing us to access deeper divine potentials within us. By holding our self in our own unique divine frequency, opening our hearts and allowing the divine to flow through us, more and more codes will unlock, transforming us into our spiritual, evolved Divine Beings. Each person has his/her own unique process and time plan for these codes to begin to unlock. It could already have happened, it could be happening now, or it could be in the future.*
>
> *As these codes begin to unlock, they will alter your reality. It will be time to release fears, doubts, worries, attachments and anger. You will begin to experience more harmony, peace, joy, bliss, synchronicity, connection with others, healing, moments of deep profoundness, awareness of Spirit, deeper levels of love for others, and more creativity.*[25]

Here is some more wisdom from Aaron about his intention for *The New Earth*: "As has been foreseen by cultures around the world, the new Earth of Light is emerging. This is a tremendous time of change on planetary and personal levels. The infinite potential within each person is bringing a new way of life to the world. The new world is now being created with love, harmony, understanding, growth, and sustainability. Never before have so many people across the world-across cultures-across races-across borders-joined together in a movement. This movement has no leader but the human heart. This movement is changing the human story, starting a new chapter. As we shift into this new cycle, fears fall away into the past and we emerge like a newborn into a world filled with new wonder. We begin to see the light within and accept each other as brothers and sisters, for we are all of One Spirit. When you find fear in your mind, breathe it out. Thank it and release it for its lesson. Align yourself with the divine that is within you, the divine that has always been there. Realize the power within you and recognize the power within others. Be grateful in each moment. Experience the love."[26]

Robby Donaghey: Awakening the Non-Dual Divine Child

In these times of transition, chaos and disillusionment, it is essential that we listen to the wisdom of the heart, for it desires to unite the rainbow tribe in health and harmony. The illuminated heart doesn't come from a place of ego and competition because it has fully claimed its beloved status. It is secure, whole, innocent and open, much like a child's heart. It comes from a place of authentic self love because it has opened to receive the tremendous gift of God's unconditional love and grace. The visionary art of Robby Donaghey works on the heart in wondrous ways. His astonishing work is filled with sacred geometry's energetic flow, and deeply insightful metaphors from a wide spectrum of the world's spiritual philosophies. His expression of spiritual metaphor invites the viewer into a divine discourse with the heart. Warm, illuminating, even enlightening, this work is truly art for the soul.

Robby spent his early years basking in the pristine beauty of Tahoe, California. These were some of the fondest memories in his life; flying down mountains on skis for days on end. He later moved to the San Francisco bay area where he was exposed to an assortment of artists and spiritual teachers. He attended the San Francisco Academy of Art Institute where he studied fine art and graphic design, then taught sacred and digital art to clients in San Francisco. He has been studying master artists his entire life and has attended seminars with some of the best art teachers.[27]

His spiritual path is quite diverse and rich. He studied Zen Buddhism in an ashram for two years, and lived in Hawaii for three years studying Huna with a master Kahuna. He studied and danced for years with a Sufi master and his community. Robby has also been blessed to train with other spiritual teachers and authors. In fact he has tutored several of them in new technologies and digital art, and they filled his mind with deeply profound

Keeper of the Cosmic Codes, Aaron Pyne, Digital Image, www.sacredvisiondesigns.com

The New Earth, Aaron Pyne, Digital Image, www.sacredvisiondesigns.com

Gaia, Robert Donaghey, Digital Image, www.artisticgenius.com

insights. He learned energetic healing and clairvoyance through the Berkeley Psychic Institute, trained with Harold Dull in Watsu, also with Louise Hay and the Church of Religious Science, with Steven Farmer, Oscar Miro-Quesada and several other shamans. Robby writes:

> *I am a lifelong spiritual seeker and artist. I can't even begin to help it--the muse is far too strong to resist. My fondest wish is to live my life on a deep spiritual path and express what I learn in my artwork along the way. Everything that touches my heart or stirs my soul is expressed visually; it's the equivalent of journaling for me. And it isn't always easy; in fact, it often requires working long days and nights until I am completely exhausted. And then I pick myself up and go back to work again, pushing myself harder, learning more, and opening deeper to the muse of creativity. My work feels like rain on the desert of my thirsty soul. I love the desert after a spring rain when the wild flowers explode into bloom.*[28]

Speaking of flowers in bloom, Robby created a beautiful digital image of *Gaia.* What I particularly love about this piece is the love emanating from her heart and eyes. Robby has captured her Bodhisattva essence in a way that brings tears to my eyes. In her hand she holds the key to new life, which is intelligent design, organic wisdom and cosmogenic brilliance. Since we don't understand this brilliance, we are constantly underestimating her transformative powers of death and rebirth. She has been trying to communicate to us that she has the knowledge of free energy that we have been seeking. It resides in her radiant heart, and because she loves us so much, she wants to offer us this gift from her heart. Her love and compassion are as vast and deep as the universe. There is no way we can fully comprehend how deep her love is for us, but we can glimpse it in the love we have for our own children.

She understands the self-hatred and illusion of separation at the root of all human suffering. This self-hatred shuts down our hearts from being able to fully receive her love. She asks that we come as reverent, humble admirers as opposed to arrogant, prideful people. When we come to her with an attitude of gratitude, it is a sign that our hearts are being transformed by her infinite abundance and grace. She has compassion for our ignorance and of-

Metamorphosis of an Indigo, Robert Donaghey, Digital Image, www.artisticgenius.com

fers us unconditional love. She holds space for all of our wounds and denials and transmutes them in the fire of her bodhisattva heart, even the most abhorrent of human frailties such as greed, pride, arrogance, self-righteousness and self-importance, for she knows that these all stem from self-hatred and inner damage. She asks that we shift our energies from guilt and shame to the opening of our hearts so that we can receive more of her love and brilliance, for her love will be our true liberation, our true awakening into the golden age and our transfiguration into divine humans.

As things become fragmented and people become more and more disillusioned by the state of the world, our hearts will begin to break open with tremendous sadness and despair at the fate we have created for ourselves, for all of us have been traumatized by the cruelty of the world -- some more than others. We all possess this kind of heartlessness or self-hatred inside of us, which is then reflected in the external world. These shadowy recesses of the human psyche are starving for loving kindness and compassion. There isn't a single soul on this planet that hasn't been damaged by human ignorance in one way or another. We trespass against ourselves and we trespass against others on a daily basis. It is in the nature of the human drama to pass on the neuroses of human ignorance, pride, arrogance and judgment.

The Hopi elders call this time that we are in the "purification time" because it is going to require a massive psychological and physical cleansing of our impurities, grudges, defense mechanisms and scarcity thinking. Part of this cleanse will be a critical self-examination or self-inventory of our individual and collective shadows. Another image by Robby that resonates with this purification is *Metamorphosis of an Indigo*. The archetype of the Divine Child wants to emerge at this time in human history, for its innocence will heal our brokenness and awaken us to a place of purity, free from pride, ego and the illusion of separation. In the upper part of the image resides a Star of David, which has a butterfly on top of it. Light and energy rays emanate out from the Source to the Divine Child in the foreground, which also has butterfly wings. The Divine child is being activated in the sacred geometry of the flower of life, which is releasing the codes in our DNA to receive the download from Source. The transmutation happens on multiple levels of awareness, but what is especially amazing is the activation of our light bodies. This isn't something I am able to talk about in depth because it is beyond the grasp of reason. We can understand it more in our hearts and intuition than in our minds. Through this metamorphosis we will grow wings of love and light. Robby offers a poem by Rumi that goes with the image:

> *God has created your wings not to be dormant As long as you are alive you must try more and more to use your wings to show you are alive These wings of yours are filled with quests and hopes. If they are not used, they will wither away and decay. You may not like what I'm going to tell you. You are stuck now. You must seek nothing but the source.*[29]

Indigo is the color of true liberation from ego and freedom from socially constructed illusions of the mind that we have been conditioned to believe in. However, we are not able to become free from the chains that bind us until we first recognize that the psychological chains exist in the first place. We have to first understand that we are products of social programming before we can go about deconstructing the illusion in our psyches. Human ignorance exists on a continuum from extreme to very little, and more often than not, the people who suffer from extreme ignorance the most are the least conscious of it. Some of these ignorant people are in positions of power and authority over others--they are in religious institutions, they are scientists or pragmatists, they are politicians and professors, they are in all walks of life.

Robby created a digital painting that speaks to the need to transcend religious dogma, but also the dogma of science (positivism), the economic materialism of capitalism and the neoconservative viewpoint that undergirds it. His image *The Release of Religious Dogma* speaks to the need to transcend all ideological barriers and religious exclusivism that keeps us from co-existing on this planet together as one rainbow tribe. Robby says "This painting is about releasing all of those old man-made ideas about God and religion, letting go of all the old rules and being true to infinite Love and pure inner knowing."[30]

Fortunately, the purification process goes much deeper than the limited constructs of ideological barriers and defense mechanisms. It will require an awakening and deep examination of the way in which knowledge has been formed and constructed from a white, male, Eurocentric bias that has marginalized the voices of women and minorities. Bob Mullaly writes "Those with power can control the language of the discourse and can therefore influence how the world is to be seen and what it will mean. Language promotes some possibilities and excludes others; it constrains what we see and what we do not see"[31] This is perhaps one of the most important assets of postmodern theory, aside from its critique of the dominant scientific ideology of positivism.

Moving beyond the illusion of separation and hierarchical dualism is at the root of the great purification. We are being asked to dive deep into our psyches and deconstruct the psychological chains that justify and maintain social inequality, social hierarchy and oppression of all kinds. There are many layers to healing and spiritual awakening, and just when you think you are done, there is always more room for growth. This is why humility is so important, for we don't know who our next teacher might be. It could be the mentally ill person living under the bridge down the street from you, a blade of grass in your back yard, a maid scrubbing your toilet or a mechanic working on your car engine. If you find yourself falling prey to spiritual elitism, you have missed the boat. The goal is to inculcate what Buddhists call "a beginner's mind" and be a student of life for eternity. It is passionate humility and devotion to spiritual growth. It is admitting that we are all works in progress and in need of healing and loving kindness. It means cultivating compassion even for arrogance, though it repels you, since

The Release of Religious Dogma, Robert Donaghey, Digital Image, www.artisticgenius.com

arrogance and self-importance are signs of a wounded ego in need of loving compassion. The goal is to shower wounded souls with love as opposed to judgment, for we suffer already from our own judgments and need to see demonstrated a different way to live.

The last image of Robby's that I would like to discuss is *Awakening*. This mind-blowing digital painting captures the non-dual state that we are seeking to attain. Many of us have had profound mystical experiences and hints of enlightenment that are beyond the strictures of language and words to describe. These types of experiences have enraptured visionary artists for centuries, since they want to be close to Spirit and to explore the universal mansion of consciousness. It is the most intriguing and mysterious thing humans have ever explored and it is what continues to humble our hearts over and over again. Robby speaks of this image in more detail below:

> *I was gazing up at the Milky Way galaxy and my soul blew open to Truth. My body was composed of an infinite array of energetic patterns that looked like fractal merkabahs. My mind's consciousness was an energetic to-*

Awakening, Robert Donaghey, Digital Image, www.artisticgenius.com

rus surrounding my head. My heart's consciousness was a larger energetic torus as well. The Earth was filled with a pattern of life force that flowed up into the center of my heart's torus. My awareness expanded to fill the entire galaxy and it was contained in each of the tiny fractals within me. As everything flowed together and became one awareness, God spoke to me as an infinitely powerful vibration that made everything resonate together as One. Glowing within this resonance I understood that this energetic resonance was the pure love that glued everything together.[32]

Robby's mystical experience of oneness is something that we all have the capacity to attain through meditation, art, dance, nature or any medium that gets us into our right brains. These kinds of mystical experiences validate and strengthen our faith in the spirit world. The Goddess wants us to experience the juiciness of life--to feel her essence, roll around in the dirt, lavish on her perfumes and sparkle in the magical glow of her aura. These are the things that nourish the soul and the feminine within all of us. The Earth is shifting and evolving in consciousness and we are being called to evolve with her. She wants us to start acting like multidimensional humans with emotional intelligence and reverence for all walks of life. She wants us to truly grasp the concepts of humility, reverence and acceptance of diversity. She wants us to become the smallness of a grain of sand teeming with the greatness of Divine Intelligence, meaning and purpose, for we are nothing and everything all at once.

Davin Infinity: Awakening the Integral Leaders

Davin Infinity is a visionary who has devoted his life to the path of the integral warrior and creating synergistic systems of change through conscious leadership. Trained in several lineages of shamanic practice, martial arts and Mystery Schools, Davin is a force to be reckoned with. He is a prime example of the new progressive, conscious, spiritual male leaders this world needs in order to create healthy changes. He is an experienced metaphysical guide in the quest for transformation. This work has influenced his visionary art, films, books, and life mastery Jedi workshops.

Davin is also the founder of the *Awakening Freedom Foundation*, a visionary culture design movement that weaves networks of unified solutions for a healthier humanity. It is home to one of the largest collection of free downloadable visionary e-books, videos and research for the co-creation of healthy communities and planetary thriving (www.AwakenFreedom.weebly.com).

Awaken the Leader, Davin Infinity, digital image, www.awakenfreedom.weebly.com

Davin compiled a free document titled *Awakening the Leader: A Hero's Journey in the Age of Innovation*, which can be accessed on his website for free. It is an innovative, nontraditional guide for people who want to become positive change agents and effective leaders in a transforming world. In this document he outlines several characteristics of the new integral leader; conscious vs. unconscious, responsive to a calling, innovative, illuminated and integrous, a shape shifter, and one who has overcome fear. Davin gave us permission to use a small excerpt from the document:

The mission of the New Earth Leader is to promote the transition towards sustainable ways of living and a global society founded on a balanced and shared ethical model. This vision will generate respect and care for the community of life, ecological integrity, universal human rights, respect for diversity, economic justice, democracy and a culture of peace. The Warrior-Leader-Hero is committed to changing the nightmare

The New Earth Avatars, Davin Infinity, digital image, www.awakenfreedom.weebly.com

Earth Avatar, Davin Infinity, digital image, www.awakenfreedom.weebly.com

of the modern world because he/she has journeyed through the darkest depths of the old world's destruction.

In confronting the shadow within, one takes the responsibility that comes with a deep transformation. This is how the world is changed--from within and then from without. There is no saving the planet or saving another human being. This is trying to control circumstances outside of your jurisdiction. If everyone traversed their fears and stepped into their highest potential, then we would not need major systems of control. This may be seen as irrational based on the size of the global population, especially in countries like China and India, but we can bring harmony back into the world through the power of innovation and sharing resources and tools that creates a fluid dialogue in small communities and giant metropolises.

We now play an active and critical role, not just in our own evolution as a human within the boundaries of our nation, but in the survival of the human race. It is important that each of us acknowledges our responsibility to become creatively engaged in the development of consciousness and the evolutionary process to help the transformation of our planet. We have the tools and the knowledge to consciously pave the way for the next seven generations. The future of leadership is more of a collaboration - a collective synergy of equally balanced elements that makes the entire whole thrive with unlimited potential.[35]

Davin is part of a dynamic group of visionary thinkers called *The Evolutionary Leaders*, who are synergistically working towards creating a new world view for humanity. In 2008 The Chopra Foundation, the Source of Synergy Foundation and the Association for Global New Thought invited a group of renowned Evolutionary Leaders to the Chopra Center in Carlsbad, California to explore their extraordinary potential as a collective. Out of this gathering came *A Call to Conscious Evolution: Our Moment of Choice*. Part of their purpose statement reads; "At this juncture in human history, urgent global crises

Pollenectar, George Atherton, digital image, www.geoglyphiks.com

challenge us to learn to live sustainably, in harmony and gratitude with one another and with the living universe. The changes required of humanity are broad, deep and far reaching. Only by acting swiftly and creatively can we birth a planetary culture that will bring well-being to every form of life in the Earth community. The good news is that a compelling new story of our potential as a whole human species is emerging--a story of collaboration, citizen action, dialogue and new understandings propelled by unprecedented levels of democratic freedom, multicultural exchange and access to communication technologies. It is nothing less than the story of our collective evolution."[34]

George Atherton: Envisioning Lotus Dome Permacultures

In response to the devastation and taxing of the Earth as a result of modernization, industrialization and the rise of population, a number of artists have attempted to envision a more sustainable way of living that is in alignment with the larger environmental movement; more specifically, permaculture and social ecology. At its crux, environmentalism is an attempt to balance relations between humans and the various natural systems on which they depend in such a way that all the components are accorded a proper degree of sustainability. In the past, environmental issues were associated with natural resources, and economic issues were associated with human activity. Advances in science, however, have led us to the understanding that environmental, economic, and even social issues are more interdependent than we realized and require a systems-thinking approach. One of the central challenges of the 21st century is how to achieve a more sustainable relationship between people and the environment.

As a result of alienation and an overall loss of community, people are longing for a more harmonious and sustainable way of living with each other and the Earth. Sustainable living integrates the cycles of nature into every aspect of our lives. Just as most creatures instinctively synchronize their daily lives according to natural cues such as sunrise and sunset, permaculture designs embrace and empower the cycles that foster sustainable living. The visionary digital art of George Atherton is touching a special place in people's hearts as they long for spiritual wisdom, tranquility, harmony and wholeness. One of the attractions of George's work for me is that he is envisioning what "home" might look like in the new golden age. For George, art is a powerful tool of envisioning, which is the first step to creating and manifesting the change we want to see in the future. He writes:

> *Art is a tool for transformation, on both a personal and planetary level. We can use the arts to express our realities, promote and reflect social change, and connect more deeply with ourselves, each other, and the Earth. From the Lascaux cave paintings, to the Egyptian hieroglyphics, to current-day infographics, it has ever been the role of the arts to preserve and promote knowledge.*

Anapurna, George Atherton, digital image, www.geoglyphiks.com

My works are designed based on the belief that what we hold in our minds eventually happens. In my art, I work with visions of a harmonious, ecologically thriving world and awakened states of being, in the hope that viewers of my work will joyfully manifest these states of being in their own lives. A truly open Internet makes it possible to share creative inspiration with vast numbers of people through the arts, and to that end I tag my own with links to the information that inspires it.

I work primarily in the digital medium. After drawing concepts in my sketchbooks and dream journals, I fully realize those concepts using an electronic drawing pad and digital ink.

I draw inspiration from a variety of related subjects, including meditation and Yoga, martial artistry, lucid dreaming, comparative mythology, culture jamming, and permaculture. Through these practices, I find the empowered center where creativity surges. [35]

Permaculture is a holistic system of design based on direct observation of nature, learning from traditional knowledge and the findings of modern science. (The word *permaculture* was coined in the mid-1970s by two Australians, Bill Mollison and David Holmgren.) Permaculture aims to restructure society by returning control of resources for living -- food, water, shelter and the means of livelihood -- to ordinary people in their communities. Stated simply, the practice of permaculture pulls the greatest possible value from the smallest possible expenditure of resources. Predicated on a deep, abiding respect for all forms of life, regenerative design embraces care for the environment and care for people. While taking care to limit consumption, it preserves valuable resources for future use. Most importantly, permaculture design is very much inherently regenerative, ensuring that we actually replenish resources at a faster rate than we use them.

Geo has created some of the most unique and spiritually nourishing digital art in the contemporary art scene, all of which resonate the high frequency of the new golden age. However, I will only mention a few that speak of Gaian wisdom, interconnectivity and conscious communities. His image *Pollenectar* is a prismatic vision of a thriving eco-community. Geo explains the intention in more detail:

This image is inspired by the symbiotic relationship between plants, pollinators and the use of bio-mimicry in design. They invoke the totems of the bee, the butterfly and the humming bird. These powerful creatures give rise to the abundance of nature by spreading the genetic information of pollen. Likewise, to assist and protect them in their mission, we must spread the information of how to transform our world, transmitting the memes of a radically sustainable society through our digital networks. In this modern age of disconnection from nature and colony collapse syndrome, we may look to the beehive for models of a thriving symbiotic society. May we live in harmony with the Earth and harvest the sweet honey of permacultural utopia. [36]

The bee has been associated with the Goddess for thousands of years. As a symbol of the Mother Goddess, bees represent fertility and healing. The most famous culture that worshiped the bee was the Minoan culture on the island of Crete. Honey was known as "the nectar of the Gods" in the ancient world and was believed to be sacred all the way back to Neolithic times. In a book by Anne Baring and Jules Cashford titled, *The Myth of the Goddess: Evolution of an Image*, they discuss the ancient connection between bees and architecture. "Bees have an ancient reputation as the bringers of order, and their hives served as models for organizing temples in many Mediterranean cultures." [37] The tombs at Mycenae were shaped like beehives, as well as the Omphalos where the famous Oracle at Delphi recited her prophecies.

Architects are now employing the use of bio-mimicry, which is a new point of view that analyzes and imitates nature's best ideas to solve human problems; "innovation inspired by nature." The conscious emulation of Gaia's genius is a survival strategy for the human race, a path to a sustainable future. Natural inspirations, bio-mimicry and biophilic design have been present in architectural history since the early 18th century. Architects, designers and engineers have returned to their natural and biological roots to investigate and seek out solutions to design and performance-based problems within architecture. Interestingly, the honeycomb is a structure that consists of cells with the shape of hexagons that are made of natural wax. The cells are used for the grubs or as depositories for honey and pollen. Because the hexagonal structure is so strong, stiff and light in weight, it's a commonly used structure in building technology products.

Advances in biotechnology and nanotechnology may completely revolutionize the way we think, design and construct our buildings, and transform our inorganic buildings into synthetic organic structures that can behave like living species and merge with the biological cycle of the planet. This change of thinking can be achieved through adopting bionic systems in our buildings and mimicking nature in the way it builds life forms.

For example, a green business that is producing environmentally conscious building materials and dome communities is *Eco Built Systems* (www.ecobuiltsystems.com). According to their website, they are "a manufacturer of modular sustainable dome homes, green building materials and bio-friendly aquaponic systems. The company specializes in producing modular green buildings designed for affordability, efficiency, disaster resistance and rapid assembly. Their designs utilize cutting edge green building systems made of nontoxic materials. They utilize natural mineral composites to produce prefab magnesium oxide based SIPs and boards. Eco Built Systems' building materials are resistant to damage by mold, fire, moisture and shrinkage. Their green building

Durga Gaia, George Atherton, digital image, www.geoglyphiks.com

composites are made of ancient natural mineral blends with a magnesium oxide (MgO) binder or a geopolymer. Today, similar blends are found in historic structures like the Greek Parthenon, the Taj Mahal and the Great Wall of China."[38]

Another digital image by Geo is *Anapurna, a Hindu Goddess of Nourishment*. *Ana* means food and grains, and *purna* means full, complete and perfect. She is a form of Parvati, the consort of Shiva. In Hindu parlance it is generally told that food should not be wasted, as Goddess Anapurna would be angry. She is considered the upholder of richness. George writes, "Goddess of nourishment, [she] reminds us that the Earth's abundance can support us all, if we rise to our role as her steward."[39]

As people living on the Earth, we have a responsibility to respect and care for it. That does not mean being perfect. It means doing what we can. If you recycle most of the time, bring your own bags to the grocery store, and in general try your hardest to be respectful of the environment and make conscious choices as a consumer, it does make an impact. Also, we might seek to become better educated consumers so that we know what we are buying and what we are exposing ourselves and our families to. Geo says, "May we tend the Earth to end world hunger and nourish our bodies with the vital chi of fresh food."[40]

Eating vital, local, organic food is an important aspect of

the new golden age, as is the Slow Food Movement.

Slow food is a resistance movement founded in 1986 by Carlo Petrini in response to the opening of a McDonald's in the Piazza di Spagna in Rome (www.slowfood.com). A nonprofit organization, slow food now counts members in more than 50 countries. Many foods we love (specific grains, vegetables, fruits, animal breeds) are disappearing due to the pervasiveness of convenience food and industrial agriculture. What's grown by industrial agribusiness is based on what's hardy, easiest to grow and easiest to ship across the continent - not necessarily taking taste and variety into account. Some people are tired of the degraded flavor of our foods and of health issues raised by an industrialized food supply, so they find the slow food message appealing.[41]

Paul Nicholson: Restoring the Sacred Hoop through Art

Paul Nicholson is a California visionary artist with a big heart and immense talent. As a nature and Goddess lover, Paul has spent his entire life in awe of Gaia, attempting to capture her beauty through painting. His artistic style falls under the category of magical realism, similar to that of Mark Henson, Jeff Bedrick and Andrew Annenberg. He did an entire series of Goddess Art in the 1990s that is extremely potent and worthy of acknowledgement. Paul believes that the reclaiming of feminine wisdom is associated with intuitive modes of knowing, which includes various forms of creativity. In our hyper-rational culture, we are taught to shut our creative centers down. Paul writes:

> *I believe that artistic expression is the birthright of every human being and that art is essential to human wellbeing. Whether it is art we make ourselves or the artwork of another, we need to have an art experience of some kind every day or we lose our higher humanity. Art making is something that distinguishes us as a species. I believe it was once as ubiquitous among us as song and nest building is among most bird species. However, we live in a culture where the importance of art and the life path of the artist are misunderstood. Few children are encouraged to take the path.*
>
> *As a result of the complexity of modern times, most of us have stopped doing art due to the demands on our time and the amount of work required by the power elite. I think there is a direct correlation between the rise of social strife, personal violence, depression and the degree to which art making has been abandoned by the people.*[42]

As a lover of Native American spirituality, Paul has a profound reverence for the Earth and all her relations. An incredibly powerful painting that speaks volumes about the demise of the Earth is titled *Cry of the Amazon*. In the painting we see Gaia rising like a Phoenix from the flames of destruction. She is holding the sacred hoop, which has been broken for many centuries. Paul writes, "I am very concerned with the human impact on the planet's environment. Before the melting of the polar ice cap, the burning of the Amazon Rain Forest was a major environmental and political issue. I sought to represent this in the form of a dancing goddess wrapped in a huge storm cloud rolling over the Amazon Basin, extinguishing the fires instigated by humans. As she dances, she is desperately trying to hold a rapidly disintegrating hoop of life together."[43]

According to rain-tree.com, an extensive website on the Amazon which features hundreds of pages, pictures and facts on rain forest plants and preservation: "The Amazon Rainforest covers over a billion acres, encompassing areas in Brazil, Venezuela, Colombia and the Eastern Andean region of Ecuador and Peru. It has been described as the 'Lungs of our Planet' because it provides the essential environmental world service of continuously recycling carbon dioxide into oxygen. More than 20 percent of the world's oxygen is produced in the Amazon Rainforest. In addition, more than half of the world's estimated 10 million species of plants, animals and insects live in the tropical rainforests. In Brazil alone, European colonists have destroyed more than 90 indigenous tribes since the 1900s. With them have gone centuries of accumulated knowledge of the medicinal value of rainforest species."[44]

The medicine wheel, originating from Native American traditions, is also referred to as the *Sacred Hoop*. The medicine wheel represents the sacred circle of life, its basic four directions and elements. Life is a circle that moves from birth to old age to death to new life. Native American traditions were not based on a fixed set of beliefs or on an interpretation of sacred writings, but on the knowledge of the rhythm of life, which they received through the observation of nature. And what they observed is that all of nature expresses itself in circular patterns. This can be seen in something as small and simple as a bird's nest as well as in things much greater, such as the cycle of the seasons or the cycle of life (birth, death, rebirth). And therefore, to Native American peoples, the circle or wheel represents Wakan-Tanka ("the Great Everything" or Universe) and also one's own personal space or personal universe.

Another striking painting is *The Dark Mother*, which

Cry of the Amazon, Paul Nicholson, 36" X 48", oil on canvas

The Dark Mother, Paul Nicholson, 24x36" oil on canvas

portrays the fierce, warrioress rising from the Earth with thunderbolts, volcanoes and torrential winds. Many Native American elders have had prophetic visions about cataclysmic Earth changes. This includes natural events, such as major earthquakes, the melting of the polar ice caps, a pole shift of the planetary axis, major weather events and solar flares, as well as huge changes of the local and global social, economic and political systems. Now, in the third millennium of the Western calendar, warnings of worldwide apocalypse are becoming more and more plentiful. But there are many other traditions that speak of a time when the Earth will undergo an upheaval that will leave it changed forever. The prophecies of the Hopi and other Native American peoples spoke of this time of great change before the European calendar was invented.

Many of the prophecies about the Purification Times have already come to pass, but there are more to come if we continue to disrespect Mother Earth. Without a new way of seeing and being that resonates with the ancient Earth-based practices of indigenous people, the human race will not continue to populate the Earth at unprecedented rates.

Kelly Hostetler: Speaking Truth to Power with Art and Poetry

A visionary artist and poet who is a seeker of universal truth and soul wisdom is Kelly Hostetler. Residing in the Florida Keys and living a simple life on a boat, he is making conscious choices to nurture his creative spirit and soul. "Kelly is a self taught artist, born in Mishawaka Indiana, lived in the southwest as a small child, but for the most part was raised in the Florida Keys. His paintings shed light upon the Southwest, Visionary, Native American, New Age and Sea Life Dreamscapes. It was in 1989 when he channeled the name Spirit Dance to represent the pictorial works, which were yet to come inspired by his writings. Kelly questioned his philosophy by way of poetry and once he felt direction this led him to express his insights through the brush. He feels painting is a good medium because it has the ability to touch all, via its silent universal language." [45]

Kelly's values are very different than the majority of humans who are unconsciously buying into the materialistic worldview and capitalistic system of social inequality, which is not only dehumanizing, but completely enslaves and de-souls individuals. Resonating with Native American spirituality and values, his artistic mission has been devoted to a spiritual and political message. Kelly has a blog that is saturated with profoundly simple truths. He is critical of our hyper-materialistic and wasteful culture. He speaks of the fulfillment that comes from feeding our soul as opposed to our pocket book, he writes, "Don't fill Your Pocket, as it will never be full, Fill Your Soul. It is the emptiness that one fills in their soul that makes them, 'want' for more. When one no longer 'wants' for more, they will truly be full. Feed your soul. Do away with the false idea of separation."

Kelly is deeply concerned about the insatiable appetite of humans to consume more than we actually need. He is also critical of the work-a-holism values endemic in Western culture. We are all slaves to the machine of global capitalism that has been built on the backs of the poor. Buying into a system that is on a suicide mission is a dead end road. He writes:

> *In order for our precious Earth Mother to mend her wounds, we must find a new form of housing and trade, one that carries a negative 'Carbon Imprint.' We should always give more then we take, as any good guest would do for their host. Man must delve deep into his soul and do away with his ego's 'Wants' and only take what he/she 'Needs.' There is plenty to go around. With our technology and equal sharing, man would no longer need money nor jobs, seldom would we need to 'work', and hence, all would once again have time to roam this beautiful 'Heavenly Garden.' It is time to re-harmonize our souls with nature--realizing our existence in the depths of Eternity.*
>
> *Humanity has been enslaved for so long that we don't even realize that we are slaves, as we march off to work. No other species charges themselves to live on an otherwise free spinning planet. The Native Americans had a difficult time comprehending land ownership. Man's ego believes that he is superior to all other species, and thus, he takes everything for himself. He has become so disconnected from nature that he doesn't even see it vanishing. Ashes to ashes, dust to dust, all that is made of matter will die, fade and rust. Man is 'Here & Now' on a spiritual journey, not a financial one.*
>
> *Humans are inherently a nomadic species. It is time to take down the fences, take a walk about, and allow Nature to once again flourish. He must keep in mind that just over 200 years ago, this grand continent of the America was free to roam--it was a national park, the Garden of Eden. Lets go on a permanent vacation and elevate our consciousness. With modern technology, it is feasible. We must only convince the 1% of our population (the money men) to allow for our "spiritual" transformation.* [46]

Big Decisions, Kelly Hostetler, 24"x30", acrylic on canvas, www.spiritdanceart.net

Inspired by Native American values, Kelly created two important works, *Big Decisions* and *Wake Up Call.* It is very clear, with all the current statistics of global climate change, the rising tide of poverty and environmental degradation, that we are at a critical junction. We are needing to make some big decisions as a human race or humanity won't continue to exist on this planet if we continue on the current path of population growth and consumption patterns of resources. The earth is giving us many wake up calls and will continue to do so in years to come if we don't make some changes to our fossil fuel addiction and consumptive patterns.

Fortunately there are a large number of nongovernment organizations that are standing up for social justice. However, it is clear that a lot of people are still very comfortable in their consumptive behaviors. Due to a serious break down in communities, it is really difficult to get people together for social activism pursuits. We are a conquered people because we are divided.

Raul Casillas: Entanglement on the Verge of Extinction

Raul Casillas Romo is a visionary steward of the Earth and a creative genius dreaming the new world into being. In the 1960s his parents emigrated from Mexico to Los Angeles, California to give birth to Raul on August 10, 1970, the seventh of nine children. Living in L.A. in the 1970s had a major impact on Raul's life as he was exposed to the multicultural California lifestyle, the hippie movement, skateboarding, world music and urban art. In 1979 his family moved back to Guadalajara, Mexico where they lived for fifteen years. It was in Mexico that Raul first discovered his passion for the arts. He later moved back to the Unites States and studied physiotherapy and marine biology, then sailed the Caribbean doing coral reef surveys for the Planetary Coral Reef Foundation while onboard the research vessel "Heraclitus." [47]

Wake up call, Kelly Hostetler, 24"x30", acrylic on canvas, www.spiritdanceart.net

Prior to his arrival in Oregon, he lived in Vancouver, Canada for fifteen years where he expanded and refined his exploration of the arts while working in the film industry decorating sets as a lead set dresser and sculptor, and creating commissioned fine art for movies. He also had the honor of painting a 16 foot mandala on the ceiling of a Buddhist Temple in Richmond, Vancouver, B.C. for the Bodhi Dharma Society.

Raul has been highly influenced by the visionary surreal fantastic arts as well as various cultural experiences in his travels globally. He has exhibited his artwork in many collective exhibitions at music and art festivals, such as Shambala in Nelson, B.C., the Visionary Art Movement in Canada and the USA, on the West Coast with Tribe 13's Interdimensional Art Show, in Los Angeles at The Temple of Visions Gallery, in Miami with the Moksha Family in conjunction with Art Basel Miami, in Hawaii at Alchemeyez Visionary Art Congress, and at The American Visionary Art Museum in Baltimore, Maryland.[48]

Raul uses his artistic gifts for the benefit of humanity and the Earth. He writes; "Expressing myself through art enables my soul to be seen, reaching deep down into my 'True Essential Self' to shine my light and share the state of interconnectedness that represents our evolving global consciousness. I meditate on global issues and I am inspired to improve my life and that of my community to help manifest a better planet where we can coexist in true sustainable abundance and synchronic harmony with each other and nature."[49]

Indigenous peoples across the globe say that we are intimately connected to all things, and what we do to the Earth, we do to ourselves. Thus, the Earth is merely reflecting all of our collective shadows and neuroses. Carole Shaffer writes in *Grandmothers Counsel the World: Women Elders Offer Their Vision for Our Planet;* "In less than one hundred years, driven by our desire for wealth, comfort and material goods, we have exploited and de-

Entanglement on the Verge of Extinction, Raul Casillas, 48"x20" oil on wood, 2007, www.raulcasillas.com

pleted vast resources, upsetting the delicate natural balance of our planet. Respect for our interdependence is cruelly lacking, and we have lost all humility before creation. Because of the arrogance, greed and indifference of so many of the Earth's children, we have reached the end of living and the beginning of survival, the Grandmothers say. Self-indulgence and delusional materialism have brought us to the brink of self-destruction."[50]

Raul created a masterpiece painting titled *Entanglement on the Verge of Extinction*, which captures this suicide mission all too well, but also the hope of a spiritual revolution. He describes his intention for the painting:

> *I created this painting as a result of meditating on how all of life seems to be interconnected at an energetic level, integrating many images that are normally not shown together. The central figure is a self-portrait that focuses on love; its hands are energized by the flaming heart of passion that nurtures the seed of our creation. One can see the mind's thoughts and prayers bursting out of the third eye throughout the entire painting. This central figure is engulfed by Gaia energy, represented by an organic Goddess above. The two central seahorses are kissing in love and they are one of the thirty animals included that are listed as endangered species on the verge of extinction, along with all feline cats, orangutan monkeys, honey bees and so on. My hope is that humanity may be able to help preserve all of these beautiful creatures by reducing our environmental footprint over their habitats.*
>
> *This painting is also autobiographical in that it includes my Leo zodiac sign, my Yellow Rhythmic Seed Mayan sign, and my Chinese Year of the Dog sign. It also includes events and places I have been, such as the Burning Man Festival, Egypt, the Mayan temple of Chichen Itza and the research vessel "Heraclitus," where I studied marine biology for two years in the Caribbean.*
>
> *This painting was completed in 2007, but I started it in 2002 just after my first Burning Man festival experience. I included symbolic events such as September 11, war, global warming and the media to show the current destructive condition on our planet, and also included the opposite positive energy that counteracts it, such as the prayers from Tibetan monks and ancient native cultures and our own love for life and well-being.*
>
> *It is a wake-up call to humanity, encouraging us to reflect on the beautiful and mysterious aspects of our life as well as on the destructive side of life, in order to guide us on a harmonious path of love and light.*[51]

"Human beings are currently causing the greatest mass extinction of species since the extinction of the dinosaurs 65 million years ago. If present trends continue, one half of all species of life on Earth will be extinct in less than 100 years as a result of habitat destruction, pollution, invasive species, and climate change."[52] There is no doubt that our planet is sick from the never-ending ravages of people, pollution, deforestation, abuse of power and hatred. The imminent demise of the Earth's ecosystems is merely a reflection of our denials, neuroses, shame and self-hatred. Raul Casillas strongly believes in transforming negative energies through prayer and ritual, for this is the ancient shamanic way of releasing fear and human

Ancient Aqua Blessing, Raul Casillas, 24"x30" Oil on Wood, 2012, www.raulcasillas.com

Sacred Organic, Raul Casillas, 23"x43" Oil on Wood, 2012, www.raulcasillas.com

suffering. Ritual and ceremony are a form of prayer, and our prayers for the world are our greatest contribution to its healing and rebirth. The Grandmothers say; "We can't just view our world from the rational, practical left side of the brain but must connect in a way that feels greater than ourselves. We must engage the intuitive, imaginative, right side of the brain with celebration, music, art, dance, games, and mythology. We are then able to connect the conscious with the unconscious, keeping open an essential connection with ourselves and driving out negativity."[53]

Raul says; "Creating art is as ancient as humanity itself. This planet is a manifestation of our collective imagination. I love to speak the ancient visual language of painting, allowing my body to become a vessel of creation to manifest a window into the soul and the imagination. I feel blessed and grateful to God and Gaia for having this talent and for living in a reality in which I can explore and express it. I am inspired to improve my life and impact my community and beyond, so I offer my being to Spirit to help manifest a better planet. I explore life with deep hope for world peace where we can co-exist in true sustainable abundance and symphonic synchronic harmony with each other and nature."[54]

As a ritual prayer to the waters, Raul created a painting called *Ancient Aqua Blessing.* The waters are the lifeblood of the Earth, and for us to pollute its waters is to pollute our own blood with toxins. "There was a time, the Grandmothers remind us, when all of our ancestors revered the Earth and used ritual to maintain the Earth's balance. It is important to reclaim that reverence and gratitude and reconstruct what has been lost. The ancients used to tell the people to go to the oceans or the rivers or the streams and call up the water spirits for healing and rebalancing. When you are feeling low, go to the Mother. Even a shower or a bath makes a difference. Now there is scientific language that explains what the Ancient Ones always knew, that negative ions from water have an impact on the brain that serves as an antidepressant."[55]

Another image by Raul is *Goddess Cave Apparition*, which was painted at a visionary art workshop with Martina Hoffmann and Robert Venosa at The Omega Institute in 2008. We are evolving in consciousness faster than ever before. However, in the process of modernization we have lost the wisdom of the ancients as well as the wisdom of the Sacred Feminine. Paradigm shifts are a long and slow process. In fact many indigenous teachers, artists, mystics and scholars agree that it can take years

Optimystic, Chris Dyer, www.positivecreations.ca

of living with images of the Goddess before the feminine face of God settles fully into human consciousness.

Chris Dyer: The Optimystic Spiritual Warrior

The global dark night of the soul is underway and every individual will be challenged to the core. If we are consciously choosing to stay in a state of false bliss, we are missing the boat. However, we also need to give ourselves permission to feel joy and hope amidst the global suffering. It is possible to be socially aware and conscious about the rampant social and environmental problems, but also laugh and cry about the absurdity of our individual and collective choices made out of ignorance, fear, denial, and pride.

Chris Dyer is a contemporary visionary artist that helps initiate some Divine comic relief in these heavy times. Chris grew up in Lima, Peru and is now based in Montreal, Canada. He first got known known for his colorful detailed spiritual expressions on recycled skateboards. His canvases have changed with the years, but his soulful blasts have only continued to progress. He has been exhibited in solo and group shows in several galleries around the world including Los Angeles, New York, Mexico, Peru, Belgium, Paris, and all over Canada and the United States. Chris' Positive Creations have been featured in several magazines, as well as a few books.[56]

Chris created a painting titled *Optimystic*, which portrays various archetypes, in a boat traveling through the ocean of imagination. He writes:

> *This is a 'Hero's Journey' about a group of archetypes traveling through the ocean of imagination, from a chaotic self-destructive world, to a harmonious, clean and peaceful world. The Archetypes I chose to be on the boat are the shaman leader, the warrior soldier, the housewife mama, the outcasted freak, the visionary artist, and the hater troll (a negative human trait we can't seem to shake, even when moving forward, and the only one looking back). Each character is a reflection of me and people in my life at the time, as well as aspects that we all carry inside.* [57]

In these chaotic times, social systems and dominant ideologies will be unraveling. We will all need to find the spiritual warrior within. Chris's painting *The Ultimate Spiritual Warrior*, is a force to be reckoned with. He writes:

> *He represents the peaceful warrior in me and my tribe who work to make this world a lighter place, equipped with the weapons of Love and mindfulness. Culturally I'd say he leans closer to an Inca, but as perusal he is an*

The Ultimate Spiritual Warrior, Chris Dyer, www.positivecreations.ca

amalgamation of several different cultures, creating oneness. He is a wise healer, an angel, a shaman, a courageous leader, a teacher, a creator, all the good in me, and what I want to grow stronger into, so I can serve better. May he guide and protect you on your own path too! Share this archetype all you want, to call his energy to you.[58]

While it is natural to sometimes feel paralyzed by grief and disillusionment over the state of the world today, the Goddess is standing at the end of the dark tunnel with her eternal promise of grace, forgiveness and unconditional love. This is a tremendous gift of hope for the human race. This is not some pie in the sky idealism. Most indigenous cultures would agree that modern westerners are constantly underestimating the brilliant intelligence of Gaia. Yet it is this ancient/future wisdom that may ultimately save humans from self-destruction.

Victoria Christian is a mystical artist, writer and eco-feminist. She holds undergraduate and Masters degrees in Sociology. She also has a Masters of Social Work, with an emphasis in the sociology of gender, social theory, the sociology of art and ecofeminism. For more information about her art, books and DVD's, you can view her website at www.victoriachristian.com. You can view this book's website at www.mysticspiritart.com

Gary Stamper has a Doctorate in Shamanic Psycho-spiritual Studies, and is an ordained Shamanic Minister and a Shamanic Priest. Gary is also a Certified Level II Reiki Practitioner, a Pastoral Counselor, and a Certified Shamanic Breathwork™ Facilitator. Gary has a degree in graphic design and Illustration and is an international award-winning artist and designer, and was also a professional singer for ten years, leading his own band in Las Vegas, nightclubs, and concerts. He has been facilitating men's workshops for the past eight years and is the creator and facilitator of The Integral Warrior: Awakening The New Masculine workshop series. Gary lives in Asheville, NC with an elderly Dachshund/Beagle who rescued him. www.awakeningthenewmasculine.com www.garystamperdesign.com http://garystamper.blogspot.com/

"When the earth is ravaged and the animals are dying, a new tribe of people shall come unto the Earth from many colors, classes, and creeds, who by their actions and deeds shall make the Earth green again. They will be known as the Warriors of the Rainbow".

– Native American Prophecy

New Eden, Morgan Mandala, www.morganmandala.com

Afterword

By Susan Stedman

Now that you, dear reader, have traveled with us on this journey of discovery where we have looked together at some of the myriad faces of the great Mother, we have learned together to appreciate the depth, variety and strength of the many aspects of the Great Mother. Without her, life would be colorless, hollow and cold. Indeed, without her we would not even exist. That is why it is so important at this time in history for us as a species to awaken again to her compassion and beauty, to honor and appreciate her in her endless forms and to protect her in her vulnerability, both in the form of women and children and also in the forms of animals, plants and our beautiful planet Earth.

In Hindu mythology, Kali is an extension of Durga, Goddess of compassion. Kali springs forth out of Durga to banish the demons that are destroying creation. Since Kali is born of compassion, there is no reason to believe that she will not be scrupulously selective, even in her wrath, for certainly the gods and goddesses have at the same time a broader and a more intimate picture of what constitutes mercy and what constitutes justice than those of us here on Earth still trapped in the blindness of unreconciled duality. So there is every reason to believe that in the times of tumultuous change that have been prophesied by so many different visionaries and mystics that we are in right now, we can know deep within us that the Great Mother will select for us what we also energetically attract to ourselves, and allow that process to unfold in the most perfect way for each of us by providing the impetus needed to evolve.

Kali has the power to destroy the demons of greed and hatred that all the male gods had failed to destroy. For all those reading this now who ever loved deeply and passionately – whether a child, a pet, a creative project or another adult – you know the depths of anger and protectiveness that can be stirred within you when what you love is threatened. Is it any wonder, then, that when our beloved Earth is threatened by those same malefic forces, Mother Earth should not be moved into her Kali nature to rise up in ferocious storms, devastating earthquakes, explosive volcanoes and terrifying tidal waves to protect her wondrous creation? And if we as a collective culture have not matured enough to protect the weak and vulnerable while simultaneously holding the principle of free will inviolate, but instead have loosed the demons of greed, avarice, malice, corruption and evil to prey upon what sustains us and gives us life--be it animal, vegetable, mineral or human--then it is Kali we will have invoked and Kali that we deserve. Yet ironically, it is Kali who may ultimately be the salvation of us all. Let me explain.

Kali, Jonathan Weber, 24x36 Oil on Canvas, www.jonathanweber.org

If this discussion brings up fear in you, then thank the Great Mother, because that fear might just save your life if you allow it to move you towards a path of healing now. And that brings me to another understanding that I would like to emphasize; that she is the Mother of all emotion, not just positive emotions, and that embracing negative emotions is just as important and necessary to healing and balance as embracing positive emotions – at least until the time when we reach true unity and balance as a species, at which time there will be no opposites that are not balanced in love. Many people grasp this concept in theory, but to put it into practice in our daily lives is another matter entirely, so let me explain further.

How many times in the last decade have you heard it said that love is all-inclusive? And how many times have you also heard it said that we must get rid of our fear? When those two concepts are placed side by side, it is easier to see how they cannot be reconciled, because if love is all-inclusive, then how can fear (or anything else, for that matter) be rightly excluded from love? You might argue that love transforms all the negative emotions or that negative emotions exclude themselves from love, and I wouldn't disagree with you. Yet in this world of apparent duality, resistance only breeds rebellion and so if we don't want to create an internal rebellion, we must learn to accept all of our thoughts and emotions without judgment.

Perhaps it would help to think of it in this way. Emotions and thoughts are as inseparable as electricity and magnetism, and we know now that they are indeed similar in that our brain clearly produces an electrical charge when we think, and our emotional body clearly magnetizes or repels things and people to us. This is evident when we say someone has a "magnetic" personality; she magnetizes people to her with the strength of her emotional vibrations.

So in the same way that the pain of burning your hand on the stove will make you less likely to place your hand on a hot stove in the future, your fears can let you know when you are in danger of violating your inner truth, of compromising your health and/or well-being or of placing yourself in a dangerous or compromising situation. In the same way, your anger can let you know when your real boundaries have been crossed and can urge you to take action against injustice or a dangerous situation. Those are just the obvious gifts that our so-called "negative" emotions bring to the table. And obviously we can't heal ourselves if we are busy judging our "negative" emotions as bad and trying to suppress them. And that is not to say that I am advocating acting out our negative emotions, but we can acknowledge them without judgment and try to understand what they are telling us instead. And since we understand now that the Great Mother represents the principle of emotion, denying our real feelings is also a denial of Her, so that we are essentially treating our inner woman and/or girl the same way the patriarchy treats women, girls and the Earth in our outer reality.

Obviously we all have mothers, yet the significance of a mother's influence on men has only recently come to consciousness in me with the birth of my first grandchild. I grew up as one of four daughters in my family of origin, and when I became a mother I gave birth to three daughters, no sons. For that reason, men seemed to spring up in my life as fully grown beings, intimidating in their physical strength and prowess. So it wasn't until my first grandchild was born -- a little boy -- that I began to see the fragility of boys and understand their utter dependence on what must seem to them as their great big mothers, whom they need in order to survive, yet who tower over them in all their terrible strength and beauty -- and also in their potential for harm, abandonment, abuse and neglect that may be carried over into their manhoods.

Many of my readers have suffered as children from angry or rageful mothers who never seemed to nurture them in ways they deeply needed and instead left them to fend for themselves, while others suffered at the hands of terrified or fearful mothers who strangled them with their own fears and paranoia and/or abandoned them in their terror to abusive fathers or step-parents. Yet if the underlying patterns of emotion in our mothers and fathers could have been fully revealed, accepted and healed, isn't it possible that a fearful mother who embraced her anger might then become more courageous, and conversely, an angry mother who embraced her fear might be gentled and made more nurturing? Maybe in this way we can move towards balance as a species one person and one family at a time.

I don't want to belabor this point, but an obvious situation where so many people completely ignored rude, even abusive behavior towards women, has been manifest in the election of Donald Trump as President of our country. That event, probably more than any other, demonstrates to me how we as a nation no longer seem to consider character as an important quality when choosing a president. In fact many of Trump's supporters said they ignored his lack of character because they thought he was going to make their life easier somehow by improving the economy and getting rid of big government. This is a sad statement on the values of today's voters, that financial matters should overcome, in their minds, the importance of honesty, integrity, respect for justice, and humility. But when we as a nation have been programmed since birth to succeed at all costs, then it shouldn't come as a surprise that basic human decency is one of those costs.

Yet the overriding truth is that we are all in this boat together when it comes to dealing with the destruction of the planet. What a way to treat our Mother Earth, who gives us everything we have, whether mineral, vegetable or animal, for nothing created by humans is made from anything that didn't originally come from the Earth. As Charles Eisenstein says in his wonderful article, The Election: Of Hate, Grief, and a New Story, "We are all victims of the same world-dominating machine, suffering different mutations of the same wound of separation. Something hurts in there. We live in a civilization that has robbed nearly all of us of deep community, intimate connection with nature, unconditional love, freedom to explore the kingdom of childhood, and so much more. The acute trauma endured by the incarcerated, the abused, the raped, the trafficked, the starved, the murdered, and the dispossessed does not exempt the perpetrators. They feel it in mirror image, adding damage to their souls atop the damage that compels them to violence. Thus it is that suicide is the leading cause of death in the U.S. military. Thus it is that addiction is rampant among the police. Thus it is that depression is epidemic in the upper middle class. We are all in this together."

So once again, the law of Karma is at play on the world scene, underlying everything as the unseen arbiter of justice. Every major religion in the world has some concept of "as you reap, so shall you sow" or some other wording that demonstrates the law of karma in action. And upon that immutable principle I personally place my hope, that with the help of Divine Mother/Father, in the end justice will prevail on earth one way or another!

In conclusion, Victoria and I would like to thank you for purchasing and reading this book. We would also like to encourage you to peruse and patronize the websites of all the talented artists who have contributed to this book and who continue to produce profound expressions of creativity, truth and beauty in a world that often rewards aggression and greed instead. We would also like to thank our contributing artists for having the heart to keep on going, sometimes in the midst of poverty and/or lack of recognition, and pray that their persistence will pay off by helping to usher in a world that rewards creativity and truth with abundance.

And last but not least, as Victoria Christian's mother, I would like to express my heartfelt gratitude and admiration for the way she never gave up on this project, no matter how daunting the challenges. It has been a long process and the roadblocks have been formidable at times, but I know that her inner passion for truth and beauty kept her going against all odds, and I am amazed at the sweetness of the love that inspired her to take on this challenge in the first place. And I would also like to thank Victoria's fiancé, John Grimshaw, who gave so generously of his many talents and technical skills to make this book possible!

We hope your journey here with us has opened your heart and mind to the wonders of the Divine Mother and all that she represents. And may the wisdom of each of these sacred archetypes and real beings fill your heart, body and soul with abundance, life, vitality, compassion and love.

Offering of Gratitude, Victoria Christian,4X4 Oil on Metite, www.victoriachristian.com

ABOUT THE EDITORS

Victoria Christian is the head editior and contributing artist and writer of several articles. As the weaver of visions, she created a lot of content for the book and produced the animated DVD, which is married to the book.

Raised in the quaint town of Ashland, Victoria was blessed to grow up in the emerald forests of Southern Oregon, learning as much as she could about the Gaian rhythms of life. She is an avid hiker and biker, which have taken her to some of the most pristine places on the West Coast.

In her early years, Victoria explored various forms of dance and started delving into art in high school. While she had some art instruction, she considers herself a self-taught painter struggling to come to terms with her identity as an artist. Art has been a circuitous path for her, amidst all her other passions. Nonetheless, she has published her art in various magazines, calendars and books, such as We' Moon, Hay House and Sage Woman to name just a few. Most of her originals are in private collections and she has done a several murals. She continues to do commissions on the side and is working on completing her "Biking Goddess" calendar.

She graduated from Southern Oregon University with a Bachelors of Science in 1996, majoring in Sociology and Women's Studies. In 2011, she graduated from Northern Arizona University in Flagstaff, Arizona with a Masters in Applied Sociology, with an emphasis in Social Theory, Sociology of Art, Sociology of Gender and Psychoanalytic Sociology (4.0 student). She did her thesis research on *Women Artists and Identity Formation in a Postmodern Society,* which turned out to be a major critique of culture and the art world. This entailed qualitative research methods and in-depth interviews with a random sample of artists (50). What emerged from her research was a developmental model of artistic identity development, which revealed the stages that most women go through in their identification process. She wrote a thesis, which was later condensed and published in academic journals and magazines. She is in the process of compiling this research into a book, as it has the potential to empower women artists in a rationally and scientifically oriented culture that is in many ways antithetical to creative and spiritual development.

Victoria started a second piece of research in 2002 on *Feminine Mysticism in Art*, which eventually led to the creation of this book. Upon interviewing several mystical artists (male and female), she discovered that most of them were extremely gifted and felt marginalized by the traditional gallery scene simply because their work was "too spiritual," "to political" and "too feminist." As a result, all of the artists felt it was necessary to harness their mission and "publish the map" in order to get their images into the world without compromising their spiritual and visionary voices. The book evolved over 12 years and includes the creative visions of over 65 emerging and established visionary writers and artists. It will no doubt be a powerful contribution to the Transcendental Art Movement, the Women's Spirituality Movement, the Inter-Spirituality Movement and the Ecological Movement.

In 2015, Victoria received a second Masters of Social Work from Portland State University and has been working in the trenches helping extremely vulnerable and oppressed people get connected to community resources and social support. She also has a thriving counseling and life coaching practice called Guanyin Healing Arts. For more information about her therapeutic modalities and counseling philosophy, please see her website: www.guanyinhealingarts.com

As a sacred activist, Victoria is fiercely devoted to improving numerous social justice issues, assisting the awakening of human consciousness, and empowering people to heal themselves and the world. She has done numerous lectures promoting the book and animated DVD . She has also lectured and done therapeutic workshops on "Healing the Feminine Wound," "Harnessing your Creative Genius," and "Artists and Identity Formation."

In 2009, Victoria produced an animated visionary art DVD titled *Feminine Mysticism in Art: Artists Envisioning the Divine,* which has been featured at various music/art festivals, theatrical performances and spiritual conferences across the globe. To see a trailer and purchase the DVD, see the website: www.mysticspiritart.com.

Susan Stedman is the assistant editor to *FMA* and devoted numerous hours doing tedious edits and being a source of emotional support for Victoria. She is a court reporter, editor, tarot/astrology counselor and the creator of oral histories documenting the lives of elderly people for future generations. She has raised three daughters, including Victoria, and had many diverse life experiences that have contributed to her wisdom and ability to work with people, including her upbringing as the daughter of a prominent theologian and minister. She draws not only on her own rich history as a preacher's kid and single mom, but also as an anthropology student at Southern Oregon University, freelance editor, and twenty years as a freelance court reporter. Susan is a respected member of the Grandmother's Council in Southern Oregon and has devoted her life to pursuing acts of compassion in her local community. She reads prodigiously and is devoted to a spiritual walk. She and her husband currently reside in Southern Oregon.

Susan Stedman and Victoria Christian

ABOUT THE CONTRIBUTORS

Contributing Writers by Chapter:

Part One: Primordial Sacred Union

Anne Baring is a writer and retired Jungian Analyst. She is the author, with Jules Cashford, of The Myth of the Goddess: Evolution of an Image and, with Andrew Harvey, of The Mystic Vision and The Divine Feminine. Her children's book, The Birds Who Flew Beyond Time, asks us to respond to the planet's need for help. She lives near Winchester, England, and has created a website www.annebaring.com to explore the ecological and spiritual issues facing us at this crucial time of choice.

Victoria Christian is a mystical artist, counselor, sociologist, writer, speaker, and sacred activist. She holds an undergraduate and Masters degree in Sociology, with an emphasis in the sociology of gender, social theory, the sociology of art and the sociology of spirituality. She received another Masters in Social Work from Portland State University in 2015 and has a private counseling practice. She is the organizer and co-editor of Feminine Mysticism in Art: Artists Envisioning the Divine and is in the midst of writer another book titled Women Artists and Identity Formation in a Postmodern Society. Her artwork, books, and private counseling can be viewed and purchased on her website at www.victoriachristian.com, www.mysticspiritart.com, and guanyinhealingarts.com

Margaret Starbird has done graduate study in European history and comparative literature, and holds a Master of Arts degree from the University of Maryland. She has studied at Christian Albrechts Universitat in Kiel, Germany, where she was a Fulbright Fellow, and at Vanderbilt University Divinity School in Nashville, Tennessee. She is the author of The Woman with the Alabaster Jar: Mary Magdalene and the Holy Grail. Her writings and books can be purchased on her website at www.margaretstarbird.com

Part Two: Rebirth of the Goddess

Chapter One: Goddess of Creation

Victoria Christian is a mystical artist, counselor, sociologist, writer, speaker, and sacred activist. She holds an undergraduate and Masters degree in Sociology, with an emphasis in the sociology of gender, social theory, the sociology of art and the sociology of spirituality. She received another Masters in Social Work from Portland State University in 2015 and has a private counseling practice. She is the organizer and co-editor of Feminine Mysticism in Art: Artists Envisioning the Divine and is in the midst of writer another book titled Women Artists and Identity Formation in a Postmodern Society. Her artwork, books, and private counseling can be viewed and purchased on her website at www.victoriachristian.com, www.mysticspiritart.com, and guanyinhealingarts.com

Arisika Razak has been a midwife, healer and spiritual dancer for over thirty years. She has provided full scope midwifery care to indigent women and women of color in the inner city of Oakland, California for over twenty years, serving as a home and hospital birth attendant, hospital based CNM, health care administrator and health educator. She currently directs the Integrative Health Studies Program at the California Institute of Integral Studies, San Francisco, California, where she is also an Associate Professor of Women's Spirituality. Arisika has led spiritual and healing workshops for women for over two decades, and her dance celebrates the physical bodies of women and the blood mysteries of childbirth, menstruation, sexuality and menopause. She is a contributor to several books, and presents at numerous conferences on the subjects of multiculturalism and diversity, women's health and healing, and embodied spirituality and movement.

Lydia Ruyle is an artist, author, scholar emerita of the Visual Arts faculty of the University of Northern Colorado in Greeley, Colorado where The Lydia Ruyle Room for Women's Art was dedicated in 2010. She has a Bachelor of Arts degree from the University of Colorado at Boulder, a Master of Arts from UNC and has studied with Syracuse University in Italy, France, Spain, and with the Art Institute of Chicago in Indonesia. She works regularly at Santa Reparata International School of Art in Florence, Italy and Columbia College Center for Book and Paper in Chicago. Her research into sacred images of women has taken her around the globe. For twenty years, Ruyle has led women's pilgrimage journeys to sacred places. Ruyle creates and exhibits her art, does workshops and is a speaker at conferences throughout the U.S. and internationally. Her website: www.lydiaruyle.com

Chapter Two: Goddess of Sexuality

Linda E. Savage, Ph.D. is a licensed psychologist and sex therapist exploring the mysteries of sexual healing for over 30 years. She is the author of Reclaiming Goddess Sexuality: The Power of the Feminine Way, a view of women's sexuality that blends the ancient wisdom of the Goddess cultures with current clinical knowledge. www.goddesstherapy.com

Azra Bertrand M.D. and Seren Bertrand are authors of the acclaimed book, Womb Awakening – Initiatory Wisdom From the Creatrix of All Life, as well as Sophia's Return: Healing the Grail Wound, and Sacred Womb Rituals. They are founders of the worldwide Womb Awakening movement, and the Fountain of Life Womb Mystery School. They hold annual in-depth Womb Awakening Apprenticeships, and share shamanic music on Sacred Sounds of the Womb, Elemental Awakening, and other albums. Visit www.thefountainoflife.org. Sophia's Return, Seren's personal story of healing from sexual abuse, is offered as a free ebook on the website: https://www.thefountainoflife.org/sophias-return-healing-grail-wound/

Vicki Noble is a feminist shamanic healer, author, scholar and wisdom teacher. Born in 1947 and raised in Iowa, she awakened to the Goddess and Women's Spirituality on her arrival in

Berkeley, California in 1976. Through a "shamanic healing crisis", she opened psychically to the healing, art, yoga, and divination processes that led to the creation of Motherpeace. Since then she has written several books, developed a powerful ritual healing process, taught and lectured internationally, and led tours of women on pilgrimage to sacred Goddess sites around the world. Learn more at her website, vickinoble.com. Vicki is the author of Motherpeace, Shakti Woman, Down is Up for Aaron Eagle, Rituals and Practices with Motherpeace Tarot, and The Double Goddess: Women Sharing Power (Inner Traditions, 2003).

Penny Slinger is a surrealist artist. She produced 50%- The Visible Woman (1971) and An Exorcism (1977), two collections of powerful and haunting collages. Her 2D collages and 3D installations incorporated images and life-casts of herself. Her media during this period included pencil and paint, printmaking, life casts and other 3-dimensional constructions, as well as photography, film and collage. Penny Slinger is also known for her erotic and Tantric work and her Caribbean/Amerindian work. She created the Secret Dakini Oracle, re-released as the Tantric Dakini Oracle. She is the co-author, illustrator or artist of the following books including Sexual Secrets- The Alchemy of Ecstasy, The Path of the Mystic Lover, Mountain Ecstasy, The Erotic Sentiment in the Paintings of India and Nepal, and The Erotic Sentiment in the Paintings of China and Japan. In 2011, Penny released an on-line version of the project she has been working on for many years, the 64 Dakini Oracle, an evolution of the Secret Dakini Oracle. Visit her websites at www.pennyslinger.com and www.64dakinioracle.org

Chapter Three: Goddess of Creativity

Claudia Connelly is a mystical painter who works intuitively, drawing inspiration from the Old Masters, particularly Sandro Botticelli, Leonardo Da Vinci and the Pre-Raphaelites. Her art is a labor of love involving perseverance and focus as the images slowly emerge, coming forward to offer remembrances-- a bridge from the past into the future. Her beautiful artwork can be viewed on her website at www.claudiaconnelly.com.

Deborah Koff-Chapin graduated with a BFA from Cooper Union in 1974. She has been practicing Touch Drawing since it came to her in an ecstatic awakening on her last day there. She teaches this simple yet profound process internationally, and has held the annual Touch Drawing Gathering since 1997. Deborah is the creator of best-selling SoulCards 1&2, timeless classic decks that are sold worldwide. She is author of Drawing Out Your Soul and The Touch Drawing Facilitator Workbook, and has published five SoulTouch Coloring Journals. Deborah has served as Interpretive Artist at numerous conferences including The Parliament of the World's Religions. She works with individuals to bring subtle dimensions of their soul into form through Inner Portraits.

Carrie Ann Baade's autobiographical oil paintings are allegorical narratives inspired by spirit, literature, and art history. These parables combine fragments of Renaissance and Baroque religious paintings, resulting in surreal landscapes inhabited by exotic flora, fauna, and figures. Baade was awarded the Florida Division of Cultural Affairs Individual Artist Fellowship in 2010, the Delaware Division of the Arts Fellowship for Established Artist in 2005, and was nominated for the prestigious United States Artist Fellowship in 2006 and the Joan Mitchell Grant in 2012. Her work has been exhibited in museums and galleries nationally and internationally, including recent solo exhibitions: the Museum of Contemporary Art in Jacksonville Florida, the Delaware Center for Contemporary Art, the Rosenfeld Gallery in Philadelphia, Billy Shire Fine Arts in Los Angeles, and the Ningbo Art Museum in China.

Chapter Four: The Goddess of Emotion

Grace is a natural artist who was blessed to have an artistic mother, and so was drawing and painting as soon as she could hold a pencil. She was always encouraged to pursue her talent, and was given many opportunities to do so. She earned a Bachelors degree in Fine Arts from the University of Oregon, studied in France with Parsons School of Design NY, and apprenticed for 8 years with NYC sculptor A. Bruce Hoheb. Grace's spiritual seeking led her to become a Tanran Reiki master with William Bagley, and this has deeply influenced her work. As a woman artist, Grace has sought to understand the Divine through the feminine, and knows that as she did this work for herself, she did it for all women who may not have had the same opportunities. Her work has been published and shown in many forms, including in the Wemoon calendar, the Ministry for the Arts catalog, and by Ascension Mastery International. She is honored to be a part of this book's collection. Grace currently lives in the Northwest with her husband and child." Visit her website: www.gracemantlestudios.com

Sherab "Shey" Khandro, a celebrated artist, speaker, and author of Creating a Healing Universe, is one of only a few Western artists to receive formal training in the spiritual arts from Tibetan masters. After spending 15 years as a Tibetan Buddhist nun, she served as artistic director for Kunzang Palyul Choeling, a Tibetan Buddhist center for practice and study in Maryland and Arizona. Many of Khandro's paintings and sculptures can be seen in private collections and galleries, or as part of sacred Buddhist monuments called stupas. To create the rich and vibrant imagery in her paintings, Khandro uses a neo-impressionist style of pointillism. As she deepens the intent of her Bodhisattva vow, each stroke of her brush holds a prayer of compassion. Each dot is offered as a jeweled universe, a prayer to end suffering in the world. Sherab Khandro is committed to living from her heart and inspires others to do the same through workshops and lectures on the spiritual arts and intentional living, which she leads across the country. Visit her website at: www.sherabkhandro.com

Victoria Christian is a mystical artist, counselor, sociologist, writer, speaker, and sacred activist. She holds an undergraduate and Masters degree in Sociology, with an emphasis in the sociology of gender, social theory, the sociology of art and the sociology of spirituality. She received another Masters in

Social Work from Portland State University in 2015 and has a private counseling practice. She is the organizer and co-editor of Feminine Mysticism in Art: Artists Envisioning the Divine and is in the midst of writer another book titled Women Artists and Identity Formation in a Postmodern Society. Her artwork, books, articles, and private counseling can be viewed and purchased on her website at www.victoriachristian.com, www.mysticspiritart.com, and guanyinhealingarts.com

Chapter Five: Goddess of Wisdom

Llewellyn Vaughan-Lee is a Sufi teacher and author. In recent years the focus of his writing and teaching has been on spiritual responsibility in our present time of transition, and the emerging global consciousness of oneness (see www.workingwithoneness.org). He has also specialized in the area of dreamwork, integrating the ancient Sufi approach to dreams with the insights of modern psychology. Llewellyn is the founder of The Golden Sufi Center (www.goldensufi.org). His most recent books include Working with Oneness and The Alchemy of Light.

Anne Scott is the founder of Dream Weather Foundation, a nonprofit organization dedicated to articulating and making more conscious the healing nature of feminine spirituality and the important role it has to play in bringing about real and lasting social change. She is the author of The Laughing Baby, Serving Fire: Food For Thought, Body and Soul, and her forthcoming book, The Treasures of Darkness. Anne has trained in dream work in the Naqshbandi Sufi Path since 1990. Visit her website at: www.dreamweather.org

Lotus Linton, PhD, has been facilitating spiritual awakening seminars for over thirty years throughout the United States, England, Bali, and Australia. She is a sound healer, a sacred dancer, a spiritual counselor and a ceremonialist. Lotus utilizes the sacred arts, stories and symbols of many cultures to elicit and express the soul's wisdom, and takes small groups on Singing the Waters Journeys to the holy springs and waters of several cultures. In her book, Soul Springs: Seeking Self in the Waters of the World, Lotus highlights her own pilgrimage to these sacred places and to the wells of her own soul's wisdom. Lotus Linton can be contacted at: soulspring@earthlink.net www.soulsprings.org

Azra Bertrand M.D. and Seren Bertrand are authors of the acclaimed book, Womb Awakening – Initiatory Wisdom From the Creatrix of All Life, as well as Sophia's Return: Healing the Grail Wound, and Sacred Womb Rituals. They are founders of the worldwide Womb Awakening movement, and the Fountain of Life Womb Mystery School. They hold annual in-depth Womb Awakening Apprenticeships, and share shamanic music on Sacred Sounds of the Womb, Elemental Awakening, and other albums. Visit www.thefountainoflife.org. Sophia's Return, Seren's personal story of healing from sexual abuse, is offered as a free ebook on the website: https://www.thefountainoflife.org/sophias-return-healing-grail-wound/

Chapter Six: Goddess of Transformation

Jacquelyn Small, MSW, is a Phi Beta Kappa graduate of the University of Texas with degrees in psychology, applied music, and clinical social work. She is the Founding Director of Eupsychia Institute, a national nonprofit service organization that certifies students in Soul-based Psychology and Integrative Breath work. Jacquelyn conducts workshops, and keynotes conferences in human consciousness and the addiction field throughout North America. She is the author of nine books on personal transformation and holistic healing of the psyche. She lives in Austin, Texas. She can be contacted via her website at www.eupsychia.com.

Uma Rhiannon Rose attended Interlochen Arts Academy and Albion College in Michigan where she majored in Art and Literature. She is primarily self-taught in the areas of painting, archetypal psychology, and mythology. Her poetry has been published (under different names) in small literary magazines. Her art has been shown in coffee houses, local bars, and small galleries. Presently she lives with her mate in Ashland, Oregon, creating out of the depths of life--her best teacher. Her artwork and poetry can be viewed at www.rhiannons-visions.com.

Anyaa T. McAndrew, M.A., L.P.C., N.C.C. psychotherapist and teacher, resides in a shamanic retreat community in the Smoky Mountains of western North Carolina. Her early work expressed through the lens of the women's movement, feminist therapy, and the rape and incest survivor's movement of the nineteen seventies and eighties as she also pioneered the integration of feminism, transpersonal psychology and spirituality in the Midwest. For the past seven years, Anyaa has facilitated several versions of The Priestess Process™ around the US and in Costa Rica, integrating a lifetime of therapeutic work with women through her own Mystery School. Anyaa is also an accomplished astrologer, tantric educator and a Bishop in the Madonna Ministry. She is a contributor to a recently released CD audio presentation called "The Priestess Within: Your Direct Divine Connection". She has written several articles which can be accessed through her website www.goddessontheloose.com .

Chapter Seven: Goddess of Interconnectivity

Cher Lyn is a visionary artist, writer and poet residing in Sedona, Arizona. Art has been a personal journey through deep inner healing and spiritual awakening for Cher Lyn. In preparation and during the process of painting, she uses meditation, sacred essences and shamanic instruments such as the didgeridoo; drum rattles and chanting to call in energies of love. She opens herself up to the grace and guidance of the Creator. Her images invite the viewer beyond the borders of the canvas into the multidimensional worlds of mysticism, myth, emotion and texture. While she paints to assist the transformation of herself and others, it is always with the intent that her paintings will illuminate and activate those who gaze upon them. Her mystical artwork can be viewed at www.mysticartmedicine.com

Sandra Ingerman, MA, is an award winning author of twelve books, including Soul Retrieval, Medicine for the Earth, Walking in Light, and The Book of Ceremony: Shamanic Wisdom for Invoking the Sacred Into Everyday Life. She is the presenter of eight audio programs produced by Sounds True, and the creator of the Transmutation App. For 35 years Sandra has been a world renowned teacher of shamanism teaching workshops internationally on shamanism and reversing environmental pollution using spiritual methods. Sandra is devoted to teaching people how we can work together as a global community to bring about positive change for the planet. She is passionate about helping people to reconnect with nature. Since the 1980's thousands of people have healed from past and present traumas through the classic cross cultural shamanic healing method Sandra teaches called Soul Retrieval. Sandra is a licensed marriage and family therapist and professional mental health counselor and a board-certified expert on traumatic stress. www.sandraingerman.com

Hank Wesselman PhD is an anthropologist who conducts research with international expeditions in Eastern Africa's Great Rift Valley, in search of answers to the mystery of human origins. He is the author of nine books on shamanism including The Journey to the Sacred Garden, Spirit Medicine (with Jill Kuykendall), the award winning Awakening to the Spirit World (with Sandra Ingerman), The Bowl of Light: Ancestral Wisdom from a Hawaiian Shaman, The Re-Enchantment: A Shamanic Path to a Life of Wonder, and his Spiritwalker Trilogy. He offers workshops at the Omega Institute in Rhinebeck NY, the Breitenbush Conference Center in northern Oregon and Mosswood Hollow in Duvall WA and lives with his family on their organic farm in south Kona, Hawaii Island. See his website at sharedwisdom.com

Martin W. Ball, PhD, is an independent researcher focused on the interface between spiritual awakening and entheogenic experience. He received his Ph.D. from UCSB in Religious Studies with an emphasis on Native American traditions, shamanism, and comparative mysticism. He is the author of several books on entheogenic spirituality, including his latest, Entheologues: Conversations with Leading Psychedelic Thinkers, Explorers and Researchers, featuring interviews from his weekly podcast, "The Entheogenic Evolution." Martin's podcast can be found at www.entheogenic.podomatic.com and his books and music can be found at his web page, www.martinball.net

Gary Stamper has a Doctorate in Shamanic Psychospiritual Studies, and is an ordained Shamanic Minister and a Shamanic Priest. Gary is also a Certified Level II Reiki Practitioner, a Pastoral Counselor, and a Certified Shamanic Breathwork™ Facilitator. Gary has a degree in graphic design and Illustration and is an international award-winning artist and designer, and was also a professional singer for ten years, leading his own band in Las Vegas, nightclubs, and concerts. He has been facilitating men's workshops for the past eight years and is the creator and facilitator of The Integral Warrior: Awakening The New Masculine workshop series. Gary lives in Asheville, NC with an elderly Dachshund/Beagle who rescued him. www.awakeningthenewmasculine.com www.garystamperdesign.com http://garystamper.blogspot.com/

Victoria Christian is a mystical artist, counselor, sociologist, writer, speaker, and sacred activist. She holds an undergraduate and Masters degree in Sociology, with an emphasis in the sociology of gender, social theory, the sociology of art and the sociology of spirituality. She received another Masters in Social Work from Portland State University in 2015 and has a private counseling practice. She is the organizer and co-editor of Feminine Mysticism in Art: Artists Envisioning the Divine and is in the midst of writer another book titled Women Artists and Identity Formation in a Postmodern Society. Her artwork, books, and private counseling can be viewed and purchased on her website at www.victoriachristian.com, www.mysticspiritart.com, and guanyinhealingarts.com

CONTRIBUTING VISUAL ARTISTS

Andrew Annenberg is a visionary artist residing in California. His sensitivity and masterful renditions have earned him the recognition and respect as one of today's foremost visionary artists, and without a doubt a significant place is reserved for him in the unfolding history of the civilized world's greatest accomplishments. His art derives from the classic tradition of European art. Much of my artistic life was spent in Hawaii, where I developed a profound love for the marine environment. Other main themes have been the allegorical, ancient civilizations and nature in general. www. aamasterworks.com

Beth Avary received her BFA cum laude from the California College For The Arts in 1964. She has shown her work throughout the United States in museums, festivals, galleries, corporations, and science fiction and fantasy conventions. Her work has received several awards, including First Place, Public Favorite and Best of Show. Paragon Fine Art, located in West Hollywood and Marina Del Rey, California, represents her. Her artwork can be viewed at: www.starfirepress.

AfraShe Asungi, HHHAS, MFA, LCSW, CSAC, is a modern day prophetess and cultural guardian who has received international acclaim as a visionary artist and pioneering creatress of "Afracentrik," Matristic Mythology and AfraGoddess(tm) Herstory. As a visionary artist, AfraShe Asungi's artistic mission has served as a powerful source of sacred imagery in the Wimmin's and AfraAmerican communities. For more information or to contact AfraShe Asungi: www.AfraSheAsungi.com and at SistahPeace@yahoo.com.

George Atherton is a graphic artist residing in Washington. In his art, he envisions a harmonious, ecologically thriving world and awakened states of being, in the hope that viewers will joyfully manifest these states of being in their own lives. He works primarily in the digital medium. After drawing concepts in my sketchbooks and dream journals, I fully realize those concepts using an electronic drawing pad and digital ink. I draw inspiration from a variety of related subjects, including meditation & Yoga, martial artistry, lucid dreaming, comparative mythology, culture jamming, and permaculture. Through these practices, I find the empowered center where creativity surges. www.geoglyphiks.com

Jose Arguelle's love of art and culture inspired him to obtain his Ph.D. in art history and aesthetics from the University of Chicago in 1969. As a prolific artist, Argüelles has provided the illustrations for a number of his books, as well as the cover art for the periodical Psychedelics: Their Uses and Implications (Osmund & Aaronson, 1969). His activity as a painter includes exhibits at the Princeton University Art Museum, 1968, and the Inner City Gallery, Los Angeles, 1969. His murals can still be seen at the Psychology Department, University of California, Davis (1969), and in the Dan Evans Library Building, The Evergreen State College, Olympia, Washington (1972). With Chögyam Trungpa Rinpoche, he assisted in the Dharma Art Exhibits in Los Angeles (1980) and San Francisco (1981). His visionary drawings were also exhibited at the Time is Art Gallery, Portland, Oregon (1999-2000) and his "Doors of Perception" paintings exhibited at the Time is Art Gallery, Ashland, Oregon (2004-2005). www.lawoftime.org

Carrie Ann Baade's autobiographical oil paintings are allegorical narratives inspired by spirit, literature, and art history. These parables combine fragments of Renaissance and Baroque religious paintings, resulting in surreal landscapes inhabited by exotic flora, fauna, and figures. Baade was awarded the Florida Division of Cultural Affairs Individual Artist Fellowship in 2010, the Delaware Division of the Arts Fellowship for Established Artist in 2005, and was nominated for the prestigious United States Artist Fellowship in 2006 and the Joan Mitchell Grant in 2012. Her work has been exhibited in museums and galleries nationally and internationally, including recent solo exhibitions: the Museum of Contemporary Art in Jacksonville Florida, the Delaware Center for Contemporary Art, the Rosenfeld Gallery in Philadelphia, Billy Shire Fine Arts in Los Angeles, and the Ningbo Art Museum in China.

Jeff Bedrick's distinguished career has spanned almost every facet of visual art and media over the last 30 years. Highlights include prestigious international exhibits and publications of his original paintings; art and art direction for numerous animated features and television specials including Shrek 2 (DreamWorks/PDI); computer games; illustrated books for Doubleday, Harper Collins, and scores of other publications. He writes and teaches courses for the digital art and animation department at the San Francisco Academy of Art University, while juggling an ongoing assortment of illustration, film, editing, and digital media projects. www.bedrickstudios.com

Turiya Bruce has been a practicing artist for the past 20 years in the beautiful Byron Shire, Northern New South Wales, Australia. Turiya has explored feminine inspired imagery drawing on the iconic and the archeological works of Marija Gimbutas. Turiya creates public installations in Mural and Mosaic and also teaches her breadth of artistic experience to children and adults. Turiya's work can be viewed at www.turiyabruce.com

Chanel Baran is an inspired visionary photographer. She is deeply passionate about creating artistic imagery that is real, raw and authentic. Chanel is driven to spread the message and awareness to inspire a powerful remembering of the innate power and potent magic women behold. Born and raised in the beautiful wet tropics of Cairns, Far North Queensland, she is currently based in Byron Bay. Chanel has discovered that photography is her medicine tool for healing. Chanel's enchanting and empowering images have deeply inspired people worldwide. For more information, see her website: www.chanelbaran.com

Krista Lynn Brown grew up inspired by the landscapes of her native Northern California and the cultural diversity of the San Francisco Bay Area. The natural world, quantum physics, folk magic, alchemical and shamanistic studies, psychedelics and plant medicines along with the joy and challenge of motherhood have all influenced the work she creates. Her art focuses on the mystic path, seeing the divine hidden in the ordinary, grounding in the symbolism of Earth and Heart. Originals, giclees, cards, books and painted artifacts, created in studio for over twenty years, are available at Deva Luna Studio online at www.devaluna.com.

Atmara Rebecca Cloe is a visionary artist and magical realist residing in Southern Oregon. She creates from an enormous breadth of subject matter, including goddesses, angels, visionary landscapes, the beauty of nature, dolphins, images of spirit and light, fractals, crystals, mandalas and more. Creating artwork is an ecstatic, mystical experience for her--there is an energy, another dimensional "beingness" that wants to be expressed through her and be given a form in this dimension. On her New World Creations website, http://www.nwcreations.com, Atmara offers prints and a variety of gifts utilizing her artwork. All her work is available for licensing, and commissions are always welcome.

Susan De Veuve is a shamanistic, visionary artist residing in Northern California. Influenced by an assortment of indigenous cultures and ancient mythology, her artistic vision incorporates her personal experiences as a woman, mother and mystic. With over twenty years experience as an artist and Shamanistic practitioner, Susan's work has graced the covers of numerous books and magazines. Her entire portfolio can be viewed on her website at: www.mcn.org/b/sdeveuve/

Robert Donaghey's astonishingly beautiful artwork is filled with sacred geometry and deeply insightful metaphor from a wide spectrum of the worlds spiritual philosophy. His expression of spiritual metaphor invites the viewer into a Divine discourse with their heart. Warm, illuminating - even enlightening, this work is truly art for the soul. View more of his work at: www.artisticgenius.com

Amoraea Dreamseed. Co-founder of The Light School, Visionary & Soul Awareness Facilitator, Sacred Ceremonialist & Spiritual Artist, Amoraea Dreamseed shares techniques and Higher Tantric teachings for awakening to Our Eternal Presence, within an emphasis on the acceleration of both personal and planetary evolution through higher-dimensional awareness and soul recalibration. Seminars, ceremonies, and intensive trainings on becoming an evolutionary ambassador in this time of Great Awakening also inspire artwork with themes of co-creative synergy, genesis and alchemy of our essence together to become the Face of Love.... and the wholeness necessary to navigate through the currents and crests of cultural rebirth. divine-blueprint.com

Chris Dyer grew up in Peru and now resides in Canada, yet he spends much time on the road. Though his work is very "visionary", he is trying to break any boxes and fuse his positive spiritual art with the different kinds of urban art cultures he navigates, from skateboarding to graffiti. His work has been shown in solo and group gallery exhibitions around the planet as well as countless magazines and a few books, including his own hardcover masterpiece by Schiffer Publications. His website can be viewed at: www.positivecreations.com

Peter Eglington is a visionary artist residing in Byron Bay, Australia. Peter's works grace the walls of homes in locations as diverse as the United States, New Zealand, Australia, Brazil, Mexico, England, Germany, the Netherlands, Canada, Hawaii, Macedonia, France, India, Brazil, Switzerland, Sweden and last but by no means least, Botswana, and in the permanent collection of the Visionary Art Museum of America in Baltimore Maryland.

Jane Evershed was born in Britain and went to live in South Africa at the age of nine. After moving to Minnesota from South Africa in 1984, she began painting and writing as a way of remembering the natural beauty of South Africa, while addressing apartheid and the horrors she had seen there. Her work has since expanded to highlight the oppression of all people, as well as that which we create for ourselves within our own minds. The Minnesota Advocates for Human Rights selected Jane Evershed for an award for promoting human rights through art. In 2005, she was voted by the MN Women's Press readership as favorite local artist. She is currently working on a book proposal titled The Time of Woman. You can view her artwork and poetry at www.janeevershed.com

Ashley Foreman attended Humboldt State University in Arcata, California, where the natural beauty and power of the land influenced her work and personal explorations. She took a leave of absence in 2010 to travel, attend music festivals, and study the mischtechnik with the students of Ernst Fuchs, Laurence Caruana, and Amanda Sage, in Torre, Italy. Primarily a painter, she also studied graphic design, and photography, graduating in 2011 with a BA in Studio Art. She is currently living in Nevada City, CA. where she works freelance in a variety of different fields, including painting, digital illustration, graphics & websites, teaching, and tattoo. www.thirteentwentystudios.com

Emma Gardner is a mystical painter, muralist and jeweler residing in Flagstaff, Arizona. She studied Fine Art as well as Art Restoration and Conservation on the east coast. She combines archaic imagery and modern icons to create an eclectic landscape of humanity. Her provocative artwork decorates the walls of the famous restaurant MartAnne's in Flagstaff and has been featured in numerous travel and art magazines. For more information on Emma and her artwork visit www.emmagardner.com or email her at spirleyes@yahoo.com.

Leslie Gibbons, M.Ed/Art, brings over 25 years of professional experience as a gifted healing arts facilitator, educator and artist. She has extensive training in indigenous wisdom traditions, Qi-Gong, energy medicine, reiki, and Eastern meditative practices. She is a Certified Life Coach and licensed Esthetician offering a unique approach to cultivating a life you Love –everyday. Leslie has served as an Educational Consultant in the fields of holistic health/wellness, creative arts and spirituality. She has offered on-site seminars and workshops for schools, universities, hospitals, multicultural centers, wellness retreats, healing centers and health spas throughout the USA. To view her sacred mosaics, visit her website at: www.sacredcreativity.com

Francene Hart is an internationally recognized visionary artist whose work has been widely published in books and magazines and hangs in the homes of art collectors and the offices of healers and seekers around the planet. She utilizes the wisdom and symbolic imagery of Sacred Geometry, reverence for the natural environment, and the interconnectedness between all things to create watercolor paintings of beauty and spirit. Her work acts as a bridge between this reality and a world of healing and transformation. She is the artist and author of the Sacred Geometry Oracle Deck. Her artwork can be viewed at: www.francenehart.com

Mark Henson, visionary artist and native of Northern California, showed artistic inclinations at an early age. After receiving his Bachelor's degree in Art from the University of California, he co-founded an art gallery, traveled to Asia and Central America, and now spends his time living and working in the rural paradise of Lake County, California, and on a small farm in the central highlands of Costa Rica. His artwork can be viewed on his website at www.markhensonart.com

Yasmin Hernandez, a Puerto Rican painter and installation artist, was born and raised in Brooklyn, New York. She attended the LaGuardia High School of Music and Art and the Performing Arts in Manhattan, and earned a BFA in Painting at Cornell University's College of Architecture, Art and Planning. As an activist, she incorporates social justice themes into her work, and has developed a workshop on the role of the arts in activism and social change, which she has offered to audiences at Cornell University, Penn State and Swarthmore College. These workshops are now being offered to youth through the Soul Rebels project at El Museo del Barrio. In 2004, Ms. Hernandez was awarded the Ramón Feliciano Social Justice Prize by the Center for Puerto Rican Studies at Hunter College, and was recognized with the Mujeres Destacadas/ Outstanding Latinas Award by New York-based Spanish-language newspaper, El Diario/La Prensa. Her painting series, Realidades de Quisqueya, inspired by a trip to the Dominican Republic and funded by a grant from the Cornell Council for the Arts (CCA), is on permanent exhibition at the Cornell Latino Studies Program Offices. Her art website www.yasminhernandez.com,

Visionary artist Paul Heussenstamm is one of the leading Mandala artists in the western hemisphere. As a renowned teacher and fourth generation artist, Paul has been sharing his unique gift of helping people discover their Soul through his paintings and Art As A Spiritual Path workshops worldwide. Paul has created over 800 unique and spiritual paintings while passionately sharing his artistic capacity to explore and create Sacred Art from many traditions such as Buddhism, Hinduism and Christianity. His Artwork can be viewed at www.mandalas.com

Martina Hoffmann, German-born, spent part of her childhood in Cameroon, West Africa. She majored in art and sculpting at the Johann Wolfgang Goethe University in Frankfurt Germany. Hoffmann currently works as a painter and sculptress. Much of her imagery addresses the sacred feminine, while her sculptural work shows undeniable African influences. Her paintings fall within the realm of Visionary Art and have been greatly inspired by a visual language generated in expanded states of consciousness such as the dream state, meditation, spontaneous visions, and from experiences with entheogenic plants. Martina has been a guest speaker at Naropa Institute, the Prophets Conference and the Mindstates Conference. Hoffmann's work has been exhibited internationally, as well as being published in books such as One Source, Sacred Journeys, The Return of The Great Goddess, Celebrating Women's Spirituality, Noospheres, Illuminatus, and Drinking Lightning. Her work can also be seen in the magazines: Magical Blend, Shaman's Drum, Wellbeing, Expose, We'Moon, and Nexus.' You can view more of her work at www.martinahoffmann.com.

Daniel B. Holeman is a visionary artist residing in the Bay Area. He invites the viewer to dive into a deeper dimension of consciousness while viewing his paintings. The imagery stirs forgotten awareness of a place felt to be HOME – a warm, familiar and heartfelt state of mind – a welcome contrast to the day-to-day world we live in. Rather than appealing only to select markets, such as "New Age" and "Spiritual", his work appeals to a good percentage of people in all categories – perhaps anyone who appreciates that heartfelt place – thus crossing race, social, gender, religious and ethnic boundaries. His Web Site, www.AwakenVisions.com, is a special world to explore and enjoy - a Domain of Beauty, Insight, Transformation and Awakening. In addition to the artwork, Awaken Visions is a haven for truth seekers, consciousness explorers and all who know, don't know, or want to know what it's all about.

Kelly Hostetler of Spirit Dance is a self taught artist, born in Mishawaka Indiana, lived in the southwest as a small child, but for most part was raised in the Florida Keys. His paintings shed light upon the Southwest, Visionary, Native American, New Age, and Sea Life Dreamscapes. Kelly questioned his philosophy by way of poetry and once he felt direction, this led him to express his insights through the brush. He feels painting is a good medium because it has the ability to touch all, via its silent universal language. For more information see his website: www.spiritdanceart.net

Davin Infinity has trained in several lineages of shamanic practice, martial arts and mystery schools. He is an experienced and powerful metaphysical guide into the Quest of human potential and transformation. This work is a major influence in his visionary art, films, books and life mastery jedi workshops (www.ShamanEyes.net). Davin is also the founder of the Awakening Freedom Foundation: a visionary culture design movement that weaves networks of unified solutions for a healthier humanity.

Hrana Janto is an artist long inhabiting the realms of History, Fantasy, Myth and The Sacred. Raised and abetted by artist-parents in, she graduated from NYC's high school of Art and Design and received a BFA from The Cooper Union. She then studied at the School of Sacred Arts while starting her career as a professional Artist and Illustrator. Painting mythology has been an ongoing longtime passion. Her commissioned works include historical paintings for the PBS series "Joseph Campbell's The Power of Myth" with Bill Moyers, numerous book covers and calendars. Hrana co-created the internationally published "The Goddess Oracle" deck, featuring her art and calligraphy, for Element Books/ HarperCollins. Most recently, Hrana created 40 illustrations for Patricia Monaghan's Encyclopedia of Goddesses and Heroines". Children's Illustration is another focus. Hrana has painted for a multitude of publishers including Cricket magazine, Macmillan/Mcgraw Hill, Pearson and Simon and Schuster. Her children's books include "King for a Day", "How Thor got his Hammer Back" and "the Slave and the Lion". She also creates portraits and private commissions. Hrana has exhibited throughout the country, including pieces at the Books of Wonder Gallery and a Society of Illustrators show. Hrana lives, paints, and dances in NY's Hudson Valley. To see more, visit: www.hranajanto.com

David Joaquin was born and raised in California, and currently resides in northern Oregon. He began painting visions and dreams, and also works with exotic woods such as milo, koa, hau, and mango. His mother, an emigrant from Colombia and an artist herself, was his first art teacher. His illustrations have appeared in numerous publications such as The Land and People of the Colorado Plateau, Dreams: Science Art and the Unconscious Mind, and most recently, Mountain Spirit: The Sheepeater Indians of the Yellowstone. His artwork can be viewed at www.twohawkstudio.com

Lindy Kehoe enjoys living a spacious and peaceful life, choosing to reflect this quality in her dream-like work. Her mediums include oil paints on canvas, acrylic, earth pigments (stoneground), clay-based eco paints, watercolors, and ink on paper. The body of work on this sight reflects a decade of painting after her studies at Ohio University, where she received her Bachelors of Fine Art, focusing on Art Education. As a certified Art Educator for kindergarten through high school, she has taught in many fashions and ages. She currently resides in the Rogue Valley of Oregon, where she fell in love and illustrated Star Hawk's "Last Wild Witch," published by Mother Tongue Ink of We'Moon. She received a silver "Nautilus Award" for her illustrations. Lindy is currently weaving together her many images into a story book called "Urial and Arianna and the Transformation of the Worlds." For more information, see her website: www.lindykehoe.com

Emily Kell is a Portland, Oregon based artist who experiences the world through travel and creativity. Her artwork takes root in ideals of divine feminine. In her artwork and in life, she celebrates women, the mystical realm, the spiritual journey of the human family, and the mysteries of the universe. She explores various spiritual realms and dimensions within her artwork and creates pieces that are intended to uplift and heal the collective with a focus on the healing of women in particular. Through her artwork and poetry, Emily endeavors to peel back the veil little by little and bring otherworldly beings and other dimensions into this world. For more information, see her website at www.emilykell.com

Sherab Khandro is a sculpture, painter and Tibetan Buddhist nun residing in Sedona, Arizona. She is one of a handful of Western ordained Buddhists who have received formal training in bringing forth sacred images of the Divine Goddess in the prescribed Tibetan way. She is also the Sacred Arts Director for the Kunzang Palyul Choling Stupa and Temple project in Sedona, Arizona. She is represented by Goldenstein Gallery in Sedona and can be contacted through their website at: www. GoldensteinArt.com.

Krystleyez: Through an ever-evolving process of intention and intuition, Krystle harnesses the power of art as a vehicle for personal and collective transformation. In a world stifled by the illusion of separation, she shares impacting visions of unity. Exploring the luminous landscapes of consciousness, her multidimensional paintings radiate transcendental light with balanced serenity. Pulsing and breathing with life, the etheric geometries that dance off her canvas disintegrate the boundaries between art and audience. Cosmic maps into the interconnected nature of existence, her artwork navigates the way between heart, mind, and the enchanting realms of spirit. Krystle humbly offers her sacred art to the world to illuminate pathways to higher consciousness and rekindle the fire of in*spirit*ation in us all. For more information, visit her website: www.krystleyez.com

Morgan Mandala was born and raised outside of Chicago, Illinois; however, she has called the front range of Colorado home for over a decade. She earned a double BFA in painting and art history with a minor in philosophy at Colorado State University. Her studies sparked her interest in the relationship between art and spirituality, and how this relationship manifests itself throughout various cultures. Morgan's early history as an artist was characterized by naturalistic drawings, however this changed as she began to focus on painting in college as a meditative and healing practice. This lead to studies in color vibrational theory, and ultimately, the creation of mandalas. For more information, see her website: www.morganmandala.com

S. Grace Mantle is from the mountains of southern Oregon. She holds a B.A. in fine arts from the University of Oregon, with courses of study at Southern Oregon University and Parsons School of Design in New York. Her training includes studies in Europe and eight years of independent training with sculptor A. Bruce Hoheb of New York City. Her work has been featured in conjunction with James Twyman's work for children. She has shown her artwork in several west coast spiritual conferences and retreat centers. She is a Tanran Reiki master/teacher, having received her training with William Bagley of Ashland, Oregon. Grace loves to teach both art and Reiki to children and teens, and has done so in schools in east Maui and Ashland, Oregon. She holds the vision for a children's world peace village for orphans and families, and she actively works to manifest this dream. You may see more of her work at www.gracemantlestudios.com.

Cathy McClelland's artwork reflects the love she has for nature, cross-cultural mythical subjects, magical and sacred places and symbols. She paints from her heart and imagination. Her medium is acrylic, using both airbrush and hand to enhance and detail her painting, giving her artwork a feeling of depth that wants to be explored. Cathymcclelland.com

Autumn Skye Morrison's meticulous and poignant paintings continue to gain expanding recognition, attracting collectors and students from around the globe. As a self-taught artist, she has dedicated innumerable hours in creative exploration. Her style gracefully weaves together refined realism, iconic imagery, profound symbolism, and subtle geometries. She teaches and exhibits worldwide, and otherwise now lives and paints on the beautiful Sunshine Coast of BC, Canada. Considering herself immensely blessed, Autumn Skye strives to support others through inspiration and creative empowerment. www.autumnskyeart.com

Tessa Mythos is a multi-disciplinary artist from Victoria and Hornby Island B.C. Canada. She has always been deeply inspired by the wild and natural beauty of the North West coast, finding her art and expressions within it from a young age. Mythos is a largely self-taught artist, believing in experience as the greatest teacher. She has experimented with many mediums and methods from the illustration of her graphic novels, oil painting, acrylics, sculpture, murals, drawings and abstract work. Her work is intuitive and inspired by, an ongoing study of mythology and spirit (personal and universal) and explores the inter-connectivity and relationship of symbol between culture and nature.

Paul Nicholson is a painter residing in Bodega Bay California. He thinks creative expression is the birthright of every human being... that artists are important to societal integrity - that the best art is that which inspires, sets wonderment in motion. It should connect artist and viewer at what i call the level of the moment - that place of oneness with all - where there is no time, no other... I feel it is the task of the artist to provide decent points of departure for this very important, very humanizing experience. View more of his work at: www.paulnicholson.com

Mariela de la Paz is a Chilean-born artist who now lives in the San Fransisco Bay Area. Primarily a self-taught painter, she later began to merge her passions for shamanism and painting into the creation of visionary artwork. After considerable travel, Mariela settled in northern California in 1989, where she attended the Mother Peace School of Female Shamanism. In 2001, after spending months in virtual solitude, and also fasting she experienced a cosmic awakening through her work with plant medicines. Today, her art is devoted to portraying shamanistic themes derived from her indigenous Mapuche ancestry and from visions obtained during plant medicine journey work. Mariela has exhibited her art extensively in the San Fransisco Bay Area, and is featured ongoing at the Rainbow Body Gallery at the Open Secret Bookstore in San Rafael, California. To see examples of her paintings visit her website at: www.marieladelapaz.com

Mauro Reátegui Perez and Juan Benavides Perez are becoming two of the most visible and sought after Peruvian visionary artists. Having trained with the renown visionary Artist, Pablo Amaringo, the shaman brothers have developed a distinctive style that has become known internationally and he has had shows through out Europe and North America. As well as being a talented painter, Mauro is also a teacher and guide and possesses an extensive knowledge of the cultural life of the Peruvian Amazon." His gallery of visionary paintings portray deep shamanic journeys and visions revealing an array of spiritual beings inhabiting the forest, the underwater and subterranean realms, and angelic realms. For more information: www.mauroart.com

Sacred Vision Designs (owned by Aaron Pyne) is a Graphic Design, Web Design, Video Design, & Visionary art company. Sacred Vision Designs works with spiritual, holistic, and eco businesses to help expand their businesses through the use of web technology and visionary design. Visit Sacred Vision Designs at www.SacredVisionDesigns.com to learn about their services and see their visionary art and designs. You can also contact them at sacredvisiondesigns@gmail.com.

Cynthia Ré Robbins earned a BFA degree from the Cleveland Institute of Art and Instituto Allende in Mexico. She later furthered her studies with Robert Venosa and Phil Rubinov Jacobson, learning the Mische technique. This method of layering transparencies over brilliant white renderings allows her to create shimmering visions and precise detail. Subject matter varies widely, with Beauty as a key focus. www.art4spirit.com

Raul Casillas Romo is a self-taught painter born in Los Angeles, California in 1970 and raised in Guadalajara Mexico, Los Angeles and London. He also lived in Vancouver, Canada for 15 years where he expanded and refined the exploration of the arts while working in the Film industry, decorating sets as a lead set dresser, sculptor and creating commissioned fine art for movies. He has exhibited his artwork in various collective exhibitions at music and art festivals, such as Shambhala, Tribe 13's Interdimensional Art Show, the Temple of Visions, Art Basel with the Moksha Family, Alchemeyez Visionary Art Congress, and The American Visionary Art Museum in Baltimore, Maryland. Raul is currently a full time Tattoo artist at Universal Rites Tattoo in Ashland, Oregon. Visit his website at: www.raulcasillas.com

Eva Sullivan Sakmar is a visionary painter and environmentalist. She spent time in both the Atlantic and Pacific Oceans, swimming with dolphins and sea turtles. Her spiritual quest and travels to sacred sites worldwide have been instrumental in transforming her work into its current form of expression. Her work is often used as a meditative journeying tool for accessing one's own portal to higher dimensions. Eva's intent is that her work serves the highest good of the viewer. You can view more of her artwork on her website at: www.stardolphin.com.

Theresa Sharrar has lived most of her life in the rural countryside of Oregon, as well as Hawaii and British Columbia. She has found great inspiration in the natural elements of these places. Her journey as a serious painter began in Hawaii, and now continues in Oregon. Much of her work is in response to being female and experiencing the wildness of the earth. Along with producing her own work, Theresa teaches art classes in her studio and works in a local co-operative gallery of which she is a founding member. While she doesn't have a website yet, she can be contacted via email at: theresasharrar@gmail.com

Rose V. Sharrar is a mystical painter and illustrator in Santa Fe, New Mexico. She grew up in northern Oregon in a family of seven siblings, all of whom discovered drawing, painting, and music at an early age. The conservative region in which she spent her childhood was incongruous with her developing sense of inner direction, so she left home at sixteen and spent her later teens and adulthood living and working in several different states, where she sought to find her creative/spiritual niche. She currently lives in New Mexico, is studying art, and aspires towards personal and planetary healing. She can be reached by email at: goldaught@yahoo.com

Penny Slinger is a surrealist artist. She produced 50%-The Visible Woman (1971) and An Exorcism (1977), two collections of powerful and haunting collages. Her 2D collages and 3D installations incorporated images and life-casts of herself. Her media during this period included pencil and paint, printmaking, life casts and other 3-dimensional constructions, as well as photography, film and collage. Penny Slinger is also known for her erotic and Tantric work and her Caribbean/ Amerindian work. She created *the Secret Dakini Oracle,* re-released as the *Tantric Dakini Oracle.* In 2011 Penny released an on-line version of the project she has been working on for many years, *the 64 Dakini Oracle,* an evolution of *the Secret Dakini Oracle.* Visit her websites at www.pennyslinger.com and www.64dakinioracle.org

Heather Taylor is a visionary artist residing in Olympia, Washington. Her art is featured in a variety of books, calendars, magazines and CD covers. She has art in clinics, hospitals, libraries, museums, and schools as well as city and state collections. Heather uses 8 different mediums in creating her 2 and 3 dimensional work. Her art is inclusive in its theme, employing sacred geometry, numerology, symbology, cultural anthropology and psychology to convey the diversity and universality of human experience. Through the mandala and the teachings it represents she seeks to align the viewer to a new appreciation of our connection, within and without, above and below, to all that is around us. Visit her website at: www.fullcirclemandalas.com

Jim Thompson is a fine and technical artist residing in Southern Oregon. My Art, Mind and Soul series represent real themes, fantasy, and extraterrestrial landscapes. I began my artistic career in advertising as a technical illustrator, then I became a freelancer and moved into fine art. My works span a broad range of subjects and have been published widely in various articles, books and magazines, as well as exhibited in numerous shows. View more of my art at: www.art-mind-soul.com or www.jt-techart.com.

The Fantastic Realism art of Robert Venosa has been exhibited worldwide and is represented in major collections, including those of noted museums, rock stars and European aristocracy. In addition to painting, sculpting and film design (pre-sketches and conceptual design for the movie Dune, and Fire in the Sky for Paramount Pictures, and the upcoming Race for Atlantis for IMAX), he has recently added computer art to his creative menu. His work has been the subject of three books, as well as being featured in numerous publications - most notably OMNI magazine - and on a number of CD covers, including those of Santana and Kitaro.Visit his amazing art at: www.venosa.com

Blaze Warrender is an Australian-born shamanistic painter. As a self-taught artist, her fascination with texture and medium led her to apprenticeships in Italy & Guernsey and a course in Chinoiserie brush techniques at Beijing University, China. In the early nineties she began painting on canvas, and found that influences from her past allowed her to express the colorful, surreal imagery of her inner world. She has exhibited in the United States, Great Britain and Australia, and has been represented in various magazines. Her artistic mission is to explore the transformative processes of art therapy, transpersonal psychology and shamanism as a means to heal herself and the planet. Her artwork can be viewed on her website at: www.blazewarrender.com

Julia Weaver, MFT, BFA, is an environmental arts educator, a licensed psychotherapist, and an exhibiting artist. She has more than 20 years experience combining the arts, and cross cultural practices, particularly the creation of mandalas and gardens for individual, community, and global healing. Since 1996, she has offered mandala workshops for adults and children in her studio in the San Francisco Bay area and across the US, as well as dolphin swims retreats in Hawaii. A passionate environmental arts educator, Julia designs and facilitates rites-of-passage ceremonies and combines the Mandala Process with tree planting, gardening, and collages to promote community revitalization and ecological healing. Her mandalas can be viewed at www.juliamandalaweaver.com.

Jonathan Weber is a visionary artist and mystic whose recent works include a meditation on the archetypes of the divine feminine. He began private tutorship for drawing and painting at the age of eight, but later left the academic realm of art to explore his emerging style on his own. His painting talents and intuitive abilities have grown alongside his passion for various spiritual traditions such as; Shamanism, Taoism, Buddhism, Yoga, Sufism, Christianity, and Advaita Vedanta. His work has been published on numerous covers of "Alternatives" magazine, the cover of Tarot and Healing; Messages From the

Archetypes, by Toni Gilbert, and in Margaret Starbird's new book Mary Magdalene; Bride In Exile. For more information, view his website at www.jonathanweber.com.

Abba Yahudah migrated to the United States in 1981 at the age of fifteen and took his first job as a sign painter, which intimately exposed him to typography and layout. He later explored and experimented with offset and screen printing techniques. While living in New York in 1985, he attended Parson's School of Design, majoring in graphic design and layout. A year later, he enrolled in The School of Visual Arts, majoring in design and illustration. His art has traveled internationally to Ethiopia, exhibiting at the Habesha and Lela Art Galleries, to the University of the West Indies in Jamaica, to the Smithsonian Museum of Natural History in Washington DC, as well as many galleries in the San Francisco Bay Area.. website: www.abbayahudah.com

REFERENCES BY CHAPTER

Introduction:

1. Christ, Carol. Rebirth of the Goddess: Finding Meaning in Feminist Spirituality, Routledge, New York, 1997, 22.
2. Gadon, Elinor. The Once and Future Goddess: A Sweeping Visual Chronicle of the Sacred Female and Her Reemergence in the Cultural Mythology of Our Time, HarperSanfrancisco,1989, 231.
3. Gimbutas, Marija. The Gods and Goddesses of Old Europe: 7000 to 3500 B.C., Myths Legends and Cult Images Berkeley, University of California Press, 1982.
4. Gimbutas, Marija. The Gods and Goddesses of Old Europe: 7000 to 3500 B.C., Myths Legends and Cult Images Berkeley, University of California Press, 1982, 11.
5. Gimbutas, Marija. The Gods and Goddesses of Old Europe: 7000 to 3500 B.C., Myths Legends and Cult Images Berkeley, University of California Press, 1982, 36.
6. Gimbutas, Marija. The Gods and Goddesses of Old Europe: 7000 to 3500 B.C., Myths Legends and Cult Images Berkeley, University of California Press, 1982, 27.
7. Stone, Merlin. When God was a Woman, New York: Dial Press, 1976, 34.
8. Orenstein, Gloria. "Recovering Her Story: Feminist Artists Reclaim the Great Goddess," in Norma Broude and Mary Garrard, The Power of Feminist Art, Harry N. Abrams, Inc., 1994.
9. Teasdale, Wayne. The Mystic Heart: Discovering a Universal Spirituality in the World's Religions,New World Library, California, 23
10. Huxley, Aldous. The Perennial Philosophy, Harper and Brothers Publishers, 1945
11. Teasdale, Wayne. The Mystic Heart: Discovering a Universal Spirituality in the World's Religions, New World Library, California, 26.
12. Kimball, Charles. When Religion Becomes Evil: Five Warning Signs, HarperCollins, New York, 2008, 13
13. Kimball, Charles. When Religion Becomes Evil: Five Warning Signs, HarperCollins, New York, 2008, 13.

Part One: The Primordial Sacred Union

The Loss of the World Soul and its Return
By Anne Baring

1. David Abram, The Spell of the Sensuous, Vintage Books, New York 1996, 250.
2. for poems to Hathor and Nut see Andrew Harvey and Anne Baring, The Divine Feminine, Conari Press 1996.
3. See Jules Cashford, The Moon: Myth and Image, Cassell Illustrated, London 2003.
4. Text by Andrew Annenberg, taken from website.
5. The phrase used by Henri Corbin in his writings on Ibn Arabi and Suhrawardi.
6. Gertrude Levy, The Gate of Horn, Faber & Faber, London 1958, 301-3.
7. Plotinus, The Enneads, transl. Stephen MacKenna, Faber and Faber, London, 1956 and 1969
8. D.H. Lawrence, Apocalypse and Other Writings, Cambridge University Press, 1931, 78
9. David Abram, The Spell of the Sensuous, Vintage Books, New York 1996, 254
10. The concept of the inferiority of woman is found in Plato's Timaeus as well as the Book of Genesis
11. Quote from Victoria Christian, image description
12. Dr. K. Ramanathan, reported in The Times, February 1, 2009
13. See Anne Baring and Jules Cashford, The Myth of the Goddess: Evolution of an Image, Viking, 1991 and Penguin Books, London and New York, 1993, chapter 13: Eve, The Mother of All Living
14. C.G. Jung, The Undiscovered Self, Collected Works Vol.10) and Man and His Symbols, Aldus Books, London, 1964.
15. See Science and the Reenchantment of the Cosmos by Ervin Laszlo, Inner Traditions, Vermont, 2006, and Richard Tarnas, Cosmos and Psyche, Viking, New York, 2006
16. Apocalypse, p. 78

Artists Envisioning the Primordial Sacred Union
By Victoria Christian

1. Carl Jung. Man and His Symbols, London: Aldus Books Ltd., 1964.
2. Alex Grey. The Mission of Art, Boston Ma: Shambala Publications, 1998, 115.
3. Sue Monk Kid. The Dance of the Dissident Daughter, New York: HarperCollins, 2002.
4. June Singer. Androgyny: The Opposites Within, York Beach, Me: Nicolas-Hays, 2000, 131.
5. Fritjof Capra. The Tao of Physics: An Exploration of the Parallels between Modern Physics and Eastern Mysticism Boston, Ma: Shambhala Publication, Inc., 1999, 29.
6. Carol Christ. Rebirth of the Goddess: Finding Meaning in Femininist Spirituality, New York: Routledge, 1997, 22.
7. Sue Monk Kid. The Dance of the Dissident Daughter, New York: HarperCollins, 2002, 137.

8. Mary Daly. Beyond God the Father: Toward a Philosophy of Women's Liberation, Boston: Beacon Press, 1973, 31.
9. Mary Daly. Beyond God the Father: Toward a Philosophy of Women's Liberation, Boston: Beacon Press, 1973, 15.
10. Elinor Gadon. The Once and Future Goddess, New York: HarperSanfransisco, 1989, 261.
11. Carl Jung. Man and His Symbols, London: Aldus Books Ltd., 1964. See also The Archetypes and the Collective Unconscious, 1959.
12. June Singer. Androgyny: The Opposites Within, York Beach, Me: Nicolas-Hays, 2000.
13. Anne Fausto-Sterling. Sexing the Body: Gender Politics and the Construction of Sexuality, New York: Basic Books, 2000.
14. June Singer. Androgyny: The Opposites Within, York Beach, Me: Nicolas-Hays, 2000.
15. Text from Jonathon Weber's website, www.alterimagestudio.com
16. Quote taken from Mark Henson website: www.markhenson.com
17.Quote taken from Amoraea Dreamseed's website: www.harmonicconvergence2012.com
18. Quote from Abbah Yahudah, book content.
19.. Tom Lowenstein. Mother Earth, Father Sky: Native American Myth, London: Barnes and Noble, 2005, Ch, 3.
20. Monica Sjoo and Barbara Mor. The Great Cosmic Mother, San Fransisco: Harper and Row, 1987.
21 Quote taken from Mark Henson's website,www.markhenson.com
22. Quote from Beth Avary's website: www.starfirepress.com
23. Monica Sjoo, and Barbara Mor. The Great Cosmic Mother, San Fransisco: Harper and Row, 1987, p. 186.
24. Monica Sjoo, and Barbara Mor. The Great Cosmic Mother, San Fransisco: Harper and Row, 1987, 192.
25. Quote from Heath Taylor, image description
26. John Macionis. Society: The Basics, New Jersey: Prentice Hall, 2000, 198.
25. Quote from Heather Taylor, image description
27. Immanuel Wallerstein. The Modern World System: Capitalist Agriculture and the Origins of the European World-Economy in the Sixteenth Century, New York: Academic Press, 1974.
28. Quote from Mark Henson's Website: www.markhenson.com
29. Quote from Mark Henson's Website. www.markhenson.com
30. Karl Marx. Selected Writings in Sociology and Social Philosophy, T. B. Bottomore, trans. New York: McGraw-Hill, 1964.
31. Max Weber. The Protestant Ethic and the Spirit of Capitalism Los Angeles, California: Roxbury Publishing, first published in 1920.
32. Carolyn Merchant. The Death of Nature: Women, Ecology and the Scientific Revolution, San Fransisco, Harper and Row, 1983.
33. Rosemary Radford Ruether. Gaia and God: An EcoFeminist Theology of Earth Healing, New York: HarperCollins, 1992, Chapter 4.
34. Evelyn Fox Keller. Reflections on Gender and Science , New Haven, Conn.: Yale University Press, 1985.
35. Sandra Harding. The Science Question in Feminism, Ithaca: Cornell University Press, 1986.
36. Max Weber. The Protestant Ethic and the Spirit of Capitalism, Los Angeles, California: Roxbury Publishing, first published in 1920.
37. Max Weber. Economy and Society. G. Roth and C. Wittich, eds., Berkeley: University of California Press, 1978.
38. Eckhart Tolle. The Power of Now: A Guide to Spiritual Enlightenment, California: Namaste Publishing, 1999, 15.
39. Herbert Marcuse. One Dimensional Man, Boston: Beacon Press, 1964.
40. Max Weber. Economy and Society. G. Roth and C. Wittich, eds. , Berkeley: University of California Press, 1978.
41. Madeleine L'Engle, 1972.
42. Rollo May. The Courage to Create, New York: W.W. Norton and Company Inc, 1975, 13.
43. Rollo May. The Courage to Create, New York: W.W. Norton and Company Inc, 1975, 14.
44. Carol Christ. Rebirth of the Goddess: Finding Meaning in Feminist Spirituality, New York: Routledge, 1997, 22.
45. Rosemary Radford Ruether. Gaia and God: An EcoFeminist Theology of Earth Healing, New York: HarperCollins, 1992, 167
46. Rosemary Radford Ruether. Gaia and God: An EcoFeminist Theology of Earth Healing, New York: HarperCollins, 1997, 167

Imaging The Divine Compliments:
By Margaret Starbird

All material taken from her own books

Part Two: Rebirth of the Goddess

Chapter One: Goddess of Creation

Envisioning the Divine in Nature
By Victoria Christian

1. Anne Baring and Andrew Harvey. The Divine Feminine. Godsfield Press and Conari Press,1996, 16.
2. See J.E. Lovelock and L. Margulis, "Gai and Geognosy," in M.B. Ramber, ed., Global Ecology: Towards a Science of the Biosphere, London: Jones and Bartlett, 1984; and J.E. Lovelock, Gaia: A New Look at Life on Earth Oxford: Oxford University Press, 1982.
3. Elisabet Sahtouris. Gaia: The Human Journey from Chaos to Cosmos. New York: Pocket Books, 1989, p. 126
4. Carole Christ. Rebirth of the Goddess: Finding Meaning in Feminist Spirituality. Routledge, New York, 1997, 106
5. Carole Christ. Rebirth of the Goddess: Finding Meaning in Feminist Spirituality Routledge, New York, 1997, 108
6. Stephanie Leland. Feminism and Ecology: Theology Connection, in Reclaim the Earth: Women Speak Out For Life on Earth. The Women's Press, 1983, p. 67
7. See Marija Gimbutas, The Language of the Goddess, HarperSanFrancisco, 1991.
8. See Elinor Gadon, The Once and Future Goddess. New York:

Harper Collins Publishers,1989.
9. See Elinor Gadon, The Once and Future Goddess, New York: Harper Collins Publishers, 1989, 133.
10. Quote from Mark Hensons website: www.markhenson.com
11. Quote from Mark Hensons website: www.markhenson.com
12. Quote from Mark Hensons website: www.markhenson.com
13. Quote from Jeffrey Bedrick's website: www.jeffreybedrick.com
14. Quote from Andrew Annenberg's website: www.andrewannenberg.com
15. Quote from Andrew Annenberg image description for Guardian of the Grail.
16. Quote for Laguna Autumn, Andrew Annenberg
17. Quote from Andrew Annenberg website: www.andrewannenberg.com
18. Quote from Paul Heussenstamm's website: www.mandalas.com
19. Quote from Paul Heussenstamm's website: www.mandalas.com
20. Quote from Paul's website: www.mandalas.com
21. Quote from Francene's website: www.francenehart.com
22. Quote from Francene's website: www.francenehart.com
23. Quote from Francene's website: www.francenehart.com
24. Quote from Francene's website: www.francenehart.com
25. Anne Baring and Andrew Harvey. The Divine Feminine. Godsfield Press and Conari Press,1996, 16.
26. Quote from Francene's website: www.francenehart.com
27. Quote from personal interview with Theresa Sharrar, 2005.
28. Quote from Beth Avary's website: www.bethavary.com
29. Quote from Beth Avary's website: www.bethavary.com
30. Quote from Beth Avary's artist statement.
31. Quote from Beth's Avary's artist statement.
32. Quote from Atmara Rebecca Cloe's website: www.nwcreations.com
33. Quote from Cynthia Ré Robbins website: www.art4spirit.com
34. Quote from Cynthia Ré Robbins website: www.art4spirit.com

Artists Reclaim the Body of Earth and Mother
By Victoria Christian

1. Ynestra King."The Ecofeminist Imperative." In Leonie Caldecott and Stephanie Leland, Reclaim the Earth: Women Speak Out for Life on Earth, The Women's Press, 1983, 11.
2. All statistics on domestic violence and women's issues were taken from John Macionis Society: The Basics, Sixth Edition, Prentice Hall, 2002.
3. Carole P. Christ. Rebirth of the Goddess: Finding Meaning in Feminist Spirituality, Routledge, New York, 1997, 78.
4. Carole P. Christ. Rebirth of the Goddess: Finding Meaning in Feminist Spirituality, Routledge, New York, 1997.
5. Gloria Orenstein. "Recovering Her Story: Feminist Artists Reclaim the Great Goddess," in Norma Broude and Mary D. Garrard, The Power of Feminist Art, Harry N. Abrams, Inc., Publishers, 1994.
6. See Marija Gimbutas, The Goddesses and Gods of Old Europe: Myths and Cult Images, Berkeley: University of California Press, 1982.
7. See Merlin Stone, When God Was a Woman, New York: Dial Press, 1976.
8. See Erich Neumann, The Great Mother, Princeton, N.J, Princeton University Press, 1963.
9. See Carl Jung. Myths and Symbols, New York: Time, Inc., 1969
10. Gloria Orenstein. "Recovering Her Story: Feminist Artists Reclaim the Great Goddess," in Norma Broude and Mary D. Garrard, The Power of Feminist Art: The American Movement of the 1970's, History and Impact, Harry N. Abrams, Inc., Publishers, 1994, 79
11. Gloria Orenstein. "Recovering Her Story: Feminist Artists Reclaim the Great Goddess," in Norma Broude and Mary D. Garrard, The Power of Feminist Art: The American Movement of the 1970's, History and Impact Harry N. Abrams, Inc., Publishers, 1994.
12. Merlin Stone. When God Was a Woman, New York: Dial Press, 1976.
13. quote from Hrana Janto website.
14. Aztec Creation Myth retrieved from: www.crytalinks.com/aztecreation.html.
15. Quote from image description provided by Hrana Janto: www.hranajanto.com
16. Quote taken from Suzanne De Veuve's artist statement.
17. Quote taken from image description, Bear Mama, Suzanne De Veuve.
18. Quote from Martina Hoffman, image description for the Goddess Triangle.
19. Quote from Jane Evershed's website.
20. Quote from Jane Evershed, image description www.janeevershed.com
21. Quote from Jane Evershed's image description, www.janeevershed.com
22. Elinor W. Gadon. The Once and Future Goddess: A Symbol For Our Time, HarperSanfransisco, 1989, 285
23. See Carole P. Christ. Rebirth of the Goddess: Finding Meaning in Feminist Spirituality, Routledge, New York, 1997)
24. Quote from person interview with Emma Gardner, 2004.
25. Quote from Emily Kell's artist biography and website.
26. Quote from Emily Kell's artist statement.
27. Quote from Emily Kell's website, www.emilykell.com
28. Quote from Emily Kell's image description for Rebirth of mother Earth.
29. Quote from Emily Tell image description for Return of Primordial Goddess.
30. Elinor W. Gadon. The Once and Future Goddess: A Symbol For Our Time, HarperSanFransisco, 1989, 285.
31. Quote from Ashley Forman's Artist Statement
32. Quote from Ashley Foreman's website: www.thirteentwentystudios.com
33. Quote taken from Autumn Skye Morrison's website: www.autumnskyemorrison.com
34. Quote taken from artist statement provided by Autumn

35. Paula Gun Allen, "The Woman I Love Is A Planet," in Irene Diamond and Gloria Orenstein (ed.), Reweaving The World: The Emergence of Ecofeminism, Sierra Club Books, San Franciso, 1990, 54.
36. Quote taken from Krista Lynn Brown's website, artist statement: www.devaluna.com
37. Quote taken from Krista Lynn Brown's website, artist statement: www.devaluna.com
38. Carole P. Christ. Rebirth of the Goddess: Finding Meaning in Feminist Spirituality, Routledge, New York, 1997.
39. Quote by Gustave Flaubert taken from Cathy's website.
40. Quote taken from Cathy's website, artist statement: www.cathymcclelland.com
41. Joanna Macy, "Working With Environmental Despair," in Theodore Rosak, Mary E. Gomes and Allen D. Kanner (eds.), Ecopsychology: Restoring the Earth, Healing the Mind, Sierra Club Books, San Francisco, 1995, 243.
42. Text on Justice, taken from Cathy's website: www.cathymcclelland.com

Contemporary Images of Spirituality and Resistance Among African Americans
By Arisika Razak

1. See: Eric Neumann. The Great Mother. Ralph Manheim (tr), Princeton: Princeton University Press, 1983; Marija Gimbutas. The Goddesses and Gods of Old Europe: Myths and Cult Images, Berkeley: University of California Press, 1982; Marija Gimbutas. The Language of the Goddess, San Francisco: Harper and Row, 1989; Hallie Austen. The Heart of the Goddess, Berkeley Wingbow Press, 1990; Elinor Gadin. The Once and Future Goddess, San Francisco: Harper and Row, 1989.
2. See: Susan Griffin. Woman and Nature, San Francisco: Harper & Row, 1978. Carolyn Merchant. The Death of Nature: Women, Ecology and the Scientific Revolution, San Francisco: Harper & Row, 1983. Christiane Northrup. Women's Bodies Women's Wisdom, New York: Bantam Books, 2002.
3. "Self hatred may be one of the deepest sources of conflict and turmoil within the African American community. This may be especially true concerning women and their bodies." Cheryl Townsend Gilkes. If It Wasn't For the Women. New York: Orbis Books, 2001, 181. Personal note: Practicing as a midwife for 23 years, I found that women of many cultures experience shame about the body. Many American women apologized for how they looked, how they smelled, and for having the bodies and genitalia of women. A fellow Black nurse-practitioner asked me once how I could be a midwife when it was so "nasty."
4. See Patricia Hill Collins. Black Feminist Thought, New York: Routledge, 2000, 69-92; Boogle, Donald. Toms, Coons, Mulattoes, Mammies and Bucks: An Interpretive History of Blacks in American Films, New York: Continuum.1994, 3-18.
5. Patricia Hill Collins. Black Feminist Thought: Knowledge, Consciousness, and the Politics of Empowerment, New York: Routledge, 2000. Defined knowledge developed by African-American women to foster Black women's empowerment as black feminist thought. Also see Beverly Guy-Sheftall's Words of Fire: An Anthology of African American Feminist Thought, New York: The New Press. 1995 documented Black feminist writing from 1831 to 1990's.
6. Alice Walker coined the term "womanist" to define "a Black feminist or feminist of color. Her four part definition praised Black women's ability to take leadership in revolutionary struggles benefiting all members of the African American community – male and female; validated our right to love, support and nurture other women "sexually and non-sexually"; honored the diversity, beauty and "roundness" of our physical forms; proclaimed the importance of rest healing and self-care, along with periodic separation when necessary in order to achieve this. (Alice Walker. In Search of Our Mothers' Gardens: Womanist Prose. San Diego: HBJ. 198. p. xi)
7. See Rosalind Jeffries "The Image of Women in African Cave Art" in Ivan Van Sertima (ed.) Black Women Antiquity, Brunswick: Transaction Publishers, 1992. And Lhote, Henri. The Search for the Tassili Frescoes, trans. Alan Brodrick, New York: E.P. Dutton, 1959.
8. Sojourner, Sabrina. "In the House of Yemanja: The Goddess Heritage of Black Women." In Gloria Wade-Gayles (ed.) My Soul is A Witness, Boston: Beacon Press, 1995, 272.
9. Reagon, Bernice. Video: The Songs Are Free with Bill Moyers, Mystic Fire Video, 1991.
10. Ani, Marimba. Yurugo, Trenton: Africa World Press Inc., 1994, 221.
11. Gilkes, Carol Townsend. If It Wasn't For the Women, New York: Orbis Books, 2001, 76-91.
12. "Colorism" refers to notions that ascribe goodness, value, or intelligence to the shade or color of one's skin. A derivative of racism, "colorism" is that system that African Americans internalized that argued that lighter skin was equivalent to greater beauty, worth, or achievement.
13. Ntozake, Shange. For colored girls who have considered suicide/when the rainbow is enuf, New York: McMillan, 1972, 63.
14. Hernandez, Yasmin. private e-mail to author, 11/20/05.
15. Asungi, AfraShe. "Afracentrik Visions." Woman of Power, Fall 1991, 42-43. "Afracentrik," "MAMAROOTS," "AfraGoddess," "MAMAROOTS: AJAMA-JEBI," are registered trademarks. All rights reserved by Asungi Productions.
16. Asungi, AfraShe. "Afracentrik Visions." Woman of Power, Fall 1991, 44.
17. Asungi, AfraShe. "Afracentrik Visions." Woman of Power, Fall 1991, 42-43.
18. Asungi. The Goddess Series . . . I notecard depicting art, 1982.
19. Asungi. The Goddess Series . . . I notecard depicting art, 1982.

20. Asungi. The Goddess Series . . . I notecard depicting art, 1982.
21. Quote taken from Lili Bernard's website: www.lilibernard.com
22. Ibid
23. Castellanos, Isabel. "A River of Many Turns: The Polysemy of Ochun in Afro-Cuban Tradition" in Osun Across the Waters: A Yoruba Goddess in Africa and the Americas. (eds.) Joseph M. Murphy & Mei-Mei Sanford. Bloomington IN: Indiana University Press, 2001, 40
24. http://lilibernard.com/Pages/About/VisualArts/Statement.html
25.http://lilibernard.com/Pages/Artwork/Paintings/Religious/ReglaYemaya.html
26. Gonzalez-Wippler, Migene. Santeria: The Religion, Saint Paul MN: Llewellyn Publications, 2001, 57
27. Hernandez, Yasmin. Private e-mail to author 12/5/05
28. Quote taken from Yasmin Hernandez website: www.yasminhernandez.com
29. Quote taken from Yasmin Hernandez website: www.yasminhernandez.com
30. Quote taken from Yasmin Hernandez website: www.yasminhernandez.com
31. Quote taken from Abba Yahudah's website: www.abbayahudah.com/gotart_site_portfolio.html
32. Excerpt from Abba Yahudah's book, A Journey to the Roots of Rastafari: The Essene Nazarite Link, not yet released
33. Excerpt from Abba Yahudah's book, A Journey to the Roots of Rastafari: The Essene Nazarite Link, not yet released
34. Revelations, Chapter 10
35. Excerpt from Abba Yahudah's book, A Journey to the Roots of Rastafari: The Essene Nazarite Link, not yet released
36. Mari Evans. "I am a Black Woman". In D.S. Madison (ed.) The Woman That I Am: The Literature and Culture of contemporary Women of Color, New York: St. Martin's Griffin, 1994, 70-71

Goddess Icons of the Dark Mother Around the Globe
By Lydia Ruyle

Atlantis La Vierge Noire sur la Terre comme au Ciel. Centre International de Recherches, d'Etudes et de Documentation sur les Civilisations d'Occident. Paris. Automne 1988.
Baring, Anne & Cashford, Jules. The Myth of the Goddess: Evolution of an Image, Viking Penguin Books, London, 1991.
Begg, Ian. The Cult of the Black Virgin, Arkana, London, 1985.
Birnbaum, Lucia Chiavola. Black Madonnas: Feminism, Religion and Politics in Italy, Northeastern University Press. Boston, 1993 and Dark mother: African origins and Godmothers, iUniverse, Inc. Lincoln, NE., 2002.
Castillo, Ana. Goddess of the Americas: Writings on the Virgin of Guadalupe, Riverhead Books, New York, 1996.
Freedberg, David. The Power of Images, The University of Chicago Press, Chicago and London, 1989.
Galland, China. Longing For Darkness. Tara and the Black Madonna, Viking Penguin, New York, 1990.
Groth-Marnat, Barbara. A Pilgrimage to the Black Madonna, Red Rose Publications, Santa Barbara, 1990.
Gustafson, Fred. The Black Madonna, Sigo Press, Boston, 1990.
Huynen, Jacques L'Enigme des Vierges Noires. Editions Jean-Michel Garnier. Chartres. 1991
Matthews, Caitlin. Sophia Goddess of Wisdom, Harper Collins, London, 1991.

Chapter Two: Goddess of Sexuality

Reclaiming Goddess Sexuality
By Linda Savage

1. Morgan, Elaine. The Descent of Woman. NY: Stein and Day, 1972, p.73..
2. Masters, William and Virginia Johnson. Human Sexual Inadequacy. NY: Little Brown, 1970.
3. Eisler, Riane. The Chalice and the Blade. NY: Harper-Collins, 1988.

The Sexual Shadow of the World
By Azra and Seren Bertrand

1. "Transcript: Donald Trump's Taped Comments About Women." The New York Times. Oct. 8, 2016. Accessed October 1, 2017: https://www.nytimes.com/2016/10/08/us/donald-trump-tape-transcript.html
2. "Game of Thrones' star Jason Momoa joked about raping 'beautiful women' on show". The Guardian. October 13, 2017. Accessed October 13, 2017: https://www.theguardian.com/tv-and-radio/2017/oct/12/jason-momoa-game-of-thrones-raping-beautiful-women.
3. Schizophrenia, autism, and some other conditions are more strongly associated with epigenetic and environmental insults before and during gestation than childhood trauma.
4.Finkelhor, D. et al. "Sexual abuse in a national survey of adult men and women: Prevalence,characteristics, and risk factors." Child Abuse and Neglect: The International Journal. 14(1), p. 19-28. (1990). Also see Singh, M. M., et al. An Epidemiological Overview of Child Sexual Abuse. Journal of Family Medicine and Primary Care, 3(4), 430–435. (2014)
5. National Research Council. 2014. Estimating the Incidence of Rape and Sexual Assault. Washington, DC: The National Academies Press. https://doi.org/10.17226/18605.
6. Menon, Preethi et al. "Childhood Sexual Abuse in Adult Patients with Borderline Personality Disorder." Industrial Psychiatry Journal 25.1 (2016): 101–106. PMC. Web. 15 Oct. 2017.
7. ibid.
8. Chu, James A; Dill, Diana L. "Dissociative Symptoms in Relation to Childhood Physical and Sexual Abuse." The American Journal of Psychiatry; Washington147.7

(Jul 1990): 887-92
9. Mulhern, S. "Satanism, Ritual Abuse, and Multiple Personality Disorder: A Sociohistorical Perspective. International Journal of Clinical and Experimental Hypnosis. 42(4),1994.
10.Patihis, Lawrence. "Are the 'Memory Wars' Over? A Scientist-Practitioner Gap in Beliefs About Repressed Memory." Psychological Science. Vol 25, Issue 2, pp. 519 – 530.
11.Anderson, MC, et al. "Neural systems underlying the suppression of unwanted memories." Science. 2004 Jan 9;303(5655):232-5. See also, Trei, L. "Psychologists offer proof of brain's ability to suppress memories." Stanford Report. Jan 8 2004. Accessed October 1 2017: https://news.stanford.edu/news/2004/january14/memory-114.html
12. Cullen, K. "More than 80 percent of victims since 1950 were male, report says." Boston Globe. 2/28/2004.
13. Bertrand and Bertrand. Womb Awakening: Initiatory Wisdom of the Creatrix of All Life. Rochester, VT: Inner Traditions, 2017, 224-227.

Yeshe Tsogyal: Awesome Yogini and Tantric Consort in Ti betan Buddhism
By Vicki Noble

1. Tarthang Tulku. Mother of Knowledge: The Enlightenment of Ye-shes mTsho-rgyal. Dharma Publishing, 1983, xxiii.
2. Tarthang Tulku. Mother of Knowledge: The Enlightenment of Ye-shes mTsho-rgyal. Dharma Publishing, 1983, 33
3. Tarthang Tulku. Mother of Knowledge: The Enlightenment of Ye-shes mTsho-rgyal. Dharma Publishing, 1983, 19.
4. Tarthang Tulku. Mother of Knowledge: The Enlightenment of Ye-shes mTsho-rgyal. Dharma Publishing, 1983, 22
5. Tarthang Tulku. Mother of Knowledge: The Enlightenment of Ye-shes mTsho-rgyal. Dharma Publishing, 1983, 23
6. Tarthang Tulku. Mother of Knowledge: The Enlightenment of Ye-shes mTsho-rgyal. Dharma Publishing, 1983, 25
7. Tarthang Tulku. Mother of Knowledge: The Enlightenment of Ye-shes mTsho-rgyal. Dharma Publishing, 1983, 30-31.
8. Dowman, Keith. Sky Dancer: The Secret Life and Songs of the Lady Yeshe Tsogyel. London: Routledge & Kegan Paul, 1984, 71.
9. Dowman, Keith. Sky Dancer: The Secret Life and Songs of the Lady Yeshe Tsogyel. London: Routledge & Kegan Paul, 1984, 201.
10. Noble, Vicki. The Double Goddess: Women Sharing Power. Rochester, VT: Inner Traditions, 2003, 3.
11. Padmakara Translation Group. Lady of the Lotus-Born: The Life and Enlightenment of Yeshe Tsogyal. Boston: Shambhala, 1999, 75.
12. Grahn, Judy. Blood, Bread, and Roses: How Menstruation Created the World. Boston: Beacon Press, 1993.
13. Simmer-Brown, Judith. Dakini's Warm Breath: The Feminine Principle in Tibetan Buddhism. Shambhala, 2001, 249.
14. Dowman, Keith. Sky Dancer: The Secret Life and Songs of the Lady Yeshe Tsogyel. London: Routledge & Kegan Paul, 1984, 224.
15. White, David Gordon. The Alchemical Body: Siddha Traditions in Medieval India. Chicago: The University of Chicago Press, 1996,5
16. White, David Gordon. The Alchemical Body: Siddha Traditions in Medieval India. Chicago: The University of Chicago Press, 1996, 4.
17. Greer, Germaine. The Female Eunuch. Mcgraw-Hill, 1971.
18. English, Elizabeth. Vajrayogini: Her Visualizations, Rituals, and Forms. Boston, Wisdom Publications, 2002, 187.
19. English, Elizabeth. Vajrayogini: Her Visualizations, Rituals, and Forms. Boston, Wisdom Publications, 2002, 149.
20. Campbell, June. Traveler in Space: In Search of Female Identity in Tibetan Buddhism. NY: George Braziller, 1996, 64.
21. Bellezza, John Vincent. Divine Dyads: Ancient Civilization in Tibet. Dharamsala, India: Library of Tibetan Works and Archives, 1997.
22. Bellezza, John Vincent. Divine Dyads: Ancient Civilization in Tibet. Dharamsala, India: Library of Tibetan Works and Archives, 1997, 134
23. Bellezza, John Vincent. Divine Dyads: Ancient Civilization in Tibet. Dharamsala, India: Library of Tibetan Works and Archives, 1997, 30
24. Bellezza, John Vincent. Divine Dyads: Ancient Civilization in Tibet. Dharamsala, India: Library of Tibetan Works and Archives, 1997, 30
25. Goettner-Abendroth, Heide. Matriarchal Societies: Studies on Indigenous Cultures Across the Globe, Peter Lang Publishing, Inc., 2012, p. 91.
26. Goettner-Abendroth, ibid. p. 95
27. Goettner-Abendroth, ibid. p. 96
28. Hua, Cai. A Society Without Fathers or Husbands: The Na of China. Zone Books, 2001.
29. Goettner-Abendroth, ibid. p. 96
30. Barber, Elizabeth Wayland. The Mummies of ürümchi, W.W. Norton & Company, 1999, 115.
31. Mallory and Mair, op cit, 2000, p. 196.
32. Campbell, June. Op cit, p. 37.
33. Davis-Kimball, Jeannine (with Mona Behan). Warrior Women: An Archaeologist's Search for History's Hidden Heroines, Warner Books, Inc., 2002.
34. Noble, 2003, op cit, p. 132.

Chapter Three: The Goddess of Creativity

The Fantastic Muse of Carrie Ann Baade
By Victoria Christian and Carrie Anne Baade

1. Quote from Carries bio, website, www.carrieannbaade.com
2. Quote from Carries bio, sent via email, 3/15/13.
3. Quote taken from an interview by Spraygraphic with Carrie, Feb., 7 2010, on School of the Art Institute of Chicago's Alumi website: www.mysaic.edu
4. Quote from Carries bio, website, www.carrieannbaade.com
5. Quote from Carries bio, website, www.carrieannbaade.com
6. Quote taken from an interview with Nancy Hightower, The Fantastic in the Fine Arts: Carrie Ann Baade's Cute

and Creepy Exhibition, Oct. 2, 2011, on Fantasy Matters website: www.fantasy-matters.com
7. Quote taken from an interview with Carrie by Nathan Spoor, on Hi Fructose: New Contemporary Art Magazine, June 22 2009, www.hifructose.com
8. Quote taken from an interview with Carrie by Nathan Spoor, on Hi Fructose: New Contemporary Art Magazine, June 22 2009, www.hifructose.com
9. Quote taken from an interview with Carrie by Nathan Spoor, on Hi Fructose: New Contemporary Art Magazine, June 22 2009, www.hifructose.com
10. Quote from Carries website, www.carrieannbaade.com
11. Quote taken from an interview with Carrie, July 2012, www.xlegion.com
12. Quote from Carries website, www.carrieannbaade.com
13. Quote from Carries website, www.carrieannbaade.com
14. Quote from Carries website, www.carrieannbaade.com
15. Quote from Carries website, www.carrieannbaade.com
16. Quote from Carries website, www.carrieannbaade.com
17. Quote by Alejandro Jodorowsky, provided by Carrie via email
18. Quote taken from an interview with Carrie by Nathan Spoor, on Hi Fructose: New Contemporary Art Magazine, June 22 2009, www.hifructose.com
19. Quote taken from an interview with Carrie by Nathan Spoor, on Hi Fructose: New Contemporary Art Magazine, June 22 2009, www.hifructose.com

Chapter Four: Goddess of Emotion

Bodhissatva of Compassion: Awakening Heart with Art
By Victoria Christian

1. Chodron, Pema. "A Bodhichitta Practice," Shambala Sun, May 2004.
2. Heather Taylor. Personal quote from an email, August 2012.
3. Heather Taylor. Personal quote from an email, August 2012.
4. Heather Taylor. Quote from her website. www.fullcirclemandalas.com
5. Julie Weaver. Quote from her website. www.mandalaweaver.com
6. See Cornell, Judith. Mandala: Luminous Symbols for Healing
7. Julia Weaver, "Ocean Goddess and Healers of the Sea," written for Feminine Mysticism in Art, 2006.
8. Quote from Julie Weaver's artist statement, 2006: www.mandalaweaver.com
9. Quote from Julia Weaver image description for Ocean of Chi
10. Quote from Eva M Sullivan-Sakmar's website, www.stardolphin.com.
11. Quote from Eva M Sullivan-Sakmar's website, www.stardolphin.com
12. Baring, Anne and Harvey, Andrew. The Divine Feminine: Exploring the Feminine Face of God Throughout The World, Godsfield Press, UK and Conari Press, USA, 1996, 54.
13. Quote from Sue Halstenberg's website. www.suehalstenberg.com
14. Quote from Doreen Virtue's website: www.angeltherapy.com
15. Quote from Sue Halstenberg, Image Description, 2007.
16. Baring, Anne and Harvery, Andrew. The Divine Feminine: Exploring the Feminine Face of God Throughout The World, Godsfield Press, UK and Conari Press, USA, 1996, 62.
17. Quote from Sue Halstenberg, Image Description, 2007.
18. Artist statement about Melanie Gendron's work, 2007
19. Artist statement about Melanie Gendron's work, 2007
20. Quote from Leslie Gibbons website: www.everydaysacredliving.com
21. Quote from personal interview with Leslie, August, 2012.
22. Mueller, RoseAnna. Virgen of Guadalupe, www.blueroadrunner.com/virgen.htm
23. Mueller, RoseAnna. Virgen of Guadalupe, www.blueroadrunner.com/virgen.htm
24. Mueller, RoseAnna. Virgen of Guadalupe, www.blueroadrunner.com/virgen.htm

Chapter Five: Goddess of Wisdom

Saraswati's Secrets: Singing the Waters for Personal and Planetary Transformation
By Lotus Linton

Bibliography:

Altman, Nathaniel, Sacred Water: The Spiritual Source of Life, Mahwah, New Jersey: Hidden Spring, 2002.

Baartmans, Frans, APAH, The Sacred Waters: An Analysis of a Primordial Symbol in Hindu Myths, Delhi: B.R. Publishing Corporation, 1990.

Emoto, Masaru, Doctor of Alternative Medicine, Messages from Water, Vols. I and II, Tokyo: HADO Kyoikusha, 2001.

Emoto, Masaru, Doctor of Alternative Medicine, The True Power of Water, Hillsboro, Oregon: Beyond Worlds Publishing, 2003.

Goldman, Jonathan, Healing Sounds: The Power of Harmonics, Boston: Element, 1996.

Hope, Jane, The Secret Language of the Soul, San Francisco: Chronicle, 1997.

Kronberger, Hans and Siegbert Lattacher, On the Track of Water's Secret: From Viktor Schauberger to Johann Grander, Vienna: Uranus, 1995.

Marks, William E., The Holy Order of Water: Healing Earth's Waters and Ourselves, Great Baring ton, MA: Bell Pond Books, 2001.

Marks, William "Healing Waters: The Stream of Life Within Us," Science of Mind, April, 2002.

Chapter Six: Goddess of Transformation

Feminine Light in the Dark Night of the Soul
By Uma Rose

1. Marion Woodman. The Pregnant Virgin:A Process of Psychological Transformations, Inner City Books, 1985, 17
2. Jack, Kornfield. A Path With Heart: A Guide Through the

Perils and Promises of the Spiritual Life, Bantam Book, 1983, 19.
3. Carl Jung, Ibid, XI, pg. 131
4. Rebecca Vassy, "Wild Women Don't Get the Blues" or "My Adventures With Baba Yaga," Sage Woman Magazine, No. 51, Autumn 2000, pg.11
5. Marcia Starck and Gynne Stern, The Dark Goddess: Dancing With the Shadow, The Crossing Press, 1993, 30
6. Marcia Starck and Gynne Stern. The Dark Goddess: Dancing With the Shadow, The Crossing Press, 1993, 82
7. Jean Shinoda Bolen, M.D. Goddesses In Older Women: Archetypes In Women Over Fifty, HarperCollins, New York, NY, 2001, 91.
8. See Eckhart Tolle, A New Earth: Awakening to Your Life's Purpose, Penguin Group Ltd., New York, NY, 2005.

Chapter Seven

The Goddess of Interconnectivity
Her One-Song: The Goddess of Interconnectivity, Shamanism and Art
By Sandra Ingerman, Hank Wesselman PhD, Martin Ball PhD, and Victoria Christian.

1. Quote from Blaze Warrender's website: www.blazewarrender.com
2. Quote from Blaze Warrender, Image Description, Healing Gift.
3. Quote from Blaze Warrender, Image Description, In the Company of Bears.
4. Quote from Blaze Warrender, Image Description, Missing You SSB.
5. Quote from Susan Seddon-Boulet website: www.turningpointgallery.com
6. Quote from Peters Eglington, image description, earth goddess.
7. Carol, Schaeffer, Grandmothers Counsel The World: Women Elders Offer Their Vision for Our Planet, Trumpeter Books, Boston, MA., 2006, pg. 4
8. Quote from Peter Eglington, image description, The Soma Tree.
9. Quote from David Joaquin's website: www.twohawkstudio.com
10. Carol, Schaeffer, Grandmothers Counsel The World: Women Elders Offer Their Vision for Our Planet (Trumpeter Books, Boston, MA., 2006) pg. 123
11. Carol, Schaeffer, Grandmothers Counsel The World: Women Elders Offer Their Vision for Our Planet (Trumpeter Books, Boston, MA., 2006) pg. 4
12. Nicholas Black Elk with Joseph Epes Brown (editor), The Sacred Pipe: Black Elk's Account of the Seven Rites of the Oglala Sioux (Norman, OK: University of Oklahoma Press, 1953, 1989), 9.
13. Quote from Tessa Mytho's website:
14. Quote from Tessa Mythos artist biography on her website,
15. Quote taken from Tessa Mythos artist statement
16. Quote taken from image description, Universal Mother.
17. Quote taken from image description for Mni Wconi: Water is Life.
18. See RH Robbins, The Encyclopedia of Witchcraft and Demonology, Spring Books, 1967
19. Quote taken from image description, As Above So Below, Tessa Mythos.
20. Quote from website: www.crystalinks.com/alchemy.html
21. Quote from Krystle's website:
22. Quote from Krystle's image description for Alchemy
23. Quote from Krystle's image description for The Arc of Grace .
24. Quote from Krystle's website:
25. from Mariela's website, image description: www.marieladelapaz.com
26. Quote from Mariela's website: www.marieladelapaz.com
27. Quote from Mariela's website, image description: www.marieladelapaz.com
28. Quote from Mariela's website, image description: www.marieladelapaz.com
29. Quote from Mariela's website, image description for New Moon Maiden.
30. Barbara Tedlock, The Woman in the Shaman's Body: Reclaiming the Feminine in Religion and Medicine, Bantom Books, New York, NY., 2005, pg. 173
31. Quote taken from Timothy White's Artist Statement
32. Quote taken from Timothy White's Bio
33. Quote taken from Timothy White's Bio
34. Quote taken from Timothy White's Bio
35. Quote taken from Timothy White's Bio
36. Sandra Ingerman and Hank Wesselman, Awakening To The Spirit World: The Shamanic Path of Direct Revelation, Sounds True, Inc., Colorado, 2010, 112.
37. Image description for Nuestra Senora de las Aguas, by Timothy White
38. Image description for Frida Kahlo's Resurrection, by Timothy White
39. Quote taken from Morgan Mandala's artist statement.
40. Quote taken from Morgan Mandalas website,
41. Quote taken from Morgan's artistic statement.
42. Quote taken from image description for Trinity.
43-54, Quotes taken from artist statement and personal interview with Martina Hoffman by Martin Ball, fall 2009.
55-58, Personal Interview with Robert Venosa by Martin Ball, 6/2011.
59. Luis Eduardo Luna and Pablo Amazing. Ayahuasca Visions: The Religious Iconography of a Peruvian Shaman, North Atlantic Books, Berkely, California, 9.
60. Luis Eduardo Luna and Pablo Amazing. Ayahuasca Visions: The Religious Iconography of a Peruvian Shaman, North Atlantic Books, Berkely, California, 9.
61. Luis Eduardo Luna and Pablo Amazing. Ayahuasca Visions: The Religious Iconography of a Peruvian Shaman, North Atlantic Books, Berkely, California, 9.
62. Quote from Mauro's website:
63. Quote from Juan Perez, artist statement.

Recommended Readings:

Sandra Ingerman and Hank Wesselman, Awakening To The Spirit World: The Shamanic Path of Direct Revelation, Sounds True, Inc., Colorado, 2010.
Martin W. Ball, Ph.D., Being Human: An Entheological Guide

to God, Evolution, and the Fractal Energetic Nature of Reality

Martin W. Ball, Ph.D., The Entheogenic Evolution: Psychedelics, Consciousness, and Awakening the Human Spirit

Rick Strassman, M.D., et al, Inner Paths to Outer Space: Journeys to Alien Worlds through Psychedelics and Other Spiritual Technologies

Thomas B. Roberts, editor, Psychoactive Sacramentals: Essays on Entheogens and Religion

Terence McKenna, Food of the Gods: The Search for the Original Tree of Knowledge – a Radical History of Plants, Drugs, and Human Evolution

Ralph Metzner, editor, Sacred Mushrooms of Visions: Teonanacatl

Jeremy Narby, The Cosmic Serpent: DNA and the Origins of Knowledge

Caludia Muller-Ebeling, et al, Shamanism and Tantra in the Himalayas

In Search of a New World View: Envisioning the Golden Era
By Victoria Christian and Gary Stamper

1. Mullaly, Bob. (2007). The New Structural Social Work. Oxford University Press, Ontario, Canada.
2. Pinchbeck, Daniel. (2006). 2012: The Return of Quetzalcoatl, Jeremy Tarcher/Penguin, New York., 56.
3. Barbara Lipman, Jeffrey Lubell, Emily Salomon. (2012). Housing an Aging Population: Are We Prepared? Center For Housing Policy, Washington, DC. Retrieved from: http://www.nhc.org/publications/index.html
4. See Buckminister Fuller Institute: www.bfi.org
5. Mullaly, Bob. (2007). The New Structural Social Work. Oxford University Press, Ontario, Canada, 153.
6. See Neale Donal Walsche, Conversations With God Series, quote used from website. http://www.nealedonaldwalsch.com/
7. McMahon, Kathy. (2007). Quotes from her blog on her website: http://www.peakoilblues.org/blog/?p=132
8. Joanna Macy, "Working With Environmental Despair," in Theodore Rosak, Mary E. Gomes and Allen D. Kanner (eds.), Ecopsychology: Restoring the Earth, Healing the Mind, Sierra Club Books, San Francisco, 1995, 243.
9. Joanna Macy, "Working With Environmental Despair," in Theodore Rosak, Mary E. Gomes and Allen D. Kanner (eds.), Ecopsychology: Restoring the Earth, Healing the Mind, Sierra Club Books, San Francisco, 1995, 243.
10. Quote from Andrew Harvey's website, The Institute for Sacred Activism: www.andrewharvey.net
11. Harvey, Andrew. The Hope: A Guide to Sacred Activism, Hay House, Inc. Carlsbad, California, 108.
12. Eisenstein, Charles. Sacred Economics: Money, Gift and Society in the Age of Transition. Evolver Editions, Berkeley, California, pg ?
13. Excerpt from Gary Stamper. (2012). Awakening the New Masculine: The Path of the Integral Warrior, IUniverse, Indiana, 1-12.
14. For more information, see the Mankind project website: www.mankindproject.org
15. Excerpt from Gary Stamper. (2012). Awakening the New Masculine: The Path of the Integral Warrior, IUniverse, Indiana, 1-12.
16. Quote from Daniel Holeman's Bio: www.awakenvisions.com
17. Quote from Daniel Holeman's Bio: www.awakenvisions.com
18. Excerpt from the Law Of Time website: www.lawoftime.org
19. Quote from Stephanie South. 2012: Biography of a Time Traveler, 2009. Foundation for the Law of Time, Ashland, Oregon.
20. Arguelles, Jose. 2011. The Manifesto for the Noosphere: The Next Stage in the Evolution of Human Consciousness. Evolver Editions, Berkeley, California, 156.
21. Excerpt from Amoraea Dreamseed's new book: The Univeral Human. For more information, see his website at: www.divine-blueprint.com.
22. Quote taken from Aaron Pyne's website: www.SacredVisionDesigns.com
23. Quote taken from Aaron Pyne's website: www.SacredVisionDesigns.com
24. Quote taken from Aaron Pyne's website: www.SacredVisionDesigns.com
25. Image description taken from Aaron Pyne's website: www.SacredVisionDesigns.com
26. Image description taken from Aaron Pyne's website: www.SacredVisionDesigns.com
27. Quote taken from Robert Donaghey's Bio: www.artisticgenius.com
28. Quote taken from Robert Donaghey's Bio: www.artisticgenius.com
29. Quote taken from a personal email, 2013.
30. Poem by Rumi, taken from Robert Donaghey's website.
31. Image description provided by Robert Donaghey: www.artisticgenius.com
32. Image description of Milky Way , robert Donaghey.
33. Davin Infinity, excerpt from Awakening the Leader: A Hero's Journey in the Age of Innovation, self published, 2012.
34. Excerpt from Mission Statement, Evolutionary Leaders, www.evolutionaryleaders.net.
35. George Atherton Bio Statement, taken from website: www.geoglyphix.com
36. Image descriptions for Pollenectar and Lotus Dome Culture, George Atherton, www.geoglyphiks.com
37. Anne Baring and Jules Cashford. The Myth of the Goddess: Evolution of an Image, Penguin: Reprint edition, 1993, 56.
38. See Eco Built Systems website: www.ecobuiltsystems.com
39. Quote from George Atherton, taken from his website: www.geoglyphiks.com
40. Quote from George Atherton, taken from his website: www.geoglyphiks.cm
41. See the Slow Food Movement website at: www.slowfood.com
42. Quote from Paul Nicholson's bio on his website:

www.paulnicholson.com
43. Image description from Paul Nicholson, 2012.
44. Amazon rainforest facts quoted from rain-tree.com for more information
45. Quote taken from Kelly Hostetler's website: www.spiritdanceart.com
46. Quote taken from Kelly's Blog: www.spiritdanceart.com
47. Quote from Raul Casillas Bio: www.raulcasillas.com
48. Quote from Raul Casilla's website: www.raulcasillas.com
49. Personal quote from Raul by email, 2012.
50. Carol, Schaeffer. Grandmothers Counsel The World: Women Elders Offer Their Vision for Our Planet, Trumpeter Books, Boston, MA., 2006, pg. 4
51. Image description provided by Raul in an email, 2012.
52. Quote taken from website: www.mysterium.com
53. Carol, Schaeffer. Grandmothers Counsel The World: Women Elders Offer Their Vision for Our Planet, Trumpeter Books, Boston, MA., 2006, 170.
54. Personal Artist Statement by Raul Casillas, website: www.raulcasillas.com
55. Carol, Schaeffer. Grandmothers Counsel The World: Women Elders Offer Their Vision for Our Planet, Trumpeter Books, Boston, MA., 2006, 172.
56. Quote from Chris Dyer website: www.positivecreations.com
57. Quote from Chris Dyer, image description for Optimystic.
58. Quote from Chris Dyer, image description, Ultimate Spiritual Warrior

IMAGE REFERENCES

Part One: The Primordial Sacred Union

The Loss of the World Soul and Its Return
by Anne Baring

1. World Soul, Robin Baring, 24"x24" oil on canvas, www.annebaring.com
2. Isis, Jonathan Weber, 24'"x30" oil on canvas, www.jonathanweber.org
3. Egyptian Enigma, Andrew Annenberg, 60"x60" oil on canvas, www.andrewannenberg.com
4. The Enchantment, Andrew Annenberg, 60" x 60 ", oil on canvas, www.andrewannenberg.com
5. The Slaying of the Dragon, Victoria Christian, 3' x 4' diptych oil on canvas, www.victoriachristian.com
6. Land of the Free, Home of the Brave, Mark Henson, 48"x64" oil on canvas, www.markhensonart.com
7. The Lovers, Mariela de la Paz, 5'x5' oil on canvas, www.marieladelapaz.com

Artists Envisioning the Primordial Sacred Union
by Victoria Christian

1. Maha Shri Yantra, Paul Heussenstamm, 24"x24" oil on canvas, www.mandalas.com
2. Emperor and Empress, Jonathan Weber, 24"x36" oil on canvas, www.jonathanweber.org
3. Double Helix, Mark Henson, 38"x52", oil on canvas, www.markhensonart.com
4. Synergenesis, Amoraea Dreamseed, 24"x 36" acrylic on canvas, www.divine-blueprint.com
5. The Gathering, Abba Yahudah, 24'"x 36" acrylic on canvas, www.abbayahudah.com
6. Mother Earth Father Sky, Atmara Rebecca Cloe, 24"x30" digital media, www.nwcreations.com
7. God Giving Birth, Monica Sjoo, 3'x5' Charcoal on paper, www.monicasjoo.weebly.com
8. Tunnel of Love, Mark Henson, 36" x 46", oil on canvas, www.markhensonart.com
9. Wonders of Nature, Mark Henson, 36" x 66", oil on canvas, www.markhensonart.com
10. Dance of Veils, Paul Nicholson, 30" x 40", oil on canvas, www.fineartamerica.com/profiles/paul-nicholson
11. Madonna, Beth Avary, 24" x 36" acrylic on canvas
12. Female Crucifixion, Martina Hoffmann, 24"x30" oil on canvas, www.martinahoffman.com
13. Homage to Women's Suffering, Victoria Christian, 24" x 24" oil on wood, www.victoriachristian.com
14. The Living Cross: A Crossroad to Transformation, Heather Taylor, 24"x36" oil on canvas, www.fullcirclemandalas.com
15. Sharing the Wealth, Mark Henson, 66"x48" oil on canvas, 2000, www.markhensonart.com
16. The March of Progress, Mark Henson, 38"x56" oil on canvas, 1995, www.markhensonart.com
17. The Iron Cage of Rationality, Victoria Christian, 24"x30" oil on canvas, www.victoriachristian.com

18. Alert...She is Waking Up, Victoria Christian, 24"X30" oil on canvas, www.victoriachristian.com
19. Creativity Under Siege, Victoria Christian, 24"x30" oil on canvas, 2004, www.victoriachristian.com

Imaging the Divine Compliments
by Margaret L. Starbird

1. God/Goddess, Claudia Connelly, 52"x13" oil on linen. www.claudiaconnelly.com
2. Mary Magdalene, Jonathan Weber, 22"x32" acrylic on canvas, 2006, www.jonathanweber.org
3. Mary of Magdala, Andrew Annenberg, www.andrewannenberg.com
4. Jesus and Mary as One, Paul Heussenstamm, oil on canvas, 2007, www.mandalas.com
5. Antahkarana, Amoraea Dreamseed, 24 x 36 acrylic on canvas, 2006 www.divine-blueprint.com

Part Two: Rebirth of the Goddess

Chapter One: Goddess of Creation

Envisioning the Divine in Nature
by Victoria Christian

1. Tree of Life, Victoria Christian, 2'x3'oil on canvas, www.victoriachristian.com
2. Creatrix, Suzanne De Veuve, 18" x 24", Oil on Canvas, www.suzannedeveuve.com
3. Ravine Rapture, Mark Henson, 86" x 48" Oil on canvas, www.markhensonart.com
4. Tree Incarnation, Mark Henson, 48" x 60", Oil on canvas, www.markhensonart.com
5. The Immortal Light, Jeffrey Bedrick, 30x40, Oil on Canvas, jeffreybedrick.com
6. Meadow Magic, Jeffrey Bedrick, 30x40, Oil on Canvas, jeffreybedrick.com
7. Guardians of the Grail, Andrew Annenberg, www.andrewannenberg.com
8. Laguna Autumn, Andrew Annenberg, www.andrewannenberg.com
9. Venus Triumphant, Andrew Annenberg, www.andrewannenberg.com
10. Women's Movement Mandala, Paul Heussenstamm, www.mandalas.com
11. Kali Mandala, Paul Heussenstamm, www.mandalas.com
12. Oceans of Change Mandala, Paul Heussenstamm, www.mandalas.com
13. Buddha Wisdom Tree, Paul Heussenstamm, www.mandalas.com
14. Twilight Dancer, Paul Heussenstamm, www.mandalas.com
15. Towards the Within, Victoria Christian, 2.5 x 3.5, Oil on Wood, Gems, 2004 www.victoriachristian.com
16. Grace, Victoria Christian, 2' x 2', Oil on Wood, Gems, 2004 www.victoriachristian.com
17. The Sunflower Goddess, Victoria Christian, 2' x 5', Acrylic on Canvas, 2002. www.victoriachristian.com
18. Forest Cathedral, Francene Hart, 18"x24", Watercolor on paper, www.francenehart.com
19. Above and Below, Francene Hart, 18"x24", watercolor on paper, www.francenehart.com
20. Ceremony of Spring, Theresa Sharrar, 24"x30", acrylic on canvas, www.lunariagallery.com/lunaria-artists/sharrar-theresa
21. Guardian of the Seeds or Demeter, Theresa Sharrar, 24"x30", oil on canvas, 1996, www.lunariagallery.com/lunaria-artists/sharrar-theresa
22. By the River, Beth Avary, 30"x40", Acrylic on canvas, 2004
23. Silent Chapel, Beth Avary, 30"x40", Acrylic on canvas, 2004
24. The Maiden Tree, Atmara Rebecca Cloe, 16"x20" digital image, 2006 www.nwcreations.com
25. Rebirth, Cynthia Ré Robbins, www.art4spirit.com
26. Shoot Star Faeries, Cynthia Ré Robbins, www.art4spirit.com
27. Pixies of Nickel Creek, Jim Thompson, 33.5X23 Digital Image, www.art-mind-soul.com

Artists Reclaim the Body of Earth and Mother
By Victoria Christian

1. Mother Nature, Andrew Annenberg, 20"x24", oil on canvas, www.andrewannenberg.com
2. Coatlique or Lady of the Serpent Skirt, Hrana Janto, 2x2 acrylic on canvas, 1996. www.hranajanto.com
3. Lady of the Beasts, Hrana Janto, 2x2 ft acrylic on canvas, 1994. www.hranajanto.com
4. Bear Mama, Suzanne DeVeuve, 20" x 24", oil on canvas, 1996.www.suzannedeveuve.com
5. Goddess Rising, Suzanne DeVeuve, www.suzannedeveuve.com
6. Salmon Goddess, Suzanne DeVeuve, www.suzannedeveuve.com
7. The Goddess Triangle, Martina Hoffman, 20'x10' multimedia installation piece, 1988-1995.

8. Raising of Women, Jane Evershed, 30"x40", acrylic
9. Who Let the Girls Out, Jane Evershed, 30"x40", acrylic
10. The Fall of Patriarchy, Jane Evershed, 60" x48", acrylic
11. American Beauty, Emma Gardner, 16'x20' acrylic on canvas, 2004.www.emmagardner.com
12. Senorita, Emma Gardner 2'x6', acrylic on wood, 2006. www.emmagardner.com
13. Show Girl, Emma Gardner, 2'x6', acrylic on wood, 2006 www.emmagardner.com
14. The Great Mother Returns, Emily Kell, www.emilykell.com
15. Return of the Primordial Goddess, Emily Kell, www.emilykell.com
16. Rebirth of Mother Earth, Emily Kell, www.emilykell.com
17. Bloom, Ashely Foreman, www.thirteentwentystudios.com
18. Fertility, Ashely Foreman, www.thirteentwentystudios.com
19. The Vital Commission, Autumn Skye Morrison, 36"x36", acrylic, 2008, www.autumnskyeart.com
20. Work in Progress, Autumn Skye Morrison, 24"x48", acrylic, 2006, www.autumnskyeart.com
21. Divine Intervention, Autumn Skye Morrison, www.autumnskyeart.com
22. Body Temple, Autumn Skye Morrison, www.autumnskyeart.com

23. Sleeping Earth, Krista Lynn Brown, 16"x20" acrylic on canvas, www.devaluna.com
24. Mother Power, Krista Lynn Brown, 18"x24" acrylic on canvas, www.devaluna.com
25. Illumination—Between the Lines, Krista Lynn Brown, 30"x40" acrylic on canvas, www.devaluna.com
26. Prayer, Cathy McClelland, 14"x20" acrylic on canvas, www.cathymcclelland.com
27. Justice, Cathy McClelland, 11"x17" acrylic on canvas, www.cathymcclelland.com
28. Earth Blessing, Heather Taylor, www.fullcirclemandalas.com

Contemporary Images of Spirituality and Resistance Among African Americans
By Arisika Razak

1. The Oracle, Return of the Sun Goddess, Victoria Christian, 24"x24", oil on wood, www.victoriachristian.com
2. Dunham's Life Story, Afra-She Asungi, 16"x20' acrylic on canvas, 1986. www.sistahpeace.com
3. Ochumare, Afra-She Asungi, 16"x20" acrylic on canvaas, 1986. www.sistahpeace.com
4. The Sale of Venus, Lili Bernard, 96"x72", Oil on Canvas, 2011, www.lilibernard.com
5. Le Virgen de Regla—Yemaya arrives in Cuba, Lili Bernard, 36"x36", Oil on Canvas, 2007, www.lilibernard.com
6. Miel De Abeja, Yasmin Hernandez, 24"x30", Acrylic on Canvas, 2003. www.yasminhernandez.com
7. Abuelita, Yasmin Hernandez, 30"x48" Oil on canvas, 1997. www.yasminhernandez.com
8. Todas Mujerous, Yasmin Hernandez, 36" x24", Mixed Media on canvas, 2004. www.yasminhernandez.com
9. First Supper, Abba Yahudah, 57"x43", Oil on canvas, 1999. www.abbayahudah.com
10. Revelation 12, Abba Yahudah, 57"x43", oil on canvas, 2002. www.abbayahudah.com

Goddess Icons of the Dark Mother Around the Globe
1. Hecate, Lydia Ruyle, Painted sewn collaged nylon fabric banner, 34" x 72"
2. Black Madonna of the Andes, Lydia Ruyle, Painted sewn collaged nylon fabric banner, 30" x 70"
3. Black Madonna of Czestochowa, Lydia Ruyle, Painted sewn collaged nylon fabric banner, 36" x 72"
4. Nuestra Senora Montserrat, Lydia Ruyle, Painted sewn collaged nylon fabric banner, 28" x 72"
5. Nuestra Senora La Virgen Guadalupe, Lydia Ruyle, Painted sewn collaged nylon fabric banner, 34" x 76"
6. Queen of Sheba, Lydia Ruyle, Painted sewn collaged nylon fabric banner, 36" x 72"
7. Crow Mother, Lydia Ruyle, Painted sewn collaged nylon fabric banner, 24" x 72"
8. Rangda, Lydia Ruyle, Painted sewn collaged nylon fabric banner, 34" x 76"
9. Maori Black Madonna, Lydia Ruyle, Painted sewn collaged nylon fabric banner, 28" x 72"

Chapter Two: Goddess of Sexuality

Reclaiming Goddess Sexuality
By Linda E. Savage, Ph.D.

1. Yoni Rose, Penny Slinger, www.pennyslinger.com
2. Nubial Bliss, Mark Henson, www.markhensonart.com
3. Yab Yum Yantra George Atherton, digital image, www.geoglyphiks.com
4. Holy Union, Heather Taylor, www.fullcirclemandalas.com
5. Wisdom of the Ages, Autumn Skye Morrison, www.autumnskyeart.com
6. Sweet Honey Wine, Heather Taylor, www.fullcirclemandalas.com

The Sexual Shadow of The World
By Azra Bertrand M.D. and Seren Bertrand

1. Lillith, Jonathan Weber, www.jonathanweber.org
2. The Rose Lineage, Chanel Baran and Shona (model), www.chanelbaran.com
3. Sophia's Return, Book Cover, Seren Bertrand, www.thefountainoflife.org/sophias-return-healing-grail-wound/

Yeshe Tsogyal: Awesome Yogini and Tantric Consort in Tibetan Buddhism
By Vicki Noble

1. Photo of a painting of Yeshe Tsogyal at the Samye Monastery in Tibet, Vicki Noble, 2007
2. Yin Yang Ecstacy, Paul Heussenstamm, www.mandalas.com
3. Photo of a painting of Yeshe Tsogyal, Samye Monastery, 2007
4. Photo of Chimphu Valley in Tibet, Vicki Noble, 2007.
5. Photo of a painting of Vajrayogini, Samye Monastery, Vicki Noble, 2007
6. Menstruation Sculpture, photo by Vicki Noble, 2007.
7. Photo of a firepit in Katmandu, Nepal. The firepit belongs to the pre-Buddhist Grandmother Goddess, Agima, Vicki Noble, 2007
8. Two Buddhist Nuns at Chimphu, where they lived like hermits in a cave-like "nun's hut," Vicki Noble, 2007.

The 64 Dakini Oracle
by Penny Slinger

1. Vajra Yogini, Penny Slinger, Digital collage, 9450 x 6300 pixels, www.64dakinioracle.org
2. Yogini Temple at Ranipur-Jharial, Orissa, India
3. Yogini, Dakini Oracle, Penny Slinger, www.64dakinioracle.org
4. Tribali, Penny Slinger, Digital collage,12600 x 8400 pixels, www.64dakinioracle.org
5. Consult the 64 Dakini Oracle at www.64dakinioracle.org
6. Enflami, Penny Slinger, Digital collage,12000 x 8000 pixels, www.64dakinioracle.org
7. Quetzakundalini, Penny Slinger, Digital collage, 10800 x 7200 pixels, www.64dakinioracle.org

Chapter Three: Goddess of Creativity

Creativity, Myth and Mysticism: Something Calls to be Remembered
By Claudia Connelly

1. Far Memory, Claudia Connelly, www.claudiaconnelly.com
2. Sacred Promise, Claudia Connelly, www.claudiaconnelly.com
2. The Gift, Claudia Connelly, www.claudiaconnelly.com
3. Sacred Moment, Claudia Connelly, www.claudiaconnelly.com
4. God/Goddess, Claudia Connelly, www.claudiaconnelly.com

A Feminine Path in Art and Life
By Deborah Koff-Chapin

1. Intuition, Deborah Koff-Chapin, www.touchdrawing.com
2. Willow Drawing in Sand, photograph, 1972, www.touchdrawing.com
3. The Uglies, watercolor on paper, 1975. www.touchdrawing.com
4. Sample of Soul Cards, Deborah Koff-Chapin, www.touchdrawing.com
5. Sample of Soul Cards, Deborah Koff-Chapin, www.touchdrawing.com

The Fantastic Muse of Carrie Ann Baade
By Victoria Christian and Carrie Anne Baade

1. Dali, Carrie Ann Baade, 10"x10" oil on panel, 2005, www.carrieannbaade.com
2. The Insomniac, Carrie Ann Baade, 14"x14" oil on panel, 2005, www.carrieannbaade.com
3. The Temptation of the Penitent Medusa, Carrie Ann Baade, 12" x 18" oil on panel, 2010, www.carrieannbaade.com
4. Our Lady of Sorrow, Carrie Ann Baade, 12"x9" oil on copper, 2005, www.carrieannbaade.com
5. The Supposedly Shared Sorrow of Magdalene, 9"x12" oil on panel, 2009, www.carrieannbaade.com
6. The Perilous Compassion Of The Honey Queen, Carrie Ann Baade, 18"x24" oil on panel, 2009, www.carrieannbaade.com
7. The Teaching of Lilith, Carrie Ann Baade, 18"x12" oil on copper, www.carrieannbaade.com
8. The Butterfly Lovers, Carrie Ann Baade, 18"x24" oil on panel, 2012, www.carrieannbaade.com

Chapter Four: Goddess of Emotion

Bodhisattvas of Compassion: Awakening Heart With Art
By Victoria Christian

1. Aphrodite, Jonathan Weber, 24"x36", Oil on Canvas, www.jonathanweber.org
2. Winged Heart, Robby Donaghey, Digital image, www.artisticgenius.com
3. Green Tara Healing, Heather Taylor, 24"x36" acrylic on canvas, www.fullcirclemandalas.com
4. Robed Mother, Heather Taylor, 24"x24" acrylic on canvas, www.fullcirclemandalas.com
5. Limitless Ocean of Chi, Julia Weaver, 18x18 pencil on black paper. www.mandalaweaver.com
6. Healing, 8x8 pencil on black paper, www.mandalaweaver.com
7. Nurturing, Julia Weaver, 8x8 pencil on black paper, www.mandalaweaver.com
8. Mermaid Dakini, 8x8 pencil on black paper, www.mandalaweaver.com
9. Sanctuary 8x8 pencil on black paper, www.mandalaweaver.com
10. Earth Balance Planetary Healing, Eva Sakmar,-Sullivan, 24"x36" acrylic on canvas, www.stardolphin.com
11. From The Heart of God, Eva Sakmar,-Sullivan 24"x30" acrylic on canvas, www.stardolphin.com
12. Pink Lotus Heart, Sue Halstenberg, 7"x22" pastel on paper, www.sue-halstenberg.pixels.com
13. Durga, Sue Halstenberg, 24"x24" pastel on paper, www.sue-halstenberg.pixels.com
14. Gaia Blessing, Melanie Gendron, www.melaniegendron.com
15. Butterfly Woman, Melanie Gendron, 3'x6' oil on wood panel, www.melaniegendron.com
16. Virgen of Guadalupe, Leslie Gibbons, 12"x18" Mosaic on wood, www.sacredcreativity.com
17. Green Mother Mary, Leslie Gibbons, 12"x18" Mosaic Triptych, www.sacredcreativity.com
18. Dark Night of the Madonna, Turiya Bruce, 91" x 107" oil on canvas. www.turiyabruce.com

Heart Of The Mother
By Grace Mantle

1. Let There be Peace in Our Hearts, Grace Mantle, 3'x 6' acrylic on wood panel, 2004, www.gracemantlestudios.com
2. Ma Mary, Grace Mantle, 3' x 5' acrylic on wood panel, 2005, www.gracemantlestudios.com
3. Makuahine o' ka La'a Aina/ Mother Maui, Grace Mantle, 3'x4' acrylic on wood, www.gracemantlestudios.com

Tara: The Savioress
By Sherab Khandro

1. Chenrezig, Buddha of Compassion, 44"x44", acrylic on canvas. www.sherabkhandro.com
2. Mother Tara: Angel of Peace, Sherab Khandro, 3'x 7' acrylic on canvas. www.sherabkhandro.com
3. Vajravarahi: Dance of the Red Dakini, Sherab Khandro, 3' x 6' acrylic on canvas. www.sherabkhandro.com
4. Red Tara: Tara of the Bodhichitta, Sherab Khandro, 28"x34", acrylic on canvas. www.sherabkhandro.com
5. Green Tara, Sue Halstenberg, www.sue-halstenberg.pixels.com

Chapter Five: Goddess of Wisdom

The Sacred Feminine and Global Transformation
By Llewellyn Vaughn Lee

1. Gaia, Suzanne De Veuve, 20x24, Acrylic on canvas, www.suzannedeveuve.com
2. Safe In Her Arms, Atmara Rebecca Cloe, 12"x12" digital image, www.nwcreations.com
3. Meditation, Cathy McClelland, www.cathymcclelland.com
4. Flower of Life, Daniel Holeman, 16'x20" digital image, www.awakenvisions.com
5. Tree of Light, Daniel Holeman, 16"x20" digital image, www.awakenvisions.com

Dreaming and the Longing For Feminine Wisdom
By Anne Scott

1. Dream Messenger, Cathy McClelland, Acrylic on illustration board, 24"x30", www.cathymcclelland.com
2. Grandmother, Cher Lyn, 39"x63"x2" Acrylic, blue corn, sage and tobacco on canvas. www.mysticartmedicine.com
3. Foxcrow, Lindy Kehoe, www.lindykehoe.com
4. Dream Guardian, Lindy Kehoe, www.lindykehoe.com

Saraswati's Secrets: Healing the Waters for Personal and Planetary Transformation
by Lotus Linton, Ph.D.

1. Saraswati, Hrana Janto, 24"x24" acrylic on canvas, www.hranajanto.com
2. Saraswati, Paul Heussenstamm, 24"x32" acrylic on canvas. www.mandalas.com
3. Water Goddess, Atmara Rebecca Cloe, 16"x20" digital image, www.nwcreations.com
4. Saraswati, Sue Halstenberg, 24"x48" acrylic on canvas, www.sue-halstenberg.pixels.com
5. Magnetic Springs Spirits.Cynthia Ré Robbins. Oil and Tempera on Panel 16" x 20". www.art4spirit.com
6. Grotto Guardians, Cynthia Ré Robbins, Oil and Egg Tempera, 12" x 16", www.art4spirit.com
7. Summoning the Spirit, Cynthia Ré Robbins, Oil and Egg Tempera, 16 x 20 www.art4spirit.com
8. Reflection, Mark Henson, 4'x6' oil on Canvas, www.markhensonart.com
9. Gateway of the Higher Heart, Tessa Mythos, www.artbymythos.com

Awakening Womb Wisdom
By Seren Bertrand and Azra Bertrand, M.D.

1. Womb Illumination, Chanal Baran and Shona(model), www.chanelbaran.com
2. The Rose Lineage, Chanel Baran, www.chanelbaran.com
3. Sophia's Return, Book Cover, Seren Bertrand, www.thefountainoflife.org/sophias-return-healing-grail-wound/

Chapter Six: Goddess of Transformation

Psyche: Goddess of Personal Transformation
By Jacquelyn Small

1. Psyche, Hrana Janto, 16"x20" acrylic on canvas, www.hranajanto.com
2. The Alchemist, Emily Kell, www.emilykell.com
3. Sanctuary, Ashley Foreman, www.thirteentwentystudios.com

Feminine Light in the Dark Night of the Soul
By Uma Rose

1. Dark Night, Uma Rose, 18"x24" acrylic on canvas.
2. Mama Yaga, Uma Rose, 24" x30" acrylic on canvas.
2. Kali-Ma, Uma Rose, 24"x 24"Acrylic on wood panel.
3. The Awakener, Uma Rose, 24"x36" acrylic on canvas.
4. Silencing of Mother's Heart, Uma Rose, 16"x20" acrylic on canvas.
5. Calm After the Storm, Uma Rose, 24"x30", acrylic on canvas
6. In the Golden Warmth of Darkness, Rose Sharrar

Reclaiming Initiation: The Priestess Path
by Anyaa T. McAndrew

1. Grandmother Moon, Suzanne DeVeuve, 20"x24" oil on canvas, www.suzannedeveuve.com
2. Pathways, Cynthia Ré Robbins, 13"x19" oil and tempera on Panel, www.art4spirit.com
3. The Healing, Cynthia Ré Robbins, 18"x24" oil and Plaka, www.art4spirit.com
4. The Beloveds, Krista Lynn Brown, 18"x24" acrylic on canvas, www.devaluna.com
5. Priestess Graduation, Ashely Foreman, www.thirteentwentystudios.com
6. Shakti, Suzanne DeVeuve, 24"x30" oil on canvas, www.suzannedeveuve.com

Chapter Seven: Goddess of Interconnectivity

The Healing Power of Art
By Cher Lyn

1. Mother Pearl, Cher Lyn,
2. Breakthrough, Cher Lyn, 24" x 30" Acrylic on Canvas, www.mysticartmedicine.com
3. Blue Oracle Woman, Cher Lyn, 30" x40" Acrylic on Canvas, www.mysticartmedicine.com
4. Creations Child, Cher Lyn, Acrylic/Mixed Media on Canvas, 50" x 50", 2001-2011, www.mysticartmedicine.com
5. RainbowActivator, Cher Lyn, 30" x 40" Acrylic/Mixed Media on Canvas, www.mysticartmedicine.com

Her One Song: Goddess of Interconnectivity, Shamanism and Art
By Daniel Mirante, Sandra Ingerman, Hank Wesselman Phd, Martin Ball PhD and Victoria Christian

1. Totem to Earth, Suzanne De Veuve, 20"x30" oil on canvas, www.suzannedeveuve.com.
2. Beings Tree, Suzanne De Veuve, 24" x 36" oil on canvas, www.suzannedeveuve.com
3. The Healing Gift, Blaze Warrender, 40" x 28" acrylic and mixed media, www.blazewarrender.com
4. In the Company of Bears, Blaze Warrender, 40" x 28" acrylic and mixed media, www.blazewarrender.com
5. Missing You SSB, Blaze Warrender, 40" x 28" acrylic and

mixed media, www.blazewarrender.com

6. Earth Goddess, Peter Eglington, 81" x 94" color pencil on canvas, www.petereglingtonart.com
7. Soma Tree, Peter Eglington, www.petereglingtonart.com
8. Holy Mother and Child, Peter Eglington, www.petereglingtonart.com
9. The Usko-Ayar Visionaries, Peter Eglington, www.petereglingtonart.com
10. Corn Mother, David Joaquin, www.theartofdavidjoaquin.com
11. Photographs by Marisol Villanueva, courtesy of the International Council of 13 Indigenous Grandmothers
12. White Buffalo Woman, David Joaquin, 24" x 36" oil on wood, www.theartofdavidjoaquin.com
13. Spirit Canoe, David Joaquin, 2' x 5' oil on wood, www.theartofdavidjoaquin.com
14. The Universal Mother, Tessa Mythos, www.artbymythos.com
15. Mni Wconi, Tessa Mythos, www.artbymythos.com
16. As Above So Below, Tessa Mythos, www.artbymythos.com
17. Alchemy, Krystleyez, www.krystleyez.com
18. The Arc of Grace , Krystleyez, www.krystleyez.com
19. La Machi, Mariela de la Paz, 5' x 5' oil on canvas, www.marieladelapaz.com
20. Ayahuaska at the Gates of San Pedro, Mariela de la Paz, 24" x 24" oil on canvas, www.marieladelapaz.com
21. The New Moon Maiden, Mariela de la Paz, 40" x 40" oil on canvas, www.marieladelapaz.com
22. Nuestra Senora de las Aguas, Timothy White, 24"x30", Acrylic on canvas, www.timothywhitefineart.com
23. Frida's Resurrection, Timothy White, 24"x30", Acrylic on canvas, www.timothywhitefineart.com
24. Seeds of Life Within, Morgan Mandala, www.morganmandala.com
25. Trinity, Morgan Mandala, www.morganmandala.com
26. Caught In The Web, Martina Hoffman, 2' x 3' oil on canvas, www.martinahoffmann.com
27. Firekeeper, Martina Hoffmann, 3' x 6' oil on canvas, www.martinahoffmann.com
28. Ayahuasca Dream, Robert Venosa, 4' x 6' oil on canvas, www.venosa.com
29. The Enlightenment, Robert Venosa, 2' x 4' oil on canvas, www.venosa.com
30. Juan Benavides Perez
31. Mauro Reátegui Perez, www.mauroart.com
32. Star Flower, Martin Ball, www.fractalimagination.com
33. Entrance to Love, Martin Ball, www.fractalimagination.com
34. Feathered Beings, Martin Ball, www.fractalimagination.com
35. Flower of the Cosmos, Martin Ball, www.fractalimagination.com
36. Spiral Dance, Martin Ball, www.fractalimagination.com

In Search of a New World View: Co-Creating a New Golden Age on Earth
By Victoria Christian M.A. and Gary Stamper Ph.D

1. Garden of Eden, Andrew Annenberg, 24"x30", oil on canvas, www.andrewannenberg.com
2. Mark Henson, New Pioneers, 48 x108" Oil on Canvas, 2010, www.markhensonart.com
3. Book Cover, Gary L. Stamper, www.awakeningthenewmasculine.com
3. Yoga Meditator, Daniel Holeman, digital image, www.awakenvisions.com
4. Bridging Heaven and Earth, Daniel Holeman, Digital Image, www.awakenvisions.com
5. Galactic Mandala, Jose Arguelles, 24"x24", acrylic on wood, www.lawoftime.org
6. Radiant Woman, Jose Arguelles, acrylic on wood door panel, www.lawoftime.org
7. Radiant Man, Jose Arguelles, acrylic on wood door panel, www.lawoftime.org
8. Homo Universalis or The Universal Human, Amoraea Dreamseed, Digital image, 2013, www.divine-blueprint.com
9. Keeper of the Cosmic Codes, Aaron Pyne, Digital Image, www.sacredvisiondesigns.com
10. The New Earth, Aaron Pyne, Digital Image, www.sacredvisiondesigns.com
11. Gaia, Robert Donaghey, Digital Image, www.artisticgenius.com
12. Metamorphosis of an Indigo, Robert Donaghey, Digital Image www.artisticgenius.com
13. The Release of Religious Dogma, Robert Donaghey, Digital Image, www.artisticgenius.com
14. Awakening, Robert Donaghey, Digital Image, www.artisticgenius.com
15. Awaken the Leader, Davin Infinity, digital image, www.awakenfreedom.weebly.com
16. The New Earth Avatars, Davin Infinity, digital image, www.awakenfreedom.weebly.com
17. Earth Avatar, Davin Infinity, digital image, www.awakenfreedom.weebly.com
18. Pollenectar, George Atherton, digital image, www.geoglyphiks.com
19. Anapurna, George Atherton, digital image, www.geoglyphiks.com
20. Durga Gaia George Atherton, digital image, www.geoglyphiks.com
21. Cry of the Amazon, Paul Nicholson, 36" X 48", oil on canvas
22. The Dark Mother, Paul Nicholson, 24x36", oil on canvas
23. Big Decisions, Kelly Hostetler, 24x30", oil on canvas, www.spiritdanceart.net
24. Wake up call, Kelly Hostetler, 24"x30", acrylic on canvas, www.spiritdanceart.net
25. Entanglement on the Verge of Extinction, Raul Casillas, 48"x20" oil on wood, 2007, www.raulcasillas.com
26. Ancient Agua Blessing, Raul Casillas, 24"x30" Oil on Wood, 2012, www.raulcasillas.com
27. Sacred Organic, Raul Casillas, 23"x43" Oil on Wood, 2012, www.raulcasillas.com
28. Optimystic, Chris Dyer, www.positivecreations.ca
29. The Ultimate Spiritual Warrior, Chris Dyer, www.positivecreations.ca
30. New Eden, Morgan Mandala, www.morganmandala.com

Afterword

By Susan Stedman

1. Kali, Jonathan Weber, 24x36 Oil on Canvas, www.altarimage.com
2. Offering of Gratitude, Victoria Christian,4X4 Oil on Metite, www.victoriachristian.com